KOPPETT'S CONCISE HISTORY OF

MAJOR LEAGUE BASEBALL

LEONARD KOPPETT

TEMPLE UNIVERSITY PRESS ◆ PHILADELPHIA

To the memory

of my mother and father,

who determined that I would become an American,

and

To all the men and women who,

over a century, made baseball what it was,

and

To everyone and anyone who is

as fascinated by it as I am.

Temple University Press, Philadelphia 19122
Copyright © 1998 by Temple University
All rights reserved
Published 1998
Printed in the United States of America

♾ The paper used in this publication meets the requirements of
the American National Standard for Information Sciences—
Permanence of Paper for Printed Library Materials,
ANSI Z39.48–1984

Text design by Kate Nichols

Library of Congress Cataloging-in-Publication Data
Koppett, Leonard.
  [Concise history of major league baseball]
  Koppett's Concise history of major league baseball / Leonard
Koppett.
    p. cm.
  Includes bibliographical references (p.   ) and index.
  ISBN 1-56639-638-7 (cloth)
  1. Baseball—United States—History. I. Title.
GV863.A1K66   1998
796.357′64′0973—dc21   98-4932

Contents

The Premise

"Narrative, it has been said, is the lifeblood of history." I read that in the introduction to a book called *Practicing History,* by Barbara Tuchman, who excelled in making history accessible to ordinary readers. She didn't say who said it. But I accept the proposition completely. History, to be of use to ordinary people (as distinct from scholars and specialists), is simply telling a story.

But why should I, after half a century of writing about baseball on a daily basis, try to retell the story of major league baseball, when library shelves are already full of such material by serious historians, tireless amateur researchers, collectors and analysts of statistics, an all-star roster of former baseball journalists, and countless single-subject explorers—not to mention the mountain of firsthand and first-person accounts of this meticulously documented subject?

For three reasons.

First of all, I simply want to tell the story on a straight-line coherent basis, as I have come to know it through wallowing in all that literature as well as from personal observation—because I believe it *is* a story that has more dramatic continuity than most people realize. I chose the adjective "concise," after much deliberation, precisely because the vast amount of available detail tends to obscure central story lines. Paying too much attention to the trees prevents you from seeing the forest (as has also been said).

The second impulse is much stronger. Increasingly, since the 1970s, I have been struck by how little present-day baseball people know about their own field's past.

That Don Mattingly could become an all-star Yankee first baseman having "never heard" of Lou Gehrig, or that Ken Griffey Jr. could be quoted (accurately or not) saying he doesn't know much about Jackie Robinson may make one shake one's head. But that's incidental. The important fact is that club owners, general managers, managers, veteran players—yes, and veteran sportswriters—and even (or especially) commissioners and their staffs seem unaware of the origins, causes, and developmental stages of the present problems they try to confront. It may not be exactly true (as has been said) that those who don't remember the past are condemned to repeat it. (That's George Santayana, I think.) But it is certainly true that if you don't know how the past formed the present, you're not likely to get to the heart of current problems. And if you don't see the similarities in recurring situations and contemplate what this or that reaction produced, you've increased the chance of stumbling into the same mistakes.

When I was developing my baseball consciousness as a teenager and then a young professional reporter (from the 1930s through the 1950s), my contemporaries and mentors had a vivid sense of baseball's past. Not only the names but the connotations of a Willie Keeler, a Napoleon Lajoie, the Players' League, Fred Merkle's boner, and each World Series melodrama from 1905 on, were all familiar to us and common conversational fodder. We weren't concerned with trivia for its own sake (although we enjoyed it), or making a conscious effort to be "learned." We simply accepted the idea of historical continuity. Just as we acquired some feeling, through school and reading, for the way George Washington, Thomas Jefferson, and Abraham Lincoln led to the world of Franklin D. Roosevelt and Dwight D. Eisenhower in which we lived, we assumed that John McGraw, the Black Sox, Babe Ruth, and Ty Cobb in their youth and the phrase "junior circuit" as applied to the American League had some relevance to the baseball we were involved with in our present.

Our whole cultural context is different today, of course. The sixties, television, and innumerable other changes have altered our attitudes about so many things, especially about relating to the past.

But I cling to the belief that one should have—and might actually enjoy—more awareness of what has gone on before.

Finally, I perceive a gap in the vast amount of material that has become available in the last couple of decades, and I feel equipped to fill it for the nonspecialist while helping specialists too.

The statistical encyclopedias, in all their forms, are absolutely marvelous and invaluable compilations—but they are devoid of narrative. They sum up every season's totals, but they tell little about the progress of events within a season.

The serious histories, now so numerous and of high quality, concentrate on off-field, behind-the-scenes, vital organizational and developmental forces, with only perfunctory reference to what was happening in the ball games and pennant races themselves—the events, after all, that are of primary interest to the baseball public.

They thoroughly explore economics, sociological contexts, personality clashes, and documentary evidence, while leaving on-field events—necessarily—to generalization or scattered anecdote.

Individual club histories and all sorts of biographies contain a wealth of fascinating information, but they are by definition subject oriented and don't pull together the whole picture—skimping on the central element of what else was going on elsewhere at that time.

And, especially in recent years, there are detailed and insightful depictions of a particular year, pennant race, or person with all the scope and overview one could hope for, yet restricted in time to the narrow chosen segment.

But I believe that the events on the field—the results of ball games and individual performances—and the off-field business decisions are inexorably linked. The one affects the other. Who wins and loses championships is often determined by what has happened in offices, where the rights to players, the procedural regulations, and even the playing rules are decided; and success or failure of particular teams determines, in turn, how those off-field decisions are made, and why, and in whose favor.

So I have two goals.

The first, aimed at everyone, is to provide a manageable—concise—overview of baseball history covering what I regard as minimal literacy in baseball lore. At the very least, it should provide one with recognizable reference points, the baseball equivalent of "Roman Empire," "Age of Exploration," "French Revolution," "Napoleon," "Churchill," and "Gorbachev" in the larger world. If this book doesn't send you scurrying to others for more information about whatever segment catches your fancy, it will have failed. And if it recalls things you already know about, their relationship to other things you may not have known about can add a dimension to your understanding.

My second purpose is to provide a convenient bridge between the statistical-factual encyclopedias and record books and the serious histories and single-topic studies. By blending the narrative (there's that key word again) of each year's pennant races and achievements with the ongoing affairs of the baseball business, we can see events in a connection to each other that the existing volumes don't show often enough; in short, a better perspective.

Those are daring goals, and here come the caveats.

I am not a trained historian and make no pretense of having done any original research. The beneficiary of work done by true historians, I am simply selecting, collating, and (I hope) clarifying what is already publicly available. My aim is to underline the main and most significant story lines—in my opinion—of baseball's development down to the present day.

I am not an academician, so I make no attempt to footnote or document every reference. I do acknowledge, at the end of the book, the sources to which I'm indebted.

I am not a controversialist. I do not try to settle disputes about one or another version of historical events but only to present, as well as I can, the way they were perceived and—of primary importance—the way those perceptions affected subsequent events. The emphasis is on what made news *then*, and on how it was remembered and retold later.

What I am is a baseball writer, of above-average experience, familiar with the frustration daily journalism imposes on those of us who care about what we cover. Cramming all the interesting and significant aspects of even one ball game into a 600-word story is possible only rarely; but at least these stories provide a minimal service. Much worse is the impossibility of covering the off-field events, which unfold over weeks and years in some sequence of meetings, statements, contradictions, arguments, and reversals of position, with no single event complete in itself (as a ball game is). And worst of all, whatever has to get left out of today's story is gone for good, in the vast majority of cases, with little occasion or opportunity for amplifying or correcting it later.

Longer pieces, such as columns, features, or magazine articles, are no less incomplete. To do them, you gather even more material than for a daily story and wind up publishing a smaller portion of what you have acquired. And in books, of which I've done a dozen or so, a strong focus on a few ideas is still necessary, although there is room to flesh out some specific themes.

Well, I've had a lot of practice at condensation, elision, selection, and deliberate excision. Now I want to describe the whole forest, not just sets of trees, and this brings us back to the term "concise."

In the process, I will observe certain boundaries. By "baseball," I mean, specifically and exclusively, major league baseball. That's the only story I'm telling. Others are very worthwhile in themselves—the minor leagues, school and amateur play, semipros, the excluded black and other minorities, women's activities, and all sorts of related aspects of society. But I am unequipped to deal with them, and they aren't part of this particular story precisely because the protagonists in it excluded them. So it is not out of disrespect or obliviousness that I ignore all these other significant elements. It is merely a matter of seeking pertinent parameters for one specific topic.

A popular formula in our time has been "everything you ever wanted to know about . . . " This exercise is the opposite. I want simply to call your attention to all the things you ought to know in order to feel you know anything. To know a lot (never mind everything), you'll have to look elsewhere, and I hope that this narrative encourages you to look.

Around ball parks, you hear certain phrases over and over:

"There's nothing new in baseball."

"Every year, you'll see something you never saw before."

"You'll never really figure this game out."

"It's really a simple game."

"Remember, baseball's a sport, not a business."

"When you tell them it's a business, they say it's a game; when you say it's a game, they say it's a business."

"Play the percentages."

"You never know what can happen in a ball game."

"A ball game is never over until the last man is out" (traditional version from the 19th century); or "It ain't over 'til it's over" (modern version, an absolutely authentic Yogi Berra quote).

None is completely true. Each is enormously suggestive and proves true an astounding proportion of the time. What follows should illustrate how, and why, and when.

The organization of this book is intended to make quick reference possible, without sacrificing the readability of straight narrative.

The sections are arranged chronologically, divided into eras defined by large-scale characteristics and external conditions. Each era is subdivided into chapters that cover a series of years dominated by certain overriding influences.

In each chapter covering the years after 1890, there are three sections. The first deals with major issues that transcend, in time frame and importance, any single year, so that a complex subject can be treated as a whole. The second chronicles, year by year, the events of each season, with cross-references to the larger issues already explained. The third is a summary bridge showing how the consequences of that segment set the stage for the next.

Any single season's content can be viewed simply by turning to that year.

The overview of larger issues—formation of leagues, club-player relations, legal problems, economic developments, evolution of playing rules and roster regulations, scandals, court cases, and so forth—is substantially self-contained in the first and third sections of each chapter and can be used without detailed reference to the year-by-year events.

A word about numbers: this book is overflowing with numerals—statistics, dollars, dates. Many of them are not correct in the sense of exactness and incontrovertible evidence, but all are true in the sense that they reflect correctly the point being made in the context at hand. One can find countless instances where a number I give as 80 is given elsewhere as 79 or 81 but never 60 or 100 or anything far enough off to make a difference. Thus, the *significance* of the number in relation to what's being discussed is entirely reliable.

There is good reason for this. Baseball records are full of discrepancies and errors. Different reference volumes give different figures for the same item, and different editions of the same reference volume contain changes. Many modern research efforts have been made to "reconcile" different sources, especially since about 1970, but none has come close to succeeding yet.

I have made no attempt to seek out "corrections," or to rely on one source to the exclusion of others to avoid contradiction. I have used many sources according to their convenience, following these general guidelines: (1) if using a record book contemporary with the event, I don't bother with researchers' corrections made decades later; (2) where modern encyclopedias differ from each other, I don't try to make them consistent; (3) the difference between batting averages of .320 and .280 is not "40 points" but the whole complex of implications about their reflection of productivity, so that the *sense* would remain valid if they were actually .318 and .282. In that respect, the numbers I use are valid and dependable—but don't try to use them to win trivia contests or settle bets.

Finally, a word about proportions. I have devoted much more space to the early part of the story than to comparable time segments of the 20th century, for two reasons. First, in order to recognize repetitive patterns, one must describe their first appearance thoroughly enough to make later reference meaningful, and, in the process, one can make those later references more concise. Second, it's the older material that's most unfamiliar to the contemporary reader, and less accessible in annual publications than more recent events. A sort of logarithmic scale comes into play: Much more baseball "has happened" since World War II than before World War I, but it doesn't take as many words to tell about its broad outlines, or to make the story coherent as it unfolds.

When all else is said and done, the essence of our fascination with baseball is that we can talk about it. More than any other game, its events can be discussed (and written about) in endless detail, not simply experienced as player or spectator. On the mental level, the involved spectator is deeply engaged during the game itself, but even more so the rest of the time. We "talk baseball" extensively all year long, year after year, sharing opinions and memories and speculations on a scale few other popular activities offer.

My hope is that this book can help us know what we're talking about.

PART I

ORIGINS

CHAPTER 1

Preliminaries

Imagine that you are a young man—say, 25—of comfortable means living in New York City in the 1840's.

It is already one of the most important cities in the world, but far more provincial than the large cities of Europe. All of it is contained within the southern third of Manhattan Island. From the Battery north to almost 30th Street, it is built-up solid. Beyond that, along Broadway and Fifth Avenue, stretch the villas of the very rich. The waterfront, along the East River (which is mostly south) and the Hudson River to the west, is a forest of masts, a maze of ferry boats, a collage of sails, ropes, barrels, wooden piers, and wooden warehouses.

A house taller than four stories is a rarity, since the only way to reach upper stories is to walk (and carry things) upstairs. The skyline's peaks, therefore, are church steeples. To get around the narrow streets, paved with cobblestones if at all, you have three alternatives: ride a horse, be pulled by a horse, or go on foot.

Your grandfather most likely fought or was otherwise involved in the Revolutionary War (which he probably calls the War of Independence), and he remembers clearly George Washington's inauguration downtown as the first president of the new country. Your father remembers vividly the anxiety and disruption of the War of 1812, when he was courting your mother. You yourself recall the financial panic of 1837 and the riots it generated, when the city's unemployed protested high rents and high food prices by sacking the city's warehouses.

But now (let's pretend the year is 1842) times are relatively peaceful and pros-

perous. The president is John Tyler because William Henry Harrison, who was selected on the slogan of "Tippecanoe and Tyler too," had died 31 days after making
his inaugural address in March 1841, during which he caught pneumonia. Tyler is a
Virginian, generally at odds with his own party, the Whigs (dominant among anti-
slavery Northerners). Abolitionists are still considered wide-eyed radicals, although
your own sympathies are basically in that direction, and the real struggle is still about
the spread of slavery to the new territories and about the slave trade, rather than
about slavery's established existence. Arkansas is the most recent, and westernmost,
of the 23 United States of America.

For heat you depend on coal or wood in a fireplace or stove. Illumination comes
from candles or torches. Among the things you have never imagined are elevators,
typewriters, cameras, sewing machines, safety razors, or safety pins.

This year, two exciting new features have been added to the bustling social life
and recreational opportunities of Little Old New York: Phineas T. Barnum has
opened his fascinating museum at Broadway and Ann Street, and the huge new
reservoir, which runs along the west side of Fifth Avenue from 40th to 42d Street, has
massive stone walls suitable for fashionable promenading along the water's edge.

But you already have a favorite entertainment, a hobby you share with your social equals. Whenever the weather is nice enough, a bunch of you get together and
play a game you have learned to call Base Ball.

It is not really new, but it has a fascination all its own. You hit a ball with a stick and
run around "bases." In some versions, it is as old as humankind. Specifically, it is an adap-
tation of two venerable English games, rounders and cricket. And that's natural enough,
because your family's roots are English or Dutch, wars notwithstanding. Almost every
"good" family in town is from this background. The waves of Irish Catholics starting to
flow into the city generate an anti-Catholicism so virulent that by 1844 New York will
elect a mayor (James Harper) from a party (the American Republican Party) that makes
anti-Catholicism one of its basic principles. You derive all your ideas—and limitations—
of "gentlemanly" behavior, your definition of social class, and your models of fashion
from contemporary England, where a young queen named Victoria has reigned for five
years and where industrialism has started upheavals that will soon cross the ocean.

For any activity, then, an exclusive "club" is as natural in this New York as in that
London, and you and your fellow Base Ball players long to form one. Among other
things, open fields on which to play are rapidly disappearing in this growing city
whose population has reached 250,000; and ferryrides to the abundant open spaces
of Brooklyn (a village of some 30,000) or New Jersey are time-consuming and hopelessly complicated if not properly organized. So when you gather at Madison Square,
where Fifth Avenue and Broadway meet at 23d Street, and play ball and argue about
what rules to use, you talk more and more of formalizing your group and its activity
into a respectable club.

Meanwhile, you become more and more captivated by the special features of the game itself: catching the ball on the run, throwing it hard and straight, the greater primitive satisfaction of smiting the ball as hard as possible with a level swing (instead of guarding a wicket against a bouncing delivery, as in cricket), the variety of having more than one station to run to after hitting the ball.

In some such fashion, it all began—baseball as we know it in New York and, therefore, baseball in America.

The ball games themselves, of course, were being played throughout New England and the Middle Atlantic states, with countless variations in local custom. Some called it Town Ball, some Goal Ball, some rounders, some One (or Two or Three) O'Cat. Their common characteristics were that the ball had to be "pitched" (that is, lobbed underhand) to the batter; that the bases (whatever their number, and whatever the shape of their layout) had to be touched in sequence on the way to a score; and that cricket's distinguishing feature, the wicket, had been abandoned. (The wicket is a three-pronged stand behind the "striker," who must prevent the "bowler's" delivery from knocking loose the "bails," two pieces of wood lodged loosely atop the wicket.)

But it was in New York that the formalization of this "child's game" took place, in a pattern that then became known as "The New York Game." And the mere act of formalization was of more than passing significance in an age when the Establishment (Protestant, mercantile in outlook, with British or Dutch roots) still felt squeamish about "frivolous" activities for responsible adults.

On September 13, 1845, the Knickerbocker Base Ball Club formalized itself. It chose a name of Dutch derivation, by way of author Washington Irving, but its officers were clearly of British stock: Duncan C. Curry, president; William B. Wheaton, vice-president; William H. Tucker, secretary and treasurer; and Alexander J. Cartwright, leader of the rules committee. Ten days later, it published its rules.

A surveyor by profession, Cartwright was 25 years old when he codified the first set of rules that would be so widely adopted. Exactly how much came out of his own head, and how much he simply recorded as common usage, is hard to say. But if any one person can be given credit for systematizing baseball into a form we now recognize, it is Cartwright, who not only wrote out the rules of procedure but also directed how the field should be laid out (as a good surveyor would).

"Rule 4—Bases shall be from home to second, and from first to third, 42 paces equidistant." This established the infield as a square—it was diamond shaped in many other versions, narrower and longer—but if did *not* put the bases that mystical distance of 90 feet apart. A "pace" meant a yard or less, so the diagonals of the square were 126 feet, and that would produce a distance of 89.1 feet from base to base. Only later was this evened off to 90 feet, and on today's fields the diagonal is 127 feet, 3⅜ inches. Some researchers say that a pace meant 2½ feet then, which would put bases only 75 feet apart.

Some other basic rules were:

If a batter missed three swings, or if a ball he hit was caught on the fly or on
   one bounce, he was "a hand out."
The lines from home through first and third were extended indefinitely, and
   any ball hit outside them was "foul," meaning that no base could be
   gained on a foul. (But a foul fly caught was an out).
Three outs retired the side.
To win a game, a team had to score 21 times by advancing a runner all the
   way around back to home. (Cartwright called such points scored "aces"
   or "counts;" we call them "runs".) But each team had to be given the
   same number of outs.
The ball had to be thrown to the batter underhand, released from below the
   line of the hip, from an area in the middle of the the diamond (that is,
   the square), whose front line was 45 feet from home.
And, of fundamental importance, there was Rule 13: "A player running the
   bases shall be out, if the ball is in the hands of an adversary on the base,
   as the runner is touched by it before he makes his base; it being understood, however, that in no instance is a ball to be thrown at him."

This key rule was not original with the Knickerbocker Club, but by institutional-
izing it, Cartwright's rules made true baseball possible.

As long as it was permissible to put a base runner out by hitting him with a thrown
ball, as in rounders and many of its variations, the ball had to be relatively soft. Otherwise, too much pain and injury would be inflicted on the player hit. But such a ball
was also too soft to be hit very far or with great velocity. (We see this, to a degree, in
softball.) Once this play was removed, the way was clear for a harder ball that could
travel farther and faster when hit, bringing into play the now traditional relationships
among the flight of the ball, the speed of the runner, the positioning of the fielders,
and the length of throws.

Another practice already widely in use but formalized for the first time in the
Knickerbocker rules was the use of flat stones for bases instead of wooden pegs or
stakes driven vertically into the ground at the "safe stations." (Goal ball was called that
because attaining each station safely was a player's "goal.") To touch a stake, a runner must slow down, if not come to a full stop, and bend down or reach out. A runner can step on a flat base without breaking stride and keep going. So flat bases also
made a crucial contribution to a faster, more graceful, more exhilarating style of play.

Two notable features did not exist in Cartwright's rules, however. There was no
such thing as a "ball" (as opposed to a strike), and therefore no such concept as a
base on balls or a "walk;" and no "called strike." The three strikes the batter had coming were three swings and misses—and even if he missed the third one, he could run

as if he had hit a fair ball if the catcher failed to catch the pitch on the fly or first bounce. (That the third strike must be caught has remained the rule, with refinements, to this day.)

This meant the batter could wait as long as he liked to get a suitably hittable pitch, and that the pitcher could throw as many "bad" deliveries as he wanted to in order to test the patience of the hitter. Why, then, wouldn't one turn at bat last all day and destroy the game? Because both men were bound by the "gentlemanly code" to avoid "unduly prolonging" the game. Besides, since the pitcher was directed, by rule, to toss the ball in a way that it could be hit, there was no point in prolonging the batter-pitcher confrontation.

The idea of *making* the batter miss hadn't yet taken hold. But it would, and soon.

A player who made out was called "a hand out." Rule 15 said, "Three hands out, all out." That defined an "inning" for the team at bat, so there had to be an equal number of innings for each side to reach the total of 21 aces—or higher.

All fall and winter, as the weather allowed, and especially through the spring, the members of the club refined these rules, practiced, and played intramural games. But not until June 19, 1846, were they able to play a formal game against a rival club.

One basic problem was that there was no other club. Since no other Base Ball Club existed, no natural pairing of social equals could be arranged. There were plenty of people playing ball passionately and well, but they simply got together and played, without "official" organization. Finally, for the sake of competition, the Knickerbockers decided to forego their social exclusivity and accepted as an opponent a team called The New York Nine, simply a collection of the better players available.

The other problem was, where to play? The grounds at Madison Square had gone the way of all Manhattan real estate: for development (in this case, a railroad terminal). No suitable spot could be found in the expanding city. But there was a place called Elysian Fields in Hoboken, across the Hudson from 14th Street, where cricket and other games were played, and the Knickerbockers booked it. There, on Friday, June 19, the first recorded regular baseball game took place.

The membership of the Knickerbocker Club consisted of merchants, bankers, brokers, insurance men, other white-collar workers, and professional men. They were not, as a group, wealthy, but well-to-do with "proper" social connections. Their playing ability was the product of zeal, not natural selection; but since they were the first to take the game seriously enough to form a club, they automatically assumed they needed expert opposition. The New York Nine was not a club at all, but a one-shot aggregation chosen on the basis of ability instead of social status.

The New York Nine won, 23–1, needing only four innings.

Right then and there, several aspects of baseball and its interaction with the American character were foreshadowed.

The "gentleman sportsmen" were no match, competitively, for more pragmatic players—and before long, the democratic nature of events on a ball field would be held up as baseball's chief virtue.

Yet the elements of snobbishness and an attempt to cling to the imagery of "the gentleman" would continue to run strongly through the organizational side of the game.

And, in the conflict between the two approaches, there was no question at all which one Americans in general favored: to win was the important thing, regardless of the pedigree of the participants. From the very start, the search by clubs for better players to recruit became a basic feature of baseball.

The Knickerbockers, having been beaten, withdrew into intramural activity and did not play another outside game for five years. They would not venture forth, officially, against a "picked nine" again and waited until another club of comparable standing would be formed.

This didn't happen until 1852, when a club called Gotham began to operate way up north, beyond the farms of mid-Manhattan, in a village called Harlem. Two years later, a third club, the Eagle, began to play regularly at Hoboken, on the same field used by the Knickerbocker. And within two years, 21 more clubs were in action, and three of them were to have lasting importance: the Atlantics, who played in the Williamsburgh section of Brooklyn and out in Jamaica, Long Island; the Excelsiors of South Brooklyn, who started out with the more vivid title of the Jolly Young Bachelors' Base Ball Club; and the Mutuals, who claimed the allegiance and identity of New York but used the grounds in the Williamsburgh section of Brooklyn.

Such clubs tended to be organized around some single occupation. The Mutuals were the firemen of the Mutual Hook and Ladder Company No. 1, for instance; the Eckfords of Brooklyn were shipbuilders; the Metropolitans were schoolteachers.

By the spring of 1858, activity was so widespread, and interest so intense, that it was time to pass beyond the unofficial leadership of the Knickerbockers. A convention was called for March 10, and, with three representatives from each of 25 clubs present, the National Association of Base Ball Players was formed. Calling itself "national" was somewhat presumptuous, since the participants in this association came from no further south than New Brunswick, New Jersey, or any further west and north than Manhattan and the Bronx. But it was the *only* formal Base Ball Association in the country at the moment, and its standardizing of some evolving rules had a pervasive and permanent effect. The "New York game" became the magnet to which all future developments would attach themselves, which is why New York is the true starting point of our story.

This convention adopted nine innings as the length of game, regardless of runs scored. It specified the circumference of ball and bat (not much different from today). It instituted the force-out, which greatly speeds up the game.

In New England, they were still playing the Massachusetts Game, which included "soaking"—runners put out by being hit with a thrown ball. In Philadelphia, a club older than the Knickerbocker, the Olympic, still clung to Town Ball. And everywhere, cricket clubs were still common. Now, with one large organization in existence, however limited geographically, the machinery for creating the nucleus of a uniform game was in place.

And life was changing. Our imaginary young man who was 25 when the Knickerbockers were first getting together is now in his 40's, living in a larger, more complicated world deep in turmoil. The waves of Irish immigrants have been joined by Germans, Scandinavians, and Central Europeans, many of them from relatively intellectual classes after Europe's political upheavals of 1848. New York City has tripled in population and is solidly built-up past 50th Street. California's Gold Rush in 1849 and statehood in 1850 have altered the psychology of a nation and made convincing Horace Greeley's advice, "Go West, young man." Florida, Iowa, Texas, and Wisconsin have become states since 1845, and Minnesota and Oregon are about to.

And, of course, war is right around the corner.

In New York (which we are now using only as an example of processes being paralleled elsewhere), several things were happening that would shape the development of baseball. In the 1850's, Boss Tweed began creating the prototype of big-city machine politics. Public transportation was expanding rapidly, with horse- drawn "trolleys" along rails and the less limited "omnibus," a high coach drawn by two horses. Steam ferries moved rapidly to Brooklyn, Staten Island, and New Jersey. Newspapers proliferated: the *Tribune,* the *Sun,* the *Herald,* a dozen others (including, in 1851, one called the *Times*). City politics, transportation patterns, newspapers, the recently invented telegraph, and the constantly improving railroads—all these would soon make possible the transformation of club baseball into serious business.

In such a society, the "gentleman's club" concept was doomed, but it had been undermined from the start by the importance of winning. Although some clubs were more expensive and more exclusive than others, all had as members some sort of wage earners, since the idle-rich population of America at that time was not large enough to fill many clubs. It was a short (not to say inevitable) step from choosing the best players from among your club members to play an outside game, to finding good players anywhere and making them members. If that meant finding a suitable job for the talented player, that wasn't too difficult in view of the fine commercial and social connections of the other members. Then it was an even shorter step to making sure the really good player got paid well for his "job" even though he seldom went near it while concentrating on practicing his ball-field skills. (American colleges make good use of this system for varsity athletes to this day, calling the salary a "scholarship.")

And from there, it was hardly any step at all to direct under-the-table payment to any good player, whether or not the formalities of "club membership" were adhered to. Full-scale professionals, unacknowledged but not uncommon, were becoming more important and more numerous.

One young man accelerated the process disproportionately. His name was Jim Creighton, he was from Brooklyn, and he was only 17 when he learned how to make that underhand "toss" nearly unhittable by imparting speed and spin to the ball by a flick of the wrist just before release. No one will ever know if he was "the first" to do so, but history tells us he was the first to get widespread recognition for doing so among the best players of his time. Even a "straight" throw moving 80 miles an hour from 45 feet reaches the batter in almost the same fraction of a second (four-tenths) as a modern 100-mile-an-hour fastball from the 60-foot-6-inch distance; in addition, spin can be controlled to make the trajectory not so straight.

Creighton burst on the scene in 1858, the first season after the formation of the association, dazzled the public as much as he baffled the hitters, and set off a cascade of effective imitators. He moved from team to team without compunction (or income tax) and became in fact, though not in name, the first professional star.

By now, the appeal of a baseball game to spectators had become clear. More games, played under stable (and therefore easily learned) rules, at fairly accessible locations, offered a many- sided blessing. The standard working time was 10 hours a day, six days a week—which meant that in summer, there were daylight hours left for recreation after 6 P.M. The mass of hard-working immigrants were not exactly in shape, physically or mentally, for elaborate athletic activity after a day's labor—but they could watch it with pleasure, and their younger and stronger sons could grow up playing the game. The more affluent classes, with more time and money to spend in a crowded city, were always looking for new diversions, especially in a culture that cared little for the traditional "artistic" interests of Europe. Baseball games to watch, to bet on, to read about, and as a focal point for pregame and postgame partying, suited them nicely. For the athletically talented youngster, here was an opportunity to escape the dullness and limitations of factory or shop; for everyone else, here was an exciting outdoor entertainment.

As proof of the game's appeal, a midsummer milestone event in 1858 started many minds spinning. The best players of New York City and Brooklyn were brought together for an all-star game. The site chosen was the Fashion Race Course, out on Long Island. To convert the field into a baseball diamond cost a lot of money, so it was decided to charge admission to defray expenses.

On July 20, no fewer than 1,500 spectators showed up, willing to pay 50 cents apiece just to watch this game. (New York won, 22–18.) Gate receipts of $750 represented an amazing sum in 1858, and the promotional possibilities were apparent immediately. Almost overnight, the equation was widely understood: better players equal stronger teams, equal more spectators, equal more revenue—which can then be used to hire better players, to generate still more revenue.

Even more important was another conclusion: those who would travel far and then pay 50 cents to watch a ball game would, undoubtedly, pay a penny or two to read about one. The newspapers, so fiercely competitive for readers and still the only medium for disseminating any kind of news, found they had a natural alliance with baseball activity. The more games, the more stories with which to entice readers. Other recreational activities weren't as useful. Those could be announced and reviewed, but a play in a theater, once reviewed, might run for months and make money for its backers without doing a newspaper any ongoing good. Athletic events, on the other hand, automatically made "new" news every time, through a score and a result, and baseball provided the largest and steadiest diet of sports news.

Exactly the same reasoning would be followed almost a hundred years later by television-set manufacturers and station operators.

Even before the Civil War, therefore, baseball heroes were well established, and at least one top-ranking baseball expert was recognized. Henry B. Chadwick, the father of baseball writing and an enormous influence on its evolving traditions, was born in England in 1824 and brought to Brooklyn by his journalist father in the 1830's. Rejecting a career as a musician, the young Chadwick committed himself to newspaper work only a couple of years after that first Knickerbocker game and soon specialized in sports-writing. Along with daily and weekly stories for regular papers and special sports papers that sprang up, Chadwick edited guides and record books throughout the remainder of the 19th century and came to wield enormous influence behind the scenes as well. The extent of his opinion-making powers is hard to exaggerate.

And so, before 1860, there was a flaming New York–Brooklyn rivalry in existence, capable of stimulating both passion and profit. There was a rapidly growing literature of baseball; and, in Creighton, the first big star as an object of adulation and wonder—and drawing power.

In the summer of 1860, he wound up with the Excelsiors of Brooklyn, who saw themselves as the social elite of their community, although creeping matrimony had long since forced them to abandon the Jolly Young Bachelors title of their club. To the snooty Knickerbockers, the Excelsiors were barely within the limits of respectability; but in Brooklyn, the well-to-do Excelsiors ranked far above such strong clubs as the Eckfords, referred to as greasy mechanics by the gentlemen of clubs that had weaker teams.

But there was nothing weak about the Excelsiors, especially with Creighton pitching. At just about the time Lincoln's first presidential campaign was beginning, they decided to show themselves to the less fortunate folk living far from the big city. They made a tour of upstate New York, and another of the Baltimore and Philadelphia areas, proudly paying all their own expenses but drawing large crowds and making money for their hosts.

What made these tours so significant was the timing, the eve of the Civil War. That the Excelsiors won all their games, and that Creighton became legendary, wasn't the point. What mattered is that they spread, by example, the virtues of the New York Game. For the first time, newspapers in many cities carried stories about the same exciting team seen elsewhere, instead of only about local heroes. Every-where the Excelsiors went, people could see for themselves (while still more could read about) the attractions of a game played with a really hard ball, flat bases that could be rounded at full stride, powerful pitching, well-drilled fielding, and a nine-inning format. In an age that had no radio, television, or even newspaper pho-tographs, such exposure would have had great impact no matter what. But in 1860, these tours planted seeds at a special moment.

It was the war that completed the fertilization. Awareness of the Excelsiors and their style came just in time for thousands of Northern soldiers to carry these rules and techniques to their camps. The inevitable boredom and waiting time all armies experience formed a perfect setting for ball games, with implements easily impro-vised. Countless Southern soldiers learned the game too, as prisoners of war or from Northern prisoners, and what they learned was The New York Game. When, after four long years, the war ended and the armies scattered, this was the style of baseball that was taken, individual by individual, to every corner of the still-growing country.

With the war over, the baseball world expanded explosively. In 1860, the Excel-siors had been one of 54 clubs in the Association. In 1865, within days of the official end of hostilities, 91 clubs sent delegates to the convention in New York. The next year, membership jumped to 202 teams (73 of them from New York State), includ-ing delegates from Maine, Oregon, and half a dozen states in between.

In 1867, all real opposition to outright professionalism collapsed. The National Association, up to then a collection of individual clubs professing amateur status, changed itself into a sort of congress of regional associations, giving each consider-able autonomy. Few, if any, of these shared the sort of gentlemanly ideals that had motivated the oldest New York clubs.

It wasn't surprising. The postwar era was a break with the past in every respect. The new cultural climate gave primary importance to commercial expansion, and the mass-entertainment aspect of baseball naturally became ascendant. That intricate in-teraction of professional player, profit-seeking investor, tie-in promoter, newspaper publicity, civic chauvinism, fan hysteria, and hero-myth manufacture was in tune with that time—and we still have it today.

With equal inevitability, these changes gave birth to two problems that would plague baseball for decades, both discoveries by the better players about how to in-crease their rewards.

One was clearly reprehensible, but hard to stop: the practice of fixing games ei-ther to collect one's own bets or bribes from gamblers or to build up the gate for next time.

The other was more open to moral argument on either side, but just as hard to live with: the practice of selling one's services to the highest bidder, month by month, week by week, or even game by game, jumping from one club to another. As early as 1864, Alfred J. Reach, an outstanding infielder with the proletarian Eckfords, accepted an offer to switch to the Philadelphia Athletic Club—and then, it was said, rejected an offer from a club in Baltimore because that was beyond commuting range from his Brooklyn home.

Fixed games, of course, were a self-defeating proposition in the long run, and in any particular area. As soon as the faith of the spectator was shaken, betting diminished and so did the gate. But "revolving," as jumping from team to team was called, couldn't go on indefinitely either. It destroyed stability, increased expenses, confused spectators who developed rooting interests, and exacerbated friction with the majority that was still amateur-minded.

What was needed, obviously, was firmer organization.

By 1868, the groundwork was there. Players, enclosed grounds, and customers were available in ever greater numbers. Increased use of the telegraph and burgeoning newspaper interest went hand in hand and made it easy to stir up hometown fans for a return match after a road game. Another key ingredient was the growth of the railroads. Regular passenger service between the Atlantic Coast and Chicago and St. Louis was established shortly before the war (Boston to St. Louis, three days). But right after it, the transcontinental connection was completed quickly. To display and cash in on glamorous teams, you must be able to transport them to distant sets of customers. This was now becoming possible. (It's no coincidence that 90 years later, major league baseball expanded to California only when jet planes cut transcontinental travel time to a few hours.)

In such circumstances, fully professional baseball was bound to flourish, one way or another, but the way it actually did was determined by an English-born New Yorker and two games played in Brooklyn.

The man was Harry Wright, son of a professional cricket player and himself the resident cricket pro at the St. George Cricket Club on Staten Island. By 1858, the year of that first convention, he had shifted his interest to baseball, but in 1865 he moved on to Cincinnati as bowler for the Union Cricket Club there. He was 30 years old. Before long, Cincinnatians developed a greater interest in baseball and wanted to form a team that was fully professional. Wright was put in charge of the operation, and the team was called the Red Stockings, for the perfectly logical and mundane reason that the uniform included red stockings.

Wright, familiar with all the top players throughout the east, signed 10 of them to season-long contracts. (That was the innovation: publicizing the fact that *every* player was committed to the team for the full year at a guaranteed salary.) Then he took the show on the road.

The Red Stockings were undefeated in 1969. They went as far as California, and the number of people who saw them play has been estimated at 200,000 in about 60 games. The next year they were finally beaten, but they had established the respectability, viability, and future of professional baseball.

The two key games took place exactly a year apart. On June 14, 1869, the Red

Stockings defeated the prestigious New York Mutuals 4–2, establishing their competitive reputation. On June 14, 1870, they were back in Brooklyn to face the Atlantics, with their winning streak intact (84 games, some sources say, but many details are in dispute).

That intensely publicized game, at the Capitoline Grounds in the Bedford-Stuyvesant area, brought out a crowd of 20,000 paying customers, and they got their money's worth. After nine innings, it was 5–5, and upon consultation with the official scorer—Chadwick—it was decided that extra innings would be proper. The Red Stockings scored two runs in the top of the 11th—but the Atlantics came back with three for an 8–7 victory that ended the streak. "The greatest game ever played!" trumpeted the New York papers the next day.

No one would ever again question the commercial possibilities of baseball, nor the preference of the public for all-out professionals playing meaningful matches. No longer was organization merely desirable; it was an irresistible necessity.

And on March 17, 1871, in Collier's Cafe on Broadway at 13th Street, it was achieved.

CHAPTER 2

The National Association

The impact the Red Stockings made in 1869 spawned imitation—that is, acknowledged professionalism—and the combined experience of 1869 and 1870 taught lessons that could not be ignored.

1. The public would pay, gladly, to watch top-flight players in action.
2. Only full-scale professionals could provide performance at that level.
3. Professionals playing amateurs, or lesser professionals, produced mismatches unable to sustain interest.
4. Therefore, top-flight professionals had to play more games with each other.
5. But the best professional teams, almost by definition and certainly as a practical matter, were based in different cities and outclassed local or nearby competition.
6. In order to play each other, these teams had to travel to each other's cities, sometimes far apart.
7. Travel cost money.

From the standpoint of most of the members of the National Association of Base Ball Players, club-based since its inception before the war, amateurism was a fundamental tenet, even if violated surreptitiously, since competition with fully staffed professional teams was not only unfair but no fun.

During 1870, the move to separate the pro's from the rest became irreversible. As the Red Stockings continued their tour, their few equals had less reason to hide—if not yet publicly avowed—their professionalism. According to Al Spalding (whom we'll meet in a moment), writing in 1911, at least a dozen teams were in reality manned by fully paid professionals, with season contracts not unlike Cincinnati's. Among these, he said, were the Athletics of Philadelphia, the Atlantics of Brooklyn (who ended Cincinnati's winning streak), the Mutuals of New York, the White Stockings of Chicago, and two teams in Washington, D.C., the Olympics and the Nationals. Smaller cities had them too: Fort Wayne, Indiana; Troy, New York; and, of special significance, Rockford, Illinois.

The Association, as it existed, had to face up to three choices: discipline the pros, expel them, or become impotent and irrelevant.

The pros saw no reason to deal with the amateur problem at all. Why couldn't they form their own association?

They could. They did.

After much informal talk and correspondence (by letter and wire, since there were no telephones yet) during late 1870, they called a meeting on St. Patrick's Day, March 17, 1870, in New York.

Harry Wright was the guiding force. After two glorious seasons, the Cincinnati Red Stockings had shown a profit of less than two dollars, and the backers decided to disband the team and return to less glorious, but less costly, amateurism. Travel and other expenses, as well salaries, had eaten up what had been considerable revenues. The risk of deficit overcame the satisfactions of fame.

All these lessons had been absorbed by Wright, along with a more subtle one. When the Red Stockings were no longer "undefeated," as early as mid-June, their power as a gate attraction visibly diminished. The magic words "national champion," mythical or not, had been attached to teams only after the event, by declaration at the conclusion of a season, when there were no more tickets to sell. What was needed was a method to let the public know how progress toward a championship was being made. If the pro's played each other and counted only such games as official, a pennant race could be created.

Just how new and brilliant such a concept was can be appreciated only in light of the sports scene of that time.

The first game of what its participants called college football, an unrecognizable variety of rugby, had been played by Princeton and Rutgers students only a few months before, on November 6, 1869.

James Naismith, who would not invent basketball until 21 years later, was an eight-year-old boy living in Canada.

Also up in Canada, they were still 15 years away from adopting any uniform rules for various hockey games played on ice, and from the manufacture of flat-bladed hockey sticks.

What was called "lawn tennis," the modern variety of long-existing racquet games, hadn't been invented yet. That wouldn't happen until 1874.

There wouldn't be a golfing club founded in America until 1888.

Prize fights were bare knuckled, disreputable, and illegal.

The established sports—horse racing, rowing, track and field—were all structured around one-shot events: you won this or that race or title, with one result having no tangible effect on the next.

And baseball, like cricket, was seen as a succession of "test matches," each competition standing on its own, until some championship pennant was awarded by decree at the end of a season.

To put all the new ideas into practice, Wright needed a compact core of teams, staffed by the best professionals. At that March 17th meeting, 10 clubs signed up and formed the National Association of Professional Base Ball Players, taking pains to emphasize the word "professional."

In almost every respect, they simply adopted the old National Association by-laws and procedures, especially the playing rules, except for the amateurism provisions. The whole idea was to exploit what was already popular and familiar, not to make revolution. They did, however, make the key provision that would define a pennant race: each team would play every other team at least five times, with the championship going to the team that accumulated the most victories. Only in case of a tie would the won-lost percentage determine the champion. Games against nonmembers simply wouldn't count.

But they also made two mistakes, sowing the seeds of failure. They left the matter of scheduling to the two teams involved, as it always had been. And they set the entry fee at $10 a club.

Self-scheduling meant that the promise to play each opponent five times could not be enforced if, for any reason, two teams failed to keep it. And with only $10 to be forfeited, a club had no reason not to drop out during an unsuccessful season, or if it was not meeting expenses. There were still lessons to be learned.

Nevertheless, the professional association was a tremendous advance and marked the birth of what would come to be known as "major league baseball."

The 10 charter members of the professional National Association (as we shall refer to it from now on, since the amateur association continued its existence until it withered away) were

> The Philadelphia Athletics
> The Washington Olympics
> The Washington Nationals
> The New York Mutuals
> The Chicago White Stockings
> The Cleveland Forest Citys

The Fort Wayne Kekiongas
The Troy Haymakers
The Rockford Forest Citys
The Boston Red Stockings

Wait. The *Boston* Red Stockings?

Right. When Cincinnati folded, Wright accepted the offer of backers in Boston to put together a team for them. He took along the now famous name, if not the actual socks, and it was from this base that he pushed for the formation of the first pro league.

He also brought with him to Boston a younger brother, George, who had been considered the best all-around player on the Red Stockings as the short fielder, and three other Cincinnati veterans. Harry had unparalleled knowledge of all the best players in the country, since he had spent two years criss-crossing the continent, observing them as opponents and hearing in detail about anyone he didn't see.

Since Asa Brainerd, his Cincinnati pitcher, had decided to join Washington Olympic, he needed a pitcher for Boston.

And he knew where to get one.

Enter Mr. Spalding, who will dominate baseball's next 40 years.

Albert Goodwill Spalding came from a prosperous Illinois farm family that settled, when he was a child, in Rockford, about 100 miles west and slightly north of Chicago. By the time he was 16, he was a good enough player to pitch for the adult Rockford team, which the town leaders backed eagerly.

In 1867, the already professional (unofficially) Washington Nationals were considered the national champions. (George Wright was their star player.) On a western tour that July, they were to play the highly regarded Chicago Excelsiors, the strongest team of that area, in a much publicized confrontation. On the way, they had beaten Columbus 90–10 and Indianapolis 106–21. The day before they were to play the Excelsiors, they accepted a warm-up game against the humble Rockford team, whose players were thrilled and honored simply to be on the same field.

Spalding, not yet 17, pitched.

Rockford won, 29–23.

The next day, the Nationals whipped Chicago 49–4.

Spalding was noticed.

The Excelsiors promptly offered him a place on their team, arranging for a grocery firm in Chicago to give him a job that would not interfere with baseball activity, at $40 a week—about eight times the going wage for an inexperienced employee. Spalding, who had a year of high school left, accepted after some soul-searching. But he played only one game in September before the grocery firm went bankrupt (not so surprising, is it?) and he went home to Rockford.

Pitching there in 1868, 1869, and 1870, he acquired a national reputation. With

Spalding and Ross Barnes, Rockford also had two outstanding hitters. They consistently defeated all the top teams in the midwest and lost 14–13 to the 1869 Red Stockings only when Cincinnati scored three runs in the ninth.

So Wright knew firsthand what Spalding could do. He persuaded the pitcher to come to Boston, paying him $1,500 a year. Wright's own salary, as boss, was only $2,500, so this was high pay at a time when the average income nationally was less than $500 a year.

Wright also signed Barnes, so with four of his former Cincinnati players his Boston team was a powerhouse, expected to win the championship right from the start.

It didn't, but before we go into what happened, let's take a snapshot of the game on the field in 1871.

The pitching distance is 45 feet. The pitcher must have both feet within the box, six feet wide and four feet deep, behind the 45-foot line, and must use a straight-armed delivery (no bent elbow) with the arm parallel to the ground and no higher than the hip. He can, however, snap his wrist to produce spin.

The batter can order a high or low delivery. High means shoulder to waist; low means waist to knees. Unless the pitch is both over the plate and in the specified area, it is not a called strike. It takes nine "unfair" balls (out of the strike zone) to get a walk.

The other rules are essentially the ones we are familiar with. But fielders don't yet have gloves, and catchers stand well back from the batter.

As the 1871 season unfolded, it became clear that the requirement of five games against each opponent wouldn't be met. It called for a minimum of 45 games for each team. None actually played more than 33. (They played many more games than that against non-Association opponents; in fact, unofficial games were too convenient and profitable to pass up.) Still, a close race developed involving Philadelphia, Boston, and Chicago.

The teams had until November 1 to complete their schedules. Chicago was ahead, and in a position to win, when the Great Fire of October 17, 1871, destroyed its ball park. The White Stockings had to play their remaining few games on the road, and lost them. Then they dropped out of the league for two years.

When the season was over, Philadelphia's record was 21–7, Boston's 20–10 and Chicago's 19–9. Philadelphia was declared champion: it had the largest number of victories. When Wright tried to argue that his team deserved the title because it had played a greater number of the required games, he got nowhere.

However, he never had to argue again. His Red Stockings won the next four championships, more and more impressively.

> In 1872, they were 39–8 to Baltimore's 35–19.
> In 1873, they were 43–16 to Philadelphia's 38–17.
> In 1874, they were 52–18 to New York's 42–23.
> In 1875, they were 71–8 to Hartford's 54–28.

In those five years, Spalding won 205 of Boston's 225 victories. He was a .325 hitter. He was young, tall, handsome, well-spoken, respectable, sociable, and vigorous. He was baseball's first true star, known and admired nationwide.

And at that point, the league died.

But not just because of Boston.

The two central flaws, unsupervised scheduling and cheap entry fee, had done their work. Of 11 teams that started the 1872 season, only four played as many as 30 official games. In 1873, only nine began and six finished. In 1874, only eight started, and all but one stuck it out. In 1875, with the glamour of major league baseball established, 13 teams tried it, including Keokuk, Iowa, and New Haven, Connecticut. But six were gone by midseason. It was too hard to stay competitive, too easy to drop out.

Through the five seasons, only Boston, Philadelphia, and New York played every year, although Chicago would have if not for the fire.

And that wasn't all. There was no mechanism for central discipline in other matters. Clubs argued about gate receipts and how they should be divided (or honestly reported). Players found to be involved in gambling or drunkenness or rowdy behavior could not be controlled—if they could play well—because they'd be hired by another team if fired. Any player could go to another team for a better deal anytime he wanted to when his contract expired, and the contract did not have to cover a full season.

Such conditions not only prevented others from matching Wright's superior organization and prestige, but confused and displeased the public.

Why was organization so loose? Because the original concept of an association of "players" had never been questioned. It was players, after all, who had formed amateur clubs. The National Association had merely accepted professionalism, not abandoned the "club" idea. The activity had evolved into a business—the business of staging baseball games—but proficiency in performance does not guarantee proficiency in business. An enormously efficient self-selection process in terms of playing ability had produced the professional performers; but those individuals could not be expected to also be skilled in running a business, or managing capital, or administering an organization. Yet all decision-making power was in player hands, and players made decisions based on what seemed good for themselves, not on what objective judgement might dictate would be good for the enterprise.

A different approach was required, and there were people who understood what that was. Even in five short years, U.S. society had undergone significant change. The war was receding, the frontier was being settled, the railroads and banks were revealing their power, immigration was gaining momentum again, technological advance was accelerating. The entrepreneur (and would-be entrepreneur) was king.

Businessmen had to take charge of the business.

It was that simple.

But how?

A fellow in Chicago had an idea.

A "national association of players" amounted to letting the inmates run the asylum. What was needed was "a national *league of clubs*" with authority vested in the club as an ongoing business firm, not in transient athletes.

Sound businessmen had to be in charge. The players had to be simply employees.

This was, after all, the year 1876: the Centennial of the United States of America, whose celebration in Philadelphia that summer would feature the world's latest technological progress; the era of men who would come to be called The Robber Barons; an age of explosive growth, opportunity, expansion, innovation. The gentleman's-club idea of a generation ago was ancient history. Its vestiges could only get in the way of the new religion—honest effort to make a lot of money wherever and however it was to be made.

The Chicagoan ready to pursue his idea was William Ambrose Hulbert. The man he needed to make it work was Albert Goodwill Spalding. When they got together, "baseball as we know it" began.

And their first order of business, as it had been for Harry Wright only five years before, was to carry out a preemptive strike against the existing order.

PART II

THE LEAGUE

CHAPTER 3

Chicago

After the Great Fire of 1871, Chicago had to be rebuilt from the ground up, and its status as one of the world's great urban centers dates from that reconstruction. William Hulbert, a coal merchant, was one of the many aggressive businessmen who took part in that rebuilding. Like many of his class and outlook, he equated a city's baseball team with boosterism, apart from the considerable enjoyment he got out of the game itself, and became a stockholder. While the National Association was establishing national interest in a pennant race, however rudimentary, Chicago had been shut out of the process in 1872 and 1873. By 1874, when a new site for a ball park had been established at 23d Street and Clark, a White Stockings team reentered National Association competition, but it was too weak to keep pace with the powerful teams in Boston, Philadelphia, and New York. When Hulbert was offered the presidency of the White Sox after the 1874 season, he turned his attention to the heart of the matter: in order to have a good team, you have to get good players.

By now, rules had been made forbidding a team to approach players on another team while a season was still in progress. But with no central authority to enforce that rule (or any other), pirating players had become common. The piracy produced a flow eastward as the strong got stronger, and when the rights to a player were in dispute, the official decision rested on internal politics. In these disputes, matters of regional chauvinism came into play, as westerners felt that the "Eastern Establishment"—the Boston–New York–Philadelphia axis—was taking advantage of them in freight rates and finances as well as snubbing them culturally and socially, far beyond baseball.

Spalding, his star persona established by his activities in Boston, came back to Rockford at the end of the 1874 season a newlywed. His mother still lived there; his younger brother, Walter, was now 19; and his sister was there with her husband. Naturally, the paths of Hulbert and Spalding crossed, and Hulbert made his pitch.

The pirating of players made it impossible, he noted, for a weak western team to build itself up against eastern opponents. The White Stockings had just lost an important infielder, Davey Force, to the Athletics. Somehow, Chicago had to engage in retaliatory piracy in a big way.

Then he said, according to Spalding: "Spalding, you've no business playing in Boston; you're a western boy, and you belong right here. If you'll come to Chicago, I'll accept the presidency of this club, and we'll give those fellows a fight for their lives."

Spalding didn't say yes—but he didn't say no. He made it clear he'd be interested and that he'd bring others with him. Hulbert took the club presidency. The alliance had been formed.

What Spalding didn't describe in his books, leaving for later historians to note, was his personal shift of focus. He had business ideas of his own, stimulated by his experience in 1874.

Even as a teenager, his eye for commercial possibilities was sharp. He noted even before he went to Boston that Harry Wright and his brother had opened a sporting-goods store in New York. He learned soon enough that Al Reach was involved in the manufacture of baseballs and had a sporting goods store in Philadelphia. And as the star attraction in the organized, if imperfect, National Association, he saw firsthand how the success of the professionals added to the popularity of baseball among amateur players (especially children and students). Well, those who wanted to play needed equipment—balls, bats, uniforms—which someone had to supply. And name recognition on the manufactured article couldn't hurt.

With all this in mind, and under the tutelage of Wright, who understood it so well, Spalding was exposed to something in 1874 that broadened his horizons.

Wright had been born in England. So had Henry Chadwick, the chief propagandist for baseball and its ranking expert, historian, and statistician. Both had roots in cricket and continuous contact with the many professional English cricketers who kept visiting the United States and drawing large crowds against local cricket teams. Wright decided it would be a good idea to display this uniquely American offshoot to the mother country.

He chose Spalding as his delegate.

Since the official schedule called for fewer than 80 games in a seven-month span (April through October), there was plenty of room for a side tour. Arranging it with his English contacts, Wright sent Spalding over to nail down the details. At home, he persuaded the Philadelphia Athletics to come along. They would play baseball games against each other, and the combined group would also (as Spalding promised, to Wright's horror) play some cricket games against English teams.

They sailed on July 17 and didn't return until September. The baseball teams played 14 games in London, Manchester, Dublin, and Sheffield and (to Spalding's delight) even won the cricket games, because the American batters, knowing no better, simply whacked away and hit the ball all over the field.

This experience gave Spalding, who turned 24 that September, enormous confidence in his management capabilities. He dealt with English nobility and snobbery, as well as hard-headed businessmen, in circumstances where he found himself comfortable socially, and smarter than most. Artistically, the tour was a success. Financially, it lost money. But the western-bred American gained sophistication.

Back home, he saw that, among other things, the National Association had no real future. If two teams could leave the country for so long in the middle of the season, the bonds at home were weak. But whether or not the Association flourished, baseball itself certainly would. Even the English seemed to enjoy it. One way or another, baseball would continue to spread—and supplying its implements was where the real money might be.

So when Hulbert approached Spalding about switching to Chicago, Spalding was already forming his plans. The Wrights' businesses in New York and Boston, and Reach's in Philadelphia, could be reproduced without competition in Chicago. His brother, Walter, was turning 20 and already working in a bank. They could set up a sporting-goods firm in Chicago that would take full advantage of the Spalding name.

Spalding made none of this explicit, although Hulbert probably felt the vibrations. At any rate, when he was ready to make a formal offer to Spalding, it was readily accepted. But it had to be kept secret, of course. The 1875 season had begun. To sign players, even for a future season, would be a violation for which they could be expelled.

All concerned had plenty of experience with secret contracts; they weren't that far removed from the "amateur" days when private deals were the rule. Spalding signed up, for Chicago, three of his best teammates—Ross Barnes, his old pal from Rockford; Cal McVey, who had been with Wright in Cincinnati; and Jim (Deacon) White, his catcher. And he also landed the best player in Philadelphia, Adrian (Cap) Anson, who had been with him on the English tour, complaining about how little money the players got for it.

But the secret couldn't be kept—and here we have, early in the story, a truth that permeates baseball to this day: there are no secrets. Everything leaks, sooner rather than later, because the whole enterprise rests on generating publicity, so that countless individuals are conditioned to have a vested interest in getting information out somehow.

When the planned defection became known, in June 1875, the Spalding coterie was vilified in Boston as "traitors." But no action was taken against them by the Association, as they were on their way to a 71–8 season, winning every single home game.

They got away with it then—but they knew they might not get away with it again. For 1876, the eastern powers could, and probably would, expel them.

Hulbert decided not to wait.

"We'll form our own association, and not wait for them to act," he and Spalding decided. And Spalding settled down at Hulbert's house to outline what became the constitution of the National League of Baseball Clubs, with emphasis on the "clubs."

It contained some radical principles.

1. The schedule would be drawn up by the League, and any club that didn't abide by it would be punished. This change set the stage for fair competition and an authentic pennant race.
2. Each club would honor every other club's contracts and—more important—abide by a blacklist: any player suspended for any reason by his own club would not be offered work by any other.
3. There would be a franchise exclusivity: only one League member in any city, and other members could not bring in other games.
4. Only cities with populations of more than 75,000 would be accepted for membership, to insure sufficient market size. (There were, in the 1870 census, only 17 such cities in the 38 United States of America, and two of them, San Francisco and New Orleans, were clearly out of transportation range.)
5. The franchise entry fee was $100. Every club would have autonomy in dealing with its own players but be subject to League authority in all interclub matters (including rights to a player).
6. The League, using the blacklist, would make a concerted effort to upgrade and maintain the "respectability" of the game, essential to broadening the customer base. In particular, severe penalties (essentially expulsion) would be imposed for gambling and fixing games, drunkenness or other rowdy behavior, contract jumping, and other violations of club-imposed discipline.
7. In that connection, no alcoholic beverages would be sold and no open betting permitted, within the grounds; no games would be played on the Sabbath; and umpires would be assigned by the League, not by local clubs.
8. The basic admission price would be 50 cents, with a fixed share to go to the visiting team. Machinery for honest accounting would be in place.

The next step was to get such a well-structured and ambitious plan accepted.

In December, Hulbert contacted three strong midwestern cities who had independent teams, Cincinnati, Louisville, and St. Louis (although St. Louis had played in the National Association in 1875 only). If they would put forth a unified proposal, the stronger eastern clubs might go along. At a meeting in Louisville, they agreed.

On February 2, 1876, Hulbert took charge of a meeting held at the Central Hotel on Broadway in New York, a few blocks from where the National Association had been formed less than five years before under Wright's leadership. The westerners had invited selected easterners to attend. Hulbert locked the door "to prevent intrusion" and made his presentation. The invited clubs—Philadelphia, New York, Boston, and Hartford—heard him out.

They bought it.

Consider Wright's position. He had every reason to feel betrayed by what Spalding had done. Instead, he understood better than anyone that the structure of the National Association was crumbling, and he was hearing, in the Hulbert plan, many of the conclusions he had come to himself. The league of clubs concept was exactly what was needed. To resist it would be foolish and self-defeating. To join it was by far the wisest course.

Thus began the National League, which was ready to play its first game in 82 days and which, in 1998, played its 123d consecutive season. It established a pattern that became the model for all commercialized spectator team sports from then on.

The League had eight charter members.

City	Team Name	Population	Chief Officer
Boston	Red Stockings	300,000	Harry Wright
New York	Mutuals	1,000,000	William Cammayer
Philadelphia	Athletics	900,000	George Thompson
Hartford	Dark Blues	40,000	Morgan G. Bulkeley
Chicago	White Stockings	400,000	William Hulbert
Cincinnati	Reds	250,000	Josiah L. Keck
St. Louis	Brown Stockings	330,000	Charles Fowle
Louisville	Grays	110,000	Walter L. Haldeman

Note: Boston ownership was represented by Nathaniel T. Appolonio, and Wright served as secretary at the February 2 meeting; but on all serious baseball decisions, Wright's prestige and experience made him de facto head of the Boston club. Fowle was the owner of the St. Louis team, but his attorney, Campbell O. Bishop, also took an active role and actually wrote out, in legal language, the National League constitution Spalding and Hulbert had outlined.

The inclusion of Hartford clearly violated the population target, but the rules provided for an exception if all the other clubs approved. They had reason to approve Hartford. Once the idea of a league was accepted, the westerners had to make political peace with the easterners, who were, all in all, still much more powerful. Bulkeley, the head of the Hartford club (which had finished a strong third behind the Red Stockings and Athletics in 1875) was an influential man. Still in his late 30's, he was the son of the founder of the Aetna Insurance Company, successful on his own as a merchant in Brooklyn and after his father's death in 1872 founder of a bank in

Hartford. That baseball team's chief backer, he eventually would become mayor of Hartford for four terms, governor of Connecticut, and a U.S. senator. He was president of Aetna from 1879 until his death in 1922.

Hulbert certainly could not have foreseen all that, but he knew a live one when he saw one. That Bulkeley gladly confessed that his interest in baseball was limited and just a hobby only made things better: Hulbert had him elected president of the new league, giving the easterners top representation without the danger of too much interference.

And the westerners went further. As secretary-treasurer—in effect, the whole administrative staff of the game—they chose Nick Young of Washington, well-known to all of them as an active participant in baseball affairs going back to the 1860's, as player and umpire as well as in business matters.

Part of the deal was for Spalding to be both captain and manager of the White Stockings. (A team captain was what we now think of as the field manager, in charge of the players. The "manager" did all the business functions, providing for the grounds, travel, payroll, advertising, ticket selling, security, and everything else we now associate with the "front office".) Five other teams also had player-captain-managers: Wright, who could still fill in as an outfield if necessary at the age of 40; Bob Ferguson, a third baseman, at Hartford; Charlie Gould, a first baseman, at Cincinnati; Chuck Fullmer, a shortstop, at Louisville; and Herman Dehlman, a first baseman, at St. Louis. The other two teams (and this would prove significant) gave their business managers field-manager duties: New York's Cammeyer (who, back in 1862, was one of the first to invest money in an enclosed playing ground so that admission could be charged), and Al Wright (no relation to the famous Wrights) in Philadelphia.

Unity achieved, the League put out its schedule. Each team was to play every other team 10 times, with no more than five of those games on its home field. That meant a 70-game campaign, three games a week between April 22 and October 21.

Creating a rational setup was one thing. Making it work was something else. Identifying problems did not make them evaporate.

The central issue was League authority, and it was tested the first year. The White Stockings, with their new lineup, were every bit as overwhelming as expected, so there was no exciting pennant race. They won 52 games and lost only 14, and the only teams within sighting distance were St. Louis (45–19) and Hartford (47–21). That these totals fell short of the 70 games scheduled reflected rained-out games that weren't made up.

But by midseason, it was evident that the New York and Philadelphia teams weren't competitive. In addition, the Athletics were constantly upstaged at home by the special events connected with the Centennial. Neither team saw any reason to make a scheduled late-season western trip to Chicago and St. Louis. They were already losing money, and this would be an added expense, while if they played nonleague games in their home areas they could recoup a little. That, after all, was the business as usual their business-manager directors had been accustomed to.

Hulbert was, in practice, the League president, while Bulkeley performed his figurehead function to perfection by staying aloof. Hulbert rejected both teams' requests to be excused. Nor would he accept offers of payment to the host clubs as compensation. The whole idea of a League-directed schedule was to establish the integrity of the competition.

Nevertheless, the Mutuals and the Athletics stayed home. New York wound up 21–35 and Philadelphia 14–45.

The showdown came at the annual meeting in December. Bulkeley, who would be resigning, didn't even attend. Hulbert, who was about to assume the League presidency officially, was in charge. The two teams that had failed to live up to their schedule commitments were expelled.

Expelled!

Did this make any sense? New York and Philadelphia were the two largest markets in the League—in the country, in fact—with the longest and richest baseball traditions. Their combined population exceeded those of the other six clubs put together, by 50 percent, and they occupied the hub of national communications and finance. What kind of "major league" could you have without them?

Was Hulbert, as president of the White Stockings, trying to eliminate potential rivals?

Would those who predicted the League would never work be proved right so quickly?

But Hulbert, of course, was the one proved right. Either the League could exert its authority over *any* club, or it couldn't. If it couldn't, it was no different than the Association had been. The rule of internal law had to prevail, not as an abstraction but as an example for the future and as a demonstration of present resolve. It took a lot of nerve for Hulbert to do what he did (and a lot of persuasiveness to make others go along), but his was a crucial decision that preserved the league concept.

Could the League continue with just six teams? It could try. It meant geographic imbalance—only Boston and Hartford as eastern clubs, with Chicago, St. Louis, Cincinnati, and Louisville in the west. (At this time the geographic center of U.S. population was a few miles *east* of Cincinnati.) It also meant a scanty schedule—10 games with each opponent made only a 50-game season, still spread over six months, an average of only two games a week (or some weeks with no games at all).

On the other hand, the League didn't abandon the New York metropolis entirely. Hartford had been an anomaly in size, included for political reasons, and Bulkeley, the biggest political reason, was stepping out anyhow. To compromise with the rule of expulsion would be unthinkable—but if, as Cammeyer arranged, the Hartford Dark Blues could play their home games as his tenant in Brooklyn, three problems would be solved at once. Brooklyn, still a separate city, had a population of more than 500,000.

That's what was done. For all practical purposes, Hartford became "Brooklyn."

The competitive situation was different too. The White Stockings, suddenly, were not the overwhelming force. Spalding had decided to pitch no more, probably because his arm was going dead but also because he was paying more attention to the sporting-goods store. (One of his biographers believed it was because he had never mastered curveball pitching, then becoming widespread; his specialty had been changes of speed.) Deacon White, the great catcher and hitter, had returned to Boston. A change in the rules (about which more presently) made Barnes ineffective. The outstanding pitcher acquired from St. Louis to replace Spalding, George Bradley, didn't pan out in Chicago. With Spalding managing from the bench, the White Stockings went through a 26–33 season. Boston, bolstered by White, went 42–18.

But the real story of 1877 was the second fundamental test: coping with the crooks.

Fixed games had been a persistent problem in the National Association, as well as in as in less formal competition. Sports automatically attract gamblers, and at least some gamblers try to arrange sure things. You can never guarantee victory, but you can guarantee defeat. A player himself might decide to bet against his own team, or have someone bet for him, or accept a bribe to insure the result. Such manipulation was hard to prove, easy to do without leaving evidence, easy to deny if accused, hard to prevent. But if the public couldn't believe that the games were on the level, both the financial and emotional underpinnings of the entertainment would be destroyed.

One of the strongest motives for forming a club-controlled league was that it could crack down on suspected players with suspensions that had teeth because of the blacklist.

During the first season, there had been rumors and suspicion—endemic to all baseball then—but no overt incident.

In 1877 one occurred.

The only team strong enough to challenge Boston was Louisville. In fact, it was in first place and well on its way to winning the pennant when it ran into a mysterious losing streak. At 27–13 in mid-August, it suddenly lost eight straight, and the team's president, Charles Chase, was alerted that foul play (no pun involved) was afoot. He investigated and forced confessions from four players, including Art Devlin, the pitcher who was the team's main strength, and George Hall, its best hitter. Louisville finished 35–25, seven games behind Boston, and when Chase unearthed telegrams proving the guilt of four players, he suspended them.

At the winter meeting that December, the League upheld the suspensions, made them life-long—and made them stick. Despite persistent and pitiful pleas, none of the guilty ever played another National League game.

And by that time, the League had faced the third fundamental threat: dropouts.

In 1876, the Cincinnati team had been the worst—nine victories, 56 defeats. In the 1877 season the club started out even worse. By mid-June the owner, meatpacker

Josiah Keck, had had enough. He simply dissolved the team. Just as it was to start an eastern trip, he called the players together and told them, "Go if you want to, at your own expense," or words to that effect.

They didn't, of course, and Hulbert found himself in an awkward position. As president of the League, he considered it essential to have the schedule played out; as president of the White Stockings, who were already losing so regularly, he wanted Charlie Jones, a hard-hitting outfielder who was Cincinnati's best players.

For more than two weeks, the Cincinnati franchise was in limbo. Then another Cincinnati businessman was found to assume Keck's baseball debts, and the team resumed play on July 3. Hulbert reluctantly returned Jones, without whom Cincinnati had no hope of retaining even a limited following. Cincinnati did finish out the season, with a 15–42 record, but the franchise was dead. At the winter meeting, the team was officially expelled for not paying its $100 dues back in June, and its games were declared null and void—although what difference that made after the season was over was hard to understand.

So the League was in bad shape approaching its third year. Only the White Stockings were in the black. But another development in 1877, proved more important in the long run than any other. The ownership of the Boston club had passed from Apollonio to Arthur Soden, who would prove second only to the Hulbert-Spalding combination in directing the shape of the baseball business for the next couple of decades.

But not right away.

Rejecting appeals from New York and Philadelphia, Hulbert decided to stick with six teams again in 1878. Three of them were new: Milwaukee, Indianapolis, and Providence. Boston and Chicago were stable. The sixth was a new franchise in Cincinnati. The League that had started out only two years before with an aggregate population of nearly 3.5 million now encompassed only 1.4 million. The Brooklyn outlet was gone. Louisville had been killed by its scandal. St. Louis was neither successful enough, nor close enough, to keep going.

The result was a nondescript season whose chief achievement was survival. Boston won again with 41–19 to 37–23 for the new Cincinnati team, managed by McVey and making the most of his identity as an original 1869 Red Stocking. Chicago, finishing fourth behind Providence, was no longer managed by Spalding, who had turned his full attention to business, but by Bob Ferguson, a name we should know. A Brooklynite born the year the Knickerbockers played their first game, he was a prominent amateur player when the National Association was formed and played in it with the Mutuals, Atlantics, and Providence. In 1872 he served as the Association's president. In 1876, he came into the League with Hartford as its manager and third baseman and moved on to Chicago, where Hulbert made him manager and shortstop.

As for Indianapolis (24–36) and Milwaukee (15–45), one year was enough. At the end of the season they dropped out.

A six-team league didn't work. The number made the official schedule too diffuse. For 1879, new entries were found and the league returned to eight, never again to have fewer members than that.

Only seven teams would make it through the season, however, focusing attention on another basic League-directed proposition and setting the stage for a solution Soden would advance.

The holdovers were Boston, Chicago, Providence, and Cincinnati. The newcomers were Cleveland (population 160,000), Buffalo (155,000), Syracuse (52,000), and Troy (50,000). The last two clearly violated the 75,000 target, but Buffalo and Syracuse fought harder against the other rule: a 50-cent admission fee. They felt it was too high for their local economies (and they were right), but the League would not budge. Again the issue was unified authority. Buffalo, with a strong team on the field, struggled along for four seasons. Syracuse packed it in halfway through its first.

But the example of strong central authority played into hands of Soden's idea. From the very beginning (that is, the Cincinnati Red Stockings), club owners tended to look upon player salaries as the controllable expense. (Other costs went up even faster, sometimes, but they couldn't control those—an approach even more devoutly believed in 100 years later.) The problem was, the owners had to give the better players more money each year, or a rival club would offer it to them. The blacklist had some effect on players who went outside the league structure, but all the players who mattered were inside it. Soden's idea went to the heart of the problem: let's stop bidding against each other.

The 1879 season ended with Providence, led by George Wright, as champion, six games ahead of Harry Wright's Boston. Buffalo and Chicago, whose managership had been turned over to Cap Anson, tied for third. Ferguson had taken over Troy and finished last. Nobody made any money but Chicago.

On September 29, 1879, at a special meeting in Buffalo, Soden's plan was adopted. It was the famous reserve system on which the baseball business would rest for the next century, and, in modified form, still does.

It was worded this way: each club would "reserve" five players from this year's team from the open market. The other League members would agree not to hire anyone on another team's reserve list. Thus, the reserved players, presumably the best on that team, would have no alternative but to stay on the owners' teams or leave the League altogether, with no comparable league to go to. Just as the League members honored each other's contracts and abided by other League regulations, they would abide by this one for the good of the whole, even if a particular case hurt a particular club.

Furthermore, the clubs agreed not to play any team, even from outside the League, that hired a reserved player.

In one sense, at this point, being reserved was a distinction: it did guarantee employment for the next season, at the expense of bargaining power for a higher salary (and, if you were one of the best players, the club had some motive to keep you at least reasonably satisfied with your wages). Also, if the reserve system stabilized the business (which it did), it was of indirect benefit to all players. If enough teams went broke, no one would have a job.

That was the practical side, in the circumstances of the time. In principle, this form of indentured service—you were tied to an employer even *after* your contract had expired, and could not work elsewhere—could not be justified and would soon be attacked. But aside from principles, it obviously invited abuse, and the invitation would be accepted in due course. Struggle over the ramifications of the reserve system set the tone for the rest of the 19th century and will permeate our story from now on.

In 1880, therefore, the League started out with unprecedented stability. Seven of the teams that had finished 1879 were in action again, with a continuity of leadership. The eighth team, replacing Syracuse, was Worcester, Massachusetts.

If you're wondering about the "major league" status at that time of cities like Providence, Hartford, Worcester, and Troy (which is on the east side of the Hudson River across from Albany, New York's state capital), look at a map. In the 1870's and 1880's, the Boston–New York corridor and the triangle formed with Albany contained the oldest, best-developed, most populous area of the United States, long since criss-crossed by railroad connections, occupied by the highest proportion of wealthy and near-wealthy citizens, a region compact, interactive, familiar. Larger cities to the west were more isolated from each other. Throughout baseball history, ease of transportation and communication has been a key factor in determining the alignment of leagues.

Thus the 1870's, which began with old baseball organization unraveling, ended with new organization finally beginning to get a firm foothold.

There was no question that the National League, entering its fifth season, was the top of the baseball pyramid.

Playing rules had kept evolving, in small ways, to make the game itself more coherent. The League established standards for the ball it would use (Spalding got that contract in 1878), how a field should be marked, how umpires should conduct games. And one rule made a fundamental difference—the one that ruined the career of Ross Barnes.

It used to be that a batted ball would be considered fair if it first touched the ground in fair territory, even if it then kicked foul before passing first or third base. Barnes was a master of this "fair-foul" type of hit. In 1877, this was changed to the rule we've had ever since: if it goes foul *before* passing first or third, it's foul. (It was not a strike, though; fouls still simply didn't count.)

Under the old rule, back in the Association and in the first year of the League, Barnes had hit .401, .422, .428, .344, .361, and .429, winning the first National League batting title in 1876. Under the new rule, he hit .272, sat out 1878, and hit .266 in 1879. Then he retired.

The pitching rules didn't change drastically in this era: the 45-foot distance, delivery release below the waist, batter ordering a high or low strike, nine balls for a walk. What was different was the caliber of pitching and defense as professionals faced one another. In 1871, when the Association began, the average game produced 20.9 runs (by both teams). By 1875, this was down to 12.27; by 1879, it was 10.62.

Gloves were coming into use (barely padded, fingers cut off, sometimes worn on both hands), and catcher's masks. Primarily, though, it was a matter of professionalism—men making their living from perfecting skills they had started to acquire before their teens, knowing what their goals were.

Consider again our imaginary original member of the Knickerbocker club. He is now 60 years old. His interest in baseball is greater than ever but satisfied entirely by watching and reading about these well-organized games. His sons are teaching their little sons to share the passion and buying Spalding's equipment for them to play with. Wives and daughters aren't generally included yet, although in this family they probably are.)

The ball parks—"grounds," as they are usually called—are all fully enclosed, equipped with turnstiles. The wooden grandstands, extending not much past first and third base, are augmented by standing-room areas beyond that. Few have dressing-room facilities for visiting teams, so the colorful procession of players in uniform from hotel to ball park is part of game-day festivity.

The League has settled on Tuesday, Thursday, and Saturday for championship games. (That's why a team can get by with one pitcher working virtually every official game.) On most other days, the team plays nonleague games, many in nonleague cities, at lower ticket prices.

Newspapers cover the local team on a daily basis. The Western Union wires deliver news of out-of-town games promptly. Weekly newspapers devoted primarily to sports news flourish. Spalding and others are publishing increasingly elaborate annual record books and instruction manuals. By 1878, the sporting-goods industry (not just Spalding) is turning out half a million bats, millions of balls, and thousands of uniforms—and selling them.

Hulbert's goal—setting up baseball on a businesslike basis—is being achieved.

CHAPTER 4

Two Leagues

The 1880's offered a foretaste of what baseball would become after the turn of the century. Formats that would eventually produce permanent prosperity displayed their practicality, but it was not yet time for them to take hold, nor did they withstand miscalculation. Six items displayed their virtue:

1. Two major leagues, with distinct characteristics, can function perfectly well as long as they don't compete for players and do share the same reserve system.
2. Two league champions create a natural matchup for a "world's championship series."
3. Playing rules must be adjusted periodically to help the offense.
4. A system of minor leagues, dominated by the majors to suit their own purposes, is both possible and necessary.
5. More teams automatically create more stars, especially when statistics are systematized and widely disseminated.
6. Beer and baseball can't be kept apart.

Also demonstrated were some things that don't work:

1. Three leagues
2. Excessive restraints on salaries
3. More than one club under the same ownership

The six positives would, in due course, become institutionalized and are imbedded in today's baseball. The three negatives arise again and again and seem to be lessons that have to be relearned periodically.

Whether or not imitation is the sincerest form of flattery, as the saying goes, it is certainly inevitable when some model becomes successful. And in 1880, the National League started to show that it really was successful. The schedule was increased to 84 games (12 against each opponent), and all eight teams completed it. And although there was no close pennant race, the dominant team created a new type of glamour. The rebuilt Chicago White Stockings, under Anson, finished 15 games ahead of Providence (67–17 to 52–32) and started a run of three straight pennants. When Boston had been a perennial champion in the National Association, it had ruined everything. But now conditions were significantly different. A comprehensive (and comprehensible) schedule; a history based on statistics; a well-oiled publicity machine, of which the Spalding, Reach, and Wright retailers were as much a part as the newspapers; a more firmly established concept of "major league," commanding nationwide reading interest beyond participation; the establishment of credibility in the integrity of the games; all these made a "superteam" and a "dynasty" an attraction instead of a turnoff, and the regularity of schedule made it possible for the other teams to cash in appropriately from visits by and to the glamorous team.

The White Stockings of the early 1880's were the first such phenomenons to be brought to its highest degree by the New York Yankees in the middle of the 20th century.

The reserve system permitted an immediate cut in salaries for 1880. That season, not all the clubs finished in the black, but it was clear they soon would. Hulbert, going into 1881, declared publicly that never before had the League been on such a sound basis financially, and it wasn't propaganda. Historians would find that club profits of 15 to 33 percent of gross revenues were not uncommon in the early 1880's.

The example was not lost on other eager entrepreneurs. Their reaction (which we'll see recur as regularly as the workings of the solar system) could be summed up in three short words: "Let me in."

The League, however, had no intention of expanding beyond eight members. Its appeal was based to a large extent on its exclusivity. It had found a size big enough for practical purposes, small enough for maximum sharing of the benefits. The last thing the insiders wanted was more partners.

So those denied entry went immediately to reaction number 2: "Let's start our own league."

After all, an enormous amount of baseball activity was still going on, with plenty of well-educated spectators, in non-League cities, including New York and Philadelphia. While the League had included some smaller cities, there were many much larger cities outside its jurisdiction.

When the Mutuals were expelled from the League and Hartford ended its one year of Brooklyn residence, New Yorkers did not lose their interest in baseball. Various local teams booked games with other professionals, and "exhibition games" with League teams. Since there was no New York League franchise, the other League members could play there without violating their own territorial and other restrictive rules.

John B. Day, a young cigar wholesaler, proved to be the most astute promoter of such an independent team. He called it the Metropolitans and hired an equally young and ambitious man named Jim Mutrie, fresh from New Bedford, Massachusetts, to run it. More important, he found a better place to play than Brooklyn, which was not yet connected to Manhattan by a bridge. Central Park had been finally completed in 1876, and immediately north of it, from 110th to 112th Street west of Fifth Avenue, was a place called "the polo grounds" because polo was played there.

Day leased it, put in a baseball field and some seats, and started drawing fine crowds for his Met games. The team played its first game there in September 1880.

A couple of months later, the National League expelled Cincinnati, over the familiar issue of League authority. The Reds had insisted on selling beer at their games—naturally enough, since their ownership was involved with a brewery, one of two dozen in a city whose citizens had German roots. Just as Hulbert would not give in to Buffalo or Syracuse on the 50-cent issue, he wouldn't give in on the prohibition of liquor. The League took in Worcester as its eighth team instead.

The outrage in Cincinnati was predictable, expressed volubly by Oliver Perry ("O.P.") Caylor, sports editor of the *Enquirer*. Also offended by the League's arrogance was Alfred H. Spink in St. Louis, who was promoting the improvement of baseball grounds on Grand Avenue, to be known as Sportsman's Park. Across the street, his good friend Chris Von der Ahe had a saloon, and although Von der Ahe knew nothing about baseball, he was extremely interested in the evident thirst of baseball spectators. Spink suggested to Caylor that they form teams carrying the famous names of the "Browns" (St. Louis) and the "Reds" (Cincinnati) and play some games. This enterprise turned out to be a big success during the summer of 1881. Other independents made comparable arrangements, in other cities.

At the same time, the Mets were playing the unheard-of total of 151 games against all comers, including 60 against league teams. (They won 18 of those, a .300 pace considerably better than the .250—40 victories, 120 defeats—produced by their namesakes 81 years later when they first faced National League competition.) Meanwhile, in the League, the White Stockings rolled along to another impressive championship, with a 56–28 record to Providence's 47–37 and Buffalo's 45–38.

The League was now making money—but so were others. The number of proficient players was increasing naturally and rapidly, as more and more young men developed their talents in hopes of a career, and as the pool of League discards, for disciplinary or other reasons, grew. Another of Spalding's bright ideas was the creation, back in 1877, of the League Alliance. Independents who had formed the International Association—the term "minor league" wasn't used yet—were invited to come under the National League's wing. The League had been picking off the International Association's improving players at will. Now it offered to honor the International Association's player contracts during a season—in return for authority over its activities. Pretty soon the League was dictating regulations, such as only one League Alliance team per city and no games against nonmembers, in the prototype of a minor league system. But a by-product was to increase the production of skilled players.

So, as 1882 approached, conditions were ripe for action. Caylor and Justus Thorner, who had been president of the Cincinnati team connected with the Sohn brewery, sought out Denny McKnight of Pittsburgh. McKnight, an iron manufacturer, had run a team called the Alleghenys in the International Association, which had just dissolved (while other minor leagues were joining the League Alliance). The three of them and Spink, who had not yet launched the *Sporting News,* the weekly paper that would become the bible of baseball, decided to form their own league.

They called it the American Association.

Cincinnati, St. Louis, Pittsburgh, and Louisville, which also had a major local brewery backing it, were charter members. So were the Brooklyn Atlantics, but they almost immediately withdrew and were replaced, before the season began, by a Baltimore team owned by Harry Vonderhorst, a—surprised?—brewer. The sixth team was called the Philadelphia Athletics, a name already used many times by different teams in that city.

They would have been delighted, of course, to have the Mets too, and Mutrie attended their organizational meetings. But the League exhibitions were too valuable to give up, so the Mets stayed out. Besides, Day already had an inkling of what might follow.

The six-team American Association set up an 80-game schedule, which meant 16 meetings for each rivalry, and did three things the League did not:

It sold beer and other beverages at the games.
It played on Sundays where local law permitted.
And it let its teams charge 25 cents, not 50 cents, as the basic ticket price.

The National League, sneering at this "beer-and-whiskey league," didn't worry too much at first and declared that it didn't recognize the upstart's existence.

But the American Association also did the one thing that to this day strikes terror into the heart of every right-thinking base-ball executive: it started to compete for players.

The League had just instituted the reserve system, limited as it was, to prevent exactly such a situation. The Association saw no reason to pay any attention to it, and since this would be its first season, had no internal problem. A signed contract had to be honored while in force—the courts would see to that—but between seasons, anyone could be approached. The result was all too plain: higher salaries.

In such circumstances, as we shall see again and again, there is only one course of action for the existing league.

First, wait and see if the new league can survive.

If it does, sue for peace. That is, co-opt it, which is what the new league wanted in the first place.

In 1882, the American Association showed it could survive. It had a larger population base than the League and drew bigger crowds. It created its own new stars automatically, through its own statistics. And while it didn't get many League players to jump, it was certainly in a position to make them attractive offers for 1883.

A series of peace conferences in the spring of 1883 settled the brief trade war. The leagues would honor each other's contracts—and their reserve lists, now increased to 11 men per club (at a time when a club only needed about 15). Agreements were reached on the disposition of disputed player rights. The blacklist would be observed by all. There would be a minimum salary ($1,000). The League Alliance was junked, and a new minor league, the North-western, also signed up (with a $750 minimum salary).

This "Tri-partite Pact" was the forerunner of the organized baseball that emerged in the next century. It was known more formally as the National Agreement.

Hulbert had died suddenly, of a heart attack, in April 1882, but he had already outlined the shape of such an agreement while the trade war was still gathering steam. It was carried through by Spalding, who assumed the presidency of the White Stockings, and by Abraham G. Mills, who became president of the National League at the end of the season after Boston's Soden had filled that position on an interim basis.

With Hulbert gone, no one was left with residual reluctance to undo the expulsions of New York and Philadelphia. Even he wouldn't have opposed them in the new situation, but his death so early in the year made it clear that those valuable franchises would be available.

John B. Day applied for the one in New York. He had shown a certain loyalty to the League by staying out of the American Association, and he had that well-placed site at the Polo Grounds.

Al Reach, insider of insiders, got the Philadelphia franchise, which has been called the Phillies ever since.

Troy and Worcester were gone, but the Troy team was moved en masse to New York, to be called the Gothams, and the Worcester roster was used to stock Philadelphia.

And where did that leave the Mets? Why, it left them free to join the Association. Columbus, Ohio, was brought in as the eighth team. Now there was a neat two-league structure with eight teams in each league. The schedule would be 98 games, 14 against each of seven fellow league members, with no interleague play except exhibitions. It would now take four championship games a week to complete the season by October, and a team would need two regular pitchers.

Two well-ordered major leagues, cooperating—and Day had a team in each.

It was a sweet set-up. The Polo Grounds was large enough for two diamonds, at opposite ends. A canvas fence separated them. One had better seats and amenities than the other. That's where the Gothams played, at 50 cents a ticket. The Mets, at 25 cents a ticket, accepted less favorable starting times when necessary and gave their spectators less comfort—but their customers could refresh themselves with libations not available to the National League clientele.

Day and Mutrie now had access to the meetings, plans, and politics of both leagues. They also had significantly attractive players on each team.

The Gothams inherited from Troy pitchers Tim Keefe and Mickey Welch; first baseman Roger Connor; and Buck Ewing, then playing third base but primarily a catcher. All are now in the Hall of Fame. So is John Montgomery Ward, a young pitcher who made his reputation in Providence but, developing arm trouble, came to New York to play the outfield and pitch part-time before settling in at shortstop.

To bolster the Mets, Day shifted Keefe to them. Weakening the Gothams would not reduce their attractiveness as league members returning to New York, while the familiar Mets playing in a new league for the first time had to be able to offer some competitiveness. Mutrie remained as manager of the Mets.

In 1883, Boston dethroned Chicago in a close race, with Providence third and Cleveland and Buffalo not far behind. New York was sixth. But the American Association race was better still: the Philadelphia Athletics won it by one game, finishing 66–32 to 65–33 for St. Louis and 62–36 for Cincinnati. The Mets were fourth, respectably over .500, with Keefe pitching 41 of their 54 victories.

By now, the baseball galaxy had plenty of nationally identifiable stars. Chicago, of course, had the biggest collection. Its infield of Cap Anson, George Gore, Tommy Burns, and Mike (King) Kelly had accounted for the three championships, with some shifts in position. In 1883, Kelly and Gore moved to the outfield, while Fred Pfeffer, after a fine rookie year in Troy, took over at second base, with Anson at first, Burns at short, and Ned Williamson in Kelly's old place at third. They would win two more pennants in 1886 and 1887, although Kelly would be gone that last year. But through 1886, Gore and Abner Dalrymple remained regular outfielders and Frank (Silver) Flint the catcher. Fred Goldsmith and Larry Corcoran were the pitchers in the first part of the decade and John Clarkson (a Hall of Famer) and Jim McCormick, who had established his stardom with Cleveland, in the second part.

Future Hall of Famers were Charles (Hoss) Radbourn and Pud Galvin, who pitched in Providence and Buffalo. So were Dan Brouthers, an outstanding hitter in Buffalo before he moved to Detroit, and Sam Thompson of Detroit.

In the American Association, pitchers like Tony Mullane and Dave Foutz in St. Louis and hitters like Harry Stovey in Philadelphia, Charlie Jones in Cincinnati, and Pete Browning in Louisville were perennial leaders, while in St. Louis Charley Comiskey hit less but revolutionized the way to play first base by not anchoring himself to the bag.

These names, and many others, were magic in their time—and beyond. Just as Mickey Mantle and Willie Mays were still figures of adulation in the 1990's to a younger generation that never actually saw them play in the 1950's and 1960's, names like Anson and Radbourn and Brouthers and Kelly retained their legendary impact in the baseball community through the first third of the 20th Century, when Ty Cobb and Babe Ruth led the then current superstars. And Cobb and Ruth, in turn, were still the universally recognized standards of stardom in the 1960's, a good 30 years after their playing days.

This longlasting fascination with heroes of the past became an indispensible feature of baseball's popularity. The young spectator, especially if exposed to the game in childhood, never forgot the first set of heroes and passed down the flavor of their names to the next generation, by written and spoken word. It proved to be an unplanned, but quickly exploited, benefit of systematized, compact, well-publicized, and well-disciplined major league play. By the 1940's, Oldtimer Days became a specific promotion, and in the 1990s their popularity remained strong.

The names that generated the most magic could command the most money—for club revenues, and for themselves. A two-tier system had come into existence: those players whose names sold tickets, and all the others necessary for the "names" to have a context in which to perform. From now on, the bitter and unending struggles over salary levels would always focus on the vast majority of ordinary players, since the few top stars always did have inherent bargaining power. By and large, the stars proved to be remarkably supportive of their teammates.

Also, at this point—after the 1883 season—we should stop and check what had been happening to the playing rules.

Two forces were constantly at work: what's fair, in the competitive sense, and what produces a game more appealing to spectators. Trial and error rather than theory was the mechanism of evolution. For every rule, professionals sought an evasion that would give them an edge, paving the way for another rule that would plug the loophole.

We noted the change in the fair-foul hit rule in 1877. The same year, home plate, which had been placed entirely in foul territory in 1875, was put back where it remains today, inside the notch where the foul lines meet, and therefore fair.

Of even greater importance was the League's decision that year that all balls would be supplied by the League instead of the home teams, assuring uniform and high-quality construction. A single ball still stayed in play until lost or almost destroyed, but it and its replacement were in the hands of the umpire. (Spectators returned fouls hit into the stands.)

Remember, in this game the pitch must be delivered from within a pitcher's box whose front line is 45 feet from home plate, a box six feet wide and six feet deep. In releasing the ball, the hand must be below the waist, and the pitcher must be facing the batter. The batter tells him, through the umpire, whether he wants high (waist to shoulder) or low (waist to knees) strikes, over the plate—and his choice for the first pitch remains in force for the entire at bat. A pitch over the plate but to the wrong vertical segment is a ball, as is any pitch that misses the plate altogether. Nine balls make a walk.

In 1879, the width of the pitcher's box is reduced from six feet to four.

In 1880, eight balls make a walk.

In 1881, the pitching distance is increased. Now the front of the box is 50 feet from the center of home plate (which is 17 inches deep). Now seven balls make a walk.

In 1883, the release point for a delivery may be as high as the shoulder (but not higher).

Back in 1877, the batter running to first was instructed to use a lane three feet wide of the foul line, to avoid interfering with a throw to first. In 1882, the League has that lane marked by the three-foot line we have today.

In 1883, the League eliminates recording an out by catching a foul ball on one bounce, but the Association does not. (Fair balls have had to be caught on the fly since 1864.)

However, in 1883, the Association is more progressive than the League in deciding that all umpires must be full-salaried employees, instead of being hired by the game.

So that's the game in 1883: 50-foot pitching distance, sidearm delivery, call for high-low strikes, fouls don't count unless caught for an out, eight balls for a walk, and three strikes for an out (but fouls aren't strikes).

Since 1877, there have been official scoring rules. The definitions of "hit" and "error" are fundamentally the same as now. But a pitcher is given an assist on a strikeout through 1882, and in 1883 a walk is charged as an error for the pitcher. There is not yet an official category for times at bat, but they are counted in order to compile batting averages.

Finally, before going on to the hectic year of 1884, let's review the locales of major league baseball to this point:

City	1880 Pop.	National Association	National League	American Association
New York*	1,900,000	1871–75	1876, 1883	1883
Boston	300,000	1871–75	1876–83	—
Philadelphia	850,000	1871–75	1876, 1883	1882–83
Chicago	500,000	1871, 1874–75	1876–83	—
Cleveland	160,000	1871–72	1879–83	—
St. Louis	350,000	1875	1876	1882–83
Cincinnati	250,000	—	1876–80	1882–83
Louisville	125,000	—	1876–77	1882–83
Baltimore	330,000	1872–74	—	1882–83

*Including Brooklyn

City	1880 Pop.	National Association	National League	American Association
Pittsburgh	235,000	—	—	1882–83
Washington	180,000	1871–73, 1875	—	—
Troy, N.Y.	50,000	1871–72	1879–82	—
Indianapolis	75,000	1871	1878	—
Hartford	40,000	1874–75	1876–77	—
Providence	105,000	—	1878–83	—
Buffalo	155,000	—	1879–83	—
Detroit	120,000	—	1881–83	—
Worcester	60,000	—	1880–82	—
Milwaukee	115,000	—	1878	—
Syracuse	52,000	—	1879	—
Columbus, Ohio	52,000	—	—	1883
Rockford, Ill.	20,000	1871	—	—
Middletown, Conn.	9,000	1872	—	—
New Haven, Conn.	70,000	1875	—	—
Keokuk, Iowa	14,000	1875	—	—
Elizabeth, N.J.	35,000	1873	—	—

That's 26 cities in a span of 13 years. But only three (New York, Philadelphia, St. Louis) were represented in all three leagues. And only Boston had continuous major league representation through all 13 years. Only nine teams had more than five years total, interrupted or not.

Of the 14 that finished 1883 on such a high note (with two teams each in New York and Philadelphia), 13 were set in among the largest population centers and Providence wasn't far behind. Only Washington went unrepresented, along with the larger but inaccessible San Francisco and New Orleans.

This list will help us understand what happened in 1884. Success again bred imitation, and again St. Louis was a focal point.

THE UNION ASSOCIATION

The National Agreement, which meant peace for the two majors and a context for minors to join, was signed on March 12, 1883. Exactly six months later, on September 12, another outside league formed itself at a meeting in Pittsburgh, the Union Association.

Its chief backer was Henry V. Lucas of St. Louis, whose family had large real-estate holdings. Lucas was also successful in transportation, which then meant trolley-car lines. He loved baseball. His brother had been president of the St. Louis

National League club of 1877. Henry Lucas yearned to be included. But the new AA franchise already existed, in the hands of Von der Ahe, and the League had just taken back New York and Philadelphia and didn't need another battleground for the 50 cent–25 cent war. The solution was to form a league of his own.

Lucas had plenty of connections and no trouble interesting backers: railroad men, manufacturers, financiers, and, of course, brewers. (One of his St. Louis investors was Adolphus Busch, head of Anheuser-Busch.)

Lucas also had an idea, one that the newly established Establishment thought was terrible: he was against the reserve.

Honoring an existing contract was one thing, and courts would enforce that anyhow. But observing the reserve restriction—joining in blacklisting a player on some other team's list *after* a contract had expired, was something else. The Union Association made a point of repudiating the practice in principle and offered no such shackles to players who would join up.

What followed in the summer of 1884 had ramifications that reverberated through baseball for the next 60 years, and their echoes still exist. Those who lived through it became convinced—and taught their descendants—that:

1. The reserve system *must* be maintained.
2. Overexposure—too many teams—hurts everyone.
3. Two leagues working together can prosper, but only if they *really* cooperate.
4. A series between two league champions for the "world's championship" is too good a promotion to ignore.
5. A serious and successful challenger who won't go away can always be absorbed.
6. Top players—but only top players—must be satisfied one way or another; the rest can be ruled with an iron hand.

At the same time, a significant playing-rule change altered the nature of the game on the field for all time—and enhanced its attractiveness. The League dropped all restrictions against overhand pitching.

Pitching technique had been evolving all along. The original idea of "put the ball in play" was doomed when Creighton popularized the wrist snap and spin. As Spalding mastered different speeds, and as others refined the arts of the breaking ball, it became harder and harder to define—let alone enforce strictly—exact limitations on the release point. "Below the hip" was as ambiguous as the strike zone, and so was "below the shoulder." Just as professionalism took root long before it was acknowledged and accepted openly, so sidearm deliveries tending toward three-quarter arm were in use before they were formally allowed.

Permitting overhand pitching amounted to letting nature take its course. The American Association didn't go along right away, but didn't wait long.

So here's what happened in 1884: The Union Association announced it would have eight teams and play a 112-game schedule (14 games against each opponent). The National League, which had played 98 the year before (12 games against each), decided to match it.

Since the Union Association was enticing some established players to jump, the National persuaded the American Association to expand from eight teams to 12. This would create more jobs in the existing leagues and place a team in Washington as a direct challenge to the Union Association team there. The 12-team league would play a 110-game schedule (10 against each).

The National League was now rock solid, with the same eight cities it had in 1883: New York, Boston, Philadelphia, Providence, Chicago, Buffalo, Cleveland, and Detroit.

The American Association also had eight holdovers: St. Louis, Cincinnati, Baltimore, Columbus, Louisville, New York, Philadelphia, and Pittsburgh. Its additions were Brooklyn, Indianapolis, Toledo, and Washington.

The Union Association had, in St. Louis, Cincinnati, Baltimore, and Washington, head-to-head competition with the American Association; in Chicago and Boston, with the National League; and in Philadelphia, with both. Its eighth team was in Altoona, Pennsylvania, a major railroad center on the Philadelphia-Pittsburgh line that was the main connection between east and west, but a much smaller city than the others.

None of the leagues made it intact into 1885.

The Union Association got off on the wrong foot. The St. Louis Maroons, the team owned by Lucas, won their first 20 games, so no illusion of competition could be created. They went on to finish with a 94–19 record, at least 20 games ahead of anyone else in the standings (which were a mess, as we shall see).

Washington, Baltimore, Boston, and Cincinnati did manage to complete their seasons, but the other three did not. The Chicago team shared time with Pittsburgh and finally gave up the ghost in September, its players shifted to St. Paul. The Philadelphia team became Wilmington in August and Milwaukee in September, each eventually listed as a separate entry (as was St. Paul). Altoona didn't make it past June, being replaced by Kansas City.

In today's history books, the one season of the Union Association is included as a "major league," since about 30 of the 250 major league players of 1883 did sign with it, and others came and went during the season. The standings show 13 different teams with Chicago-Pittsburgh counted as one, five of them playing less than 70 games (down to St. Paul's nine).

Three player moves had far-reaching effects. Mullane was the biggest name to sign up originally, headed for St. Louis, but before the season began he jumped back to the American Association with the new Toledo team. The first time Toledo came to St. Louis to play, Mullane played one game before Lucas got a court order preventing from playing in that city. When the Unions tried the same tactic at the next stop, Cincinnati, another court dismissed the issue as too trivial to deal with because baseball was "a sport, not a business"—a judicial view met by derisive press comment even in 1884, but endlessly repeated for the next century.

The real effect, however, was to make the Unions go after players *already* under contract to the established clubs, setting off precisely the kind of war that had ruined the National Association and that would mark future attempts to start rival leagues.

That led to the Cleveland situation. By June, this was clearly the weak sister of the National League, and its owner refused to spend any more money. But the League had astute leadership by this time, in Spalding and in Abraham G. Mills, who had succeeded Hulbert as League president. If the Cleveland club folded, its players would add to the prestige and population of the Unions, so the League *itself* had to keep the club functioning. Mills funneled money and players to it, establishing a principle of League aid to a weak member that would become standard practice into the middle of the next century. "Revenue sharing," the buzzword of the 1990's, has a longer pedigree than people think.

Nevertheless, the Cincinnati Unions raided the Cleveland club for three prominent players, bringing the matter to a head. Cleveland finished the season (35–77, but even so ahead of Detroit) and then disbanded, its players being assigned to Brooklyn of the American Association without difficulty, because by that time the Union Association was gone.

The third case involved the opposite end of the National League, the top. Providence had the strongest team. In 1881, Harry Wright himself had come down from Boston to take charge, and he quickly built a winner, finishing third in a close race with Boston and Chicago in 1883. The Grays had a star pitcher, Charles "Old Hoss" Radbourn, 29 years old, who had won 25, 33, and 48 games in the preceding three seasons. But the new rules and schedule—overhand pitching and four games a week—made it prudent to have another pitcher, and the Grays did: Charles Sweeney. By June, he had a 17–8 record with an earned run average modern researchers have computed as 1.55. (There would be no official such statistic until 28 years later.)

At that point, Sweeney jumped to the St. Louis Maroons.

Radbourn, taking over all the remaining pitching assignments, posted his famous total of 60 victories, working 679 innings with an earned run average of 1.38.

The human arm can't do that, overhand, and survive. Radbourn's career record, as he turned 30 at that point, was 166–68. He pitched seven more years and remained a great pitcher, but the rest of the time his record was 143–129 and he was soon working half as many innings. And he didn't throw overhand *all* the time.

The two-starter system was becoming standard.

Providence, never letting up after its good start, won the National League pennant by 10½ games over Boston, even though Wright had turned over the managing to Frank Bancroft. Chicago finished fourth, but in noteworthy circumstances.

The White Stockings had moved into a new ball park, Lake Front Park, in 1883. It was on the same site as their previous one (which had burned down) but with unusual dimensions: 186 feet down the left-field line, 190 down the right-field line, 300 in deepest center. In 1883, balls hit over the left-field fence were ground-rule doubles—but since ground rules were up to the home team, Cap Anson (star and manager) and Spalding decided that in 1884 these would be home runs.

As a result, the 1884 Chicagos, already the most powerful offensive team in the League, hit 142 home runs instead of the 13 they totaled the year before. (No other team hit more than Buffalo's 39.) Four Chicago players hit 20 or more, led by Ned Williamson's 27, which remained the record until Babe Ruth broke it in 1919. (No one else in the League hit more homers than the 14 Dan Brouthers produced for Buffalo.) In 1883, Chicago had hit 277 doubles; in 1884, only 162. But the total of homers plus doubles was virtually the same, so the ground rule made the whole difference.

But this idea of maximizing a team's assets by ground rules did not pay off. The White Stockings had three outstanding pitchers, not two—Corcoran, Clarkson, and Goldsmith—but they were tagged for 83 homers instead of the previous year's 21, and the team wound up only a little over .500.

The lesson was, you can go only so far in manipulating your home field, because both teams have to play on it. When Yankee Stadium was built, 40 years later, with its right-field contour tailored to Ruth's left-handed drives, the distortion was kept within reasonable bounds and the Yankee need for outstanding left-handed *pitchers* was recognized from the start.

Meanwhile, in the American Association, the New York Metropolitans won the pennant. John Day, with a team entering each league in 1883, had made a straightforward (and cold-blooded) entrepreneurial analysis, as we have seen. His Gothams would be playing on one side of the fence dividing the Polo Grounds for 50 cents a ticket, the Metropolitans on the other side for 25 cents. Simply the return to National League membership would sustain interest in the first year of the Gothams, but the Mets would have to earn attention by winning in the younger and less prestigious American Association. So he had moved the best pitcher on the Gotham roster (inherited from Troy), Tim Keefe, to the Mets and kept his "good" manager, Mutrie, with the Mets. And it had worked. That the Gothams finished sixth did no harm (and that was better than the other returnee, Philadelphia, who finished eighth and last). As for the Mets, they ran a respectable fourth, with Keefe providing 41 of their 54 victories and building up his star identity.

The 1884 Gothams did better, crossing .500 and tying the celebrated Chicagos for fourth place. The Mets did better still. They had found a partner for Keefe in Jack Lynch and finished first by 6½ games. Each pitcher won 37, accounting for all but one of their victories.

The public, always ahead of the promoters in understanding what it wanted, had been clamoring for a postseason meeting between the two League champions to settle the "world's" championship. It had been tried briefly in 1882, when Chicago (NL) and Cincinnati (AA) played two games and split them, but at that point no peace treaty with the upstart league had yet been negotiated (as it would be the next spring), and the teams were told to back off and consider the games as exhibitions. In 1883, Philadelphia (AA) was regarded as so much weaker than Boston (NL), which had dethroned the mighty Chicagos, that nothing was arranged.

But now you had New York involved, still the largest area of intense baseball interest. And you had Day, with a foot in each camp. And you had a common enemy, the Union Association—the factor that probably tilted the balance. Matching the two champions would automatically snub the Union St. Louis Maroons, who won more games than anyone.

So the first World's Series (the apostrophe was always used then) was held in October 1884. The weather was miserable, the crowd small, and the Mets quickly beaten in the three scheduled games, but the excitement generated was authentic and widespread—and produced fodder for the hot-stove-league talk all winter, a factor that was emerging as baseball's great asset. As a concept, a postseason climax would never die.

When it was over, it was time to sort out the wreckage. The Union Association was dead, but Lucas and his Maroons had established their value. They were taken in by the National League for 1885 to replace Cleveland.

The American Association was bitter. It had been talked into expanding by the League as a war measure against the Unions and had suffered for it. The Washington team, which was supposed to fight the Union entry there, had been forced to move to Richmond in August and had no reason to continue. Indianapolis and Toledo were also failed experiments. Only Brooklyn proved viable, so it stayed in the Association as a replacement for Columbus, which was not really in a position to compete in what had become a big-city circuit. What's more, letting the Maroons into St. Louis Browns territory clearly broke the National Agreement.

The real fights, however, were over rights to players who, by joining the Unions, now had to be redistributed by negotiation. The reserve system, emerging stronger than ever, left all these decisions to club owners, and in making them, economic and political power counted. Bickering continued through 1885, and the practice of selling a player's *reserve* rights (beyond the actual unfinished contract) became institutionalized. Being reserved by the team he signed with, had left a player in an ambiguous position if his contract was sold. Once it was established that the "reserve" went *with* the contract the system was complete. The player was tied up forever until discarded. But one overriding reality made all detailed squabbles secondary. There was more money to be made from cooperation than from warfare, and enough money all around. A new National Agreement was adopted, and the two-league format was back in place.

The 1885 season was one of readjustment, with order restored in competitive terms for followers of the game. In the League, the Colts (eventually the Cubs), regained their throne after moving into West Side Park, an oval-shaped field with short foul lines (216 feet) but sensible ground rules. They had their famous sluggers—Anson, Kelly, Dalrymple, Williamson—and led the League in homers again, with 54; but their pitchers gave up only 37 and Clarkson himself won 53 games, pitching 623 innings. Pitchers were only gradually learning about arm limitations.

But Chicago had to fight off the Gothams, right down to the wire, because Day took full advantage of his double ownership.

Winning an American Association pennant with the Mets wasn't nearly as profitable as doing well in the National League, at double the ticket price, would be. So he moved Keefe to the Gothams, to join the already outstanding Mickey Welch, and brought along the best everyday player on the Mets, Duke Esterbrook, his third baseman. What's more, he shifted Mutrie to the other end of the Polo Grounds to manage what was now an imposing lineup. New York finished 85–27, a 23-game improvement in one year, only two games behind Chicago.

The stripped-down Mets, naturally enough, fell to seventh in the Association, winning only 44 games, a 31-game drop. But Day knew what he was doing. Having no more use for the team he had created when New York had no National League outlet, he was about to sell it now that he was achieving League power.

At the top of the Association standings were Von der Ahe's St. Louis Browns, winners by 16 games over Cincinnati. This result healed some wounds. Letting Lucas's St. Louis Maroons enter the National League had been an economic blow to Von der Ahe and created a potential rival for local prestige. But the Maroons, so dominant in the thinned-out Union Association, could win only 36 games in League competition and finished dead last.

The World's Series idea, now accepted and expected, was still not fully formed. Chicago and St. Louis scheduled seven games: the first in Chicago, the next three in St. Louis, then one in Pittsburgh and two in Cincinnati. The "championship" was still more appealing to followers everywhere than to ticket buyers in northern-climate cities in the last two weeks of October.

This Series ended tie with a 3–3 and highlighted two of baseball's unsolved problems: resistance to an umpire's authority and the absence of any interleague authority. Both would become increasingly serious until finally confronted after the turn of the century, holding back faster development, and, when eventually solved, making possible full-scale success.

Both problems had affected the Providence-Met Series of 1884, billed as a two of three. The third game became irrelevant when the Grays won the first two, but it went on as scheduled, anyhow—at the Polo Grounds on October 25 in frigid weather. Only a few hundred spectators showed up, so there was no money to be made, and the Providence players had no desire to play at all.

The umpire, under the rules, had to be approved by both teams. The Grays' strategy was to object to every umpire the Mets, as the home team, proposed. So the Mets, "not to allow them any loophole to postpone the game," the *New York Times* reported, told Providence to pick anyone, even its own manager. The manager, Bancroft, went them one better: he chose Keefe, who had pitched the first two games against Radbourn. New York's substitute pitcher was hammered early, and with the score 11–2 in the sixth inning, Keefe—always a smart pitcher—called the game on account of darkness.

In the 1885 Series, the umpire trouble erupted in the second game, after darkness ended the first as a 5–5 tie after eight innings. Now, in St. Louis, the hometown Browns were trailing 5–4 in the sixth inning. They were so displeased with the umpiring of Dave Sullivan that their manager and first baseman, Comiskey, pulled his team off the field—at which point Sullivan declared Chicago the winner by forfeit.

Using other umpires, the teams then played four ordinary games, St. Louis winning the first two, Chicago the next two. Before the seventh game, Chicago's manager, Anson, apparently agreed that the forfeit shouldn't count, which would make the series 2–2 with a tie and allow this last game to decide the championship. But after St. Louis won it 13–2, Anson insisted that the forfeit had been legitimate after all, and today's record books list it as a 3–3–1 Series.

In 1886, Chicago won a close race again, holding off Detroit by 2½ games, with New York a distant third. Detroit had been strengthened by four players, including Dan Brouthers, acquired when Buffalo folded. Buffalo had never fully accepted the 50-cent ticket scale, finding it too high. At the same time, Providence also dropped out. Their places were taken by Washington and Kansas City, as the League became more and more a big-market enterprise.

In the Association, St. Louis remained as powerful as ever, and unthreatened domestically as the League's St. Louis team finished sixth, ahead of only the two new teams.

This time Comiskey and Anson decided, with owner approval, of course, on a real World Series: winner-take-all prize money (the gate after expenses) to the team that first won four games. The first two were split at Chicago, and the White Sockings won the third game there. The Browns won the next two at home, then ended the Series there with a 10th-inning 4–3 victory on a steal of home against Clarkson, whose delivery was too wide even though catcher King Kelly had called for a pitchout.

Now *there* was fuel for the hot-stove league.

Going into the 1887 season, therefore, major league baseball was enjoying unprecedented prosperity, popularity, artistic success (in terms of great players of high visibility), publicity (as the rotary press made daily newspapers a larger and more aggressive industry seeking mass circulation), and stability. Its growing pains seemed to be behind it. The future looked bright.

The rules seemed well understood. On the field, the era of major change seemed over. The National League had tried six balls for a walk in 1884 and 1885, but in 1886 had returned to seven, from which the American Association had never strayed. The pitcher was now required to face the batter before he began his delivery but enjoyed the new freedom of throwing overhand. And off the field, the whole complex of regulations summed up by the word "reserve" were now the accepted way of doing business.

Accepted, but not unchallenged.

CHAPTER 5

The Revolt of
the Players

THE BROTHERHOOD

Success breeds imitation—but it also breeds arrogance. Those who enjoy it, especially if they had little to do with laying its groundwork but came into control of a going proposition, start to believe they can do pretty much as they like. Worse, they think they know what would be good for their business without fully grasping, or thinking through, all the consequences of a particular action.

One small and unimportant sign of this kind of thinking appeared in 1887. Baseball's increasing audience seemed fascinated with batting stars, like the ones in Chicago, New York, and Detroit. Batting stars were usually identified by their high batting averages, as the dissemination of annual and daily statistics continued to grow, making comparisons to the past more possible and popular.

Therefore, higher batting averages must be good for business, right? Okay, let's count walks as hits. That'll make higher averages.

That bit of silliness lasted only one year and represented the arrogant aspect of manipulating the product. But other steps to build up the offense—which, evidently, sold tickets—were more fundamental.

Five balls for a walk—a drastic drop from seven.

Four *called* strikes before you're out.

However, the batter can no longer order a high or low delivery: anything over the plate not higher than the shoulders and not lower than the knees is a strike.

If a batter fouls off a pitch *clearly on purpose,* it can be ruled a strike—umpire's judgment.

If a pitch hits the batter or any part of his uniform, he's entitled to first base, just like a walk.

The fourth strike, like the scoring of walks as hits, was a one-year mistake, but the other rules represented permanent change. By 1889, it was four balls for a walk, as it has remained since. The foul-strike rules would change gradually over the next 15 years. The hit-by-pitch rule is intact.

As a result, 1887 produced offensive statistics as aberrent for league totals as the 1883 ground-rule homers had produced for one Chicago club. The League aggregate batting average jumped 18 points to .269, and the Association's 30 points to .273—and that's using the standard method. At the time, the walks-included averages came out as .321 and .330. James (Tip) O'Neill, the Association's batting champion, hit a legitimate .435 that was recorded then as .485. Detroit's Sam Thompson led the League with a real .372 that was published as .407.

The influential factor, no doubt, was the fourth strike. The next year, when that was abandoned and pitchers had learned how to adjust to five balls for a walk, the rebound downward was even more extreme: the League hit .239 and the Association .238, as O'Neill won his batting title again—at .335, a full 100 points lower than the previous year. Anson led the League at .344.

And the year after that, 1889, both league averages were back up in the .260's, as the walk requirement went down to four balls, only to settle into the .250's after that as the pitchers adjusted again.

But the real arrogance and miscalculation were manifesting themselves off the field.

Commercial success has two inseparable aspects. Profits flow from increased attendance, which results from the publicized performance of outstanding players—who then demand a larger portion of the profit they can see being generated. Club owners welcome the increased revenue but detest the increased salaries.

That's the dichotomy that created the drama—some may call it tragedy—that was played out in 1890 and replayed, with only the language modernized, a century later.

It started modestly enough in the aftermath of the tumultuous events of 1884. The contraction from 28 teams to 16 in 1885 left a lot of players without major league jobs, friends and former teammates of the remaining major leaguers among them. None of them had made all that much money before, and the tightened reserve made it harder for the ordinary player to make much from now on.

John Montgomery Ward—"Johnny" to his contemporaries but referred to as "Monte" in most baseball literature until recently—felt something should be done. He was 25 years old, fresh out of Columbia Law School, a highly respected infielder on the suddenly improved New York Gothams. He had credentials. As a 19-year-old pitcher in Providence, he had won 47 games in 1879 and the next year pitched a perfect game. When his arm went bad, he moved to the outfield, teaching himself to throw *left*-handed, and remained a good left-handed hitter. When the arm healed, he did a little more pitching but settled in at shortstop. In 1885, when Mutrie came over from the Mets to take charge of the Gothams, he made Ward his field captain.

Aware of the problems of indigent, blacklisted, and otherwise unfortunate professional ball players, Ward took the lead in organizing the Brotherhood of Professional Baseball Players. It was to be a benevolent organization, less to help those already in need than to create a structure that might keep players from falling into need.

In the United States of the 1880's labor unions were in their first period of growth, engendering fierce opposition in society's conservative and business elements. Many used the idea and language of "brotherhood" in their organization, among them the railroad workers. But Ward had no such intention in 1885; he simply felt that players needed some organization to look after their common interests, not against employers but beyond what employers dealt with routinely.

The best way to grasp what happened is to follow the chronology.

At the end of 1884, after the Union Association folded and the new National League–American Association relationship was established, Abraham Mills resigns as National League president and is replaced by Nick Young, long associated with baseball administration in Washington. But Spalding, as president of the Chicago team, remains the de facto leader when key decisions have to be made.

In October 1885, Ward and eight Giant teammates (including Keefe, Connor, and Ewing) create the New York chapter of the Brotherhood of Professional Base Ball Players, formalizing it.

At about the same time, the owners adopt a $2,000 salary limit but neither publicize it nor enforce it. Most top players get more than that from payments outside the official contract.

In the 1886 season, Chicago wins another pennant, but only by 2½ games over Detroit, which has put together an equally powerful hitting team.

That September, the Brotherhood makes public its existence. The League says "welcome;" the American Association is hostile.

In October, the World Series between Chicago and St. Louis ends in the dispute and acrimony already described.

Between seasons, Spalding makes a move that alters a lot of perceptions all around. Its details are enlightening, and the following version is Spalding's own, from in his 1911 book.

Even though his team has now won five pennants in seven years, he thinks it needs to be shaken up. Among other things, its fans are starting to take victory for granted and attendance is falling off. There have already been cases of a player being "traded" or, in baseball language, having his contract (with its reserve rights) "assigned" to another club in exchange for a player—or money. But these have been isolated, low-key transactions.

Spalding decides to sell a star.

He asks Anson if he can spare Kelly, the most flamboyant and popular of the stars. Anson says sure, we're good enough to spare anybody.

Spalding asks Kelly how he'd like to play for Boston. Kelly says he likes it in Chicago. Spalding asks him how much money he'd want to play in Boston.

Kelly, who is making $3,000 (50 percent above the official limit), says, "$4,000."

"How would you like $5,000?" asks Spalding.

Kelly beams.

"But then you don't care how much I get for your contract, do you?" asks Spalding.

"If you get me $5,000, I don't care if you sell me for $100,000," says Kelly.

"All right, just remember: you ask for $5,000, not $4,000."

Spalding then offers Boston Kelly's contract for $10,000. Boston accepts quickly and gives Kelly a three-year contract for $5,000 a year—$2,000 to play baseball, $3,000 for the use of his picture.

As Spalding describes the fallout from this transaction:

It was understood between us that he was at liberty to play "the poor baseball slave" act to the limit. . . . The whole Chicago press called me names. . . . I replied by having the check received from Boston published in facsimile in the Chicago papers. . . . I had learned the value of good newspaper advertising, and it came good and plenty as long as Kelly remained to weep and wail over his sad fate in being sold away from a city he loved so well.

But other members of the team soon caught on, and I found myself besieged by players begging to be sold into a slavery that would help them to redoubled salaries.

As the 1887 season is beginning, a new figure enters the scene unobtrusively. John T. Brush, who is in the clothing business in Indianapolis, acquires the failed Kansas City franchise and moves it to Indianapolis. No one anticipates how important he will prove to be.

At the League's annual meeting, the Brotherhood, claiming 90 members (in a league that has about 120 altogether), asks for a hearing. Represented by Ward, Ned Hanlon, and Dan Brouthers, it seeks formal recognition, which is denied, and two contract reforms, which are taken under consideration. The reforms are: (1) write the *true* salary into each contract, and (2) eliminate the reserve for any player who is offered a cut in pay.

The first point creates a problem. It would expose the unobserved $2,000 limitation. The League tells the players it's willing to repeal the limitation and accept their request, but that it can't get the American Association to go along, tsk tsk.

As for the second point, which sounds fair, sure.

During the 1887 season, with offense artificially heightened by the "walk is a hit," a fourth strike, and only five balls for a walk, Detroit's hitters bring it in first, ahead of Philadelphia and Chicago in a good race. (Even with Kelly, Boston is fifth.)

But in midseason, Ward publishes an inflammatory article in a magazine. He attacks blacklisting of nonsigners, stresses the "slavery" issue, calls the reserve a product of the distrust club owners have for each other, and advocates letting "supply and demand" regulate salaries.

Spalding's sale of Kelly combined with Ward's outspokenness alter the conversational climate. Papers now routinely refer to trades and sales as "slave traffic." The real conflict of interest between the players' desire for maximum earning power (which the reserve prevents) and the owners' desire for holding salaries down (which the reserve makes possible) is out in the open.

In October 1887, a Detroit–St. Louis World Series shows how you can have too much of what you think is a good thing. It's a 15-game set that drags on through 10 different cities, starting out with crowds that average 5,000 a game for the first seven and end with 378 (in Chicago) and 659 (in St. Louis) for the last two.

For the 1888 season, Brush proposes a "classification" system: a salary cap with a vengeance. It would take into account the player's "habits, earnestness, and special qualities" (and presumably performance) in the previous season to determine his "class." Class A would be paid $2,500; B, $2,250; C, $2,000; D, $1,750; E, $1,500. In short, "conduct," as judged subjectively by the owner, would determine salary. The League adopts the system in principle but holds off applying it.

During 1888, Spalding makes another big sale (pitcher Clarkson to Boston), while Fred (Sure Shot) Dunlap, Detroit's reserve second baseman, stirs owner outrage by asking for a share of the sales price when his contract is sold to Pittsburgh.

The Giants win the 1888 National League pennant with players who are the backbone of the Brotherhood, and they go on to beat St. Louis in the best World Series so far. (The Gothams have been renamed the Giants by manager Mutried.)

Immediately afterward, Spalding sets out on another foreign tour. His Chicago team and a group of invited all-stars are to play exhibitions on the West Coast and in Hawaii, New Zealand, and Australia, demonstrating the great American game to the Pacific region, just as the 1874 tour had to Britain. (In Honolulu, one of the hosts is Alexander Cartwright, the man who had written that first rule book for the Knickerbockers in 1845, now in his 70's.) But since it's about the same distance from Australia to New York in either direction, it is decided to continue westward—to Ceylon, through the new Suez Canal to Cairo (playing "in the shadow of the pyramids"), to Naples ("under the shadow of Vesuvius") and Rome, to Paris ("in the shadow of the Eiffel Tower then under construction"), to England, and across the Atlantic back to New York just in time for the start of the 1889 season in April.

Among the all-stars are Ward and Hanlon.

While Spalding and these Brotherhood leaders are out of the country, the League decides to enforce Brush's classification plan for the 1889 season.

When the boat docks in New York, a delegation of players led by Keefe is waiting for Ward. They have been betrayed. They want to strike. But after discussion, they adopt a different plan.

They will play out the 1889 season and use the time to set up a league of their own. On May 19, they form an official grievance committee.

In June, they appeal to Young, as League president, to end the classification system and the selling of players. Young refers it to a three-man committee headed by Spalding. On June 25, when Spalding and Ward meet alone, Spalding brushes Ward off. These matters can wait until the season is over, says Spalding. That's what *you* think, says Ward.

Many players want to call a strike for the Fourth of July (the biggest gate receipts day for baseball); owners call the threat "nonsense" and "absurd." But the Brotherhood actually takes a vote and decides not to strike but to pursue its own plans, while talking about strikes as a diversion.

They start assigning themselves in secret to the new, so far nonexistent, clubs.

In September, the story breaks: the players will form their own league in 1890. Surprisingly, the two most important sports newspapers of the time, *The Sporting News* in St. Louis and *Sporting Life* in Philadelphia, come out in support of the players.

In October, as the Giants defeat Brooklyn (the American Association champion, having dethroned St. Louis) in the World Series amid more turmoil about umpiring, the Brotherhood makes an official announcement: it will field its own teams in 1890.

On November 4 and 5, about three dozen players meet in New York, lining up financial backers for the teams.

In December, Ward tells the American Association not to worry, the Players League won't go after its players, and it should consider expanding to 10 teams. The fight is against the National League.

Meanwhile, the Players League announces its format:

1. Teams will be in New York, Brooklyn, Boston, Philadelphia, Pittsburgh, Cleveland, Chicago, and Buffalo.
2. Each player will sign for three years at his 1889 salary.
3. There will be no reserve clause.
4. The League will be governed by a senate of 16 members, two from each club, one chosen by players, the other by backers. The senate will choose a president and vice-president from its own ranks and hire an outsider as secretary-treasurer.
5. Gross gate receipts will be shared 50–50 with the visiting team. The home team will keep all money from concessions.

6. From its receipts, each club will pay obligations in this order: (a) running expenses; (b) player salaries, if not guaranteed personally by backers; (c) $2,500 to the League for a prize-money fund of $20,000 to be distributed by order of finish, with $7,000 for first place; (d) of additional profits, if any, the first $10,000 go to the backers and the next $10,000 to *all* the League's players, divided equally; (e) beyond that, half to the clubs and half to the players.

7. A player may purchase stock in his own club.

8. A player can't be released until the season is over.

Also in December:

The National League drops Washington, Indianapolis and Cincinnati taking in Brooklyn from the American Association.

The Players League tries to negotiate for National League leases, and the National League tries to buy stock in Players League teams. Neither tactic works. The Players League builds its own ball parks (which can be done quickly and easily in a day of plentiful empty lots and wooden-stands construction).

By January 1, 1890, the Players League says it has 71 National League, 16 American Association, and four minor league players signed up.

The stage is set. The war is on.

SEASONS 1890–91

1890

As the 1890 baseball season approached, the public impact of baseball news reached unprecedented heights. In proportion to population and media capabilities, the attention paid to off-field and business-related developments was just as great then as it would be a century later, with just as many passionately held opposing positions and just as many dire predictions about the survival of the game. Fans familiar with star players felt strong attachments to them, felt little animosity to the idea of players having their own league, and were interested in its possibilities. Clearly, its level of play would be the highest, and they had seen three leagues come into existence from scratch in the last 15 years, so it wasn't the kind of "unthinkable" innovation an "outside" league would come to suggest subsequently. At this point, fans of American Association teams were affected only marginally, as the onslaught focused on the National League. The question was, could the players actually manage their business and financial affairs in the way outlined? Doubters could remember that it was their inability to do so that had ended the National Association and created the National League, within living memory, only 15 years before.

It was plain, however, that emotion and a desire for victory were overcoming common business sense. The players chose outright head-to-head confrontation by placing their teams in National League cities and finding nearby playing sites. They made up their schedule and sent a copy to the National League so that conflicting dates could be avoided "if the League so chose," and offered to play exhibition games before and after the season. The National League responded by scheduling its *own* games on the same dates and spurned the exhibition offer. In keeping with the climate of the times, businessmen still saw success in terms of driving a rival out of business—as the National League had done with the Union Association and had tried to do with the American Association before it had proved strong enough to be worth accommodating.

The American Association had its own internal conflicts, and in November 1889, Cincinnati and Brooklyn broke away and applied for membership in the National League. Anxious to drop failing situations in Indianapolis and Washington, the National accepted them. It bought back the Indianapolis franchise from Brush (setting in motion repercussions that would be felt for years) and shifted the players to Cincinnati. Since Kansas City also pulled out, the American Association filled out by downsizing below what had become accepted market-size standards: Toledo, Rochester, and Syracuse, to go with Columbus, Louisville, and a new franchise in Brooklyn. Its only holdovers in major markets were St. Louis and Philadelphia.

This, then, was how the 1890 season started in April:

City	National League	Players League	American Association
New York	Giants	Giants	—
Brooklyn	Bridge-grooms	Wonders	Gladiators
Boston	Beaneaters	Reds	—
Philadelphia	Phillies	Quakers	Athletics
Chicago	White Stockings (or Colts)	Pirates	—
Pittsburgh	Innocents	Burghers	—
Cleveland	Spiders	Infants	—
Cincinnati	Reds	—	—
Buffalo	—	Bisons	—
Louisville	—	—	Colonels (or Eclipse)
St. Louis	—	—	Brown Stockings
Columbus	—	—	Solons
Toledo	—	—	Maumees
Rochester	—	—	Hop Bitters
Syracuse	—	—	Stars

Buffalo's roster was essentially the Washington team that had been disbanded.

Brooklyn's Brotherhood team was called the Wonders because it was backed by Ward's Wonder Bread, a major Brooklyn bakery (but no rela-

tion to John Montgomery Ward, the team's player-manager). Corporate sponsorship is not a recent invention.

Note that all the National League franchises except Cleveland have survived, uninterrupted, to this day, although they've had name changes to Dodgers, Braves, Cubs, and Pirates, and the Boston entry has moved on to Atlanta by way of Milwaukee.

Note also that Brooklyn and Philadelphia were presenting *three* major league teams each. New York and Brooklyn were still separate cities (until 1898), but the metropolitan area was trying to support *five* teams.

The new teams had to have places to play. Buffalo took over Olympic Stadium, which had been used as the National League park in the years 1884–85. The Chicago Pirates took a South Side location (near today's Comiskey Park) used by the Union Association team in 1884. Boston played at Congress Street, near the waterfront, a field also used by the Unions in 1884. Pittsburgh moved into old Exposition Park, the city's oldest such facility—where Three Rivers Stadium is now. Cleveland and Philadelphia built new parks.

But the center of the struggle was New York, coming into a class of its own as a communications and financial hub, steeped in the oldest of baseball traditions and, currently, the home of both 1889 league champions.

Brooklyn was all set, in Washington Park, named after the adjacent site of George Washington's headquarters during the Revolutionary War. The ball park had burned down in May of 1889 but was rebuilt and open for business within four weeks. Its accessibility was attested to by the name "Trolley Dodgers" given the team in its early American Association years (1884 on), although it was now called the Bridegrooms because several players had married during the year.

The Brotherhood Brooklynites set themselves up in East New York, building their own Eastern Park, in a section of the borough far on the other side of Prospect Park from Washington Park. And the new American Association Gladiators moved into Ridgewood Park, on the Brooklyn-Queens border, where the Dodgers had played Sunday games in recent years.

But in Manhattan it wasn't so simple.

Remember the Polo Grounds, which Day's Giants and Mets shared? Day had sold the Mets back in 1886, and they had gone to Staten Island and then out of existence. But after the 1888 season, even though the Giants were the toast of the town, having won their first pennant and World's Series, they were being evicted. The city had finally decided to run 111th Street through the middle of the site. (This, too, will have significance later.)

Day found a spot two miles farther uptown, something called Manhattan Field, at 155th Street and Eighth Avenue, where the Sixth Avenue Elevated Line (connecting to Wall Street) ended. At the southwest corner of this tract, backed by a huge hill called Coogan's Bluff and facing the Harlem River (just past the El), he built a brand new ball park—and took the familiar name Polo Grounds with him.

It wasn't ready for the start of the 1889 season, so the Giants played on Staten Island (where the Mets had died), and in Jersey City. On July 8, they moved into the New Polo Grounds and completed another year of triumph. Their first full season in their new home would be 1890.

And what did the Brotherhood Giants do? They not only appropriated the team name— Giants—with which their players were already identified, they built a brand new park of their own right next door.

Using the northwest corner of the same Manhattan Field lot, they built a bigger grandstand, with more seats, housing a fancy bar beneath the grandstand. They called it Brotherhood Park, and its canvas fence in right center bordered on left center of the Polo Grounds. (Almost every baseball history ever written cites the day that Mike Tiernan, in the Polo Grounds, hit a homer over that fence while a Brotherhood game was also in progress, and got an ovation from both sets of fans.)

While all this was going on, the courts brushed aside several cases in which clubs tried to hold players to reserve rights. The baseball contract was so patently unfair—a club could cancel it on 10 days' notice, but the player was bound for years if not life—that most judges treated it with contempt. Still, efforts to get players to come back to the National League never let up. Spalding offered Kelly, who would now manage the Brotherhood Boston team

while playing for it, a blank contract (you fill in the salary) *plus* a $10,000 bonus to sign it. Only three years before, Kelly had been delighted to be traded for $5,000 total salary; now he turned down at least three times as much. "I can't go back on the boys," he told Spalding. "My mother and father would never look at me again if I proved a traitor to the boys."

The on-field events of the 1890 baseball season deserve an entire book, but all we can do here is mention them in passing and stick to the main story line. The fact is, those games disappeared quickly from baseball consciousness, and that demonstrates how fundamentally important context is. What the Players League did to the structure and future behavior of baseball operations was of permanent significance, but the ball games themselves had no lasting impact because they weren't part of anything that continued. Today's record books contain all the results and accomplishments of the 1890 Players League, dutifully recorded—nine 20-game winners, a batting champion (Pete Browning, Cleveland, .387), a home-run leader (Roger Connor, New York, 13)—and the career records of all individuals include their Players League performances. But legends about those games are virtually nonexistent, because they weren't part of anything for comparison. The one enduring anecdote mentioned in most history books is Tiernan's home run, so that oddity is better known than the pennant race itself.

Boston, managed by Kelly, won the pennant, with Brooklyn, managed by Ward, 6½ games back. Then came New York (managed by Ewing), Chicago, Philadelphia, Pittsburgh, Cleveland, and Buffalo. Chicago's manager was Comiskey, one of the several stars who did leave the American Association. (Batting champion Browning was another.) Hanlon managed Pittsburgh.

In the National League, Brooklyn finished first with substantially its 1889 American Association team, beating out Chicago (where Anson remained as player-manager at the age of 39; he would retire only after hitting .302 at the age of 46 in 1897). What remained of the Giants finished sixth, but stripped of talent more than anyone was Pittsburgh. The team finished with a record of 23–113, which is why it was called the Innocents. In the totally unreliable and admittedly inflated attendance figures announced by both leagues after the season, the home attendance for Pittsburgh's entire year is given as 16,064—with home games abandoned entirely after July. (The Pittsburgh team in the Players League claimed 117,123.) The Innocents were outscored, 1,235 runs to 597.

The American Association pennant went to Louisville, 88–44, with more or less the same lineup, minus Browning, that had gone 27–111 the year before. That indicates what happened to quality of play.

By June, there were strong (and accurate) reports of financial difficulties for the Players League. Backdoor negotiations by backers—not players—began. The National League, considering New York its worst problem, had other teams chip in money and transfer players to keep it respectable, a step that would cause serious problems later on. In the American Association, the Brooklyn team folded in midseason and was replaced by Baltimore, which had pulled out of the Association during the winter of turmoil in 1889–90 and had played the first part of 1890 in an independent league.

And the disaster spread downward. Minor league teams struggled as they lost personnel, who became "replacement players" (to use the current term) in the majors. The Texas, Indiana State, International, Pennsylvania State, Western New York, Michigan State, Interstate, and Tri-State Leagues could not complete their seasons.

The war of words never let up. The League position was publicized by all the publications controlled by Spalding and the sporting-goods cartel and generally supported by conservative elements of society in general. The players had their champions among fans and liberals.

In the final analysis, however, the players were either betrayed by their backers or had chosen the wrong ones. Everyone in baseball had losses that year, but the League losses were undoubtedly greater than the Brotherhood's. If the new league's backers had been willing (or able) to try another year, the League and its dedication to the reserve might have given in and sought coexistence.

Instead, backers tried to cut their losses by seeking private deals that would end the war and perhaps give them an interest in future teams. Spalding, as commander-in-chief of League forces (with Day and Brooklyn's Charley Byrne as his war committee) was once again the key figure.

Just as the season was ending, Aaron Stern, owner of the League's Cincinnati club (acquired from Indianapolis), sold the franchise to a group of Players League investors.

Ward called for a peace conference, along the lines of the one that had given the American Association recognition by the National League back in 1883. While this was being arranged, Spalding went to a meeting with three Players League owners at which they revealed the size of their losses. Sensing their weakness while fully aware of his own, he pulled a "bluff"—to use his own word—and said the National League demanded "unconditional surrender." To his amazement, it worked: they accepted, and all subsequent discussions dealt with how to dismantle the Players League—although the members of the Brotherhood themselves didn't know that yet.

They suspected, of course, but they couldn't do anything about it. Spalding bought the Chicago team. Others took what they could get. By the end of November, the Players League was dead.

The National League had won—but it was a Pyrrhic victory from which baseball would not really recover for nearly two decades.

1891

Five immediate issues had to be faced:
Which teams would survive and who would own them?
Which players would be assigned to which teams?
Which ball parks would be used?
What format would reconstructed leagues take?
How should playing rules be adjusted?

The last point, which received by far the least attention at the time, turned out to be the most lasting effect of the Brotherhood

War, because it pushed the game on the field toward the form that became standard right after the turn of the century.

We saw how, during the 1880's, the rules were constantly in flux in pursuit of an optimum level of offense. Pitchers kept improving their techniques, and more and more highly skilled pitchers were coming into existence. Fielding was improving as rudimentary gloves came into use. Improved groundskeeping also helped fielders. Yet it was clear that spectators, however much they might lionize an outstanding individual pitcher, preferred lots of hitting, scoring, action on the bases, and so forth. And the players, no less than club officials, understood that the name of the game was pleasing the public.

When the Players League was forming, it knew that it would consist of the best players, in even greater density (per lineup) than the League or Association had in the late 1880's. The gimmicks to help hitters—phony batting averages counting walks as hits, a fourth strike—hadn't worked. Dropping to five balls for a walk and abolishing a hitter's right to call for high or low deliveries had the net result of making pitchers tougher than ever. And in 1889, the walk requirement had been brought down to four balls (but fouls still did not count as strikes).

The front of the pitcher's box had been set at 50 feet back in 1880. Since the front foot, after delivery, had to come down inside it, the "effective" distance—the spot where the pivot foot had to be planted—was about 53½ feet. But in 1886, the National League had made an important change. The box was now 5½ feet deep (and, as always, four feet wide), and the pitcher had to keep his back foot in contact with the *back* line until he let go of the ball. The back foot *is* the pivot foot. So the effective distance became 55½ feet.

The Players League decided to move the whole box back a foot. The front of the box would be 51 feet from the plate and six feet deep, so that the effective (pivot-foot) distance would be 57 feet. All these measurements were to the *center* of home base.

The desired result was achieved. The National League and American Association kept the old rule, with inferior players, and here's what happened:

	Runs Per Game (both teams)	League Batting Average
Players League	13.8	.274
National League	11.2	.254
American Association	11.2	.253

For 1891 and 1892, the National League, back in command, retained its 50-foot, 5½ foot-deep pitcher's box. But the Players League had shown not only that the longer pitching distance produced more scoring, but that—far more important—top pitchers could adjust to it without serious loss of effectiveness or physical difficulty.

The Players League experiment, therefore, paved the way for, and hastened, the 60-foot 6-inch pitching *slab*—instead of a back line—that has been standard ever since. The slab appeared in 1893, and we'll discuss its significance when we get there.

Meanwhile, the four business considerations were on the front burner.

Everyone had lost money, including many players who had invested in their clubs, and some who hadn't been fully paid. Simply sending every player back to his 1889 club wasn't always possible; among other things, some had now been managers, and over the winter some had defected back sooner than others. And before you could determine the rights to a player, you had to determine who had which team.

Essentially, the National League teams absorbed the rosters and some of the backers of the Brotherhood teams in their cities. There were two exceptions: the Brotherhood Philadelphia team merged with the American Association's Athletics, while the Boston Brotherhood team joined the American Association. Cleveland absorbed both the Cleveland and Buffalo clubs from the Players League.

In New York, Brooklyn, and Pittsburgh, the new Brotherhood parks were better than the ones the National League teams had, so the League teams took them over (The name

Polo Grounds was transferred to the more lux-urious Brotherhood Park, and Day's New Polo Grounds, less than two years old, was torn down. (What the baseball world came to know as the odd shape of Polo Grounds III and IV—as historians refer to it—with such short foul lines and long center field, was the result of the original need to fit that diamond in the northwest corner of the lot alongside the other park). The Dodgers moved to East New York, away from the trolleys, and the Pitts-burgh Pirates into Exposition Park. Chicago, Boston, Philadelphia, and Cincinnati re-mained in their own National League parks, while Cleveland built itself a new park alto-gether, even farther out at East 70th Street.

But wait a minute. Pittsburgh *Pirates?*

That's right. In the redistribution of play-ers, Pittsburgh signed two good ones the As-sociation Athletics had neglected to reserve. An arbitration commission, set up to adjudi-cate disputes about rights to players, ruled for Pittsburgh, but the press and public consid-ered it "piracy." Well, "pirates" was a suitably aggressive image for a competitive team, es-pecially after being the Innocents, and they've been the Pirates ever since.

The real loser, of course, was the Associa-tion. The League had found it profitable to cooperate with Association throughout the 1880's but had always considered itself supe-rior and, realistically, it was on a higher level with its 50-cent basic admission price instead of the Association's 25-cent ticket. Now that the player revolt had failed, there was no need to cater to the lesser league any longer. The League was in no mood to help anyone but it-self, or to be "fair."

So the Association was left with St. Louis, Louisville, Philadelphia, and Columbus, and the Baltimore club that had replaced Brooklyn during 1890. It had the Players League Boston franchise (but not its players), with a promise to abide by the 50-cent rule. And it filled out with new teams in Washington and Cincinnati, discarding Toledo, Rochester, and Syracuse.

The Cincinnati situation was a tangle. The National League franchise had been sold to the Players League, as we saw, but the League sim-ply issued a new one and gave it to Brush, as part payment for his contributions to keeping Day's New York team going. The Association wanted a Cincinnati team too, and got Von der Ahe of St. Louis to back it. (The Cincinnati–St. Louis axis had always been a strong counter-weight to the League's Chicago–Boston–New York triangle.) They got King Kelly to manage it and called the team Kelly's Killers; they played in the outskirts of Cincinnati in Pendle-ton, Ohio.

Eventually, Brush and Von der Ahe became part of committees negotiating some sort of settlement. But midsummer, Columbus and Louisville were going broke. In August, the Cincinnati team was moved to Milwaukee, and Kelly went to the American Association Boston club, which was abrogating its agreement and selling 25-cent tickets. Then, in September, Kelly jumped back to the Beaneaters.

The season lurched on to completion. Both Boston teams won pennants, the Beaneaters by 3½ games over Anson's Chicago, the Reds (or Red Stockings) 8½ over St. Louis (where Comiskey was back at first base and manag-ing). A Brooklyn-Louisville "World Series" in 1890, ending 3-3-1, had been a farce without the Brotherhood stars. There seemed to be no point in trying one now.

The social climate of the time prevailed. The key to business success was monopoly. This was so unquestioned a principle, and so vigorously (and often viciously) pursued, that Congress had just passed the Sherman Anti-Trust Act because monopolistic abuses were so widespread and so evident to the electorate.

The originators of the National League in 1876 had felt that one league was enough, and that it had to have absolute control of business affairs free of player—or other—interference. Their 1891 counterparts—including still ac-tive original participants like Spalding, Reach and Wright—felt the same way now.

In December 1891, the National League accepted applications for membership from St. Louis, Louisville, Baltimore, and Washing-ton of the American Association. The first three simply transferred with their existing ownership. Washington, it was agreed, would be bought by J. Earl Wagner, the Philadelphia butcher who had bailed out the Brotherhood team there in 1890 and had operated the American Association Athletics in 1891. The Athletics as such simply disappeared, while the owners of the disappearing Boston, Columbus, and Cincinnati-Milwaukee clubs were bought off for $130,000, to be paid by the new 12-team circuit.

The League would have a single 12-team standing and play a 154-game schedule, each team playing 14 games (seven home, seven away) with each of 11 opponents. Since Sunday games were still outlawed in many places, teams had to average six *championship* games a week to complete a schedule in the 25 weeks between mid-April and early October, the only period weather made practical in what was still only the northeast quadrant of the country. *Everyday* baseball was here to stay, and there was no shortage of experienced pitchers to make a three-day rotation work.

How things seemed then can be gathered from the 1893 edition of the *World Almanac*. A 16-page section devoted to sports starts with the laws of "American whist"—bridge—adopted in 1892. Then come chess, English horse racing, game laws (hunting), American horse racing, weight-throwing records, and university boat

racing. Finally, "Baseball Records" list past National League and American Association pennant winners, batting champions, and "Championship of America" results—the World's Series, not using that name. After a summary of the 1892 professional and college seasons, a section headed "Important Baseball Events" includes this entry:

1890—Players League organized. Its object was to conduct baseball on broader principles than those of the League and Association. The competition was disastrous to both sides, and at the conclusion of playing season the new League was *dismembered by the superior diplomacy of the old magnates.* (my italics)

So it took less than two years to reduce the Players League to a historical footnote.

And the "old magnates," whose superior diplomacy had now eliminated the American Association as well, looked forward to unfettered exploitation of their monopoly, with no more outside challenges, no obstacles to runaway prosperity, no trouble with players, and unquestioned prestige and public approval.

That's what *they* thought.

CHAPTER 6

The Monopoly

When the 1892 baseball season opened in April, what Hulbert and Spalding had envisioned only 16 years before seemed to have come true. The National League, at the very beginning, was supposed to be a monopoly of major league presentation, but the industry itself had not yet taken form. As soon as the idea of a well-run major league had proved itself, it ceased to be a monopoly because others wanted to imitate its success and could not be fought off. Then the players, against whom the whole league concept was directed as a result of the pre-league experience with chaos, had revolted because the control measures—the very essence of the system—had been applied too harshly and undiplomatically. Now the players had been forced back into submission, the rival league had been disbanded, and the National League was free to operate the way it had always wanted to: with minimum outside interference for maximum profit.

And as always, baseball was part of the times, reflecting and responding to the larger social forces around it. The men who ran it, in the 40–60 age group, had grown up in a commercial climate that considered monopolies and cartels the natural goal of entrepreneurs. The damaging side effects of such arrangements were already recognized so widely that federal antitrust laws had been passed in 1890, so in this sense these club owners were behind the times. But in their view of labor as commodity, unionism as a radicalism to be suppressed, and the inherent right of an employer to make any rules he wanted (and it was always "he" in their thoughts), they were still mainstream.

That spring, economic times were still good. The Depression that would persist through much of the 1890's did not get started until the following year. But change was in the air. In the 1890 election, the Democrats had taken control of Congress, for the first time since the Civil War, by a huge margin. The 1892 presidential campaign, typical for those days, didn't gather steam until midsummer, but President Benjamin Harrison, who had unseated Grover Cleveland in 1888, would be facing him again (and losing). The West had been settled so rapidly, in the last 20 years, that there were now 44 states, with only Oklahoma, Utah, Arizona, and New Mexico territories still moving toward statehood. Immigration, which had peaked at the beginning of the 1880's, was rapidly rising again. The Civil War and its direct aftermath were receding into history, with more than half the present population not even born when it had ended. The two oceans provided a sense of isolation from foreign affairs.

In such a climate, why shouldn't honest businessmen fully expect to arrange their affairs to suit themselves?

And what suited them was profit. The game itself, its rules and conduct, could be left to the professionals, the managers and players. From this viewpoint, an odd mixture emerged: rigid control of the business, loose discipline on the field. And in a pattern we'll see again and again, right through to the end of the 20th century, the part club owners concentrated on got progressively messier, while the part they left alone thrived. The business end of baseball, in the 1890's, was disastrous. The game itself developed the rules and techniques that would become permanent and, in the artistic sense, "right." Perhaps that's not as contradictory as it sounds. The performers (players and managers) knew what they were doing, understood their craft, and were constantly tested by reality and competition. The owners didn't know what they were doing, because few really understood the product they were selling but only guessed and groped for what seemed like short-term return, and, as monopolists, had no competitive forces to set them straight.

The men who had been most influential at the beginning—Spalding, the Wright brothers, Reach, the Jim Mutrie–John Day combination in New York—had brought field experience to business decisions, providing balance for the purely commerce-minded investors. Now the decisive leaders were people like Soden and Brush who, for all the time they had spent in baseball, possessed a merchant mentality. The first group kept seeking ways to make the product—ball games—more attractive to the customers. The new monopolists took the product for granted—people loved it, didn't they?—and focused on how best to cash in. The ironic result was that as the product improved under their benign neglect, their efforts to milk it eventually prevented them from cashing in, the way they expected.

Here, too, is a pattern we'll see repeated, especially in the period around World War I, the 1960's, and the 1990's.

The big story of the 1890's, then, is on the business side. The on-field events, exciting as they were at the time, were quickly (and deliberately) pushed out of the general public consciousness when the new century began, as an entirely new two-league system arose, anxious to disassociate itself from the troubled past and build up its own new importance. What happened on the business side, however, set up all the elements of the next century's success—not deliberately, but by painful experience.

Even before the 1892 season started, the powers that be made a major mistake. They decided on a split season. That is, the won-lost records for the first half of the campaign would determine a first-half champion. Then in the second half everyone would start from zero again. If different teams won the two halves, they could have a postseason playoff and make still more money.

Businessmen may think like that. If one pennant race is good, wouldn't two be better? Wasn't the hot feature of the late 1880's the World Series, and when there is no second league to have it with, wouldn't this replace it?

Any player or experienced fan, of course, could spot the flaw right away. If you win the first half, why should you win the second and kill off interest in a championship playoff? And even if the first-half winner doesn't think that way, will the public at large really believe that it isn't thinking that way?

But when the 1892 season began, the owners were convinced they were on the right track.

The 1892 season started this way:

Team	President	Manager	Ball Park
Baltimore Orioles	Harry Vonderhorst	George Van Haltren	AA Park (1891)
Boston Beaneaters	Arthur Soden	Frank Selee	Old NL Park (1871)
Brooklyn Bridegrooms	Charles Byrne	John M.Ward	Brotherhood Park (1890)
Chicago Colts	Jim Hart	Cap Anson	Brotherhood Park (1890)
Cincinnati Reds	John Brush	Charles Comiskey	AA Park (1884)
Cleveland Spiders	Frank Robison	Patsy Tebeau	NL Park (1891)
Louisville Colonels		Jack Chapman	AA Park (1882)
New York Giants	John Day	Pat Powers	Brotherhood Park (1890) (Polo Grounds III)
Philadelphia	John Rogers	Bill Sharsig	NL Park (1887)
Pittsburgh	William Temple	Tom Burns	NL Park (1891)
St. Louis Cardinals	Chris Von der Ahe	Chris Von der Ahe	AA Park (1882)
Washington Senators	Earl Wagner	Billy Barnie	New Park (1892)

This list tells us a great deal. I list team "presidents" rather than "owners" because actual ownership almost always involves many shareholders with varying degrees of influence. Those with the corporate title of president were the ones, with some exceptions, actually attending meetings and making day-to-day decisions, and almost always owners of major shares.

Hart has just been made president of the Chicago team by Spalding, who has assured Anson that he, Spalding, is still making all the key decisions. He was the chief architect of the successful struggle against the players, and a leader in what is now referred to as "the Second Association War;" but at the age of 42, his attention is more on the sporting-goods business. The still secret but every expanding Spalding–Reach–Wright Bros. cartel continues to grow.

Reach, in similar fashion, has let Rogers take more responsibility for the Phillies (or has Rogers pushed him aside? Reach is no Spalding). And although aging Harry Wright remains dedicated to baseball, younger brother George, the great shortshop, has become a preacher for the new religion of golf. Think of it: 18 people playing a baseball game need one bat; one person playing a round of golf needs half a dozen or more clubs, each more expensive than a plain wooden bat. (Tennis, with one racket per player and a faster rate of using up balls, lies in between.)

Vonderhorst and Von der Ahe are brewers and original members of the now defunct "beer-and-whiskey league." Byrne and Rogers are real-estate people. Wagner and his brother, who made their money as butchers, came in as backers of the Players League team in Philadelphia, took the American Association franchise in 1891, and were allowed to take Washington in the 1892 shakeout—owning three teams in three leagues in three years. Brush is a clothing and department-store merchant. Robison (and his brother Matt) are from the closely related fields of urban transportation (streetcars) and urban real estate (whose value follows the car lines). Soden had acquired the Boston club in the National League's second year, was looked upon as the inventor of the reserve system in 1879, and is a hard-line economizer from the word "go." Day had left the cigar business as a young man to form the original Mets and had made baseball his chief concern for 10 years, but he is now in debt to Soden and Brush.

The managers are six established players (Ward, Anson, Comiskey, Burns, Tebeau, and Van Haltren); five have previous major league managing experience, although they weren't major league players (Selee, Chapman, Powers, Sharsig, and Barnie), and the flamboyant, totally unqualified Von der Ahe, who has decided to manage his own club.

The home fields include three built (or refurbished) for the Brotherhood in 1890; four used by the American Association (the one in Baltimore new in 1891); two established National League locations and two League parks new in 1891; and a new park in Washington. In other words, seven of the 12 parks are less than three years old, and only three (Boston, Louisville, St. Louis) have been in use for as long as 10 years. This means that only one "traditional" National League facility is still in use—

Boston's South End Grounds. It's an indication of how competition, considered ruinous financially at the time and beaten off at all costs, leaves a residue of major improvements. We'll see this happening again and again.

Finally, look at the list of 12 teams. Eight of those franchises are still in business, more than 100 years later, their continuous operation unbroken. They've changed hands, of course, many times; and the Boston team moved on to Milwaukee and Atlanta, while Brooklyn and New York emigrated to California. But their permanence *as franchises* demonstrates the truth of a phrase that the players used as a battle cry in the labor wars of the 1990s when management warned of imminent disaster: "Ball clubs don't go bankrupt, ball club *owners* do; but the clubs go on."

During the 1892 season, two highly significant managerial changes took place. Van Haltren was replaced in Baltimore by Ned Hanlon, and Barnie left Washington, taking over Louisville in 1893. Both had enormous influence on what transpired in the next 10 years as they became part owners as well as field leaders.

But the balance was shifting more and more to the nonbaseball owners. Day, in New York, who had been kept going through the Brotherhood War only by loans from other clubs, now was broke. The franchise was, for all intents and purposes, owned by other teams and operated by the League. "Lending" players (who were now under total control) didn't help. Day had been able to keep Mutrie in charge in 1891 but had been forced by his stockholders to replace him with Powers in 1892. In 1893, Day himself was out, given some menial duties. The new club president was C. C. Van-Cott, but the stockholders who counted were Eddie Talbott in New York and Brush.

At the same time, Byrne, who owned Brooklyn, had also been bled in the economic warfare. In the settlement with the Players League, he accepted financing from George Chauncey, a principal backer of the Brooklyn Brotherhood team, and had to yield to Chauncey's insistence that Ward be made the manager, even though the team had just won two straight pennants (in two leagues!) under Bill McGunnigle. Now, for 1893, Talbott wanted Ward in New York, where he had been so prominent a part of the Giant glory of 1888–89, as a stimulus to the gate. That was okay with Byrne, who made Dave Foutz, one of his outfielders, the Brooklyn manager.

This was just one example of how the owners began to run baseball with a cartel mentality, shifting personnel and stock shares around at will in response to expediency, with no concern for what the long-range effect might be on the perceptions of their customers.

The customers didn't like the split season. Boston, with the best team, won the first half handily. When it finished second to Cleveland in the second half, there was widespread speculation that the Beaneaters hadn't done their best. When Boston polished off Cleveland in the playoff, four games to none with one tie, suspicions did not evaporate. But what got the owners' attention was the way crowds dwindled in the second half. The first-half tailenders, instead of being looked upon as getting another chance, were perceived as proven losers. The Boston fans had nothing to do but wait for the playoff. When it was over, the 12-team league had drawn about 1.8 million customers—150,000 per team (not evenly distributed, of course). Even in the war-ravaged year of 1891, with the Association in its death throes, the 16 teams had averaged well above 160,000. The bonanza had not arrived on schedule.

So the split season was abandoned. For the rest of the decade, the 12-team league played in a single standing, and its deficiencies became evident. The essential feature of a pennant race is the battle to finish first as the schedule gets into its later stages; and at any point, the better attractions, on the road as well as at home, are the teams perceived to be in contention. Suppose you consider any team as high as fourth as being in contention—the "first division," as it used to be called in the eight-team leagues. If you are one of the top four, you have the benefit of that status, and play 43 percent of your games against another contender; if you're not, at least 57 percent of opponents in an eight team league are. But in a 12-team league, two-thirds of the teams are *not* contenders (or perceived as such). So the four top teams play only 27 percent of their games ($\frac{3}{11}$) against other contenders, and the eight noncontenders play 64 percent of their games against other noncontenders.

Besides, if there's only one league with one standing, what do you do for a post-season climax? Boston's third straight pennant in 1893 was an anticlimax.

William Temple, who stepped down as president but remained a major stock-holder of the Pittsburgh Pirates in 1893, had an idea. Why not have the top two finishers play each other? For what? A good question. His answer was, "For the Temple Cup," which, in a fit of modesty, he put up. The governor-general of Canada, Lord Stanley, put up his hockey championship cup the same year; tennis didn't get around to the Davis Cup (donated by Dwight Davis, whose grandson would become an investor in the Amazin' Mets in 1962) until 1900.

But to have a postseason series, you must have players willing to play, and they play for pay. Salaries stop when the season ends. So the gate receipts were earmarked for the players, with 65 percent to the winning club, which was entrusted with passing it on to its players.

To Baltimore, the 1894 pennant winner now being run by Hanlon, this didn't seem right. Hanlon wanted a 50–50 split because, after all, his Orioles were already champions. Temple insisted on 65–35, however, and the second-place Giants, under Ward, won four straight games by an aggregate score of 33–11. The possibility that the players themselves had decided privately on a 50–50 split lingered in the air. (Incidentally, New York's centerfielder, who hit .500 in this series, was Van Haltren, (the former Baltimore manager.)

But now it was time to get serious about cutting salaries.

In 1890, the year of the revolt, the reserve system was essentially not functioning. By 1892, top salaries were in the $3,000–$4,000 range. The player revolt had been against a $2,500 ceiling. But in 1890, 24 major league teams had been in action, which meant that almost 400 positions had to be filled. Now there were half that many, and there was no need to make a formal maximum of $2,400; it became a *de facto* maximum, enforced by both market forces and owner cooperation (blacklisting recalcitrants). The 1893 Phillies, who finished fourth, had an outfield of Ed Delehanty, Sam Thompson, and Billy Hamilton, all eventual Hall of Famers, and pitcher Tim Keefe, also in the Hall of Fame. They had averaged $3,000 apiece in 1892; they played for $1,800 each in 1893.

In the agreement that formed the 12-team League for 1892, rosters were set at 15 men. Halfway through the 1892 season, they were cut to 13, so there wasn't much sense in resisting the lower 1893 offers.

And attendance did pick up in 1893, to 185,000 a club, and in 1894 to 200,000. Eliminating the split-season nonsense helped (if the first-half attendance rate of 1892 had been matched by the second half, attendance would have finished at 185,000.) Being the only game available to the public helped even more.

So with salaries slashed an average of 40 percent and revenue up, the $130,000 owed to the bought-out Association teams was paid off by 1894. Eleven of the 12 teams finished in the black. The country had fallen into a Depression that showed no sign of letting up, but baseball was enjoying unprecedented prosperity.

Now the monopoly would pay off, wouldn't it?

Well, not exactly.

Can you guess the first thing that happened? That's right, success bred imitation. There was a move to revive the American Association in September of 1894.

Barnie in Louisville and Al Buckenberger, the Pittsburgh manager, were involved in it. A prime mover was Francis Richter, editor of the *Sporting Life* in Philadelphia, the eastern equivalent of the *Sporting News* in St. Louis. At an organizational meeting in October, they awarded franchises to New York, Brooklyn, Philadelphia, Pittsburgh, Chicago, Milwaukee, and Washington.

They thought they could sell 25-cent admissions and Sunday games, without a reserve system. And there were certainly enough unemployed professional players to stock the teams.

The monopoly, however, was too entrenched. It had its National Agreement with the minor leagues, and the two most important minors, the Eastern and the Western, stood by it. So did most of the sporting and establishment press: more turmoil like that of 1890, so fresh in recent memory, was the last thing anyone wanted. Declaring the project a threat to the National Agreement, the League ordered anyone connected with it blacklisted—namely, Barnie and Buckenberger. They backed down, and that plan died without reaching the point of financing a club, signing a player, or making a schedule.

Meanwhile, the serious moneymaking business involved real estate. As attendance climbed modestly (to 240,000 a club in 1895 and 1896), building new ball parks was the thing to do, and the key question about a ball park is location. The Robison brothers, in both Cleveland and St. Louis, dealt with trolley-car lines. A ball park built along or at the end of such a line would give the transport line many riders and raise the value of property along that line. In other cities, the relationship might not be as obvious, but the combination of real estate, political influence, and the baseball operation as a come-on with built-in publicity existed everywhere in some form. An increasing flow of immigrants created booming populations in precisely those cities that had teams, and improved transportation technology hastened the geographic expansion of city boundaries.

And necessity frequently intervened. These wooden grandstands were easy prey to fire.

In 1891, in Cleveland, the Robisons rejected the Brotherhood Park on East 55th Street and built their own, farther out on the line at 70th Street. They called it League Park.

In New York, the Giants had taken over the better Polo Grounds in 1891 and were there to stay.

In Pittsburgh, the 1891 amalgamation with the Players League team had taken over their new facility, Exposition Park.

In 1892, the new Washington team set up shop at Boundary Field on Seventh Street, where Griffith Stadium would someday stand.

In 1893, Louisville moved into a new version of Eclipse Park, across the street from the original, damaged by fire in September of 1892.

The same year in St. Louis, the Robisons built Robison Field only a few blocks from Sportsman's Park, where Von der Ahe had always operated; he was now their tenant.

Also in 1893, Chicago had to vacate West Side Park, occupied since 1885, because the great Columbian Exposition was to be built on that site. The Colts played a year in South Side Park (where Comiskey is now) and then moved to West Side Grounds, a new field farther west, between Polk and Taylor Streets, which run east-west from midtown. The team would stay there until 1915, when it took over Wrigley Field.

Baltimore had occupied the third version of Oriole Park, originally built for the Association Orioles in 1882, when they became National Leaguers in 1892. After a fire in May of 1894, it was rebuilt in July and made smaller, because affordable insurance wouldn't cover a larger one.

In 1894, Cincinnati had a new playing field at League Park, opened in 1884. It was turned around so that first base was to the south instead of to the east, to get the sun out of the hitter's eyes, and the stands had to be rebuilt accordingly. The next year, it became the first park to paint the center-field fence black, to help a hitter's vision.

In 1895, the Phillies moved into Baker Bowl, which would become legendary in the next century. At Broad Street and Huntingdon, it was called The Huntingdon Street Grounds until 1915, two years after William F. Baker bought the team.

Finally, in 1898, Brooklyn abandoned the Eastern Parkway location forced upon it by its deal with the Players League and moved back to the center of the borough into a new Washington Park, dodging trolleys again.

So in a span of eight years, each of the 12 teams had acquired a new ball park. That used up a lot of managerial attention. Control of salaries and players remained firm, but attendance stagnated, then started to dip. It stayed at 250,000 a club for three more years but fell alarmingly in 1898 below 200,000. By this time, there were bewildering interlocking ownerships, a situation never envisioned by the creators of "orderly competition." There was no strong leadership after Spalding's withdrawal, since the league president, Nick Young, was simply a caretaker and superclerk in his own eyes as well as in the view of his employers, the autonomous owners. No one was in a position to say to these "magnates," as they had come to be called, that public belief in the integrity of the competition might be undermined.

Nor was any aura of integrity enhanced by the widespread awareness that players, managers, and even owners were betting on games, while open betting in the stands returned, reminiscent of the pool-selling days that had seemed so troublesome 20 years before.

And with no strong central league organization, umpires were at the mercy of intimidation and abuse from players and managers, who learned quickly that persistent rowdiness and outright cheating (with only two umpires on the field) could help them win.

In this deteriorating moral climate, however, the ball game itself was taking shape and being polished to a high professional gloss. Owners absorbed with financial matters rubber-stamped playing-rule changes suggested by people focused on what made a good game—and that benign neglect turned out to be the best thing they ever did.

For the 1892 season, the playing rules are already mostly those we're familiar with: four balls for a walk, three strikes for an out, a batted ball caught on the fly is an out, force plays (touching the base, not the runner, when the runner is forced to advance), and so forth.

There are two very important differences, however. The pitching distance and method of delivery are not yet stabilized, and a foul does not count as a strike (if it's not caught on the fly for an out).

The pitching rules have been changing almost every year and have been different in different leagues. The four-ball walk, reduced from five, was adopted only in 1889. The "pitcher's box" (a term we still use) is exactly that, a box, whose width has remained at four feet but whose depth has varied from 5½ to seven feet. Since 1887, the pitcher has been required to keep his back foot in contact with the back line and to start his delivery facing the batter, with the ball held clearly visible to the umpire and batter. Now the box is 5½ feet deep, and its front line is 50 feet from the middle of home base, which is a 12-inch square set into the intersection of the foul lines.

Therefore, the effective pitching distance is 54 feet 9½ inches, from the back line of the pitcher's box to the front corner of home plate. This is *not* the distance from the release point of the delivery, which varies with each individual's stride and motion. It is the limiting point where the back foot must remain during delivery.

Since this is marked with chalk, it's easy enough during a game for a pitcher to cheat occasionally by inching forward in a way the umpire might not notice.

But the back line, even if scrupulously observed, is four feet wide, and the pitcher may keep contact with any part of it. He then has a wide choice of angles from which to deliver the ball and can adjust this on each pitch to his preference, giving the hitter a greater variety of trajectories to react to.

What's more, full overhand pitching has been allowed for nine years now, and there are more and more pitchers (especially young ones) who can throw harder that way. And the harder a pitcher throws, the more intimidating he is, because being hit by the ball hurts.

All this has been tilting the offense-defense balance in favor of the pitcher.

The Players League, run by players, tried moving the pitcher's box back one foot and had success. But in 1891, the two surviving leagues stuck with their existing rules, which carried over in 1892 to the monopoly league.

But spectators and most players—the nonpitchers—prefer more hitting. While everyone had been so absorbed with the business turmoil of 1889–91, the League batting average had been dropping, from .264 to .254 to .252. (The Players League had hit .274, remember?)

Now, in 1892, the League batting average fell to .245.

So for 1893, the whole pitching rule is redesigned in favor of the hitter.

The back line is replaced by a rubber slab, 12 inches wide and four inches deep, and the rest of the "box" erased. The pitcher's foot must be in contact with the slab when he releases the ball.

And the front of the slab is to be 60 feet 6 inches from the *rear corner*—not the center—of home base. That makes the effective pitching distance to the front corner of the plate 59 feet 1 inch.

That's 4 feet 3½ inches farther.

That's about a 7 percent increase in air-flight distance, translating an 85-mile-an-hour fastball into about five miles less.

But that's not the main thing. Pitchers can adjust to throwing a bit farther and can learn to make their breaking balls break at a different point. The even bigger help to the hitter is that the pitcher is now pinned down to one spot horizontally, right in line with home plate. He can no longer come at the hitter from two feet to either side.

The hitters respond, and even feast. In 1893 the league hits .280, and in 1894 it hits .309.

So a final adjustment is needed, and Hanlon is the one who pushes for it. The 12-inch slab is too narrow, he says, because each pitcher's forward stride creates a hole (he calls it a "bank"). The tall man, with a longer stride, creates this hole farther forward, and when a shorter man takes his turn, his step hits the slope, not the bottom, of this bank, and he slips, causing injury and ineffectiveness. This is not fair. If the slab is made wider, allowing different pitchers to choose their own starting point, each can make his own "bank" and not be bothered by the others'. Also, the four-inch depth of the slab isn't enough for good footing.

So in 1895, the slab becomes 24 inches wide and six inches deep.

It still is.

There is no formalized "mound" at this point, but it gradually is coming into use. Overhand pitchers have learned that pitching from a hill is an advantage, and home groundskeepers accommodate them, but there are no set rules about it. The slab, instead of a box, will hasten systematization of the mound.

Meanwhile, the hitter has retained a great advantage in that fouls don't count. There are exceptions. If a batter plainly fouls off a pitch "deliberately," the umpire has the right to call a strike; but that's subjective and not often done. A bunt, however, is certainly a deliberate act. So in 1894, the rules redefine what constitutes a bunt and automatically make foul bunts count as strikes.

Rules are made to be broken, and professionals, as a matter of pride as well as for advantage, push every rule to the limit to see what they can get away with. The loose discipline of the 1890's, characterized by rough language and physical confrontations on the field, brings to light other necessary refinements.

In 1896, the requirement that a pitcher hold the ball in plain view is dropped. The slab, pinning him in the middle of the field and changing his motion, has made the rule unnecessary.

In 1897, he is forbidden to intentionally discolor the ball (which stays in play many innings at a time), either by rubbing dirt on it or by other means.

The foul hit is also redefined. The umpire used to rule a ball foul as soon as it hit foul ground. Now it won't be foul until it *comes to rest* (or hits an obstruction, including player or umpire) on foul ground before passing first or third base. That is, a ball can bounce back and be fair *before* reaching first or third; if its first bounce is foul *beyond* first or third, it's foul; if it passes either bag fair, it's fair for good.

In 1898, the specifications for what constitutes a balk by the pitcher are spelled out. In 1899, a balk (that is, an illegal motion by the pitcher) gives the batter first base, but that's dropped after one year. The balk is to protect base runners; the batter can be protected by calling an illegal pitch a ball or no play.

And in 1900, the front corners of home base are filled in, to give the pitcher (and umpire) a better target for calling strikes, and the five-sided home plate has arrived.

Only one more step has to be taken to create "modern baseball," and that's coming up in the next chapter. In the 1890's, however, a nonbunt foul is not a strike: it's simply no play.

But while the game itself is improving, while spectators are responding to the sight of heavy hitting and readers are being attracted to it, while fireballing pitchers are becoming heroes in a heavy-hitting age, the boys in the back room—the owners—are brewing a bigger mess than ever.

In 1895, the debt-ridden New York Giants are purchased by Andrew Freedman, who has strong ties to the corrupt Tammany Hall political machine. He is flamboyant, autocratic, and prone to conflict with his employees and with his fellow owners. The franchise, of such key importance to the league as a whole, flounders.

The same year, Von der Ahe is in so much trouble in his personal life—debt, divorce, drunkenness—that he is losing control of his St. Louis franchise.

The owners of Cincinnati (Brush) and Boston (Soden) remain significant stockholders in the Giants.

In 1898, the Robison brothers acquire St. Louis. They still have Cleveland, having been refused permission to sell that team to Detroit. Controlling both teams and thinking like businessmen, they transfer the best Cleveland players to St. Louis, to create one strong team in a better market. Baltimore's Vonderhorst and Hanlon have bought into the Brooklyn team and transfer the best Baltimore players there, with Hanlon now president of the Orioles and manager of the Dodgers, simultaneously.

The 1899 season is a disaster on many levels. Boston or Baltimore has won all seven of the 12-team League pennants so far. The Temple Cup has been abandoned after 1897. Now the artificially strengthened Brooklyn team wins the pennant by eight games over Boston, with Baltimore fourth, 15 games back. St. Louis, even with Cy Young added, rises only to fifth, while the stripped Cleveland Spiders compile a 20–134 record that not even the 1962 Mets will be able to match for futility. The attendance average inches back up over 200,000, but it is concentrated almost entirely in seven solid cities: Chicago, Philadelphia, Boston, Cincinnati, and, with special player help, St. Louis, Brooklyn, and Pittsburgh. These account for 80 percent of the total.

Something has to give, and it will at the annual League meeting in December of 1899.

SEASONS 1892–99

1892

Boston had emerged from the Brotherhood War and the American Association's demise with by far the best roster. It had kept some Players League stars and now inherited some players from the AA franchise. It had an aging King Kelly and a young Hugh Duffy, who would become a Hall of Fame hitter and outfielder. The shortstop, Herman (Germany) Long, was an outstanding base stealer. The first baseman, Tommy Tucker, was outstanding defensively. Its top pitcher, Kid Nichols, was in only the third full year of what would be a Hall of Fame career. And No. 2 was Jack Stivetts, not only one of the new fireball pitchers but a good hitter.

Boston's manager, Frank Selee, was a man ahead of his time, a nonplayer (at any high level) who was nevertheless a fully qualified judge of talent, tactics, strategy, and handling players. He was 31 years old when given a chance to manage the denuded League team in Boston in 1890, and finished fifth; but when the stars came back in 1891, he won the National League pennant. He would go on to have one of the most brilliant, and least recognized, managerial records in baseball history, cut short by ill health.

So Boston's fast start of 11–2 was not surprising, and continuing to win at a .700 pace, the team clinched the first half of the split season, to end July 15, before the end of June. It wound up 52–22. The second strongest team, Cleveland, was 40–33.

And that spelled trouble.

If Boston did that again in the second half, it

would be undisputed champion, and in 11 other cities there would be nothing to get excited about. If it didn't, people would think the team wasn't trying, since it could still win the championship in a play-off. Management, drunk with monopoly power, compounded the problem by cutting salaries and releasing aging stars like Kelly and pitcher John Clarkson to save money. So when Cleveland started the second half 23–5 and built an 8½-game lead by mid-August, the public's worst suspicions seemed to be confirmed. Attendance everywhere dropped precipitously.

Boston then re-signed Kelly (while Clarkson joined Cleveland) and resumed winning. A 28–9 finish made its second-half record 50–26, but still three games behind Cleveland's 53–23. There would indeed be a play-off for the championship.

The situation was unsatisfactory all around. Boston's full-season mark of 102–48 was clearly the best, and Brooklyn (95–56) had a better record than Cleveland (93–56) even though it won neither half. And Cleveland's success had been made possible by Clarkson, who posted a 17–10 record after coming over from Boston to join Cleveland's young phenom, Denton True (Cy for Cyclone) Young, now in his third season.

The first game of the best-of-nine play-off, in Cleveland, was an 11-inning scoreless tie, hailed as one of the greatest games ever played, in terms of skill. Young allowed four singles, Stivetts (who had pitched a no-hitter on August 6 against Brooklyn) six. But then Boston beat Clarkson 4–3 and Young 3–2, and won the next three games 4–0, 12–7, and 8–3, confirming the public's impression that the superior Boston team had been playing more possum than baseball during late July and August.

The first three games, in Cleveland, had drawn an average of almost 7,000. The fourth, in Boston, drew 6,500. But the last two brought in 3,376 and 1,812. On the final day, a Monday, it was as cold as one might expect in Boston on October 24.

The split-season format was dead.

1893

Along with severe cuts in salaries across the board, the owners cut the schedule back to 132 games in 1893. It would be a straight-up 12-team pennant race, with no talk of postseason play for the first time in 11 years. But the new pitching distance of 60 feet 6 inches would stimulate offense and therefore, it was hoped, attendance.

A continuation of the Boston-Cleveland rivalry was expected, and the Spiders did lead the league through May. But by the end of June, Boston, Brooklyn, and Philadelphia were tied for first place, with Cleveland 5½ games back. Baltimore, rebuilding under Hanlon, was put in its place when Boston swept a five-game series July 27–29. The Beaneaters then took two of three from Philadelphia, whose season was wrecked when Billy Hamilton got typhoid fever and was through for the year. Boston followed that series with a nine-game winning streak, and its 35–5 stretch to a 13-game lead let it clinch the pennant in Cleveland September 20.

Even this far back in the game's history, it turned out that the absence of postseason attention and glamour deprived a team of lasting appreciation. This Boston team, under Selee's direction, perfected the hit-and run play and intensive use of signals, for which Baltimore would get all the credit in subsequent years (until modern historians went to work). The disproportionate effect World Series events have on reputations is an unfair, and perhaps irrational, phenomenon; but it was at work even then. The 1893 team was even stronger than the 1892 version because Bobby Lowe, when moved from the outfield to second base, suddenly emerged as a home-run hitter in the new offense-friendly world.

The pitching changes had the desired effect. The league batting average jumped from .245 to .280. Runs per game went from 10.2 to 13.1. Strikeouts were reduced by a third, but walks went up only one-sixth. Home runs were still rare—about one homer every two games—but up 30 percent from 1892.

The rest of the 1890s would continue to be hitters' years.

Boston's final margin was only five games, because Pittsburgh put on a 19–4 spurt to take second place from Cleveland. Philadelphia, limping after losing Hamilton, was fourth, while New York, Brooklyn, and Cincinnati were closely bunched just above .500. But Baltimore, although eighth with 60–70, was getting its pieces into place.

1894

The Orioles started 1894 with only one regular left from the 1892 team Hanlon had taken over, which finished last. That was Wilbert Robinson, the catcher, a 30-year-old New Englander starting his ninth big-league season. At first base was Joe Kelley, a bright young prospect for whom Hanlon had sent George Van Haltren, the Baltimore manager he had succeeded, to Pittsburgh. But when a trade with Brooklyn before the 1894 season brought him Dan Brouthers and Willie Keeler, he moved Kelley to the outfield and put Brouthers, a well-established slugger, at first. (Brooklyn considered Keeler a throw-in because he was "too small.") In center between Keeler and Kelley he had Steve Brodie, a solid all-around player acquired from St. Louis late in 1893.

Another trade, with Louisville, brought Hanlon a young shortstop named Hughie Jennings, moving an even younger John McGraw over to third. The second baseman was Henry (Heinie) Reitz, also in his mid-20s, installed there in 1893. The chief pitchers were Sadie McMahon, Kid Gleason, Bill Hawke, and Duke Esper—a four-man rotation indicating Hanlon's rapid response to the new pitching conditions and the absence of workhorses like Nichols and Young.

This team became the "Old Orioles," one of baseball's most enduring legends. McGraw, Jennings, Robinson, Gleason, and Kelley became prominent managers, the first four winning pennants; all but Gleason, along with Keeler, Brouthers, and Hanlon himself, are in the Hall of Fame.

This group adopted, refined, and made permanently popular the techniques Selee's Boston team had developed, especially the teamwork represented by elaborate signals and the hit-and-run aggressive offense, so well suited to the new pitching conditions. To these it added physical aggressiveness to the point of viciousness, endless verbal abuse heaped on opponents and umpires, and outright fighting at the least provocation. But the underlying attitude consisted of cleverness and alertness applied with more constant intensity than others had maintained. What can be called the "tempo" of modern big-league baseball was established in everyone's consciousness by these Orioles.

All the way to September they battled Boston on even terms, and that month began with the teams tied for the lead. Then the Orioles won 18 straight and the pennant by three games over New York, which overtook fading Boston. In Hanlon's rotation, McMahon had won 25 games, Hawke 16, and Gleason and Esper 15 each.

But of course that wasn't the end of it. The Temple Cup had been highly publicized all season long, so the Orioles had to face a series with the Giants.

What happened was the opposite of 1892: the favorite was beaten soundly, while the series was a great financial success.

New York had the game's most powerful pitcher, Amos Rusie, whose devastating fastball had encouraged the idea of moving the mound back, and Monte Ward as player-manager. McMahon, his arm sore, couldn't pitch for the Orioles, who didn't want to play anyhow. The Giants swept them 4–1, 9–6, 4–1, 16–3, but the attendance figures were eye-openers: 11,000 for each of the first two games in Baltimore, 22,000 and 12,000 in New York.

1895

Baltimore, New York, Boston, and Cleveland were looked upon as the contenders going into the 1895 season. But the Giants, having passed into Freedman's hands, used three managers after dropping Ward, started 15–17, never got better, and finished 66–65. Boston, showing wear and tear in its distinguished lineup, wound up tied for fifth with Brooklyn. The season turned into a two-team race between Baltimore and Cleveland.

September arrived with Cleveland ahead by half a game, so the Orioles repeated their 1894 routine: a 20–7 September gave them first place by a three-game margin. Hanlon had made two significant changes: he turned Gleason, a .500 pitcher, into his regular second baseman, keeping Reitz in a utility role (when this, too, was a relatively new concept) and he relied on young pitchers—a fastballing rookie (Billy Hoffer, 31–6) and a journeyman (George Hemming, 20–13), keeping McMahon (10–4) as a spot starter.

This was the third year of the longer pitching distance, and the hitters were feasting. The league batting average was up to .296. The Orioles scored 1,009 runs—7.6 a game—as Kelley and Brodie knocked in 134 runs each and Jennings 125. (We know that now, thanks to modern researchers; there were no official or publicized RBI figures in those days, but of course the fans could see what was going on even if they didn't have hand calculators.) Third-place Philadelphia scored even more, 1,068 runs, but Baltimore's strength lay in scoring differential: the Orioles scored 363 more runs than they allowed and led the league in pitching.

All this meant more identifiable heroes. Lowe, who had unexpectedly tied for third in the league with 14 homers in 1893, had hit four in one game on May 30, 1894, but still wasn't the leader with 17, because teammate Duffy hit 18 while hitting .440—still a record. Philadelphia had Ed Delehanty, the 1893 champion, and Sam Thompson, the 1895 champion, with 18. Hamilton, back in action as the third member of the outfield, hit .380, .404, and .389 in those three seasons and was outhit by both Delehanty and Thompson in two of those years. That's why the Phillies scored 1,068 runs.

But pitchers, while giving up more runs, held up their glamour quotient in terms of victories. In those three seasons, Rusie won 33, 36, and 22; Nichols, 34, 32, and 30; and Young, 34, 25, and 35.

One of the benefits of monopoly was that with fewer players to keep track of, fans could focus fully on the biggest stars. Cleveland's two standouts were Jesse Burkett, the 1895 batting champion at .409 (beating out Delehanty's .404), and Young. That's what the Orioles had to overcome in the second Temple Cup series.

They couldn't and didn't. Young beat them 5–4 (thanks to two runs in the bottom of the ninth), 7–1, and 5–2 in alternate games, and Cleveland beat Hoffer in the second game 7–2. The Orioles avoided a sweep only by winning the fourth game 5–0 behind Esper. Burkett conducted business as usual, hitting .476.

But two straight triumphs for the runner-up weren't doing much to enhance the validity of—and need for—the Temple Cup.

1896

The batting barrage continued in 1896, as the league hit .290. On July 13, Delehanty matched Lowe's feat of hitting four home runs in one game. (It wouldn't happen again until Lou Gehrig did it 36 years later.) But he hit only nine others and shared the homer title at 13. Burkett hit over .400 again, winning the title at .410. They didn't mind that Rusie, in a salary dispute with Freedman, held out the entire 1896 season.

The Orioles (who hit .328 as a team) stuck to their September magic. Pittsburgh, Philadelphia, Baltimore, and Cleveland all started well, and when Cincinnati had a 25–6 stretch in July, it surged to a six-game lead over the field. But the Reds cooled off, were passed by Cleveland, and the Spiders, in turn, were overtaken by the Orioles, who wound up 9½ games ahead. For the third straight year. Baltimore not only finished first but won more than two-thirds of its games. Cincinnati settled for third, and Boston, showing signs of revival, was fourth.

However, an equally firm pattern had developed at the other end of the league. Louisville finished 12th and last for the third year in a row, failing to win 30 percent of its games each time. In the five years of the 12-team league, Washington and St. Louis had never finished higher than ninth—that is, in the "third division," if one spoke in what would become baseball language (counting the top four teams in an eight-team league as the "first division"). In 1895, Chicago, never a contender, drew 380,000 while finishing fourth. Louisville drew fewer than that for its four-year total, 1892–95. The gap was widening.

Meanwhile, another Temple Cup series was coming up, with virtually the same Baltimore and Cleveland teams that had met the year before. This time the Orioles were determined to take it more seriously. They had won three straight pennants but were 1–8 in the Temple Cup and no longer wiling to be embarrassed. Their task was made easier when the very first batter, McGraw, hit a line drive that struck Young on his right wrist. Young finished the game but was unable to pitch again in the series. Baltimore went on to sweep four straight, 7–1, 7–2, 6–2, 5–0, with a clearly superior team playing up to its potential. A top-form Young might have postponed the outcome, but probably could not have altered the final result.

As for the public, however, it was losing interest. The first two games in Cleveland drew 4,000 and 3,000, the last two in Baltimore, 4,000 and 1,200. Only three years before, when the Orioles had been swept by the Giants, a four-game series pulled in 56,720; now a similar set had produced only 12,200. When your sales drop off 78 percent in two years, it's time to worry about your product.

1897

A great pennant race and the final blow to the Temple Cup marked the 1897 season. The hated-but-admired Orioles and the revived Beaneaters slugged it out all year long. After a 1–6 start, Boston got straightened out and in June took the lead with a 22–2 spurt. From then on, it was neck and neck, and through September the teams were never more than one game apart. In a late-September showdown series, Boston took first place by winning the opener, but Baltimore won the next day. Boston moved ahead again by winning the rubber game 19–10 and went on to finish first by two games, 93–39 to Baltimore's 90–40.

Boston now had Jimmy Collins (Hall of Fame) playing third base, and Hamilton in center field. Duffy, Lowe, Long, and Nichols were still going strong. The team scored 1,025 runs, 360 more than it allowed, and had a batting average of .318. Baltimore hit .325 as Keeler led the league with a .432 average, hitting safely in the first 44 games. This would be a forgotten streak until DiMaggio's 56 in 1941 focused attention on it. But the Orioles scored a bit less than Boston and didn't have as good pitching. The four-man rotation was now well established, and each team had three 20-game winners.

However, neither team displayed any intensity in the postseason series. Rumors were abroad again that the Baltimore and Cleveland players had agreed to split the money the year before, and that the teams were doing it again. Pitchers complained of sore arms, the fielding was described as lackadaisical, and the batters had as fine a time as one would expect if major leaguers weren't bearing down. Boston won the opener 13–12, then lost 13–11. Baltimore went ahead with an 8–3 victory in seven innings. With two days off before resuming the series in Baltimore, the teams stopped off for exhibition games against each other in Worcester and Springfield (evidently going south by heading

west), indicating that the Temple Cup competition was something less than all-important. Baltimore won those games, and the next cup game 12–11. One more victory would close it out for the Orioles, and they managed one, 9–3, in one hour and 20 minutes before some 750 home-town fans on October 11.

The runner-up had won again, but everyone knew that Boston was the real champion and that the Temple Cup games were pointless. That three-game series in Baltimore in September had drawn 57,000 customers. The Temple Cup crowds, each markedly smaller than the one before, totaled 23,000 for five games.

At the winter meeting, it was decided to retire the cup.

1898

The schedule went back up to 154 games in 1898 (14 against each opponent instead of 12), since there would be no postseason. Boston, stronger than ever, won 102 games—as it had in the 154-game schedule of 1892—and finished six games ahead of Baltimore. Cincinnati was 11½ games out, with no one else within 17, while St. Louis, last for the second straight year, finished 63½ games behind. The two-year record of the Cardinals was 68–213, a fact that would soon take on enormous significance.

For all the imbalance, however, bright new stars were rising. Louisville had a young shortstop, incredibly fast and a terrific hitter, Honus (Hans) Wagner. In Philadelphia, Napoleon Lajoie was a dazzling new second baseman. Rusie, who had returned to the Giants in 1897 with 28 victories, won 20 again in 1898, while a wily little right-hander in Chicago, Clark Griffith, relying on trick pitches, had just reeled off his fifth straight 20-victory season with a winning percentage of .672 over that span. In the race for the batting title, Keeler had beaten out Hamilton .379 to .369, and as the pitchers had begun to master the new conditions, the league batting average went down to a more reasonable .271.

Fans had plenty of personalities and outstanding performances to interest them, but too many noncompetitive teams and the persistent rowdiness, fomented by the Orioles but actually widespread in the absence of league discipline, tarnished the scene.

The problem, for the owners, was something that fans a century later would hear about ad nauseum: there was too great a discrepancy between "big" (or "good") markets and "small" (or "bad") markets.

Weaker clubs seeking finances, as we've seen, had led to interlocking ownerships. In particular, Baltimore had bought into Brooklyn and Cleveland into St. Louis. In 1898, Brooklyn, an independent city, had become part of Greater New York, one of five boroughs of a world-class metropolis challenging the great European capitals. Obviously, it was a better market than Baltimore, fading at the end of a decade of depressed economy. Baltimore had lots of good ball players; Brooklyn had lots of good customers. What would you do? That's what Hanlon, Vonderhorst, and Byrne did: they shipped good players to Brooklyn.

As for St. Louis, it had been wrecked by the protracted ruin of Von der Ahe himself, but it had a baseball tradition and appetite the equal of Chicago's. Cleveland, on the other hand, hadn't supported its Spiders when they were winners in the first half of the decade; why should Burkett and Young, superstars, languish there? Ship them to St. Louis and create a contender where people appreciate one.

"Syndicate baseball!" cried press and public.

"Sure," replied the honest and upright monopolists. "What's wrong with that?"

1899

Hanlon himself went to Brooklyn as field manager in 1899, bringing along Keeler, Kelley, Jennings, and first baseman Dan McGann. The Dodgers had finished 10th the year before, so disorganized that owner Byrne and his protégé, Charlie Ebbets, took turns at managing. Now they finished first, eight games ahead of Boston and nine ahead of Philadelphia. In Baltimore, where McGraw and Robinson had refused to leave because they had a profitable cafe business there, McGraw was mollified by being made manager. The team had enough left to finish a strong fourth.

But the Baltimore-Brooklyn shift worked as it was supposed to. Brooklyn drew 270,000, not only more than double its 1898 attendance but more than double Baltimore's 1898 figure in its season-long battle for first place. Baltimore, with half a team, drew the same 120,000 it had the year before. Net gain: almost 150,000.

The shift of Young, Burkett, and some others from Cleveland to St. Louis did not work so well. The Cardinals got out of the basement, but no higher than fifth, even though Young won 26 games and Burkett barely lost the batting title to Delehanty. Nevertheless, attendance more than doubled, to a hefty 370,000, second only to Philadelphia and more than perennially profitable Chicago.

However, the effect on Cleveland was devastating. Even with the club's stars and a respectable fifth-place finish in 1898, League Park had a *season* total of only 70,000, which meant precious few passengers for that trolley line. Now, the totally stripped Spiders won only 20 games and lost 134—and reported a season total of 6,088 for 42 home games, an average crowd of 145. The remaining 35 scheduled home games were farmed out elsewhere, so the team's road record was 11–101.

That tore it.

AFTERMATH

At their December 1899, meeting, the owners brought into the open the issue that had been percolating in private: the strong must jettison the weak; they had to get rid of some clubs.

Freedman had been outspoken in previous meetings and private conversations. His New York franchise was of key importance to the league as a whole, and it was sick often in the 1890s. It had been kept alive, at the beginning, by the infusion of money and players from other teams. To end Rusie's one-year holdout, other clubs had contributed to his salary. But, Freedman insisted, he'd do nothing to promote his own team unless the league slimmed down; he wouldn't spend his money to keep weak teams alive so that others could profit.

Results on the field had aggravated the instability. The same teams won, the same teams lost, every year. Artificial attempts at postseason excitement, like the Temple Cup, only underlined the fact that people outside the two cities involved didn't care, since they knew who the "real" champion was—and if they didn't care about the post-season, they didn't care about the late stages of the regular season once it took shape, since those led to nothing else.

Game results, abstract economic theory, and hard-headed, short-term, profit-loss considerations coalesced toward the same conclusion: the 12-team league didn't work.

Four teams had to go. Baltimore and Cleveland were easy to let go of: their owners now had Brooklyn and St. Louis. The other two expendables were Louisville and Washington, which had finished higher than 10th only once in 16 tries (Washington, seventh in 1897). Their 1899 attendance figures had been 109,000 and 86,000. In addition, Louisville's best players, the young Wagner and an outstanding outfielder named Fred Clarke, had already been trans-ferred to Pittsburgh by Barney Dreyfuss, who had emerged as Louisville's top officer in recent years and then bought a piece of the financially troubled Pittsburgh team and become its president for 1900.

At the same time, there was much talk of a renewed effort to revive an American Association (about which more in the next chapter), so it was important to keep the abandoned cities from joining a new league. A buyout was the way to go: it had worked beautifully only eight years before in the execution of the old Association. The four teams to be expelled asked for a plan that would cost $150,000. They settled in March for one that came to $105,000, to be raised by having each of the remaining eight earmark 5 percent of gross revenue for the next two years.

This left a circuit of Boston, Brooklyn, New York, and Philadelphia in the "east" and Pittsburgh, Cincinnati, Chicago, and St. Louis in the "West." It would stay intact for 53 years.

PART III

THE MAJORS

CHAPTER 7

War

Amerian life in the 1890's was still localized to a degree we can't imagine these days. Telegraph wires did carry major news (and sports results) from coast to coast within minutes, but by and large people's attention was focused on events in their own immediate town and region. While the monopolized National League did represent big-league play for baseball followers everywhere and controlled many minor leagues through interlocking agreements, its full impact was limited to the cities it occupied. Elsewhere, baseball activity could thrive without the need for broader awareness.

One minor league was particularly successful. It was called the Western League.

In the wreckage of 1890–92, minor league baseball had suffered also, especially as the new monopoly paid so little heed to past major-minor agreements. The Western League, consisting of Indianapolis, Sioux City, Detroit, Toledo, Kansas City, Milwaukee, Minneapolis, and Grand Rapids, was one of the failing minors. For its 1894 season it acquired a new president, a Cincinnati newspaperman named Bancroft (Ban) Johnson. As a baseball writer, he had become an acquaintance of, and irritant to, John Brush, the Cincinnati club's owner, and Charles Comiskey, the Cincinnati manager who had been the great first baseman of the St. Louis Browns of the 1880's.

Brush, who also owned the Indianapolis club, helped promote Johnson's presidency as a way of getting him out of Cincinnati. A year later, when Brush fired Comiskey, Johnson welcomed Comiskey as manager in Sioux City. A year after that, Comiskey bought the team and moved it to St. Paul.

Johnson, a big man physically, bursting with energy and conviviality, and a brilliant strategist, put the league on its feet. In the abortive attempt to start another American Association in 1894, Johnson had remained loyal to the National League by sticking to the major-minor agreements. He built up his own league, stressing support for umpires and strong discipline against rowdiness, the two troublesome aspects of the monopoly major league that bothered the public. He also fought with Brush, who would draft players for Cincinnati (as the majors could from the minors) and assign them to Indianapolis.

In 1897, when a catcher named Connie Mack was fired (or quit) as manager in Pittsburgh, Johnson recruited him for Milwaukee, giving him an interest in the club. Johnson already had long-range plans to challenge the National for major status.

In the fall of 1899, when the National was deciding to drop four teams, a new move to restart the American Association developed. Its backers offered the Western League a merger. Johnson refused. He had plans of his own. His league now had Indianapolis, Detroit, Columbus, Milwaukee, Kansas City, and Buffalo—all one-time National League members—and both Minneapolis and St. Paul. He wanted Cleveland, being dropped by the National, and was ready to put a team in Chicago, where baseball fans continued to flock to the Colts in their lackluster years.

In 1900, therefore, he changed the league's name to the American League and negotiated with the National to allow a move into Chicago but did not, pointedly, abrogate the major-minor agreement that gave the National draft rights and other privileges. Worried more about a possible American Association, the National accepted sharing Chicago, because it, too, had plans of its own.

Comiskey's St.Paul team moved to Chicago's South Side and became the White Stockings. The Grand Rapids team moved into vacated Cleveland. Now seven of the eight American League teams had former National League identities, and a move east was the next step.

During the 1900 season, Brooklyn won the National League pennant again, fighting off the greatly strengthened Pittsburgh team. In the American League, Comiskey's White Sox finished first, four games ahead of Mack's Milwaukee, and drew 120,000, about half as much as the National League's Chicago team did while finishing fifth in its slimmed-down eight-team circuit.

In December 1900, Johnson was stalling about signing on again for a major-minor agreement, and the National, feeling strong in its tightened monopoly, was not living up to provisions intended to protect the minors. Dropping its weak members had pushed average attendance back to the 250,000 range and made salary control even easier. It would do as it liked. Still another try at an American Association didn't worry it now.

Johnson thereupon announced that the American League would move into Baltimore, Washington, Philadelphia, and Boston, dropping Kansas City, Indianapolis, Minneapolis, and Buffalo. It would now be "national" in scope (since the great mass of the population was still concentrated in the Northeast and bordering the Great Lakes); it would claim major status and not allow its players to be drafted; and while it would observe all player contracts where they were valid, it would sign any player who was merely "reserved" by a National League club without a fresh contract.

Johnson, Comiskey, and Mack had acquired two important allies: Griffith, the star pitcher of the Chicago Nationals, who switched sides and became manager of the White Sox under Comiskey; and McGraw, betrayed by the Brooklyn deal and a participant in the previous year's attempts to form an American Association, who had abandoned that course and cast his lot with Johnson on the promise that a team would be placed in New York with McGraw as manager. McGraw and Wilbert Robinson, meanwhile, were traded by Baltimore to St. Louis, where they refused to report until they won the right to play out the 1900 season without being bound by the reserve clause after that.

This group began recruiting National Leaguers for the American, and it was easy: they simply offered more money. The strict salary limits the monopoly had imposed made it a sitting duck for this approach, since its best players were significantly underpaid in terms of what a successful baseball operation could afford. And it didn't take many big names to give the American League credibility with most of the press and public. Actually, almost two-thirds of the American's players were former National Leaguers, about 110 out of 180.

Money men were needed to finance such a start-up, and Johnson had found two: Charles Somers and John Kilfoyle in Cleveland. Somers was a coal dealer who took the Boston franchise and supplied the backing for Cleveland, Chicago, and Philadelphia as well. Kilfoyle took the Cleveland team. In Philadelphia, the owner-operator was Ben Shibe, whose company made the machines that made baseballs, and who was therefore a business partner of Al Reach, who owned part of the National League Phillies. (And Reach, of course, was part of the Spalding-Wright Brothers sporting-goods cartel.)

Now the battleground became ball parks. Finding suitable locations meant delving deep into city politics. (Building the wooden structures was simple and neither time-consuming nor terribly expensive; a park could be ready in months or even weeks. But buying or leasing the land or an existing park was another story.) In Chicago, the stockyards area had been deemed too unfavorable to worry about. In Cleveland, the Robisons didn't mind being landlords, and those trolleys needed riders. In Detroit, a site was found that would still be in use in the 1990's as Tiger Stadium. In Philadelphia, Mack got a 10-year lease at 29th and Oxford Streets just weeks before the season started. Boston (with Mack doing the scouting) found a Huntington Avenue site not far from the National's South End Grounds. In Baltimore and Washington, no existing parks were made available, so new locations were found; the one in Washington would be used for the next 60 years.

New York was the hang-up. Freedman, with his Tammany connections, could threaten to "run a street through" any site rivals might pursue. Overcoming this obstacle would turn out to be the final step in creating the format for the 20th century baseball.

In 1901, Griffith led the White Stockings to the championship of the American League's first self-declared major league season, a status the public accepted. They finished four games ahead of the Boston Puritans (also referred to as Somersets because of Somers). The National League pennant went to the new powerhouse, Pittsburgh, well ahead of Philadelphia and Brooklyn in a league whose player talent was notably thinned out.

And the new league came within striking distance of the old one in attendance, with 1.7 million to the National's 1.9 million. It clearly had a future.

Still, the National's club owners remained focused on how to maximize a monopoly they no longer had. In their December 1901 deliberations, they produced one of the most bizarre series of incidents the baseball business has ever known.

Freedman and Brush had been pushing their pet idea, a National Baseball Trust, for some time. It would make the National League a single corporation instead of eight independent clubs, moving players around to wherever they could generate most revenue as gate attractions and produce competitive pennant races. This was the plan:

New York (Freedman) would hold 30 percent of the stock. Cincinnati (Brush), St. Louis (Robison), and Boston (Soden) would have 12 percent each. Philadelphia (John Rogers and Reach) and Chicago (Hart and Spalding) would have 10 percent each. Pittsburgh (Dreyfuss and William Kerr) was assigned 8 percent and Brooklyn (Ebbets and Hanlon) 6 percent. A five-man board of regents would be elected by the stockholders (of whom the top three would constitute a majority). The board would hire a president and all team managers and would "license" players.

Does it surprise you that the first four clubs were in favor of this scheme and the other four opposed it?

A 4–4 split meant no action could be taken. A key question was whether to re-elect Nick Young as league president, so that business could proceed. As the deadlock continued, Spalding himself was brought in to speak and was proposed and drafted a candidate for the presidency. When the four syndicate backers left the room, they left the other four without a quorum, according to Young. Nevertheless, these voted 4–0 for Spalding, who in the middle of the night promptly marched over to Young's hotel room to physically take charge of the records. While Young argued that he wouldn't give them up, Spalding's porters carried them off. Spalding had kidnapped the league he had started a quarter of a century before.

This move was, needless to say, of doubtful legality, so Spalding called a league meeting. Only his four supporters showed up, but when Spalding spotted a New York official, Fred Knowles, observing from the doorway, he declared that club "represented," ruled that he had a quorum, and had the syndicate proposal voted down.

Also needless to say, Freedman took the case to court, and the deadlock persisted for months. Spalding, with the records in his possession, got out of New York State and set up shop in South Carolina. The main exchanges took place between him and Brush. Finally, as March was turning into April, the adoption of a 1902 playing schedule could not be delayed any longer, and a compromise was reached. Freedman would sell the Giants to Brush, who would sell Cincinnati to Gary Herrmann, an associate of George Cox, political boss of Hamilton County, and to Julius Fleischmann (of Fleischmann's yeast). They would admit the syndicate plan was dead. But all this depended on Spalding stepping aside. Brush, Soden, and Hart (who was Spalding's man) would run the league as an executive committee in 1902 and choose a president later.

All this was done, and the 1902 season proceeded, with more National Leaguers jumping to the American and with the National raiding all minor leagues everywhere for any players it could get. Amid the confusion, the American moved its Milwaukee team to St. Louis, giving it the venerable name Browns, and creating a fourth head-to-head confrontation with the National.

This, then, was the picture in 1902:

City	Population	NL Attendance	AL Attendance
New York*	2,100,000	303,000	——
Philadelphia	1,300,000	112,000	420,000
Boston	600,000	117,000	349,000
Brooklyn**	1,300,000	200,000	——
Washington	300,000	——	188,000
Baltimore	500,000	——	175,000
Chicago	1,700,000	264,000	338,000
St. Louis	600,000	226,000	272,000
Pittsburgh	500,000	243,000	——
Cincinnati	300,000	217,000	——
Cleveland	400,000	——	275,000
Detroit	300,000	——	189,000
Totals NL:	8,400,000	1,700,000	——
AL:	5,700,000	——	2,200,000

*Manhattan-Bronx only
**Brooklyn-Queens only

Consider what this table shows.

1. The new league's attendance was almost 30 percent higher than the old league's.
2. The American did better than the National in each of the four two-team cities, by devastating margins in Philadelphia and Boston.

3. With a population base 2.7 million smaller, the new league drew half a million more customers than the old league.

4. The National, except in Philadelphia and Boston, had achieved the most even distribution of attendance it had ever known.

5. In the one-team cities, the National did better, on the whole, than the American.

6. New York (including Brooklyn) is of unique importance. The American *must* get a team in there for long-range success. The National can't afford to have happen there what has happened in Philadelphia and Boston.

7. The baseball map is now full. The smallest members of the two leagues have 300,000 populations. Only two other cities in the United States are that big: San Francisco, which is several days away from the others by train and therefore inaccessible; and Buffalo, recently shut out. And neither of them is as big as 400,000.

The battle for New York is now fully engaged. McGraw, as field manager in Baltimore, is constantly in conflict with Johnson, who won't tolerate the umpire baiting McGraw considers a necessary part of the game (as well as a part of his nature). But there is also secrecy, subterfuge, and public playacting on both sides. At least two versions of what actually happened have been widely discussed.

The more standard story is that Johnson was looking for a way to get rid of McGraw and, when able to move Baltimore to New York, planned to leave him out. McGraw learned of this plan and, in a preventive strike, made a deal to become manager of the Giants. Freedman was still in charge during 1902, but his departure had already been agreed to, and the one who really had to be satisfied was Brush—and Brush saw this as a strong blow against Johnson and the new league, both of which he hated. In July, McGraw suddenly appeared at the Polo Grounds with a sensational deal: four years at $11,000 a year. (The official salary cap for players was still $2,400.) Had McGraw jumped his Baltimore contract to do this? No. He had laid out $7,000 of his own money to meet Baltimore payrolls. By demanding immediate repayment of that loan, he negotiated an honest release from his contract there.

The other version is that the Johnson-McGraw feud, while real enough as a personality clash, was overplayed for effect, that letting the Giants have McGraw was part of a back room deal to let the American League into New York, with all those involved well aware of what they were doing.

Think back to Spalding's actions in trading King Kelley in 1888, and his comments on it afterwards. Understanding the true nature of sports promotion better than most, he had not opposed with any real enthusiasm the growth of the American League and had tried to act as peacemaker. He knew that controversy and conflict make news and sell tickets. He had seen how two solid leagues are a better setup than one. His idea of monopoly, a concept to which he was as dedicated as anyone, was broader than a tight coterie of club owners in one league. The more teams, up to a point, the more attention, and the better for the cartel he really cared about, selling sporting goods. His weird campaign to save the National League from the syndicalists was rooted in his vision of what a second league could do for business—if the two worked together.

But they shouldn't be *seen*, too soon, to be working together. Until, in private, every issue had been worked out and all agreements were ready to be signed, let the public enjoy the spectacle of war. On this principle (with no suggestion of Spalding's direct participation) the fight over McGraw, in the middle of the ongoing fight over star players, could be played up for maximum effect.

At any rate, in mid-July McGraw took over a Giant team in last place with a 23–50 record and immediately began cleaning house. He was popular right away with the fans who had hated him as a Baltimore opponent—as Giant fans would, nearly half a century later, take to Leo Durocher when he suddenly switched, also in July, from the detested Dodgers. McGraw could make a team win, and that's all the fans really cared about.

McGraw's move stirred things up, but even more important elements were falling into place. A New York club would need a place to play, and owners. Freedman's political influence would mean less once he left the club, but influence was still needed. As owners, Johnson found Bill Devery, a former police chief notorious for shady dealings, and Frank Farrell, a major gambler and casino operator, both with Tammany connections of their own. They bought Baltimore for $18,000 at the end of the 1902 season.

By May of 1903 they had their ballpark, a 16,000-seat wooden structure atop a hill at 168th Street (where Columbia University's medical center is now), less than a mile northwest of the Polo Grounds. To have a respectable front man, they made Joseph Gordon, a prominent coal dealer, the club president.

The New York deal was only one facet of the true change: the two leagues were talking to each other. Once again it was time to get rid of that supreme evil, rival baseball teams bidding for the talents of outstanding players. The American League had doubled salary levels everywhere by its mere existence. Peace was a necessity.

In December 1902, the formal peace process began. The National appointed Herrmann, Hart, and Frank Robison as its delegation, and elected Harry Pulliam, secretary of the Pittsburgh club and a protégé of Dreyfuss's from Louisville, to the vacant League presidency. Johnson brought along Somers and Kilfoyle. In January, at a meeting in Cincinnati, a National League feeler about going back to a 12-team National League was quickly brushed aside and what we now call Organized Baseball was set up.

Each league would observe the other's reserve system. They would coordinate schedules and adopt the same playing rules. They would enter into a new National Agreement with the minors.

They would eschew rhetoric about "monopoly" and "trusts" and concentrate on solidifying the new buzz phrase, "national pastime."

And this time, they got it right.

SEASONS 1900–1902

1900

As defending champions, the Brooklyn Superbas had players whose names would remain famous for decades; most 19th-century names did not. They were now called the Superbas because of Hanlon. Vaudeville then was as ubiquitous as television is now, and there was a famous troupe of acrobats called Hanlon's Superbas. The law of publicity is that whatever is hot spills over to other associations. Headline writers and the rest of the media world—like all print media still—used anything that came to hand.

"Superb" was a good word. Keeler was in right field, a native Brooklynite, still only 28 years old. He got more than 200 hits for the seventh straight year, and his .368 average—good enough for third in the league behind Wagner and Elmer Flick—was the *lowest* of his career so far. In left was Joe Kelley, only 29, slowing up a bit: his ninth straight over-.300 average was only .319, and he played outfield half the time, filling in at first and third in other games. Jennings had been shifted to first base when an established star shortstop, Bill Dahlen, had come over from Chicago in 1899. The third baseman was Lave Cross, a 14-year veteran who had come over from St. Louis early in the season ("Lave" was short for Lafayette Napoleon). The center fielder was Fielder (his real name, not a nickname) Jones, a young player outstanding offensively and defensively. The top pitcher (29–9) was "Iron Man" Joe McGinnity. He did pitch and win doubleheaders now and then, but that was not the reason for the title: in the off-season, he told the Brooklyn writers that year, he worked in his father-in-law's iron foundry. "I'm an iron man," he said, the way one would say "I'm a railroad man." The name stuck.

With eight teams, the schedule was set at 140 games (20 with each of seven opponents). This was the third year that the Superbas were back in Washington Park, in Brooklyn's heart, and the team's chief officer now was Charlie Ebbets, just past 30, who had started as a minor stockholder in 1890 and had become Charlie Byrne's right-hand man.

Dreyfuss had brought to Pittsburgh the blos-

soming Wagner, whose .381 led the league; Clarke, whom he made playing manager; and pitchers Deacon Phillippe and Rube Waddell. The team's strong finish behind Brooklyn provoked another try at postseason play, a best-of-five series to be played entirely at Pittsburgh, for a cup put up by the *Chronicle-Telegraph* newspaper. Brooklyn won 4–2 and 5–2, lost 10–0, and won 6–1, without generating much interest. The four games drew less than 11,000 altogether.

All these Brooklyn and Pittsburgh names continued to mean something to baseball people well beyond the middle of the 20th century, and they dot today's encyclopedias, record books, and numerous histories. The same is true of Burkett, Young, and McGraw, playing for St. Louis, where McGraw hit .344 in completing his nonreserve contract while Burkett hit .363; of Duffy, Long, Lowe, Collins, Hamilton, and Nichols, still playing for Boston; and even Kid Gleason on the last-place and hapless Giants, who were managed by the now legendary Buck Ewing until Freedman fired him. Philadelphians had Napoleon Lajoie, Ed Delehanty, and batting champion Flick to cheer for.

Whatever else the consolidation had done, it had increased star density to a degree baseball had never before experienced, creating a public-relations impact out of proportion to the direct economic benefit.

It wouldn't last.

1901

In 1901, the American's first raid on the National's talent directly affected the National's pennant race. The two-time champion Brooklyns lost McGinnity to Baltimore, Cross to Philadelphia, and Jones to Chicago, while Pittsburgh remained essentially intact, and that was enough to account for a 14-game swing in the relative standings of the two teams. The Pirates, who had finished 4½ games behind Brooklyn the year before, finished 9½ ahead of them, while Philadelphia slipped into second place, two games ahead of Brooklyn.

However, the big story was in Philadelphia. Lajoie, the city's biggest baseball hero, stayed in town but switched to the new American team, bearing the historic name Athletics and managed by Mack. The Phillies were paying Lajoie $2,600. Mack gave him $4,000. The Phillies sought an injunction to enforce the reserve clause, and lost. (Courts uniformly cited the lack of mutuality in baseball contracts, which tried to bind a player for life while letting the club fire him on 10 days' notice.) Lajoie proceeded to lead the league with .422, with 14 homers and (retroactively, when statisticians went to work) 125 runs batted in. He was its first triple-crown winner before there was a triple crown.

Even so, the Athletics finished only fourth, nine games behind Chicago, for whom manager-pitcher Griffith produced a 24–7 record. Boston, having picked off Cy Young, finished second as he went 33–10, and also persuaded Jimmy Collins to switch leagues in Boston the way Lajoie did in Philadelphia.

That's why attendance swung in those two cities the way it did.

Meanwhile, the National League had refined a rule: foul balls, regardless of intent, would count as strikes up to two strikes. This was the final step in creating the game we know. The American League didn't adopt the change, so Lajoie's high average wasn't comparable to subsequent averages. His was the 12th batting average of .400 or better in the nine seasons since the pitching distance had been increased. Once the foul-strike rule was adopted, and before the hitting revolution of 1920, that level would be achieved only by Ty Cobb twice and Joe Jackson once.

1902

Two days before the 1902 season was to start, a Pennsylvania appeals court ruled in favor of the Phillies in the Lajoie case. It turned out that his particular contract, signed for 1900, was for three years. He was enjoined from playing for any other club, and the National League exulted at its legal victory. But the American noted that this court's jurisdiction covered only Pennsylvania, and that Lajoie could play anywhere else. Mack sold his contract to Cleveland, where Lajoie signed a three-year deal for $25,000 or more. In other cases, the National lost, running afoul of the Sherman Anti-Trust Act and the 14th Amendment (outlawing involuntary servitude). But the dollars in Lajoie's new contract, more than legal decisions, intensified the pressure on both leagues to come to some sort of anticompetitive agreement.

Lajoie, skipping whatever games Cleveland played in Philadelphia, didn't get into action the first few weeks and wound up hitting .378, winning another batting title by only two points over Delehanty, his one-time teammate, who had gone over to Washington.

But Mack, even without Lajoie, won the American League pennant. He had added Rube Waddell, who had been traded by Pittsburgh to the Chicago Nationals early in 1901 and had started the 1902 season in the Pacific Coast League. Rube had a 12–7 record there when Mack brought him to Philadelphia, and he won 23 games for the A's (Athletics) in the last two-thirds of the season.

In midseason, when McGraw went to New York, he made a snide remark about how Mack was spending money on players and called the Athletics "White Elephants." Mack's cheerful response was to adopt the image as a mascot, and the A's were referred to as White Elephants through many successful seasons, the way a fat man might be called "Slim." Ninety years later the management of the A's, then domiciled in Oakland, California, made a big deal out of reviving the White Elephant identity.

In the National League, Pittsburgh had put together a terrific pitching staff with the emergence of Jack Chesbro (28–6) along with Phillippe (20–9) and Jesse Tannehill (20–6). It also had the best offense, with Wagner and Clarke and the new batting champion, outfielder Ginger Beaumont. The Pirates won 103 games and lost only 36, a .741 pace, and finished 27½ games ahead of Brooklyn. The Giants, even with McGraw taking over in July, finished last, 53½ games out of first place at 48–88.

AFTERMATH

The peace agreement included a provision for uniform rules, so the American League adopted the foul-strike rule that establishes the modern version of the game. The mound, tailored by the home team to its own pitchers' needs, was limited by rule to a height of 15 inches. The National continued to use a Spalding labeled ball and the American one with a Reach label, and although the winding was all done on Shibe's machines, the covers and the way they were sewn were somewhat different, so that there was an authentic, though slight, difference between the two leagues' balls.

Resolving disputes always presented a problem. The prime desire was to avoid recourse to the courts at all costs. If the conflict were between a player and his club, the situation was simple: the league president could rule, assuring total player control (since the president was responsible only to the owners who elected him). If two or more clubs had a disagreement—usually over who actually held the rights to a particular player—the league president could arbitrate. But what if clubs in different leagues had a dispute? In the 1880s, this issue remained vague and unsatisfactory, but because the National League was more powerful than the American Association, things got settled somehow (almost always in the League's favor). However, the whole point of the new agreement was that the leagues were to be *equals*. A new mechanism was needed.

Thus was created the National Commission. It would consist of the two league presidents and a third member chosen by them. Johnson, now the most powerful individual in the game (with Spalding back out of the limelight), could make decisions as he pleased. Pulliam, the new National League head (with Nick Young staying on in the subordinate position of secretary), was much more a representative at best, an errand boy at worst, of his very strong-minded owners, especially Brush, Rogers, Dreyfuss, Ebbets, and Hart. The third commissioner would be the swing vote.

They chose Herrmann. As president of the Cincinnati club, he was acceptable to the National League. As an old friend of Johnson from the Cincinnati newspaper days, he was acceptable to him. If baseball was going to be one happy family, these certainly seemed to be the kind of people who could preside over it.

It wouldn't turn out to be that easy. Like the late great monopoly, the Commission system didn't live up to expectations in the long run, but its existence made possible a decade of growth that put the "industry"—a familiar term now that would have been looked upon with horror then—on a sound footing once and for all.

CHAPTER 8

Peace

Peace, it's wonderful. But the end of external war does not guarantee domestic tranquility, as the larger world would learn when the new century unfolded. Three problems that had plagued baseball from the beginning remained virulent: (1) controlling gambling and its accompanying threat of fixed games; (2) finding a salary scale low enough to assure profit but high enough to prevent players from rebelling; and (3) reaching an orderly resolution of disputes about the rights to a particular player. Throughout the prosperity of the next decade, these clouds would hang over the horizon, sometimes larger and darker, sometimes seeming lighter, but always there.

On the other hand, peacetime made it possible to conduct business and make it flourish, and the positive developments of this period greatly outweighed the problems.

New ball parks, of ultramodern steel-and-concrete construction, sprang up everywhere. Systematic promotion and marketing of the major league product was invented and expanded. Relations with the minor leagues, to suit the needs of the majors, were stabilized. The Spalding empire created and promoted a romanticized history for "the national game." A new and improved World Series started to cash in on all its inherent benefits. And with Johnson unquestionably the strongest individual with the greatest influence in the entire baseball sphere, his campaign to reduce rowdiness took hold.

More important in the long run than the visible clouds or the growing brilliance was the fundamental weakness of the three-man Commission, a setup good enough for routine business but incapable of dealing with serious conflict. The consequences of this weakness would not come to the surface until later, but they would.

The main story line of this period, 1903 through 1912, was how splendidly foundations were built.

THE WORLD SERIES

When the 1901 and 1902 seasons ended with two clear-cut champions, there was no possibility of their meeting because the two leagues were fighting each other. But in 1903, they had reached complete agreement, so a resumption of the popular World Series feature was feasible. However, no formal structure for such a competition had ever existed. The arrangements in the 1880s had been left to the participating teams, as long as certain provisions demanded by the leagues were observed. That was the procedure followed in 1903.

Pittsburgh had won its third straight National League pennant and was the most powerful team in baseball. Boston had won the third American League race, which had, naturally, no comparable prestige. Dreyfuss made the proposal to Boston. In addition to his good promotional sense, Dreyfuss had the usual motives for postseason play: it could provide some welcome extra money to his players beyond their salaries, and perhaps a little extra profit for the club along with the significant asset of great free publicity.

Boston got Johnson's approval, and the two clubs made their arrangements: five of nine, split the receipts, use no players added after September 1, and take care of their own player shares. Since Pittsburgh's contracts ran to October 15, with the series starting October 1, Dreyfuss had no problem; but Boston's contracts ended October 1, so to avoid a strike the club had to promise an extra two weeks' pay as well as some share of the receipts.

The National hoped, of course, to show up the inferiority of the upstart rival; the American hoped to show off its equality. But not everyone was enthusiastic, and Brush in particular, who opposed the peace treaty altogether and still resented the invasion of New York, was openly hostile.

Pittsburgh, after winning three of the first four games, lost the next four, two to Young and two to Bill Dinneen, a National League star in Boston in 1900 and 1901 who had switched leagues in 1902. The eight games drew 100,000, a healthy 12,000 average compared to a regular-season major league average of about 7,500. But Boston's deal with its own players gave them less money ($1,182 apiece) than Pittsburgh's got ($1,316) because Dreyfuss shared more of his profits—showing why his team had been less susceptible to the American's raids from the beginning.

That year, his first in full charge of the Giants, McGraw had lifted New York to a strong second. New York's American League entry, turned over to Griffith as manager, was a routine fourth, over .500 but not particularly exciting even though the popular Keeler came over from Brooklyn and Jack Chesbro, the star pitcher, moved in from Pittsburgh, where he had been 21–9 and 28–6 in its first two pennant-winning years.

The head-on collision came in 1904. The Giants ran away with the National League pennant by 13 games, and Griffith's team was challenging Boston neck and neck from August on. Much as the Superba name had been attached to Hanlon's Brooklyn team, New York's team was called the Highlanders because the Scottish Highlanders were touring America and their commander was named Gordon and so was the ball club's president. But the name had a dual meaning, since the team was also called the Hilltoppers, referring to its new 168th Street Park with its grand view of the Hudson River and the Palisades. The Boston team was now called Pilgrims, and every once in a while someone tried to attach the word "Yankee" to either or both.

Brush made it clear that his team was not interested in facing any American League upstart, least of all the Highlanders, and McGraw made all the appropriate derogatory pronouncements, although his players didn't like the idea of losing out on extra money. Both 1903 shares, well publicized, represented half a year's pay. Press and public were furious: they loved the World Series idea, and the prospect of two New Yorks, walking-distance apart, was intriguing.

As it happened, the Highlanders lost the pennant on the last day to Boston. Both had offered to play the Giants, but Brush was adamant. The National was too prestigious for its champion to play a "minor" team.

So there was no World Series in 1904.

The criticism of Brush's stance was so severe, and his logic so preposterous, that Brush himself took the lead in setting up a format for the future. He may have been combative in all his baseball years, but he wasn't stupid. If the public so wildly desires an event, one must not refuse to cash in. When customers clamor, the wise merchant acts.

For 1905, then, the two leagues formally agreed on a format for a World Series: four of seven; the games to be conducted by the interleague Commission, which would be financed by a share of the receipts; the players to get their shares out of a large slice of the receipts for the first four games only—to show that they had no reason to prolong a Series if one team was in command—with a 75–25 split in favor of the winners. This was soon adjusted to 60–40, but in all other basic respects, this pattern is still in use. It was referred to as "the Brush rules."

The 1905 World Series was a spectacular success, catching the national imagination: McGraw's Giants against Mack's Athletics, every game a shutout, three of them by the first true superstar, Christy Mathewson of the Giants. The next World Series involved both Chicago teams, with the underdog White Sox winning, but the Cubs (as they were now called) defeated Detroit in the next two. Then the Pirates also beat Detroit, and the Cubs were back in 1910 to lose to the Athletics. In 1911, it was Mack versus McGraw again, with the A's winning in six games. And 1912 was the best yet: the Giants versus Boston (now the Red Sox), going to the 10th inning of the final and deciding game—actually the eighth game, because one had been a tie ended by darkness.

Notice a creeping change in the above paragraph. I stopped referring to the teams by their city names and switched to nicknames. This reflects how this decade instilled such identifications in the public mind. Finally, for the first time, the city locations were stable: the circuits from 1903 on, and five cities had two teams. Also, the World Series, both as a goal all season long and as the most glamorous sports event ever presented up to that time, helped solidify these identities.

The 1905 Series, in the nation's two largest cities, had averaged 18,000 a game. The same two teams in 1911 averaged 30,000, and the player shares were up to $3,600 for winners and $2,400 for losers. In 1912, the eight games brought in more than a quarter of a million customers, 31,500 a game, and the winner's share reached $4,000.

One cannot exaggerate the benefits that flowed from the firm establishment of what soon came to be called "the Fall Classic." It worked in both directions: it gave the current season the tangible goal of a supercompetition in a superspotlight, not merely possession of a flag; and it guaranteed excited anticipation for what the next year's drama would bring. Historically speaking, the World Series was, and remains, the best single sports promotion ever conceived.

BALL PARKS

Wooden stands could be put up quickly and cheaply, and serve spectators well enough. (Seat cushions were a big concessions item.) But they were susceptible to fire, and many burned. As the skyscraper age began, however, new materials and methods were available for sturdier and larger parks, more extensively double-decked. While the investment was greater, the anticipated return was greater still.

Philadelphia's Baker Bowl was constructed in 1895, after the wooden stands burned down. Built over a railroad tunnel near the North Philadelphia station, it wasn't much larger in capacity than wooden parks of that day. The revolution really began in 1909.

In St. Louis, the first three versions of Sportsman's Park, dating back to the 1870's, were of wood. The new steel-and-concrete structure was ready for the American League Browns when they opened the 1909 season on April 14. That was two days after Mack and Shibe had opened their spectacular palace in Philadelphia, Shibe Park, flaunting a round tower (containing offices) behind the home plate corner and block-long outer facades to the right and left adorned with columns and arched openings like some huge government building.

Forbes Field in Pittsburgh was occupied that June 30. Cleveland's new League Park was ready for the 1910 opener, and on July 1 the White Sox had their Comiskey Park. Washington and New York joined the parade in 1911, Washington's known as National Park until it became Griffith Stadium a decade later. The Polo

Grounds, now called Brush Stadium, took its new form in record time after fire destroyed the old grandstand in April; it was reoccupied (not quite completed) by June 28. It wouldn't get its final bathtub shape, with the double deck curving around both outfields to meet the center-field clubhouse, until 1923.

Cincinnati, Detroit, and Boston got their new parks in 1912 (Redland Field, Navin Field, and Fenway Park, respectively). The last two, much changed but never moved, are still in use in the 1990's. With Brooklyn's Ebbets Field in 1913, a Federal League park built in Chicago in 1914 (which became Wrigley Field later), and Braves Field in Boston in 1915, modern facilities had been provided for 13 of the 16 teams in a seven-year period. When the Yankees moved into the Polo Grounds in 1913, that made 14. The Cardinals didn't shift from Robison Field to Sportsman's Park until 1920, at which point the Phillies, who had been ahead of the pack, were left with the most antiquated building when a new Golden Age dawned.

The new rules (foul-strikes), new administration (the Commission uniting two leagues), and new parks (with reachable fences, as outfield bleachers were inserted and enlarged) created "baseball as we know it."

GAMBLING

From the beginning, gambling was a problem for baseball, as it would be for all money sports, and part of the National League's success lay in meeting the issue head on in its second year. The dedicated audience—those willing to buy tickets—always included a disproportionate number of fans who liked to bet, and even if individuals bet only for "fun," an infrastructure of professional gambling would automatically develop and grow to sustain, and profit from, that recreational urge. And where there is gambling, there is always the possibility that someone will try to prearrange a result, to take the risk out of risk taking. Since no one can guarantee victory over an opponent, the fix took the form of guaranteeing a loss, which anyone can arrange. The trick (and not so difficult a trick) is to avoid making deliberate misplay obvious.

The promoter, then, had to walk a tightrope. He had to condemn, publicly and perhaps in his own mind, betting on his games, without doing anything that would have the practical effect of discouraging his best customers from buying tickets or following the daily free publicity newspapers provided.

Players, beyond the simple honesty that most people live by, also had a realistic motive for playing "on the square"; they understood that public *perception* of a likely fix would kill the goose laying their golden eggs: salaries derived from gate receipts. A rough formula developed as professionalism took hold: an adequate salary level also deterred players' accepting bribes or betting on the side. The more the legitimate a player's income, the less likely he was to risk doing something crooked.

Since there are always some rotten apples in any barrel, the problem never really disappeared, but it was pretty well under control in the major leagues from the 1880s on. In the minor and independent leagues, it was more common. The best indicators of this are the plot lines of the boys' books that were the standard popular fare of the premovie and pretelevision generations: Frank Merriwell, Baseball Joe, and so forth. Time and again those stories centered on foiling the nefarious plans of gamblers trying to fix a game by kidnapping or otherwise harrassing the hero, or by corrupting an evil or morally weak character. If readers found that scenario so believable, they must have been aware of the reality bubbling under the surface of the sport.

During the first two decades of the 20th century, the gambling problem grew as the baseball industry expanded. As we shall see, the Black Sox of 1919 were not an anomaly, but the culmination of a process.

Organized Baseball's response during the increasing prosperity of the two-league system was a deliberate policy of sweeping the dirt under the rug. It whitewashed cases it couldn't ignore and ignored as much as it could. Praising itself as publicly as possible for presenting "clean sport," it chose concealment over cleaning up the instances that arose. At the same time, the gambling proclivities of managers and club owners were well known, especially at racetracks and gaming clubs, and condoned by their fellow authorities.

Refusal to confront this problem or recognize its seriousness would have devastating consequences eventually. But during the 1903–12 era of peace, it was shunted aside in the propaganda blitz of selling "our national pastime." In Harold Seymour's second volume of baseball history, published in 1971, the chapter on this subject lists at least a dozen specific cases that *were* public issues before the Black Sox. But even these were overwhelmed by the aura of glory baseball was enjoying under a unified administration.

And the tendency to see no evil was encouraged by promulgating the Doubleday myth about baseball's origins, promoted by Spalding.

THE DOUBLEDAY MYTH

In the late 19th century, nationalistic chauvinism and jingoism were mainstream philosophies of Euro-American culture, and Americans in particular were sensitive about their cultural identity in the face of so much older and elaborate European heritage. Spalding, exposed to English snobbery at an early age during the 1874 tour with Harry Wright's expedition, felt deeply the peculiarly "American" virtues of his game: individuality, initiative, creative teamwork, clever alertness, and so forth. A game so wonderful *must* be the product of uniquely American ingenuity. As early as 1889, at a banquet at the conclusion of the famous world tour, the game's American origins were asserted with high passion, as well as in a book by Monte Ward.

In 1903, Spalding was back in retirement from baseball after fighting the Syndicate

War in the National League, having contributed to the peace treaty informally. The fruits of the two-league system were about to be enjoyed. At that point, Henry Chadwick wrote another essay on baseball's derivation from the English child's game of rounders.

Chadwick was English-born, accepted universally as the country's greatest authority on baseball, the "father" of baseball writing, architect of many playing rules, developer of the box score and statistics, supporter of the Establishment, and editor of the *Spalding Guides* since 1881. He and Spalding had argued about the game's history on and off for more than 20 years.

This time, Spalding reacted. He called for a "conclusive" settlement of the question. A blue-ribbon panel of seven prominent baseball experts was formed, chaired by Abraham G. Mills, who as a former president of the National League, had made that ringing speech at the 1889 banquet and had been so important a figure in baseball affairs in the first Golden Age of the 1880's.

Mills came up with one Abner Graves, who declared that, 68 years before, in 1839 in Cooperstown, New York, his schoolmate Abner Doubleday "invented" baseball by "improving" town ball. In a report published early in 1908, Mills cited that improvement as evidence of baseball's U.S. origin.

This totally fabricated proposition was accepted by the public and endlessly repeated for the next 30 years, unquestioned by the press and dutifully recorded in books. By the late 1930's, it was known that (1) literature published back in the 1700's made explicit the derivation from rounders; (2) Abner Doubleday was at West Point during the spring of 1839 and became a prominent general who never gave the slightest indication of interest in, connection to, or knowledge of baseball, even to personal friends, who included Abraham G. Mills; and (3) the nationalistic issue of baseball's "invention" as a reflection of "patriotism" meant nothing in post–World War I America. Nevertheless, when a patron in Cooperstown offered a site for a baseball museum, organized baseball jumped at it, reiterated the myth, and in 1936 set in motion the whole glorious Cooperstown mechanism, whose celebration of baseball's roots and continuity has become an incomparable asset. It is the crown-jewel example of the cynical journalistic credo, "Never let a [historical] fact interfere with a good story." The splendor of the Hall of Fame complex transcends the irrelevancy of the myth.

But the "Americanism" of baseball was taken very seriously in the early years of the century, and patriotism would become a practical question only a few years down the road.

OUTLAW LEAGUES AND PLAYER RELATIONS

The major-minor agreement, fundamental to the doing of orderly baseball business, did not yet include all minor leagues. If a player on an Organized-Baseball reserve list played in an "outlaw" league, he could be blacklisted—or reinstated with a slap on the wrist, if Organized Baseball wanted it that way. Meanwhile, he and others who never did have pro contracts could play for pay. This did provide an escape hatch, at least temporarily, for someone who wouldn't accept the terms offered by an Organized-Baseball team.

Realistically, however, players remained prisoners of the reserve system and understood they couldn't bargain against it (or under it) individually. The Brotherhood experiment hadn't worked, and its backlash produced lower salaries and arbitrary restrictions. In 1900, when the National had cut back to eight teams, the American wasn't yet claiming major status, and talk of a new American Association was heating up, the players had made another try at unionizing, led by Griffith, Jennings, and Chief Zimmer. But even with loud vocal support from Sam Gompers and his American Federation of Labor, this effort dissolved within months, for the best of reasons: the American-National war began, creating jobs and doubling salaries for everyone. Griffith went from being a leading pitcher of the Chicago Nationals to pitcher-manager of the Chicago Americans; Jennings stayed in the National League as a player but wound up managing Detroit from 1907 on; and Zimmer, past 40, finished out his career as the backup catcher for Pittsburgh's pennant winners.

With the peace agreement of 1903, however, the players were back in their box. The two majors and the top minors had the ironbound reserve in place again, and salaries leveled off quickly after the escalations produced by the war. More important than the general level of salaries was that no individual player could get satisfaction for a grievance, whether or not it involved pay.

Theoretically, a player could turn to the Commission for adjudication, but the futility of that effort was self-evident.

David Fultz had been a journeyman infielder with both Philadelphias and Baltimore at the turn of the century and wound up with the Yankees (as the Hilltoppers were sometimes called) in 1903. He went through New York University Law School and set up shop as an attorney in 1905, at the end of his baseball career.

Players would come to him for advice, if not formal representation, and by 1908 he was well known throughout the baseball community. By 1910, he was being urged to accept the leadership of a new union, the Baseball Fraternity. In September of 1912 it was formalized, and by November it had 300 members. Its emphasis was on dealing with individual problems rather than collective bargaining, and helping needy players.

What happened to the Fraternity belongs to the next chapter, but its formation was one more sign that the peak of popularity and prosperity reached in the 1912 World Series concealed problems—gambling, player unrest, and overextended finances—that weren't being faced.

SEASONS 1903-12

1903

Both 1903 pennant races were runaways, leaving plenty of time to arrange the championship series between the winners.

NL—Pittsburgh cruised to its third straight pennant even though its two top pitchers, Jack Chesbro and Jesse Tannehill, switched to the American League. Sam Leever took up the slack, while Wagner won another batting title at .355, Clarke hit .351 while managing and playing 100 games in the outfield, and Ginger Beaumont hit .341. During July, the Pirates pulled away from the Cubs and the Giants, but these three teams would dominate the rest of the decade. Under McGraw for a full year for the first time, the Giants won 84 games, 36 more than the year before, and established a legendary tandem of pitchers: Mathewson, 30–13 in his first year of stardom (and third with the team), and McGinnity, 31–20 in his first full season as a Giant. The Cubs had acquired a new manager in 1902, none other than Frank Selee, whose Boston clubs had matched Baltimore's success in the 1890s. That year Chicago finished one game under .500, but in 1903 Selee put in place the nucleus of a lineup that would be known as one of the finest ever, to this day: Frank Chance at first, Johnny Evers at second, Joe Tinker at short, Johnny Kling catching. The Cubs won 82 but, even with three 20-game winners, couldn't match the quality of pitching the Giants and Pirates offered.

AL—Boston took command in mid-July and won by 14½ games over the defending champion Athletics. Cleveland, now known as the Naps in honor of Lajoie (who led the league again with .355, new foul-strike rule and all), was third. On July 2, Ed Delehanty, now with last-place Washington, died in mysterious circumstances when he fell or was thrown off a train near Niagara Falls. Whether this was suicide, accident, or foul play was not established. The 35-year-old slugger was still hitting .388, and his lifetime average of .346 has him in the Hall of Fame.

WS—National League superiority was taken for granted by all but dedicated American Leaguers, and it seemed beyond question after Pittsburgh won three of the first four games in the best-of-nine series. Phillippe pitched those victories in six days, 7–3 at Boston October 1 and 4–2 there October 3 after Dinneen had beaten Leever 3–0 the day between, and then 5–4 in the first game played at Pittsburgh October 6. He had outpitched Young in the first game and Dinneen in the fourth.

But the Young-Dinneen combination prevailed. They swept the three remaining games in Pittsburgh, played on alternate days, 11–2, 8–3, and 7–3, beating Phillippe on October 10. Now Boston led, four games to three, and on October 13, after a rainout at Boston, Dinneen wrapped it up by beating Phillippe, 3–0.

1904

The 1904 American League race between Boston and New York, going down to the final day, established the new league once and for all in the Big City, even though New York lost; and the rise of the Giants to dominance under McGraw cemented baseball's status in what was emerging as the most important of all opinion-formation and entertainment centers. That the refusal to have a World Series produced the storm of protest that it did only emphasized this new attraction's public impact.

NL—McGraw's Giants won 106 games, 35 by McGinnity, 31 by Mathewson. Chicago finished 13 games behind, and Pittsburgh fell to fourth (behind Cincinnati), as Phillippe was injured and Clarke and Beaumont fell off sharply, even though Wagner won his third batting title (hitting .349 and stealing 53 bases).

AL—It all came down to the last weekend. Boston and New York had jockeyed for the lead all season long, with Cleveland and Philadelphia also in contention until September and Chicago hanging on as late as September 30. On Friday, October 7, Boston came to New York with a half-game lead. Chesbro, at the age of 30, had just mastered the spitball to add to the equipment that had already made him such a big winner in Pittsburgh, and was able to start after two days of rest most of the time. In his 50th start, he produced his 41st victory and 47th complete game, and the 3–2 decision put the Highlanders in first place.

But on Saturday, Boston swept a doubleheader, 13–2 and 1–0, to lead by a game and a half. Sunday ball was still prohibited, so a doubleheader Monday would end the season. The Highlanders had to win both games to win the pennant, the Pilgrims either one.

Chesbro faced Dinneen in the opener, and Boston had Cy Young available for the second game if necessary. The teams were tied 2–2 in the top of the ninth, which Lou Crigar opened with a single. A sacrifice bunt and groundout moved him to third with two out—and a wild pitch (presumably a spitball) let him score. The game ended 3–2, and the Boston Pilgrims were champions again, of a league bristling with stars, whatever pretensions the National League Giants professed. Lajoie was batting champion again, with .381. On May 5, Young had pitched the first "true" perfect game, under foul-strike rules at the 60-foot distance. Philadelphia had Waddell, the free spirit and left-hander who struck out 349 batters but had the same 26–17 won-lost record as his left-handed teammate Eddie Plank. Willie Keeler with the Highlanders, Sam Crawford in Detroit, the aging Jesse Burkett in St. Louis, Elmer Flick in Cleveland, and other batting leaders were much appreciated. And a 24-year-old right-hander in Cleveland named Addie Joss was catching the eye of insiders.

If there had been a World Series, it would have opened with Cy Young facing Mathewson or McGinnity.

1905

The first confrontation of mental giants, McGraw and Mack, raised national consciousness of baseball's appeal to an unprecedented level in 1905.

NL—McGraw's Giants were a continuation of the 1904 team. They won 105 games for a two-year total of 211, took the lead at the start, and never trailed. Mathewson, now fully mature, had a 32–8 season, including a no-hitter; and although McGinnity won "only" 22, so did 22-year-old Red Ames. They were strongly supported by Hooks Wiltse and Dummy Taylor, a deaf mute whose needs brought refinements to McGraw's hand-signal techniques. Roger Bresnahan, a budding star at 26, and Frank Bowerman, 10

years older and from a background that included the Old Orioles, did the catching. Dan McGann, another Old Oriole, was at first, Billy Gilbert at second, Bill Dahlen at short, Arlie Latham at third—all would be household names for years to come. So would Mike Donlin's, the slugger and flamboyant outfielder. In later years, McGraw would refer to this as his best team ever.

Pittsburgh finished second, nine games out, as Wagner hit another .363 and stole 57 more bases. The Cubs were third, undergoing a managerial change in midseason when Selee, forced to step down by illness, handed the reins to 27-year-old Chance. But a measure of the changing times was this: Boston and Brooklyn, who had fought it out at the top in 1899, only six years before, finished 51–103 and 48–104.

AL—Mack's A's made it only after a terrific struggle. Cleveland led the early part of the season, now under Lajoie as manager, but it had little pitching beyond Joss and wound up fifth. Ahead by seven games on September 5, the A's were caught by the White Sox, now managed by Fielder Jones, on September 27. On Thursday, September 28 in Philadelphia, the A's defeated the Sox 6–2, and the next day 11–1. Even though Chicago won the last game of the series 4–3, the A's reeled off five straight against tailenders St. Louis and Washington and finished with a two-game margin.

Waddell won 26, Plank 25, Andy Coakley 20, and Chief Bender 16, as Mack, like McGraw, kept moving toward a full four-man starting rotation. This team's strength was primarily its pitching. Detroit was a distant third, heading a group that included Cleveland, Boston, and New York. The late-season arrival of an 18-year-old outfielder from Georgia named Ty Cobb got little notice.

WS—New York and Philadelphia, the two largest cities and the country's main commercial centers, squared off in the first official World Series under the Brush rules: this was the greatest peace dividend yet. And from it emerged the first true superstar of the American sports scene.

October 9 at Philadelphia, Mathewson faced Plank and won 3–0. The next day, McGinnity faced Bender and lost 3–0. There was no game on

October 11, so Mathewson started with two days' rest at the Polo Grounds on the 12th, pitched another four-hit shutout, and won 9–0, as Philadelphia's defense fell apart behind Coakley. On the 13th, McGinnity and Plank squared off and McGinnity won 1–0 on a fourth-inning run produced by a fumbled grounder, an infield out, and a single.

Then, on Saturday, October 14, Mathewson went out again with *one* day's rest and pitched his third shutout, this time a five-hitter. If McGraw, with a 3–1 lead in games, had let someone else pitch, with no game on Sunday, both Mathewson and McGinnity would have been ready if needed for a sixth and seventh game with normal rest. Such thinking would become prevalent in baseball minds, but not in McGraw's, not then.

If baseball's peculiar advantage was that you could talk (and read and write) about it endlessly through what was becoming known as the "hot-stove league" winter months, Mathewson's performance lifted that aspect of it to its highest plateau so far. His All-America persona—tall, handsome, college trained, forthrightly Christian, clean-living sportsman yet fierce competitor—combined with his achievements to give professional baseball a degree of respectability much higher than it had every enjoyed. A case can be made that 1905 marks the real beginning of "baseball as we know it."

1906

Chicago, birthplace of the National League, was firmly established as the nation's most important metropolis after New York and Philadelphia, and well on its way to being the Second City. When both its teams won pennants in 1906, it became the center of gravity in the baseball world and remain so until 1921.

NL—What Selee had been building jelled under Chance, who became known as "the Peerless Leader." By July 29, the Cubs had a 61–26 record. The rest of the way, they picked up the pace to 55–10. That 116–36 remains the best pennant-winning mark ever, a .763 winning percentage. Until then, the Cubs had not been able to match the top-quality pitching of the Pirates and Giants. Now they had put together, over three years,

Mordecai (Three-Fingered) Brown, Ed Reulbach, Jack Pfeister, and a strong backup staff. The Giants and Pirates, not much weaker than before, were left 20 and 23½ games behind, even though they won more than 90 games themselves. (Last-place Boston finished 66½ games out.)

AL—While there was no suspense amid all the glory on Chicago's North Side, it was all suspense and no glory on the less fashionable South Side. In an era of pitching ascendancy, the White Sox were dubbed the "Hitless Wonders." The team batting average was .230, lowest in the league. No regular had star identity, not even outfielder-manager Fielder Jones (who played every day and hit exactly .230). Two White Sox pitchers would become enduring names, Doc White and Ed Walsh; but the two who actually won 20 games were Frank Owen and Nick Altrock. Altrock, in due course, became famous for his clowning act as coach in the 1920s and 1930s, but the 43 games he won in 1905 and 1906 amounted to more than half his lifetime total.

By the end of July, the Sox were only a little over .500, watching Cleveland, New York, and Philadelphia conduct a pennant race far above them. Then they started to win, while the others leveled off. A 19-game winning streak in August put them into first place, but the Highlanders took it back in September, lost it, and took it back again. In the final week, however, New York faltered, the Sox pitchers came through, and Chicago won by a three-game margin.

WS—No contest, right? The Cubs certainly had reason to think so. But games have to be played on the field, not on paper (a cliché then in the making, given life by what occurred). In the first game, at West Side Grounds (the Cubs' home), Altrock beat Brown 2–1. In the second, at South Side Park, the Cubs asserted themselves 7–1, behind a one-hitter by Ruelbach. With the sites alternating, the visiting team continued to win. Walsh's two-hitter beat Pfeister (who allowed only four) 3–0; then Brown produced a two-hitter to beat Altrock 1–0.

Back at West Side, it was time for the Cubs to take command, right? Wrong. Up to now, the games had been played in very cold weather, making it tougher on hitters. For this game it was warmer, and the field was small: an overflow crowd of 23,000 was allowed to stand behind ropes in the outfield.

Hits into the crowd were ground-rule doubles. Trailing 3–1 after the first inning, the Sox pulled even in the fourth on two such hits. Then they hammered out four runs in the fourth, without reaching the crowd, and went on to win 8–6.

One game from elimination. Chance chose Brown to start the sixth game on one day's rest. It didn't work. The Hitless Wonders scored seven runs in the first two innings, won 8–3, and were champions of the world.

The hot-stove league had plenty of fuel that winter.

1907

Despite the World Series upset, by 1907 the Cubs had a dynasty going and this time didn't stumble.

NL—The Cubs finished 107–45, ahead of Pittsburgh by 17 games and the fourth-place Giants by 25½, with Philadelphia third. Their pitching leader now was Orvie Overall, heading a five-man rotation, and the team was simply too strong in every respect for its opposition. At Pittsburgh, Wagner won another batting title (.350 with 61 stolen bases), and McGraw was engaged in some rebuilding at New York, but Chicago owned the league.

AL—A new champion emerged, as Detroit, managed by Hughie Jennings, nosed out Mack's A's and the defending champion White Sox. Ty Cobb, now 20, won the batting title at .350, stole 49 bases, and batted cleanup behind Crawford, so that was one reason. But a pitching staff led by Wild Bill Donovan and Ed Killian, with 25 victories each, and George Mullin (20) and Ed Siever (19) was a bigger one.

The four-team race involved Philadelphia, Chicago, and Cleveland, as well as the Tigers. September started with Cleveland ahead by percentage points. On the 20th, the A's and Tigers were tied. On the 27th, the Tigers won at Philadelphia 5–4 to take a 1½-game lead. The next day it rained, and the next was Sunday. On Monday, the teams played a 17-inning, 9–9 tie; the Tigers left town with the lead, whereupon they won four games in

Washington and clinched the pennant by beating St. Louis.

WS—The Series began in Chicago with a 3–3 tie, ended by darkness after 12 innings. Detroit's Donovan took a 3–1 lead into the bottom of the ninth and led 3–2, with two out and men on second and third. He struck out the next man, but his catcher, Boss Schmidt, couldn't catch the ball, and the batter made it to first while the tying run scored. (When they say there's nothing new in baseball, they're right; the far more famous missed third strike by Mickey Owen in the 1941 World Series, which so traumatized Dodger fans, had its precedent.)

Then the Cubs reeled off four straight. Pfeister beat Mullin 3–1, Ruelbach pitched a 5–1 six-hitter, and, in Detroit, Overall delivered a 6–1 five-hitter and Brown a 2–0 seven-hit shutout. The Tigers failed to score in 45 of their 48 turns at bat, and Cobb's three singles and a triple in 20 tries (.200) didn't help. The Cubs were undisputed "world champions."

1908

The 1908 season has been called the best baseball season ever, and nearly a century later it would be hard to argue against the claim. Both pennant races went down to the last day and beyond, because of the greatest on-field-result controversy in baseball history, the famous "Merkle game." Whole books have been written about it; here we can have only a sketchy summary.

NL—The Cubs started off as fast as ever but hit a two-month stretch of .500 ball through July and August. The Pirates caught them by the end of June and led a close race into late August. The Giants, starting slowly, came on strong after mid-June and passed the Pirates early in September, and by that time the Cubs had resumed winning.

A game in Pittsburgh on September 4 drew little attention, although it set the stage for the later drama. In the bottom of the 10th of a scoreless game, the Pirates had bases full and two out. Owen Wilson lined a clean single to center, and as soon as the ball landed, the winning run scored, and Hank O'Day, umpiring the game alone, started off the field. But the man on first, a recently arrived minor leaguer named Warren Gill, also left the field, without going down to touch second. Evers called for the ball from the outfield and tagged second for a third-out force but couldn't get O'Day's attention. The Cubs protested—correctly—that the run couldn't count, but the league eventually ruled that since O'Day did see a runner score but didn't see Evers tag second, the result would stand.

Eighteen days later the Cubs arrived in New York for their final series with the Giants. Having lost 2–1 to the Pirates the day before, the Giants were still in first place at 87–48. The Cubs were 2½ games behind, 87–53, and Pittsburgh was third at 87–54. On Tuesday, September 22, the Cubs swept a doubleheader at the Polo Grounds. On Wednesday, the score was 1–1 in the bottom of the ninth. With two out, the Giants had Moose McCormick on third and Fred Merkle, a rookie who had just singled, on first. Al Bridwell lined a clean hit to center.

McCormick scored.

The overflow crowd of 20,000 poured onto the field.

Merkle, halfway to second, took off for the center-field clubhouse. Evers called for the ball. McGinnity, who had been coaching at third, retrieved the ball, which had been thrown past Evers. As Cub players converged on him to get it back, he threw it far into the crowd beyond third base. Somehow, the Cubs produced a ball and tagged second.

The umpire was Hank O'Day, this time working with a partner, Bob Emslie. Chance urged them to call Merkle out, nullifying the run. Surrounded by the crowd, both flustered umpires refused to issue a clear decision. It seemed to be a 2–1 Giant victory.

But that night O'Day filed his report with Harry Pulliam, the league president, upholding the force play and calling the game a 1–1 tie. He said it couldn't have been continued because the crowd could not be cleared from the field.

By the time all this was official, the Giants had won Thursday's game 5–4. The teams had no mutual open dates left, so Pulliam ruled that the tie would be replayed the day after the schedule ended if needed to determine the final standing.

On Tuesday, October 6, the schedule ended with the Giants and Cubs tied 98–55 and Pitts-

burgh eliminated at 98–56. The "Merkle boner" game would have to be made up. If it had been a Giant victory instead of a tie, the Giants would have been pennant winners by a one-game margin. As it was, the special play-off game would decide it.

The Cubs won it 4–2, with Brown defeating Mathewson.

One of baseball's most enduring legends was born.

AL—With less turmoil, the American League race was no less dramatic. The Tigers, as defending champions, seemed to be taking command in August, but the St. Louis Browns, having added Waddell and Dinneen to their pitching staff, stayed close. By Labor Day, Chicago was even with St. Louis on Detroit's heels, and shortly after that Cleveland produced a 16–2 spurt that gave it the lead. As the Browns faltered, the other three went down to the wire.

On Friday, October 2, with Detroit in first place, Chicago's Walsh faced Joss in Cleveland. Walsh struck out 15 but permitted a run; Joss pitched a perfect game. But Chicago won the next day and then beat Detroit twice, while Cleveland split with St. Louis.

So the final day came with Detroit half a game ahead of the other two; the Tigers had a rained-out game that, under the rules, would not have to be made up once the schedule ended. (The Giant-Cub postschedule game was the replay of a tie, not the makeup of a rainout.) Donovan shut out the White Sox 7–0, and that was enough to clinch the pennant, even though Cleveland defeated St. Louis. Cleveland's complaints that the rain out should be played, giving it a chance to play off a tie if Detroit lost, got nowhere.

Walsh had won 40 games for Chicago, pitching 464 innings. What did that do to his arm? Well, he pitched 969 more innings in the next three seasons, and 393 the year after that. But Joss was the most respected by his peers, with a 24–11 record and an earned run average subsequently computed at 1.18. In such a league, which had seven regular pitchers with earned run averages under 2.00, Cobb's .324 was high enough to win the batting title.

WS—After all that, the World Series rematch between the Cubs and Tigers was an anticlimax and another decisive victory for the Cubs, this time in five games. The Cubs won 10–6 at Detroit, won 6–1 and lost 8–3 at home, then produced shutouts by Brown (3–0, four hits) and Overall (2–0, three hits) in Detroit. Cobb had a more characteristic .368 average, but no other Tiger did better than Crawford's .238, while Chance did the best thing any manager can do, hitting .421 himself.

1909

A third straight Chicago-Detroit Series didn't materialize because Pittsburgh, upstaged by its two rivals in 1908, surpassed them in 1909, even though they didn't fall back much.

NL—The Pirates won 110 games and lost 42, so Chicago's 104–49 wasn't good enough, and New York's 92 victories left it 18½ games off the pace. Wagner, now 35, won his sixth batting title in seven years at .339. Manager Clarke, at 36, was still spry enough to play 150 games. But the real strength was a deep pitching staff, with six different men making at least 12 starts. The leaders were Howie Camnitz and Vic Willis, both veterans, who were 25–6 and 22–11, while Leever (8–1) and Phillippe (8–3) were still able to contribute at 37. This was to be the last triumph for one of baseball's least appreciated outstanding teams.

AL—Detroit's third straight pennant was the easiest of the three. The Tigers led all season except for a few days in August, and the final margin was 3½ games only because Philadelphia, in a rebuilding phase, finished so well. Cobb and Crawford were now the most feared one-two punch, Cobb leading the league with .377, and the pitching remained strong.

But Mack was putting something together. He had three young infielders, 22 or 23 years old— Eddie Collins, Jack Barry, and Frank Baker. Plank and Bender, still top pitchers, had Jack Coombs coming into his own in his mid-20s.

But a recurring pattern had developed, one endemic to baseball and a hot topic again in the 1990s: a widening gap between haves and have-nots, based as much on quality of team management as on financial or population resources. This was the American League's ninth season. Boston, Chicago, and Philadelphia had won two

pennants each, and Detroit three. But Washington had been last four times, seventh three times, and sixth twice and had lost 686 games in the last seven seasons. St. Louis, despite its one moment of contention in 1908, was a second-division team the rest of the time, now sinking: it would lose 315 games in the next three years. Cleveland contended often, New York twice, but neither had won and both seemed to be going downhill.

And even in the National League, as the Cubs, Pirates, and Giants piled up their victories, Boston, Brooklyn, and St. Louis were becoming laughingstocks. In the last five years, Boston had lost 494 games, Brooklyn 461, and St. Louis 498. Peace was not producing parity.

One consequence of these won-lost records was an imbalance of political power within baseball's councils, since losers are neither listened to nor worried about by their peers. This would soon prove important in shaping the future.

WS—The Detroit-Pittsburgh set was the first to go the full seven games. Its anticipated feature was Cobb versus Wagner, the batting champions, but the hero turned out to be Babe Adams, Pittsburgh's fifth-ranking pitcher during the season. He pitched complete-game victories in games one and five, and an 8–0 shutout in the decisive seventh game. Detroit had won games two and four, losing game three at home 8–6, so the fifth game was pivotal. The home-field pattern tried this time was 2-2-1-2, so the last two games were back in Detroit. The Tigers won the sixth 5–4 but then couldn't handle Adams. In these games, spectators in the outfield behind ropes had become the rule, requiring unsatisfactory ground rules and hastening the impulse to build new parks.

1910

Mack and McGraw were making rapid progress toward new dynasties, but the Cubs weren't dead yet. Winning their fourth pennant in five years, the Cubs completed a sequence of 530 victories in five seasons, never approached since by anyone.

Meanwhile, an artistic problem was getting out of control. After 17 seasons of the 60-foot distance and seven of the foul-strike rule, offense was dying again as more and more pitchers perfected their craft. The combined major league batting average had fallen below .250 in 1904 and bottomed out at .239 in 1908. It was .244 in 1909, and run production over the last three seasons was below seven runs—by both teams—a game. No one wanted to tinker with the rules, which had become not only satisfactory in themselves but a force for stability, but something could be done. The ball itself could be made livelier.

During the 1910 season, with no fanfare and to a limited degree, a new ball was introduced. It had a cork center inside its rubber core. Its full effect wasn't felt until 1911, when it went into regular use, but that effect was distinct and far-reaching. It was still not like the modern lively ball introduced in 1920, but a step in that direction and an indicator that this was the direction to go. In 1911 and 1912, the aggregate batting average would jump to .266 and .269, and runs per game to nine instead of seven.

NL—The Giants stayed close to the Cubs into mid-July, then spent the rest of the season fighting off Pittsburgh for second place. At 104–50, Chicago finished 13 games ahead of New York and 17½ ahead of Pittsburgh.

AL—Between unusual events on the first and last days, the Athletics marched majestically to their third pennant. The first American League team to win 100 games, their 102–48 record left them 14½ games ahead of New York, where an interesting situation was developing, and 18 ahead of dethroned Detroit.

The Opening Day occasion took place in Washington, where President William Howard Taft agreed to "throw out the first ball," a ceremony that became an annual affair and solidified baseball's claim to its "national game" status.

The final day was as sordid as the opener had been uplifting. The pennant race had long been settled, but Cobb and Lajoie were in a tight battle for the batting title, which now had a tangible stake: a fancy new automobile (the Chalmers Award) would go to the winner. In a last-day doubleheader at St. Louis, Lajoie got eight hits in eight times at bat—six of them bunts toward a rookie third baseman instructed to play deep against this 34-year-old nonspeedster. This raised Lajoie to .384, and Cobb had decided to sit out

his last two games with a .385 average. Lajoie would have won the title if his last attempt, also a bunt scored as a sacrifice (no hit, no time at bat), had been a hit.

Cobb was already widely detested through the league, and Lajoie well liked as a league pioneer. There were allegations of bribery involving the official scorer, and an investigation in which the third baseman blamed the manager, who also caught the second game and lauded Lajoie's cleverness. The attempt to deprive Cobb of the car didn't work, but it did persuade the Chalmers Company to (1) give a car to each and (2) change the prize to a Most Valuable Player Award selected by a panel.

While this did not involve gambling as such, it was clearly the sort of game manipulation always feared. At the same time, a managerial change in New York during the last two weeks of the season aroused the same spectre.

The Yankee owners had long been squabbling in public, distracting readers from on-field events. Farrell, the gambling-house operator, and Devery, the police chief of ill repute, were a two-man version of George Steinbrenner, in public-relations terms. (Yes, there's nothing new in baseball.) Most of all, they second-guessed their managers, often in contradictory fashion. Halfway through 1908, with the team in last place, Griffith couldn't stand it any more and quit, becoming Cincinnati's manager for 1909. In 1909, the Yankees were turned over to George Stallings, who lifted them to fifth and, in 1910, to second.

His first baseman, in place since 1905, was a fielding wizard named Hal Chase, still cited as a model of defensive skills 50 years later. But Chase was also notorious for gambling, attempting fixes, corrupting other players, and undermining his managers. His rapport with the Yankee owners was not surprising, and with 11 games to go they fired Stallings and appointed Chase.

This move marked the beginning of the end for the Farrell-Devery regime, and both Chase and their successors would play major roles in the events leading to baseball's cataclysmic upheaval of 1920.

WS—The Cub dynasty ended with a five-game loss to Mack's youth-movement A's. Plank had a sore arm, so Bender and Coombs did all the pitching, while the rest of the lineup hit. Philadelphia's team batting average of .316 was a World Series record not surpassed until 1960.

In their sumptuous new Shibe Park, the A's won the first game 4–1 behind Bender's three-hitter and the second 9–3 behind Coombs. This was so easy that, after a travel day, Coombs pitched another complete game in Chicago and won 12–5, after being staked to an 8–3 lead in the third inning. The Cubs salvaged Game Four by tying it in the bottom of the ninth and beating Bender in the 10th, 4–3, but Coombs closed it out with his third nine-inning job in seven days. He was leading only 2–1 into the eighth, when the A's scored five more runs and the game ended 7–2.

The new cork-center ball was used in this Series, helping account for Philadelphia's scoring (but not, obviously, doing Chicago any good). This demonstrated a truth that would become more and more evident over the rest of the century: a livelier ball will help hitters only if they can hit it.

The average attendance of 25,000 and winning player share of $2,000 were unprecedented, measures of the new prosperity.

1911

In 1911, the second McGraw-Mack confrontation had plenty of buildup, since both teams took command of their pennant races in August.

NL—After the first two games of the season, the Polo Grounds grandstand, home of the Giants, was destroyed by fire. The Yankees immediately made Hilltop Park available, and since one of the benefits of the peace treaty was interlocking schedules in two-team cities, that was no problem. A new steel-and-concrete grandstand was built in record time, connecting up with the Polo Ground's 10,000 intact bleacher seats and center-field clubhouse, and on June 28 the Giants moved back in. At that point they were in a close race with Chicago and Philadelphia, which lasted another month. They pulled away from the Cubs in September and won by 7½ games, while the Phillies fell to fourth behind Pittsburgh.

Mathewson had a new second banana, purchased for $11,000 by McGraw in 1908 when McGinnity's career was running out. Rube Marquard hadn't done much for two years, but now he went 24–7 to back up Mathewson's 26–13, and the staff still had Wiltse, Ames, and Doc Crandall as a spot starter. But it was the daily lineup that contained new heroes. Merkle, still only 22 and always supported by McGraw despite the deathless persistence of the "boner" label, was the first baseman. Larry Doyle at second, Bridwell at short, and Art Devlin at third completed an infield as impressive as Chicago's. Chief Meyers was the catcher, and all three outfielders—Red Murray, Fred Snodgrass, (in center), and Josh Devore—could hit. All but Devlin, Myers, Mathewson, and Wiltse were in their 20s, and Mathewson was the oldest at 32. In midseason, Buck Herzog, 26, came from Boston to play third, and Art Fletcher, 26, took over at short.

Meanwhile, Wagner added another batting title at .334 (by one point over Boston's Doc Miller), while Chicago's Frank (Wildfire) Schulte, who had led the league with 10 home runs in 1910, led it with 21 now that the new ball was in use. In Philadelphia, the league's most exciting new pitcher was a 24-year-old right-hander, Grover Cleveland (Pete) Alexander. He posted a 28–13 record, in hitter-friendly Baker Bowl, for a fourth-place team that was 51–60 in its other games.

AL—The new ball really showed up here. Cobb hit .420 and Cleveland's Joe Jackson .408, while the whole Philadelphia team hit .296. The A's trailed the Tigers until the first week in August, then pulled away to a final 13½-game margin as Detroit played only .500 ball the rest of the way. The Yankees, managed by Chase and overshadowed by the Giants, fell to sixth as their owners bickered more than ever. In Washington, still seventh, Alexander's counterpart was dazzling everyone: Walter Johnson, 23, had won 25 games in 1910 and did it again in 1911, accounting for 50 victories in two years on a team that won only 80 other games.

WS—New ball or not, the name of the game has always been pitching, and Philadelphia had the better of it. On October 14 at New York, Mathewson defeated Bender 2–1 in a completed Polo Grounds, renamed Brush Stadium, that now accommodated 38,000. Two days later in Philadelphia, Plank defeated Marquard 3–1, and the next day in New York, Coombs and Mathewson got to the 11th inning 1–1. Two errors helped the A's score twice in their half, and an error that gave the Giants a run in the bottom half wasn't enough, so Philadelphia had a 3–2 victory.

Then it rained for six days.

When play resumed on October 24 in Philadelphia, Bender beat Mathewson 4–2, and the A's led three games to one. On the verge of elimination in the ninth inning of the next game at New York, trailing 3–1, the Giants rallied: with two out, they scored twice to tie and won in the 10th on a scoring fly by Merkle. But when Ames started against Bender in the sixth game at Philadelphia, it turned into no contest. The A's broke a 1–1 tie with a four-run fourth, added a seven-run seventh, and won 13–2.

In game two, Frank Baker, whose 11 home runs had led the American League, hit one off Marquard with a man on to provide the winning margin. The next day he hit another off Mathewson, producing a 1–1 tie in the ninth. Forever afterwards, he was known as Home Run Baker.

1912

As statistics became more and more conversational currency after a decade of team and schedule stability, the 1912 season bristled with spectacular individual achievements and wound up with the delectable Boston–New York World Series matchup rejected by the Giants in 1904.

NL—To the team that won 99 games in 1911, McGraw added only Jeff Tesreau, a rookie spitball pitcher, and won 103. After Cincinnati, which started out 22–6, cooled off (and finished fourth, under .500), there was no competition. The final margin was 10 games over Pittsburgh, 11½ over Chicago—the last time these teams would be one-two-three until 1929. Marquard was 26–11, Mathewson 23–12, and Tesreau 17–7. Meyers, their catcher, hit .358, second only to Chicago's Heinie Zimmerman, who led with .372 and 14 homers and missed a triple crown by three runs batted in: Wagner had 102 and Zim 99. The earned run averages, accepted as official for the first time, made Tesreau the leader at 1.96.

AL—Here the numbers were more sensational. Boston's 105 victories set a league record,

and its top pitcher, Smoky Joe Wood, went 34–5 with 10 shutouts. Cobb's batting-title average was .410, and the next three were Jackson (.395), Boston's Tris Speaker (.383), and Lajoie (.368 at the age of 36). Washington's Clyde Milan stole 88 bases, a record.

Washington was the surprise club. Griffith had come over from Cincinnati to manage it and finished second, 14 games behind Boston but one ahead of defending champion Philadelphia. Johnson had a 32–12 season and a 1.39 earned run average, although it wouldn't be official in this league until the following year. (Wood's ERA was 1.91.)

Boston was now called the Red Sox. The National League team had switched to white stockings in 1908 and called itself the Doves (because its owners were brothers named Dove), and the American Leaguers jumped at the chance to appropriate so hallowed a name. The Red Sox also moved into their brand new ball park, Fenway, and Detroit, Cleveland, Chicago, Washington, Philadelphia, and St. Louis were playing in new homes. Only the Yankees still had an old wooden facility, and they wouldn't be there long.

WS—In the euphoric atmosphere throughout the baseball world, the World Series lived up to all expectations, and beyond.

It started in New York, in the rebuilt Polo Grounds, now called Brush Stadium. Wood beat Tesreau 4–3, striking out the last two batters with the tying run on third and lead run on second, before 36,000.

The next day they were in Boston, and 30,000 watched a 6–6 tie ended by darkness after 11 innings. Then the Giants evened the series with a 2–1 squeaker behind Marquard, who had a shutout until the ninth. It ended with the tying run at third, the lead run on second, on a line drive out. Attendance: 35,000.

Back in New York, Wood beat Tesreau again, 3–1, before 36,500. And in another pitchers' duel at Fenway (35,000 again), Mathewson lost to Hugh Bedient 2–1. But the Giants weren't through. In New York, a five-run first gave them a 5–2 decision behind Marquard, and in Boston they knocked out Wood with a six-run first, gave Tesreau an 11–4 victory, and brought the issue down to a final game.

On October 16 in Boston, Mathewson started against Bedient. The Giants got him a run in the third. Boston tied it in the seventh on a pinch-hit double by Olaf Henriksen, a 24-year-old reserve outfielder. Wood took over on the mound and ninth ended 1–1.

In the 10th, the Giants scored. Red Murray doubled with one out, and Merkle's single drove him in. Now Mathewson, 33, working his 339th inning of that season, needed three outs.

Clyde Engle, hitting for Wood, hit a soft fly to short center—and Snodgrass dropped it. Engle wound up on second.

Harry Hooper drove a sure extra-base hit to right center—where Snodgrass made a sensational running catch. Engle was able to take third.

Mathewson walked Steve Yerkes, a right-handed .250 hitter. That made a double play possible, but it brought up Speaker, no less.

Mathewson made him pop it up, foul, just wide of first.

Merkle and Meyers converged on it, shied off, and it dropped, giving Speaker another chance.

Speaker lined a single to right, tying the score and sending Yerkes to third, taking second himself on the throw-in.

Well, Matty had pitched three outs, but two of them hadn't been caught. Now, with one out, he walked Duffy Lewis on purpose to fill the bases and set up a force at home.

Larry Gardner, third baseman, left-handed hitter (.315 during the season), stepped up.

He produced a fly to right long enough to score Yerkes.

Those bases on balls will kill you.

Do all these details matter? They did then. They blazed through the hot-stove league for many years. That dropped fly became "Snodgrass's $30,000 muff," representing the difference between the winning and losing team's prize money. Merkle's 1908 transgression took on new life after the messed-up foul. McGraw's bitter defeat brought joy to all the McGraw haters. Jake Stahl, the first-year Boston manager, was New England's hero.

Baseball fever—a phrase that would be invented 60 years later—was reaching epidemic proportions.

AFTERMATH

Success generates its own problems, cyclically.

First of all, it breeds imitation. If baseball is so popular and profitable, why don't we form more teams and cash in? Just as in 1881 and 1884 and 1890 and 1901, other entrepreneurs got interested, and the seeds of the Federal League were planted.

Second, such evident good times, large crowds, and mammoth publicity convince the best players that they are underpaid in the totally restrictive, no-bargaining-power system. So they join in efforts to organize.

Third, anything that might rock the happy boat, such as dealing with crookedness, rogue owners, and people like Chase, must be suppressed, denied, ignored, deflected, avoided like the plague. This is no time for bad publicity.

Fourth, major capital investment in expensive new ball parks can strain previously sufficient financial resources.

Fifth, success creates power, which leads to power struggles, which lead to factionalism, which leads to victory for somebody, which promotes arrogance in winners.

On the other hand, and outweighing all the negatives, was the simple fact that 10 seasons of peace and order, under common leadership had built so strong a foundation that the next ten stormy years could not tear it down.

CHAPTER 9

The Feds

The Federal League's indirect influence on baseball has been continuous in various ways ever since its brief existence, and remains alive in the antitrust question.

It started modestly enough.

A key provision of the National Agreement was observance of the territorial rights of all clubs, major and minor. No town could house more than one Organized-Baseball (OB) representative unless the host team and league agreed to it. The opportunity to start up new teams, therefore, was restricted to unoccupied territory or OB permission. Leagues that didn't sign up with OB, run by the National Commission for the benefit of the majors, were considered "outlaws:" the Pacific Coast, the Atlantic, the Tidewater, the California State, and so forth.

Big-league players could also make extra money by barnstorming after the World Series, and in "city series" in the two-team cities (Chicago, St. Louis, New York, Boston, Philadelphia) not involved in the World Series.

So talk of new leagues popped up all the time. A United States League actually started play in 1912, only to evaporate before June 1, and tried again in 1913, dying in mid-May.

In March 1913, a Federal League of Baseball Clubs announced it would play in Chicago, Cleveland, Pittsburgh, St. Louis, Cincinnati (across the Ohio River in Covington, Kentucky), and Indianapolis. It had no major league pretensions in calibre of play but was pointedly violating territorial rights.

But you can't compete in major league cities while advertising your own inferiority. By August, the Fed had plans to "go major" in 1914. That meant trying to sign up players off the reserve lists when their current contracts expired.

In other words (horrors!), competition for talent.

James A. Gilmore of Chicago emerged as leader of this enterprise. There were plenty of interested investors, turned on by the glittering magnificence of the majors. Among them was Hanlon, long since gone from a Brooklyn operation taken over by Ebbets after Byrne's death. But the three who proved important were Charles Weeghman in Chicago, who ran a chain of newly popular cafeterias, where patrons served themselves; Robert B. Ward, who owned the Tip Top Bakeries in Brooklyn; and Phil Ball, who built artificial-ice plants in St. Louis. These millionaires had to be taken seriously.

The 1914 circuit would include Chicago, Brooklyn, Pittsburgh, and St. Louis, in direct competition with the majors, and Indianapolis, Baltimore, Buffalo, and Kansas City, abandoned by the National League in the 1880's and 1890's, within living memory.

And players were receptive. Fultz's Fraternity was not only collecting members, but creating a climate. In May of 1912, when Cobb went into the stands at Philadelphia to attack a heckling fan and was suspended, his teammates staged a one-day strike in protest, forcing the Tigers to recruit local amateurs to avoid forfeiting a game (which the Athletics won 23–2).

Even before the 1912 season began, Cobb and three teammates (including Crawford) staged a collective holdout, and antitrust questions were discussed in league councils. Cobb, seeking $15,000 instead of the $9,000 he'd been getting for three years without raises while winning batting titles, settled for $12,000. And all players were well aware of such negotiations.

In December 1913, Tinker jumped to the Feds. The Cubs had passed him on to Cincinnati in 1913, and Cincinnati sold him to Brooklyn. When he was refused a share of the $15,000 sales price, he signed with Weeghman's Chicago Whales as manager and became a prime recruiter for the new league.

Weeghman built a new ball park at Addison and Clark on the residential North Side. Ward's Brooklyn team occupied Washington Park, now that Ebbets had opened his magnificent Ebbets Field for the 1913 season. Pittsburgh also took over Exposition Park, abandoned by the Pirates for Forbes Field.

In January 1914, Gilmore offered Cobb $75,000 for five years, but Cobb had already signed with Detroit. Later, Walter Johnson was a recruitment target in Washington, but Griffith (with Ban Johnson's urging) was ready to match any offer and tied him down. St. Louis signed Mordecai Brown as Manager, then replaced him with Fielder Jones.

John Montgomery Ward, in 1912 part of a syndicate that bought the Boston Nationals and named them the Braves, as an inside-joke reference to the Tammany Hall political machine connections of his group, suddenly popped up as business manager of the Brooklyn Feds.

These were important baseball names, and there were others. In the 1914 and 1915 seasons, the Federal League received major league treatment in most of the press. According to baseball historian Harold Seymour, of the league's 264 players in the two seasons, 81 were from the majors, 140 from the minors. More important, however, was the effect on those who stayed in the two established majors: their salaries doubled, and their bargaining power made the Fraternity stillborn as a labor union, although it continued to help minor leaguers.

In 1915, the Federal League shifted one franchise: Indianapolis became Newark, backed by Harry Sinclair, the oil millionaire who would later be connected to the Teapot Dome scandal in the Harding administration.

But most important of all was this: On January 5, 1915, the Federal League sued Organized Baseball under federal antitrust law, for interfering with its attempt to hire major league stars between contracts (that is, when they were bound only by the reserve). The judge getting the case was Kenesaw Mountain Landis, with a reputation as a "trustbuster" because of his $29 million judgment against Standard Oil (later overturned). But Landis, it turned out, was also a rabid Cub fan, a bigot, a wild-eyed jingoist patriot (as he would prove during World War I), and a whiz, not at jurisprudence, but at public relations.

He would consider any "blow at baseball," he declared, "a blow to a national institution," and he urged an out-of-court settlement. Knowing that applying the law would leave him no alternative but to rule against OB, Landis did the next best thing: He took the case under advisement and sat on it, refusing to make any ruling.

The 1915 season, then, took care of the problem. Three major leagues hadn't worked in 1884 and 1890, and they didn't work now. It was oversaturation. The war in Europe had begun in August 1914, and by 1915 the U.S. economy was feeling its effects in general, while the public as a whole was developing other concerns (like staying out of the war) than following sports. The three-league situation, which would have been a difficulty for baseball in the best of times, became acute. However, the established leagues had achieved a firm foundation; the new league was going broke. The new league sought accommodation, and the old leagues were only too glad to find a way to restore their monopoly.

This was the lineup in 1915:

City	American League	National League	Federal League
New York	Yankees	Giants	Newark Peppers
Brooklyn	—	Dodgers	Brookfeds
Chicago	White sox	Cubs	Whales
St. Louis	Browns	Cardinals	Terriers
Pittsburgh	—	Pirates	Rebels
Buffalo	—	—	Buffeds
Baltimore	—	—	Terrapins

City	American League	National League	Federal League
Kansas City	—	—	Packers
Philadelphia	Athletics	Phillies	—
Detroit	Tigers	—	—
Cleveland	Indians	—	—
Boston	Red Sox	Braves	—
Washington	Senators	—	—
Cincinnati	—	Reds	—
Attendance	2,435,000	2,430,000	—
1913 Attendance	3,529,000	2,832,000	—

In planning for 1916, the Feds had some bright ideas. They would move the Kansas City franchise to New York, backed by Sinclair (who would sell Newark), and build a new park with no view-obstructing posts about half a mile south of the Polo Grounds in Harlem, with a capacity expandable to 55,000 seats. And Brooklyn would try to play night games on weekdays if a lighting experiment that fall proved successful.

But that was talk. On October 9, 1915, secret peace negotiations took place in Philadelphia. On October 19, Robert Ward died, removing one of the strongest supporters of continuing the fight. After the World Series, there were more meetings. In December, agreement was reached.

The Feds asked Landis to dismiss the antitrust case. He was happy to do so, his protection of the old leagues accomplished.

The peace terms were:

Weeghman would buy the Cubs, combine Cub and Whale rosters, move the team into the Federal park, and make Tinker the manager.

Ball would buy the St. Louis Browns, combine rosters, fire Branch Rickey, and have Fielder Jones take over as manager.

The Pittsburgh, Brooklyn, and Newark ownerships would be paid off, with Sinclair allowed to sell his players.

Buffalo and Kansas City, recipients of league subsidies to finish out 1915, were given nothing.

All the Fed players were reinstated by OB, after much posturing by Ban Johnson against it.

That seemed to satisfy everyone. Well, not quite everyone. There was Baltimore.

The Terrapin stockholders tried to buy a major league franchise, unspecified, but presumably St. Louis, for $250,000. They were rebuffed. Then they tried to get their team into the International League, the top minor. They were rebuffed again. When the Federal League dissolved itself on February 16, 1916, the Baltimore people refused to take part in the proceedings. On March 29, 1916, they filed an antitrust suit charging conspiracy to destroy the Federal League, seeking $900,000 in damages.

On June 11, 1917, when the case came up in federal court in Philadelphia, the suit was dropped. Three months later, it was filed again in Washington, this time with Weeghman, Sinclair, and Gilmore added as defendants. In April 1919, the District court awarded Baltimore $240,000. An appellate court heard arguments in October 1920 (when the Black Sox revelations were at their height) but didn't rule until April 1921. It overturned the lower-court decision, buying the argument that baseball "was not the kind of commerce" federal law was intended to regulate.

On May 22, 1922, the Supreme Court upheld the appellate decision in an opinion written by Oliver Wendell Holmes, an opinion considered by many (including future Supreme Court justices) one of the most ludicrous decisions in the Courts history.

In 1952 and 1972, the Supreme Court would let the 1922 decision stand, criticizing it but insisting it was up to Congress to straighten out this "anomaly"—which Congress had not created in the first place.

The anomaly would still be there in 1994, playing a role in prolonging baseball's most devastating labor war.

But look at what the settlement of 1916 consisted of. Two favored owners, Weegham and Ball, were made insiders. Others were paid off. (And if Baltimore had been, there would have been no antitrust suit.) This had been the approach at the end of the Brotherhood War in 1891 and 1892. It was what had been done in the consolidation from 12 to eight teams in 1900. It was what would be done when another third-league threat would arise in 1958. The only alternative—employed in 1903 and repeated in the 1960's—is to accept expansion, another way of buying off challengers.

Only one circumstance is intolerable: competing with each other for players. And a time bomb was ticking loudly on that front, in the form of a sweet-natured, ordinary-sized, well-brought-up, and mild-mannered young Ohioan named George Sisler.

Back in the spring of 1911, around Akron, Ohio, a 17-year-old high school senior was displaying remarkable skills as a pitcher and infielder and especially as a hitter. The minor league team in Akron offered him a contract, and he signed it, but he never joined the team or played in a game. In September, he entered the University of Michigan at Ann Arbor, and, although freshmen were not eligible for varsity teams, the baseball coach there knew about him and sought him out. The coach, a recently retired catcher of marginal ability who had already been a college football coach, was Branch Rickey.

The signed contract was not valid, since Sisler was underage, and his father, who didn't know at the time that it had been signed, wrote a letter to the Commission asking for formal acknowledgment of its invalidity. The family and Rickey were afraid a taint of professionalism might interfere with George's college eligibility.

The Akron contract was acquired by Columbus, a higher-ranking minor league club, and in March 1912 Columbus asked Sisler to report for spring training. That's what provoked the correspondence. But the college authorities had no problem with Sisler's eligibility, and the Commission saw no reason to worry about the case.

In August, Columbus sold the contract to Pittsburgh for $5,000. On September

1, the Commission approved the sale and declared that the Sisler request for its nullification was "dormant."

In the spring of 1913, as a sophomore, Sisler showed that he was one of the best college players in the country, a magnet for all scouts. In 1914, he was even better, and the Federal League had just declared itself major, and professional players were changing teams and getting big money. A Detroit judge, on behalf of the Sislers, asked the Commission to declare officially that Sisler was a free agent. By October, he was threatening to sue and using the words "antitrust" and "triple damages." On January 5, 1915, the Commission declared Sisler a free agent.

That spring, Sisler was clearly the best college player and most sought after amateur in the country. Barney Dreyfuss, the Pittsburgh owner, insisted he should have first crack at him, since he had paid $5,000 in good faith for that invalid contract.

By this time, Branch Rickey was the manager of the St. Louis Browns.

On June 1, Sisler notified the Commission that he would listen to Pittsburgh's offer but make no commitments.

On June 18, he told Dreyfuss that he would be joining the Browns.

Dreyfuss accused the Browns of tampering and complained to the Commission. Ban Johnson, as American League president and a member of the Commission, suspended Sisler pending a hearing.

Judge George Codd, the Sisler representative, threatened another lawsuit.

Sisler was promptly reinstated and made his debut June 28. On July 3 he pitched a 3–1 victory over Cleveland. But he was too good a hitter to be wasted as a pitcher, as Rickey realized even before Boston came to that conclusion about Babe Ruth. He was installed at first base and, spending the next 13 years with the Browns, became one of the greatest players ever, mentioned always along with Ruth, Cobb, Speaker, Wagner, and Lajoie when all-time all-star teams were discussed. He compiled a lifetime average of .340 and, in 1939, was only the 10th player to be named to the Hall of Fame. Those who fought over him knew what they were fighting over.

Dreyfuss never forgave Herrmann, chairman of the Commission, or Johnson, with whom he'd had better relations than other National Leaguers did in the peace-treaty years. He began agitating for a "neutral" chairman—Herrmann was still an owner of the Reds—and got increasing support from other dissatisfied owners long before the Black Sox case arose.

It wasn't until June 10, 1916, that the Commission formally rejected Pittsburgh's complaint. The unraveling of the Commission was under way. Three more key player-control cases in 1918 and 1919 would complete the process, but the Sisler story launched the forces and created the momentum for restructuring baseball administration. It ran parallel to, and was indirectly affected by, the Federal League story, adding a volatile element to the underlying issue of player movement and control.

That process, however, was to be sidetracked and delayed by the larger world. War—not baseball war over players by leagues, but the real thing—was coming.

SEASONS 1913–15

1913

Another Mack-McGraw confrontation in the 1913 World Series helped keep the Federal League a secondary story.

NL—McGraw's third straight pennant was an item of familiarity in a year full of great changes. Brush had died shortly after the 1912 World Series, and there was much speculation about who might purchase the Giants. But the family, led by son-in-law Harry Hempstead, decided to retain the team, making McGraw more than ever the one completely in charge. In Brooklyn, Ebbets Field with its gaudy rotunda entrance had a gala opening. In Chicago, Chance decided to retire and Johnny Evers took over as manager, while Tinker and Three-Fingered Brown were traded to Cincinnati. In Pittsburgh, the 39-year-old Wagner hit a mere .300, while Clarke was in his second year as a bench manager. The new batting champion was Jake Daubert, Brooklyn's first baseman, and the new second-place team was Philadelphia, a noncontender since 1901 and the arrival in town of the A's. The rise of the Phillies resulted from help for Alexander, who put up a 22–8 record, in the form of another young pitcher, Tom Seaton, 27–12, and a slugging first baseman, Gavvy Cravath, who hit .341 and 19 home runs. And in Brooklyn, a rookie outfielder named Casey Stengel was being platooned by the manager, Bill Dahlen, who had learned that strategy while playing for McGraw before becoming Brooklyn's pilot in 1908.

The Giants overtook the fast-starting Phillies around July 1 and went on to win 101 games and finish 12½ games ahead. Their lineup was the same, their pitching superior, as Mathewson won 25, Marquard 23, and Tesreau 22.

AL—Boston could not repeat its 1912 glory, largely because Wood suffered a broken hand and could contribute only 11 victories. It fell to fourth. So it was the Athletics who held off Griffith's suddenly competitive Senators, by 6½ games, but they were never really threatened. In fact, Cleveland was the second-place club most of the year, until the Senators overtook it at the end. Washington's success rested on Johnson, who had perhaps his greatest year: 36–7 with 12 shutouts and an earned run average of 1.09. But Mack's approach with the A's was exactly the opposite: he used 13 different starters, and everyone relieved regularly. His six top pitchers, who started 135 games, also made 95 relief appearances.

The A's made an important lineup change, putting Stuffy McInnis at first base. With Collins, Barry, and Baker, he completed what came to be called "the $100,000 infield," a number reflecting the limits of the 1913 imagination.

Cleveland's challenge was based on offense, always insufficient by itself, as Jackson hit .373 (but still trailed Cobb's title-winning .390) and Lajoie, at 37, hit .335. And the New York situation remained bizarre. Chance, having left the Cubs to retire to California, was persuaded to come back and manage the Yankees, who had passed Chase on to the White Sox. Chance found the two owners irritating and the club untalented, and finished seventh.

WS—Once again, the A's handled the Giants easily, winning in five games. The A's won the first game 6–4 in what was again called the Polo Grounds, with Bender beating Marquard. (Illness kept Coombs out all year.) The Giants took the second at Philadelphia, scoring three runs in the 10th inning after Mathewson and Plank had thrown nine innings of zeroes, with Mathewson himself driving in the first run. It was to be his last moment of supreme glory.

The A's then pounded Tesreau 8–2 in New York and built a 6–0 early-inning lead against Al Demaree and Marquard in Philadelphia, hanging on for a 6–5 victory behind Bender. They wrapped it up at the Polo Grounds as Plank produced a two-hitter and outpitched Mathewson 3–1. Mathewson got one of the hits.

After the Series, a bitter fight developed between McGraw and Wilbert Robinson, his oldest friend and, since 1911, one of his coaches. It had to do, apparently, with something about missed signs, but it was really McGraw's increasing megalomania becoming intolerable to the older and benign "Uncle Robby." Within weeks Robinson was in Brooklyn, replacing Dahlen, and he would put his stamp on the Dodgers for the next 20 years so firmly that they would be called the Robins, or The Flock. The true intensity of the unique Giant-Dodger rivalry grew out of those years.

Meanwhile, McGraw and Comiskey took the Giants and White Sox on a postseason world tour, so once again, as in 1888–89, influential figures and important players were out of the country while significant business decisions were being made in secret. When they returned in March, the Federal League operation was well under way.

1914

The year 1914 was baseball's most pivotal since 1901. The A's continued their dynasty, making it four pennants in five years, while the Braves produced a miracle run that has never been equaled, going from last place in midseason to a four-game sweep of the World Series. The Federal League, with all its ramifications, established its authenticity, and in August Europe went to war. In a world that would never be the same, baseball also could hardly escape fundamental change.

NL—George Stallings, who had kept the 1910 Yankees in contention so unexpectedly, had been appointed manager of the Braves in 1913 by their new New York–based owners, who were aware of his ability. The team had finished last four years in a row, losing 108, 100, 101, and 107 games under five managers and three ownerships. In 1913, Stallings brought it in fifth, with only 82 losses. When the games of July 15, 1914, were complete, the Braves were back in last place, 33–43, while the Giants seemed to be cruising comfortably to a fourth straight pennant. Boston had an unimposing lineup but some pretty good pitchers. The three best were Dick Rudolph, Lefty Tyler, and Bill James.

On July 16, the Braves started a six-game winning streak, leapfrogging over four other clubs into fourth place. Since the Giants won six straight at the same time, the Braves didn't get much attention. But after losing a couple, the team won 18 of the next 20 and found themselves in a tie for the lead with the suddenly floundering Giants. They had gone from last to first in 37 days. For the next two weeks the two were neck and neck, but on September 8 the Braves took the lead for good by winning the rubber game of a three-game series from the Giants at Boston. In the remaining four weeks, the Giants played .500 while the Braves lost only six more games and won by a 10½-game margin.

Stallings did it by using his three hot pitchers. From July 16 on, James went 18–1, Rudolph 17–1, and Tyler 10–6—and when Stallings had to use someone else, right after that early September Giant series, George Davis gave him a no-hitter against the Phillies. In their spurt, the Braves won 61 games and lost 16 in exactly half the 154-game schedule. For the full season, Rudolph was 27–10, James 26–7, and Tyler 16–14.

In a culture passionately devoted to rooting for the underdog, at a time of sobering news from abroad, the Braves were the nation's darlings.

The downfall of the Giants was due largely to the loss of Marquard's effectiveness. While Tesreau won 26 and Mathewson 24, Marquard fell to 12–22 and never regained his 1911–13 form, although he pitched until 1925. Perhaps a 21-inning game he pitched in 1914 had something to do with it.

Alexander was 27–15 for the Phillies, but Seaton had gone over to the Federal League, so even though Cravath hit 19 home runs again, the team dropped all the way to sixth. Uncle Robby's Dodgers were fifth, the Cubs under a new manager fourth, and the perennial tailender St. Louis suddenly third under a young manager named Miller Huggins. Johnny Evers? He had moved on to the Braves, where he was the only regular over 30 and Stallings's chief nonpitching asset.

AL—The A's, now being hailed as the greatest baseball team ever assembled, stuck with the opposite approach to pitching. They had no 20-game winner, but seven 10-game winners. In addition to Bender and Plank, they had three newcomers who would become famous: Herb Pennock, Bob Shawkey, and Joe Bush. Unthreatened after June, they won by 8½ games over Boston, with no one else closer than 19. Boston's strong second half in the second year of a new regime (Bill Carrigan, manager; Joseph Lannin, owner) didn't get much attention, nor did its rookie pitcher, a kid from Baltimore named George Herman Ruth and called "Babe." This 19 year old started three games, won two, got to bat 10 times, hit one single and one double, and struck out four times. No hint of greatness there.

Cobb had a normal year in Detroit: .388 and the batting title. Walter Johnson's record "fell" to 28–18, 10 shutouts and a 1.71 ERA, but what really hurt was that Bob Groom, who had supplied an additional 40 victories the two previous seasons, had gone over to the Feds (where he lost 20 games for last-place St. Louis). In New York, Chance was fighting more and more publicly with owners Farrell and Devery; he finally walked out on the seventh-place team with three weeks to go, giving his 23-year-old shortstop, Roger Peckinpaugh, a chance to manage 17 games and forever carry the label of "youngest" major league manager. Cleveland, with Lajoie finally wearing out and with no pitching at all, fell to last.

WS—For all the melodrama and fascination surrounding the Braves, the World Series was supposed to be a walkover for the A's. Instead, they were brushed aside in four straight, stifled by the three hot pitchers. Rudolph held them to six hits in the 7–1 first game and five in the 3–1 fourth. James gave them only two in outpitching Plank 1–0 in the second. The first two games had been played at Shibe Park, a symbol of modernity, and the Boston games were played in Fenway Park, where the Braves had been tenants since August. (They had abandoned South End Grounds, their home since 1894, and were building their own new stadium for 1915.) The first Fenway game, third of the Series, pitted Tyler against Bullet Joe Bush. It was 2–2 after nine innings, and each team scored two runs in the 10th. Boston won in the 12th, 5–4, when Bush made a wild throw past third after fielding a bunt with two on and none out.

The greatest team ever assembled had hit .172, scored six runs in four games, and produced nothing longer than a double. Mack blamed it, later, on the distraction of offers, overt and implied, from the Feds. "They started to think only of money," he complained, "instead of baseball." It was a complaint already 30 years old then, and

it would be repeated louder than ever 80 years later.

A better explanation was a different cliché, applied to the Braves: "When you're hot, you're hot."

Federal League—The Feds staged quite a pennant race of their own. Five of the eight teams were in contention as late as September 10, and the race boiled down to Chicago versus Indiana, the Whales ahead by two games into the final week. But the Hoosiers were on a final eight-game winning streak, while the Whales lost twice to sixth-place Kansas City, and Indiana won by a game and a half. That championship didn't lead to anything, of course, and by that time the World Series, from which the Feds were excluded, was starting. Here was one more piece of evidence of the importance of a World Series.

The new league also had its own superstar, Benny Kauff of Indianapolis, a 24-year-old outfielder who hit .370, stole 75 bases, and compared himself loudly to Cobb. He wore fancy clothes and lots of jewelry (but not earrings, I think) and strutted his stuff as much as possible, in a society that did not yet honor brashness. The Hoosiers also had a 25-game winner in Cy Falkenberg, a 34-year-old right-hander, who had won 23 games for Cleveland the year before after a nondescript 10-year career in the American League.

1915

The Federal League's existence shook up rosters in the established leagues and hastened shifts of power. Both the A's and the Giants fell all the way to last place, while the Braves, Phillies, Dodgers, and White Sox, noncontenders for so many years, rose into the first division. The Feds staged the closest kind of pennant race, but by the time it ended the league's dissolution was already being discussed.

The finish reminded people of the 1908 American League windup and the complaints about Detroit's unplayed rainout. This time, St. Louis and Kansas City, such failures in 1914, were part of a five-team scramble in September with Pittsburgh, Chicago, and Newark (the transplanted Indianapolis team). In the last two weeks, Newark and Kansas City dropped out, but the other three started the next to last day with Pittsburgh a game and a half ahead of Chicago and St. Louis. That Saturday, Chicago swept a doubleheader from Pittsburgh, while St. Louis, losing at Kansas City, found itself eliminated because the teams would not have an equal number of games played. Chicago's Whales and Pittsburgh's Rebels had another doubleheader to play, St. Louis just one game at Kansas City—but it would be its 154th. The doubleheader in Chicago was split, after the Whales clinched first place by winning the opener, so the final standing was:

	Won	Lost	%	Games Behind
Chicago	86	66	.5658	—
St. Louis	87	67	.5649	0
Pittsburgh	86	67	.562	½

Here was something to build on for next year—except that there wasn't going to be any next year for them.

NL—Of the three National League franchises that had never won a pennant, Philadelphia was the oldest, entering the league in 1883 and now in its 33rd season. (St. Louis and Cincinnati, the other two nonwinners, had come in during the 1890s from American Association backgrounds.) Philadelphia's Alexander putting up with Walter Johnson–like numbers—31–10, 12 shutouts, a 1.22 ERA—and Cravath hitting what was considered a record 24 home runs (ignoring Williamson's 26 in 1884), manager Pat Moran's Phillies took command in the second half. Uncle Robby's Dodgers made a run at the Phillies in August, and the Braves, coming from last place again in July, finished fast enough to overtake the Dodgers for second, but Philadelphia's final margin was a comfortable seven games, pretty much intact through September.

It was at the other end of the standings that the reversal of power was best demonstrated. The Cubs, Pirates, and Giants fought it out for last place. The Cubs, now managed by Bresnahan, were league leaders in June, seventh in September, and bounced up to finish fourth—but only 3½ games out of eighth. The Giants started badly, touched .500 at the end of July, then sank like a stone and took last place one game below Cincin-

nati. Pittsburgh, in a campaign much like New York's, wound up fifth, half a game ahead of St. Louis, half a game behind the Cubs, and only three above the Giants. The three dominators had become doormats.

Time was the main reason. The Giants' Mathewson, at 36, finally gave out: he was 8–14, and that was enough to unravel the Giants. Pittsburgh's Wagner was 41, and although he still played a full season, a Wagner hitting .274 wasn't going to carry a club, and Clarke had long since become a bench manager. In Chicago, three-quarters of the players from Chance's last team of 1912 were gone.

AL—Philadelphia's A's went from top to bottom for a different reason: Mack and Shibe sold off their best players. They couldn't match salary demands in a competitive market and hadn't cashed in all that much during the five fat years. In 1914, attendance had dropped nearly 40 percent from the average of the preceding four years, primarily because fans start to take winning for granted after a certain point—a phenomenon that "dynasty" teams would experience again and again in the future. So Collins went to the White Sox for the amazing sum of $50,000 (and got a $15,000 contract for himself); Plank and Bender went to the Federal League, and the supposedly recovering Coombs was released. Barry and Pennock were sold to Boston, Shawkey to New York. Baker decided to retire, a euphemism for not getting his price. The stripped down A's finished 43–109, a full 14 games below seventh place. They would stay at the bottom for many years.

At the top, meanwhile, the Red Sox realized their 1914 promise, but only by winning a three-month sprint against Detroit. The Tigers won 100 games; the Red Sox won 101 and lost only 50, while Detroit lost 54. Boston never did yield the lead, but it was close all the way.

Young pitchers were Boston's strength. Rube Foster, 27, was 20–8; Ernie Shore, 24, was 19–8; Ruth, 20, was 18–6 (and led the team with four home runs in 92 at bats, hitting .315; only eight players in the league hit more homers). But the main cog was Speaker, center fielder par excellence, a .322 hitter (with *no* homers), still flanked by Hooper and Lewis.

At Detroit, this was the year Cobb stole 96

bases, a record no one would ever approach, the baseball world believed for the next 45 years—until Maury Wills beat it and others followed. Cobb's .369 gave him his ninth straight batting title, while Sam Crawford and Bobby Veach completed an outfield to rival Boston's. And Jennings finally had strong pitchers available, as Harry Covaleski and Hooks Dauss won 23 games each. The White Sox, finishing a strong third, also had improved pitching and Collins, who delivered a .332 average, stole 46 bases, and took 119 walks while striking out 27 times. And yes, he was outstanding defensively, too. That's why he got the big bucks.

WS—In Baker Bowl, a hitter's paradise, Alexander outpitched Shore 3–1, as the Phillies broke a 1–1 tie in the eighth with infield hits. Foster evened matters the next day, winning 2–1 as Boston scored in the ninth on two singles.

Moving to Boston, the teams did not go to Fenway. Braves Field had been built, with 8,000 more seats than Fenway Park. So a record crowd of 42,000 watched Alexander and Dutch Leonard battle 1–1 into the last of the ninth. Hooper's single, a sacrifice, an intentional pass to Speaker, and a single by Lewis (his third hit) produced a 2–1 Red Sox victory, highlighting that wonderful outfield. And it was 2–1 Boston again the next day, Shore beating George Chalmers.

Back in Philadelphia, Boston closed it out 5–4, behind Foster, when Lewis hit a two-run homer to tie the game in the eighth and Hooper hit his second of the game to break the tie in the ninth. Car-rigan didn't even have to use Ruth (who pinch-hit once and lined out), but it's easy to see why the Red Sox thought of him only as a pitcher. They didn't need another outfielder.

Federal League—Uninvolved in the close pennant race was Kauff, who won the batting title again at .342 and stole 55 bases. Rejecting a $5,000 bonus offer from McGraw, he moved to the Brooklyn Feds, where he provided some excitement for a seventh-place team and held the attention of the New York press. In the settlement, after Robert Ward's death, Kauff's contract came into Sinclair's hands and was sold to McGraw for $35,000, none of which went to Kauff. He spent the next four years playing productively for the Giants.

AFTERMATH

The immediate effect of the Federal League, aside from the longer-range consequences, can be summed up in one word: disruption. The neat arrangements fashioned in the peace of 1903 and enjoyed for a decade could not be put back together the same way. Ban Johnson was no longer the unopposed leader of baseball's business philosophy. The antitrust questions raised were terrifying. The need to redistribute returning players exacerbated inter- and intraleague frictions in the American and National. And the possibility of U.S. involvement in the war, so passionately opposed by most of the country, could not be ignored. Difficulties lay ahead.

CHAPTER 10

Real War

Up to now, we've used the word "war" to refer to conflicts between leagues competing for players, because that's the word contemporaries used. The First Association War, 1882–83; the Union Association War, 1884; the Brotherhood War, 1890; the Second Association War, 1891; and the American-National War that led to the peace of 1903 were all referred to in such terms at the time and by subsequent historians. They were "trade wars," true enough. But during baseball's organized existence, from 1870 on, the nation had not been involved in a real war. There were plenty of military actions taking place—in the Far West, along the Mexican border, and in dealing with pirates—but not anything that threatened the security of the United States or impacted civilian life. The Spanish-American War, contained entirely within calendar year 1898, was an overseas news event, not a disruption of daily life, and that year baseball prestige was at a low point anyhow.

But in 1916, the situation was quite different. Baseball had become the immensely publicized and accepted "national pastime." Presidents attended opening ceremonies each baseball season. The recently implanted myth of the game's U.S. origin had jingoist overtones. And the war in Europe was impinging on daily life in many ways. In August of 1914, the fighting was expected to be over in a few months, at most; by January of 1916, the dimensions of the on-going slaughter on the Western Front were well understood. The *Lusitania*'s sinking by a German submarine in May 1915 was an American trauma. During 1916, U.S. loans to European countries and U.S. trade with Europe grew so large that the domestic economy became deeply involved. The tide that would pull the United States into more direct participation against Germany was increasingly discernible. But through 1916, it seemed America might keep its distance after all.

Not in 1917. On February 1, the Germans announced unrestricted submarine warfare against neutral—that is, U.S.—shipping. On April 6, President Woodrow Wilson asked Congress for, and got, a declaration of war. On May 18, Congress passed the first universal military draft in U.S. history. On June 5, men between the ages of 21 and 30 had to register. And on July 20, the first draft was held.

In manpower terms, therefore, baseball was unaffected in 1916 and touched lightly while the 1917 season was still on. But from the very beginning of 1917, clubs engaged heavily in promotions to raise money for Liberty Bonds, the Red Cross, and various charities. Teams did close-order drill in spring training, staged military parades at ball parks, let servicemen into games for free, and promoted patriotism at every turn.

In New York, there arose a particularly close connection to the war effort that would lead to fundamental changes in baseball. When Brush died in 1912, the Giants were the most desirable property, and McGraw was baseball's best-known personage. A magnet for New York's social and theatrical celebrities, McGraw had friends everywhere, and two of them were Jacob Ruppert, heir to a brewery fortune, and Tillinghast L'Hommedieu Huston, a self-made millionaire engineer-contractor. Both had some military experience; Ruppert was known as "Colonel" and Huston as "Cap" (for captain). Both loved baseball, both knew McGraw, both wanted to own a ball club. McGraw introduced Huston to Ruppert and told them the Giants were not for sale but suggested they buy the Yankees. In 1913, with Brush's old animosities no longer an issue, the Yankees had moved into the rebuilt Polo Grounds as tenants, obviously no competitor of the host Giants as an attraction, but increasing their value as a property.

In January 1915, Ruppert and Huston took charge as co-owners of the Yankees, having paid Farrell and Devery $460,000 for their $18,000 investment of 12 years before.

Two important circumstances changed overnight, and a third would come to light more slowly. In the league's largest city, a franchise hitherto mismanaged was now in the hands of men richer and sharper than other owners. Furthermore, these were strong men who owed absolutely nothing to Ban Johnson, who had handpicked owners and even field managers for the whole league during its first decade; these men had no patience with the autocratic behavior of one they considered an employee (which Johnson was). Finally, Ruppert and Huston were complete opposites in temperament and ideas, equally strong-willed, so their eventual split was preordained, and it would alter baseball fortunes in fundamental ways.

On top of that, there was the war. Huston, the gregarious one, was close to players and press; Ruppert was reclusive. But as soon as war was declared, Huston took off for France with an engineering unit, leaving Ruppert in charge of the club. They had chosen as their manager, in 1915, Wild Bill Donovan, the former Tiger pitcher, who pulled the team up to fifth that year and over .500 in 1916, when he persuaded Home Run

Baker to unretire and found a 24-game winner in Shawkey, purchased from the A's during the 1915 season. But the team fell back to sixth in 1917, and the two colonels (now that Huston had been promoted) didn't consider that good enough progress.

Huston, in France, knew whom he wanted: Uncle Robby, who had won a pennant in Brooklyn in 1916 and was a buddy. Ruppert, in New York, had a different view, looking for a younger and fresher mind. On Ban Johnson's recommendation, he interviewed Miller Huggins, manager of the St. Louis Cardinals since 1913 and doing well there. They hit if off. When Ruppert hired Huggins, Huston was outraged that it wasn't Robinson and told all his newspaper friends how he felt. The rift between the two owners would rapidly grow wider, and that, too, would have leaguewide ramifications.

Other major ownership changes were taking place. Weeghman took over the Cubs in 1916. Ball, the other inductee from the Federal League, took over the St. Louis Browns the same year from Bob Hedges, who had bought the team when it first came to St. Louis from Milwaukee in 1902. At the same time, Sam Breadon, a transplanted New Yorker making his fortune as a car dealer, started investing in the Cardinals, whose operation was turned over to Rickey when Ball fired him as manager of the Browns. By 1920, Breadon would be the one in charge, with Rickey definitely a subordinate.

That wasn't all. Also in 1916, the Braves were sold again, to a Boston syndicate headed by Percy Haughton, the celebrated Harvard football coach, then sold again in 1919. The Phillies were acquired by William F. Baker in 1913, after a succession of ownerships since 1903, when Reach and Rogers had sold out.

And in Cleveland, Somers, chief bankroller of the American League at its beginning, was finally going bankrupt. Before the 1916 season started, he sold Joe Jackson to the White Sox for $15,000, then the whole club to James Dunn—who promptly bought Speaker from the Red Sox for $55,000. Boston's Lannin, willing to make such an unpopular sale, had acquired the Red Sox only in 1913, and in 1917 he sold the club to a New York theatrical producer named Harry Frazee.

All this meant that at the beginning of 1917, when baseball confronted those unprecedented wartime conditions, only six of the 16 clubs were being run by men who had been there for the peace treaty of 1903—Mack (Philadelphia), Griffith (Washington), and Comiskey (Chicago) in the American; Dreyfuss (Pittsburgh), Hermann (Cincinnati), and Ebbets (Brooklyn) in the National. The control of Ban Johnson was waning, if not yet his influence. The newcomers, except Ball, had no personal ties or obligations to him, and Dreyfuss had become an enemy over the Sisler matter, while Johnson and Comiskey had become alienated for other reasons. For the first time since 1903, baseball was not functioning under strong and unified leadership.

On the field, the 1916 season was normal enough and 1917 almost so (a comparable year would come in 1942, when the military draft also had not yet reached a majority of the players). But 1918 was seriously disrupted.

Should baseball close down altogether? The government said no, it had a positive morale value as entertainment for the public. Should the schedule be shortened to 140 games? Johnson advocated that in October of 1917 and, after much argument, prevailed. Players with low draft numbers would be lost, of course, but those with high numbers and various exemptions would staff teams well enough.

On May 18, 1918, the rules changed. A German offensive in March, after the Russian Revolution had led to surrender on the Eastern Front, put extreme pressure on the Allies. General Enoch Crowder, in charge of Selective Service, issued his "work or fight" order: by July 1, anyone between the ages of 21 and 31 in a "nonessential" occupation must enlist, get a war-related job, or be reclassified with a lower draft number. By September, the draft would be extended to the 18-to-45 age range.

Baseball was nonessential. Players who didn't enlist or face an early call-up rushed to take exempt jobs in shipyards, steel mills, other factories, or farming. Industrial teams stocked with major leaguers generated great interest and criticism. Some minor leagues simply closed down.

The Commission appealed to the authorities to give baseball until October 15, instead of July 1, to comply. The government said they could have until September 1. Did that date mean end of season or end of World Series? Johnson argued for an August 20 close of the regular schedule, to leave time for a World Series. But the new ownership mix overruled him and chose September 2 as the closing date, because September 1 was Labor Day and meant big holiday gates. The government went along and extended the cutoff date to September 15 for the two World Series participants only.

So the 1918 season had an abrupt and tumultuous ending with an early Cubs–Red Sox World Series, and it was expected that the 1919 season would have to be canceled altogether.

However, on November 11 the war ended, and by the time the 1919 season started—with another shortened 140-game schedule—all the war workers were back in action and most of the servicemen had been demobilized. In all, about 220 major leaguers served in the armed forces during the two-year period.

From the standpoint of major league history, the World War I era obscured, rather than caused, the enormous changes taking place in the wake of the Federal League challenge.

SEASONS 1916–18

1916

A return to the normality of the two-league system in 1916 was marked by two close pennant races. The Red Sox won again, even after trading away Speaker, and Brooklyn fought off Philadelphia and Boston, continuing the revolt of the recent underdogs in that league.

NL—The Dodgers managed to stay on top almost without interruption. To Jeff Pfeffer, their best pitcher (25–11), they had added and rehabilitated Coombs and Marquard, who contributed 13 victories each. Zack Wheat and Daubert led a good offense, while Larry Cheney and Sherry Smith completed a strong pitching staff. But Philadelphia still had Alexander (33–12 this time, with an astounding 16 shutouts and a 1.55 ERA) and Eppa Rixey (22–10), and the

Braves still had Rudolph (19–12), Tyler (17–10), and, instead of James, a 32-year-old veteran, Tom Hughes, who went 16–3. Around Labor Day, they were in a virtual three-way tie. On September 28, the Phils beat the Dodgers to close within one game, then caught them by winning the first game of a doubleheader on September 30; but the Dodgers won the second game 6–1 and the next two from the Giants to clinch, while the Phillies and Braves were beating each other.

The Giants, however, were as remarkable a story as the contenders. They had winning streaks of 17 games (all on the road) and 26 games (the last 23 at home), and yet finished fourth. The first streak was preceded by a 2–13 start of the season and followed by a protracted slump. At that point, Mc-Graw revamped the team. Mathewson went to Cincinnati to become manager, and Edd Roush went with him; Merkle was sent to Brooklyn, Doyle to Chicago, and Bill McKechnie also to Cincinnati. (Roush and McKechnie had been Federal League standouts; Kauff, whom McGraw kept, hit only .264 but did steal 40 bases.) In their place came Slim Sallee, a left-handed pitcher, Buck Herzog (who had been managing Cincinnati), and Heinie Zimmerman from Chicago. Below .500 on September 6, this group won 26 in a row, tying Boston for third place before losing four of its last five. McGraw declared that the new lineup was the "best" he ever had, and next year it would prove him at least arguably right.

The batting champion was none other than Hal Chase, now at Cincinnati and still suspect, while Max Carey, the closest thing Pittsburgh had to a successor to Wagner as a base runner, stole 63 bases, giving him a four-year total of 198.

AL—Boston's pitching was even stronger than before. Ruth was the ace now, 23–12 with a 1.75 ERA, while Dutch Leonard and Carl Mays won 18 each, Shore 17, and Foster 13. Gardner was now playing third and Barry, shortstop of the great A's, was at second, because Everett Scott, the shortstop, was on his way to a consecutive-games record that Lou Gehrig would someday break. Tilly Walker, playing between Hooper and Lewis, proved good enough.

But it wasn't easy. Chicago and Detroit were the challengers, and during July the Yankees led them all before fading. The White Sox now had Jackson, hitting .341, as well as Eddie Collins, and a well-balanced pitching staff under a second-year manager, Clarence (Pants) Rowland. Detroit was still sound, although Crawford was winding down, and Cobb, for once, didn't win the batting title even though he hit .371 (and stole 68 bases). Speaker, revitalizing Cleveland's baseball scene despite the team's sixth-place finish, won the crown with .388.

September 19–21, the Red Sox swept three games in Detroit after winning two of three in Chicago, and went from there to a final margin of two games over Chicago and four over Detroit. A remarkable feature of this season was that six of the eight teams finished at .500 or better, and the seventh was only one game under. That's because the dismantled A's posted a 36–117 record, which was even that good only because they won their last two games from Boston after the pennant was clinched. A 20-game losing streak in July and August helped, but it wasn't all that different from the rest of the season.

WS—The Red Sox again used Braves Field, with its larger capacity, for home games. They built a 6–1 lead for Shore against the Dodgers' Marquard in the first game, but Mays had to come in to get the last two outs as the Dodgers rallied in a 6–5 defeat. The next day Ruth started, and the third batter, Hi Myers, got an inside-the-park home run. Ruth then started a 29-inning scoreless streak that would be a World Series record until Whitey Ford broke it in 1961, only a week after Roger Maris had broken Ruth's record of 60 homers. ("It's been a tough week for the Babe," observed Whitey.) In this game, Ruth knocked in the tying run with a groundout in the third inning after a triple by Scott, and neither team scored again until the 14th. Then Smith walked the first batter, and a sacrifice and a pinch single by Del Gainer gave Boston a 2–1 decision.

In Brooklyn, the original version of Ebbets Field had only about 22,000 seats and a huge left-field area. The Dodgers built a 4–0 lead for Coombs in five innings against Mays, but Boston got two in the sixth and when Gardner homered over the right-field wall in the seventh, Pfeffer came in and set down the last eight men in order, holding it at 4–3. Dodgers manager Robinson, sticking to his plan to start left-handers (which is why Pfeffer, his big winner, was in the bull pen), went back to Marquard, who was beaten 6–2 by Leonard.

Finally, in game five at Boston, Pfeffer started, but it was too late. Shore pitched a 4–1 three-hitter, and the Red Sox were world champions again.

1917

In 1917, the rebuilt Giants, reasserting manager McGraw's status as a genius, won the pennant for the sixth time in his regime, while the White Sox, beneficiaries of the financial troubles of others (in the form of Collins and Jackson), had what looked like the beginning of a dynasty.

NL—While the Giants went from last to first in one year, the Dodgers went from first to next-to-last, and the interborough rivalry flourished. The Giants simply took up where they left off in that 26-game winning streak of September 1916. With one of their best-balanced teams, less star-dependent than usual, they finished 10 games ahead of Philadelphia, which didn't have enough to back up Alexander's 30–13 (8 shutouts, 1.86 ERA). Huggins brought the Cardinals home third, and Mathewson finished fourth with Cincinnati, where Roush won the batting title at .341 and Chase seemed to behave himself (but not really). Matty had two football greats on this Reds team: Jim Thorpe, the Carlisle Indian and medal-deprived Olympian, and Greasy Neale, who would become better known as coach of the Philadelphia Eagles in the National Football League.

On May 2 in Chicago, there was a remarkable game. Hippo Vaughn of the Cubs pitched against Fred Toney of the Reds, and after nine innings, neither had allowed a hit. With one out in the top of the 10th, the Reds' Larry Kopf singled, and when Chase's liner to center was dropped by Cy Williams, Kopf made third. Thorpe then hit a high hopper in front of the plate and Vaughn, seeing how fast Thorpe was going toward first, threw home and took his own catcher by surprise—but he wasn't too surprised to retrieve the ball and tag Chase, also trying to score. Now Toney had to complete his no-hitter, and he started with a strikeout. The next batter, Merkle, blasted what looked like a game-tying homer until it was caught against the fence. (The story of Merkle's life, right?) Toney then fanned Williams—the only man who had reached base against him, on two earlier walks.

AL—The White Sox, who had been getting stronger gradually, now were simply better than Boston, which was no weaker. The two were in a class by themselves, and Chicago pulled away in September to win by nine games, with 100 victories. Eddie Cicotte, a late bloomer at 33, had a 28–12 season, ERA 1.53, and the lineup behind him was approaching all-star quality. For Boston, Ruth's 24–13 (ERA 2.02) was his best yet, and Mays was even better, 22–9 and 1.74. But with virtually the same record as the year before, the Red Sox were simply trumped by Chicago's growth.

On June 23, the American League had its remarkable game, at Boston. Ruth started the opener of a doubleheader against Washington by walking the Senators' Ray Morgan. Ruth didn't like how umpire Brick Owen called balls and strikes, and Owen didn't like the way Ruth said so and threw him out of the game. Shore had to replace him, and Morgan was promptly thrown out trying to steal. Thereupon Shore retired the remaining 26 batters in order. Was this a true "perfect game"? It was certainly considered so at the time and was listed in record books that way for decades, with or without an asterisk. Modern statisticians reclassify it somehow, but the point is, it's something to *talk* about endlessly, like the double no-hitter. That's what baseball had going for it and what the two-league system had made so universally available.

Cobb regained his batting title in 1917 at .389, and Sisler, who had hit .305 in his first full season in 1916, hit .353 this time, intensifying Dreyfuss's bitterness, a feeling that was beginning to matter.

WS—McGraw had not won a World Series since 1905, had needed all shutouts to win that one, and he was overmatched again. In Chicago, the White Sox's Cicotte outpitched Sallee 2–1, and the Sox broke a 2–2 tie with a five-run fourth in the 7–2 second game. After a two-day break, in New York Cicotte tried again, but Rube Benton pitched a five-hit shutout and made two fourth-inning runs stand up. Another shutout, 5–0 by the Giants' Fred Schupp, evened the Series at 2–2. But the Sox won the fifth game, in Chicago, 8–5 with a late-inning attack, and game six was back in New York. Red Faber won it 4–2, after one of those plays that was becoming the stuff of baseball legend, another incident overemphasized and misinterpreted but never allowed to die because it happened in such a spotlight.

It was 0–0 when the fourth inning began with the Giants' Zimmerman throwing high to first on a grounder by Collins. Jackson hit a fly to right that Dave Robertson dropped, Collins racing to third. At this point, Benton had just made two of the greatest hitters in baseball history hit "outs" but had nothing to show for it but trouble; now he had to face Happy Felsch, another toughie (.308, 102 runs batted in during the season). He made Felsch tap back to the mound, saw Collins far off third, and threw to Zimmerman there. Collins broke for the plate, and Zim threw to catcher Bill Rariden, who chased Collins back toward third before flipping the ball back to Zimmerman. But Rariden had gone too far, so as Collins went by him, heading home again, Zimmerman had no choice but to chase Collins all the way across the plate—because Benton wasn't covering it.

Giant fans blamed Zimmerman, and a book published in 1976 still refers to him "foolishly" chasing Collins. What else could he have done with no one to throw to? Benton, upset by nonsupport and perhaps at himself, served up a two-run single to Chick Gandil, and the 3–0 lead held.

Merkle's boner, Snodgrass's muff, Zim's chase—hot-stove-league fuel of the highest order, for years to come.

1918

The aborted 1918 season had no orderly ending, and the Cubs and Red Sox wound up in a tarnished World Series.

NL—Since the Cubs had been pulling away from the Giants since June and were 10½ games ahead when play ended after Labor Day, there was nothing tarnished about their fifth pennant in 13 years. They had bought Alexander from the Phillies, but he was drafted three games into the season. Vaughn, Claude Hendrix, and Lefty Tyler (of Miracle Braves fame) were their top pitchers, Merkle their first baseman, Fred Mitchell their manager. The Giants lost Benton to enlistment, Tesreau to war work, and Kauff to the draft in midseason.

Cincinnati was third, lots of hitting, no pitching, and Chase acting up again. Mathewson

couldn't stand him, since by now his betting, fixing, and corrupting others was so blatant. On August 9, with the hearty approval of his players, Mathewson suspended Chase. Before the month was out, Matty was in the army, where he would be seriously wounded (by gas) in France later in the year. What happened next belongs in the next chapter.

AL—The Red Sox were in first place by 2½ games over Cleveland and four over Washington when play stopped, but since they'd been leading from April on, their pennant was legitimate enough. The new owner, Frazee, had made Jack Barry playing-manager in 1917, but Barry was in the army so Ed Barrow managed. Barrow had a rich baseball background and had been president of the International League during the Federal League War, essentially a front-office man with little field experience but astute judgment. He didn't see why Ruth couldn't play the outfield on days he didn't pitch, so the Babe's pitching record was only 13–7 (with a 2.22 ERA), but 59 games in the outfield and 13 at first base provided him with 317 times at bat, plus 57 walks. He hit .300, with 26 doubles, 11 triples, and 11 homers. That tied him for the home-run lead with Tilly Walker, now in Philadelphia, who had almost 100 more at bats. Meanwhile, Mays was 21–13, a suddenly effective Sam Jones 16–5, and Joe Bush, bought from the A's, 15–15. The Red Sox had no pitching problems.

The Yankees, in their first year under Huggins, came in a respectable fourth. The White Sox, with half their team in war work or service, fell to sixth. Sisler, with fifth-place St. Louis, hit .341, second only to Cobb's .382, but led the league with 45 stolen bases (to Cobb's 34). Dreyfuss fumed.

WS—Here the real mess began. The curtailed schedule, unplanned, meant that, among other things, players would lose four to six weeks of expected pay, or nearly 20 percent of a year's total. In addition, they learned that, without their having been consulted or informed, the World Series prize-money formula had been changed, so that teams finishing second, third, and fourth could get some prize money too. Furthermore, anticipating less interest, the owners decided to charge regular ticket prices instead of the customary higher ones, lowering the player pool total (60 percent of the receipts of the first four games), and the players had already pledged 10 percent of their share to the Red Cross. The Commission estimated that the winner-loser shares would be $2,000 and $1,400. The three preceding years they had averaged $3,800 and $2,600.

Grumbling, the players began the Series in Chicago September 5. Ruth faced Vaughn. The Red Sox scored in the fourth (walk, single, single) and that was enough. Ruth won 1–0. Then Bush faced Tyler. The Cubs had a three-run second, with Tyler delivering a two-run single, and Tyler won 3–1. Then Boston won 2–1, with Mays and Vaughn (on one day's rest) allowing seven hits each.

The attendance, at low prices, had been 19,000, 20,000, and 27,000. The Commission announced that the player shares would be cut to $1,200 and $800. On the train back to Boston, the players got together and formed a four-man committee to talk to the Commission. They met the morning of the fourth game, September 9. The players said either postpone the plan for sharing with other first-division teams until after the war, or give us the originally promised shares ($2,000 and $1,400). The Commission pleaded poverty—receipts were half what was expected—and claimed that only the leagues themselves could change rules. Interpreting that as stalling, the players decided to play no more games.

At game time, there were 22,000 people in Fenway Park but no players on the field. American League president Ban Johnson, apparently drunk, appealed to them. With Johnson clearly in no condition to talk seriously, the players decided to go ahead, for the sake of the public and their own feeling for the game, exacting only a promise of no retribution for the brief but undeniable strike action.

Starting an hour late (which mattered, since there were no lights), Ruth faced Tyler. In the fourth, Ruth knocked in two runs with a triple. In the eighth, his scoreless streak ended at 29 innings plus: walk, single, wild pitch, groundout, groundout, single. But Boston made it 3–2 in its half on a single, passed ball, and wild throw to third on a bunt. In the ninth, Ruth needed Bush's help to nail it down.

Chicago won the next day 3–0, on Vaughn's five-hitter against Jones. The sixth game followed the same pattern: a three-hitter by Mays, beating Tyler 2–1 on two unearned runs.

The Red Sox had been in five World Series—1903, 1912, 1915, 1916, 1918—and had won them all. They would not be able to do that again for at least 80 years as of 1998. Baseball, as they say, is a humbling game.

AFTERMATH

The end of World War I marked a new age in every part of the world, in every aspect of various cultures. Baseball could not be exempt. But the war years demonstrated two points in particular to players: that discipline, as exerted by owners, was weakening and that promises could not be relied upon: the 1918 shares came in at $1,100 and $670, below even the last worst-case projection, and the "no reprisals" promise was honored by "fining" them their championship emblems, which they never did receive. And the season provoked the owners into desperate measures to recoup, as quickly as possible, their wartime losses.

Player distrust of the game's leadership contributed to an atmosphere of looseness that only a minority of players acted upon, but that minority's response was in the direction of crookedness, rationalized as legitimate self-interest.

Owner panic led to a familiar cycle destined to be repeated many times: slash salaries, as the only significant reduction in outlays; justify the cuts to the public by calling the players greedy, adding insult to injury; seek remedies city by city, regardless of the effect on the whole; don't look beyond the end of your own nose, and sneer at those who do, so that the time horizon for action is months and weeks, with no thought of side effects or long-range planning; and most of all, show no faith in the quality of your own product, thus not recognizing prosperity when it really is around the corner.

Owners had proceeded along such lines in the 1880s and 1890s, and in the Federal settlement. They would do it again in the 1920s, 1950s, 1960s, 1970s, and 1980s, and one more time in the 1990s. Critics (not many at first) called them "stupid," "selfish," and worse, but that wasn't the case at all. They were simply shortsighted and, in too many instances, recent investors ill-versed in the history, realities, and peculiar qualities of their own business.

But there had been a difference between the

two leagues. The National, originally, had strong presidents: Hulbert, Soden, Mills, and also Spalding, always behind the scenes without title. In the 1890s, when Spalding withdrew, Nick Young was more office manager than chief executive, and order deteriorated to the point where Spalding had to return to quash syndicalism. Harry Pulliam (1903–9), Dreyfuss's protégé, never possessed much power as the third member of the Commission, outranked by one of his own club owners (Herrmann as chairman), and was destroyed by the Merkle incident's fallout. Tom Lynch, a former umpire, was concerned mainly (and properly) with upholding and increasing the authority of umpires, as his opposite number had done all along in the American. He was a nonparticipant in business decisions. John K. Tener, who had been governor of Pennsylvania, was the strong outsider many turned to in the difficult period starting in 1913, but he was resisted by the people he tried to lead and by Johnson, and he quit in 1918. The new president was John Heydler, whose first contact had been with Young in Washington. He was hired in 1903 by Pulliam as a league statistician, then served under Lynch and Tener as secretary-treasurer, a position that in those days constituted virtually the entire administrative staff of the president's office. He totally accepted his function as servant of his owners, not their guide.

In contrast, Johnson had created the American League, ruled it with an iron hand, and selected its members. Right or wrong on any particular issue, he was completely in command and completely supported—until so much began to change around 1913, especially as new ownerships came in.

Then the Federal League, the real war, and accumulated animosities had eroded his power as league president and as Commission member, so that when leadership and vision were so desperately needed for the postwar world, he couldn't supply them either.

Like an atom bomb, which explodes when the unstable atoms at the center reach critical mass, the explosive elements within baseball were already rushing toward critical mass, invisible from outside. The war years had set in motion irresistible forces. And, like atomic forces, these were unfamiliar, poorly understood, frightening to the public of that time, unexpectedly powerful, and very hard to control.

CHAPTER 11

The Blowup

The myth is: America was shocked to learn that Chicago White Sox players had thrown the 1919 World Series, shattering the purity of the "national game," and was ready to turn its back on baseball forever. Desperate club owners then hired Judge Landis, a monument of no-nonsense morality, to be their "czar," and he saved the sport by banning the crooked players for life. At the same time, Babe Ruth started hitting home runs, and the combination of Ruth's superhuman feats on the field and the judge's iron-handed rule restored the public's faith and brought about a Golden Age.

But it wasn't quite like that. In fact, it wasn't anything like that.

A better description would go like this: pressure had been building for years to find a neutral chairman for the three-man Commission, presided over from the beginning by an owner of the Cincinnati Reds and dominated by the American League president. Disputes over the rights to a particular player, supposed to be resolved by the Commission, led only to bitterness and factionalism. New club owners had little patience with Ban Johnson's autocracy, and a fight over the rights to pitcher Carl Mays brought things to a boil after the 1919 season. Infighting prevented prompt action on the World Series fix, of which authorities were aware at the time. Landis was chosen for the commissionership, which he insisted become a one-man office, because he had bailed baseball out of an antitrust suit back in 1915. His disposition of conflicting claims to players, not his banning of crooks, constituted his power. Meanwhile, having seen the benefits of introducing a livelier ball in 1911, the owners adopted a *much* livelier ball and other offense-aiding changes for the 1920 season, *before* the Black Sox scandal broke and without any real awareness of what Ruth would do under the more favorable conditions. The success that followed was the result of the Landis *image* as keeper of the flame, and the playing-style revolution wrought by Ruth's home runs, which showed what could be done by others as well, if not to the same extent.

I believe the second version is realistic, and it is well described in all serious baseball histories.

I know, firsthand, that the myth version is what the vast majority of people in the baseball business and baseball fans have always believed.

But for many years, they believed the Doubleday Myth too.

This characteristic runs through all baseball affairs, even to some theories of hitting and pitching: a simple story, however inaccurate or misleading, is preferred to a complicated explanation, however true. Perhaps it's a general human characteristic. But it certainly applies to baseball.

So let's go through the period of the Big Blowup one step at a time.

The 1919 baseball season began in an atmosphere of excitement and anticipation, fed by pent-up hunger for a return to normal life. The type of euphoria associated with the phrase "the war is over" is hard to describe to anyone who has not lived through it. In 1919, along with this universal sense of relief and survival, the specific belief that the world had been "made safe for democracy" increased the momentary optimism. Such feelings spilled over into the prime mass-spectator interest of that time: baseball, unrivaled as yet by other sports, talking pictures, radio, or television.

The great White Sox champions of 1917 were reassembled, and all the other teams had their established stars back. Huston was back from the war, alongside Ruppert, and whatever their private differences, it was clear that the Yankees would be made important somehow—in a New York where both the Giants and Dodgers had been recent pennant winners. The Cubs had been purchased by William Wrigley of the great chewing-gum company, so Chicago also had a power base in both leagues. The activism of Phil Ball and Sam Breadon in St. Louis gave that city new life in both leagues. Boston and Philadelphia had recent champions in both leagues; Detroit had Ty Cobb; Cleveland had Tris Speaker; Washington had Walter Johnson.

Of the 16 clubs, 14 were playing in fancy modern parks less than 10 years old. (The exceptions were the Phillies and the St. Louis Cardinals.) And mass-circulation newspapers, prime disseminators of baseball material, were entering their peak period of influence and market penetration.

Fans could hardly wait.

Behind the scenes, things didn't look quite so rosy. Underestimating the public's eagerness to respond, the owners had chosen a 140-game schedule, giving away 10 percent of the money they could have made. The search for a "neutral" Commission chairman was fully under way, reflecting and exacerbating political infighting. Making up for the wartime financial losses as quickly as possible was an obsession with some.

A simple chronology sheds light on the tangled story.

1918—Wrigley buys the Cubs and hires William Veeck Sr., a sportswriter, as general manager. The second-largest stockholder is Albert Lasker, a prominent retailer who is also a major backroom power in national Republican politics. He becomes the leading proponent of finding a "neutral" Commission chairman not connected with baseball.

1918—Early in the war-disrupted season, the A's sign a minor-league pitcher named Scott Perry, who wins 20 games in the shortened schedule.

1918—Midway through the season, the White Sox sign a 35-year-old journeyman pitcher named John Picus Quinn, who wins five games.

August 1918—Braves claim they bought Perry's contract from minors. Commission upholds claim, but Mack (with Johnson's backing) gets it overturned in court. John K. Tener, National League president (and former governor of Pennsylvania), resigns the Commission and then the League presidency over this issue.

September 1918—The one-hour strike of the World Series is put down.

November 1918—William Howard Taft, ex-president of the United States, now teaching law at Yale, turns down approach to become Commission chairman.

December 1918—Formal committee created to find a Commission chairman. Judge Landis has strong backing in Chicago and among other owners grateful for his actions in the Federal League case. Heydler now officially National League president.

Early 1919—Quinn joins Yankees. White Sox appeal to Commission, which awards him to Yankees, with Johnson (who in effect also controls Herrmann's vote) siding against Comiskey.

July 1919—Carl Mays walks off the mound in Chicago and leaves Red Sox without permission. Without being suspended, he is traded by Frazee to Yankees two weeks later. Johnson voids the deal, insisting the player must be disciplined first to preserve the integrity of player contracts.

August 1919—Ruppert and Huston get court injunctions to prevent Johnson from interfering. Mays pitches the rest of the season for New York, winning nine games.

September 1919—Yankees overtake Tigers for third place, as White Sox win pennant with Cleveland second. Cincinnati pulls away from Giants for upset victory in National League race.

October 1919—Heavily favored White Sox upset by Cincinnati in World Series, five games to three. (The nine-game format was adopted to increase receipts.) Rumors fly that the Series was fixed, and, it turns out, both White Sox officials and Johnson have strong evidence of a fix at the time and immediately afterwards, but sweep it under the rug.

November 1919—Johnson rules Yankees must forfeit all games pitched by Mays, holds up third-place money (About $13,000 to be divided among Yankee players).

December 1919—American League is now split. Yankees, White Sox (Comiskey), and Boston (Frazee) are determined to get rid of Johnson, who is backed by the "Loyal Five"—Mack (Philadelphia), Griffith (Washington), Ball (St. Louis), Navin (Detroit), and Dunn (Cleveland). Since Johnson helped finance Dunn and is therefore a part-owner of Cleveland, and since Comiskey knows that Johnson is also part of a group trying to force Comiskey to sell them the White Sox at a low price, this civil war is for real.

December 1919—The Loyal Five vote the three "Insurrectionists" off the League's board of directors, where they had held a 3–2 edge over Johnson and Dunn. This meeting breaks up as papers are served on Johnson in three lawsuits filed by the Insurrectionists.

February 1920—When the League reconvenes, the civil war is resolved. The terms: the Yankees keep Mays and third place; the Yankees drop all lawsuits (including some against Johnson personally); a two-year arbitration committee consisting of Griffith and Ruppert will review all Johnson's disciplinary decisions and, if unable to agree, will put the matter before "a federal judge in Chicago"; Johnson drops his claim that he was given a 20-year contract in 1910, which newer owners have never seen.

The era of Ban Johnson as "czar" is over.

Meanwhile:

January 3, 1920—Frazee sells Babe Ruth to the Yankees for $125,000 and a $350,000 personal loan from Ruppert.

At this point, we must pause for some background. The Red Sox, originally financed by Somers of Cleveland, were sold in 1903 to Henry Killilea, of Milwaukee, and the next year to John Taylor, whose father was publisher of the *Boston Globe.* After the 1911 season, Jimmy McAleer and Robert McRoy, close friends of Johnson, acquired the team. (McAleer had been a prominent player and manager.) After the 1913 season, they sold control to Joseph Lannin, the man who eventually sold Speaker to Cleveland, the club in which Johnson had such an interest.

Frazee's main business was producing Broadway shows. When he had a hit, he was flush; when he had a flop, he was broke. Right after the 1916 World Series, he was flush and bought the Red Sox from Lannin. It was the first sale of any American League franchise in which Johnson had no part or advance knowledge.

Ruppert, very much a man-about-town in New York's wealthy social circles, was quite familiar with Frazee and the theater world. In 1919, Frazee had produced some flops. In 1919, Ed Barrow had decided Ruth should be a full-time hitter. He pitched only 17 times, played 111 games in the outfield—and hit 29 home runs, an "incredible" all-time record. The 1920 *Spalding Baseball Guide,* in marveling at that feat, predicted he might never approach that total again.

So Frazee knows how to convert his biggest asset into much-needed cash. He does so now, while League affairs are in legal limbo.

Now back to chronology.

February 1920—Amid all the turmoil, the owners have paid a bit of attention to the game itself. They notice Ruth's effect on crowds. They remember the increase in interest when the ball was made livelier in 1910–11 and note the gradual decrease in offense since. So they adopt some new rules:

1. The ball will be made livelier (without public acknowledgment).
2. Umpires will be instructed to keep a fresh ball in play at all times. (In 1916, a whole game had been played using one ball.)
3. Trick pitches will be forbidden (spitballs or any action that roughs up or applies a foreign substance to the baseball's surface). However, certified "spitball pitchers" will be allowed to practice their specialty for the balance of their careers. (Burleigh Grimes will be the last, in 1934.)

At the same time, the trend of filling in outfield spaces with additional bleacher seats will have the side effect of bringing fences closer.

Thus the lively-ball era—still with us—begins.

February 1920—Johnson tries to get control of the Polo Grounds lease to use it as a weapon against Ruppert and Huston. The lease is now in the hands of Charles H. Stoneham, who had bought the Giants from the Brush heirs in 1919, with a small share assigned to McGraw. Stoneham was known as a "stock broker" (we'll get a better description further on) and, like McGraw, associated with Arnold Rothstein, a well-known professional gambler with strong Tammany Hall connections.

Johnson does not succeed, but Ruppert and Huston are already planning to build their own park, as their League has been urging them to do for some time.

April–September 1920—Despite persistent but little-publicized rumors about the 1919 World Series, the season itself is a sensational success. Ruth, as a Yankee in the Polo Grounds, hits not 29 homers, but 54. Sisler, with the St. Louis Browns, hits .407, and Rogers Hornsby, on the other St. Louis team, wins the first of six straight batting titles at .370. The White Sox seem headed for another pennant, in a tight race with Cleveland and the Yankees, while the National has a good three-team race going with the Dodgers, Giants, and defending-champion Reds. With the schedule back up to 154 games, attendance exceeds 9 million—25 percent more than the previous record, set in 1909. The major league batting average, which had been .248 in the last 154-game season (1917), jumps to .276 in 1920. The lively-ball, no-trick-pitch measures are working just the way they are supposed to.

August 16, 1920—A tragic moment occurs. Ray Chapman, Cleveland's shortstop, is hit in the head by a Mays pitch. He dies the next day. It is the only death in baseball combat in major league history, although many careers, before and since, are ended by beanball injury.

September 4, 1920—News breaks in Chicago that an August 31 game at Wrigley Field may have been fixed for last-place Philadelphia to win. Veeck calls for a full-scale investigation.

September 7, 1920—A Cook County grand jury, Judge Charles MacDonald presiding, will probe that game and baseball gambling in general. Speculation about the 1919 Series gets new life.

September 22, 1920—The grand jury convenes. Johnson and Comiskey are among the first witnesses. The whole Black Sox story, and their early awareness of it, goes on record.

September 27, 1920—The public gets the story when a Philadelphia paper breaks it with the headline, "Gamblers Promised White Sox $100,000 to Lose Series."

September 28, 1920—Eight White Sox players are indicted by the grand jury. Al Cicotte and Joe Jackson confess to agreeing to the fix (but not to carrying it out). All eight are immediately suspended from baseball. At that point the White Sox trail Cleveland by half a game with three games left, but Cleveland has six to go and wins five of them, finishing two games ahead of Chicago and three ahead of the Yankees.

October 1920—Cleveland defeats Brooklyn, five games to two, in a World Series marked by two unprecedented plays: a grand-slam home run by Cleveland's Elmer Smith, and an unassisted triple play by Cleveland's second baseman, Bill Wambsganss. The grand-jury hearings continue.

October 18, 1920—The National League invites the American to a meeting to adopt the Lasker plan for a Commission chairman, to be Landis (Another candidate, favored by Ban Johnson, is Judge MacDonald, conducting the grand-jury hearings.) Only the three Insurrectionists show up.

October 22, 1920—The grand jury hands down indictments.

November 2, 1920—Election day.

Time out again for more background. Wrigley and Lasker were among the early backers of Sen. Warren G. Harding (R-Ohio) for president. With Harding's election being celebrated, they learn that Will Hays, chairman of the Republican National Committee and at this moment greatly empowered by victory, had tried to exert influence in favor of MacDonald over Landis. Since MacDonald is Johnson's candidate, this complicates the situation.

At the October 18 meeting, which Johnson and the Loyal Five had snubbed, a November 1 deadline had been set for their acceptance of the Lasker plan: a three-man commission on which no member is connected to baseball. Now the deadline has passed.

But elections are not only presidential. Local offices are at stake too. And Cook County has just elected Robert Crowe state's attorney, making MacClay Hoyne, the prosecutor handling the Black Sox case, a lame duck.

Back to chronology.

November 3, 1920—Heydler invites the Loyal Five to meet with the other 11 on November 8 in Chicago.

November 8, 1920—The two groups meet in separate rooms, making no progress for hours. The other 11 acts: the National League dissolves, the Insurrectionists withdraw from the American League, and a new 12-team National League is formed, the 12th team to be whichever Loyal Five member comes over first. If none does, a new team will be placed in Detroit. The new league will be governed by a three-man commission, chaired by Landis.

November 9, 1920—Overnight, all the clubs have moved on to Kansas City, where the annual minor league meetings are opening. Johnson addresses the minor league convention, urging its members not to go along with the Lasker plan, while at the very same moment Griffith is meeting with Ebbets to talk peace. The next day, November 12 is set for a reorganization meeting back in Chicago.

November 12, 1920—The owners, with Heydler and Johnson pointedly excluded, meet and agree: the National and American circuits are restored; there will be a one-man Commission, and Landis will be it.

The owners taxi to the federal courthouse, to Landis's chambers. Upon being satisfied that he will have unlimited authority, Landis accepts. They offer $50,000 a year. He says, make it $42,500 because I will keep my $7,500 judgeship. Then they throw in the other $7,500 as expenses, a better tax break than salary.

Landis is the new Czar.

December 1920—The case against the players, ready since November 6, has not come to trial. Why not? The new state's attorney has discovered that the evidence, including the player confessions, is no longer in the files.

January 12, 1921—A new National Agreement, to which the minors do sign on, is formally adopted. It gives Landis, for seven years, absolute power to investigate, punish, and act as final arbitrator of all disputes; it renounces the right to go to court against any of his decisions, or even to complain publicly about any decision an owner thinks is wrong.

February 1921—The eight Black Sox players, having repudiated their confessions, are arraigned, and in the absence of evidence, the case is dismissed.

March 1921—Johnson embarks on a two-month journey to collect testimony and recreate the missing material and gathers enough for a new indictment.

June 27, 1921—The players go on trial.

August 2, 1921—The jury finds them not guilty.

August 3, 1921—Landis bans (that is, blacklists) the players for life from Organized Baseball, in a ringing declaration of his judicial temperament, starting with the words "Regardless of the verdict of juries. . . ."

The country applauds. And it regards him as a heroic figure to this day.

That Landis became, for the next two decades, the defining force in baseball (and therefore in all professional sports) is beyond dispute. Whether or not his influence was good and admirable, better for the baseball business or worse, and the foundation of future prosperity or an obstacle to what might have been faster and more worthy development, one must judge from subsequent chapters. That he was perceived as a savior when such an image was needed must not be doubted, and must be respected; that such a perception, in and of itself, created increasing difficulties after his death, especially after 1960, is also true.

In the context of this entire sequence of events, let's zero in on the Black Sox scandal itself.

First of all, it was not entirely the shock to baseball people that later literature has made it appear. Crooked games had been a worry and an acknowledged possibility for 50 years. Rumors about fixes were a steady undertone in baseball themes, never fully out of the consciousness of the game's followers. The open connection to gambling interests and political corruption of club owners and player-managers as prominent as John McGraw was not news.

What was truly shocking was (1) the scale of the caper—"$100,000" and the "World Series," (2) the *substantiation* of rumors, and (3) the willingness and attempt to keep the whole story hidden for nearly a year.

But the larger impact went beyond the knowledgeable baseball public of that time. For all its growing glamour in the early years of the century, baseball activity was still a minority interest before World War I. The wider public was only beginning to be aware of it during the 1910s, saturated with "national pastime" propaganda, absorbing its culture from first-generation children of immigrants. The war and especially the immediate postwar period intensified both cultural unity and news (including fads) readership. The baseball scene, through 1919 and into September of 1920, got unprecedented publicity throughout the general population of nonfans. To them, the shock was complete and unique.

Second, the details themselves—as they came out then and were repeated for a generation, before real historians went to work—were incomplete, contradictory, and twisted by self-interest in several directions. Exactly what was planned when, and what was actually *done*, remained vague. Just the concept of "throwing a game" was enough to trigger visceral reactions.

Third, the whole business was *used* for various power-building purposes far beyond the impetus to "clean up" the game. Fix attempts would take place in the 1920s and be hushed up even more effectively than in the 1910s; they would eventually evaporate not because of vigilance but because legitimate earning power became significant and—

not to be underestimated—because football and basketball with their point spreads were easier to manipulate once they reached a large enough public following.

Rumors of a World Series fix go back to 1905. Fix rumors flourished about the famous 1908 National League pennant race. There were reports of teams "lying down" to help friends or foil enemies. The attempt to rig the 1910 batting race was no secret.

In the White Sox scandal, specifically, team members apparently bribed Detroit to lose some important games to them in September 1917, and perhaps St. Louis too. In 1919, on a visit to Boston, the Sox play was so suspicious that Collins complained to Comiskey when they got home. Rumors of a fixed Series were circulating in gambling circles *before* it began.

Which gambling circles? Well, the word was that the financier and master fixer was Rothstein, the new Giant owner's associate. Voluntarily appearing before the grand jury, Rothstein denied any complicity, said he loved baseball, flaunted his friendship with the respected McGraw, and was declared clean by prosecutor Hoyne. (Rothstein had, in fact, refused to finance those who first suggested the fix, then used his knowledge that the fix was in to cash in through his own operations; but no baseball or legal authority ever fingered him.) The active go-between was Abe Attell, a former boxing champion who was a well-known Rothstein associate, acting on his own with a Philadelphia group; he got out of the country and avoided testifying.

At any rate, eight players were accused of agreeing in advance to throw the Series. Chick Gandil, the first baseman, was the ringleader. Outfielders Jackson and Happy Felsch, shortstop Swede Risberg, and pitchers Eddie Cicotte and Claude Williams confessed. Buck Weaver, third baseman, insisted he refused to take part, but was in on all the plans and didn't report them. Fred McMullin, the utility infielder, was the eighth. It was the players who first approached the gamblers.

Gandil, in California, sat out the 1920 season. The others were back, at roughly double their 1919 salaries (because Comiskey knew the situation). Once suspended, when the grand jury called them on September 28, 1920, they never worked in Organized Baseball again. Landis not only made his ban stick, he threatened reprisals against any player who appeared on the same field (in independent ball) with the eight exiles or any affiliated club that allowed its field to be used for any game involving them.

SEASONS 1919–21

1919

The actual 1919 pennant races, as seen by a public unaware of the revelations to come, had both champions taking command in the final month.

NL—Cincinnati had never been a serious pennant contender in its entire National League history. Its third-place finish in the war-shortened 1918 season was considered an aberration. The Cubs, as defending champions, and the Giants, the 1917 champions, were the teams to watch. While the Cubs floundered, the Giants seemed to build a comfortable lead through June. But the Reds had a new manager, Pat Moran, who had taken the 1915 Phillies to the World Series, and some emerging assets: Edd Roush, the 1917 batting champion, regaining his crown; Heinie Groh, whose .310 was fourth highest in the league; Jake Daubert, at 35 an anchor at first base instead of Chase (who wound up playing full time for McGraw's Giants under the new owners, who had no antipathy, to say the least, to gamblers); and, as the essential ingredient, good pitchers— ex-Giant Slim Sallee (21–7); their own young Hod Eller (20–9); Dutch Ruether (19–6), the future Dodger; and a 29-year-old Cuban, Dolph Luque, just starting what would be a 20-year career.

The Reds, five games above .500 at the beginning of June, started climbing and never stopped. They caught and passed the Giants at the beginning of August and won by nine games with a 96–44 record, which means they played 47 over .500 the last four months. The Cubs, in third, were 21 games out.

Alexander, back from service, was now with the Cubs, and although he won only 16, nine were shutouts and his ERA was 1.72. But most of the attention-getting names were new, as a younger generation was taking command.

AL—The White Sox started fast, slumped seriously in June while the Yankees spurted into the lead, then got going again as the Yankees faded. Cleveland and Detroit were Chicago's chief pursuers through August, then the Tigers sagged and only Cleveland kept pace. But the Indians never really closed the gap and finished 3½ games out, while the Yankees (thanks to Mays) overtook the Tigers for third place at the very end. Were subsequent rumors true that the Sox, watching the scoreboard, lost games on purpose to keep the race close when Cleveland lost? We don't know.

Cobb was a batting champion again at .384, with Veach, Sisler, and Jackson clustered just over .350, but Ruth's 29 homers were what set the world agog. Next best was 10, by Sisler, Home Run Baker (a Yankee now), and Tilly Walker (with the A's). Speaker had an off-year hitting, at .296, but took over as manager of the Indians at midseason.

The White Sox also had a new manager, Kid Gleason, onetime Old Oriole, ex-Giant, early jumper to the American League, and never before a big league manager. His two top pitchers, Cicotte and Williams, made 75 starts (in the 140-game schedule), completed 56, and had records of 29–7 and 23–11. One can see why gamblers would be confident these two could control the World Series. The Yankees already had two players acquired from Frazee—Ernie Shore (5–8) and Duffy Lewis, playing the outfield—before picking up Mays.

WS—At Cincinnati, the Reds won the first game 9–1, knocking out Cicotte in a five-run fourth. They beat Williams in the second game 4–2, leading 4–0 into the seventh. Ray Schalk, Chicago's catcher, was the one most upset by what his pitchers seemed to be doing (crossing him up and showing uncharacteristically bad control), and he complained to Gleason. Writers were expressing their suspicions. Bettors knew that the odds were going crazy with money coming in on Cincinnati. Comiskey, Heydler, and Johnson were alerted in varying degrees.

But the public knew nothing.

In Chicago, Dickie Kerr, a rookie left-hander, pitched a shutout for the Sox, who won 3–0. (He was too unimportant to include in any fix.) But Cicotte and Williams lost the next two games, while their teammates didn't score at all, 2–0 and 5–0. Cincinnati now needed only one more victory in four games to close it out.

In Cincinnati, the Sox won two straight, 5–4 in 10 innings after trailing 4–0, and 4–1 behind Cicotte. (We know now there was confusion about who got money, who was being double-crossed, which player was trying to do what, and whether every game went as intended; conflicting versions abound.)

But game eight, back in Chicago, delivered the goods. Williams gave up four runs in the top of the first, and the Reds built a 9–1 lead within six innings. It ended 10–5.

Kerr was a momentary hero in Chicago for his two victories (he had pitched the whole 10-inning game), and he won 41 games the next two seasons. But he was no hero to Comiskey. Unable to get a raise for 1922, Kerr refused to sign and spent the rest of his baseball life as a semipro, minor league pitcher, college coach, and minor league manager. More than 20 years later, he was in the spotlight again when Stan Musial identified him as the manager who had befriended and counseled him as a 20-year-old rookie in Daytona

Beach. Musial showed his gratitude by buying Kerr a home in 1958.

1920

In the first season of the lively-ball era, 1920, the public was in the dark both ways—it didn't know about the ball or about the brewing scandal until the final week of the season.

NL—The Reds and Dodgers were neck and neck from the start. The Giants, on the other hand, couldn't even get back to .500 until August 1 but played better than .700 the rest of the way. By the second week in September, the three teams were bunched, but the Dodgers had begun a 16–2 spurt on September 7 that carried them through. They finished seven games ahead of the Giants and 10½ ahead of the fading Reds.

Grimes was Uncle Robby's chief pitcher, 23–11, and everyone in the regular lineup was older than 30 except Pete Kilduff, the 27-year-old second baseman. Zach Wheat's .328 was fourth in the league, behind Hornsby's .370, the .351 posted by the new Giant star, Ross Youngs, and Roush's .339. But the home-run leader, Cy Williams of the Phillies, hit only 15. The leagues did not use identical balls, and although both juiced theirs up, the National's wasn't quite as lively as the American's. Still, in one year the league's batting average leaped from .258 to .270, a scale of change almost always associated with changes in the ball.

On May 1, a historic game took place. Brooklyn's Leon Cadore started against Boston's Jim Oeschger at Braves Field before about 2,000 spectators. A pregame drizzle was just letting up. In the fifth inning, a walk, a missed double-play opportunity, and a single gave the Dodgers a run. In the sixth, a triple and a single enabled the Braves to tie.

And that's how it stayed through the 9th inning—and the 12th, 15th, 18th, 21st, 24th. Since neither pitcher was having any trouble, neither manager (Boston's was still Stallings) took his out. After 26 innings, umpire Harry McCormick decided it was too dark to continue. The tie game remains, as of 1997, the longest ever played in the majors.

Longest by innings, that is. It lasted three hours 50 minutes. In the 1990s, a considerable number of nine-inning games would take that long.

On July 1, the Cardinals moved into St. Louis's Sportsman's Park as tenants of the Browns, who had changed it to steel and concrete back in 1909. The abandonment of Robison Field marked the end of wooden ball parks in the majors.

AL—The Indians stayed ahead of the White Sox from mid-May to mid-August, and the Yankees caught the Indians in mid-June and hung on. The White Sox caught both in early September and effectively pushed out the Yankees by beating them September 17–18. September 23–25, when the grand jury had been convened but no specific information had yet been released, the Sox won two of three in Cleveland, cutting the Indians' lead to half a game. Chicago then won two from Detroit while Cleveland won two from St. Louis, so the margin was the same on September 28 when the White Sox players were suspended. The Indians completed a four-game sweep of the Browns while Chicago was idle. On the final weekend, the White Sox, with a makeshift lineup, lost two of three to St. Louis, while the Indians, after splitting a Friday doubleheader with Detroit, clinched on Saturday, October 2. What if the decimated White Sox had made it into the World Series? Comiskey's fellow club owners, Ruppert and Frazee, declared publicly that they were ready to lend him their players.

Those were strange times.

Cleveland's transformation under Speaker was due to outstanding pitchers. Jim Bagby was 31–12, Stan Covaleski 24–14, Ray Caldwell 20–10. They started 109 games, completed 76, relieved 14 times. All were right-handers. The only lefty, Duster Mails, brought up from the minors in August, made eight starts and won seven of them without a loss.

But the transformation that counted, and the new excitement, was happening in New York. Could Ruth, in a Yankee uniform, hit 29 homers again? He hit 54. He broke his own record in only the 88th game of the season, on July 19 at the Polo Grounds—off Kerr, of all people. In fact, he hit two off him that day. (Imagine! This was exactly *double* the record of only two years before, and that old record, set by Williamson in 1884, was phony because of that one-year short fence in

Chicago—a fact the baseball fans of 1920 were not told.) People were fascinated not only by the frequency of Ruth's homers, but by their majestic flight, taking long seconds in a high arc before landing at a distance from home plate considered prodigious. The 1920 *Guide* article that marveled at his record of 29 devoted its first half to a description of a home run he had hit in an *exhibition* game in Tampa, because of its length. (As the legend grew, it went more than 600 feet.) He had been called "Babe" in the sarcastic sense, because he was so big a man (for those days—six feet two inches tall, over 200 pounds); but now it was with awe that he was called "Sultan of Swat," "Home Run King," and onomatopoeically, the "Great Bambino with the emphasis on 'Bam'!"

In 1919, McGraw's Giants had pulled 709,000 customers into the Polo Grounds, a total that had been exceeded only in the remarkable seasons of 1908 and 1909. The Yankees, improving and building a following, had drawn 619,000, their best by a wide margin. In 1920, with Ruth, the Yankees doubled their audience to an unheard of 1.3 million, the first team to cross the million mark. The Giants, also pennant contenders, with tradition, social status, and habit on their side, drew 929,000—a record for them, and higher than any team had ever enjoyed in baseball history, yet 30 percent short of what their tenant had done.

That's the kind of lesson baseball people *never* ignore. It led to two obvious conclusions: more home runs are good for business, and the Yankees ought to pay more rent.

WS—Overshadowed by the sensational developments breaking in Chicago, the best-of-nine Series opened in Brooklyn. Uncle Robby chose Marquard to start for Brooklyn, because he was a left-hander and because in Cleveland's platooned outfield, the right-handed pair seemed less dangerous. The theory wasn't wrong, since Cleveland got only five hits, but Covaleski also gave up only five hits and won 3–1. Then big winner Grimes produced a 3–0 shutout against the Indians' Bagby, and Brooklyn's Sherry Smith, another left-hander, made two first-inning runs stand up in a 2–1 three-hitter, so the teams moved on to Cleveland with the Dodgers ahead two games to one.

·Covaleski won again, 5–1, and the fifth game proved pivotal. Elmer Smith hit a grand-slam homer—the first in Series history—off Grimes in the first inning. Bagby added a three-run homer—the first by a pitcher—in the fourth. And when the first two Dodgers reached base in the fifth, Wambsganss speared a line drive, stepped on second, and tagged the runner coming from first for an unassisted triple play—still the only one ever in World Series play. The final score was 8–1.

Mails then kept his perfect season intact with a 1–0 three-hitter against Smith, and Covaleski, producing his third straight five-hitter, beat Grimes 3–0. So it was unnecessary to go back to Brooklyn.

By now, a World Series tradition had taken root: someone must be blamed for defeat. The story was that Kilduff, the youngest Dodger, had tipped off Grimes's spitball by grabbing a handful of dirt every time the catcher called for it, in case he had to field the wet ball.

No one voiced suspicions about this Series.

1921

In 1921, the first Yankee pennant produced the first of many all–New York World Series, the first to be played entirely in one ball park, and the last to use the nine-game format. Both the Yankees and Giants had to come from behind in early September to get there.

NL—The Giants' McGraw had rebuilt again, into what would be his greatest period of success: four straight National League pennants, unmatched before or since. What he lacked, he bought, often in midseason. And if a lively ball meant more hitting and less bunt and steal, so be it. He had George (High Pockets) Kelly, 25, at first base; Dave (Beauty) Bancroft, 30, at shortstop; Frankie Frisch (the Fordham Flash), 22, at second or third, the best player to come out of college (in 1919) since Sisler; Frank (Pancho) Snyder, 28, a catcher who hit .320; and Ross Youngs, still only 24, and George Burns, 31, in his tenth season as a Giant, in the outfield. His starters were left-handed Art Nehf (20–10), Fred Toney (18–11, the double no-hitter winner who had come from Cincinnati during 1918), Jesse Barnes (15–9), and Phil Douglas (15–10)—and Sallee was back in New York as a relief specialist.

When he needed outfield help in midseason, he got Irish Meusel and Casey Stengel from Philadelphia, and platooned them.

Most of the season, the Giants chased Pittsburgh, now managed by George Gibson, who had ended his playing career as a reserve catcher for McGraw in 1917–18. The Pirates had a 22-year-old first baseman, Charlie Grimm, and Max Carey, who was still only 31. But the Giants swept them in a five-game series in August and went on to win by a four-game margin. St. Louis, with Branch Rickey acting as field manager, came in a strong third, as Hornsby hit .397 while filling in at four other positions and playing 142 games at second base. Brooklyn fell to fifth and Cincinnati to sixth.

AL—Ruth had what is still considered the best single year any hitter has ever had. He raised his home-run total to 59, batted in 170 runs (now an official statistic), scored 177, walked 144 times, hit .378, and posted a slugging average (total bases divided by at bats) of .846. He also tied for the team lead with 17 stolen bases and, making two token starts as a pitcher, won both games.

But he was also surrounded by a well-balanced cast: Wally Pipp at first, Aaron Ward at second, Roger Peckinpaugh at short, and Home Run Baker at third, Wally Schang catching, Bob Meusel in the sun field (Ruth played left or right to avoid that problem). Mays had a 27–9 season and Shawkey 18–12, and the pipeline from Boston was still open. Waite Hoyt, a New York high school flash rejected by McGraw at age 18, was now 21. He came from the Red Sox with Schang and promptly won 19 games. That made seven regulars sold by Frazee to Ruppert in four years, and Frazee wasn't finished.

Cleveland was still favored, however, and did lead the season-long close race into mid-September. Then injuries to Speaker and catcher Steve O'Neill helped slow down the Indians, and the Yankees won by 4½ games. The Indians' Coveleski won 23 games, but Bagby only 14. Chapman's place at shortstop was taken by 22-year-old Joey Sewell, who hit .318 and played every game.

St. Louis was third, largely because of Sisler (.371 with 35 stolen bases) and Urban Shocker, one of the licensed spitballers, who went 27–12. Ty Cobb, who succeeded Hughie Jennings as manager of the Tigers, hit .389 but lost the bat-

ting title to his young teammate Harry Heilmann, who hit .394 (making Ruth third).

WS—The Giants had broken their own attendance record by drawing 973,000, but the Yankees had drawn 1.2 million. That was the Ruth factor in its most dramatic form. With all World Series games taking place in the Polo Grounds, which held 35,000, one would expect all sellouts; but the first and eighth games did not sell out, because the art of the advanced sale was not yet fully developed. Still, the gate (270,000), receipts ($900,000), and player shares ($5,300 and $3,500) were all records.

Each team batted last in alternate games, the Giants first. Mays started the Yankees off with a 3–0 five-hit shutout, Frisch getting four of the hits, including a triple. The Yankees' Hoyt did even better, a 3–0 two-hitter (one by Frisch), while Nehf, giving the Yankees only three hits, paid the price of three Giant errors.

The Giants won the next two, 13–5 with an eight-run seventh and 4–2 against Mays, despite Ruth's first World Series homer. But when Hoyt and Nehf squared off again in the fifth game, Ruth beat out a bunt to start a two-run rally that gave the Yankees a 3–1 decision. At that point, however, Ruth was unable to play anymore because of an arm infection and bad knee, and the Giants swept the next three games to win the championship. They came from behind to win Game Six 8–5. Douglas beat Mays 2–1, and Nehf beat Hoyt 1–0 on a first-inning unearned run.

In their last 25 innings without Ruth, the Yankees scored just one run. He pinch-hit in the last inning of the last game but grounded out.

AFTERMATH

All three masterplans worked the way they were supposed to: (1) the installation of Landis ended owner infighting (and reflected the willingness to end hostilities); (2) treatment of the Black Sox as an aberration, vigorously cleaned up, was accepted by the public, aided by the Landis mystique; (3) the lively ball and other offense-aiding measures succeeded beyond expectations.

The third point was by far the most important. Ruth was its symbol and chief beneficiary, and would have been head and shoulders above his peers with any ball (as he was in 1919). What made the difference, though, was the perception that *others* could also produce home-run excitement. Ruth alone would not have been enough. The new style had to be universal. It would take a few years for the effect to spread, because already successful players can't change habits and techniques overnight, or perhaps at all. (Cobb never did.) But even the start of the process was dramatic:

	1919	1921
Aggregate batting average	.263	.291
Runs per game (both teams)	7.75	9.71
Home runs per 10 games	3.9	7.6
Shutouts pitched	190	123

What's involved is how batters approach their craft. The conventional wisdom, from baseball's beginning to 1920, was summed up frequently by Chadwick, the most respected theorist of the game and intimate friend of its leading practitioners. Good hitting, he wrote, consisted of *forwarding runners on bases:* place-hitting means "a safe tap over the heads of infielders," not far enough for outfielders to have a chance to catch it; "a hard hit *daisy-cutter* or a twisting hard-hit *bounder,*" just out of reach of infielders; a well-placed bunt; or a sharply hit, low line drive that might go *between* outfielders. Weak batting is "to slug at a swiftly pitched ball with all your force, in order to make a chance hit to the deep outfield"; hitting hard "from the shoulder," which will cause a high fly (which can be caught); or a complete miss.

These precepts, honed by trial and error, meant: develop a level swing emphasizing wrist snap, lay off high pitches, *don't* hit long flies. The pitcher's goal, conversely, is to make the batter hit the ball in the air.

As long as the ball was relatively dead (and in use for long periods of time), with outfield fences too far away to reach, this advice made sense. A lively ball and growing bleachers alter the cost-benefit ratio. If you *can* reach or clear the fences, it becomes worth trying. But to do that, you must

develop an *uppercut* type of swing, as Ruth did, instead of the dead-even stroke of Cobb, Sisler, and the like, and a high pitch is one you can hit far. When enough hitters learn (or try) to do that, pitchers start to *avoid* high pitches and look for outs on grounders instead of on flies.

Awareness of Ruth made the next generation of young players try. Meanwhile, even the level swingers benefited from the lively-ball conditions, not only in terms of batting average but in extra-base-run production.

It also takes a while for managers to change their thinking, not only because successful habits of thought die hard, but because the raw material—new players—able to perform the new tasks must come to hand.

The first result of the new rules and ball, therefore, was a period of transition to ever greater offense.

The aftermath of the installation of Landis, and the owner attitudes that led to it, combined with the Black Sox trauma resulted in a concentration of power in Landis himself that no one intended or anticipated. Quickly regretted, it was hard to escape. Landis was a complicated man: very shrewd, quick witted, skilled at public relations, opportunistic, sincerely devoted to "the good of baseball" as he saw it without the conflicts of interest that undermined Johnson in that respect—but also self-righteous, a racial bigot, an ideological jingoist, a prude, a hypocrite, selfish, often vindictive, and single-minded in the consolidation of his own power.

Landis understood, better than anyone, that baseball affairs must be kept out of the courts at any cost, as they had not been for the preceding 20 years. He realized that the core of his power lay not in banning or disciplining players—which he did to reap public-relations benefits—but in *disposing* of the rights to players wanted by more than one owner. And he knew that moralistic posturing, particularly about gambling, brings greater rewards than actually trying to do something about the vice in question.

His viewpoints would dominate baseball's next 20 years.

PART IV

THE GOLDEN AGE

CHAPTER 12

Lively Ball Baseball

SELLING THE OFFENSE

Within baseball, the first reaction to Babe Ruth was largely negative. What he was doing was "unscientific," a display of "brute strength." What's more, professionals were sure it would prove counterproductive; the odds were against winning by free-swinging. After all, "he struck out a lot," and that was the ultimate shame for any hitter.

The baseball brains weren't wrong—yet—and their view of "inside baseball" was exactly what existing fans liked. The art and science of bunt, steal, hit-and-run, "hit 'em where they ain't," one-run-at-a-time counterclockwise baseball, all appealed to baseball connoisseurs the way clean high notes appealed to opera buffs or good poetry to literary types.

Trouble was, the truly dedicated and educated baseball fans, however sincere, were a small fraction of the total population.

In the 1920's, baseball owners suddenly discovered what so much of American business was discovering: in the enlarged modern marketplace, you can't live off your "dedicated" customers alone; you have to reach out.

And what that larger potential market had just been exposed to, whatever its degree of previous interest, was a crooked World Series.

The larger market of potential new customers had better be given something else to think about. And if Babe Ruth is getting their attention, who are we, the owners, to look such a gift horse in the mouth?

In making the 1920 rule changes, they thought they were simply adjusting an imbalance to promote attractiveness. They didn't think they were "revolutionizing" their sacred game. Well, James Watt probably didn't think he was revolutionizing all social relations and industry when he tried to improve the steam engine, but he set in motion the forces that did. In baseball, the indirect results showed up much quicker.

Now, the unique drama of the home run was that it produced an immediate change in the score—the thing the whole game was about—without preliminaries. It provided, in a phrase not then in use, instant gratification. It was baseball's equivalent of a long touchdown run on the football field, a knockout in the ring, a stretch-drive victory by a racehorse. You didn't need to know any "fine points" to be thrilled by it. You just had to sit and watch and wait until it happened. The flight of the ball took long enough to be savored, its descent beyond a fence was fulfillment (or despair, if it was an enemy homer), and the effect on the contest was indelible.

And if, while waiting for this climax to occur, you watched everything else that was going on during the two-hour game, you might learn to be a baseball fan too.

Systematic promotion of home-run baseball began. The central hero in the baseball story had always been the pitcher. Now it became the home-run hitter. The best batsmen, the .400 hitters, had always been admired and honored, but no instant charisma was attached to being a batting champion—a status that could be determined only after the season was over. But a home run was *now*, and if the hero could deliver it 20, or 30, or even 40 times a year, at unpredictable moments—well, there was a reason to go to the ball park as often as possible to enjoy that moment.

Whether or not the home team was winning.

That was the extra ingredient. Selling victories is an automatically self-limiting process, since half of all games must be lost and only one of eight teams can finish in first place. A great pitching performance is sheer frustration if it ends in defeat. But a home run, any home run that adds to a significant personal total, is satisfying in and of itself, however the game comes out. If it helps win, so much the better; but it offers some solace even in defeat.

How do you promote the new game? Simply by talking about it. Baseball writers write about what baseball people say. They can't do anything else. People then discuss what they have read. Even oldtimer diatribes *against* the new free-swingers become positive items in this context, by stimulating argument.

And the fact is, baseball *is* more fun to watch when there's lots of scoring, with the ball hit hard, fielders running after it, runners whizzing around the bases, the score changing hands, and the outcome potentially in doubt right to the last inning. It was that way in the 1880's and the 1890's, and it's that way today.

Here, then, is a chart of the years 1919–25, and, for comparison, 1992.

	Batting Average	Runs per Game	Shutout Games (%)
1919	.263	7.75	16.9
1920	.276	8.73	14.8
1921	.291	9.71	10.0
1922	.288	9.74	11.7
1923	.284	9.63	10.3
1924	.286	9.50	10.9
1925	.292	10.25	8.7
1992	.256	8.23	14.2

By the middle of the 1920's, these offensive levels were considered normal, reflected in minor league play as well, and scouts were scouring the country for someone "who can hit the ball a mile."

And the public ate it up. Attendance stabilized at the nine-million-a-year level, almost three times the prewar average.

NEW OWNERS

The events leading up to Landis, as we saw, followed major shifts in the characteristics as well as identity of team ownerships. The process was not finished.

We have been using the word "owner" in a vague and not always accurate sense. Actual ownership of a majority of the shares is not a matter of public record, and, for our purposes, it is irrelevant. In sports, an "owner" is whoever appears, in public, to be making the significant decisions and who attends meetings. Silent partners are just that, silent—in public. In so endlessly publicized a business as sports, where publicity is so fundamental a part of the business itself, whoever puts himself forth as the "owner" is it, whatever the private arrangements may be.

Right after the war, the unstable situations were in New York, St. Louis, Boston, and Cleveland, involving seven clubs.

New York Yankees—Ruppert had assumed command when Huston went to France in 1917. They fell out over the hiring of Miller Huggins as manager. When Ruppert acquired Ruth and Huggins finally won a pennant in 1921, Ruppert had prevailed. Now Ruppert wanted to go ahead with building his own ball park, right across the Harlem River from the Polo Grounds, and Huston didn't agree with that. On May 21, 1922, Ruppert bought out Huston, and Yankee Stadium was ready for play (but not fully built) for the 1923 season.

New York Giants—As the new owner of the Giants in 1919, Stoneham was not yet embarrassed by his business connections with Rothstein. By the fall of 1920, when the scandal broke, he was. But in 1921, the embarrassment was worse.

Stoneham's brokerage was what was called a "bucket shop." It took orders for transactions but didn't execute them, in effect betting on how the securities would move. This was not illegal then, but neither was it widely admired by conservative businesspeople. Rothstein was associated with Stoneham in that enterprise. Rothstein also acted as middleman when McGraw found Stoneham as a purchaser of the Giants from the Brush heirs; another minority-share buyer in the Giants (with McGraw) was Judge Francis X. McQuade, a Tammany buddy of Rothstein. At the same time (1919), McGraw, Stoneham, and Rothstein bought a race track and casino in Havana.

Here's how Harold Seymour, the first serious and thorough historian of the baseball business, describes Rothstein in *Baseball, the Golden Age,* published in 1971: "He bet on horses, ball games, elections and prize fights. . . . He was involved in a vast illegal drug trade and was a fence for expensive stolen goods as well as a banker for racketeers. He operated a number of plush gambling houses."

So when Stoneham prominently displayed Rothstein as his guest in the Polo Grounds in 1921—after the scandal, after Landis had taken office—Landis issued a "reprimand." He had already told Stoneham to get rid of the Havana track and casino or get out of baseball; Landis was determined to divorce baseball from even the word "gambling"—in public. Stoneham promised to behave, but in 1923 he was embarrassed again. He had sold his brokerage and passed on his clients to other houses, which went bankrupt, losing everyone's money. When he was indicted for perjury and mail fraud, National League president Heydler wondered aloud if Stoneham should sell the Giants "for the good of baseball." Actually, however, the owners added Stoneham to the league board of directors while he was under indictment, citing the innocent-until-proven-guilty philosophy, and were relieved when he was eventually acquitted. The contrast between this approach and the Landis principle of guilty even after found innocent, applied to the Black Sox, did not go unnoticed, and we'll see more of such Landisism in the next chapter. Owners and players are not held to the same standard.

Boston—George Grant had bought the Braves from the Percy Haughton (Harvard) group in 1918. It was rumored that Grant had some kind of ties to Stoneham. When some of his better players kept being sold or traded to the Giants (Art Nehf and Jesse Barnes among them) while his own team sank to the bottom the impression was not dispelled. Nor did it disappear when he sold the team to Christy Mathewson, McGraw's darling, and Judge Emil Fuchs, who just happened to be one of Rothstein's attorneys. Matty, who had still been in France in 1919 recovering from his gas wounds, was not in good health and would die of complications (tuberculosis and pneumonia) in 1925.

Meanwhile, Frazee was selling talent to the Yankees faster than Grant was to the Giants. In 1922 he shipped along pitchers Sam Jones and Joe Bush and shortstop Everett Scott (whose consecutive-games streak was intact and passing 1,000). In 1921, Ed Barrow had become Ruppert's general manager as Huston moved out and the Yankees' former business manager, Harry Sparrow had died. Barrow would have more to do with what became the Yankee dynasty than anyone else, even Ruth.

By 1923, Frazee was out of players as well as money, so he sold the team altogether to Bob Quinn, vice-president and general manager of the St. Louis Browns under Ball. The Red Sox were already in last place and would stay there all through the decade except for 1924, when they beat out the White Sox for seventh place by half a game.

St. Louis—Ball had a firm grip on the Browns, but the situation in town wasn't so simple. He had discarded Rickey as soon as he could, and the Cardinals, in terrible shape, hired Rickey as president on the recommendation of the sportswriting community. The resulting mutual lawsuits were eventually settled, but by 1919, the Cards were in such bad shape that they gave Sam Breadon stock in return for a loan to keep going. Breadon, who also didn't like Rickey, still left him in charge of baseball operations, including managing from the dugout. In league councils, however, Breadon became a louder voice from 1921 on and kept Rickey out of policy matters.

Cleveland—The revolt against Johnson had left the Indians' owner, Dunn, brought in and backed financially by Johnson in 1916, in a weakened position. The team was still strong but hard to maintain. Dunn's assistant, Eugene S. Barnard, was given an increasing role in league and club affairs.

In Washington, Griffith had obtained a larger share of the ownership in 1919, and in 1920 he took himself out of the dugout to be a full-time magnate. The 16-unit ownership group was becoming more hardheaded, less fractious, and more ready to take orderly advantage of good times (which were taking hold of the country after a brief postwar boom-and-bust cycle)—and found themselves thoroughly under the thumb of their new commissioner.

On May 22, 1922, Landis's freedom of action (and the owners', for that matter) was codified by law. The Supreme Court ruled unanimously that the federal antitrust laws did not apply to baseball because it was an activity not constituting "interstate trade or commerce," which was the only sort the Constitution empowered Congress to regulate. Each game was a "local" event, and the transport of players from city to city was "incidental."

This was the final resolution of the suit brought by the excluded owners of the Baltimore Federal League club when they were denied a piece of the action in 1916. It was the very issue Landis had prevented from going forward in the earlier Federal League suit, because he was sure it would lose; he had first gained support for becoming commissioner by sitting on the case until the Federal League folded; now, in an illogical decision condemned by legal scholars ever since, the Supreme Court wiped out the threat from which he had protected baseball and, in the process, certified baseball's right (and therefore his) to act outside the law.

Club owners hailed the decision as a great victory and would fight hard to retain the exemption 70 years later in the turmoil of the 1990's, having had it reaffirmed twice. But it also, at that point, solidified the Landis autocracy not only by insulating the industry from external challenge but also by putting off indefinitely any need to reexamine the underlying issues and their consequences for the industry itself.

SEASONS 1922–25

1922

The Yankees and Giants made it to the World Series again in 1922. This time, the most serious opposition came from the two St. Louis clubs, especially the Browns.

NL—Except for the July spurt that brought the Cardinals to first place for a few days, the Giants were not threatened. They ended up seven games ahead of Cincinnati, which had a late-season drive, and eight ahead of St. Louis and Pittsburgh, tied for third. The only new Giant regular was Heinie Groh, installed at third with Frisch at second. Casey Stengel played center on a platoon basis and hit .368. The pitching staff, led by Nehf and Rosy Ryan, was deep: McGraw gave 14 different men starting assignments, half of them at least 10 each.

Pittsburgh got going when Bill McKechnie replaced Gibson as manager in June. Grimm and a rookie third baseman, Pie Traynor, anchored an infield that had Rabbit Maranville (of the 1914 Miracle Braves) at shortstop. Pittsburgh's Max Carey led the league again with 51 stolen bases. St. Louis was led by the full blossoming of Hornsby, the first official triple-crown winner, with 42 home runs (more than Ruth's 35), 152 runs batted in, and a .401 average. But neither team, nor Cincinnati, had the pitching consistency to stay with the Giants.

AL—The Yankees had to play until May 20 without Ruth and Meusel, because Landis had suspended them for making a postseason barnstorming tour without permission after the 1921 World Series. (More on this in the next chapter.) But the new arrivals from Boston created a monster pitching staff. Bullet Joe Bush was 26–7 and Sad Sam Jones 13–13; their earlier teammates also did their thing: Hoyt 19–12 and Mays 12–14. The four one-time Red Sox and Shawkey (20–12) started 151 of the 154 games and supplied 90 of the 94 victories. But the suspension cost Ruth another home-run title: he hit 35 in 110 games, while Ken Williams of the St. Louis Browns hit 39 in 153.

Williams and Sisler, who led the league in batting average (.420) and stolen bases (51), were the mainsprings of the Brownies. The lead seesawed until mid-August, when the Yankees took a one-game lead and never let go. Detroit was third, with Cobb's .401 not good enough for a title, and Cleveland, slowly sinking, was fourth.

WS—The format was returned to best of seven, and again the teams alternated batting last. With the new stadium under construction and plainly visible, this would be the end of the shared arrangement at the Polo Grounds.

Lively ball or not, it turned out to be a pitchers' Series, and all Giants. A three-run eighth off Bush gave the Giants the opener, 3–2, and the next game was called for darkness at a 3–3 tie after 10 innings—when it was not yet five o'clock. Fans showered the field with debris, and Landis ordered the receipts turned over to charity, a public-relations masterstroke.

Then Jack Scott pitched a 3–0 four-hitter, Hugh McQuillan beat Mays 4–3, and Nehf beat Bush 5–3, as the Giants produced another three-run eighth. McGraw had figured out a way to pitch to Ruth, holding him to one single and one double in 17 at bats (.118), striking him out three times, and walking him only twice. The Yankees had not figured out a way to pitch to Groh, Frisch, and Youngs, who hit .442 collectively.

This time, every game sold out.

1923

The third straight Yankee-Giant confrontation, in 1923, could accurately be called a Subway Series for the first time, since one had to take the subway or the El (elevated train) to get to one park from the other. It was easy to anticipate, too, since the Yankees had a runaway and the Giants, by a smaller margin, were still on top from start to finish.

NL—Same lineup as 1922, same formula, same result for the Giants. No 20-game winners, no batting champions, no pitcher working more than 220 innings, team hitting .295—balance, balance, balance. Cincinnati second by 4½ games, but not that close; Pittsburgh, Chicago, St. Louis, Brooklyn spaced out evenly below. One promising new face on the Giants, a 19-year-old infield reserve named Travis Jackson.

AL—The 16-game margin over Detroit, with Cleveland half a game behind that, is the most one-sided victory in American League history so far. The Yankees are also sticking to their formula. Herb Pennock has been added from

Boston, and the stylish left-hander goes 19–6 in the new stadium, whose contours are built to favor Ruth—and therefore, incidentally, left-handed pitchers.

Jones is 21–8, Bush 19–15, Hoyt 17–9, Mays 5–2—81 of the 98 victories from ex-Bostonians. Home Run Baker has retired, his place at third taken by Jumping Joe Dugan, who also came from Boston in the middle of 1922 after going there from Philadelphia.

Up for a look in September is a rookie of local repute, Lou Gehrig, a Columbia dropout. In 26 at bats he gets five singles, four doubles, a triple, and a homer (.423) and knocks in nine runs. It's decided he's not ready, and he goes back to the minors for 1924.

It's Heilmann's turn to be batting champion, at .403, and Cobb, 36 years old, falls off all the way to .340. Speaker, at 35, hits .380. When managers can hit like that themselves, they are automatically smarter than other managers.

The Browns? Sisler is out all year with a serious eye ailment, and the Browns drop to fifth. Ruth regains the home-run crown with 41 to Ken Williams's 29. No one else has more than Heilmann's 18.

WS—We open at still incomplete Yankee Stadium, with its capacity of 62,000 not quite filled. (Attendance is 55,000, a record of course.) In the ninth inning with the score 4–4, the Giants' Stengel hits one into that endless left-center-field alley and makes an inside-the-park home run on his aging legs. Giants win 5–4, their eighth straight World Series–game victory over the Yankees.

At the Polo Grounds, Pennock pitches, Ruth hits two homers (one over the right-field roof), Yankees win 4–2.

At the Stadium, the Giants' Nehf outpitches Jones 1–0, as Stengel hits a seventh-inning homer into the bleachers built for Ruth.

At the Polo Grounds, the Yankees have a six-run second, build an 8–0 lead, win 8–4.

At the Stadium, the Yankees unload: three in the first, four in the second, an 8–1 victory as Bush hurls a three-hitter.

At the Polo Grounds, Nehf leads 4–1 into the top of the eighth. He forces in a run on a bases-loaded walk with one out, and McGraw brings in Ryan, who walks in another and faces Ruth with a one-run lead. Strike one. Strike two. Time out.

McGraw sends instructions: throw it in the dirt, the big guy will swing at anything now. Ryan does, Ruth does. Strike three. Brilliant managing.

But Meusel bounces one up the middle, past Ryan, over second, to Bill Cunningham (Stengel's right-handed platoon mate) in center. Two runs score, and a third on Cunningham's wild throw past third. Yankees lead, 6–4. Pitcher Sam Jones keeps it that way. Yanks win Series. So much for brilliant managing.

And all this is being broadcast by that newfangled gadget, the radio. Attendance: 300,000 (the other two Yankee Stadium games did sell out). Winner's share: $6,100, loser's: $4,100. Extended audience: uncountable but immense. Things are looking good.

1924

The Giants made it four straight in a three-team struggle in September 1924, but the Yankees couldn't catch a surprising Washington team.

NL—In mid-August, it looked like the Giants would win by a larger margin than ever. Pittsburgh was 10 games behind, and no one else seemed to matter. But as the Giants leveled off, Pittsburgh started to climb, and all of a sudden, here came Brooklyn from nowhere. On August 25, the Robins began a 15-game winning streak, winning 11 in one week by sweeping four straight doubleheaders from Philadelphia and Boston. The 15th nosed them half a game ahead of the Giants. But the Giants won 13 of their remaining 20, including a three-game sweep of the Pirates at the Polo Grounds during the final week. The Robins won only half of the 18 following the winning streak and were eliminated on the next to last day. The final margin was a game and a half, with Pittsburgh a game and a half behind that.

Veterans led Brooklyn's unexpected charge. Dazzy Vance, 33, was the league's best pitcher, 28–6 and a 2.16 ERA when the league's average was 3.87. Grimes, 30, was 22–13. Wheat, 38, hit .375. Jacques Fournier, 31, hit .334 with 27 homers, the league's best.

But the Giants had added young blood to their championship roster. Jackson was installed at shortstop, Hack Wilson in the outfield. Joining a Kelly-Frisch-Groh infield and Youngs-Meusel outfield, they constituted an all-star lineup. Pitching was still being done nicely by committee, with six men getting at least 16 starts.

Pittsburgh's challenge was also based on the arrival of future stars, Glen Wright at shortstop and Kiki Cuyler in the outfield (he hit .354). But the player of the year was clearly the St. Louis Cardinals' Hornsby. He peaked at .424 in taking his fifth straight batting title—the highest average ever under modern rules—and was second in homers with 25. Nevertheless, the Cards finished sixth.

AL—The Yankees also met an unexpected challenger, but couldn't catch Washington once the Senators pulled ahead in August. They came up two games short.

Griffith had made his 27-year-old second baseman, Bucky Harris, playing-manager, replacing Donie Bush. Griff had been putting together a strong team quietly: Joe Judge at first, Peckinpaugh at short, Sam Rice in center, Goose Goslin in right. Walter Johnson was now 36 years old but still sharp enough to have a 23–7 season and provide leadership for the rest of the staff. Then there was Firpo Marberry, a 25-year-old right-hander who became the first fully exploited—and publicized as such—relief specialist (although he also started).

Whatever falloff the Yankees had was in pitching. Mays was gone, to Cincinnati (where he won 20). Pennock was 21–9, but the others didn't get much above .500. Ruth hit 46 home runs and .378, but the other hitters, except Meusel, had subpar years.

The Tigers, in contention until September, finished a strong third. Sisler was back with the Browns, as their manager, but still not right physically and hitting "only" .305. They were fourth and, lo and behold, Mack's Athletics were fifth. After 1914, Philadelphia had been last for seven straight years, then seventh and in 1923 sixth. The A's would bear watching. The old man with the scorecard, waving it to position fielders, was putting something together.

WS—Now unquestionably the nation's focus of attention as the Fall Classic, a World Series involving the nation's capital had a special panache. It had McGraw, the supreme general ("Little Napoleon"), and Harris, "the Boy Wonder." And it had, for the first time in his long career, Walter Johnson. At last. Even President Calvin Coolidge showed up to throw out the first ball.

Johnson and Nehf battled 2–2 for 11 innings, the Senators having averted a 2–1 loss in the ninth. Then Johnson yielded two runs in the 12th, and the Giants won 4–3. The Senators won the next day by the same score, after the Giants had pulled to a 3–3 tie in the ninth. In the bottom half, with one out and Judge on second, Peckinpaugh lined a double past the 18-year-old third baseman, Freddie Lindstrom, who had displaced Groh late in the season.

The Polo Grounds had been enlarged that year, with double decking around both outfield corners, so the games there drew 49,000. The Giants won 6–4, lost 7–4, won 6–2, and returned to Washington needing one victory.

They didn't get it on October 9, although Nehf allowed only four hits and Ryan none in relief, because Tom Zachary outpitched them, 2–1, thanks to a two-run single by manager Harris in the fifth. (This was the Cobb-Speaker school of managing.)

And they didn't get it on October 10 either, despite a 3–1 lead in the eighth inning.

Harris, who had hit a home run in the fourth, came up with two out and produced a two-run single, a grounder right at Lindstrom at third that suddenly took a bad hop over his head. With the score 3–3, Harris brought in Johnson to pitch the ninth, and, despite a one-out triple by Frisch, the Big Train, as Johnson was called, put up a zero. And another. And another. And another.

In the bottom of the 12th, with one out, Muddy Ruel hit a high foul pop-up and catcher Hank Gowdy, tripping over his discarded mask, dropped it. Ruel then doubled to left. (Old-time Giant fans had apprehensive flashbacks to 1912, only 12 years earlier, which proved well-founded.) Johnson, batting for himself, hit a grounder to short, and Jackson bobbled the ball, getting no one out and leaving Ruel on second.

Earl McNeely also hit a grounder—a possible double-play grounder—right at Lindstrom, and again the ball took a big bounce over his head down the left-field line. Ruel raced home with the winning run.

Thus two new World Series legends were created, to be repeated for decades: Gowdy's misstep, and that "same pebble" at third base. And along with that, the legendary (perhaps apocryphal) quote: "I guess the Good Lord just couldn't stand to see Big Train not win another time."

1925

The Pirates ended New York's National League streak in 1925, while Washington retained its American League title as the Yankees self-destructed and the A's jumped to second place. A quarter of a century after the birth of the American League, four of the chief actors in that old drama suddenly occupied the top of the baseball world: Griffith, Mack, McGraw, and Barney Dreyfuss, owner of the Pirates.

NL—Pittsburgh started slowly but climbed steadily from mid-June on. The Giants broke on top, but did little better than break even after mid-May. They were overtaken in July and left 8½ games behind at the end.

McKechnie's leaders were Carey and Cuyler. Max, at 35, stole 46 bases and hit .343, while Kiki, ten years younger, hit .357 and stole 41. Almost all the other regulars also hit .300 or better (well, almost; one hit .298). You don't need 20-game winners with such support, so McKechnie used a five-man rotation that gave him a 19 (Lee Meadows), three 17's, and a 15. The sixth starter was Babe Adams, 43, the hero of Pittsburgh's last World Series appearance in 1909.

The Giants were in transition. Bill Terry was replacing Kelly at first, Billy Southworth was playing outfield more than Hack Wilson, and no pitcher won more than 15 games. In fact, the whole league had only three 20-game winners: Rixey and Pete Donohue, 21 each for Cincinnati (a distant third) and Vance, 22–9 for a Dodger team back in sixth place and starting to be called the Daffiness Boys.

For St. Louis, Hornsby hit .402 for his sixth straight batting title and took over as Cardinals manager in mid-May, as Rickey moved into the front office full time. He also led the league in homers with 39 and runs batted in with 143—another triple crown. The Cobb-Speaker-Harris approach to managing was getting a good workout.

AL—Sisler was using that approach in St. Louis too, his eyesight improving, and his .345 average helped the Browns finish third. But the Washington Senators' Harris was finishing first

while hitting only .287, so there must have been more to it. The biggest "more" was Stan Covaleski, acquired from Cleveland, who posted a 20–5 for the Senators alongside Johnson's 20–7, and another was Dutch Reuther, acquired from Brooklyn, 18–7. Marberry pitched 55 times, all in relief.

Philadelphia seesawed with Washington right through August, then fell back and lost by 8½ games. Connie Mack had a 22-year-old catcher named Mickey Cochrane; a 23-year-old outfielder, renamed Al Simmons (actually Szymanski); a 25-year-old pitcher bought from Baltimore named Bob (Lefty) Grove; a 28-year-old infielder named Jimmy Dykes; a 17-year-old catcher (who got into one game) named Jimmie Foxx; and a 25-year-old second baseman named Max Bishop. They would soon be very familiar names indeed.

The Yankee story was something else. Ruth got sick during spring training ("the world's most important stomach ache," the papers said). He couldn't start the season, and when he did play, he was weak and ineffective. The team showed other weaknesses too, and by the end of July was 15 games under .500 in seventh place. Ruth was hitting less than .250, with only 15 homers. He had lost interest and was concentrating on carousing, showing up late if at all, having bitter arguments in public as well as in private with Huggins, the Yankee manager. In August, in St. Louis, he showed up late once too often. Huggins fined him $5,000. Ruth hurried back to New York and appealed to Ruppert and Barrow. They backed Huggins, the manager's authority. Ruth learned a lesson in discipline that helped him forever afterwards. He got his final average up to .290 and 25 homers during September. But the Yankees finished seventh.

Historic events, however, are not always obvious and don't always get attention at the time.

On May 6, Huggins took the slumping Scott out of the lineup and put Pee Wee Wanninger at short. Scott hadn't missed a game since June 20, 1916, so his consecutive-games streak ended at 1,307—perhaps never to be equaled, his contemporaries thought.

Less than four weeks later, on June 2, Pipp showed up with a bad headache, having been beaned some time before. Gehrig had to play first base. He had pinch-hit for Wanninger the day before, so this became No. 2 in Lou's streak of 2,130 straight games, which would end in May of 1939.

To this day, players not otherwise steeped in historical lore tease a teammate who has to sit out a game about Wally Pipp.

WS—The Series opened in Pittsburgh, and the Senators' Johnson was in full glory: a five-hit, 10-strikeout, 4–1 victory. (That night, Mathewson died, and players donned black armbands for the remaining games.)

The Pirates got even when Vic Aldridge beat Covaleskie 3–2.

In Washington, the Senators won 4–3, and Johnson's second start was even stronger, a 4–0, six-hit shutout.

No team had ever survived a 3–1 deficit in a World Series, and few have since, but the Pirates became the first. They won the last game in Washington 6–3, behind Aldridge, and Game Six in Pittsburgh 3–2, behind Remy Kremer.

Rain produced a day off, and it was still drizzling when Johnson and Aldridge started the seventh game. The Senators knocked out Aldridge in a four-run first, but Johnson, who would be 38 in about three weeks, was nearing the end of the line. He gave up three runs in the third, clung to a 6–4 lead into the seventh, and was tied in the eighth on two unearned runs following Peckinpaugh's muff of a pop fly. Peck hit a home run to regain the lead, 7–6, in the top of the eighth, but Johnson was running down. The league's best relief pitcher was available, but you just don't take out Walter Johnson; at least, Harris wouldn't. And Johnson did get the first two outs in the eighth. But two doubles tied the score. After a walk, Johnson got Carey to bounce to short, only to have Peckinpaugh's throw for the force at second go wide, leaving bases loaded instead of ending the inning.

It was Peckinpaugh's *eighth* error of the Series.

Cuyler was next, and he drove a ground-rule double into the crowd in right field, making the score 9–7, which is the way it ended.

AFTERMATH

The change in playing style was taking hold, and the game would never go back to a nonhomer psychology. The czarist regime of Landis was having the desired effect: greater public confidence that the "integrity of the game" was being protected, and less internecine warfare. The new Yankee Stadium, the enlarged Polo Grounds, the addition of seats in many other ball parks, and the Cardinals' move into Sportsman's Park ushered in an era of stable and adequate playing sites for everyone.

The three all–New York Series played perfectly into the search for expanding markets through maximum publicity, because New York was now in a class of its own as the communications center of the nation, if not the world. Among other things, this positioned both baseball and the infant radio industry for giving serious consideration to their possible interaction.

Ruth's status as supercelebrity was changing perceptions of what "stardom" could really mean, beyond the activity in question. It paralleled, and enhanced, the excitement being created by Jack Dempsey, heavyweight champion of the world; Red Grange, the University of Illinois football star who was opening doors to new commercial possibilities for pro football; and Bobby Jones and Bill Tilden, reigning giants of the country-club sports of golf and tennis, not yet commercialized but extensively covered in print.

The years 1921–25 carried one overriding message for baseball people: we're on the right track.

CHAPTER 13

The Commissioner

Judge Landis was everything a judge should never be. His prejudices, strong ones, dictated his decisions. He ignored the law. He expressed openly, as well as practiced mercilessly, extreme partisanship. He had no use for objectivity, although he didn't mind pretending it if convenient; or for facts that conflicted with his already established desire. If he had any ethics at all, which is doubtful, they were summed up by a common but hardly admirable formula: "If I want to do it, it is good and pure. If it's something I don't like, it is evil and God ought to punish it, and if He doesn't, I'll try." His rulings from the bench were regularly overturned by higher courts and oscillated wildly from excessively harsh to unaccountably lenient. He was condemned by the American Bar Association, threatened with impeachment by Congress.

His view of the world was shallow, bigoted, and ill informed, based on a poor education and thoroughly selfish impulses. He could be devious and vengeful.

Landis also had brains and an exceptional instinct for sensing the popular mood, especially the mood of the lowest common denominator. He knew which stance, in a controversy, would make him look good at that moment. He knew the value of taking either an absolutely firm and simplistic stand or no stand at all, but nothing in between.

How can one say, therefore, that such a man was "good for baseball"—or for anything? The truth is that he *was* good for that industry at that particular time in those particular circumstances. He had all the characteristics of an effective dictator—and civil wars, sooner or later, produce a dictator to restore order.

Baseball's club owners had been engaging in civil war—fighting among themselves over player contracts and franchises—for more than a decade. Turmoil at their level permitted, and perhaps encouraged, "civil" disorder—fixed games and lax discipline. At some point, the need for orderly authority becomes paramount, and the warring factions become willing to accept it from anyone who can exert it.

Landis knew how to exert it. And he enjoyed doing it.

Would a less arbitrary ruler have been preferable? Of course. Would baseball's future have been better under wiser and more benevolent leadership? Probably. Would baseball in 1921 have prospered the way it did without someone like Landis taking charge? Almost certainly no.

A common observation about historical process goes, "If it [something crucial] didn't exist, they'd have had to invent it." Well, a strong central authority *didn't* exist, so they *did* invent it.

But Landis, the person, collaborated in his own invention.

Landis spent the first half of the 1920s organizing and consolidating his personal power. He spent the next 10 years exercising it to the fullest, and his final few years—up to and during World War II—hanging on to it.

Everything exacts its price. The price of having a dictator impose order is that initiative and progress are stifled, a bad example is set, and disorder returns when the dictator is gone. In baseball, the operative phrase became "If Judge Landis were alive today . . ." when subsequent problems arose. That fantasy in itself did as much harm as any absence of Landis-like action.

Well, if Landis were alive today, given his characteristics and background, he wouldn't be a judge at all, but a highly successful radio talk-show host of right-wing persuasion. His talents, in this respect, were ahead of their time.

But it is important *not* to evaluate Landis by 1990 standards, politically correct or otherwise. His biases against blacks, immigrants, union labor, pacifists, and anyone he considered "radical" were not unusual in his time, and expressing them openly was quite acceptable in "decent" society. What now seems like shocking insensitivity was perfectly ordinary intercourse then. He was well within the mainstream of passive bigotry, untainted by the militancy that was also tolerated in that society (like the Ku Klux Klan, racially selective immigration laws, and avowed quotas on Jews in higher education). The men who hired him were, as a group, no less conservative than he.

What he could be blamed for, then and now, was his total lack of judicial integrity. The men who hired him were soon appalled by his arbitrary decisions, but they were stuck with him. They had renounced the right to oppose him in any way, by public statement or recourse to the courts, so they were all subject to retaliation if they fought him in private. And since they had staked everything on his public relations value—convincing fans that he was the instrument of cleansing and vigilance—they could not afford to fire him or force him to resign. Whom they could not depose they had to obey. (It's not unusual for businessmen to find themselves in that position with respect to a dictator whose ascension they supported.)

So the first order of business for Landis was to establish his autocracy. For nearly 20 years, Ban Johnson had been the autocrat, and it was the unraveling of his power in recent years that had brought about the entry of Landis. Still, Ban remained president of the American League and had considerable residual influence, backed by his Loyal Five even after their surrender. Step No. 1: chop down what remains of Ban Johnson.

The immediate storm centered on the Black Sox, which meant gambling. Step No. 2: display total intolerance for this sinful activity by (1) banning for life any player to whom suspicion (not proof) can be attached; (2) loudly forbidding owners to have gambling connections, like owning or frequenting racetracks and casinos (but scrupulously avoiding any action against them); (3) calling on newspapers to stop printing the run-scoring tables on which betting pools were based (but making sure that newspapers understood he would never actually do anything to interfere with the free flow of free publicity).

Step No. 3: simultaneously feather and fortify his own nest.

To carry out Step 2, Landis didn't stop with his condemnation of the Black Sox, before and after trial and "regardless of the verdict of juries." Between 1921 and 1925, he banned a dozen other players for life, with or without allegations of crookedness. Upon taking office in 1921, one of his first acts was to blacklist Benny Kauff because he was under indictment for improprieties in his automobile agency, unconnected to baseball in any way; when Kauff was acquitted, Landis didn't agree with the verdict and never allowed him to return to baseball. That June he blacklisted Ray Fisher for the crime of seeking employment outside of baseball (as coach at Michigan) while the Cincinnati Reds still wanted him to pitch. He banned Phil Douglas, right after the 1922 World Series, because this notorious drunk had once written a letter saying he wanted to be traded away from the Giants because if he stayed "I am afraid I'll win the pennant for him," meaning McGraw.

But in the case of Rube Benton, another pitcher on record as knowing of the 1919 fix and declared undesirable by National League president Heydler, Landis cleared Benton to put Heydler in his place. Heydler was no Ban Johnson, but the new commissioner was intent on making the point that *any* league president was now irrelevant.

Just before the 1924 World Series, the Cozy Dolan case broke. Jimmy O'Connell, a 23-year-old outfield substitute on the Giants, offered a Philadelphia player $500 to take it easy the day the Giants needed to win to clinch the pennant. The Phillie told his manager, Art Fletcher (once McGraw's shortstop), who told Heydler, who told Landis. O'Connell admitted it, saying he was carrying out instructions from Cozy Dolan, the coach who was McGraw's close friend and stooge, and said Giants players Frisch, Youngs, and Kelly knew about it. Landis immediately banned O'Connell and Dolan but cleared the three star players, ruling that O'Connell and Dolan acted on their own.

And so it went. Wherever Landis saw an opportunity to score public-relations points, he made a decision in that direction. But the showdown didn't come until 1926. Then he could complete Step 1 by using Step 2: destroy Johnson by crusading against gambling.

A chronology is useful again:

September 1926—Johnson receives documents accusing Cobb, Speaker, and Joe Wood (then an outfielder with Cleveland, after his pitching arm had gone dead) of conspiring to fix a game in 1919, to help Detroit finish third ahead of the Yankees, and of also betting on the sure thing. Johnson has other evidence of betting activity by Cobb and Sisler. The league decides to handle the matter quietly, to avoid disgracing the stars and itself.

October—The league forwards the file to Landis.

November 2—Cobb resigns as player-manager of the Tigers.

December 2—Speaker resigns as player-manager of the Indians.

December 15—The American League gives Johnson a vote of confidence.

December 21—Landis is reelected for another seven-year term with a $15,000 raise to $65,000 (plus expenses).

December 21—Landis makes public all the Cobb and Speaker material and says he'll investigate further.

January 6–7, 1927—Swede Risberg, one of the Black Sox, has said he has a lot of information about fixed games in 1917 as well as 1919. Landis brings him to Chicago to confront 35 players and decides to believe them, not him.

January 13—Johnson gives out an interview attacking Landis for reopening the Cobb-Sisler case and declares the two will never again play in the American League.

January 23—American League owners repudiate Johnson's criticism of Landis. Johnson appears seriously ill and distracted at this meeting in Chicago. He is given a leave of absence, and Navin (Detroit owner) becomes acting president.

January 27—Landis issues a statement completely exonerating Cobb and Speaker, restoring them to the eligible list, and allowing all *American League* clubs to seek their services. The league proviso is important: it negates Johnson's assertion of January 13. Remember how Landis put down Heydler by clearing Benton? This is a stronger version of the same president-neutralizing maneuver.

Cobb signed as a player with the Athletics, Speaker with the Senators. It was not a random result. Detroit and Cleveland didn't want them back, while Philadelphia's Mack and Washington's Griffith were the two oldest, most respected figures of "integrity" the league had, implying acceptability. Cobb played two more seasons with the A's, and Speaker joined him the second year, 1928. Then both retired.

The Cobb-Speaker affair was pivotal in several respects. It marked the final defeat of Johnson, who agreed to resign in July and formally stepped down in October. He was succeeded by Barnard, who had been running Cleveland for Dunn (who died in 1926), and the Cleveland club was sold to Alva Bradley. From now on, the American League president would have no more real power than National League presidents had had since 1903, and that was all right with Barnard.

It also put the fixed-game controversies to rest. The public and the press were fed up with them, and the inconsistency of Landis's rulings had blurred the issue beyond recognition. The game on the field was going great guns. Wall Street was booming. The Jazz Age was in full swing. Enough already. Which was fine with Landis. Stoneham, Navin, and other owners who liked racetracks (and sometimes owned horses) did as they pleased. So did players of the stature of Hornsby, a notorious horseplayer. But anyone below that level of influence would be cut down at any moment, on almost any pretext, if he crossed the czar in some way, or if the czar saw something to gain by picking on him.

Landis's Step 3 produced an element that had a profound effect on the way baseball developed. The simple part was money. Landis wanted $50,000 and got it (with the expense gimmick) in 1921, when no player had ever been paid that much and the president of the United States got $75,000. He also kept his federal judgeship at $7,500, a clear conflict of interest since the Baltimore Federal Baseball case was still working its way up to the Supreme Court. Besides, either job was supposed to be a full-time occupation. First the House, then the Senate, threatened impeachment, and the American Bar Association issued an "unqualified condemnation" of his conduct. Not until March 1922, did Landis resign the judgeship. The Supreme Court's decision, freeing baseball of antitrust law, came two months later.

To keep the money, however, Landis had to keep the power, and he used two methods. One was to hold the staff of his all-powerful office to a minimum: Leslie O'Connor, a young lawyer, was, in effect, the whole staff, and his loyalty was guaranteed. Landis could move as slowly (or as quickly) as he liked on any question, and there could be no nuclei for "factions." The smaller the inner circle, with the least delegation of duties, the tighter the control.

The bigger weapon was player control. As part of Landis's public-relations image as czar of all baseball, he could be portrayed as protector of players with grievances—and could "set free" a player as arbitrarily as banish him. This meant he had the power to manipulate a club's assets: its player contracts. Every owner had a strong motive to court his goodwill, especially when they saw how capricious and perhaps vindictive his rulings could be. Landis, for this part, "freed" enough players to bolster the protector image, yet not so many as to upset the business.

Players, as well as owners, had to be shown forcefully who was boss, and the chance to do that came after the 1921 World Series. Landis had issued an edict that no postseason barnstorming tours could be arranged without his permission. (Club owners never liked the idea of others collecting gate receipts for "their" players; there was the real danger of injury; and, in the post–Black Sox atmosphere, players might make "disreputable" contacts.) Ruth, Bob Meusel, and some others went ahead anyhow, as was the custom. Landis shocked them, and everyone, by suspending them for the first month of the 1922 season. Free-lancing players didn't challenge his authority after that.

By 1927, then, the commissioner was in full command, and the public—getting a better product on the field than it had ever seen—approved wholeheartedly. Most players, buying the myth that they could "appeal" to the judge, liked the system too. Owners found it increasingly chafing, but preferable to the recently remembered anarchy.

And didn't everyone know only too vividly in the 1920's that the alternative to czarism was bolshevism?

SEASONS 1926–28

1926

The Yankees returned to the top in 1926, stronger than ever, while the St. Louis Cardinals, with Hornsby taking his turn at the player-manager trick, gave their city a pennant for the first time since 1888, when the Brown Stockings led by Charley Comiskey had won the American Association championship and lost a World Series to New York (Jim Mutrie's Giants).

NL—For the first time, the whole western half of the league—St. Louis, Chicago, Pittsburgh, and Cincinnati—constituted the pennant race, and the schedule had all four ending the season with a trip through the East. At that point, it was down to the Cards and Reds, tied as late as September 17. Then the Cardinals won four from last-place Philadelphia, 23–3, 10–2, 10–1, 7–3, just before Cincinnati lost three straight to seventh-place Boston, and finished two games ahead.

Hornsby, after a five-year combined batting average of .401 through nearly 700 games, hit only .317 under the weight of thinking. But he ran the club well enough, while fighting bitterly and openly with Breadon over unwanted advice. His main pitchers were Flint Rhem (20–7), Bill Sherdel (16–12), and Jesse Haines (13–4), with a big lift from Grover Cleveland Alexander, now 39 years old, acquired from the Cubs during the first half of the season. Alex won nine games and saved two others. The big bat belonged to Jim Bottomley, the first baseman, who drove in 120 runs.

Defending champion Pittsburgh's problem was internal: Dreyfuss had brought back Fred Clarke as the Pirates' "vice-president and assistant manager," and Clarke's second-guessing of McKechnie on the bench split the players and undercut the manger. Dreyfuss reacted by sending Carey, of the Clarke faction, to Brooklyn, buying out Clarke, releasing some other players—and letting McKechnie go. In the confusion, the Pirates unveiled a rookie outfielder who hit .336: Paul Waner.

The Cubs had a new manager who had never played a major league game but had established a minor league managing reputation in Louisville, Joe McCarthy. The Reds still had Roush (.323), Mays, Donohue, Rixey, and Luque to pitch, and Wally Pipp—unneeded by the Yankees—at first base. Bubbles Hargrove, who caught only 83 games, hit .353 and was awarded the batting title with only 328 at bats, prompting revision of rules about minimum appearances for that honor.

McGraw's temper and weaker pitching were undoing the Giants. Frisch, widely regarded as being groomed as the next manager when and if McGraw ever retired, couldn't stand his constant carping and walked out in midseason. No pitcher won more than the 14 posted by young Fred Fitzsimmons. The pendulum of prestige in celebrity and success-minded New York was shifting to the Yankees.

AL—Babe Ruth's 1925 blowup cleared the air for all concerned. Huggins was clearly boss, the Babe had better control of himself (and good health), and that Gehrig fellow wasn't doing the batting order any harm. Leading from start to finish, the Yankees opened a 10-game lead, then coasted, and when Cleveland started to close in during September, locked it up. Ruth hit 47 homers, batted .372, knocked in 155 runs. The new second baseman, San Franciscan Tony Lazzeri, hit 18 homers and got New York's Italian community all excited. The new shortstop, Mark Koenig, fit nicely, and so did the center fielder, Earle Combs, little noticed in the wreckage of 1925 although he had hit .342 as a rookie.

Also in 1925, the Yankees had regained Urban Shocker, traded away by Huggins when he first took over the Yankees to St. Louis Browns, where Shocker became a 20-game winner. In 1926, Pennock won 23, Shocker 19, and Hoyt 16.

Cleveland's charge was led by George Uhle, a veteran pitcher exploiting a newly popular pitch we now call a "slider." He was 27–11. Speaker, at 38, still played 150 games and hit .304, which made his season-end resignation that much more inexplicable to the public. (Cobb, with sixth-place Detroit, played only half the time but hit .339, while his second-year outfielder, Heinie Manush, won the batting title at .378 and Heilmann hit .367. But you still need pitching.)

In Philadelphia, the A's, in third place, were gaining experience. And in Washington, Johnson showed that the 1925 World Series wasn't exactly his swan song. On Opening Day, he pitched a 15-inning, six-hit, 12-strikeout, three-walk, 1–0 victory over the A's and Ed Rommel. Time of game: two hours, 33 minutes.

WS—At Yankee Stadium, Pennock won a three-hitter for the Yankees 2–1. The tie-breaking run in the sixth was suggestively old-fashioned: Ruth singled through the left side, Muesel sacrificed, Gehrig singled to right to score Ruth.

Alexander defeated Shocker in the second game 6–2, and the Cardinals' Haines won in St. Louis 4–0. At this point, the Yankees had 15 hits, all singles, in three games. In game four, they got 14, including three home runs by Ruth and five doubles by others, for a 10–5 victory for Hoyt, who also allowed 14 hits but only one double. And the Yankees won the fifth game in 10 innings 3–2, with Pennock beating Sherdel again and Lazzeri providing the winning run with a bases-loaded sacrifice fly.

Back in New York, Alexander pitched a complete-game 10–2 victory, creating a seventh-game showdown for the third straight year, Haines versus Hoyt. Ruth homered in the third, but two Yankee errors gave St. Louis three runs in the fourth. The Yankees scored in the sixth and filled the bases with two out in the seventh.

Hornsby called in Alexander, who had celebrated the end of his season the night before, to face Lazzeri. On a 1–1 count, "Poosh 'em up Tony" lined one into the left-field stands—foul. Then he struck out. One of the most dramatic of all World Series moments would certainly be made into a movie some day, but who knew that the actor portraying Alexander would go on to become the president of the United States? (Yes, Ronald Reagan.)

But this was not a movie, and the game wasn't over.

Pennock held the Cards scoreless the last three innings. Alex got the side in order in the eighth and retired Combs and Koenig on grounders in the ninth, bringing up Ruth. On a 3–2 pitch, Alex wouldn't give in and threw ball four, Ruth's 11th walk in the Series. In stepped Meusel, with Gehrig on deck.

Ruth took off for second. Catcher Bob O'Farrell threw him out. Series over.

They asked the Babe why he tried to steal second. "Well, I wasn't going to do any blanking good on first base, was I?"

The old-style habits of thought were not yet gone from baseball.

1927

The Yankees had their best year ever in 1927, and the Pirates, regaining first place under a new manager, were no match for them in the now hysterically ballyhooed Fall Classic.

NL—Dreyfuss had restored peace to his Pittsburgh ball club by cleaning house. His new manager was Donie Bush, McKechnie having gone to St. Louis as pitching coach for O'Farrell, made manger when Hornsby was traded to the Giants for Frisch. Bush had been Hughie Jennings's shortstop all those years in Detroit, and Washington's manager before Bucky Harris. Paul Waner, batting champion at .380, now had his younger brother Lloyd (.355) alongside: "Big Poison" and "Little Poison," they were called. Trayner and Wright were fixtures. Kremer and Meadows won

19 each, Aldridge 15, and a 31-year-old right-hander named Carmen Hill, who had won only nine games in parts of six previous major league season over an 11-year span, suddenly won 22 and lost 11. (He would be 16–10 the following year, 3–3 over the next two, then gone from the scene.) Nickname: "Bunker."

Bush did have conflict, however, with Cuyler, playing him only half the time.

The Cardinals didn't make it, but not because they missed Hornsby, since Frisch hit .337 and stole 38 bases. Alex still had it (21–10 at age 40), and Hines was 24–10. On Labor Day, the Pirates, Cards, Cubs, and Giants were still closely bunched. Then the Pirates won 11 straight and the Cubs dropped out, but the Giants and Cards kept coming. In the next to last week, the Pirates lost the last three of a four-game series to the Giants at Forbes Field, letting the Cards climb to within two games. But they won the next four at Chicago while the Cards lost two of three in Cincinnati, and Pittsburgh finished a game and a half ahead of St. Louis and two ahead of New York.

Hornsby didn't get along with McGraw any better than he had with Breadon or Rickey, and when McGraw got ill and let Hornsby function as manager, "the Rajah" didn't get along with Stoneham either. He did hit .361, of course, with 26 homers. McGraw had also acquired Roush, who had hated him as a young player before being traded to Cincinnati with Mathewson in 1917, and Burleigh Grimes, who won 19 games. But basically the pitching wasn't there, as the Giants tried 22 different men.

On May 30, Cub shortstop Jimmy Cooney made an unassisted triple play, only the sixth in major league history. The next day, Tiger first baseman Johnny Neun made one. There wasn't another for 41 years.

AL—They called it Murderers' Row. The Yankees won 110 games. Ruth hit 60 home runs, breaking his 1921 record, Gehrig 47, Lazzeri 18—and they were 1-2-3 in the league. Gehrig hit .373 and knocked in 175 runs. Ruth and Combs hit .356 each, Ruth driving in 164. Meusel at .337 was overshadowed despite 47 doubles (Gehrig had 52), and Combs had 23 triples. The team batting average was .307.

But all that went with terrific pitching. Huggins had latched on to the relief-specialist idea, using Wilcy Moore the way the Senators had Marberry, as a "closer" (a term not yet invented). So the chart showed Hoyt 22–7, Moore 19–7 (13–3 of it in relief with 13 saves, also not yet invented), Pennock 19–8, Shocker 18–6, Reuther 13–6, George Pipgras 10–3. Moore, at 30, was in the big leagues for the first time after years in the minors.

There was, naturally, no pennant race. The final margin was 19 games. The big suspense factor was Ruth's holdout during spring training. Amid maximum coast-to-coast publicity (Ruth was moviemaking in Hollywood), he demanded $100,000 a year for two years. Ruppert and Barrow finally persuaded him to take $210,000 for three.

Meanwhile, the A's had built their own victory total to 91 and finished seven games ahead of everyone else. They were almost ready. Grove became a 20-game winner in a league that had only two others (Hoyt and Chicago's Ted Lyons). Simmons hit .392 (but Heilmann, true to his odd-numbered-year pattern, was batting champion at .398). Cobb, playing full-time at age 40, hit .357, a point higher than Ruth. Nobody was bothering much with base stealing any more (Why risk an out when the next man can hit?), so Sisler's 27 led the league.

WS—The myth-making machinery now didn't even have to wait for a game to take place. America was told that Yankee batting practice in Forbes Field the day before the Series opened so intimidated the Pirates that they were beaten then and there. More mundane, and relevant, was the fact that all the Pittsburgh pitchers were right-handers while Combs, Ruth, and Gehrig hit left-handed.

The Yankees got only six hits in the first game but won 5–4 for Hoyt with Moore's help. They won the second 6–2 behind Pipgras. Not a single ball was hit over a Forbes Field fence.

Ruth hit one in Yankee Stadium, though, as Pennock's three-hitter marked an 8–1 Yankee victory. And he hit another the next day, as Moore started and couldn't hold a 3–1 lead in the seventh when two errors (his own and Lazzeri's) enabled the Pirates to tie. In the bottom of the ninth, a walk, a safe bunt, a wild pitch, and an intentional pass to Ruth filled the bases with none out. Johnny Miljus was Pittsburgh's pitcher.

He struck out Gehrig. He struck out Meusel.

He threw strike one to Lazzeri. Then he made another wild pitch.

That's how Murderers' Row completed its World Series sweep. Intimidation indeed.

1928

"Break up the Yankees!" was the cry in 1928, as they won 101 games and swept another World Series, while the Cardinals, managed by McKechnie, won another close National League race over Chicago and New York.

NL—McKechnie was Rickey's preference and was made manager because Breadon second-guessed O'Farrell's handling of pitchers. They gave O'Farrell a big raise to return to just catching, and in May shipped him to the Giants. It was a constructive move, because pitching made the difference. Alexander, at 41, was 16–9, Haines 20–8, Sherdel 21–10. Bottomly led the league with 31 homers and 135 runs batted in. Frisch's new keystone partner at short was Maranville, now 36. Chick Hafey hit .337 and knocked in 111 runs.

Stoneham traded Hornsby to hapless Boston, where he won another batting title at .387 and became manager halfway through the season. From June on, his first baseman was Sisler, who hit .340, but only one Braves pitcher could win 13 games and no other won more than nine. Still, the 103 defeats were exceeded by Philadelphia's 109.

The Giants replaced Hornsby with Andy Cohen and made a big deal of promoting his Jewishness (in imitation of Lazzeri's hold on New York Italians). But the rest of the infield was terrific: Terry, Jackson, Lindstrom. Mel Ott, playing regularly now that he was 18, produced 18 homers and hit .322. Lefty O'Doul, who had failed with the Yankees as a pitcher, was back as a hard-hitting outfielder. Larry Benton (25–9) and Fitzsimmons (20–9) were top pitchers, but the rest of the staff could not match the Cardinals' depth.

McCarthy had built well in Chicago. Wilson hit 31 homers, tying Bottomley for the league lead, and drove in 120. Cuyler had come over from Pittsburgh and stole 37 bases, and the third outfielder, Riggs Stephenson, hit .324. Gabby Hartnett, the catcher, could also hit, and Charlie "Jolly Cholly" Grimm was an immensely popular and smooth first baseman. But the pitching was inadequate. Pittsburgh had the best hitting team (.309) with the Waners posting .370 and .335 and Traynor .337, and it had a 25-game winner in Grimes, but not enough else.

The race boiled down to the Giants chasing the Cardinals through September. In the final week the Cubs, who had dropped back, took three of four from the Giants at the Polo Grounds while the Cards swept three in Boston, and that did it. The final margin was two games over the Giants, four over the Cubs.

AL—It was going to be shamefully easy. The Yankees started 39–9, were 30 games over .500 by June 10, were 12 games ahead around July 4—and Ruth was ahead of his 60-homer pace. But the A's had matured, and the Yankees slowed down. Philadelphia won 25 games in July, had the lead down to 3½ on August 5, and took first place by half a game on September 8. The next day, a Sunday, the Yankees beat them in a doubleheader before a stadium crowd they called 85,000 and split the remaining two games of that series. The A's got back to a tie on September 15, as both teams finished the season on western trips, where the Yankees nosed ahead again and prevailed by 2½ games, clinching on the final Friday in Detroit.

This Yankee team was less balanced. Pipgras was 24–13 and Hoyt 23–7, but Moore faded to 4–4. Shocker, taken ill, died September 9. Ruth finished with 54 homers, Gehrig with 27, as each drove in 142 and Meusel placed third in the league with 113. Gehrig's .374 was a close third to Goslin's .379 (Washington) and Manush's .378 (St. Louis).

Simmons led Philadelphia's hitters at .354, and Grove had a 24–8 season, backed up by impressive geriatric assistance. Cobb, 41, played half the time and still hit .323. Speaker played less, and Eddie Collins just pinch-hit, while John Picus Quinn, at 44, took his regular turn and won 18 games.

The third-place Browns finished 19 games out, and no other team finished above .500.

WS—What Murderers' Row was supposed to do to the Pirates in 1927, it did to the Cardinals in 1928. The cumulative score in the four-game sweep was 27–10.

Hoyt pitched a three-hitter in the Stadium opener, the Yankees winning 4–1 as Ruth and Gehrig got five of the seven Yankee hits. Pipgras followed with a four-hitter, while the Yankees raked Alexander for eight runs in the first three innings in a 9–3 decision. Gehrig hit a homer, and Ruth a double and single.

In Sportsman's Park, Gehrig hit two homers during a 7–3 victory, and the fourth game ended with the same score as Gehrig hit another and Ruth hit three. They had a combined batting average for the Series of .595 and a slugging average of 1.509. The Series ended with Ruth making a great running catch of Frisch's fly in foul territory in front of the grandstand.

AFTERMATH

At the end of 1928, U.S. prosperity was peaking, there was no visible trouble in Europe, even the Soviets had eased into an early version of pere-stroika, the Empire of Japan had not yet begun to expand, and optimism reigned. In baseball, this was truly the best of times—financially, artistically, competitively, administratively, prestige-wise. And the absolute rule Landis had attained was a central factor in all these good things.

But seeds had been sown. Wonderful seeds, like a new generation of stars (Gehrig, Waner, Grove, and teenagers in the dugout like Foxx and McGraw's Mel Ott, yet to be heard from); and dangerous seeds, like the opposition of Landis to a new talent-procurement approach called "farm systems" that Rickey was developing in St. Louis. And, perhaps less noticeable even than seeds or weeds, a pollutant that can ruin fertile soil. Call it complacency.

CHAPTER 14

Boom and Bust

The Great Depression changed America even more than World War I did. The stock-market crash of October 1929 became identified as the end of the boom times of the 1920's, although in reality the preconditions were there well before. The year 1933, in which both Franklin D. Roosevelt and Adolph Hitler became their countries' chief executives, didn't end the Depression but marked radical changes in the approach to coping with it. The changes in baseball's microcosm were also profound and permanent, directly related to the conditions of the outside world but largely invisible to outsiders because the game on the field did not change. On the contrary, baseball was looked upon as an island of welcome stability, not only a respite from real-world difficulties but a gratifying affirmation of "traditional American values."

But changes there were, and they were profound.

First was the full flowering of minor league farm systems, a trend strongly resisted at first but ultimately the only way to keep the minors going amid the general economic wreckage.

Second was another cycle of turnover among club ownerships, forming a different mix of viewpoints and purposes in that group.

Third was a deep freeze on anything and everything to do with labor's—that is, the players'—resistance to ownership exploitation. Anybody who had a job in this era knew they were lucky to be working at all.

Fourth was a willingness, born of necessity, to contemplate—but not yet act upon—significantly nontraditional arrangements.

The three main story lines of this five-year period are: (1) the economic consequences of the Depression; (2) the growth of the farm system; and (3) the rise and
fall of the Yankee and Athletic dynasties.

HARD TIMES

The 16 league clubs entered the business downturn with some significant advantages.
Thanks to the 1922 Supreme Court decision exempting them from antitrust law, they
were secure against challenges from outsiders wanting to imitate their success (as
they had not been for the 40 years before 1922) and from players chafing under contract restrictions. Nor did they have to fight for "the entertainment dollar," an emerging concept, when depression conditions crippled professional enterprises in other
sports that seemed to be getting a foothold in the marketplace in the 1920's. Most
owned their stadiums and the land they stood on, or at least had long-term favorable
leases on the land, so that financing was not a major problem. And that valuable in-
tangible, goodwill, was at a peak. In hard times, they were equipped to weather
storms. The storms came, and they did weather them.

However, while a ball club—the franchise—has a continuous existence, ownership changes, and at any point, the exact composition of that ownership determines
the industry's path.

During the 1920's boom, there were only four transfers, and only one of these
was driven by the owner's need for money. In 1923, Frazee finally sold the Red Sox,
having sold off all marketable players, to finance more shows and clean up his debt.
The buyer was Bob Quinn, who had been working for Phil Ball and the Browns in St.
Louis.

In 1925, in April, Charlie Ebbets died. He had sold a half interest in the Brooklyn Dodgers to the McKeever brothers in order to finance the building of Ebbets
field. Ed McKeever, the brother he got along with, died two weeks later. Steve Mc-
Keever, with whom he had fallen out, controlled exactly 50 percent, and the Ebbets
heirs and McKeever families were in conflict. It was decided to make Uncle Robby
president of the club as well as manager, in effect removing Brooklyn from any influential position in league councils it had held through Ebbets.

In 1926, Dunn, who had turned over direction of Cleveland to Ernest Barnard,
died. The heirs sold the team to Alva Bradley in 1927, while Barnard was elected
American League president to succeed Johnson.

In 1927, Herrmann stepped down as president of the Cincinnati Reds, the last
tie to the pre-Landis Commission, and Sidney Weil, one of the owners, became the
active figure.

But the next few years were different. Baker sold the Phillies in 1930, and they
were resold in 1932 to Gerry Nugent, their 10th different owner in 30 years. In 1933

Quinn, having been unable to lift the Red Sox off the floor, sold them to Thomas Yawkey. These were hardship sales.

Meanwhile, in 1931, Comiskey had died, his widow and heirs taking over the White Sox, and in 1932, when Dreyfuss died, he left the Pirates to his son-in-law, Bill Benswanger. As family operations, the White Sox and Pirates had no significant resources outside of baseball: their patriarchs had spent their whole lives in baseball and accumulated some wealth, but not like a Ruppert, Stoneham, Wrigley, or Powell Crosley, who bought the Reds from Weil in 1934. Yawkey, on the other hand, with a childhood passion for baseball, was heir to a fortune and was the nephew of a former owner of the Tigers. The differences in these situations would shape the fortunes of many teams for the next two decades and more.

When Bill Veeck Sr. died in 1933, Phil Wrigley, who had inherited the Cubs, became their decision maker in policy matters without running the club day-to-day. Also in 1933, Phil Ball died, and his estate couldn't find buyers for the St. Louis Browns until November 1936, when Donald Barnes and Bill DeWitt (whose baseball career began as an office boy for Rickey) took the team on.

In Brooklyn, after Wilbert Robinson was finally deposed as president in 1929 and manager in 1931, McKeever brought in Bob Quinn to run the club as soon as Quinn had disposed of the Red Sox.

And in 1935, when Judge Fuchs could no longer hang on to the Braves, the purchaser was Quinn. The same year, Detroit Tigers owner Navin died, and Walter Briggs, who had owned 25 percent, acquired the rest. Detroit's Navin Field became Briggs Stadium.

Thus, by 1935, only five of the 16 clubs were represented by men who had preceded Landis: Mack, Griffith, Ruppert, Stoneham, and Breadon. The commissioner was more entrenched than ever.

THE FARM SYSTEM

Consider what a baseball club's business really is.

You seek out the best players you can find, that is, those who help win games and whose individual performances please spectators. When you sign a player to his first contract, his services become your property forever through the reserve system (then). Therefore, player contracts are your main asset, buttressed by two others: the franchise itself, which is a territorial monopoly for selling that product (your league's baseball games), and whatever real estate and stadium structure the club owns.

The franchise and stadium are fixed assets as long as you own the club. Player contracts, however, can be sold, traded, or voided—at a profit or a loss.

But where can you find a player proficient enough, well enough trained and experienced, to play at a major league level? With very few exceptions, only in the minors.

And where can minor league teams find new players? In the lower minors, the basic entry level for sandlot, semipro, and school and college players.

And how can a major league team acquire the contract of a minor league player? By buying it.

This is the system we saw evolve in the 19th century. Minor league teams made their living by selling their better players to the majors. Major league teams needed minors to provide a flow of talent. Their symbiotic relationship depended on observing the sanctity of the ownership of a contract, just as the existence of any league depended on it.

Remember the basic idea: to avoid having one club bid against another for the services of a desired player.

Honoring contracts—not making an offer to a player under contract to someone else *or on someone's reserve list even if the contract has expired*—is the key to the whole business. Agreements among leagues (not teams, leagues) go back to 1879 and the League Alliance.

In 1903, when the American and National agreed on peace, that was the peace, and the minors joined in creating Organized Baseball. By then, certain problems were so evident that regulations were adopted to deal with them.

A good player could be kept by a minor league club forever, if it refused to sell him, killing his chance to advance and, more important, depriving a higher-classification team of his services. A "draft" system gave the major club the right to buy any minor player at a stipulated price (and a higher minor could draft from a lower minor).

A major club with a surplus—a second good player at a position—could sell that player to the minors, not only for a good price, but to keep him away from a rival major club in the same league. This demoted the player but, more important, kept another club from getting a good one. The "waiver" system took care of that: before selling a player outside the league, you had to get every other league team to "waive" its right to purchase the player at a stipulated price.

Draft and waivers served as some protection to a player's advancement and career, but their main purpose was to keep the talent-supply pipeline open for *clubs*.

The 1903 agreement incorporated draft and waivers, and also committed teams not to enter into secret deals to "cover up" players—a sale, for instance, involving a promise to return the player later.

As with all regulations, their adoption was a signal to evade them. By 1905, "working agreements"—mutual promises between a higher and lower club—were common, and the "option sale" was in use: a major league club sells a player to the minors with an option to buy him back at a stipulated price.

By 1907, clubs were allowed to option a player.

By 1909, six major clubs controlled at least 50 players each.

By 1911, it was necessary to set a limit of 8 optioned players at any one time by any one team.

By 1912, the agreement with the minors was being revised so that a major league team could control only 35 players (including those out on option) on its own roster. And teams that had bought an interest in a lower-classification club (thus controlling all the players on *that* roster) had to divest themselves of the lower club.

But in 1913, the Federal League started up and all the regulations went by the boards as the ogre returned: competition for players.

Then came World War I, and more turmoil in contract matters, and by 1919 the major-minor agreement was dead. In this realm, as in others (gambling, fights like the one over Sisler, the ineffectual Commission, players talking about unions), anarchy reigned.

In 1921, as part of the reform that installed Landis, a new major-minor agreement was adopted. It allowed a minor league to escape having its players drafted if it gave up the right to draft from lower leagues.

Five important minors chose that course. Their complaint had been that the stipulated draft prices were much too low and that they didn't get fair market value for their best players. The majors hated this, since it drove up the price, and Landis in particular pushed for an unrestricted draft. But the top minors got their way.

At this point, Rickey, in St. Louis, had embarked upon a plan he began devising during his days with the Browns, 1913–19. If you had enough working agreements and ownership of minor clubs, you could stock them with developing players, give them good instruction, let the cream rise to the top, keep what you needed, and sell off the surplus. You would "grow" your own talent on your "farm."

His central point was this: it is extremely difficult to predict the eventual productivity of a young athlete, no matter how wise and skilled the evaluator is, because so much can happen between the ages of 18 and 25—injury, life experience, illness, character flaws, and limitations not visible until higher competition is met (physically, reflexively, mentally). Some scouts (like Rickey himself) may be substantially better than others, but all deal with uncertainty. A superior talent like Sisler is not hard to recognize; but team success depends on dozens of lesser talents, whose gradations of ability must be identified correctly.

But if you start with a very large group of potentially good players, weeding out only the evidently nontalented, and let them play for a few years under adequate supervision, the actual major leaguers will identify themselves by what they do. In that top group (10 percent, let's say), you have not only the pieces you need to fill gaps on your own team, but a surplus of players who have demonstrated their capability to everyone. These can be sold to other clubs, just the way independent operators have always done, with the profit going to your own major league club.

This system reduces the "gamble" in early player development, and you *receive* instead of *pay* seller's-market prices for top minor leagues.

The essential feature of this reasoning—that relying on any *individual's* future performance is hazardous—would be even less generally understood by club owners in the 1980's and 1990's than in the 1920's.

In the 1921 agreement, exemption from the draft enabled minor league teams to raise prices for their best prospects, which is why they wanted it. Landis and the majors wanted an unrestricted draft, which would set (lower) prices. But they didn't bother to forbid Rickey's new activity of buying into minor league clubs, in part because Dreyfuss and Navin assured Landis that the Rickey plan was economically unfeasible: money would be lost investing in minor league operations, and they would fall under their own weight.

By 1928, they had changed their minds. Thirteen minor league teams, at different levels, were owned by major league clubs, five of them by the Cardinals (none by the Yankees), while independents were getting $50,000 to $100,000 for top prospects. The Cardinals, who had gotten nowhere for some 30 years by orthodox means, had just won two pennants in three years with the products of their farm system.

Landis, his contract just renewed for seven more years, kept opposing the idea. The minors had accepted a modified draft in 1923, and Landis was carrying on guerrilla warfare against farms by "freeing" players any time he could find a pretext for ruling "cover-up." This enhanced his image with players and public and gave him a weapon to use against any owner.

In 1929, National League teams owned 12 farms and American Leaguers six. Ruppert—owner of the Yankees and the richest, most successful, most powerful of them all—was declaring loudly that he "couldn't afford" to pay the outrageous prices minor leagues were getting for top talent. St. Louis Cardinals owner Breadon challenged Landis publicly and backed up his argument with statements from seven top minor leagues that *they* preferred farm-system arrangements themselves.

So after the 1930 season, the permissible number of optioned players went to 15 from eight; requests to raise the draft-price levels were rejected; and farm systems began to spread.

What Landis had failed to take into account was the Depression. The majors, though hurt, were surviving. The minors, as in previous bad economic times, could not. They *needed* the infusion of parent-club money, not only in actual dollars but for some guarantee of stability for next year and current cash flow. The parent club supplemented player salaries, supplied coaches and equipment, and helped with administration, even under a "working agreement." If it owned the minor league team outright, it took all responsibility, and the local operators became, in effect, concessionaires.

And Landis's defeat on this issue revealed a reality about "czarism" little understood by public and players, but fully grasped by the club owners, who had inherited a commissionership with much more authority than had ever been intended. On matters involving *property rights*—contracts and franchises—the commissioner did *not* have veto power, because he had no investment; he was, truly, only an employee. If he tampered with property rights, he would have been taken to court, and Landis knew he could never win there.

So the ascendancy of the farm systems, hastened by the Depression, marked the beginning of the end of the commissionership's absolute power.

It also changed the balance of power on the field. Before long, the teams that would do most of the winning would be teams that built the best farm systems, not the ones that shopped best in the open market, as the Yankees and Giants of the 1920's had done. Ruppert had openly bought all of the Red Sox assets, but McGraw had also "bought" his pennants in a different way. In the second half of a season, when involved in a pennant race, he could buy a top-quality player from some team hopelessly out of contention, because that team needed the money and McGraw had it to spend.

In August 1919, he had bought Nehf from the Braves. In June of 1920, he bought Bancroft from Philadelphia. In June of 1921, he got Emil (Irish) Meusel from Philadelphia. And in July of 1922, he got much needed help in the form of Hugh Mc-Quillan, the best pitcher on the Braves, when Phil Douglas was self-destructing.

In 1923, the June 15 Rule was adopted: no sales or trades could be made after that date except through waivers, so that teams ranked below the potential buyer could prevent such an acquisition. (The waiver system worked in reverse order of the standing, giving lower teams priority.) The rule made moving optioned players back forth that much more important and added to the power of farm systems.

YANKEES AND A'S

That late spurt by the A's in 1928 signaled a change at the top. As Mack's team reached full maturity, an aging Yankee team was shaken by the sudden death of Huggins late in the 1929 season. So the three straight Yankee pennants were followed by three straight Philadelphia pennants, 1929–31. The A's won their first two World Series and lost in seven games to the Cardinals in 1931, just as the Yankees had in 1926. The symmetry of those six years was perfect, and forever afterwards, arguments about "the best team of all time" would begin by comparing the 1927–28 Yankees to the 1929–30 A's. The Yankees represented ultimate batting power, with a Ruth-Gehrig-Meusel core flanked by Lazzeri and Combs, with outstanding pitching (Hoyt, Pennock, Pipgras) and good defense. The A's displayed less home-run power but equal, if less explosive, scoring machinery through a Cochrane-Foxx-Simmons-Haas-Miller batting order, and even more brilliant pitching with Grove, Earnshaw, and Walberg, with a superior defense. Despite their World Series defeats, these two teams were "at the next level," in today's terminology, above all the rest.

But when the Yankees fell from the top, Ruppert had the resources to put them back. He hired a winning manager, Joe McCarthy, from the Cubs, bought new pitchers (Red Ruffing from the Red Sox, Lofty Gomez from the minors), and went about building a farm system rapidly. As a result, the Yankees were back on top quickly and dominated baseball for the next 30 years.

Mack, the A's owner, had no resources, so when the depression hit he had to sell off his stars to stay solvent, just as he had back in 1915, with the same result: the A's hit bottom and stayed there. Their revival in the mid-1920's was made possible by unprecedented prosperity in baseball and the nation, following 1920: they were one of all the boats raised by a rising tide. With enough operating money—not a lot, but enough to avoid team-destroying sales—Mack's baseball brilliance asserted itself as it had in the early years of the century, when the economic playing field was more level. When it became uneven again after 1930, he was doomed. Not only did he have to sell his stars, but he could not invest in a farm system. The A's never again became a contender in his lifetime and beyond, until they landed 3,000 miles away almost 40 years later, in Oakland, California.

The instructive part of their story is that the fates of these two teams, among the greatest ever assembled, were determined by *unequal financial resources*—the very same "competitive balance" argument that would tear baseball apart in the 1990's in a "big market–small market" guise. The premise is correct: those with insufficient resources cannot compete in the long run. What was false in the labor war rhetoric from the 1980's on was the implication that this imbalance had ever been otherwise, or that it was peculiar to or caused by "free agency." The problem, even for Mack, was not "high salaries," but low revenue and cash flow. Cheaper labor could not solve it but would always be passionately pursued. A more realistic appraisal in the 1990s of the perennial nature of this problem might have led to more constructive proposals than the quick-fix solutions offered, which were certain to cause the management-player strife they did.

SEASONS 1929–33

1929

The A's took up in 1929 where they had left off and won their pennant by 18 games, while the Cubs won theirs by 10½ and were far ahead by mid-August. It was the first time since 1912 that both winners had double-digit margins, producing no pennant-race suspense at all during September.

NL—Despite denials, the 1929 league ball was even livelier than before (a fact admitted eventually). The whole league hit .294, while the Cubs and second-place Pirates hit .303 and the fifth-place Phillies topped them with .309. What Mc-

Carthy had in Chicago was better pitching and defense to go along with that terrific hitting.

And it really was terrific. Hornsby was now Chicago's second baseman, and even his .380 was not good enough to win the batting title, taken by Philadelphia's Lefty O'Doul at .398. In the outfield, Stephenson hit .362, Cuyler .360, and Wilson .345, while Hornsby produced 40 homers and Wilson 39. (That wasn't good enough to lead the league either. Philadelphia's 24-year-old Chuck Klein hit 43 and the Giant's 20-year-old Ott 42.) The three outfielders and Hornsby drove in 502 runs. Pat Malone, Charlie Root, Guy Bush, and Sheriff Blake formed McCarthy's all-right-handed starting rotation, and Bush got first call for key relief assignments. Malone, 22–10, was the only 20-game winner in the whole league, which posted an earned run average of 4.71.

AL—The American League ball, lively enough, hadn't changed much, as the league hit .284, so the A's hit "only" .296 (behind sixth-place Detroit's .299). Foxx, now 21, was installed at first base and hit .354 with 33 homers. Simmons hit .365 with 34 homers. But the most important player was Cochrane, the fiery and intelligent catcher, who added a .331 batting average to his defensive skills. The other outfielders were Bing Miller (.335) and Mule Haas (.313), while the middle infielders were there for defense: Max Bishop at second, Joe Boley at short.

The pitcher who dazzled people with his fastball was Bob (Lefty) Grove. He led the league with a 2.82 earned run average when the league's figure was 4.24 and led in strikeouts (170). His right-handed teammate, George Earnshaw, actually had more victories (24–8 to 20–6) and was second in strikeouts. Walberg, the other left-hander, was 18–11.

Among the Yankees, Ruth, at 34, wasn't slowing down much, hitting .345 with 46 homers and 154 runs batted in, to which Gehrig added 35 and 126. Lazzeri outhit all of them at .354, and a rookie catcher, Bill Dickey, had Cochrane-like characteristics: brilliant defense with a .324 average. But the pitching had worn out. Pipgras, Hoyt, and Pennock, among them, were 37–32. In August, Huggins fell ill, and Art Fletcher, who had become his third-base coach in 1927 after managing the Phillies and playing for McGraw, had to take over in the last two weeks. On September 25, Huggins died.

WS—A's manager Mack opened the Series with a stratagem that became instant legend. Instead of starting Grove, he gave the assignment to Howard Ehmke, a 35-year-old right-hander who had been in only 11 games all year. Knowing so far ahead who the Series opponent would be, he had sent Ehmke to follow the Cubs in September and scout their hitters. Ehmke noted that they were all free-swingers and all (except Grimm) right-handed. He and Mack (and later McCarthy, as he also admitted) knew that soft stuff would tie them into knots, so that's what Ehmke fed them—and struck out 13, a Series record. Foxx hit a homer off Root in the seventh, Miller made it 3–0 with a

bases-full single in the ninth, and Ehmke walked off with a 3–1 victory.

The next day, Mack started Earnshaw, who had a 6–0 lead in the fifth when the Cubs stroked five singles for three runs. In came Grove to get the third out (on strikes), and he finished the 9–3 game.

After a travel day, Earnshaw started again in Philadelphia. He struck out 10, raising the Cub total to 36 in three games, but lost 3–1 to Bush. And Root apparently had the Cubs even as he went into the seventh inning of the fourth game with an 8–0 lead. But, starting with a home run by Simmons to the left-field roof, the A's scored 10 runs—the biggest inning in Series history to this day—and in came Grove, no less, to get the last six outs (four on strikes) in a 10–8 triumph.

Ehmke started again and was replaced by Walberg when the Cubs got two runs in the fourth. The Cubs' Malone had a two-hit shutout going with one out in the ninth. Then Bishop singled, Haas homered, Cochrane grounded out, Simmons doubled, Foxx was purposely passed, and Miller smacked a double to end the Series.

At that point, counting the World Series, the A's had won 167 games and lost only 74 from July 1, 1928, on.

1930

The A's were dominant again in 1930 and won another World Series, this time beating a Cardinal team that had survived another wild National League September.

NL—This was the season the National League ball was *really* juiced, as never before or since. The whole league hit .303, the Giants leading at .319. The Phillies were second, hitting .315—and finished last. The earned run average was 4.97. The Cubs hit 171 home runs—legitimate ones, in Wrigley Field—as Wilson set a league record with 56. (But there wasn't much talk of his threatening Ruth's 60, because he had only 46 with 20 games to play and hit six in the last 10.) Bill Terry's .401 won the batting title over Babe Herman's .393 for Brooklyn, and at least 25 regulars hit better than .333. The Phillies' Klein hit 40 homers, and a Boston rookie, Wally Berger, 38 (a record for rookies). Wilson batted in 190 runs for the Cubs (still a major league record), Klein 170. The

Cubs' Cuyler, with 37 stolen bases, was the only man in the league with more than 18. The Cardinals scored 1,004 runs—and the Phillies allowed 1,199.

The fans loved it. Attendance of 5.4 million broke a league record set in 1927.

They loved the race even more. First the Pirates, then the Dodgers took early leads, but by the end of June the defending-champion Cubs were back in first place. Then they fell back as the Dodgers forged ahead, until Brooklyn fell into a terrible August slump, leaving the Cubs with a sizable lead over the Giants. On August 30, the Cubs were 5½ games ahead of the Giants, 7 ahead of the Dodgers. The Cards, who had been barely above .500 in mid-August, were now right behind the Dodgers, having begun what would be a 36–10 run to the pennant, full of late-inning rallies.

September 9–11, the Dodgers swept a three-game series from the Cubs at Ebbets Field, creating a three-way tie for first with the onrushing Cardinals. On September 16, the Cards arrived in Brooklyn one game behind and swept three low-scoring (for that year) games, 1–0, 5–3, 4–2. They won the next day in Philadelphia, split a double-header, then pounded the Phils 15–7 and 19–16. Two days later they clinched. The Cubs, reeling after they left Brooklyn, revived enough to win their last seven and finish two games out. The Giants, winning 10 of their last 12, took third, as the Dodgers wound up fourth.

For their third pennant in five years, the Cards could thank the farm system and a midseason trade with Boston for Burleigh Grimes, who gave them 13 victories in the second half. The farms had provided Charley Gelbert, a brilliant shortstop to play alongside Frisch; Gus Mancuso, a young catcher able to take over when Jimmy Wilson got hurt; and Wild Bill Hallahan, their biggest winner with 15. They still had Bottomley, Hafey, and Frisch at their best, Haines and Rhem still pitching, and another rookie outfielder, a 30-year-old long-toiling farm product named George Watkins, who broke in by hitting .373.

Their manager was Gabby Street, once a well-known catcher, later a popular broadcaster. Breadon had humiliated McKechnie in 1929 by demoting him to Rochester and bringing up Southworth, then had brought McKechnie back in midseason. McKechnie moved on to Boston in 1930, and Street, who had been a coach, inherited the Cardinal job and made it a great success.

The Cubs fell short because their pitching wasn't good enough, and Wrigley proved an impatient owner too. When McCarthy was fired in the final week, less than a year after opening a World Series, Hornsby took over. For Brooklyn's Uncle Robby, in his last real shot, 39-year-old Vance led the league with a 2.61 earned run average—more than two full runs below the league norm—but the pitching didn't stand up or get much defense help, despite heavy hitting. The Giants, too, didn't have the pitching to match a fine lineup.

AL—If the A's seemed invincible, that's because they were. There was Grove: 32 starts, 18 relief appearances, a 28–5 won-lost record with 9 (retroactively computed) saves, a 2.54 earned run average, more than two runs below the league. (Next best was the 3.31 of Cleveland's Wes Ferrell.) Earnshaw was 22–13, with the team's other 52 victories evenly distributed among five veterans. Simmons was batting champion at .381 (beating out Gehrig by two points), and the infield now had Jimmy Dykes at third, 33 years old and for the previous 10 seasons used full-time as a utility infielder by Mack. Cochrane, along with all his other assets, including wit, hit .357, while Foxx outhomered Simmons, 37 to 36.

The Yankees had as much power as ever, but not as much pitching. Ruth and Gehrig hit 90 homers (49 by the Babe) and drove in 327 runs (174 by Gehrig), with Lazzeri adding 121. Combs hit .344, Dickey .339, Ruth .359. But Hoyt was gone (to Detroit), Pipgras won only 15, and Pennock only 11. The best record belonged to Ruffing, whose record with the 1929 Red Sox had been 9–22 and who was already 0–3 in May of this year when traded for an undistinguished outfielder, Cedric Durst. Ruffing went 15–5 the rest of the year for the Yankees and became the mainstay of their next dynasty. Shawkey, on the basis of his long Yankee association, had been made manager, and was neither a problem nor an inspiration.

Washington was the surprise, finishing second ahead of the Yankees. Walter Johnson had become manager in 1929, when Bucky Harris moved to Detroit, and finished an unnoticed fifth. The Senators showed an outstanding infield, with a spectacular 23-year-old shortstop from San Francisco, Joe Cronin. Sam Rice could still hit .349, and in mid-season Manush came back from St. Louis. No one pitcher stood out, but the team's 3.96 earned run average was the only one under 4.00 in either league. This team had a future.

WS—The A's Mack wasn't doing any tricks this time around. He started Grove, who beat the Cardinals' Grimes 5–2, and Earnshaw, who beat Rhem 6–1, in Philadelphia. In St. Louis, Hallahan shut out the A's 5–0, and Haines outpitched Grove 3–1 with a four-hitter. In the fifth game, Grimes had a four-hit shutout into the ninth inning with one out when Foxx hit a two-run homer, breaking a scoreless tie. But the Cards had managed only two hits off Earnshaw in seven innings, and one off Grove when he took over in the eighth, so 2–0 it was.

Back in Philadelphia, Earnshaw made his third start in seven days, breezed through a 7–1 five-hitter, and that was that.

1931

The 1931 World Series was a rematch, both teams reaching it without difficulty, and this time the Cardinals won it in seven games. Both leagues decided it was time to deaden the ball to restore some offense-defense balance, and league averages dropped to the .276 level. The sacrifice fly was abolished.

NL—The Cardinals, with essentially their 1930 team, finished 13 games ahead of New York and 17 ahead of Chicago, where the manager now was Rogers Hornsby. A young outfielder named Pepper Martin took Taylor Douthit's job in St. Louis, and a rookie pitcher named Paul Derringer went 18–8. The rest of the cast was the same. Hafey nosed out New York's Terry for the batting title, .3489 to .3486, while Bottomly hit .3482. The Rickey system had produced four pennants in six years, and was delivering a bigger profit from player sales than from gate receipts.

AL—The Yankees grabbed McCarthy as manager to replace Shawkey, but that wasn't going to make any difference to the A's, who reeled off 107 victories. Their 3½-year record now stood at 372–170, a .687 pace maintained through more than 500 games, plus 8–3 in the World Series. Their 1931 margin was 13½ games.

Simmons of the A's led the league with .390 and might have had .400 if the sacrifice-fly rule were still operative, but there were no "might haves" about the season Grove had: 31–4 with a 2.06 earned run average in a 4.38 league, and a league-leading 175 strikeouts—the pitching triple crown. He completed 27 of his 30 starts, relieved 11 times. Earnshaw's 21–7 and Walberg's 20–12 were overshadowed.

Other pitching stars were coming to the fore. Ferrell, in Cleveland, was 22–12, giving him 68 victories in three seasons. Gomez, who had been in only 15 games as a 21-year-old rookie the year before, went 21–9 for the Yankees with a 2.63 ERA, second only to Grove's, and was being compared to Grove for his speed.

Ruth and Gehrig hit 46 homers apiece for the Yankees, and Gehrig drove in 184, an American League record, while Ruth added 163. A new Yankee outfielder, Ben Chapman, could run, and McCarthy let him. He stole 61 bases, the highest total in the majors since 1920. All this let the Yankees finish second, two games ahead of Washington.

But the Depression was starting to bite, and statistics were no substitute for pennant races. The A's had drawn 840,000 in 1929; now they were down to 630,000 while winning their third straight pennant and two World Series. League attendance, exceeding 5 million in the middle 1920s, slipped below 4 million in 1931. Even the Yankees dropped below one million after surpassing that figure in nine of the 11 years of the Ruth era, and they would not return to it until after the war.

WS—For the myth and legend makers, the 1931 World Series was one of the best. Against the invincible A's, the Cards were surefire underdogs, and the worsening times made the public root for the underdog more than ever. And no one symbolized underdogism better than Pepper Martin, small in size, scruffy in appearance, no spring chicken, playing his first big-league season at the age of 27, and a native of Oklahoma, where Okies were bearing the brunt of drought and Depression and starting to migrate. He was associated with the Dust Bowl, and his uniform reflected it after his head-first slides.

Martin did hit .300 and steal 16 bases during the season, but half his teammates had better years. When he hit a double and two singles off Grove and stole a base against Cochrane in the first game, he was just a footnote to Grove's 6–2 victory in St. Louis. Against Earnshaw the next day, however, he was the difference: in the second, he doubled, stole third, scored on a fly; in the seventh, he singled, stole second, took third on a groundout, and scored on a squeeze bunt. Those were the only runs, as Hallahan pitched a three-hit 2–0 shutout.

Radio was now making every World Series play instantly available to the whole country. In game three, Martin's single off Grove in the second keyed a two-run rally. Next time up, he just missed a homer, hitting the top of the scoreboard for a double that moved a man to third, and Grimes himself knocked them in with a two-out single. With two out in the ninth, Grimes still had a one-hit shutout when he walked Cochrane and Simmons hit a homer, but he fanned Foxx and settled for a 5–2 two-hitter.

Earnshaw took the hint and produced a two-hit shutout himself to even the Series. The two hits were a single and double by Martin, who also stole a base. Pepper certainly had the spotlight now.

Hallahan started against Hoyt, who had joined the A's in midseason. In the first inning, Martin was just short of a home run on what became a scoring fly. In the sixth, after a double by Frisch, he did hit a home run, making the score 3–0. In the eighth inning, with the score 3–1, he singled home a run, tying a Series record with his 12th hit, and was thrown out stealing—finally. The Cards won 5–1.

In St. Louis, Grove put a stop to the nonsense, held Martin hitless, turned in a five-hitter, and won 8–1. That brought it down to the seventh game.

Now they were calling Martin "the Wild Horse of the Osage." In a two-run first off Earnshaw, his contribution was a walk and a stolen base. In the third, a two-run homer by Watkins made it 4–0, and the rest was up to Grimes. He got as far as two out in the ninth when a bases-loaded single by Doc Cramer reduced the Cards' lead to 4–2, so Hallahan came in and got the third out.

The Cardinals, led by Martin, had beaten the unbeatable. An "unlikely" World Series hero was becoming a tradition in itself, and Martin was as unlikely as they come.

1932

The Yankees traded places with the A's in 1932, and McCarthy found himself opposing in the World Series the very Cubs he had managed only three years before. The big story, however, was John McGraw's decision to retire as manager of the Giants in midseason, 30 years after he had taken them over in midseason.

NL—On Memorial Day, the Giants were in last place. Four days later, McGraw announced his resignation, handing the baton to Bill Terry, his 33-year-old acerbic first baseman. It made no difference then, but it would soon enough.

It was a topsy-turvy season in other ways, too. The Cubs started strong, slipped behind Pittsburgh, and had just regained the lead on August 2 when Veeck fired Hornsby and made *his* first baseman, Charlie Grimm, the manager. Hornsby's record of talking himself out of four leadership roles in seven years with four different ownerships (Cards, Giants, Braves, Cubs) has never been equaled, not even by Billy Martin, who had George Steinbrenner as a recurrent sparring partner.

Grimm had no problems. The Cubs kept winning and finished four games ahead of the Pirates. Much of the 1929 Cub team was intact. Billy Herman replaced Hornsby at second, Wilson (ineffective in 1931) had moved on to Brooklyn, and Lon Warneke, in his first full season, was the league's leading pitcher at 22–6 with a 2.37 earned run average.

Pittsburgh had a new manager, George Gibson; a new hard-hitting shortstop, Arky Vaughan; those potent Waner and Traynor bats; and a workhorse left-hander, Larry French. But its campaign was a series of long stretches of winning, losing, winning, losing.

Brooklyn also had a new manager, Robinson having been retired. It was Max Carey, who brought in Stengel as a coach, and it took them until late July to get the club going. Then it moved up so fast for so long that it passed the Pirates and came within a game and a half of the Cubs in late August, before subsiding to a respectable third, nine games out. The Dodgers had acquired O'Doul, who emerged as batting champion at .368, and a hard-throwing right-hander named Van Lingle Mungo.

The Phillies, who had not been out of the second division since finishing second in 1917, came in fourth, in what would be their only first-division finish in a 31-year span extending to 1949. The Braves, under McKechnie, posted a .500 record for the first time in 11 years. The limping Giants and totally collapsed Cardinals tied for sixth, but the Cardinal system churned up a right-hander who won 18 games, led the league in innings pitched and strikeouts, never stopped talking, and was properly called "Dizzy" Dean.

It was an odd year, but only one year. The next season, most teams went back to their accustomed niches.

AL—McCarthy liked to deal in basics. In 1931, the A's had won 107 games and the Yankees only 94, so this time he had the Yankees win 107—and sure enough, the A's won only 94. Ruth, at 37, wasn't done yet: .341, 41 homers, 137 runs batted in. Gehrig, at 29, was still learning: .349, 34 homers, 151 runs batted in. Combs and Chapman completed the outfield; Dickey was second only to Cochrane, if second at all, among catchers; and a new young shortstop from California, Frank Crosetti, settled in alongside Lazzeri. Gomez went 24–7, Ruffing 18–7, newcomer Johnny Allen 17–4, Pipgras and Pennock 25–14 between them. Joey Sewell, who had taken over third base in 1931, had fallen short of Scott's record for consecutive games played but did reach 1,103. He is still one of only six players to reach a thousand. Gehrig had started 1932 with 1,153 and was closing in on Scott's 1,307.

On June 3, at Shibe Park, Gehrig hit four home runs on consecutive turns at bat, a feat managed before only by Bobby Lowe in 1894. It didn't get much attention. That was the day McGraw announced he was stepping down.

Washington, finishing strong, ended up only one game behind the A's, winning one more game than its 1924 championship team had.

And the A's Foxx made an assault on Ruth's record of 60 homers. As other challengers would find out, the trick was that in 1927 Ruth had hit 17 in September, so "being ahead of Ruth's pace"—which became the popular and eventually mandatory comparison—didn't guarantee much. With only seven games left, Foxx had 53, so although a final burst of five in the last five games gave him a

total of 58, he hadn't come that close. (It would be different for Hank Greenberg in a few years.)

One other specific game deserves mention for the light it sheds on frames of mind. On July 10, a Sunday, Ed Rommel pitched 17 innings *as a reliever* for the A's in Cleveland. He won the game 18–17 in 18 innings, having been touched for 29 hits and given up nine walks. Foxx hit three homers in that one. Rommel was 34 years old.

Why in the world would anyone, let alone Connie Mack, leave an aging pitcher in for 17 innings, giving up 29 hits? Well, the Sunday game was in Cleveland because Pennsylvania still prohibited Sunday baseball (until 1934). The teams played in Philadelphia on Saturday, took an overnight train to Cleveland, played Sunday, took a train back, and played a doubleheader in Philadelphia on Monday.

Connie, as manager and owner, took only 15 players to Cleveland—to save train fare. Only two were pitchers. The first one gave up three runs in the first inning. Rommel started the second inning.

To save train fare. Think about it.

WS—On its merits, this is the most overplayed, overdramatized, overrepeated World Series story of them all.

It was no contest. The Yankees won four straight over the Chicago Cubs, 12–6 and 5–2 in the Stadium, 7–5 and 13–6 at Wrigley.

But it contained Ruth's last World Series homer and it became the story.

The third game was tied 4–4 when Ruth came up with one out in the fifth. He made some sort of gesture, pointing at the outfield, or maybe the mound, or maybe just waggling a finger. But when he hit his second homer of the game into the center-field bleachers, the story circulated that he had "called his shot" in an exchange of insults with the Cubs.

Insults? Mark Koenig had been the shortstop on Murderers' Row in 1927, popular among teammates. In 1932, he had joined the Cubs late in the season and hit .353 to help them nail down the pennant. They voted him only a half share of Series money. The Yankees, led by Ruth, called the Cubs "cheapskates." That was the "hatred" supposedly permeating the competition.

A called shot was too good a story to pass up, whatever Ruth actually intended or did. Once it got going, he didn't flatly deny it, and it became a mandatory feature of every story (especially on film) about Ruth, 1932, or American culture. Most teammates, as well as Cubs, say nothing of the sort took place. ("What a chump I would have been to do that," Ruth told a teammate. "What if I missed?") But the arguments, explanations, and conflicting versions have taken on a life of their own, and *whether* he called the shot or not has become a cottage industry of its own.

The truth: It was a dull World Series. For the Yankees, Gehrig hit three homers, Ruth and Lazzeri two each, Gomez pitched the only really good game (5–2 over Warneke), and Koenig's half share came to $2,122.50.

1933

The old let-the-manager-make-his-own-key-hits trick worked in 1933 for both the Senators and the Giants, who had rookie managers at that. Of more lasting value was the inauguration of the midsummer All-Star Game, one of baseball's crown jewels in the eyes of the public, adopted against the heartfelt resistance of the club owners.

NL—Terry, managing the Giants from first base, had a starting rotation any manager would envy. Carl Hubbell, at 30, was ready to come into his own, having mastered the screwball (a left-handed version of Mathewson's fadeaway, that is, a reverse curve) and every other facet of the pitching art. His 23–15 record included 10 shutouts and a league-best 1.66 earned run average, by far the lowest since dead-ball days. Hal Schumacher, 22 and right-handed, was 19–12. Fitzsimmons was 16–11, and Roy Parmelee won 13. Luque, at 42, was used strictly in relief, winning eight games and saving four. To catch them, Terry had Mancuso, acquired from St. Louis. By mid-June the Giants were in command and won by five games over Pittsburgh and six over Chicago, after leading by more than that most of the time. Terry, at .322, was the only .300 hitter, while Ott supplied 23 homers and 103 runs batted in.

Does this suggest they deadened the ball some more? Yes, but the real change had been made in 1931 and the effect is cumulative. Philadelphia's Chuck Klein took the triple crown with .368, 28

homers, 120 runs batted in—numbers far lower than his statistics in years when he didn't win it.

Pittsburgh hit 22 points higher than the Giants but had no comparable pitching. Chicago, managed by Grimm all year, had better pitching (Bush 20–12, Warneke 18–13, Root 15–10) but not as much hitting. Grimm wasn't as smart a manager as Terry because he hit 75 points less, .247. McKechnie, a whiz at teaching and handling pitchers, brought the Braves in fourth with an undistinguished roster, while the Cardinals, finishing fifth, switched to the playing-manager mode in midseason by having Frisch take over from Street. Brooklyn fell to sixth.

Was making a star player the manager a way to save a salary? You bet.

AL—The A's weakened themselves by selling Simmons, Haas, and Dykes to the White Sox, just to raise cash, and became a noncontending third even though Foxx had a triple crown and Grove had a 24–8 season. Foxx hit 48 homers, knocked in 163 runs, batted .356—and was still only 25 years old. But only Cochrane also held his own offensively (.322), and no other pitcher won as many as 14. (With two triple-crown winners on display Philadelphia drew a total of 450,000 to two parks; so much for star appeal.)

Ruth was finally slowing down—.301, 34 homers—but the real Yankee problem was mass failure by the pitchers. All had off years so that Gomez's 16–10 led the staff.

That left the field clear for the Senators. Joe Kuhel at first, Buddy Myer at second, and Cronin at short all hit over .300, and Ossie Bluege at third completed an excellent infield. Manush, Goslin, and Fred Schulte, the outfielders, hit .336, .297, and .295 respectively. Luke Sewell, Joey's younger brother, was a first-rate defensive catcher, and the pitchers he caught were of high quality, led by Alvin (General) Crowder (24–15) and lefty Earl Whitehill (22–8). (As a child, I wondered why Crowder was called "General"; now I know the connection was to the head of the World War I military draft, Gen. Enoch B. Crowder.) The Senators couldn't shake the Yankees until August, but then pulled away decisively.

When the season ended, Mack proceeded with dismantling the A's by selling Grove, Walberg, and Bishop to the new owner of the Red Sox, the millionaire Yawkey.

All-Star Game—Chicago had a World's Fair in 1933, "A Century of Progress," celebrating its centennial. Arch Ward, sports editor of the influential *Chicago Tribune,* wanted to stage an all-star extravaganza in connection with the fair. Landis, based in Chicago, went along. Comiskey Park was the site, July 6 the date. The managers would be Mack and McGraw. Fans would vote for players.

Of all games, baseball is ideal for an all-star contest, because each player does his thing individually, not dependent on intricate teamwork. It's truly a Dream Game for fans, whatever happens, just from the glamour generated by the presence on one field of the greatest players.

For club owners, it was sheer nuisance. There was danger of injury to a star (as events would prove) in a game that didn't count in the standings. They got none of the receipts, which were earmarked for charity. It interrupted the schedule and created expenses. It interfered with their own profitable exhibition games played on open dates. Who needed it?

Players appreciated the honor and the festive occasion, but it meant injury risk and extra travel, for no direct reward.

It turned out to be such a rousing success that it could never be abandoned.

Gomez, Crowder, and Grove pitched three innings each. Ruth hit a two-run homer in the third off Warneke (following Hallahan) for a 3–0 lead. Frisch hit one for the National League, but the Americans won 4–2. McGraw made sure everyone played; Mack played to win. Oh, yes: 49,000 people paid to get in. That was hard to ignore. Maybe there would be another, maybe not.

WS—By the time the Fall Classic came around in October, Roosevelt's New Deal was in full swing, the country's mood was more optimistic than a year before, and Washington was full of eager new faces hoping to remake the social and economic order. It was fitting that the Senators were in the Series. Naturally, they would win it.

However, Hubbell and Schumacher delivered five-hitters for 4–2 and 6–1 Giant victories at the Polo Grounds, so Whitehill's 4–0 six-hitter for the Senators at Griffith Stadium made the fourth game pivotal. Hubbell and Monte Weaver battled 1–1 through 10 innings. In the 11th, Blondy Ryan, New York's late-season call-up reserve infielder, knocked in a run with a single and then started a game-ending double play with the bases loaded in the bottom half, preserving the 2–1 victory. The fifth game also went into extra innings, 3–3. Ott's two-out home run in the tenth made the Giants world champions, once Luque, who had relieved Schumacher back in the sixth, struck out Kuhel with the tying and winning runs on base.

AFTERMATH

The five transition years 1929–33 set baseball on an entirely different course. That its break with the past happened gradually, and off the field, didn't make it any less drastic.

First, the farm system triumphed not only because it was good for the selfish goals of the majors, but because it was an economic necessity for the minors. In their struggle to stay alive, the minors had turned to night games in 1930, tapping the pool of potential customers who were at work in the daytime. In 1933, Frank Shaughnessy, president of the International League (the strongest of the top minors), instituted a postseason play-off system involving the top four clubs in the eight-team league, a play-off format quickly adopted by others and the prototype for playoffs, which are the big moneymakers in all sports. The play-offs themselves, for championship stakes, sold out (as if they were mini–World Series); but far more important, they created a season-long incentive to qualify for the play-offs for teams (and their fans) who had no hope of finishing first.

These two constructive steps would be adopted, in due course, by the majors, but not quickly.

Second, the triumph of the farm system, as a defeat for Landis, became a de facto curtailment of his arbitrary power: it made him less aggressive about using the power he retained. That meant that ideas other than his could circulate in the baseball hierarchy, especially as new club owners came in.

Third, hard times made owners pay attention to simple marketing principles, namely customer comfort and involvement. In 1929, the Yankees introduced numbers on uniforms; numbers had been used only sporadically before. They simply used their batting order: Combs, 1; Koenig, 2; Ruth, 3; Gehrig, 4; Meusel, 5; Lazzeri, 6; Dickey, 8; and pitchers starting with 10, 11, 12 and so forth. For 1930, the American League made numbers mandatory for every team, and the National soon went along. In 1929, the Giants installed amplifiers—a public address system—in the Polo Grounds. The still dimly understood ramifications of radio broadcasts were being confronted, and left to local option in one annual league meeting after another, making experimentation and comparison possible.

At the December 1928 annual meeting, Heydler proposed a designated hitter (DH)—a permanent pinch-hitter for the pitcher. "It will speed up the game and promote interest," he said. Commented the *Guide:* the idea was "heard with profound interest and caused widespread comment, but the National League took no action on it for this year." It still hasn't, although the American League adopted the idea a mere 44 years later, an example of the glacial movement of new ideas in baseball.

Particularly amusing, from today's viewpoint, was the concern with "long games." While Heydler was suggesting a DH would speed things up, Barnard, his opposite number, was congratulating himself by pointing out that "his specific instructions to umpires had resulted in measurably shortening the time for completing a game." There was no reason, he felt, why an ordinary game should take longer than one hour and 45 minutes, he declared at the 1930 meeting, two years later.

The year-by-year tinkering with the baseball was part of this concern, seeking a balance most favorable for spectators. They were coming out in fewer numbers—as more and more urban residents couldn't afford to—even as *interest* in baseball, measured by reading and talking, was growing faster than ever.

Attendance figures were alarming. All through the 1920s the major league average had been around 9 million a season, peaking at 10 million in 1930. The next three years brought 8.5, 7.0, and 6.1 million. Mack's A's, in 1932, were down to 400,000, less than half their 1929 gate, which is why he started selling off players. His next two years were 300,000, and by 1935 he had 230,000—a predictable result of dismantling, but one to which he had no alternative. The 1933 St. Louis Browns had a *season* total of 88,000, the first sub-100,000 in American League history and less than Louisville did in 1895.

To get the full impact of such figures we must remember that attendance was still the only significant form of revenue: ticket sales and concessions and a bit of signage, with no radio or licensing rights that might alter the picture. Day-of-game gate sale was crucial, since there was little advance sale, and it was entirely at the mercy of the home team's fortunes, a visiting star, and unreliable weather.

Nevertheless, the clubs found ways to survive. In a report to Congress in 1951, it says that in the years 1931–34 teams showed a net profit in 18 cases and a net loss in 46. Yet, 68 years later, every single one of those 16 franchises is in existence and worth at least $100 million on the open market, without ever having missed a day of operation.

Club *owners* can go bankrupt, and do; ball *clubs* do not.

Ultimately, the most important effect of hard times was the destruction of complacency. The antitrust exemption, the Landis mystique, the sensational game on the field produced by Ruth and a plethora of new stars, the doubled attendance, the arrival of radio, the prospering minors—all these combined in the 1920s to feed a self-satisfied arrogance among baseball operators. When Ruth's three-year contract for $70,000 a year ran out at the end of 1929, he signed a two-year pact for $80,000 a year, a number that became as celebrated as his 60 home runs. By then, the Babe had personal managers and scriptwriters, and when asked if he knew that he was getting more money than the president of the United States (salary $75,000), he is supposed to have replied, "Why not, I had a better year than he did."

That anecdote, embedded permanently in the literature, reflects the attitude not so much of Ruth as of the baseball community. The shocks of the Depression brought it back to reality and prompted the one thing it has always resisted (and still does): a willingness to try something new.

CHAPTER 15

An Age of Glory

For the baseball fan, the 1930's were a true Golden Age. The clusters of stars were as dense as the center of a galaxy. More and more games became available on the radio, enabling one to follow events more closely than newspaper accounts made possible, and whetting the appetite for more reading matter. The introduction of occasional night games added a note of exotic glamour. The All-Star Game became a fixture. Other sports did not yet usurp any portion of the major league spotlight. The 16 teams, in place since the start of the century, had clear cut identities. Their population of fewer than 400 players put their names, numbers, and characteristics within the memorizing capacity of dedicated fans, especially teenagers. The terrible events of the outside world were only beginning to, slightly, impinge on the age of innocence in which spectator sports held a pure emotional importance never again possible.

The Yankees produced the most awesome dynasty yet, while the National League produced more stirring home-stretch races. And all this was formalized, officially blessed, and glorified by saturation publicity with the establishment of the Hall of Fame at Cooperstown and its annual election of baseball gods to the pantheon.

Stars, lights, radio, Cooperstown, Yankees. Those were the main themes before all were engulfed in a war whose scale made World War I, so vivid then in adult memory, seem like a skirmish.

THE NEW STARS

Lou Gehrig, Joe DiMaggio, Ted Williams, and Bob Feller became the enduring symbols of the prewar glory, recognizable identities more than half a century later to millions not yet born when their careers ended. Gehrig was the Tragic Hero, a marvel of endurance ("the Iron Horse") struck down by an unheard-of disease before the age of 40, his story immortalized in a movie when movies were at their peak of cultural impact. DiMaggio was associated with unmatched Yankee triumphs, a 56-game hitting streak, and—subsequently—his marriage to Marilyn Monroe, and television commercials stressing his personal dignity; he represented the idea of "class." Williams, at once irascible and charming, stood for perfection of craft, the best "pure hitter," whose .406 average in 1941 set him apart from mortals. Feller, the fireballing "Strikeout King," burst on the baseball world as a 17-year-old Iowa schoolboy, joining the Cleveland Indians in 1936 and striking out 76 big-league batters in his first 62 innings pitched. The strikeout was to pitching what the home run was to hitting, and the superfast fastball was what made strikeouts. Feller picked up where Johnson and Grove left off, adding the fascination of precociousness.

But these were the tips of tall icebergs filling an ocean. Every franchise had an abundance of what later decades would call superstars, to the point where they were taken for granted but not unappreciated.

Among the big home-run hitters, defined as capable of hitting 35 or more in a season, were Hal Trosky in Cleveland, Hank Greenberg in Detroit, Simmons in Chicago after Philadelphia, Foxx in Boston after Philadelphia, John Mize in St. Louis, and of course Gehrig, DiMaggio, and Ott in New York. But aside from homers, every team had hitters who excited their fans: Luke Appling on the White Sox, Cecil Travis on the Senators, Earl Averill on the Indians, the young Williams, Harlond Clift on the lowly Browns, the Waners in Pittsburgh, Ernie Lombardi in Cincinnati, Joe Medwick in St. Louis, and so on and so on.

Yet there were just as many pitchers as ever to be dazzled by, whether the general earned run average was higher or not: Schoolboy Rowe and Tommy Bridges in Detroit, Mel Harder and Feller in Cleveland, Ted Lyons in Chicago, Wes Ferrell in Cleveland and Boston, Ruffing and Gomez with the Yankees, Hubbell and Schumacher with the Giants, Mungo with the Dodgers, French, Bill Lee, and Warneke with the Cubs, Dizzy Dean and his brother Paul with the Cardinals, Paul Derringer and Bucky Walters in Cincinnati, Grove in Boston after Philadelphia, Bobo Newsom popping up everywhere—these were magic names then and longer-lived in trivia discussions than many who played a generation later.

Gehrig's paralytic illness struck in 1939, and he died in June of 1941. DiMaggio and Feller played almost as long after returning from the war as before it and added considerably to their records, while Williams played only four years before going into

World War II and then had his long career interrupted again by service in the Korean War, playing until 1960. But their images were fully formed, and made permanent before they went away in 1942. They were products of the Golden Age, though not confined to it.

The personalities as well as the exploits of these stars were made more vivid and detailed by radio than those of the preceding generation, described only in print. Their own words could be heard in interviews. Every at bat and field play was reported specifically. With only eight box scores to study each morning, always there because all the games had been completed early enough the day before, a fan could acquire intimate knowledge of a whole league to a degree feasible later only for divisions or home teams. One's mind could encompass the whole, from year to year.

The game on the field was never more satisfying than it was in the 1930's. And never, before or since, did the off-field events cause as little distraction.

RADIO

A 1922 World Series game was the first to be broadcast. Would broadcasting regular games keep ticket buyers away, since they could get the play-by-play for free? (This wasn't a dumb question on the face of it: everybody understood that a large fraction of the spectators came to bet, and they could satisfy that urge just as well around a radio giving play-by-play.) No one had an answer or a solid basis for judgment, and that was fortunate. In the absence of certainty, all the owners could do in league meetings was leave the matter to "local option." Let each club decide for itself, without interference from the visiting club. (This would become a major sticking point, but not until later.) The beneficent result was that different patterns could be tried by different teams, and a body of knowledge created.

In 1925, Wrigley offered Cub games, without fee, to any Chicago station wanting them. Breadon soon followed suit in St. Louis. They had the idea, ultimately proved correct, that the free advertising sold more tickets than it negated.

But there was a problem in the two-team cities: when an away game was broadcast at home (by recreating a wire report in the studio), it would conflict with the actual game in town. So St. Louis, Chicago, Boston, and Philadelphia agreed not to broadcast away games. In New York, however, there were three teams. They agreed, in 1932, to ban all broadcasts, home or away.

In Cincinnati, Powell Crosley bought the Reds on February 5, 1934. Larry MacPhail had been brought in on Rickey's recommendation to straighten out the franchise failing under Weil. Crosley owned two radio stations in Cincinnati, so there was no reluctance to broadcast. MacPhail found a young Floridian with a gift for language and explanation and brought him in to do the Reds' games. The kid's name was Walter (Red) Barber.

That was 1934. In 1938, MacPhail moved to Brooklyn, to straighten out a franchise in shambles there. He learned of the New York agreement—and repudiated it. He brought Barber in to do all Dodger games, home and away, and Red's soft tones became the medium of education for Brooklyn housewives and children in the moment-to-moment intricacies of baseball, while also humanizing the players themselves.

The next year, the Yankees and Giants gave in, sharing home-game-only broadcasts, unveiling another articulate southerner, Mel Allen. Now all teams were broadcasting at least some of their games.

The World Series, of course, had no conflict problems. In 1935, Landis made a deal with all three radio networks (RCA's Red and Blue, and Columbia), which paid baseball $400,000 for the rights for four years.

Since minor league games were also being broadcast locally, and major league games picked up by some small-town stations, a generation was growing up learning how to take baseball by ear. Once again, a most beneficent innovation had come into being against the resistance of the people benefitting from it.

LIGHTS

MacPhail did something of far greater importance in resuscitating Cincinnati. He asked the National League's permission to play night games, and got it. His idea was to create "another Sunday" in midweek. Baseball's big crowds had always turned out on Saturdays and Sundays, when people were off work. They were off work on a weekday nights, too. If you played seven such games, one against each visitor, you'd have the equivalent of seven extra Sundays.

This was radicalism indeed. Play baseball at *night?* The quality of artificial light was suspect (and minor league experience showed that it could be pretty bad). What would it do to a player's reactions to a fastball, or a fly ball? Wouldn't only the top of the ball be lit? Wouldn't shadows be unnatural? And what about the next game? When would players sleep (as if some of them weren't going without sleep after day games anyhow, eh?)

The last question was resolved by a rule making the day following a night game an open date. The others produced a solemn decision to keep "strictly separate" statistical records for night games.

The seven games drew 130,000. The other 61 dates (including eight doubleheaders) drew 318,000. The 448,000 total was more than double each of the two preceding years, and twice what Mack's A's drew in Philadelphia. And the Reds, after four straight seasons in last place, rose to sixth.

Would you call that experiment a success? Baseball didn't. The American League promptly went on record forbidding its teams to try it.

Nobody else tried it, although the Browns talked about it. When MacPhail moved to Brooklyn in 1938, the first thing he did was order lights for Ebbets Field. On June 15, at the first night game, there was the one in which Johnny Vander Meer, who had pitched a no-hitter for the Reds in Boston four days before, pitched another one— the only second straight no-hitter by anyone in baseball history. Red Barber described every bit of the drama. Dodger attendance, under 500,000 the last three years, came in at 660,000 in 1938.

That December, the American League approved night games.

In 1939, American League parks in Philadelphia, Cleveland, and Chicago had lights. Since the Phillies had abandoned Baker Bowl in the middle of 1938 and moved in as tenants at Shibe Park, they played night games too. So three teams in each league had night games that season.

In 1940, both St. Louis teams (in the same park), the Giants, and Pittsburgh came on line, leaving only the Cubs and Braves without lights in the National League. Washington's Griffith Stadium got lights in 1941. All the others had to wait until after the war.

The seven-game limit remained in force. No sense rushing into something new.

THE HALL OF FAME

True to the Doubleday Myth, 1939 was designated as a centennial year for baseball. But the commitment to a Hall of Fame at Cooperstown was made in 1936, and electing players began before there was a home for their plaques. The Baseball Writers Association of America was assigned the task of choosing the players, and its election (requiring 75 percent of the votes cast) produced five: Cobb, Ruth, Wagner, Walter Johnson, and Mathewson.

The next year, Speaker, Lajoie, and Cy Young were added. In 1938, they voted in Alexander, and in 1939 Sisler, Eddie Collins, and Willie Keeler, along with Gehrig in a special election after his retirement. Meanwhile, a special commission named others to be honored not as contemporary players but as "contributors to the game:" George Wright (not Harry!), Ban Johnson, McGraw, and Mack in 1937; Morgan G. Bulkeley, the National League's first president, Henry Chadwick, and Alexander Cartwright in 1938; and Spalding, Anson, Buck Ewing, Comiskey, Hoss Radbourn, and Candy Cummings in 1939.

If you've been reading this book, the qualifications of those named are self-evident, with three exceptions. Bulkeley was a figurehead for the actual creator of the National League, William Ambrose Hulbert, and doesn't belong at all; incredibly, they didn't get around to including Hulbert until 1995, after decades of stone-walled appeals on his behalf. Cummings was the early pitcher credited with "inventing" the curve ball and certainly had a major impact in his time. George Wright belongs on his merits but is far less important than Harry, the originator and prototype of the position of manager. The commission didn't catch up with Harry until 1953.

The small brick building that would house the Museum and Hall of Fame was opened with elaborate ceremony on June 12, 1939. All of baseball's brass and all living members of the Hall of Fame were present on the steps, before a crowd of 10,000 (in a village whose population was 3,000). It became the core of what is now a sprawling state-of-the-art museum and library, full of sophisticated exhibits. Behind it is Doubleday Field, where two major league teams play an exhibition every year the day after installation ceremonies.

FARM SYSTEMS AND ADMINISTRATION

Once opposition to the farm-system concept collapsed, their growth was phenomenal. The Yankees, first and foremost, built one that eclipsed the Cardinal system in productivity. After the 1931 season, they bought the Newark club in the International League and hired George Weiss to run it. He urged Barrow to go whole hog into a farm system, and with Ruppert's money, it was easy. By 1937, the Newark Bears were so powerful that many considered them of major league second-division calibre. At the same time, the Yankees had Kansas City in the American Association, and a full complement of teams in lower classifications.

The 1937 Bears, finishing first by 25½ games, had such soon-to-be stars as Joe Gordon and Charlie Keller, along with two catchers, two first basemen, and five pitchers who would soon play in a World Series. In the Little World Series (between International League and American Association play-off winners) they defeated Columbus, the Cardinal farm, which included Enos Slaughter and Morton Cooper, soon to face the Yankees in a World Series. In 1940, when Kansas City finished first in the Association, three infielders (including Phil Rizzuto) and a pitcher (Ernie Bonham) moved up to become Yankee regulars in the next two World Series.

Other clubs moved in the same direction, if not as fast. In 1928, with virtually all clubs independent, 31 minor leagues started the season and only three failed to finish. By 1931, only 19 started and 16 finished. In 1933, only 14 leagues existed, but all completed the season, and by 1936 two-thirds of all minor league teams had a major league affiliation—and the failures had stopped. From 1935 through 1941, the number of leagues grew from 21 to 41, and in the 247 league-seasons involved, there was only one failure (in 1940).

Rickey, Weiss, and MacPhail were the three leading promoters of farm systems, sneeringly called "chain gangs" by those who disapproved. In 1936, St. Louis had 28 teams, Cincinnati 16, the Yankees and Tigers 11 each, while the Phillies and Senators had only one each and the Giants (who had the money but not the wisdom) only two. In 1940, the score was St. Louis, 29; Brooklyn, 18; Yankees, 14; Browns (surprisingly),

11; and everyone else at least 5 except for the A's, 4; Senators, 4; Phillies, 3; and (amazingly, not just surprisingly) the Cubs, 2.

Now and then Landis would set a bunch of farm hands free, charging clubs with holding back their advancement. (The Yankees got Tommy Henrich this way out of the Cleveland organization.) But the commissioner was shoveling against the tide.

As any good monopolist can tell you, you have to control your source of supply if you can.

In this period, some interesting "housekeeping" decisions were made. In 1937, home plate acquired its beveled edges, to eliminate a hazard the sharp edge had constituted for a runner sliding in. In 1939, the active player list went up from 23 to 25. In 1940, the American League, frustrated by the Yankee run of pennants, barred the pennant-winning team from making any trades the next year except through waivers. Also in 1940, the first 60-day disabled list was adopted, a device to add roster room. The American was for it, the National against, and Landis cast the deciding vote.

The position of league president was now well-defined: totally subservient to the commissionership. Run the umpires, get out the schedule, rubber-stamp contracts (after checking their technical correctness under the rules), impose discipline and fines in minor matters only, and make the annual spring-training prediction that there would be an eight-team race. Charisma was not part of the job description; in fact, if discovered it would call for disqualification.

In 1927, Barnard had become American League president when Johnson retired. When he died in 1931, his assistant, Will Harridge, moved up. (Harridge, among other things, had great experience with railroad schedules, so important to scheduling.) He was given a three-year term, then reelected for five years, then (in December 1938) for 10 more.

Heydler had become National League president, promoted from assistant in 1919 when Tener resigned. Late in 1933, he announced his retirement because of ill health. That spring, the league had hired a publicity man for the first time, Ford Frick, prominent sportswriter and radio commentator, particularly close to Ruth. Now they elected Frick league president for one year, then two, then three, then four.

As for Landis, his original seven-year term was followed by another (with a rise to $65,000) and another. In 1940, his contract was extended to 1946.

One mustn't think that the club owners, in their meetings, lacked humanitarian and magnanimous impulses. At the December 1934 meeting, they felt they should do something nice for players. The Depression was at its deepest, big-league salaries of $4,000 were common, the iron-bound reserve was no longer being challenged even in conversation, and no one gave any thought to pensions, severance pay, or moving expenses for a traded player. But players deserved something, so the owners passed a resolution. Every former player who had spent at least 10 years in the National League was given a lifetime free pass to National League games.

And Frick, the sophisticated public-relations expert, lobbied hard at the 1936 meeting (over which he presided) for more water fountains in ball parks.

His idea was taken under advisement.

"BREAK UP THE YANKEES"

The cry to "break up the Yankees" had been heard in 1928, and the Athletics took care of it very nicely. Before anyone could apply it to them, Mack did the breaking up himself, and one result of that—his sale of Cochrane to Detroit—held off Yankee domination two more years. But starting in 1936, the Yankees won the World Series four straight years. After coming up just short in a a three-team race in 1940, they won three more pennants in a row. Some details will be given year by year, but the degree of dominance can be seen best in summary.

DiMaggio was the key ingredient, arriving in 1936 as the result of a minor league purchase completed in 1935. Gomez, Ruffing, and reliever Johnny Murphy led a pitching staff that became increasingly diffuse as farm products moved up. When Gehrig couldn't play after 1938, four different first basemen got the job done. When Lazzeri gave out, Joe Gordon took his place. At shortstop, Crosetti was followed by Rizzuto. Red Rolfe was at third throughout. Henrich joined DiMaggio in the outfield in 1937 and Charley Keller in 1939.

That's why they called McCarthy a push-button manager, an inappropriate put-down because that's all a manager is supposed to do: make best use of his resources. Barrow and Weiss were providing resources, and McCarthy knew exactly how best to use them. In winning seven pennants in eight years, his final-standing margins in games ahead were 19½, 13, 9½, 17, 17, 9, and 13½. The year the Yankees lost, 1940, they missed by two.

Not even the Cubs of 1906–10 had dominated by that much for that long, and in the 1930's there was little disposition to make comparisons to anything before 1920.

Legislative counterattacks, like the no-trade rule of 1940 aimed specifically at the Yankees, had little effect. That cycle ended only because the war leveled everything, and the postwar Yankee dominance, which actually lasted longer than the prewar run, had entirely different parameters. Hot-stove arguments boiled down to comparing the 1927 and 1936 teams for which deserved to be designated "greatest."

For the American League, the Yankees constituted a two-edged sword. Their glamour made money for every other club, since they drew big crowds as visitors and gave visiting teams a fat check when they came to New York. But by killing the *perception* as well as the fact of competitiveness, they hurt the gate for all non-Yankee games.

Worst of all, they created a frame of mind in too many of their competitors that was harmful: they could live off what their Yankee games provided. Why spend money on improving your own team if you couldn't improve it enough to catch the Yankees anyhow? You might as well adjust to the "New York plus seven" economy, relax, and enjoy it. Not every club reacted that way, of course—certainly not Boston, Detroit, and Cleveland. But some did, and this weakened the entire league.

But as long as the Yankees were the Yankees, the American would look stronger than the National, winning most World Series and All Star Games and producing the statistics so dear to baseball fans.

Perhaps the Age wasn't quite as Golden as it appeared in New York.

SEASONS 1934–41

1934

Anyone attracted to the 1931 Cardinals must have flipped out over the 1934 edition, which made a great pennant drive and then defeated the Tigers in a seven-game World Series loaded with incident.

NL—The pennant race actually began long before Opening Day. In February, the defending-champion manager, Terry, was predicting the Giants would win again. Pittsburgh, St. Louis, and Chicago would be the teams to beat, he said, but they would be beaten.

"What about Brooklyn?" he was asked.

"Is Brooklyn still in the league?" he replied, and smiled.

Brooklyn didn't smile. Its team had finished sixth in 1933, hadn't won a pennant since 1920. It needed no insults from across the bridges. Bob Quinn, having sold the Red Sox, had taken over as Dodger general manager. He wanted his field manager, Max Carey, to snap back, make waves, cause a fuss, inflame the populace, and make it easier to sell a few tickets. Carey, in Florida, was not the type. He was a solid old baseball man who knew the game was on the field, not in the newspapers.

That's not what Quinn wanted. He fired Carey and made Stengel manager. Stengel *was* the type. As it turned out, Casey didn't sell many more tickets, and the team finished no higher. But Stengel didn't let anyone forget the "still in the league" crack, and he knew how to steam people up.

The season began. The Giants got ahead in mid-June and seemed to be building a comfortable lead over the Cubs and Cardinals while the Pirates dropped out. But the Cardinals were even better talkers than Stengel.

They were called the Gashouse Gang, flaunting their aggressive disreputability, after a remark made by their shortstop, "Lippy Leo" Durocher. Frisch, their manager–second baseman, had never been shy. Their top pitcher, Dizzy Dean, was in a class of his own as an attention-getting rabble rouser, but also on his way to 30 victories while expounding his philosophy that "it ain't bragging if you can do it." His brother Paul, as quiet as Diz was garrulous, was promptly dubbed "Daffy," just to go with "Dizzy."

Pepper Martin was now the third baseman. A terrific hitter in left field, a New Jersey Hungarian named Joe Medwick, was known as Ducky Wucky. Their third starter was Tex Carlton. Catcher Spud Davis was backed up by the rookie, Bill DeLancey, who had made Mancuso expendable.

Best of all, they fought among themselves, drove Frisch crazy, got suspensions, quit and came back, pulled outrageous practical jokes on the public as well as each other—and all of it got in the papers. As far back as spring training, Diz had predicted "me an' Paul" would win 45 games.

With about seven weeks to go, the Cards started what would be a 33–12 run to the wire. On September 13, they arrived at the Polo Grounds trailing by 5½ games, split two games with the Giants, then swept a doubleheader before 62,000, the biggest crowd the league had ever drawn, as Dizzy outpitched Hubbell and Daffy beat Schumacher. On September 21, they had to return to Brooklyn for a rain-makeup doubleheader. Diz pitched a three-hitter, and Paul followed with a no hitter. "If I'd-a known he was going to do that, I'd have pitched one too," declared Diz.

By the final Saturday, the Cards had achieved a

tie for first. Both teams were at home for the final two games, the Cards against Cincinnati, and the Giants against—Brooklyn. The faithful trekked to Harlem to avenge the preseason insult.

Mungo stifled the Giants 5–1. Paul Dean beat the Reds 6–1. The Cards were assured of a tie. On Sunday, even before Dizzy completed shutting out the Reds 9–0, the Dodgers had won again, 8–5, making sure the Giants were dead.

The cry "Brooklyn is still in the league" echoed through baseball lore, and not just in New York, for decades.

Rip Collins, the switch-hitting first baseman of the Cardinals, had tied Ott for the home-run title with 35. Paul Waner was batting champ at .362. Dizzy Dean's record was 30–7, brother Paul's 19–11 (for a total of 49, so it hadn't been "boasting"); Hubbell, Schumacher, and Warneke were the league's other 20-game winners.

Yet, in what was one of the most eventful seasons the league has ever had, attendance remained at the 3.2 million low point reached in 1933. Times were tough.

AL—By comparison, the American League season was routine. Mack had sold Cochrane to Detroit, to be player-manager. There Mickey had an all-star second baseman in Charlie Gehringer, a slugging second-year first baseman in Hank Greenberg, Goose Goslin acquired from Washington along with Firpo Marberry, and three fine starting pitchers in Schoolboy Rowe (fastball), Tommy Bridges (curves), and Eldon Auker (underhand). From August on, the Tigers pulled away from the Yankees and won by seven games.

The Yankees were in transition. Gomez and Gehrig both won Triple Crowns, Lefty with 26–5, 2.33, and 158 strikeouts, Gehrig with .363, 49 home runs, and 165 runs batted in. But Ruth was finally done. At age 40, he could deliver only 22 homers and a .288 average. It was time to hang it up, and he wanted McCarthy's job as manager, something Barrow and Ruppert had no intention of giving him. His release left a lot of ill feeling all around, but there really wasn't much alternative.

Foxx, still with the A's, hit 44 home runs as Philadelphia managed to finish fifth with some younger talent—infielders Pinky Higgins and Eric McNair, center fielder Doc Cramer, and outfielder Bob Johnson, with 34 homers—but no

pitching. Washington also had a pitching collapse despite its intact daily lineup and fell to seventh.

And attendance was even worse than the National's. At 2.8 million, it was below the 1917 level, and the third lowest in 30 years. Only 1915, with Federal League competition, and 1918, cut short by war, had produced lower figures.

All-Star Game—They had to have another All-Star Game, of course, and this one was at the Polo Grounds. Hubbell started against Gomez. The managers were the previous year's World Series managers, Terry and Cronin, setting a permanent pattern, and both not only started but played the entire game.

Gehringer opened the game with a single and continued to second on the outfielder's bobble. Manush walked. Hubbell then struck out Ruth, Gehrig, and Foxx in succession. He started the second inning by striking out Simmons and Cronin before Dickey singled; then he struck out Gomez.

The five straight strikeouts of those Hall of Famers has lived on as one of the supreme feats of individual mastery. Gomez boasted about his own strikeout for the rest of his life: "That day I was as good as the greatest hitters ever."

Lefty gave up a lead-off homer to Frisch and a three-run homer to Medwick in the third, but the Americans scored nine runs in the three middle innings and won 9–7. A crowd of 48,000 turned out, and the money, as decided the previous year, went to a fund for needy players, called the Association of Professional Baseball Players, not to be confused with a union or pension plan.

WS—Since Cleveland in 1920, the American League representative at the World Series had always been New York, Philadelphia, or Washington, so Detroit, as a "western" team, facing St. Louis, involved mid-America as never before. (The last "all-west" World Series had been the one in 1919, best left unmentioned.) The strong identities of so many of the players was just what national radio needed.

Cochrane started Crowder against Diz in Detroit, and it didn't work. The Cards won 8–3. Medwick and Greenberg hit homers, and Medwick got three other hits.

The next day, Rowe gave up single runs in the second and third, Hallahan a run in the fourth. The Tigers didn't tie it until the ninth, aided by an uncaught, windblown pop-up, and they won it in the 12th when Goslin singled after two walks. Rowe had allowed only two hits over those last nine scoreless innings.

In St. Louis, Paul Dean won the third game 4–1, and Detroit the fourth 10–5, with a five-run eighth. When Bridges beat Diz 3–1 in the fifth game, the Tigers headed home with victory in their grasp. But Paul Dean won the duel with Rowe 4–3, driving in the winning run himself in the seventh. And the seventh game turned into a rout when the Cards scored seven runs in the third inning, and Diz closed out an 11–0 Shutout.

In the sixth inning, the rout had turned into a riot. Medwick hit a triple and slid high into third baseman Marvin Owen. They scuffled, and when Medwick went to his position in left field, the fans showered him with so much debris (mostly vegetables) that Commissioner Landis himself, from his box seat, had to order Medwick removed from the game so that it could continue. It was a great moment for the imagery of czarism, referred to ad nauseum for the next few years.

In November, Mack led a group of American League stars, with Ruth as manager, on a tour of Japan. The game was already popular and well organized in Japan, but this visit was a major step forward in mutual appreciation and set the pattern for many such trips in the future.

The same month, the National League elected Frick president.

1935

The Tigers repeated in 1935, and this time beat the Cubs in the World Series. But the big stories were the 21-game winning streak the Cubs used to dethrone the Cardinals, and the final few games of Babe Ruth's career.

NL—Once again, the Giants led into late August, when the Cards caught and passed them. On the morning of Labor Day (September 1), the Cards were two games ahead of the Giants, and the Cubs, who had been paralleling the St. Louis rise were half a game behind the Giants. That day, the Cubs began four consecutive four-game sweeps of the eastern teams (outscoring the Giants 34–10 in four games) and stretched the streak to 18 by beating Pittsburgh twice. So they took a three-game lead into the last five games, all against St. Louis, and clinched by winning the first three. Losing the

last two meaningless ones left them four ahead of the Cards and 8½ ahead of the Giants.

Grimm was now a bench manager, letting 18-year-old Phil Cavaretta take care of first base in a brilliant infield: Billy Herman at second, Bill Jurges at short, Stan Hack at third. Gabby Hartnett, at 34, was a great defensive catcher who also hit .344. Chuck Klein, who had come from Philadelphia the year before, and Augie Galan were the full-time outfielders. Reserves included Cuyler (before he went to Cincinnati in midseason) and Lindstrom. And all this support was applied to strong pitching: Bil Lee, a hard-throwing newcomer, 20–6; Warneke, 20–13; French, 17–10; Root, 15–8; Tex Carlton, 11–8; lefty Roy Henshaw, 13–5. This team won 100 games, and the surprise is that it needed the September streak to win.

Pittsburgh's Arky Vaughan was batting champion at .385, Boston's Berger led Ott in homers, 34 to 31, Galan's 22 steals were enough to lead the league in the new let-'em-hit style. Dizzy Dean went 28–12, Daffy 19–12, giving "me an' Paul" exactly 100 victories in two seasons (counting the World Series). Medwick's .353 was second only to Vaughan, and the Cards actually won one more game than in 1934. The difference was the quality of the Cubs.

Cut loose by the Yankees, Ruth signed with the Boston Braves, a dying franchise under Judge Fuchs. He was to be vice-president, assistant manager (to McKechnie), and part-time player. On May 25 in Pittsburgh, he hit three home runs in one game—the 72d time he had hit two or more in a game, still the record—and never hit another. Early in June he announced his retirement, having hit six homers in 72 at bats, but only seven other safeties, all singles, for an average of .181.

By early August, Fuchs was gone too, as a syndicate headed by Bob Quinn took over the club to reorganize it. Reorganization was needed. The Braves finished 38–115, 61½ games out, 26 games behind the *seventh*-place Phillies. Not even the famous Original Mets of 1962 would have so bad a record.

AL—The Tigers and Yankees again outdistanced the rest of their league. Once more, the Tigers built a commanding lead in August and September, and a final Yankee spurt came too late. But there was an interesting angle that caused no fuss whatever at the time, or since.

Detroit's final record was 93–58, New York's 89–60, a three-game margin. But the Yankees had five rained-out games left un-played, and the Tigers three. Obviously, if those had been made up, the result could have been different.

Now look back at 1908. Supposedly, the un-played-game element in that race had led to a rule that all such games must be made up if they can affect the league championship. In 1935, no-body said a word. It was the Depression. Trying to play them would mean extra travel, and eight games is a lot. The World Series was to start in two days, and radio was paying good money for that. Besides, the Yankees would have to win four and the Tigers lose two to create a tie, which would then mean a playoff.

Forget it.

Those who imagine ideological purity in base-ball's past should contemplate this and many other examples of its nonexistence.

The Tigers had their 1934 team intact. The Yankees, with Red Rolfe installed at third and George Selkirk taking Ruth's place (and wearing his No. 3, also without much fuss), were no weaker in everyday lineup. The whole difference was pitching. Detroit had Bridges (21–10), Rowe (19–13), Auker (18–7), and Crowder (16–10). For the Yankees, Gomez fell to 12–15, and no one did better than Ruffing's 16–11.

Foxx and Greenberg tied for the home-run lead at 36, while Greenberg was in a class of his own with 170 runs batted in. Washington's Myer nosed out Cleveland's Joe Vosmik for the batting title, .349 to .348, with Foxx right behind at .346. Boston had two top pitchers, Ferrell (from Cleve-land the year before), 25–14, and Grove, 20–12, with a league-leading 2.70 earned run average but not enough else to do better than fourth.

But Yawkey was trying. He had bought Cronin from Griffith for $250,000, getting not only a shortstop-manager but Griffith's son-in-law. Bucky Harris, who had been managing the Red Sox, went back to Washington, so in effect this was a trade of managers.

Cleveland, finishing third, replaced Walter Johnson in midseason with Steve O'Neill. The Browns, in their second full season under Hornsby, were floundering in sixth and seventh. Dykes was managing the White Sox, giving the league a managerial lineup of five middle in-fielders and three catchers (including Mack, who was back in last place with the A's).

One good sign: attendance graph was starting to turn up—not by a lot, but in the right direc-tion. The Depression was easing a bit.

All-Star Game—No. 3 was assigned to Cleve-land's huge Municipal Stadium, built in 1931 and used by the Indians only for Sunday games. It drew just under 70,000 people, who produced just under $100,000 in receipts, which should tell you something about ticket prices. Player selec-tion was left to the managers. Cochrane let Gomez pitch the first six innings and Mel Harder worked the last three in a 4–1 American victory, leading to the formalization of the three-innings-maximum rule (no All-Star pitcher is allowed to work more than three innings). Foxx's two-run homer in the first (there was no interior false fence then) was enough.

WS—Warneke's four-hit 3–0 shutout gave Chicago the lead as the Series opened again in Detroit, violating the alternate-year site pattern. But the Tigers won the next three games, 8–3, 6–5 in 11 innings, and 2–1 behind Crowder. When Warneke won again, 3–1, backed by a two-run homer by Klein, the teams had to return to De-troit.

There the Tigers won it in the 10th inning 4–3, when Goslin's single off French drove in Mickey Cochrane from second. Mickey had now been the catcher on five pennant-winning teams in seven years, cementing his status as the best in the game. But true fans knew that. Back in October of 1931, despite Pepper Martin's steals, a mine worker in Commerce, Oklahoma, had named his newborn son Mickey in Cochrane's honor. The family's name was Mantle.

1936

The arrival of DiMaggio in 1936 changed the bal-ance of power in the American League for good, while Terry's Giants stopped merely flirting with championships and actually got one.

NL—By mid-July, the Cards and Cubs were even with each other at the top, while the Giants were tied with the Reds for fifth. The Cubs had had a 15-game winning streak; the Cards just moved steadily upward. Then, in August, the Gi-ants put together their own 15-game winning streak with Hubbell starting a personal 16-game streak to the end of the season. The Giants took the lead in the last week of August, held it, and finished five games ahead of the other two, who tied for second.

This was the year that both leagues changed the schedule pattern to four western (and eastern) trips instead of three. This meant shorter home stands and road trips and fewer four-game series, affecting starting-pitcher matchups. This pattern would become "normal" for the duration of the eight-team leagues, changed only when the 162-game schedule forced by expansion had to be adopted in 1961.

Hubbell, now referred to as "King Karl" more often than as the more mundane "Mealticket," was at his peak: 26–6 with a 2.31 earned run average that was half a run better than anyone else's in the majors. (Grove and Danny MacFayden of the Braves were the only others below 3.00.) He carried a staff whose next best record was Harry Gumbert's 11–3 and whose next biggest winner was lefty Al Smith, 14–13. Terry managed from the bench, so the infield of Sam Leslie (first), Burgess Whitehead (second), Dick Bartell (short), Jackson (third) was totally revamped. Ott and Jo-Jo Moore had Hank Lieber between them in the outfield. Mancuso was still catching.

The Cardinal farm system was producing: John Mize; Stu Martin to share time with Frisch at second; Terry Moore, a spectacular center fielder. Paul Dean came down with a sore arm, so Dizzy's 24–13 season (with a league-leading 195 strikeouts) wasn't enough. The Cubs had their 1935 lineup intact, but none of the pitchers reached 20 victories or matched French's 18–9 winning percentage. Pittsburgh had the best hitting team, Paul Waner taking the batting title with .373, while Ott led in homers (33) and Medwick in runs batted in (138). Charles Stoneham died this year, and his son Horace took over direction of the Giants.

AL—The Tigers were undone early when a broken wrist put Greenberg out of action after only 12 games, and Cochrane had to leave the club because of illness in June. Bridges (23–11), Rowe (19–10), and Gehringer (.354) were themselves, but that couldn't make up for the lost leaders.

It wouldn't have mattered. The Yankees were supercharged. They hit 182 home runs, a record.

They added Monte Pearson, from Cleveland, and Bump Hadley, from Washington, to their pitching staff. Once DiMaggio could play (he missed the first couple of weeks because of injury), they traded Ben Chapman to Washington for Jake Powell. They were out of sight by July 1, won 102 games, and probably could have won 112 or 120 if necessary.

Gehrig hit 49 homers and knocked in 152 runs, but his .354 average wasn't good enough for a Triple Crown because Luke Appling, the White Sox shortstop, hit .388, and even Lou's roommate, Dickey, outhit Gehrig at .362. Cleveland's Earl Averill was second at .378. What's more, Trosky in Cleveland knocked in 162 with 42 homers.

Mack had made his last big sale: Foxx, Cramer, McNair, and pitcher Johnny Marcum to the Red Sox for $300,000. They didn't keep the Sox from finishing sixth, but they soon would.

Foxx, in Boston's Fenway, had 41 homers and hit .338. So why get excited about DiMaggio's .323 with 29 homers and 125 runs batted in? Well, for one thing, he was still a 21-year-old rookie. For another, there was the way he fielded, which was something else. "Gliding perfection" was one way to describe it.

For the Yankees, Ruffing finally reached 20 victories, while Pearson and Hadley were 33–11 between them, taking up the slack of Gomez's 13–7 off year. The Yankees clinched on September 9, the earliest in league history for a full season.

All-Star Game—In Braves Field, the Nationals finally won, 4–3, and it was no fun for DiMaggio. He missed a shoestring catch in the second, leading to two runs, bobbled a single during a two-run fifth, and lined out to Durocher with the bases loaded and two out after the Americans had scored three runs in the seventh. Then he popped up for the final out of the game, giving him an 0-for-5 horse collar.

The experience had no permanent effect on his career.

WS—In a steady downpour at the Polo Grounds, the Giants' Hubbell stifled the Yankees 6–1, a close game broken up by a four-run eighth. They had to postpone the next day's game to let the field dry out. Then, in the presence of President Roosevelt, the Yankees unloaded 18–4 behind Gomez, producing a seven-run third capped by Lazzeri's grand-slam homer, only the second in Series history. (Elmer Smith, who hit the first in 1920, "congratulated Lazzeri by wire the moment he heard the news," the *Guide* reported.)

Although held to four hits, the Yankees beat Fitzsimmons at the Stadium 2–1. Crosetti knocked in the tie-breaking winning run with two out in the eighth by hitting a line drive off Fitz's glove and beating the throw to first while Powell scored from third. We'll recall this in 1941.

Pearson won 5–2, but Schumacher wouldn't let it end at Yankee Stadium. He hung in for all 10 innings and a 5–4 decision. So the long trip (about a mile) back to the Polo Grounds was required. The Yankees led 5–2 but then only 6–5 going into the ninth, when they added seven runs for a 13–5 final. The dynasty was officially under way.

After the season, Landis had to make a ruling. The Indians had signed Feller, underage and not a member of any organized high school team, to a minor league contract that they then acquired. The Des Moines club claimed this violated rules that reserved sandlot players (Feller's classification) for minor league teams only, and that it had been deprived of a chance to compete for him.

The judge ruled for Cleveland. Baseball's "Great Emancipator" knew how not to go too far. But he did award Des Moines $7,500. Hush money? Perhaps.

1937

The Yankees and Giants made it to the Series again in 1937, and this time the Yankees won more decisively, as DiMaggio displayed what made those who raved about him rave so much.

NL—The Cubs and Giants had a two-team race all the way. The Cubs pulled ahead during August, then slumped. The Giants got ahead just before September and stayed there, winning by three games.

Hubbell kept it up. His carryover winning streak reached 24, and he wound up 22–6. A new left-hander, Cliff Melton, was 20–9. Johnny McCarthy was now the first baseman, Jimmy Ripple the center fielder, Harry Danning the catcher. The Cubs were substantially the same as the year before, and again the pitching wasn't quite good enough.

St. Louis was fourth, behind Pittsburgh, but Medwick won a triple crown, or at least five-

sixths of one: he led in average (.374) and runs batted in (154) and tied Ott with 31 homers. It was not a pitchers' year: five of the clubs had no pitcher winning more than 16 games, and the only 20-game winners besides the Giant pair were Lou Fette and Jim Turner in Boston, for a fifth-place club. Warneke led St. Louis, 18–11, and Dean's season was wrecked in the All-Star Game.

MacPhail, taking over Brooklyn, fired Stengel and brought in Burleigh Grimes. It didn't make much difference, but MacPhail had plans.

AL—Whatever competition the Tigers might have given the Yankees disappeared May 25, when a Hadley pitch fractured Cochrane's skull. He survived, and returned to managing late in the year, but his career was over. Since Rowe was also out all year with a bad arm, Greenberg's 40 homers and Gehringer's .371 batting title didn't matter.

The Yankees won 102 again. Gomez returned to form, 21–11, and Ruffing was 20–7. Gehrig had his last great year—.351, 37 homers, 159 runs batted in—and Dickey hit .332 with 29 homers! (What numbers that Gehrig-Dickey room had!) But the spotlight was on DiMaggio. In July, he was making a run at that "Ruth's 1927 pace," even in Yankee Stadium, considered impossible for right-handed home runs in quantity. He would up with 46, hit .346, and knocked in 167 runs. He went to bat 592 times (64 walks, five times hit by pitch, two sacrifice bunts) and struck out 37.

"Oh," said those withholding judgment. "See what you mean."

Behind Detroit came the White Sox (a tribute to Dykes), Cleveland, and Boston. The only pitcher with more than 16 victories in this group was Grove, 17–9. The Browns, replacing Hornsby in midseason with Jim Bottomley, had no pitcher win 10.

Greenberg, with 183 runs batted in, missed Gehrig's record by one.

All-Star Game—In Washington, Gomez started against Dizzy Dean. Diz fanned Gehrig in the first inning but served up a two-run homer to him in the third. The next batter, Averill, hit a liner off Dean's foot, which Diz fielded for the third out. But he had a broken toe. When he tried to resume pitching too soon afterwards, the unnatural stride favoring the injured foot resulted in a sore arm. He never had his fastball again. He was 12–2 before the All-Star Game, 1–8 the rest of the year.

The Americans went on to an 8–3 victory, even though Medwick got four hits, two of them doubles.

WS—It was no contest. At Yankee Stadium, a seven-run sixth gave Gomez an 8–1 victory over Hubbell. It was the same score the next day, as Ruffing beat Melton. At the Polo Grounds, Pearson needed Murphy's help only for the last out in a 5–1 game. Finally, on Saturday, the Giants had a six-run second and Hubbell won 7–3. Then Gomez closed it out on Sunday 4–2, driving in the tie-breaking run himself in the fifth.

1938

As the Yankees rolled along, the Cubs in 1938 added another dramatic last-ditch pennant drive to their long list but got swept ignominiously by the Yankees.

NL—The Pirates seemed to take control of a four-team race during August, but the Cubs started coming at them as September began. Hartnett had replaced Grimm as manager at almost the exact midpoint of the campaign, when a 45–36 record was no cause for alarm. On Labor Day, the Pirates had a seven-game lead but lost a doubleheader to the Cubs. A hurricane interrupted the schedule for three days when the western teams were making their last eastern swing (through Philadelphia, New York, and Boston), and the delay provided a fortuitous rest for a tired Cub pitching staff. They then started a 10-game winning streak that moved them ahead of Pittsburgh and set up a high-drama finale.

Pittsburgh came to Wrigley Field September 27 leading by a game and a half. Dizzy Dean, bought between seasons by the Cubs partly for sentimental reasons despite his dead arm, had been in only 12 games all year, but had a 6–1 record. Yet he beat the Pirates 2–1, with some ninth-inning help from Lee. The next game was 6–6 after eight innings. Dark clouds and dusk were rapidly extinguishing the remaining daylight. The umpires declared that one more inning would be it, whatever happened. The Pirates didn't score. The first two Cubs went out. Then Hartnett hit a 1–1 pitch into the left-field bleach-

ers for a home run, a 7–6 victory and a half-game lead with four to play.

That manager-with-a-bat-in-his-hand stuff really works.

In retrospect, that left the Pirates in shock and won the pennant for the Cubs. Of course, it didn't. It took a 10–1 complete game victory by Lee, pitching for the fourth straight day, to put Pittsburgh a game and a half behind. On Friday, the Pirates split in Cincinnati while the Cubs played a tie in St. Louis. On Saturday, the Cubs lost the opener of their doubleheader, but when Pittsburgh lost at Cincinnati, Chicago won its second game 10–3 and clinched the pennant.

Lee was the key man, 22–9 with nine shutouts and the iron-man stunt at the end. Clay Bryant, 19–11, pitched as much. Rip Collins was now their first baseman (Mize having arrived in St. Louis), and Lazzeri, displaced by Gordon on the Yankees, was a reserve. Pittsburgh, managed by Pie Traynor, had its usual strong hitting but no pitcher better than Mace Brown's 15–9. Paul Derringer, 21–14 in Cincinnati, was the only 20-game winner besides Lee, and his catcher, Ernie Lombardi, was batting champion at .342 even though he was so slow that infielders played him well out on the outfield grass. Ott (36) and Medwick (122) were leaders again in homers and runs batted in.

In Brooklyn, MacPhail was collecting: Durocher from St. Louis, Dolph Camilli from Philadelphia, Cookie Lavagetto from Pittsburgh, Fitzsimmons from the Giants. Wait 'til next year. Vander Meer pitched his first no-hitter June 11 at Boston, beating the Braves 11–0 and setting up his June 15 climax with the only second-straight no-hitter anyone has ever pitched.

AL—Yawkey's collecting was starting to pay off for the Boston Red Sox. Foxx hit 50 homers. A 20-year-old Bobby Doerr came from the minors and took charge of second base. Cronin hit .325, becoming a good manager again. Higgins came from the A's, Ben Chapman from Washington, Joe Vosmik from Cleveland. Even with inadequate pitching (Grove was wearing out at 38), the Red Sox won 88 games, their highest total since 1917, the year Frazee got them.

But that only left them 9½ games behind the Yankees, who outdistanced the pack in July. New York's keynote was balance, not impressive individual averages. No one hit more homers than DiMaggio's 32, but four others were over 20 and the other three had 9 or 10 each. Ruffing was 21–7, Gomez 18–12, Pearson 16–7, Spud Chandler 14–5.

In Detroit, excitement centered on Greenberg, who really did make an assault on Ruth's record. He reached 50 with 20 games to go and 54 with 13 left. But he was being walked too often and could add only two more in game no. 146 (out of 155) and another pair in game no. 150. He ended with 58.

All-Star Game—At Cincinnati, the Nationals won for the second time. Vander Meer, fresh from his two no-hitters, Lee, and Brown stifled the Americans 4–1. Gomez, yielding an unearned run in the first (on Cronin's error), was the losing pitcher for the first time. At this point, his combined World Series and All Star record was 8–1, and by the fall it would be 9–1. More errors (the Americans made four) gave the Nationals a 3–0 lead.

WS—The Yankees' Ruffing outpitched the Cubs' Lee 3–1 in the Wrigley Field opener. Dizzy Dean made a gallant try against Gomez in the second game and took a 3–2 lead into the eighth. But with two out, Crosetti hit a two-run homer on a 3–2 pitch, and in the ninth DiMaggio hit a two-run homer, so it ended 6–3 Yankees.

It was Pearson's turn in New York, and the Yankee pitcher checked in with a 5–2 five-hitter (home runs by Dickey and Gordon). The fourth game was 8–3 for Ruffing (home run by Henrich, four runs batted in by Crosetti with a double and triple).

The Yankees now had a 24–3 record in World Series games starting with 1927. They were having some unsuccessful summers, but no unsuccessful autumns.

1939

The Lou Gehrig story touched everyone. The Yankee player response was to win more games than ever (in this cycle), 106. Cincinnati emerged as the National League winner and Brooklyn as a contender, as the machinations of MacPhail in both cities began to pay off.

NL—It was as if the National League had a by-law that the Cardinals must make a second-half surge. Cincinnati, hitting its stride during May, went to the top and stayed there. The Cards, in the last two months, went 41–21, closed to within 2½ games and finished 4½ out. Brooklyn hovered around .500 until September, made a smaller, later rush, and nosed out the Cubs for third.

McKechnie, in his second year at Cincinnati, found the missing piece in Bucky Walters, an infielder converted to pitcher by the Phillies before they traded him. Mastering the art at age 30 for the first time, Walters posted a league-leading 2.29 earned run average and a 27–11 record. Derringer, in his sixth year with the Reds, was 25–7. The big hitter was Frank McCormick, at first base, leading the league with 128 runs batted in.

Frisch was gone, replaced by Ray Blades, as Rickey promoted from within the system. All the St. Louis position players were in their 20s. The pitching staff was older, led by 35-year-old Curt Davis (22–16).

MacPhail had made Durocher manager in Brooklyn, installed Camilli (26 homers) at first and Lavagetto at third. New pitchers turned up, Luke Hamlin winning 20 games, Hugh Casey 15. Thanks to the seven night games and Barber's broadcasts, the Dodgers outdrew even the mighty Yankees, 960,000 to 860,000, with the sagging Giants a poor third at 700,000.

AL—Gehrig's string ran out at 2,130 games when he told McCarthy he couldn't play as the team was to start a western trip in Detroit on May 2. Babe Dahlgren took his place and hit two home runs as the Yankees won 22–2 that day. They were 24–4 in May while Lou went to the Mayo clinic and learned he had ALS, amyotrophic lateral sclerosis, unheard of then by the public, now called Lou Gehrig's disease. He announced his retirement June 21 but stayed with the club to act as captain and take the lineup to the umpires. On July 4, when he made his famous speech ("I consider myself the luckiest man on the face of the earth") before a gathering of old teammates in a packed Yankee Stadium, the Yankees had an 11½ game lead.

DiMaggio was batting champ at .381. He was over .400 in September when he kept playing despite a sinus infection that interfered with his vision. Ruffing was 21–7, and seven other starters had a combined record of 78–32. The 106–45 record meant a .702 pace for an entire season.

The Red Sox unveiled 20-year-old Ted Williams (.327, 31 homers, a league-leading 145 runs batted in), backed up by Foxx's .360 and 35 homers. Grove, at 39, led the league again with a 2.54 earned run average and was 15–4, but the rest of the pitching was ordinary. Feller, now 20, broke out with a 24–9 season for the third-place Indians, managed by Ossie Vitt, who had been manager of that 1937 Newark farm of the Yankees. Del Baker, who had been Cochrane's chief coach and fill-in manager, had the Tigers and finished fifth.

All-Star Game—At Yankee Stadium, six Yankees were in McCarthy's starting lineup, including Ruffing. Two runs in the fourth and DiMaggio's homer in the fifth gave the Americans a 3–1 lead, but the Nationals threatened in the sixth. With the bases full and one out, McCarthy brought in Feller, who got Vaughan to hit into a double play. Then (contrary to the rules) he pitched three more scoreless innings for a 3–1 victory.

WS—The games were close, but the result was another sweep. Ruffing beat the Reds' Derringer 2–1, when Charlie Keller tripled and Dickey singled with one out in the bottom of the ninth. Pearson took a no-hitter into the eighth inning and completed a 4–0 two-hitter for the Yankees, equaling a World Series record. In Cincinnati, two home runs by Keller and one each by DiMaggio and Dickey marked a 7–3 Yankee victory.

In the fourth game, the Yankees scored twice in the ninth for a 4–4 tie, and three in the tenth on play that became, unjustly, World Series legend.

With two on and one out, DiMaggio lined a single to right, scoring a run. When Ival Goodman let the ball get away, Keller (called King Kong because of his muscular build) kept going and slammed into Lombardi as the ball arrived at home. Lombardi was stunned, and as he lay there with the ball a few feet away, DiMaggio picked up speed and scored too. Lombardi was vilified for "going to sleep," when (a) he was actually stunned and (b) the deciding runs had scored anyhow. The final score was 7–4.

No team previously had won more than two straight World Series. The Yankees now had four in a row, and there was no reason to think they would stop there.

1940

Cincinnati proved to be a repeater champion in 1940, while Detroit edged out Cleveland and the Yankees in the first three-way race the American League had seen since that traumatic last week of 1920, when the Black Sox scandal broke.

NL—The Reds were so solid that they won by 12 games, with no challenge after July. Staying with them for the first half were the Dodgers, to whom MacPhail had made significant additions. He bought shortstop Pee Wee Reese, the jewel of the Red Sox farm system at Louisville, to replace Durocher on the field; it was a Red Sox mistake that weakened their future for many years, in a way similar to the Ruth sale if not of the same magnitude. MacPhail got Dixie Walker, 29, considered a possible Ruth successor in the Yankee chain before a serious injury set him back, on waivers. Before trading deadline he got Medwick and Curt Davis from the Cardinals, who had a glut of farm products. Whitlow Wyatt, at 32, was turning into a winning pitcher, 15–14, while Fitzsimmons had a 16–2 season. Brooklyn's 88 victories, its highest total since the pennant race of 1924, caused excitement well beyond the borough, because "Brooklyn" was every comedian's laugh word, and the Dodger reputation for underdog inept zaniness appealed to the country in the heyday of "screwball comedy" in the movies.

The Cardinals made their usual second-half drive but started from too deep a hole. They were 15–29 when Billy Southworth took over as manager, and 69–40 the rest of the way. Their new shortstop, Marty Marion, was considered exceptionally tall for that position (a skinny 6 foot 2). Mize led the league with 43 homers and 137 runs batted in, and there was a controversial batting champion. Debs Garms, a reserve outfielder at Pittsburgh, hit .355 in only 358 official at bats, but he appeared in 105 games and the rule then classified as a "regular" anyone in more than 75. However, since the top two batters with a normal 500–600 at bats were Hack at .317 and Mize at .314, it wasn't such a terrible injustice. They soon changed the rule to require 400 at bats to qualify for the title, but if you gave Garms 400 with no more than his 127 actual hits, he'd still have .318.

Frisch, who had spent 1939 broadcasting games in Boston and watched Garms play there, had become the Pirate manager and brought him to Pittsburgh. The Boston manager who let him go was Stengel, hired again by Quinn to follow McKechnie in 1938. Quinn had also changed the name of the Boston Braves to the Bees and called Braves Field the Beehive, but that wouldn't last long.

AL—Whether it was a delayed reaction to Gehrig, now home in Westchester and slowly dying (which his friends knew although the public didn't), or something else, the Yankees got off to their worst start since 1925. In mid-May they were in last place, and they didn't get over .500 until July. The Red Sox, off to an early lead, played only .500 ball for the last four months and got nowhere. So it became a race between Cleveland (for whom Feller opened the season with a no-hitter) and Detroit.

In August, the Yankees found themselves and launched a 19–4 spurt in which they defeated both leaders in dramatic games. On September 11 there was a virtual three-way tie, but the Yankees lost the second game of a rain-shortened doubleheader in Cleveland, two out of three in Detroit, and all three in St. Louis, so their final nine-game winning streak left them in third place, two games out.

Meanwhile, the Tigers and Indians were going head-to-head. September 4–6 the Tigers swept a three-game set in Detroit. September 20–22, the Indians were there again, and the Tigers won the first two before losing to Feller. The final three games of the season were in Cleveland, which the Tigers reached with a two-game lead. Feller, 27–10, was rested and ready; the Detroit staff was worn out. Tiger manager Del Baker started a 30-year-old right-hander named Floyd Giebell, whose major league experience consisted of 24 innings pitched in 10 games over two seasons—obviously a give-up move against Feller, hoping for a victory in one of the other two games.

So Giebell shut out the Indians, Rudy York hit a two-run homer off Feller, and the Tigers clinched the pennant 2–0.

Cleveland's defeat was all the more traumatic because the players had been feuding with manager Vitt all season, once presenting a petition to owner Alva Bradley asking for his dismissal. Their complaint was that he kept harping on "the Yankee system" and making comparisons to the 1937 Newark team he had managed. The players were dubbed "Crybabies" by Bradley and the press, and the label stuck.

Baker, as Cochrane's successor, had made a bold move. He sent Greenberg to left field, moved catcher York to first, and made Birdie Tebbetts the first-string catcher. It worked perfectly. Greenberg hit 41 homers, knocked in 150 runs, and won the Most Valuable Player Award (even though DiMaggio won another batting title at .352; Greenberg hit .340). York added 33 homers, and even Tebbetts, in there for his receiving, hit .296. Bobo Newson, 21–5, and Rowe, 16–3, were phenomenally effective. Al Benton, the relief specialist, was not: he had 17 saves but 10 losses. As for Giebell, he never won another game. But Tebbetts's ability to handle pitchers paid off.

All-Star Game—In Sportsman's Park in St. Louis, the Nationals were the home team and won 4–0, the seventh time in the eight-game series that the home team won. Derringer, Walters, Wyatt, French, and Hubbell shut out the Americans, yielding only three hits. The first three batters to face Ruffing went single, single, homer (by Max West of Stengel's Boston Bees, who knocked himself out of the game the next inning by crashing into the right-field wall). It was over then and there.

WS—A five-run second inning gave the Tigers the first game 7–2, behind Bobo Newsom. The Reds' Bucky Walters beat Rowe in the second 5–2. At Detroit, the Tigers' Bridges won 7–4, but Derringer, the first-game loser, evened matters, 5–2. Newsom's three-hit 8–0 shutout then gave Detroit the lead going back to Cincinnati.

Now it was elemental for the Reds: Walters and Derringer. Bucky produced a five-hit shutout (all singles in different innings) and hit a home run in a 4–0 victory. That left it up to Derringer and Newsom. Bobo led 1–0 in the seventh when McCormick hit the left-field fence for a double, Jimmy Ripple hit the right-field fence for a double, and after a sacrifice bunt, Billy Myers, a .202 hitter during the season, delivered the long fly that let Ripple trot home with the winning run. The Reds had their second world championship, and this one, unlike 1919's, was untarnished.

1941

Brooklyn finally made it. In 1941, the first Dodger pennant since 1920 triggered joyful celebrations and the tabloid headline, "WE WIN!" Referring to them as "Dem Bums" had become a compliment. But the Yankees, getting over whatever ailed them in 1940, were back and asserted themselves again in the World Series.

NL—In hand-to-hand combat from start to finish, the Dodgers and Cardinals left the rest of the league behind early, seesawed in and out of first place, and were never more than a couple of games apart all the way to the wire. The Dodgers pulled out of the last tie on Labor Day, September 1, protected the lead by winning two of three epic struggles in St. Louis September 11–13, clinched in Boston with two games to go, and finished up by 2½ games. The Dodgers won 100, the Cards 97, and dethroned Cincinnati, in third, 88.

It was a triumph of MacPhail's collection of veterans at Brooklyn over Rickey's farm system at St. Louis. Camilli, whose 34 homers led the league, had come from the Phillies. Billy Herman, discarded in May by the Cubs, was at second. Reese, tutored by Durocher the year before, was full-time shortstop, with Lavagetto, from Pittsburgh, at third. Dixie Walker and Joe Medick were the corner outfielders and Mickey Owen, another Cardinal product, the catcher.

But the key man was Pete Reiser in center, a 22-year-old phenom plucked out of the Cardinal system in 1939 when Landis freed about 100 players. The switch-hitter's .3443 took the batting title, while speed and fearlessness made him a superb outfielder and base runner. Wyatt, 22–10, was joined by Kirby Higbe, 22–9, acquired from the Phillies. Hugh Casey started 18 times, relieved 27, and had a 14–11 record. Curt Davis, at 37, contributed 13–7. And during the season, MacPhail picked up Larry French, Johnny Allen, and Mace Brown. No half measures for Leland Stanford MacPhail.

The Cards had Mize, Frank Crespi, Marion, and Jimmy Brown around the infield; Slaughter, Moore, and Johnny Hopp in the outfield; Mancuso back with them catching (having displaced Mickey Owen)—all their own farm products. So were pitchers Ernie White, Morton Cooper, Max Lanier, Howie Krist, and, in the closing weeks,

Howie Pollet. The only exception was Warneke, a 17-game winner along with White.

It was a great race, and there would be an encore.

AL—The Yankees turned to their farm system for replenishment. The Kansas City infield had been Johnny Sturm at first, Gerry Priddy second, Phil Rizzuto at short. Priddy couldn't displace Gordon, of course, so he became utility; the other two started. Behind Ruffing and Gomez, who won 15 each, were all recent farmhands: Marius Russo, Spud Chandler, Atley Donald, Marv Breuer, Ernie Bonham. Dickey was aging but still the game's best catcher. And the DiMaggio-Keller-Henrich outfield hit 94 home runs, each getting at least 30.

But it was DiMaggio who ignited everything with his 56-game hitting streak. It started May 15 and ran to July 17, and the Yankees won 41, tied two, and lost only 13 of their games in that stretch. They started 5½ games out of the lead and had control of the race before it ended. While it was on, Gehrig died on June 2; Joe Louis beat Billy Conn in one of the most famous of all heavyweight championship fights on June 18 (they stopped a Giant game at Forbes Field for 45 minutes to let the crowd listen to the broadcast); Nazi armies launched their invasion of Russia on June 22; and the Yankees set a record by hitting at least one home run in each of 25 straight games, a record tied but still not surpassed 56 years later. But nothing kept DiMaggio's streak off the front pages and radio news bulletins once he got into the 30s.

The drama of the streak and Yankee dominance overshadowed what Ted Williams was doing in Boston, and what became fully appreciated only in retrospect. He hit .406, the first player to reach .400 since Terry's .401 in 1930, and the last to this day. And he did it decisively, insisting on playing a doubleheader on the last day when his .39955 average would have been recorded as .400. He got six hits. He led DiMaggio (and the league) in homers, 37–33, but trailed in runs batted in, 125–120. He also finished second to DiMaggio in the Most Valuable Player balloting—not unreasonable in view of how their teams finished.

Feller had a 25–13 season with the fourth-place Indians, but that was obscured along with everything else by the events in New York and

Brooklyn. The Yankees clinched on September 4, the earliest date ever.

All-Star Game—This one, in Detroit, established the extravaganza's special quality just when the novelty was starting to wear off. The Americans took a 2–1 lead into the seventh, but a pair of two-run homers by Arky Vaughan in the seventh and eighth sent the Nationals into the ninth ahead 5–3.

With one out, an infield hit, a sharp single, and a walk filled the bases for DiMaggio, who had preserved the honor of his streak with an earlier double. He hit a sharp grounder to short and beat the relay to first, avoiding a game-ending double play, while a run scored on the force-out. Whereupon Williams blasted Claude Passeau's 2–1 pitch into the top deck of the right-field stands for a three-run homer and a 7–5 victory. Storybook stuff.

WS—The streak was over, Williams had his .400, Brooklyn had survived its wild pennant celebration, and now the Dodgers were clearly sentimental favorites against the not-broken-up-after-all Yankees.

At the Stadium, Ruffing beat Davis 3–2 for the Yankees, then Wyatt beat Chandler 3–2 for the Dodgers, so they went to Ebbets Field all even. Russo and Fitzsimmons were locked in a 0–0 duel in the top of the seventh when Russo, with two out, hit a line drive that cracked Fitz's kneecap and bounced high enough for Reese to catch. Remember the hit off Fitz's glove that let the Yankees beat him 2–1 in the third game of 1936? This shot also changed the direction of the Series. When Casey took over in the eighth, DiMaggio and Keller reached him for run-scoring singles, and the Yankees went on to win 2–1.

But the Dodgers seemed to have pulled even the next day, Sunday, leading 4–3 with two out in the ninth, and Casey holding the Yankees scoreless since relieving in the fifth. His wide-breaking curve was missed by Henrich for strike three—but also by Owen, and Henrich reached first safely.

It was a shock, but not yet a disaster. All the Dodgers needed was one more out. But DiMaggio lined a single to left, Keller hit an 0–2 pitch off the right-field wall for a two-run double that put the Yankees ahead, Dickey walked, and Gordon socked a two-run double to left. Yankees 7, Dodgers 4.

Now it was shock *and* disaster. Murphy set the side down in order, and the Yankees had a three-games-to-one grip on the Series. Bonham's 3–1 victory over Wyatt the next day seemed preordained.

AFTERMATH

The 1941 World Series marks the end of "prewar" baseball, the end of that particular Golden Age. Although the 1942 season would be relatively normal as players left for military service only gradually, the war years would be understandably abnormal, and everything—but everything—would be different in American life after the war was won.

On September 16, 1940, Congress enacted the first peacetime military draft in the country's history. Hitler had conquered Europe and was bombing Britain. The first draft numbers were drawn October 29, after the baseball season was over. Fans were focused on major league stars, but baseball people knew that the impact on the minors, their lifeblood, would be immediate.

In May 1941, Hank Greenberg became the first big leaguer to be called up, just 19 games into the season. His departure helped wreck whatever hopes the Tigers had that season, but few other teams were affected. The machinery for war takes time to get rolling, and besides, the United States wasn't at war, just rebuilding neglected defenses. Deferments for many reasons—school, family support, useful job—seemed likely.

December 7 and Pearl Harbor changed all that instantly. But the atmosphere was quite different from World War I days, which anyone over 35 could remember perfectly well. Then the world "war" still had connotations of glory, adventure, flaming patriotism, and moral force for many people. It was a war "for Democracy," a "war to end all wars," suffused with idealism. And those who didn't share the idealism avoided service if they could, in "essential occupations." Factory and military-base teams composed of major leaguers were seen as scandalous, but were plentiful. The bottom line was that the country itself had not been attacked and wasn't threatened.

Now it was different. Japan *had* attacked, and Hitler was out to conquer the world, and our "way of life" was directly threatened with no assurance it could be preserved. Going into service or war work was seen much more realistically as an ugly necessity, "a job to be done"; the war was an unspeakable horror for civilians as well as on the battlefield. Less idealism and more determination and acceptance of responsibility formed the prevailing mood.

President Roosevelt made it explicit right away that he wanted major league baseball to continue: entertainment on the home front was essential to morale, and a nation of citizen-soldiers cared about reading the scores. If we were fighting to preserve "our" civilization, baseball was part of what we were hoping to save and come back to. All sorts of practical adjustments could be made about travel, personnel, etc.; but continuity should not be broken as a matter of public policy.

Entering such a period, some of the conclusions drawn from the preceding decade had to be put in storage for the duration. Night baseball had to be made universal, but later. Reaction to changing demographics—the growth of western and West Coast cities—would have to be recognized, but later. Television, in the experimental stage, would have to be confronted, but later. (Barber had done a telecast of a Dodger game as early as 1939.) The farm-system concept, totally triumphant, could be expanded further, but later.

In the present, only one thing mattered: there was a war to be won.

PART V

A CHANGING WORLD

CHAPTER 16

Wartime Baseball

Of all American institutions, the two fundamental items of mass entertainment, Hollywood movies and major league baseball, probably changed the least during World War II. Men went into military service, women went into the workplace, everyday life dealt with rationing, racial segregation began to weaken amid mass migration out of the South and into the military, global awareness became permanent, centralized government power increased dramatically and forever, individual lives and viewpoints were altered in countless ways. Even the mass medium of radio, accepted primarily as entertainment before the war in Europe began, became more basically an instant conveyor of news.

Baseball and the movies were also greatly affected, of course, and made their adjustments, but they retained their familiar forms in remarkable fashion. The content of movies shifted to reflect patriotic themes or total escapism, and the calibre of baseball played was inevitably lower. But each season was completed on schedule, each World Series was played, all records were duly recorded, and anyone who enjoyed "following" baseball could do so in traditional fashion.

On January 15, 1942, barely a month after Pearl Harbor, President Roosevelt sent Commissioner Landis a letter urging baseball to proceed as usual. The war effort would make everyone work harder for longer hours, and people would need relaxation. "Baseball provides a recreation which does not last over two hours or two hours and a half and which can be got for very little cost," wrote the president of the United States.

Think about *that* premise in the light of the 1990's. Two hours? Little cost? Well, it was perfectly true then.

In the spring of 1942, training camps were run as usual in Florida, Arizona, and California. The wartime transportation crunch (not enough trains, gasoline shortages for cars and buses) had not yet kicked in. The 1942 schedule was also played out as planned. But in December 1942, Washington asked for a plan to cut travel mileage, and two steps were taken. All training camps were shifted to within 500 miles of the home city. The two Chicago teams, Detroit, Cleveland, Cincinnati, and Pittsburgh found places in Indiana. New York's Giants and Yankees went down to the Jersey shore and the Dodgers to Bear Mountain, alongside West Point up the Hudson. The others found adjacent sites in Connecticut, Delaware, Maryland, Missouri (Browns), and Illinois (Cardinals), while the Red Sox, at Tufts College, were only a trolley-car ride away from Fenway Park.

The regular-season schedule went back to three western-eastern trips instead of four. More night games were permitted, 14 to a club and 21 for the Senators, to accommodate war workers. An extra All Star Game was scheduled for 1942, with the winner of the regular game facing an All Star service team, the money from both to be passed on to relief and other war-related funds.

By 1943, some 100 major leaguers and 1,400 minor leaguers were in service, and over the next couple of years, baseball turned over to the government several million dollars raised through special promotions, war-bond drives, and other contributions.

For 1944, the Senators were granted unlimited night-game rights and other teams 21 games. As "dimout" regulations to save energy took hold, most night games became in fact twilight games, because year-round Daylight Savings Time made full darkness occur later on the clock.

At the end of the 1944 season, about 500 players from major league rosters were listed on honor rolls of those in service. And finally, in 1945, the All-Star Game had to be canceled because travel restrictions had become so severe—even though, as it turned out, the war in Europe ended in May. The game had been scheduled for July 10, which would have been just six days before the first test of the atomic bomb in the New Mexico desert.

Meanwhile, in the winter of 1944–45, five different units of baseball celebrities, mostly older players and managers, went to war theaters as part of USO (United Service Organizations, providing recreation for servicemen) tours. The mere fact that these were wanted shows how firmly baseball was embedded in the cultural fabric of the time. The tours involved 23 people in a seven-week period.

All this was significantly different than the reactions to, and actual activities during the World War I experience. (Contrast it with Chapter 10.)

Meanwhile, the baseball business itself continued. In February of 1943, the Phillies were sold. Gerry Nugent, who owned them for 10 years, had made his living by selling off every one of his better players as soon as he became marketable and had been trying to unload the team for some time. As of the end of the 1942 season, the Phillies had finished last five years in a row, and last or next-to-last 10 straight years, losing at least 100 games six times. Finally, the league office took charge of the franchise and within weeks found a buyer: Bill Cox, a New Yorker described as a "sportsman." That he was: he liked to bet, including on the Phillies (but only to win, he insisted). Landis promptly banned him from baseball, and before the year was over the new owner was Bob Carpenter Jr., a member of the DuPont family and a true baseball fan. He paid the same $400,000 Cox had paid Nugent and would soon demonstrate what a difference intelligent ownership (with cash available, of course) could make.

A change in Brooklyn made bigger waves. At the end of the 1942 season, MacPhail resigned to go back into service. (He was famous for a World War I escapade in which he had taken part in kidnapping the kaiser in November 1918.) In St. Louis, Rickey and Breadon had not been getting along for years. The Brooklyn bankers who actually controlled the club (and had brought in MacPhail) offered the job and part ownership to Rickey. He took it, and from 1943 on the Rickey System was transferred to Brooklyn while it purred along on its own momentum in St. Louis for years and years. Training young leaders and executives was part of the system.

On November 25, 1944, Landis died at the age of 78 after a short illness. The commissioner's office was put into the hands of Frick and Harridge, the league presidents, and of O'Connor, who had actually been running the Landis office in day-to-day affairs from the beginning. While they performed the routine caretaker functions, the owners wasted no time in rewriting the Major League Agreement (the document that rules interleague matters) to get rid of the arbitrary powers never intended for Landis but never pried out of his grip. The next commissioner would have two limitations. He could not, by definition, find anything "detrimental to baseball" that a majority of club owners or a written rule permitted—in other words, no blank check. Furthermore, they eliminated the agreement forbidding an owner to go to court to oppose a commissioner's decision. In other words, not only no blank check, but the powerful deterrent of threatening to sue—the very right that had created the mess that led to Landis in 1919.

The new commissioner would have to be elected by a three-quarter vote (12 of 16), not a simple majority, and would have a seven-year term at $50,000.

The new Major League Agreement was adopted in February 1945, and a search committee went to work. In April, MacPhail, who now owned the Yankees, suggested the name of Albert B. (Happy) Chandler, U.S. senator from Kentucky, a Democrat. The idea of influence in Washington seemed highly desirable in the new, central-government civilization and amid the uncertainties created by President Roosevelt's death that month. Chandler accepted, took office July 12, resigned the Senate October 29. He brought with him Walter Mulbry, his administrative assistant, to be his O'Connor, while O'Connor stayed on as a "senior advisor." The commissioner's office, which had been in Chicago (as Landis originally insisted) was moved to Cincinnati, the major league site closest to Kentucky, and remained a small-staff, essentially secretive, closely held operation.

MacPhail, back in civilian life at the beginning of 1945, when the war in Europe had turned irreversibly against Germany, had pulled a coup. Colonel Ruppert had died in January of 1939 (he never knew of the Gehrig tragedy). He was childless. His heirs were sisters and other relatives. Barrow continued to run the club for them, but they really had no interest in owning it and faced inheritance-tax problems if they did. Barrow himself was now 77 and often ill. The price was set at $3 million—for the Yankees, the whole farm system, the Stadium and the land under it, and ball parks in Newark and Kansas City. MacPhail got Dan Topping, heir to a tin fortune and previously involved in sports promotion, and Del Webb, an engineer-contractor who built much of Las Vegas, to put in $1.4 million each for equal one-third shares along with his own $200,000, and to be silent partners with him in charge. The sale was completed January 25, 1945, and MacPhail was not only back in baseball but one of its chief movers and shakers in what was suddenly the post-Landis era.

By now, there were no restrictions on night games, except for Sundays. MacPhail had two immediate projects for the "House that Ruth Built and Larry Now Ran": lights for the roof, and a "stadium club" under the stands, an elaborate restaurant-bar for season-ticket buyers and other upscale customers.

Germany surrendered in May. Two atom bombs fell on Japan in August. Victory in the Pacific was declared August 14, and Japan formally surrendered on September 2. Hank Greenberg, the first star to leave, was one of the first to return, in July, and he led the Tigers to a pennant with a last-day home run and starred in the October World Series. In December, a new major and minor league agreement was fashioned, to fit the new Major League Agreement, completing the new structure of Organized Baseball.

The decks were clear for the post-war era.

SEASONS 1942–45

1942

The Cardinals, with a second-half rush that outdid all their previous efforts, in 1942 turned the tables on the Dodgers and then, in a clash of top farm systems, upset the Yankees in the World Series. Relatively few players had gone into service before this season began, but there was steady attrition of regular lineups by draft calls and enlistments. The two pennant winners, however, were basically at full strength for the Series.

NL—The Dodgers, their lineup intact, won 70 of their first 100 games and had a 10½-game lead in mid-August. But MacPhail must have seen something: at a team meeting, he warned them that if they got complacent they wouldn't hold it. The Cards had swept a doubleheader from the Dodgers on August 4, and from that point on won 43 of their last 51 games, many of them with ninth-inning rallies.

They caught the Dodgers September 11–12 at Ebbets Field, winning 3–0 and 2–1. Both lost the next day, then the Cards won 12 of their remaining 13, while the Dodgers lost three of their next five, then won eight straight. St. Louis finished with 106 victories, the Dodgers with 104—the highest total ever not good enough to finish first, matched only by the 1909 Cubs.

St. Louis's farm supply seemed bottomless. Rickey had traded Mize, his best hitter, to the Giants at age 29, and put Johnny Hopp at first. Whitey Kurowski took over third, Walker Cooper (Mort's younger brother) became the catcher, Stan Musial played left—all recent farm graduates. Mort Cooper was 22–7, a rookie right-hander named Johnny Beazley 21–6, and all the other significant pitchers were young farmhands except Harry Gumbert. Southworth had managed many of them in the minors.

The rest of the league was outclassed. Lombardi, traded to Boston, won another batting title at .330, slow-footed or not. Ott, taking over from Terry as Giants manager, hit 30 homers, with Mize second in the league with 26. Mize nosed out Brooklyn's Camilli in runs batted in, 110–109, but Cardinal pitching led the league with a 2.58 earned run average and 18 shutouts.

It would not be the last time the Dodgers were nipped at the tape.

AL—The Yankees had no trouble at all, with their final margin at nine games only because the Red Sox had a hot last two months. Buddy Hassett at first was the Yankees' only lineup change, and the younger pitchers took over: Bonham 21–5, Chandler 16–5, Hank Borowy 15–4.

Williams produced a Triple Crown: .356, 36 homers, 137 runs batted in. Tex Hughson had a 22–6 year for the Red Sox, and a Washington outfielder, George Case, stole 44 bases. Feller was in the navy. Luke Sewell, managing the Browns, surprised everyone by bringing them in third.

All-Star Game—At the Polo Grounds, in a twilight start, the Americans won 3–1, as Lou Boudreau, now Cleveland's shortstop-manager at age 24, and York hit first-inning homers for all the runs. The next night in Cleveland, the Americans defeated the service team managed by Cochrane 5–0, raking Feller for three runs in the first two innings. The two games produced $161,000 for the Bat and Ball Fund (supplies for service teams) and war relief.

WS—The ninth inning of the first game foretold an end to Yankee dominance. Ruffing had a no-hitter for seven innings and a 7–0 Yankee lead into the ninth. Then the Cards scored four runs

and had the bases loaded with Musial up before Chandler got him to ground out. The Cards' Beazley beat Bonham the next day 4–3, on a two-out double by Slaughter and single by Musial.

In New York, the Cards' White beat Chandler 2–0, the first World Series shutout suffered by the Yankees since 1926. The next game was a 9–6 Cardinal victory and the fifth a 4–2 victory for Beazley over Ruffing. The Yankees had won eight World Series in a row since last losing in 1926—to the Cardinals, in Yankee Stadium. In the same 17-year span, the Cards had won four of six.

1943

The Yankees and Cardinals reached the World Series again in 1943, with the opposite result, as all lineups became increasingly haphazard and unfamiliar. Not only the quality of play but the quality of the baseball itself was in decline, as high-grade wool became less available. In 1941, the last normal year, the majors had hit .262, scored nine runs a game, and averaged 1.1 homers a game. In 1943, they hit .253, scored 7.8 runs, and hit 20 percent fewer homers. The difference was not just in talent.

NL—Their line-up was disrupted, but minor league replacements kept coming as the Cards ran off and won by 18 games over Cincinnati and 23½ over Brooklyn. Cooper's 21–6 and Lanier's 15–7 led the way to 105 St. Louis victories. Musial's .357 gave him the first of his seven batting titles. Ott and his Giants fell to last place, while the Cubs came up with a new home-run champion, Bill Nicholson (29). Bucky Harris, who was kept as Phillies' manager when Cox bought the team from Nugent, was replaced by Fitzsimmons when Carpenter took over.

All-Star Game—Played fully under lights for the first time, at Philadelphia, the 11th in the All-Star series was won for the eighth time by the Americans, 5–3. Bobby Doerr hit a three-run homer off Cooper in the second, and three pitchers made it stand up: Dutch Leonard, a Washington knuckleballer not to be confused with the one-time Boston pitcher of that name; Hal Newhouser, a young Detroit left-hander, and Hughson.

AL—The Yankees still had Keller, Gordon, Dickey, and some pitchers (Chandler 20–4, Bonham 15–8, Borowy 14–9, Murphy bouncing back from a bad year at 34). Their new first baseman was Nick Etten, from the Phillies, and he batted in 107 runs. Washington, managed by Ossie Bluege, stayed close for a while but finished 13½ games back.

WS—At the Stadium, the Yankees' Chandler started by beating the Cards' Lanier 4–2, but Cooper evened matters with a 4–3 decision over Bonham.

The third game was also in New York, since only one change of cities was adopted as a transportation-saving device. Alpha Brazle, another of the endless line of good St. Louis pitchers cultivated on the farm, was beating Borowy 2–1 until the Yankees had a five-run eighth, featuring a three-run triple by Billy Johnson, New York's farm-grown third baseman. That was the pivotal play. In St. Louis, Russo beat Lanier 2–1, scoring the winning run himself after hitting a double in the eighth, and Chandler's 10-hit 2–0 shutout needed only Dickey's two-run homer off Cooper in a final game marked by 20 men left on base. The Yankees had their revenge, for what it was worth.

1944

An all–St. Louis World Series, that most unlikely of baseball occurrences, came up in 1944 when the world at war was going through its most intensive phase and didn't get the kind of attention it would have commanded under other circumstances. But then, without the war, it probably would never have happened at all.

NL—The Cardinals still had their core—the Cooper brothers, Musial, Kurowski, Marion, Hopp, Lanier—and won 105 again, with a 73–27 start. Frisch's Pirates took second, 14½ games out, a game and a half ahead of McKechnie's Cincinnati. The following figures convey an idea of the imbalance: the Dodgers, finishing seventh, used 54 different players; the Reds used 41, including 15-year-old Joe Nuxhall (who pitched one inning); two other teams used 40, one 39. The Cards got by with 27.

Dixie Walker outhit Musial for the batting title, .357 to .347, while some pitchers had outstanding years: the Cards' Cooper 22–7, Pittsburgh's Rip Sewell 21–12, the Reds' Walters 23–8.

The Cubs' Nicholson remained the power king—33 homers, 122 runs batted in—and had a remarkable day on July 23 at the Polo Grounds. He hit four home runs in consecutive turns at bat, two in the first game of a doubleheader and two in the second, and was paid the ultimate compliment by opposing manager Ott, who certainly understood home runs and that 257-foot right-field foul line. With the Giants leading 10–7 in the eighth inning, the bases full, and Nicholson up, Ott ordered an intentional walk, forcing in a run—but only one run. As it happened, the Cubs tied the score anyhow, but the Giants finally won the game 12–10. Although few were on hand to see it, the story was told and retold for years.

AL—At the end of May, the Yankees were in their usual position, well ahead. Then they had a slump that lasted three months while the Browns opened a big lead, fell back, and survived a September stretch run with the Tigers. On Labor Day, the Browns and Yankees were virtually tied, the Tigers and Red Sox a couple of games back. On September 15, a five-game losing streak pulled the Yankees back, after the Red Sox had dropped out. The final weekend found the Tigers one game ahead facing Washington, the Browns hosting a four-game set with the Yankees.

All season, of course, baseball news was secondary. In June the Allies invaded Normandy. In July they broke out, in August they liberated Paris, in September the race to the Rhine began. But Armed Forces Radio brought word of that last American League weekend to outposts everywhere.

On Friday, the Browns' Jack Kramer and Nelson Potter beat the Yankees, 4–1 and 1–0, while the Tigers lost the second game of their twin bill, creating a tie. On Saturday, Denny Galehouse blanked the Yankees 2–0, while Hal Newhouser kept the Tigers even with his 29th victory. On Sunday, Detroit's Dizzy Trout, who had 27 victories, lost 4–1 to knuckleballer Leonard while the game in St. Louis was still on. The Browns broke a 2–2 tie in the fifth and went on to win 5–2, behind Sig Jakucki, a 34-year-old right-hander spending his first full season in the majors after having failed on his first try eight years earlier.

The statistics were taking on wartime colors. Cleveland's Boudreau was batting champion at .327, the Yankees' Etten led in homers with 22, and St. Louis shortstop Vern Stephens in runs batted in with 109. Etten's total was the lowest for a major league home-run leader since 1918, the year before Ruth's record 29; Stephens had the lowest since 1920; Boudreau was only one point lower than Appling the year before, but that made his average the lowest since 1919. They were producing dead-ball numbers, at least in part because the wartime ball was in fact relatively dead.

All-Star Game—At Pittsburgh's Forbes Field, under the lights, the Nationals pulled away in the late innings of a 7–1 victory, their most one-sided of the series.

WS—On paper, this Cardinals-Browns series was a mismatch, but the Browns gave it a good try. Galehouse beat Cooper in the opener 2–1, and the Cards had to go 11 innings to win the second 3–2. Then Kramer put the Browns ahead again 6–2.

That was all, however. Harry (the Cat) Brecheen won 5–1, Cooper beat Galehouse, 2–0, and Lanier and Ted Wilks combined on a 3–1 three-hitter to wrap it up.

1945

As "real" big leaguers began drifting back from service, the Cubs ended the reign of the Cardinals and faced Detroit, survivor of another last-day decision, in the Series. It went seven games, had the nation's full attention, and was won by the Tigers.

NL—Charlie Grimm had returned to the Cub dugout early in 1944, and now got them breaking out of the pack in July. The Cards, in their patented fashion, came along. With a week to go, the Cards came to Wrigley Field trailing by a game and a half. The Cubs, in July, had acquired Borowy from the Yankees in a "waiver" deal, although Borowy was 10–5 in the American League at that time. He did even better in the National and now stopped the Cards 6–5. Although the Cards won the second game of the series, the Cubs proceeded to win doubleheaders from the Reds and Pirates and finished three games ahead. Borowy wound up 11–2 as a Cub for a 21–12 season across two leagues, and the Cubs wound up with 20 doubleheader sweeps.

Cavaretta, 10 years after being a teenage phenom for the Cubs, won the batting title at .355,

three points better than Tommy Holmes of Boston, who had a 37-game hitting streak and led in homers with 28. Along with Borowy, the Cubs had Hank Wyse (22–10), Passeau (17–9), and Derringer (16–11). Cardinal pitchers were led by Red Barrett, acquired in May from the Braves, who had a 23–12 season (21 victories for the Cards), and Ken Burkhart (18–9).

AL—Greenberg, the first star to leave, was the first to come back, a civilian again on July 1 (as the defeat of Germany allowed some demobilization to begin). The Tigers were already well ahead of the Yankees and Senators at that point, managed by Steve O'Neill for the third year, relying on Newhouser and Trout, with an otherwise undistinguished lineup except for York. Newhouser was putting a 25–9 season behind his 29–9 of 1944, and Trout would be 18–15 after 27–14.

In the last 72 games, Greenberg hit .311 with 13 homers. In August, it was the Senators who made up ground, and on September 15 the Tigers came to Washington for a five-game series, with the teams tied for first place. The Tigers won three of them, but then staggered. In the abnormal schedule, the Senators completed their games a week early, their record 87–67. The Tigers were 86–64 with four to go and had to win two to clinch. On Wednesday, they split a doubleheader with Cleveland. That left two in St. Louis.

Rain forced everything into a Sunday doubleheader, and rain delayed the first game so long that it was evident that only one would be able to be completed. They finally started with Potter facing the Tigers' Virgil Trucks, fresh out of the navy. In the ninth-inning darkness, trailing 3–2, the Tigers filled the bases with one out—and Greenberg hit a grand-slam home run that meant the pennant.

This was the year, the only year, that there was no All-Star Game.

WS—The wartime pattern of three games in one city, four in the other, was still in force. But the war was officially over and the October 3 opener symbolized a return to the "way of Life" for which the war had been fought.

In Detroit, the Cubs scored seven runs off Newhouser in the first three innings, and Borowy pitched a six-hit shutout, 9–0. That could be ascribed to letdown after the Pennant drama, and sure enough, Trucks defeated Wyse 4–1, on the strength of a three-run homer by Greenberg. But the Cubs' Passeau produced a one-hitter, the best World Series game ever pitched so far, and the 3–0 victory sent the Cubs back to Chicago in good shape. (The hit was a second-inning single by York, so there wasn't any no-hit suspense.)

A four-run fourth was all Trout needed to get the Tigers even, 4–1. Greenberg contributed three doubles to an 8–4 victory for Newhouser, and the sixth game became a dogfight. The Cubs couldn't hold 5–1 and 7–3 leads, and when the eighth ended 7–7, Grimm brought in Borowy. He pitched four scoreless innings, and the Cubs won in the 12th on a run-scoring double by Hack.

There was a day off before the seventh game, so Borowy started on one day's rest against Newhouser. It was too soon. Three straight singles brought in Derringer, and a three-run double by 38-year-old Tiger catcher Paul Richards completed a five-run first. It ended 9–3.

AFTERMATH

To most people, including players and baseball's working population, "coming back from the war" meant picking up where they left off, the yearned-for return to "normal" life the way it used to be. In reality, of course, nothing could ever be the same, and the postwar world would be uncharted territory. A famous award-winning movie, *The Time of Our Lives,* dealt with this theme of misplaced expectations and bewildering new times.

That theme applied equally to baseball. On the surface, the returned stars would restore the old romance in the familiar way. Underneath, everything had changed. Landis was gone, and czarism gone with him. Night baseball was here. Independent minors were gone, and "organizations" were supreme (and profoundly influenced in their operations by military-industrial experience and models). MacPhail's Stadium Club was the entering wedge of modern marketing, for all its basic similarity to the beer-hall connections of the 1880s; difference in scale is difference in kind. Television's development would alter everything—not just the introduction of televised baseball games or other televised sports, but the very existence of television, which would permeate daily life. The Yankees, Dodgers, Phillies, and Braves were enter-

ing 1946 with drastically different ownerships than they had in 1942, and within months Cleveland and Pittsburgh would have comparable upheavals.

And, of course, steps to break the color line, in the person of Jackie Robinson but on a much larger scale, had been in the works for some time.

All this had happened out of the spotlight during the war years. The results would become visible only gradually at first, then overwhelmingly. But the break with the past was a greater break, more complete and more far-reaching, than those of 1920 or 1901.

Between the end of the 1945 World Series and the opening of the 1946 baseball season, steps were taken to form the All-America Football Conference (AAFC) to challenge the National Football League, and the Basketball Association of America, which would become the National Basketball Association and make viable big-league professional basketball. These would, in time and because of television, erode baseball's exclusivity as a "major league" sport. Also, some wealthy Mexicans decided to recruit U.S. players for a baseball league in Mexico. And the West Coast, its population exploding because of wartime and Dust Bowl migration, entered actively into the sports scene: the NFL champion Cleveland Rams moved to Los Angeles, the AAFC put two of its teams in California, and civilian air transport started to eliminate the word "inaccessible."

Amid these developments, perhaps the most important and subtle change in the national pastime was simply night baseball itself. It moved baseball across the imperceptible line between "sport" and "entertainment," pushing the business into competition with other businesses in ways it had not been forced to confront before, especially movies and television. It was a line that once crossed could not be recrossed, and since among all professional sports only baseball had enjoyed the cachet of "national game," only baseball could lose it. The others were in the entertainment business from their beginnings.

For many years, this fundamental change in psychological status went unrecognized or denied by the baseball world, resisted and mishandled. Nevertheless, it was all-encompassing. The original idea, 75 years before, had been to put this "game" on an efficient business basis to make money from it. Now began its evolution into a moneymaking business that happened to be using baseball games as its currency. In another 50 years, the difference in attitude would be reflected by a slogan for which the club owners paid a couple of million dollars to repair the public-relations damage done by the strike of 1994 and the cancellation of that year's World Series: "Welcome to the Show." Perhaps some advertising wizard believed that because the dialogue in a popular movie had minor league players referring to The Majors as "the Show" as short for "the Big Show," this was inside baseball talk with which the "audience" could be hooked. But before television, the *last* thing any baseball promoter would want to suggest was that the "game" was a "show"—a word that implies pre-arrangement and rehearsal. (Actually, ball players aspiring to the majors talked about getting to "the Bigs," not to "the Show.")

The atomic bomb had introduced a new word to public consciousness: "fallout." What happened in baseball from 1946 on was fallout from what the years 1941–45 had already set in motion.

CHAPTER 17

The Stars Are Back—and on TV!

B etween January 1, 1946, and December 31, 1953, the following were only some of the occurrences that made this the most eventful eight-year period in baseball history:

1. The racial barrier was broken, and black players, long recognized by their white peers as equal in ability, entered the organized-baseball mainstream.
2. The Mexican League signed players at inflated salaries (not always delivered) with no regard to the reserve, and Organized Baseball responded by blacklisting such players and anyone who played against them or dealt with them in any way.
3. The Second Commissionership, under a Happy Chandler given less authority, failed in several respects and ended with his being fired.
4. The 1922 antitrust exemption, upset by an appeals court, was reaffirmed by the Supreme Court, making the reserve system invulnerable.
5. An unsuccessful attempt to unionize the Pittsburgh Pirates nevertheless led to the first offer of working-condition agreements by the owners, intended to relieve pressure for labor militancy.
6. The elevation of National League president Ford Frick to the commissionership gave baseball, for the first time, "one of its own" in that position.

7. Attendance, and therefore revenue, took a roller-coaster ride, soaring to double all previous records in the immediate postwar boom, plunging halfway back to prewar levels when the boom ran out, despite the preponderance of night games.

8. Local telecasts became common, and the shape of national television became discernible.

9. Bill Veeck Jr., as owner-operator of the Indians and then the Browns, spread revolutionary promotional ideas and brought to the surface the possibility of moving franchises, a thought moribund since 1903.

10. Every club acquired a farm system.

11. The Pacific Coast League's request for "major status" was turned down, but a new high level of minors—Triple A—was created.

12. Nationally circulated radio broadcasts of major league games paved the way for television and started to undermine the minors.

13. The Yankees created a new dynasty, stronger than any previous one, while the Dodgers replaced the Cardinals as the other chief operator of farm-system methodology.

14. A major league team actually did move for the first time in 50 years when the Braves went from Boston to Milwaukee.

There were other changes, but let's take these one at a time.

INTEGRATION

Jim Crow segregation settled into baseball, as it did in the rest of U.S. society, in the last decade of the 19th century. Even before that, the founders of the National League, just 11 years after the Civil War and 13 years after the Emancipation Proclamation, had a gentleman's agreement not to use "colored" players, defined almost exclusively by the tint of one's skin. A light enough Negro might pass, at least for a while, as "Indian" or "Cuban," and if really light enough, might pass into the white world altogether. In the absence of genetic tests, only appearance mattered, unless specific family history turned up.

Baseball was no different than the culture in which it was embedded. In segregated times, it was rigidly segregated. Black baseball, during the early 20th century, developed along its own lines and found its own important cultural niche in the black community.

However, segregation didn't mean no contact between black and white players. Outside the Organized-Baseball context, they played as opponents and even teammates in barnstorming exhibitions and semipro circumstances. White stars often expressed their respect for the best black players as equals, although such remarks were not publicized by an equally segregated media world.

In the 1930's, two Negro leagues, the National and American, gave black base-ball a strong structure (and a Negro World Series) and widespread off-season exhi-bition action with the most prominent white players—who nevertheless did not ques-tion (at least out loud) segregation as such. The fact that Negro league teams used major league parks, drew big crowds, and were valuable tenants helped make their players much more familiar to the professional baseball community than to the white world at large.

In 1942 the first serious attempts at integration began. "Manpower shortage" was a problem in every phase of civilian life, and with more and more professional play-ers going into service, the need for replacement was weakening traditional avoidance of an obvious talent pool.

That spring, Jackie Robinson and one of his UCLA teammates got a look from manager Dykes at the White Sox training camp in Pasadena. Dykes was impressed by Robinson. On the other coast, manager Durocher of the Dodgers declared he'd be perfectly willing to manage "them." For his public remark, he was promptly rebuked by Landis.

That December, Paul Robeson, the great singer and fighter for equal rights, sought to discuss matters with the club owners at their winter meeting. Landis ruled that the subject would not be pursued and cut him short. At the same time, in strict privacy, Rickey notified the Brooklyn directors who had just brought him in as MacPhail's successor that he would be signing "colored" players before long.

Not while Landis was alive, however. When the Pirates gave Roy Campanella a tryout, Campanella heard no more about it. When Griffith, owner of the Washing-ton Senators, approached Josh Gibson and Buck Leonard, two of the biggest Negro stars, they said yes, but he never got back to them. When Bill Veeck Jr. tried to buy the Philadelphia Phillies, the team the league was eager to peddle for Gerry Nugent, he intended to stock them with Negro league players. Suddenly the Phillies weren't available, and soon they were sold to Carpenter of the DuPonts. This was 1943.

The source of all the backstage pressure was Landis. He was not only a bigot but also a hypocrite, making public statements that "no regulations" barred Negroes from Organized Baseball while making it clear that any club trying to hire one would have to deal with him. In the late stages of czarism, on top of all the problems of De-pression and war, no owner was prepared to engage in that fight.

Minor league clubs were especially interested in 1942 and 1943, in breaking the color line. But they, too were in no position to buck the commissioner's known views.

So nothing happened. In this, as in many of his other autocratic practices, Lan-dis did baseball a tremendous disservice. If the opportunity to integrate the game had been grasped in the middle of the 1930's, great financial and performance benefits might have flowed into baseball when help was needed.

But perhaps not, as we'll see in a moment.

In any case, nothing happened until Landis died in 1944.

In 1945, with the end of the war in sight, Rickey was scouting black players intensively, all over the Caribbean area as well as in the United States. He pretended he was going to start another Negro league but he was actually looking for the right man to handle what he knew would be a horribly difficult situation. By August, he had settled on Robinson. On August 28, in the Dodger office in Brooklyn, he signed Robinson to a 1946 contract with Montreal, the top Dodger farm club—secretly.

He made the announcement on October 23, after the 1945 World Series, and it got a generally hostile reception outside New York. For the 1946 season, he signed four other black players: Campanella and Don Newcombe, for Nashua, New Hampshire, in the class B New England League, and John Wright and Roy Partlow, pitchers, who tried out at Montreal before going down to Three Rivers in the Class C Canadian-American League.

Robinson broke in with a four-hit performance at Roosevelt Stadium in Jersey City and had a spectacular season at Montreal, which went on to win the Little World Series. Three Rivers finished first in its league. Nashua finished second but won the postseason play-off.

How did major league club owners react? That August, at a meeting to discuss the situation, they took no official action but expressed alarm that the presence of Negroes on their teams might "lessen franchise value." This "property value" rationalization for maintaining segregated neighborhoods would be used throughout American society for the next 20 years at least, and it still exists.

So it can't all be blamed on Landis, a creature of his time.

In spring training of 1947, Dixie Walker led a petition drive to keep Robinson from being promoted to the Dodgers. Younger players like Reese and Reiser refused to go along with that. Rickey having hoped to avoid such a split, announced on April 10 that Robinson would be a Dodger—and play first base. (He had played second at Montreal, but the Dodgers had Eddie Stanky, a Durocher favorite, at second and no star at first.) After the season, Rickey traded Walker away, and Stanky too.

The day before the Robinson announcement, Durocher had been suspended for the season by Commissioner Chandler (we'll come to that in a moment), so Robinson's first big-league manager was Burt Shotton, an old associate of Rickey's.

In Montreal, Robinson had been abused to the point of breakdown by opposing players: thrown at, spiked, vilified verbally. He faced the same treatment in the majors. But Rickey had chosen his man well: Robinson could handle it.

A crisis moment came in May. Rumors reached Frick, the league president, that the Cardinal players were planning to refuse to play against Robinson. (St. Louis and Cincinnati were the two cities most "southern" in their prevailing attitudes.) He told them directly: do anything like that, and you're suspended for good. No protest materialized.

By July, Veeck had brought Larry Doby to Cleveland, and the brothers DeWitt, owners of the Browns, signed Henry Thompson and Willard Brown. None of these blacks did well, but they helped make the point that there was no turning back. On August 25, Dan Bankhead made his debut as a Dodger pitcher. Fewer than a dozen black players were scattered through the minors—but at least there were some.

Robinson had a great first year. The Dodgers won the pennant. Doby became a regular in 1948, and Cleveland won that year's pennant, aided from July on by 42-year-old Satchel Paige.

In 1949, the Giants brought up Monte Irvin and Henry Thompson, who would soon help them win two pennants. All three Triple A leagues had outstanding black players, and seven of the 16 major league clubs had broken their own farm system's color line: Giants, Dodgers, Yankees, Cubs, Braves, Indians, and Browns.

For 1950, the Braves paid the Dodgers $100,000 for Sam Jethroe, center fielder and base-stealing whiz, who became Rookie of the Year. In 1951, the Giants brought up Willie Mays, and the White Sox, Minnie Minoso. Yet by August of 1953, there were still no black players on 10 of the 16 major league teams. The next month, the Cubs brought up Ernie Banks, and in 1954 there were only four all-white teams. Progress would be slow. Only the best talents were welcome, unwritten quotas existed, and off-field segregation was still virulent. But the issue, as an issue, was settled. Baseball on the field was racially integrated.

This killed, naturally, the Negro leagues, although it represented justice and opportunity for individual players. But what it really showed to white society was the full extent of the deprivation to which it had subjected itself by clinging to segregation as long as it did.

COMMISSIONER CHANDLER

On the integration issue, Chandler was a benign semineutral. He didn't promote integration, but he didn't resist it, and he supported Rickey and Frick in showdowns. He was from a segregated state, Kentucky, but he was also a Roosevelt Democrat. His troubles came from entirely different directions.

His employers wanted four things: a strong public image, which Landis had provided; noninterference in their business decisions, which Landis overrode in ways the new contract now prevented; efficient administration in carrying out policies *they* chose; and avoidance of lawsuits, combined with influence in Washington as necessary.

Chandler flunked on all four counts. His image was wrong. His rulings, though few, were unwelcome when important (as in the Durocher case, the beginning of his undoing). He wasn't very efficient, and—here we have the fatal flaw—he didn't keep them out of court.

The Landis image—hands folded on a box-seat railing, chin resting on hands, all under a floppy hat—suggested an independent autocrat protecting the public from squabbling and potentially dishonest club owners and players. Chandler was the prototype of a glad-handing politician, offending no one, sometimes clownish, enthusiastic but not credibly authoritative. The New York Baseball Writers at their annual dinner, which was, in the 1930–1960 period, baseball's foremost social function, portrayed him as a Senator Claghorn type (from the *Fred Allen Comedy Hour*) shouting, "Ah loves baseball!" at the least provocation.

The Leo Durocher incident in 1947 went as follows: MacPhail had signed Charlie Dressen and Red Corriden, Leo's coaches in Brooklyn, for the Yankees for the 1947 season, and there were rumors that he wanted Leo to manage, since Joe McCarthy had left in the middle of the 1946 season. Leo's behavior had long been under fire—fights with fans and umpires, public condemnation by church groups about his divorce and life-style, racetrack visits frowned upon by Landis—and Rickey, in his heart, wouldn't have minded his leaving Brooklyn. At a spring-training exhibition in Havana, Leo pointed to some prominent gambling (horse-racing) figures sitting in MacPhail's box, presumably his guests. "If that was my box, I'd be barred from baseball," Durocher told the sportswriters, or something like that.

MacPhail demanded that the commissioner do something about this insult and implied attack on his integrity. (All Leo had actually done, of course, was claim he was being subjected to a double standard, which he was, in spades, as Chandler promptly proved.) Chandler held a hearing on March 24, another on March 28, and on April 9, just before the season was to open, suspended Durocher for one year.

The baseball public—fans as well as other club owners—found this shocking. To suddenly ban an outstanding manager from a pennant contender on the eve of the season, for an undefined crime that didn't seem terrible no matter how you described it, did the exact opposite of "uphold the integrity of the competition." Making it worse was everyone's awareness that MacPhail had been Chandler's champion and was in conflict with Rickey, so Chandler's decision looked like a political favor returned.

(And what's wrong with that? a U.S. senator might ask.)

For at least some other owners, it displayed poor judgment and unreliability on the part of their new commissioner. What if he acted so arbitrarily in something involving *them?*

Rickey was not so perturbed. He called in Burt Shotton, who had recently managed the Phillies, to manage the Dodgers. He and Shotton had been close for 30 years or more; Rickey used Shotton as his "Sunday manager" when Rickey ran the Browns before World War I and was living up to his family vow not to work baseball games on Sundays. Shotton knew the system, knew baseball, was totally loyal and, ultimately, highly successful. Durocher suffered no visible damage from his year off and returned to scale greater heights than ever. MacPhail self-destructed over other issues before the year was out. The loser was Chandler.

Finally, though, there was the Mexican League and its fallout. Chandler followed the book by blacklisting for five years those who went to the league, called contract jumpers even if it was only the reserve clause they were violating. But he could do nothing, by persuasion or intimidation or creative compromise (the Landis methods), to keep the affected players from suing. This strengthened and encouraged other minor leaguers, not involved in the Mexican caper, to press their cases against farm-system abuses. (As for influence in Washington, it turned out not to be needed, and not possessed by Chandler anyhow.)

Danny Gardella, a Giant outfielder, had the strongest antitrust case as a Mexican League refugee. He played in an outlaw Canadian league in 1947 and filed suit in October. In February 1949, an appeals court ruled 2–1 that the case merited going to trial, where it seemed like Gardella would win. In April, another court rejected an appeal from players for immediate reinstatement—whereupon Chandler lifted the ban, saying he could do that now that the courts weren't "forcing" him to.

But the Gardella case and others were still working their way up to the Supreme Court amid widely held legal opinions that the 1922 antitrust exemption could not survive reexamination. In October 1949, Gardella settled secretly for $60,000 (some said it was $300,000), but other cases continued.

By 1950, a substantial minority of the owners wanted Chandler out. He hadn't delivered, he was spending their money on settlements while still facing millions in punitive damages, and his image wasn't doing them any good. What they wanted, after Landis, was the image of czarism without its substance; now they had neither.

At the December 1950 winter meetings, an earlier promise to extend Chandler's contract (which would expire in 1952) came up for a vote. It needed 12 yesses. It got only nine. Chandler vowed to finish his term. In March, another vote came out 9–7 again. Against him were the Yankees, White Sox, and Pirates (alienated by player-deal rulings), Cards and Browns, Phils and Braves, and eventually Cleveland. In April, he offered his buy-out terms. In June, they were accepted. In July, he resigned. In August, a search committee pared its candidate list from 60 to nine, including four generals, a governor of Ohio, a college president, Frick, and Warren Giles, general manager of the Cincinnati Reds.

On September 20 in Chicago, at a nine-hour meeting, Frick and Giles were deadlocked through 16 ballots. Then Giles withdrew, Frick was elected 14–2, and Giles was named his successor as president of the National League.

Now, for the first time since the Ban Johnson Commission evaporated in 1920, they had "a baseball man" at the top of the hierarchy.

THE MEXICAN LEAGUE

Five Pascual brothers belonged to one of Mexico's richest and most politically powerful families. Jorge was the one determined to upgrade Mexican baseball by attracting major leaguers with fabulous (by that day's standards) offers of wealth. Many of the top black stars, barred from U.S. baseball, had been playing in Mexico for years.

In February of 1946, the Pascuals signed eight players from major league rosters, only one of whom was a U.S. citizen: Gardella. In April, Michey Owen, the Dodger catcher, was the most prominent player to go. Offers of $100,000 a year for three years to Williams and Feller were turned down. The season began with 27 U.S. players, seven of whom had played 100 or more games in the majors in 1945. The Pascuals brought Babe Ruth down to "consider" being commissioner or a manger. (He was polite, then went home.) In June, Breadon went down to talk to Pascual, who had made overtures to Musial, and received a promise that no more Cardinal players would be touched. (Pitchers Max Lanier and Fred Martin had gone to Mexico.) Chandler wanted to fine Breadon $5,000 for, evidently, "talking to the enemy," but Frick persuaded him not to do it. Chalk up another vote against Chandler; remember, Breadon had made even Landis back down on the farm-system issue.)

Vern Stephens, the heavy-hitting shortstop of the Browns, accepted a $250,000 deal, found life impossible in Mexico, had to sneak out of the country (Pascual influence included police and military), and returned on the promise that the Browns would trade him to a contender. They did: the Red Sox.

In August, Mickey Owen also came back and asked Chandler for reinstatement. He was turned down, and all the lawsuits followed. By 1948, the Mexican League was a dead issue on both sides of the border, a financial as well as artistic failure.

It had made vivid, however, the omnipresent and overriding fear club owners live with: competing employers, whoever and wherever they are, can drive up salaries.

ANTITRUST

The 1922 decision written by Justice Oliver Wendell Holmes took the position that staging baseball games was essentially a "local" enterprise, even if players were transported across state lines, and therefore not "interstate commerce," the only commerce Congress was allowed to regulate. Therefore, laws passed by Congress (the Sherman and Clayton Anti-Trust Acts) could not apply to baseball. Baseball was exempt.

This reasoning was soon held ludicrous by most of the legal community, but there it was. In 1922, baseball was the only major commercial team sport. In the 1940s, the Supreme Court explicitly rejected comparable status for pro football, boxing, moviemaking, and anything else that came its way, making clear its view that mistaken reasoning in the past was no reason to repeat it.

Baseball's powerful publicity and myth-making machinery put a different spin on the situation. It told everyone that the highest court in the land had declared that baseball was "a sport, not a business" (quite the opposite of what the court actually said), and therefore on a higher moral plane (in some ill-defined manner). The phrase took root by repetition and evolved into the player complaint, "If you tell them it's a game, they tell you it's a business; if you say it's a business, they tell you it's a game."

That it is obviously both, without internal contradiction, became obscured. Playing baseball is a game. Staging games is a business. To play the game *for money* one must operate the business.

Heck, they had that figured out in 1876.

But the exemption gave baseball a free ride in three respects. It shut off the practical possibility of challenge by another league (like the Federal). It removed complications from farm-system and radio-television arrangements. And it protected the reserve system from attack on the grounds of abusive monopolistic practice.

In 1949, after the Gardella opinion by such distinguished jurists as Learned Hand and Jerome N. Frank, it was being taken for granted that the exemption would not survive another visit to the Supreme Court. Gardella was bought off, but others weren't (or didn't seem important enough), and the case that got there involved a Yankee farmhand named George Toolson, claiming he was blacklisted for refusing to report to a club to which he had been assigned against his will.

Anticipating defeat, baseball's friends in Congress prepared various bills to make the exemption explicit. Hearings before a House judiciary subcommittee headed by Emmanuel Celler, Democrat from Brooklyn, took place during the summer and fall of 1951, got massive publicity, and produced the first well-documented material about baseball finances. The Committee's recommendation: wait and see.

Almost two years later, on November 9, 1953, the Court ruled on Toolson. By 7–2, it upheld the exemption, while agreeing that it made no sense. However, since the baseball business had been allowed to develop for 30 years thinking that it *was* exempt, with investments made accordingly, the Court would not upset the earlier decision and create retroactive problems. It urged Congress to legislate whatever status it thought baseball should have.

The dissenting opinions by Judges Burton and Reed were scathing. The majority had decided that since Congress had not, in 30 years, specifically revoked the 1922 result, it was apparently okay with Congress. The dissenters pointed out that Congress had not, in 30 years, enacted any exemption to its own laws, which contained no exemption to begin with. The majority excused itself from looking at "underlying principles." The dissenters said they should.

In my own opinion—wholly personal and shared by few if any—the victory was a Pyrrhic one for baseball. It gave ownership a false sense of security and fed its arrogance, and fighting endlessly to preserve the exemption deflected its attention from devising needed and constructive reforms.

If forced to conform to the law under the conditions that existed in 1953, baseball might have developed patterns far more favorable to management than those forced upon it by organized players 20 years later. All the other sports proved they could thrive within the antitrust laws. Baseball could have too and perhaps have escaped the path that led eventually to protracted labor war and the debacle of 1994.

But that's just my peculiar opinion.

UNIONIZATION

War industry had greatly strengthened the power and appeal of union labor. Pittsburgh, home of the steel industry, was a strong union town. Early in 1946, an attorney named Robert Murphy organized the American Baseball Guild among Pirate Players. In June his call for a strike vote carried by only 20–16, short of the two-thirds needed for union certification. That movement died.

But the warning it represented, along with the Mexican League, moved the owners to give the players something—unilaterally and voluntarily, of course. The player contract and league regulations were rewritten to provide for:

A minimum salary of $5,000

A maximum cut of 25 percent in a renewed contract

A moving allowance of $500 if traded in season, and expense money to go home at the end of a season

Medical coverage for game-related injuries

Full pay if injured or sent to the minors

Expense money of $25 a week during spring training (when there is no salary), quickly named "Murphy money"

Expansion to 30 days from 10 days for permissible postseason barnstorming

Consideration of some sort of pension plan, to be funded from World Series and All-Star Game receipts in some way. (A plan was adopted in 1947.)

Simply looking at the "improvements" granted by that list tells you the kind of things players *didn't* have up to that time.

The pension idea—a hot topic on everyone's mind after military experience and in organized-labor bargaining so soon after the 1935 establishment of Social Security—turned out to be the acorn out of which the oak of player labor organization would grow.

FORD FRICK

Frick was the first (and I would argue the last) baseball commissioner who really understood the job's function and limitations. He held the office for 15 years and was often vilified by outsiders for "knuckling under" to club-owner demands, especially when teams started moving out of old cities for greener pastures. But that was the whole point: he was *supposed* to carry out their wishes, seeing that they acted in an orderly manner with due regard for public relations, health of the whole, and minimum friction, using maximum persuasion in private for whatever particular action seemed preferable in his best judgment. He had no illusions about "ruling;" he knew his job was to "guide."

"That's not in my jurisdiction," a characteristic Frick remark that became a club in the hands of those who wished to beat him over the head, was actually the core of his success. He knew baseball inside out, as reporter, as intimate of players, as publicity man, and, after being National League president, as administrator dealing with diverse club owners. He knew that ultimate power resided in the only people who had money invested and property rights, the owners; that they didn't want any commissioner at all except for public-relations purposes and to settle small-scale disagreements that didn't touch vital interests; that whatever Landis had done, the new contract didn't permit; that they needed, wanted, and would tolerate only a peacekeeper, not a dictator.

And since the business was a protected monopoly, a peacekeeper was all it required.

Frick had credibility because of his media background and long personal contact with so many in the business. His public manner was pompous enough, but not too pompous. He had no empire-building tendencies as a bureaucrat, keeping the office small. He did all right as a congressional witness, and better than that in behind-the-scenes talk.

He would leave baseball in 1965 healthier than he found it in 1951.

ATTENDANCE

Before 1946, baseball's peak attendance was 10.1 million in 1930. In 1940, before the war, it was about the same: 9.8 million. Pent-up demand, especially for entertainment, and unspent wages created a business boom in the years 1946–48. Then an economic reaction set in, a recession. Here's what happened:

Year	Attendance (in millions)	Change from Previous Year	
1945	10.8	—	—
1946	18.5	Up 71%	—
1947	19.9	Up 7.6%	—
1948	20.9	Up 5%	—
1949	20.2	—	Down 3%
1950	17.5	—	Down 13.4%
1951	16.1	—	Down 8%
1952	14.6	—	Down 9.3%
1953	14.4	—	Down 1.4%

The drop from the 1948 peak to 1953 is 31 percent. But 1953 includes the huge increase in Milwaukee. The 1948 attendance was 1.3 million per club—a level not reached again until 1976. In all of baseball's previous history, a team had drawn one million only 18 times, exactly half of them by Babe Ruth's Yankees. In the period 1946–49, that milestone was reached 43 times in four years. With lights added, Yankee Stadium had 2.27 million customers in 1946, and Veeck's well-promoted and champion Indians of 1948 went to 2.62 million. The next time the Indians won a pennant, six years later in 1954, they drew only 1.33 million.

The rise and fall had very little to do with "baseball's appeal to the public." It reflected general economic conditions, particular marketing situations, variations in quality of club management, and the advent of television. Similar fluctuations had occurred between the two great wars. This should be noted when we get to the hysterical pronouncements that accompanied the aftermath of the 1994 shutdown.

But the new rule of thumb was: you had to draw a million people to have a prosperous season.

TELEVISION AND RADIO

In 1947, every team but Pittsburgh had a local television deal, carrying home games. (Line charges for away games were still too expensive.) Teams got between $15,000 and $75,000 for the rights. The Giants had a $400,000 package for radio and television combined. In 1949, a new World Series radio deal with the Gillette Razor Company amounted to just under $200,000 a year for seven years, some of it earmarked for the pension fund. In December of 1950, while he was being given his no-confidence vote, Chandler concluded a World Series television deal with Gillette for $1 million a year for six years.

Along with the income from inflated attendance, this meant baseball was rolling in wealth. But the owners were in no mood to share it. The players had to beg for any improvement in the pension fund, and all their other requests were ignored. Nor would owners share with each other, as Veeck would learn. The irony was, they persistently underpriced their product. David Sarnoff, head of RCA, revealed this in a speech years later. The television industry's problem, he said, was to get enough sets into people's homes to create an audience large enough for advertisers' needs. What would make people buy sets? What programs would entice them? "We had to have baseball games," he said, "and if they had demanded millions for the rights, we would have had to give it to them."

Then attendance started to decline, and broadcast money loomed more important as gate receipts fell. Local radio rights increased. Since 1948, the Liberty Radio Network had been doing a "game of the day" nationally by studio re-creation, reaching 240 stations in 33 states, but the majors kept their live broadcasts out of minor league venues. However, the Giant-Dodger pennant playoff of 1951—the one climaxed by Bobby Thomson's homer—was televised nationally, and five days later all restrictions on major league radio and television broadcasts were dropped. A new source of income had opened up.

In 1952, saturation broadcasting began killing the minors. In 1953, the White Sox, Indians, and athletics entered an agreement with the ABC network for a Saturday "Game of the Week." Every team except Milwaukee had its own television deal and gave reciprocal permission to the home team when it was a visitor, although both St. Louis teams asked for a share of the local rights fees. The Mutual Radio Network picked up the failed Liberty operation, for a fee. The basic shift away from total dependence on ticket sales had begun.

The 1952 estimate for aggregate TV-only income for the majors was $5 million. Newark, New Jersey, provided an early example of the effect on the minors. As the crown jewel of the Yankee farm system, in a city whose own population was 440,000, a half hour from Manhattan, the Newark Bears got full coverage in New York newspapers, had a flourishing radio network even before the Giants and Yankees did any broadcasting, and sold 300,000 tickets in 1946. In 1949, they sold 88,000, and in January of 1950 the Yankees sold the team to the Cubs, who moved it to Springfield, Massachusetts.

In other words, even the most successful minor league team was dead if it lived in the "television shadow" of a major team. National radio and television would spread this process through the less-populated hinterlands as time went on.

FARM SYSTEMS

The whole minor league story is best told by a table.

Year	No. of Leagues	No. of Farm Clubs	Attendance (in Millions)
1945	12	68	10
1946	43	197	33
1947	52	243	40.5
1948	58	281	41.5
1949	59	243	42
1950	58	210	35
1951	50	172	28
1952	43	166	25
1953	38	150	22

In 1945, only the White Sox had no farm club. Brooklyn had the most, nine.

By 1948, no club had fewer than 10 (the Athletics). Brooklyn (26) and the Yankees (24) had the most.

By 1953 everyone had a system and knew it didn't have to be too big. Sizes ranged between 6 (Red Sox) and 16 (Cardinals).

By 1961, when major league expansion began, the minors settled in at an average of 19 leagues, steady to the present day.

The issue was stability. Between 1922 and 1932, under independent operation, in a total of 187 league-seasons 30 minor leagues failed to finish a year they started. After that, in more than 500 league-seasons through 1953, there was only one year in which more than one league failed, and only six times did that happen. The exception was 1942, during the military buildup, when five leagues failed.

But Dreyfuss and Navin had not been totally wrong in their assessment to Landis in 1921. A farm system was *not* economically viable if allowed to grow too large to fit Rickey's idea of the quantity producing cream to skim. It had to be trimmed to concentrate *only* on developing promising talent, sloughing off career minor leaguers and local followings. That realization accounts for the contraction that began in 1950. During the Depression, only farm systems kept the minors alive. In the postwar boom, everything thrived. Then the new real world began to manifest itself.

VEECK AS IN WRECK

No individual, not even Rickey, had as great an impact on the modern baseball business as Bill Veeck Jr., son of the man who ran the Cubs for William Wrigley. His promotional genius altered the way all others did business, either by imitation or by dealing with the consequences of their opposition to him, his methods, and his ideas. His activities will pop up again and again in our year-by-year sections, but his key period was the postwar era and his influence must be summarized.

The name is pronounced "Veck." People saw its spelling and inevitably said "Veek." When he wrote his first book, in 1962, he called it *Veeck as in Wreck,* which is what he used to tell people to straighten them out. So of course book buyers asked for "Veek as in Wreck." Failure to get others to accept an eminently sensible concept was the story of his life.

As a wounded marine with a wooden leg, he was back in the States in 1944 and operated the Milwaukee Brewers of the American Association. When his old buddy Jolly Cholly Grimm was called back to manage the Cubs for the third time, Veeck brought in Casey Stengel as manager. In 1946, he figured out a way to take advantage of new tax laws to finance a club through capital gains and depreciation provisions (when wealthy people were in a 91 percent income-tax bracket and eager for legal tax breaks). He formed a syndicate that bought the Indians. Within a year and a half, he had them winning the World Series and outdrawing the mighty Yankees. He had that rarest of combinations, excellent baseball judgment and a circus mentality for promotion. He sold fun, giveaways, and special events instead of dignity while delivering the basic product, a winning team. After the 1949 season, he sold the Indians and set his sights on the Browns. He believed he could drive the Cardinals, who had deteriorated after Breadon sold out, out of town. He bought the Browns in June of 1951 and started building them up. But in February 1953, the Cardinals were acquired by Anheuser Busch, the local corporate gorilla and national business giant, and Veeck's belief that St. Louis was a one-team city meant that the Browns would have to be the ones to leave.

Things he advocated made enemies among his peers. He wanted a visitor's share of local radio-television money (for providing half the show). He wanted an unrestricted draft of minor league players after one year (which would cut into farm-system stockpiling). And his promotions either showed up others as stodgy or forced them to prove they weren't by expending effort and money.

The Establishment decided baseball would be better off without him. The only to get rid of him was to make him go broke. The way to do that was to keep him in St. Louis.

Milwaukee was now the top farm club of the Boston Braves. Baltimore had an independent International League team ever since the Old Orioles had become the New York Yankees in 1903. Veeck was ready to move to either city. Milwaukee was already building a new stadium, but Lou Perini, who owned the Braves, had a failing situation in Boston. If anyone was going to Milwaukee, it would be him. Fine, said Veeck, I'll go to Baltimore.

In March 1953, his fellow American League owners vetoed the move, claiming it was too near the opening of the season to make such a drastic change. Two days later, the National League voted 8–0 to let Perini take the Braves to Milwaukee immediately. Stuck for a lame-duck season in St. Louis, Veeck hocked everything in sight (including his Arizona ranch) and sold good players to get through the year so that he could move to Baltimore in 1954. When the time came, he was turned down again: only if you sell the team, was the message. He had no choice. He sold it to a Baltimore group, and the Establishment, led by the Yankees, and breathed easier.

The significance of Veeck is that he forced an end to 50 years of franchise stagnation, just as Rickey had forced an end to segregation. Sooner or later, it would have happened anyhow, but they actually *did* it.

Del Webb, of the Yankees, had been pushing for a team in Los Angeles. Veeck would have been happy to take the Browns there, but no park was available, and the Cubs, who owned the minor league Angels, wouldn't permit it anyhow. Veeck forced

Perini to go to Milwaukee before Perini wanted to, and the runaway success there un-plugged franchise moves for everyone. Webb, meanwhile, got his league to commit to expansion. Without Veeck's goading, baseball history would have taken quite different turns.

We'll hear from him again and again as the story goes on.

THE PACIFIC COAST LEAGUE

Explosive population growth in California after the war stimulated longstanding Pacific Coast League desires for higher status. Requests to become a third major league—that is, free from draft and other provisions—were rebuffed annually. Finally, when the PCL threatened to pull out of Organized Baseball in 1952, it was granted an "open" classification—still Triple A, but with greater rights to hang onto players it wanted. But once talk began of moving existing teams, and the Braves actually moved, Los Angeles was no longer interested in a promoted PCL but in the real thing: a major league franchise, new or acquired, of its own. Veeck's talk of moving the Browns had the indirect effect of dooming the Pacific Coast League.

RADIO AND THE MINORS

The main issues here have already been discussed, but a significant difference between radio and television in the 1950s should be noted. The TV signal extended only in a radius of a few miles, and hooking in distant stations was expensive. Regular AM radio stations had a much longer reach, and putting networks together was easy and cheap. So radio, at this point, was hurting the rural minors while making more money for the majors than television was.

A NEW YANKEE DYNASTY

In the 1920s and 1930s, the Yankees had won 11 pennants in 20 years and provoked the cry to "Break Up the Yankees." They won three more in the 1941–43 seasons and were stopped, apparently, only by the war. They threatened no one in 1946 but won going away in 1947 and lost only on the final day in 1948. Then they won 14 of the next 16 years, and no one said break up anything. There were three reasons for the different reactions. First, while dominant consecutively, they were not so dominant within a season so often, providing more close races than one-sided ones. Second, others had become accustomed to living off the money the Yankees generated.

Third, the television age put a premium on *national, simultaneous, supralocal,* star-celebrity appeal, and that's what the Yankees had. All the forces already mentioned—farm systems, broadcast, weakened commissionership, night games, ironclad reserve—worked to strengthen the elements of self-perpetuation in the Yankee operation.

BOSTON TO MILWAUKEE

The move of the Braves, only semivoluntary, is the crossroads event of 20th-century baseball. It demonstrated conclusively that (1) a team *can* move, even at the last minute; (2) unimagined riches can be found in a new location; (3) a new ball park is the key magnet in attracting a team to move—or stay; (4) a city classified historically and demographically as "minor league" can become major merely by changing the label (opening the door to the inclusion of so many smaller makets that the market-size disparities would eventually tear baseball apart); (5) not only is tradition expendable but abandoning it may actually be profitable.

Perini was one of three Boston contractors who bought the failing Braves in 1942. Their operation was turned over to John Quinn, Bob's son, who built a first-class farm system as soon as the war ended and money became available. In 1948, the Braves won their first pennant since the 1914 miracle while the neighboring Red Sox were losing theirs in a play-off, and drawing 1.45 million to the Red Sox's 1.55 million. Then, as quickly as they rose, they fell: manager Billy Southworth self-destructed, the players rebelled, the recession hit everyone, the Red Sox stayed glamorous, a bad trade made things worse, promising newcomers weren't quite ready. In four seasons the Braves dropped to seventh place and a 1952 attendance of 280,000, in a deteriorating facility.

Once Veeck started talking about Milwaukee, it was impossible to sell minor league baseball there—and the Braves, as owners of the Brewers, would be the ones keeping major league baseball out. By now, Perini and his brothers were sole owners of the team. Milwaukee was their escape hatch. Even if they wanted (as they said) to stay in Boston longer, they couldn't let someone else go to Milwaukee and find themselves locked out. Milwaukee had one thing they didn't, a new stadium almost completed.

So they went—apprehensively, motivated by other agendas (including the internal war against Veeck), with no idea of how much history they would make.

In 1953, with better players and amid civic enthusiasm that surpassed even Brooklyn's, they became a contending team and drew 1.83 million, the highest ever in the National League's 78 years of existence. Over the next five years, they would win two pennants and a World Series and sell more than 10 million tickets.

The effect on baseball was much like the effect of the California Gold Rush on America: it changed the map forever.

So much for our list of 1946–53 developments. Among the "others" two need mentioning: the bonus problem, and a comprehensive list of ownership changes.

BONUS PLAYERS

The farm-system approach had an Achilles' heel. Before, players used to enter the professional ranks thorough the minors. Now major league scouts were competing for top high school and college talent to *assign* them to the minors. In the postwar world, a good prospect could demand—and get—a bonus for signing, since the reserve system meant his first contract tied him up for life.

The bonuses got out of hand right away. By 1940, the Tigers were giving Dick Wakefield, coming out of Michigan, $52,000. By 1947, there was a "bonus rule" in place: a player who received $6,000 or more could not be optioned out. The club he signed with (it could be a minor league club) had to keep him or subject him to the draft-waiver system.

Such a rule was hard to police, and in 1950 it was repealed. By 1952, a total of $4.5 million was being laid out for bonuses to untried players, almost as much as was coming in from television. A new bonus rule was adopted: at $4,000 and above, the player had to stay on the major league active roster for two years or be put up for grabs. (That's how Sandy Koufax spent his first two seasons with the Dodgers.)

The underlying problem was less a matter of dollars, as such, than the inherent unpredictability of talent development. Here's an example. In 1952, Pittsburgh had two teenage pitchers on its Bristol team in the Class D Appalachian League. In May, Ron Neccai struck out 27 batters (one walked, on was hit by a pitch, one was safe on a fumbled grounder, and one grounded out), and Bill Bell pitched two consecutive no-hitters, striking out 17 and 20. That this earned them a premature trip to the sad-sack Pirates was simply exploitation, and both got hammered by major leaguers. But the point is that neither had any kind of career later, despite the innate ability they certainly had. On the other hand, bonus babies Harey Kuenn and Dick Groat became instant major leaguers of great value.

Giving bonuses to untried players was shooting dice, pure and simple—blind gambling. The problem would never go away, but it became institutionalized in this period.

Now the ownerships:

June 1946—Veeck buys the Indians.

August 1946—A group headed by Frank McKinney of Indianapolis, including Bing Crosby and John Galbreath (a prominent racehorse owner), buys the Pirates from Benswanger, ending the Dreyfuss heritage.

October 1947—At the Yankee victory party the night they won the World Series, MacPhail resigns, leaving Dan Topping and Del Webb as sole owners of the Yankees.

They promote George Weiss to the position Barrow and MacPhail had held as operating head.

November 1947—Bob Hannegan, a major figure in national politics as a Democrat, buys the St. Louis Cardinals from Breadon for $4 million, then the highest price ever paid for a ball club. Fred Saigh of St. Louis is one of his partners.

January 1948—Saigh buys out Hannegan.

February 1948—The DeWitt brothers acquire 58 percent of the stock and full control of the Browns.

November 1948—Veeck sells the Indians to a group headed by Ellis Ryan.

July 1950—Galbrath buys out McKinney for full control of Pittsburgh.

October 1950—Connie Mack retires, leaving effective control of the franchise in the hands of his sons and Shibe heirs.

October 1950—Walter O'Malley and John L. Smith buy out Rickey's share of the Dodgers and dismiss him as general manager. O'Malley is now in total control of Brooklyn.

June 1951—Veeck buys the Browns from the DeWitts.

January 1952—Spike Briggs inherits the Tigers upon the death of his father, Walter Briggs.

November 1952—Perini acquires sole control of the Boston Braves.

December 1952—Cleveland's new head is Mike Wilson, after a conflict between Ryan and general manager Hank Greenberg is resolved by the stockholders.

January 1953—Saigh is indicted for income-tax evasion.

February 1953—The Cardinals are bought from Saigh by the Budweiser Beer brewery, headed by Gussie Busch, for $2.5 million and debts.

April 1953—Veeck, prevented from moving to Milwaukee or Baltimore, sells Sportsmans's Park to the Cardinals for $800,000. It became Busch Stadium.

September 1953—Veeck, refused permission to move to Baltimore, sells the Browns to a Baltimore syndicate.

October 1953—The American League approves the move to Baltimore.

We now have the following groupings going into 1954:

National League—Stoneham (New York), Wrigley (Chicago), and Crosley (Cincinnati) continue their prewar properties. The other five are newcomers to baseball since 1942.

American League—Yawkey (Boston), the Comiskey family (Chicago), and Griffith (Washington) represent continuity. The Tigers and Athletics have just passed into the hands of a younger generation in prewar families. New York, Cleveland, and Baltimore are postwar ownerships.

League presidents Harridge and Giles and Commissioner Frick, however, are lifelong baseball people.

It's less than 30 years since Ban Johnson stepped down, but in a joint meeting of the major leagues, Griffith is the only person left who ever had any substantial dealings with him (although Harridge had worked in Johnson's office from 1911 on, mostly on arranging schedules).

So what? So this: baseball was entering an era of enormous and fundamental change with increasing inattention to its own past experience. Not only were lessons that should have been learned not applied to repetitive problems, but an atmosphere had evolved in which the customers—fans—had a better sense of the historical tradition they were buying than the operators trying to sell it. That's why the upheavals to come—franchise shifts, expansion, schedule changes, response to unionization—would be plunged into with so little thinking-through of long-range consequences or consideration of better alternatives.

A similar, and bigger, shift in ownership population in the 1980's would lead to similar responses and bigger trouble.

SEASONS 1946–52

1946

The first full year of regulars back from the war in 1946 produced a total runaway by the Boston Red Sox and the first flat-out tie for a pennant between the Dodgers and Cardinals. (The 1908 play-off had been a makeup game.) The Cardinals won the play-off and, as was their habit, the seven-game World Series.

NL—The Dodgers and Cardinals took up where they left off in 1942, with major cast changes but the same story line. The Cards had a rookie manager, Eddie Dyer, promoted from within. Musial now played first base, switch-hitting Red Schoendienst played second, with Marion and Kurowski completing the infield. Slaughter, Moore, and Harry Walker, Dixie's younger brother, were the outfielders. A 20-year-old local kid, Joe Garagiola, did half the catching. The Cooper brothers were gone, Mort to Boston and Walker to the Giants, but there was an abundance of pitching anyhow: Howie Pollet, Murry Dickson, Harry Brecheen, Alpha Brazle, Ted Wilks. At Brooklyn, Durocher had Reese and Reiser back, Carl Furillo and Walker flanking Reiser, Higbe, Casey, and a flock of younger pitchers.

Never far apart, the Dodgers led through June and July, the Cards through September after a dead-heat August. The final Sunday dawned with them tied, 96–57. At Ebbets Field, Cooper shut out the Dodgers for the Braves, giving his old

team a chance, but the Cards lost to the Cubs at St. Louis a little later. That called for a two-of-three playoff.

Pollet won the first game 4–2, beating a Dodger rookie who had shut out the Cards in September, 20-year-old Ralph Branca. That was in St. Louis, and the rest of the series was to be in Brooklyn. It lasted only one more game, the Cards winning 8–4.

AL—When Feller came out of the navy in September of 1945, he was determined to make up for lost time. He won five for Cleveland, lost three before the season ended, then embarked on an elaborate barnstorming tour. Then he produced a 26–15 season, striking out 348 batters in 371 innings, with 10 shutouts, the first of which was a no-hitter at Yankee Stadium April 30. But he didn't get the pitching triple crown because his 2.18 earned run average was surpassed by Hal Newhouser's 1.94 in Detroit. Newhouser's 26–9 record gave him 70 victories in three seasons.

Such numbers underlined the return of glamour. Feller was hailed for setting a strikeout record, surpassing the 343 the record book gave Rube Waddell in 1904. Other statisticians claimed the correct number was 349, and a controversy raged that had to be settled by the league. Since no official sheets from 1904 existed, the league accepted Feller's mark as the record. Nowadays the 349 is accepted for Waddell, but to understand the scope of what Feller did, it should be noted that only one other pitcher had ever reached 300 at that time: Walter Johnson in 1910 with 313.

That superstars were performing superfeats was an important aspect of 1946. But the Red Sox performed like a superteam. They won 104 games, beating Detroit by 12 and the Yankees by 17. Boo Ferriss, whose 21–10 as a rookie in 1945 was shrugged off as "wartime," went 25–6 against the returned regulars, and Tex Hughson was 20–11. Williams hit .342 (second to Mickey Vernon's .353), knocked in 123 (second to Hank Greenberg's 127), and hit 38 homers (second to Greenberg's 44). Rudy York had replaced Foxx at first, Doerr was back at second, Johnny Pesky was the new shortstop, Dom DiMaggio was back in center. These Red Sox had less sheer power than the Yankee pursuers of before the war, but better pitching and defense.

The Tigers actually won more games than they had as 1945 champions, but the opposition was different. The Yankee machine, under MacPhail's hectic guidance, came apart: McCarthy, who had health and drinking problems, resigned in May. MacPhail made Dickey playing-manager, and that didn't work, so Johnny Neun (who had managed in Newark) had to finish out September. If MacPhail really was pursuing Durocher, it was understandable. None of the returned Yankee stars approached normal production except Chandler, who had a 20–8 season.

All-Star Game—At Fenway Park, the Americans wiped out the Nationals 12–0, with Williams the star among stars. He hit two homers, and the memorable one was off Rip Sewell, who tossed up his celebrated "ephus pitch"—a high-arching slower-than-slow ball—which Williams timed and crushed.

WS—St. Louis to New York was a 21-hour train ride, to Boston 26. The Cards had ended their season in St. Louis on Sunday, started the play-offs there Monday, traveled Tuesday, won in Brooklyn Wednesday, and were back in St. Louis "well rested" to open the World Series on Saturday against a Boston team that hadn't played a meaningful game in weeks. When a 10th-inning homer by York off Pollet gave Boston a 3–2 victory, eventual triumph for the Red Sox seemed assured. But Brecheen's four-hit 3–0 shutout sent the teams back to Boston all even.

Ferriss won 4–0, the Cards won 12–2, and the Red Sox won 6–2, so it was back to the long train ride with the Red Sox again apparently in command. But Brecheen evened matters again, 4–1, so it came down to Game Seven—which the Cardinals had won in 1926, 1931, and 1934, every time they had reached one.

They did it again. Dickson took a 3–1 lead into the top of the eighth, but when it opened with a single and double, Dyer brought in Brecheen, who couldn't stop DiMaggio from tying the score with a two-run double, but held it there by making Williams pop up. The Cards had held Williams to five singles in 25 at bats.

In the bottom half, Slaughter singled and raced all the way home on Walker's double to left center, beating the relay from Pesky. When Brecheen wormed his way out of the ninth after the Red Sox got the first two men on, he had his third victory of the Series and the Red Sox had a memory that would rankle for decades.

1947

The Yankees in 1947 launched what would be their new dynasty, in which he Dodgers would be their most dramatic rival. Jackie Robinson's debut was a historic success, Williams won a Triple Crown, the Giants broke all home-run records, and Greenberg got a $100,000 salary in moving to Pittsburgh.

NL—The first half of the season was dominated by everyone's adjustment to Robinson, whose play was spectacular from the start. Then the Dodgers ran away from the pack, winding up five games ahead of the Cardinals and the oncoming Braves. Durocher's absence wasn't felt, because Shotton had an even better Dodgers lineup. Robinson, Stanky, and Reese anchored a fine infield, Walker had a productive year at 36 despite his antiblack feelings, Reiser (who had missed the last three weeks of 1946) was able to play most of the season, Carl Furillo was establishing himself, and Bruce Edwards was no longer a rookie catcher. Branca, in his first full year, went 21–12 on a staff full of young pitchers, with the older Casey now strictly a relief specialist.

The Cards had a squad composed almost entirely of their farm graduates. They traded Harry Walker to Philadelphia, where he proceeded to win the batting title at .363, while those they kept had a slightly off year—but the cloud on the horizon was that the next generation of farmhands wasn't of the same quality after Rickey left. The Braves rose to third place behind the Johnny Sain (21–12, righty) and Warren Spahn (21–10, lefty) combination that inspired the prayerful formula, "Spahn and Sain and two days of rain."

The fourth-place Giants, despite a 21–5 performance by rookie pitcher Larry Jansen, lacked the pitching to take advantage of 221 home runs, a team record eclipsing anything the Yankees had ever been able to do. Mize hit 51, Willard Marshall 36, Walker Cooper 35, a rookie named Bobby Thomson 29. They became the perennially cited example of why "pitching is the name of the game."

And Pittsburgh made news while finishing tied for last with Philadelphia. In January, Greenberg, dissatisfied in Detroit, had been able to make a $100,000 deal with Pittsburgh's new ownership, a move that required waivers, which all other clubs dutifully gave. A false fence cutting down the home-run distance in spacious Forbes Field created Greenberg Gardens and helped him hit 25 home runs; but it was his 24-year-old sophomore and protégé, Ralph Kiner, who tied Mize with 51 and began a seven-year span of home-run production of Ruthian proportions. The Pirates had also brought in Billy Herman as manager. Their decade of failure was under way.

AL—MacPhail had settled on Bucky Harris as Yankee manager, and Bucky had never had such talent at his disposal. In a major trade, the Yankees had sent Joe Gordon to Cleveland for a power pitcher, Allie Reynolds (on DiMaggio's recommendation about which pitcher to take). Joe Page emerged as a spectacular reliever (with the aid of a lecture by DiMaggio), and suddenly the Yankees had strong pitching to go with their other assets. A 19-game winning streak in July, equaling a league record set by the Hitless Wonder White Sox of 1906, launched them to a final 12-game margin over Detroit and 14 over Boston. Red Sox pitching fell apart so completely, largely because of injuries, that a Triple Crown for Williams—.343 with 114 runs batted in and 32 homers—couldn't overcome it. Feller, 20–11, was the league's only 20-game winner, but the cumulative effect of his 1946 effort would soon begin to show.

All-Star Game—At Wrigley Field, the Americans won 2–1, taking a 10–4 lead in the series.

WS—Extensive film footage of this one is still being shown, the first of comparable dramas to be available in such quantity.

It started in the Bronx. A five-run fifth inning gave the Yankees the first game 5–3, as Page pitched the last four innings for Spec Shea, the rookie who had shared the staff leadership with Reynolds. Reynolds won the second game 10–3. But in the third game the Dodgers had a six-run second and hung on, behind Casey's last two innings, for a 9–8 victory at Ebbets Field, and Bill Bevens started the next game for the Yankees.

He took a no-hitter into the ninth inning, leading 2–1, since two of his eight walks, a sacrifice, and an infield out had given Brooklyn a run in the fifth. He retired Edwards on a long fly, walked Furillo, and got Spider Jorgensen on a foul pop-up. At that point, Al Gionfriddo ran for Furillo and stole second, while Reiser, hobbled by a bad ankle, pinch-hit for Casey. Harris decided to walk Reiser on purpose, so Shotton sent Eddie Miksis in to run for Reiser and Cookie Lavagetto to bat for Stanky.

Lavagetto hit one high off the right-field wall for a double, breaking up the no-hitter and winning the game 3–2. That moment has been reshown as much as any one play in baseball history.

But Shea pitched a four-hitter the next day, for a 2–1 Yankee victory secured by DiMaggio's home run, and the Yankees went back to the Stadium one game up.

In game six the Yankees fell behind 4–0, took a 5–4 lead, then ran into a four-run Dodger sixth. In the bottom half, DiMaggio came up with two on and two out, trailing 8–5, and blasted a high drive toward the left-field bull-pen gate, where the sign says 415 feet. Gionfriddo raced back, turned, and made an acrobatic catch just short of the wall—another moment reshown endlessly ever since. (It probably would not have been a home run, but it was close enough to make that the accepted assumption; why look a gift melodrama in the mouth?) The Dodgers went on to win 8–6.

Shea started the seventh game for the Yankees, fell behind 2–1, and was replaced by Bevens in the third. In the bottom of the fourth, with two on and two out, Yankees manager Harris had Bobby Brown bat for Bevens, and his double tied the score. A single by Henrich put the Yankees ahead 3–2, so Harris called on Page again, with five innings to go. The left-hander retired 13 men in a row, yielded a single, and got a game-ending double play as the Yankees won the game 5–2.

That wasn't on national TV yet, but it was seen in the New York area, where all the media executives were concentrated. As much as any other single circumstance, the 1947 World Series—the details just cited—committed television to baseball, and vice versa.

That night, the victory party at the Biltmore Hotel was going full blast when MacPhail started punching people, including his road secretary, Jack MacDonald, and tearfully announced his resignation. It was formalized in a press conference the next day.

1948

In 1948 the spotlight shifted to Boston and Cleveland, while all three New York teams went through internal upheavals that would lead to their complete domination of the next decade. Babe Ruth's death on August 16 brought 100,000 people out to file past his coffin at the Stadium and marked a conscious passing into a new era. Single-minded awe at feats on the field itself, which had been the public reaction to Mathewson, Cobb, Ruth, Walter Johnson, and the rest of the prewar, all-white baseball world, was giving way to increasing awareness of off-field aspects, such as Veeck's promotions, television availability, and, before long, franchise moves. Ruth had changed the "old game," but what he had changed it into had remained stable for a generation. Now that stability was unraveling, and his passing symbolized the process.

NL—A rookie shortstop, Alvin Dark, and a rookie pitcher, Vern Bickford, helped put Southworth's Braves over the top. Sain won 24, Spahn only 15, but Bickford's 14–5 was a big help on a staff loaded with veterans spotted judiciously by Southworth. The Braves started to pull away at the end of June and wound up comfortably ahead of St. Louis, Brooklyn, and Pittsburgh, bunched between 6½ and 8½ games out.

The Cardinals were pretty much as they had been, but a bombshell exploded in New York.

Leo Durocher, his suspension over, had a Dodger team in transition. Robinson was at second, his natural position, with Stanky gone to Boston; Gil Hodges, a converted catcher, was in-

stalled at first base. Reiser, only 29, had been destroyed by his accumulated injuries, including a fractured skull in a collision with a concrete wall. (Padding? Owners scoffed when players suggested such a thing.) On July 16, the Dodgers were 36–37 and the Giants, under Ott, 27–38, both going nowhere. Stoneham and Rickey talked, and then came the announcement:

Durocher was the new manager of the Giants, effective immediately.

Ott was out.

Shotton was back as manager of the Dodgers.

One can't exaggerate the trauma for passionate followers of both teams. In a rivalry built on a hatred nurtured since the 1880s Durocher was the most hated Brooklyn Bum, and Ott the best-loved favorite, among Giant fans. And while Leo had detractors as well as fervent boosters in Brooklyn, the idea of his going *there* upset everyone. The emotional wrench can be compared to having Ulysses S. Grant suddenly replace Robert E. Lee as head of the Confederate Army in the middle of the Civil War. It would appall both sides.

But this was, after all, only baseball. Hadn't McGraw suddenly switched from American League Baltimore to the Giants in 1902, at the height of that baseball war? Hadn't Lajoie switched Philadelphias? Hadn't the Red Sox sold Babe Ruth to the Yankees? Hadn't Griffith sold his manager-shortstop (and son-in-law) to the Red Sox? Hadn't Mack unloaded all his stars to his rivals? No, Leo's move had plenty of precedent—but the fans then, as now, were not concerned with history. All they knew was that the world had turned upside down.

The immediate effects weren't great. The Dodgers called up Roy Campanella from St. Paul, picked up their pace, and finished third. The Giants did even better (51–38 after Leo took over) but still finished fifth. But a new balance of power was in the making.

Meanwhile, Musial just missed a Triple Crown, hitting .376 with 131 runs batted in, but one homer less at 39 than Mize and Kiner, who hit 40 each. Brecheen, 20–7, was the only 20-game winner besides Sain. The Phillies fired Ben Chapman as manager the same day as the Durocher move and soon brought in Eddie Sawyer, while a couple of weeks later at Cincinnati, Neun was replaced by Bucky Walters, who had practically stopped pitching anyhow. The Old Order was changing rapidly.

AL—Veeck didn't think much of his shortstop-manager for the Cleveland Indians, now 30 years old, and tried to trade Boudreau to the Browns. Veeck had hired McKechnie as a pitching coach when he left Cincinnati and wanted him to manage. But Boudreau was such a hero in Cleveland that Veeck backed down and added Muddy Ruel and Mel Harder to a coaches' brain trust. Doby was ready to play full time, and Gordon was acclimated to his new team. Feller was wearing down, but a left-handed rookie, Gene Bearden, and a converted infielder, Bob Lemon, could more than take up the slack. And midway through the season Veeck brought in Satchel Paige. Promoting like crazy, he had a contender and sold 2.6 million tickets, doubling the best the Yankees had ever done with Ruth, surpassing by more than a million any previous year in Cleveland.

The Yankees had management problems. Weiss, now in charge, had not chosen Harris. When developments called for quick promotion from the minors to give the Yankees immediate help, Weiss stuck by his farm-system timetables, and if that turned out to cost Harris his job, too bad. He had traded for one good pitcher, Eddie Lopat, from the White Sox. He had brought up Vic Raschi. That was enough. That both Shea and Page turned ineffective was not his farm system's fault. Eventually, he did let pitcher Bob Porterfield come up, and outfielders Hank Bauer and Cliff Mapes after the minor league season ended, but that was too late.

And the Red Sox? Cronin had moved into the front office and hired Joe McCarthy, Boston's old Yankee nemesis, to manage. After a 14–23 start, the Sox won 62 and lost only 25 for the next three months and entered September leading a three-team scramble. With a week to go, all three were tied. On the final Saturday Cleveland was a game ahead of both Yankees and Red Sox, with two games to go. At Fenway, the Red Sox beat the Yankees 5–1 behind Jack Kramer, so when Bearden blanked Detroit 8–0, the Yankees were eliminated. The Red Sox won again on Sunday 10–5, and when Newhouser finished beating Feller 7–1, the race ended in a tie. For the second time in three years, what had never happened before had occurred.

The American League rules called for a one-game play-off. The Indians came to Boston. McCarthy started Denny Galehouse, 8–8 and 36 years old. Boudreau started Bearden for the second time in 48 hours. Who was the better manager? Boudreau, of course: he hit two home runs and two singles in an 8–3 victory, while all McCarthy did was sit in the dugout. Managing with a bat in your hands had triumphed again. (But it would be the last time.)

All-Star Game—In St. Louis, Musial hit a two-run homer in the first inning, but the Nationals couldn't score again and lost 5–2.

WS—Already in Boston, the Indians simply had to go to the other ball park after one day off. Cleveland's Feller and the Braves' Sain matched zeroes until the bottom of the eighth. With two out and men on first and second, Feller's throw to second apparently had Phil Masi picked off—but umpire Bill Stewart ruled safe. Tommy Holmes thereupon lined a single to center, only the second hit off Feller, and Sain closed out a 1–0 four-hitter.

The rest of it can be summed up, from Boston's point of view, this way: it didn't rain. Lemon beat Spahn 4–1, and in Cleveland, Bearden won 2–0 and Steve Gromek, facing Sain, won 2–1. Feller was hit hard as Spahn posted an 11–5 victory that forced the teams to return to Boston, so it was Bearden again, pitching his fourth complete game in 10 days and winning 4–3. Veeck had hit the jackpot in his second full season as a big-league owner, and the Braves had aroused excessive expectations that would magnify the effect of their failure to repeat.

A final note on 1948: Cleveland's 2.6 million was in a 78,000-seat stadium. The Yankees did 2.3 million with 70,000 seats. But the Dodgers, in Robinson's first year, 1947, set a National League record of 1.8 million with 32,111 as the capacity of Ebbets Field. In 70 dates, they filled 80 percent of their available seats, and in the years 1948–49 they would average 60 percent. Such levels would not be approached again until the new ball parks of the 1990's came on line.

1949

Such elaborate and excellent descriptions of the 1949 season are available in whole books and countless fine chapters, in other books, only the sketchiest review is needed here.

NL—Another race went down to the last day.

The Cardinals and Dodgers were neck and neck all season long, Brooklyn ahead into July, the Cards clinging to a narrow lead through most of September. In the final week, the Cards lost four straight, two each at Pittsburgh and Chicago, enabling the Dodgers to take the lead by winning a doubleheader in Boston. On Saturday, the Cards loss to the Cubs prevented them from overtaking the Dodgers, who lost at Philadelphia, but their victory in Chicago on Sunday meant they'd tie if the Dodgers lost. But the Dodgers managed to win 9–7 in 10 innings, after blowing a 5–0 lead.

Robinson, in his third year, peaked: batting champion at .342, stolen-base leader with 37, second only to Ralph Kiner in runs batted in (124 to 127), even though Kiner hit 54 home runs to Robinson's 16. Robinson won the Most Valuable Player Award.

When Rickey had to dispose of Dixie Walker in 1948 because he objected to Robinson's presence, he got Preacher Roe, a left-handed pitcher, and Billy Cox, a defensive whiz at third, from Pittsburgh. These two and the full-time use of Campanella and Newcombe made the 1949 Dodgers nearly an all-star team. Reiser, wrecked by injuries, was replaced in center by an exciting rookie slugger named Duke Snider. Hodges turned out to be a superb first baseman as well as a home-run threat. Reese was now the veteran at short, Furillo in the outfield. Newcombe went 17–6, Roe 15–6, Branca 13–5, and behind them a deep but not brilliant pitching staff shared the load. Shotton's low-key managing, effective in 1947, was just as effective now.

The Cardinals, all farm grown, were as good as ever, if aging. Philadelphia, managed by Eddie Sawyer and also stocked with youngsters, came in a distant third—its highest finish in 32 years. The Braves, defending champions, were in disarray as Southworth lost control while dealing with personal tragedy (his son's death) and a recurrence of his drinking problem. (That Sain had a 10–17 season and Holmes hit .266 didn't help.) The Giants, in their first full season under Durocher, were still an all-power, no-pitching team that fell below .500.

Spahn (21–14) and Pollet (20–9) were the only 20-game winners. The last-place Cubs switched managers in June, from Grimm to Frisch.

AL—A Yankee–Red Sox race upstaged anything and everything that happened in the other league. The Yankees led all season long, fell behind in the last week, then beat the Red Sox in the last two games at Yankee Stadium to finish one game ahead.

Back in 1947, when MacPhail was pursuing Durocher, he had hired Bucky Harris as a front-office advisor, then made him manager. Weiss, in charge in 1948 after MacPhail quit, didn't want Harris, and the last-day loss of 1948 was enough excuse to drop him. He wanted his own man, and he chose Casey Stengel, who had just won a Pacific Coast League pennant in Oakland. Casey hadn't been in the majors since being fired in Boston, and was considered a clown by the New York baseball community—well loved, but little respected.

Now, for the first time, Stengel had real playing talent at his disposal—and it kept getting hurt. Arthur Patterson, the publicity director brought in by MacPhail (when most clubs didn't have one), started counting "injuries" and got up to 71. DiMaggio missed the whole first half of the season because of a damaged heel. Nevertheless, the Yankees got off well and kept winning as Stengel juggled lineups and brought the term "platooning" into prominence. (He was simply applying what McGraw had taught him, while wartime experience made the public receptive to "a right-handed platoon" and "a left-handed platoon" terminology.)

The Red Sox, frustrated by their play-off loss in 1948, had trouble getting started but clearly had the more powerful lineup. In late June, DiMaggio came back, still limping, and exploded for four homers in a three-game sweep at Boston. But the Red Sox, 24–8 in August, kept coming on. On September 18, DiMaggio went out again with viral pneumonia, with the Red Sox 2½ games behind. On the final Monday, Boston took the lead with a third straight victory over the Yankees. On the final Saturday, trailing by one game with two to play, the Yankees fell behind 4–0 but won 5–4, thanks to a six-inning relief turn by Joe Page and an eighth-inning tie-breaking home run by Johnny Lindell.

With the race tied on Sunday, the Yankees behind, Vic Raschi nursed a 1–0 lead until Henrich's home run started, and Jerry Coleman's three-run bloop double-ended, a four-run eighth. They won 5–3.

Williams led the league with 43 homers and shared the RBI lead with his shortstop, Vern Stephens, at 159; but he lost the batting title to Detroit's George Kell, .3429 to .3427, even though Williams had 15 more hits and 162 walks (in 155 games!) to Kell's 71. DiMaggio, in the 76 games he played, hit .346.

Boston had Mel Parnell at 25–7 and Ellis Kinder 23–6, but no reliever to match Page, who had 27 saves (while no one else in the league had more than 10). Raschi (21–10) and Allie Reynolds (17–6) led the Yankee starters. Cleveland's Bob Lemon (22–10) and Philadelphia's Alex Kellner (20–12) were the other 20-game winners.

In August, in a "waiver" deal, the Yankees bought Mize from the Giants, but he was injured almost immediately and was no factor—until the World Series.

All-Star Game—At Ebbets Field, the hitters made the most of the cozy confines. The Americans won 11–7 in a game with 30 hits, 11 walks, and six errors, five by the Nationals. That gave the American League an 11–4 lead in the series.

WS—For the third time in nine years, it was Yankees vs. Dodgers, the new version of the Subway Series. The first game, at the Stadium, was a 0–0 duel between Brooklyn's Newcombe and Reynolds until Henrich led off the bottom of the ninth with a home run. But Roe matched that with a 1–0 victory for the Dodgers, who got a second-inning run off Raschi on Robinson's double and Hodges's single.

At Ebbets Field, it was 1–1 into the top of the ninth, when the Yankees scored three runs with two out, the last two on a pinch-hit by Mize. That withstood ninth-inning homers off Page by Campanella and Luis Olma, so the Yankees won 4–3. They won the fourth game 6–4, beating Newcombe with Reynolds saving Eddie Lopat in the sixth, and closed the Series out 10–6 for Raschi, after building a 10–1 lead.

Snider, at 22, struck out eight times, tying a Series record, an embarrassment he was not allowed to forget for years (even though the record he tied was held by Rogers Hornsby). Bobby Brown, hitting .500 with five runs batted in, had his peak moments as a Yankee.

1950

Between the 1949–50 seasons, the rule book was completely rewritten and recodified into the form it now has, although no actual changes in playing rules were involved.

Once again in 1950, both races went down to the wire, with the Yankees and Phillies emerging as winners.

NL—The Phillies, breaking away from the pack during August, were called the Whiz Kids, after a radio and television panel show featuring precocious youngsters. Pitchers Robin Roberts and left-handed Curt Simmons, infielders Mike Goliat, Granny Hamner, and Willie Jones, and outfielders Richie Ashburn and Del Ennis were all 25 or younger. Catcher Andy Seminick and outfielder Dick Sisler were 29. Eddie Waitkus, the first baseman who had been shot the year before by a lovesick fan, was 30 and fully recovered. Only Jim Konstanty, appearing in 74 games strictly as a reliever, was "old" at 33—and this was only his second full year in the majors, after a decade in the minors.

The Dodgers, their championship team intact, sputtered. The Phils opened up a nine-game lead in September and were still ahead by seven with 12 to play. Then they lost successive doubleheaders to the Giants while the Dodgers were winning four of six from the Braves, so the Phillies arrived in Brooklyn leading by two with two to play. Simmons, called to reserve military duty, was unavailable down the stretch.

On Saturday, Erv Palica beat them 7–3. Another loss would create a tie. Roberts, starting for the third time in five days, faced Newcombe. They were 1–1 in the ninth when the Phillies' Ashburn threw out Cal Abrams at the plate on Snider's single with one out. An intentional pass to Robinson filled the bases, but Roberts made Furillo pop up and Hodges fly out. Then Sisler hit a three-run homer in the top of the 10th, and the Whiz Kids were champions.

Overshadowed was the transformation of Durocher's Giants. A trade with Boston brought Alvin Dark and Eddie Stanky to New York, for their infield and subtle run-making skills, in exchange for the slow-footed power represented by Sid Gordon and Willard Marshall (Mize and Walker Cooper also having been discarded). Sal Maglie, reinstated after a period of Mexican League exile, joined Larry Jansen as a top pitcher. It took until August to put it all together, but the Giants won 41 of their last 62 games and finished third.

Musial regained his batting title (.346), Kiner

hit his 47 home runs for the last-place Pirates, Ennis led with 125 runs batted in, while Sam Jethroe, another new black star acquired by the Braves from the Dodger farm system, led in stolen bases with 35. (At Montreal the year before, at the age of 27, he had stolen 89.) The only 20-game winners were Roberts (20–11), Sain (20–13), and Spahn (21–17).

AL—Was Stengel's first-season victory a fluke? If so, he did it again. In a three-way battle with the Red Sox and Tigers, the Yankees pulled away in the last 10 days, finishing three games ahead of Detroit (managed by Red Rolfe) and four ahead of Boston. To the Raschi, Reynolds, and Lopat rotation the Yankees added, in midseason, 21-year-old Whitey Ford. Page's arm gave out so they made a trading-deadline deal for Tom Ferrick, who took over prime relief responsibilities. Mize, healthy, played halftime, pinch-hit the rest, and supplied 25 homers. When an August lift was needed, another waiver deal brought them Johnny Hopp from Pittsburgh, where he had been hitting .340 and fighting Musial for the batting title. DiMaggio, his aching body starting to give out, still produced 32 homers and hit .301, while Rizzuto (.324), Yogi Berra (.322), and Hank Bauer (.320) outhit him. Yogi, now that Bill Dickey as coach had "learned me his experiences," was the regular catcher. Rizzuto was most valuable player (MVP).

Rolfe, the ex-Yankee in his second year as Tiger manager, had lots of starters (Newhouser, Fred Hutchinson, Art Houtteman, Dizzy Trout, Ted Gray) and good hitters (George Kell .340, Hoot Evers .323, Vic Wertz 27 homers), but not quite good enough bull pen or defense. The Red Sox were a batting powerhouse: a team batting average of .302 and 1,027 runs scored. But the pitching staff, while deep, was shaky, and other problems arose. McCarthy, depressed and criticized after two near misses, resigned on June 23, after a 2–11 stretch that made the record 32–30. He was replaced by Steve O'Neill. Three weeks later Williams fractured his elbow in the All-Star Game and was out for two months. Nevertheless, the Sox had a 24–6 August and got to within half a game of the Yankees on September 19 before falling back. Billy Goodman, a utility infielder who took the place of Williams in left field, won the batting title at .354, Stephens and Walt

Dropo shared the runs batted in lead with 144, and Williams hit 28 homers in the 86 games he played.

Only Raschi (21–8) and Lemon (23–11) were 20-game winners. Bucky Harris was back in uniform, managing Washington to sixth place, and Connie Mack finally stepped down after his Athletics finished last with 102 losses, having managed them for 50 years. As for Boudreau, the manage-with-a-bat technique was evaporating. Only two years after hitting .355 to help himself win a World Series, he hit only .269 playing half-time (at 32) and finished fourth. The day of the successful player-manager was done.

All-Star Game—Back in Comiskey Park, where it had all started in 1933, the game went into extra innings for the first time—lots of them. In the very first inning, Williams cracked his elbow against the left-field wall hauling in a drive by Kiner. He continued to play and actually singled home a run that gave his team a 3–2 lead in the fifth. But he had to quit in the ninth inning and only afterwards did X-rays show the fracture that required an operation to remove bone fragments.

Kiner led off the ninth with a homer that tied the game, and Red Schoendienst led off the 14th with a homer that stood up for a 4–3 National League victory, its first since 1944 and first as a visiting team.

WS—A four-game sweep seems one-sided, but the individual games in this Yankee triumph over Philadelphia were close. Konstanty, National League MVP for his relief work, was pressed into a starting role and almost matched Raschi as the World Series opener ended 1–0 for the third straight year. The Yankee run came in the fourth on Bobby Brown's double followed by two outfield flies, while Raschi allowed just two singles and one walk. Also in Philadelphia, Roberts and Reynolds went 1–1 through nine innings in the second game. Then DiMaggio's home run leading off the 10th stood up.

In New York, it was left-handers Lopat for the Yankees and Ken Heintzelman for the Phils. The Phils went ahead 2–1, with single runs in the sixth and seventh. But with two out in the eighth, Heintzelman walked three in a row. Konstanty came in and made Brown, pinch-hitting, hit a grounder—which Hamner fumbled, tying the score. In the ninth, with two out, two infield singles and a clean one to left center by Jerry Coleman gave the Yankees a 3–2 decision.

Ford pitched the fourth game and had a 5–0 shutout in the ninth. But Woodling couldn't hold a drive near the left-field fence with two on and two out, letting two runs score, and when a single brought the potential tying run to bat, Stengel waved in Reynolds, who fanned Stan Lopata.

1951

If 1949 was well documented in subsequent literature, 1951 was even more so. Of all baseball seasons, this one has been given the most exhaustive and accessible examination, forever to be referred to as the year of Bobby Thomson's homer.

NL—The Dodgers had new direction at the top. Walter O'Malley had bought out Rickey, fired Shotten, and made Charlie Dressen manager of the talent-laden roster. The only position not occupied by a recognized star was left field, and just before the June trading deadline, O'Malley filled it with Andy Pafko, an established star, from the Cubs. The Phillies, having overachieved in 1950, could not keep pace with such a crew. The Dodgers started well enough and got better: 24–15 by June 1, 42–25 by July 1, 63–32 by August 1 with a 9½ game lead. The Phillies fell below .500 in early May and stayed there.

The Giants were a different story.

They won, lost, won, then lost 11 straight. They didn't get over .500 until May 27. And they kept losing ground to the Dodgers in June and July. But on May 21, they had called up Willie Mays from Minneapolis (where he was hitting .477!) and Durocher began rearranging his forces. He had started the season with Bobby Thomson ("the Flying Scot") in center, Monte Irvin at first, and Whitey Lockman in left. Irvin, now 31, had been an established Negro league player whose first two years with the Giants were diminished by injury. Henry Thompson, who had been given that brief trial by the Browns in 1948 when the color line was broken, had been installed at third after Sid Gordon was traded away. And midway through 1950, Durocher had acquired a third right-handed starter, Jim Hearn, from St. Louis, who had wound up leading the league in earned run average.

Now Leo put Mays in center and left him there, whether he hit or not; moved Irvin to left,

helping Mays with positioning, and Lockman to first, where he proved better defensively. That left Bobby Thomson on the bench until, in July, Thompson got hurt and Bobby took over at third base. For the rest of the year, Thomson hit .357.

On August 11, by winning the first game of a doubleheader, the Dodgers made their record 70–35 and their lead 13½ games. They lost the second game. The next day, the Giants started a 16-game winning streak that cut the margin to five. But the Dodgers were also winning regularly and still had a 4½-game lead on September 20. The Giants, with only seven games left, had six more defeats on their record; the Dodgers had 10 to play. The Giants won their next five; the Dodgers lost six of their next eight. With two days to go, the race was tied.

On Saturday, the Giants won a day game in Boston, the Dodgers a night game in Philadelphia. On Sunday, the Giants won their game and took the train to New York. In Philadelphia, the Dodgers battled through 14 innings before winning 9–8 on Robinson's home run, after he had made a game-saving catch in the 12th. En route home, the Giants learned there would have to be a three-game play-off.

Monday, at Ebbets Field, Hearn beat Branca 3–1 on the strength of a two-run homer by Thomson in the fourth. (Pafko and Irvin hit solos.) Tuesday at the Polo Grounds, a rookie, Clem Labine, pitched a six-hit, 10–0 shutout for the Dodgers, who hammered Sheldon Jones and two relievers. Wednesday at the Polo Grounds, Maglie gave up a run to Brooklyn in the first, and Newcombe nursed it until the seventh. In the top of the eighth, four singles, a walk, and a wild pitch gave Brooklyn a 4–1 lead, and Newcombe took a four-hitter into the ninth.

The Giants' Dark and Don Mueller hit ground singles to right. Irvin popped up. Lockman's double made it 4–2 with men on second and third. Dressen brought in Branca to face Thomson with Mays on deck. Thomson lined the second pitch into the left-field stands, over Pafko's head, for a three-run homer, a 5–4 victory, the pennant, and a legend.

The dramatic impact of this climax to a two-month comeback cannot be over-emphasized. It was telecast nationally, and Russ Hodges screaming "The Giants win the pennant, the Giants win the pennant!" in a radio broadcast became folk-lore. And it wasn't just because this was New York, the media hub, and the cast of characters, from Durocher through Robinson, so fascinating. It was the ultimate fictional situation actualized in real life, a championship *reversed*—not simply won—by one swing of the bat. It had never happened before and has happened only once since (in 1992). In fiction, of course, it's always two out with the bases loaded and a three-run deficit. But this was good enough.

They called it "the shot heard around the world" and, more to the point, "the miracle of Coogan's Bluff," that being the name of the cliff that overlooked the west side of the Polo Grounds.

The Giants had won 39 of their last 47 games. Maglie and Jansen (who had pitched the top of the ninth before Thomson's homer) had posted 23 victories each. Stanky and catcher Wes Westrum were the less-sung heroes. Irvin's 121 runs batted in led the league.

But the rest of the league also played. Musial, at .355, and Kiner, with 42 homers, led their departments again. The Dodgers *had* spectacular statistics—Hodges with 40 homers, Campanella 33, Roe 22–3, Newcombe 20–9, Robinson .338—but they were no solace. The Cards, under new ownership, came in third with a new manager, Marty Marion. The deteriorating Braves, placing fourth, switched managers from Southworth to Tommy Holmes June 19. The Phils, with Simmons in service all year, fell to fifth even though Ashburn hit .344 and Roberts won 21. (Spahn won 22 and Murry Dickson 20 for seventh-place Pittsburgh, where Rickey had been put in charge after leaving Brooklyn to O'Malley.) The Cubs, finishing last, replaced Frisch with Phil Cavaretta (their boy wonder of 1935, now 34 and still able to hit .311 in 89 games) on July 21.

Jethroe led again in base stealing with 35. Campanella was MVP.

AL—Stengel's Yankees made it three straight by a more comfortable margin, five games over Cleveland. With DiMaggio on his last legs (literally), the team's strength had shifted to pitching: Lopat 21–9, Raschi 21–10, Reynolds 17–8 with seven saves. A rookie sensation in training camp, 19-year-old Mickey Mantle, was hailed as DiMaggio's successor, but he had to be sent back to the minors for a month in midseason. The annual great midsea-son pickup was Sain, available because he was 5–13 with the Braves, who became a vital bull-pen presence. Reynolds pitched a 1–0 no-hitter against Feller in Cleveland July 12 and another at Yankee Stadium September 28 against the Red Sox, in a game that clinched a pennant tie. Berra, with 27 home runs, was the league's MVP.

The Indians, having let Boudreau go, promoted Al Lopez from Indianapolis, and he too had a pitcher-oriented club: Feller 22–8, Mike Garcia and Early Wynn 20–13 each, Lemon 17–14. Luke Easter hit 27 homers, Al Rosen 24, Doby 20. Boudreau went to Boston as a player, with the understanding that he would be made manager eventually.

The Red Sox, their pitching shot and their offense down to merely human, were third by 11 games. Paul Richards, a rookie manager in Chicago, brought the White Sox in an unexpected fourth. Jimmy Dykes replaced Mack in Philadelphia and finished sixth, as Ferris Fain, his fiery first baseman, won the batting title at .344 while his left fielder, Gus Zernial, led the league in homers (33), runs batted in (129), and strikeouts (101).

Ned Garver, with the last-place Browns, was 20–12, giving the league six 20-game winners for the first time since 1922. The National League's seven was the most since 1923, and the total of 13 the most in the majors in 31 years—since the adoption of the lively ball and of trick-pitch restrictions.

All-Star Game—The National, winning 8–3 at Detroit, showed a shift in balance of power: its larger and faster infusion of black players was making it a stronger league, although only Robinson, Campanella, and Newcombe contributed to this particular game. Kiner, Hodges, Musial, and Bob Elliot hit home runs for the Nationals, Wertz and Kell for the Americans.

WS—It started on Thursday, the day after Thomson's homer, across the Harlem in Yankee Stadium. The Yankees were well rested, having clinched the Friday before. The Giants had no choice but to start Dave Koslo, their left-hander who'd had a 10–9 season. So Koslow outpitched Reynolds 5–1, backed by a three-run homer by Dark. The Yankees' Lopat beat Jansen 3–1 the next day, but at the Polo Grounds Hearn, for the Giants, prevailed over Raschi 6–2, thanks to a five-run fifth triggered by Stanky kicking the ball out of Rizzuto's hands on a steal attempt (a hit and run, actually) and completed, after another error, by Lockman's three-run homer.

The team of destiny was rolling. The Yankees were out of regular starters, while the Giants had Maglie ready.

But on Sunday it rained.

That meant Reynolds could start Monday, and he won 6–2, backed by a two-run homer by DiMaggio that made the score 4–1 in the fifth.

The fifth game was 1–1 in the third, DiMaggio having singled with two out to tie the game, when Gil McDougald followed with a grand slam off Jansen. It ended 13–1 on Lopat's five-hitter.

Destiny was unraveling.

The sixth game was back at Yankee Stadium, Koslo against Raschi. A three-run, two-out triple by Bauer in the sixth broke a 1–1 tie, and when Mays and Koslo opened the seventh with singles, Sain came in to rescue Raschi. The Giants filled the bases in the eighth, but Sain got a called third strike past Ray Noble and escaped. When they filled them again with nobody out in the ninth, Stengel brought in Bob Kuzava, a left-hander, to face the right-handed Irvin. A long fly to the Stadium's deep left field let every runner move up. Thomson did the same, bringing in the run that cut the lead to 4–3 with the tying run on second. Durocher sent up Sal Yvars to bat for the left-handed-hitter Thompson, and Yvars hit a sharp liner to right, which Bauer caught sitting down after racing in and losing his balance.

Miracles have their limits.

So the Yankees had their third straight, and the Giants, still aglow with Thomson euphoria, couldn't mind too much.

Back in Game Two, a play occurred whose historic import could be seen only in retrospect. On a fly ball to right center, the right fielder hurrying over to help the center fielder stepped on a drain and tore up his knee. He was Mickey Mantle. The man who caught the ball was DiMaggio. The man who hit it was Mays. That was the last and only intersection of those three careers.

1952

Military service, now a continuous aspect of American life, had deprived the 1950 and 1951 Phillies of Curt Simmons when they needed him. Now in 1952, with the Korean War going on, the reserve callups were more noticeable: Ted Williams, the biggest star of all, went back into the marines as a combat pilot, as did Jerry Coleman, so recently a late-season Yankee hero. The Giants lost Willie Mays to ordinary army duty early in the season, and all clubs, especially in their farm systems, had to adjust their plans to conscription.

In pennant races less eventful than the previous four, the Yankees and Dodgers emerged to give their World Series rivalry new intensity.

NL—The shock of 1951 had no lingering aftereffects for the Dodgers. They took charge with a 39–16 May and June, overtook a 27–10 start by the Giants, and moved steadily to a final 4½-game margin. Once Mays left for the army after 34 games (in which he hit only .236), the Giants were essentially a .500 club, especially since Irvin had broken his ankle in spring training and didn't play until August.

The Dodgers, however, had to do without Newcombe, who also went into the army. They came up with a 28-year-old rookie, Joe Black, who did his remarkable work out of the bull pen: a 15–4 record with 15 saves. Dressen used 15 different starters (including Black twice), as the Dodgers swept along on their terrific hitting and defense.

Another departed Giant was Stanky, hired as manager by the Cardinals, who came in third as Musial won another batting title with a modest .338. Philadelphia, in fourth, had nothing remarkable except a 28–7 for Roberts, who worked 330 innings and completed 37 of his 39 starts. On June 28, with the club in sixth, the Phils replaced Sawyer with Steve O'Neill. Cavaretta, as a bench manager, brought the Cubs in at exactly .500. The Braves, in what would be their last Boston season, switched from Holmes to Grimm on May 31, and the Pirates, with Rickey concentrating entirely on trying to build a farm system, lost 112 games while providing their catcher, Joe Garagiola, with anecdotes that would launch his more brilliant career as a speaker and broadcaster. Even so, Kiner's 37 homers tied him with Chicago's Hank Sauer for the league lead.

AL—Stengel went into the season with two goals for the Yankees: to match the record of four straight pennants achieved only by McGraw (1921–24) and McCarthy (1936–39), and McCarthy's four straight World Series victories.

DiMaggio had retired. Mantle was not yet fully healthy. Those starting pitchers were aging, Ford was in the army, the bull pen was a mishmash, Coleman was gone. Bobby Brown would be going soon. Mize was done at 39. Cleveland's pitching and power were clearly superior. The master juggler would really have to juggle to pull this off.

He juggled. Brash Billy Martin took over second. Gil McDougald, a bright rookie in 1951, took full possession of third, Joe Collins of first. To play center until Mantle's knee was 100 percent, Weiss traded Jackie Jensen to Washington for Irv Noren, a hot Dodger prospect who had been stymied by Snider. But the key piece was Sain, for whom the Yankees had given a good prospect named Lew Burdette. Stengel had Sain split his time equally between starting and relieving, did the same with left-handed Kuzava, lightened the load on the big three and, like his good friend Dressen, didn't hesitate to give 14 different men starting assignments, with only Reynolds and Raschi getting more than 19. The result was a staff earned run average of 3.14, the league's best.

With all that, the Yankees led by 2½ games on Labor Day, facing 18 of their remaining 21 games on the road while the Indians had 20 of 22 at home. But both posted 19–5 September records, and the Yankee lead held. For Cleveland, Wynn wound up 23–12, Lemon and Garcia 22–11 each—but Feller, now 33, had his first losing year, 9–13. In the last three weeks, Lopez started the top three in 18 of 19 games and won 16 of them, but it wasn't enough. Stengel's pitching by committee prevailed over Lopez's orthodoxy.

Richards caused great excitement by bringing the White Sox in third, while Dykes got the A's up to fourth, thanks to a little left-hander named Bobby Shantz who went 24–7, fielded brilliantly, hit some, and won the MVP Award.

Boudreau became bench manager at Boston and got nowhere without Williams and with a pitching staff whose top winner, Parnell, had 12 victories. Veeck, knowing he faced disaster when Busch bought the Cardinals, tried bringing back Hornsby as manager, but by June 10 the players couldn't stand him and Veeck had to replace him with Marion. Detroit, falling to last place for the first time in its history, dropped Rolfe July 5 and made Fred Hutchinson, still pitching and 32 years old, the manager.

All-Star Game—It rained on this one in Philadelphia. There was no batting practice (a big attraction at All-Star Games) and a 20-minute delay. Robinson hit a homer off Raschi in the first inning, the American scored two in the top of the fourth, and Sauer belted a two-run homer off Lemon in the bottom half. By now it was raining harder and the field was a swamp. Two pitches into the sixth inning, the umpires stopped it, waited less than an hour, and called it a 3–2 National victory.

WS—Now on national television, World Series plays had a greater impact than ever on the larger public. And this series was a beauty. It opened at Ebbets Field. Dodgers manager Dressen made Black his World Series starter—and won, 4–2, as Robinson and Snider hit homers off Reynolds, Snider with a man on. Then the Yankees won 7–1, on Raschi's three-hitter and a five-run sixth. At the Stadium, Brooklyn's Roe outlasted the Yankees' Lopat 5–3, but Reynolds got even with Black, 2–0, as Mize hit a homer and Mantle a triple for the Yankee runs.

This made the fifth game pivotal, and the Dodgers won it in 11 innings 6–5, as Carl Erskine pitched the distance, allowing four hits (including a three-run homer by Mize) in the fifth inning but only one in the other 10.

Back in Ebbets Field, the Dodgers sent Billy Loes against Raschi. Snider homered in the sixth, Berra matched it leading off the seventh, and the Yankees emerged with a 2–1 lead when Raschi bounced a single off Loes's knee. Mantle homered in the eighth, Snider hit another in the bottom half, and Reynolds came in to get the last four outs of a 3–2 Yankee victory. The Series was tied and headed for a seventh game for the first time since 1947.

The Yankees started Lopat, then used Reynolds and Raschi. The Dodgers followed Black with Roe and Erskine. Mantle's sixth-inning homer and seventh-inning single gave the Yankees a 4–2 lead, but the Dogers filled the bases with one out in the bottom of the seventh, and Kuzava replaced Raschi to face Snider. He made Snider pop up to McDougald, and Robinson pop up to the right of the mound. Collins, who had replaced Mize at first for defensive purposes, lost sight of the ball and froze. Martin, racing in from second, caught the ball off his shoe tops at the last moment. Kuzava pitched two more hitless innings and the deed was done: four straight World Championships for Stengel the Clown and his platoons, matching the push-button perfection of McCarthy and his Aristocrats.

AFTERMATH

For baseball fans, the 1952 season was only the middle of a story, the fabulous New York decade of 1947–56 in which the city's three teams finished first 15 times (counting the 1951 tie). Its ending would be the moving away of the Giants and Dodgers after 1957.

In reality, however, the season marked the end of stability, even if the major forces at work were not so visible to the public. The congressional hearings of 1951 had brought to light so much previously closely held information that baseball authorities had to face up to change. The monopoly could not be maintained without some accommodation to population growth in other areas (since it was assumed the Supreme Court would overturn the antitrust exemption). New owners, notably O'Malley, Veeck, and Busch, had their own diverse agendas. Frick as commissioner would understand his role as a facilitator, not dictator. The postwar recession following the postwar boom, plus television, was making two-team cities impractical. The West Coast could not be ignored much longer, as new airplanes, already on the drawing board, would make it accessible. If the hallowed "48 states" could be expanding to include Alaska and Hawaii, how could baseball

hope to sit still? Football was proving a more attractive television product. Scandals had blown up college basketball, but that just showed how big it had become, and it seemed the basketball pros might benefit and survive. DiMaggio was gone, no one knew if Williams would be back, Feller was fading, and no marquee names of comparable magnitude seemed at hand. And while the concentration on New York was well and good for media moguls and their advertising-world buddies, the effect on the rest of the baseball public, traditionally local and regional, was not so clear.

Europe had recovered. The cold war was on. The atom bomb's existence terrified everyone. The war in Korea was being fought under United Nations auspices. General Eisenhower was being elected president, ending the reign of Roosevelt Democrats, and the political and cultural center was clearly shifting from inner cities to suburbs. It was a new age, and baseball would have to find a new place in it.

Fans did not think about such things, but owners and executives, however glibly referred to as "dumb" by media critics, realized them.

And even in sheer baseball terms, on the field, what Stengel had done with the Yankees demonstrated that new approaches to winning might work.

Like an earthquake centered offshore under the ocean, the forces set in motion in the period 1951–52 would make themselves felt after some time lag and be fully grasped only in retrospect.

CHAPTER 18

Movement

For 50 years, since 1903, the 16 major league baseball teams had lived in the same locations: two in Chicago, Boston, Philadelphia, and St. Louis; three in New York, counting Brooklyn; and one each in Cincinnati, Pittsburgh, Detroit, Cleveland, and Washington. Every one of those communities had also housed a National League team in the 1890's, when that was the only major league. If people thought that alignment was immutable, it wasn't surprising.

In the next five years, five new cities appeared on the major league map, and Chicago was the only two-team city left. As startling as it seemed at the time, it is even more remarkable in retrospect. This mass migration involved only existing clubs, moving to greener pastures, in a shuffle unparalleled before or since. Later, almost all new venues were added through expansion. In the next 40 years, only five teams would actually change locations, three of them from the original group of 16, while 12 new teams were created. But that first cracking of the glacier, in 1953–57, altered forever the character of baseball as a business, as an entertainment, and as an idealistic concept. It shattered two beliefs that the fans of 1952 had always taken for granted: that a team somehow "belonged" to its hometown, and that baseball records were legitimately comparable from year to year. The first made it safe to invest life-long emotional attachment to the home team. The second was a uniquely satisfying component of one's intellectual interest in traditional numbers. Destruction of these two core convictions, so deep that they were seldom even mentioned, began changes in fan perception that created, through the need to adapt, further changes. While most of the baseball experience, for fan and participant, retained familiar form, one aspect of it was gone forever: stability.

THE MOVES

Veeck was the immediate problem. He had bought the Browns because the Cards seemed weak, only to have the Cards bought by a huge economic and local power. He *had* to move somewhere, and fast. He was also an annoyance to the other members of the ownership club, not only because his flamboyant promotion was showing up the stolid incompetence of some of the others, but because he was asking for types of revenue sharing (of radio-television receipts) that the big boys would not countenance. One way to get rid of him—perhaps the only way—was to not let him move.

But how? Since Los Angeles was not yet reachable (the passenger jets wouldn't come on line until late in the decade), he set his sights, publicly, on Milwaukee. A new park was being built there, suitable for major league standards. It was a political and public-relations impossibility to simply say no to Veeck. The Supreme Court had not yet ruled on the antitrust exemption now before it. Congress had shown, in the 1951 hearings, willingness to get involved. Anticipation aroused in Milwaukee could not be ignored. The toothpaste could not be squeezed back into the tube.

But Milwaukee had the Brewers, in the Triple-A American Association, the top farm team of the Boston Braves. And the Braves, now owned entirely by the Perini brothers, needed an escape hatch themselves. In four seasons they had gone from first place to seventh, from drawing 1.45 million to 280,000, in a city more and more fascinated by the Red Sox.

The only thing to do was to have the Braves go to Milwaukee themselves, in last-minute circumstances already described.

What no one expected, or could even imagine, was the response.

The Milwaukee Braves drew 1.82 million, the highest total ever in the National League, breaking the record the Dodgers had set in Jackie Robinson's first year. But that Dodger team was a pennant winner, in the country's biggest market, tapping into a major social revolution with maximum publicity. This team had no marquee names, no established stars except Spahn, no local ties, and no hint of contention, and it operated in the smallest market, in the shadow of Chicago.

In the first 13 dates, attendance exceeded the previous year's total. The team on the field did make a spectacular improvement, helped as much by the unprecedented fan support as by the arrival of fine young talent, and finished second (although 13 games out). But the crowds averaging 30,000 were coming out long before the August winning streaks that secured that high finish.

The next year, finishing third behind the Giants and Dodgers, Milwaukee drew 2.1 million. Only the Yankees and Indians, in stadiums twice as big during the peak of the postwar economic boom, had ever done that.

If that's what opening up the store in a new location meant in Milwaukee, what would it do elsewhere?

The key element, it was recognized, was the availability of a new ball park. The one in Milwaukee wasn't fancy, following the standard design established 40 years before, but it was surrounded by lots of parking spaces and easily accessible from downtown and surrounding suburbs. It also became a focus of identification for the whole state of Wisconsin, drawing customers from a large hinterland. And, of course, it made the Braves the biggest thing in town, which they had not been in Boston.

So the formulas were clear. Build us a ball park, and we'll come. You want us to stay where we are, build us a ball park.

Baltimore was next, a commitment made even before Milwaukee's dazzling display of the possibilities. Veeck wanted to move the Browns there in 1953, when Perini claimed Milwaukee, but was kept in St. Louis to be forced to go broke. When he agreed to sell the franchise—that is, not go with the team—the club was allowed to go to Baltimore for the 1954 season, where its name because the Orioles.

And for 1955, the revered Philadelphia Athletics became the Kansas City Athletics. Under Carpenter, the Phillies had become a contender and the bigger attraction in town, sharing Shibe Park with the A's since 1938, drawing twice as many customers as the landlord in the 1950's. Once Mack retired, it made sense for the family to sell, and there were no buyers in Philadelphia. In 1953, the ball park was renamed Connie Mack Stadium and bought by the Phillies. The franchise went to Kansas City, where Municipal Stadium, expandable to major league standards, had existed since 1923 on a suitable site. It was enlarged from 17,000 to 30,000 between seasons and graced by the scoreboard that used to be at Braves Field.

As the Milwaukee Braves evolved into pennant winners, they drew 2 million every year. Baltimore and Kansas City didn't match such numbers (or provide contenders) but drew two, three, and four times as much as they had as parties of the second part in their old cities.

O'Malley, in Brooklyn, was most outspoken about the new situation of the Braves. Their suddenly enormous revenue would allow them to invest in players through bonuses and farm systems on a scale he couldn't match with his Ebbets Field income, good as that was. The parking problem was crucial for a team whose regular customers came increasingly from the suburbs, and Milwaukee demonstrated that too.

Stoneham faced the same realities in the Polo Grounds. The historic parks, built originally in upscale middle-class residential neighborhoods, were now deep within deteriorating slum areas. New facilities were needed.

If not in New York, elsewhere.

O'Malley sought a futuristic domed stadium in downtown Brooklyn, privately built and owned but with the city and state paying for land acquisition and surrounding infrastructure. Stoneham listened to plans for a project on Manhattan's middle west side. Both were quickly rejected by politicians and public opinion.

O.K., elsewhere. Stoneham's top farm club was in Minneapolis, a longtime American Association partner of Milwaukee and Kansas City. Minnesotans could read handwriting on walls. They started building a ball park near the airport that could easily grow to major league qualifications, and the Millers started playing there in 1956. Stoneham prepared to move the Giants there for 1958.

O'Malley had bigger ideas. To drive home the point that he wouldn't stay at Ebbets Field no matter what, he (1) sold it and (2) scheduled seven home games a year in 1956 and 1957 in Jersey City's 32,000 seat Municipal Stadium, empty since the International League Jersey Giants had departed in 1951. His goal, and his suitor, was Los Angeles. Clearly, it was the best market imaginable, and the jet planes would soon be available. But being the only team on the West Coast, nearly 2,000 miles from the nearest rival, wasn't a good idea. What if Stoneham, who was going to leave New York in any case, made a deal in San Francisco?

Each city would have to provide a brand-new ball park, of course, even if not immediately. And there was another enticement. Cable television was coming, and that would mean pay television, a potential bonanza. In the built-up East, where all cable had to be put underground, it would be a long time before it reached enough homes. But in California, telephone and other wires were still strung on poles, to which cable lines could be added quickly and easily at much less cost.

Horace Stoneham went to San Francisco, liked it, saw the value of keeping the great rivalry intact, and went along. So in 1958, they became the Los Angeles Dodgers and the San Francisco Giants. When O'Malley had first asked for permission to go to Los Angeles, the other owners wouldn't give it. Once Stoneham agreed to make it a two-club move, they approved.

Whatever emotional agonies may have plagued dedicated fans of the Braves, Browns, and Athletics in their own cities, those not involved paid little attention, wasted little sympathy on them, and accepted the logic of economics. The abandonment of New York caused a different reaction: widespread outrage. Beyond the direct loss to followers of those teams, this was a tearing of the fabric of history, a repudiation of traditional values, a betrayal, a crime, a disgrace. There was no visible economic necessity, and local buyers would have come forth if Stoneham and O'Malley had offered to sell. And it was all happening in the lap of that dominant media-advertising establishment, striking at the fan attachments of those individuals and their children.

Gone forever was a feeling fans seldom thought about but always depended on: a sense of certainty that one knew exactly what major league baseball was and how it operated. New patterns could be (and would be) learned quickly, but certainty could never be recaptured.

Four centuries earlier, the idea that it was the earth going around the sun instead of the other way around shook a whole culture's sense of mankind's central importance. In baseball's miniuniverse, the franchise shifts of the 1950's had an analogous impact. The situation is best summed up in tables.

City	1903 Population	1952 Population	Teams
New York	2,500,000	7,900,000	3
Chicago	1,700,000	3,700,000	2
Philadelphia	1,300,000	2,100,000	2
Boston	600,000	800,000	2
St. Louis	600,000	900,000	2
Pittsburgh	500,000	700,000	1
Cleveland	400,000	1,000,000	1
Detroit	300,000	2,000,000	1
Washington	300,000	800,000	1
Cincinnati	300,000	500,000	1
Baltimore	500,000	1,000,000	0
Milwaukee	300,000	700,000	0
Kansas City	200,000	500,000	0

In 1903, the circuits reflect population perfectly, with the exception of Baltimore, victim of an insider deal to put a third team (the Yankees) in New York.

By 1952, Baltimore, Milwaukee, and Kansas City are every bit as viable, in population-market terms, as all the one-team cities except explosively enlarged Detroit, while Boston and St. Louis obviously belong in the one-team category.

The three moves of 1953–55 might have been predicted by someone with no knowledge of baseball or sports in general, just from looking at the census.

The 1957 move to California is different. Los Angeles, a village of 100,000 in 1903, has grown to 2 million—long since desirable, only now accessible. San Francisco, 400,000 in 1903, was a great city then, but out of reach. In 1952, at 800,000, it's ideal for pairing with Los Angeles.

Population pressure is as inexorable as the force of gravity. When we look at 1960, we use a different set of numbers. The Census Bureau now lists "metropolitan areas." Up to 1950, considering only the legal boundaries of large cities made sense in commercial terms, but with the advent of the private automobile and extended suburbs, the *actual* relevant market is the circle within easy transportation reach of the center. The metropolitan populations look like this:

City	1960 Population (in Millions)	Teams
New York–New Jersey	10.7	1
Los Angeles–Riverside	6.0	1

City	1960 Population (in Millions)	Teams
Chicago	6.2	2
Philadelphia	4.3	1
Detroit	3.8	1
San Francisco–Oakland	2.6	1
Boston–New England	2.6	1
Pittsburgh	2.4	1
St. Louis	2.1	1
Washington	2.0	1
Cleveland	1.9	1
Baltimore	1.8	1
Dallas–Fort Worth	1.7	0
Minneapolis–St. Paul	1.5	0
Houston	1.4	0
Cincinnati	1.3	1
Milwaukee	1.3	1
Kansas City	1.1	1
Seattle	1.1	0
San Diego	1.0	0
Atlanta	1.0	0

The vacuum in New York and Los Angeles, sucking in a second team, is obvious. So is the increasingly attractive force of Dallas, Houston, and Minneapolis, and the rising tide in Seattle and San Diego, the northern and southern extremities of the opened-up West Coast. It will take longer, but all seven openings will be filled in another decade or so.

But an even more important process is at work: trend lines. Between 1950 and 1960, all the original 10 cities undergo a *decrease* in central-city population (except Cincinnati, which stays the same). So do Baltimore and San Francisco. But Milwaukee, Kansas City, and Los Angeles show slight increases, even within the city limits. And Houston, Dallas, San Diego, and Seattle are growing at enormous rates (but Minneapolis–St. Paul is not). On the horizon, smaller but growing even faster, are Denver, Miami, Tampa, and Phoenix—who will become the new members of the 1990's—and Atlanta, occupied in 1966. And the only two great Canadian metropolises, Montreal and Toronto, so long successful in Triple A, can't be ignored either: Canadians have television sets too.

What was happening was expansion. Perceived only as "moving franchises" at the time, baseball was really expanding the size of its market, making more "outlets" inevitable.

What does all this have to do with baseball games? Everything. Whether the press and public were paying attention or not, the decision makers were thoroughly aware of market reality, and, it is impossible to understand what has been happening to the game's organization ever since without keeping these basic patterns in mind.

	In 1903	In 1952	In 1960
Major league cities	10	10	15
Total population	8.5 million	20.4 million	25 million
Total attendance	4.7 million	14.6 million	19.9 million
Future members	15*	17	12
Their population	2.2 million	10.4 million	7.4 million

*Excluding Montreal and Toronto

In other words, the franchise shifts of the 1950's skimmed the cream of the unoccupied areas, while making everyone aware that the bottle was not yet empty.

THE FRICK ADMINISTRATION

The new commissioner, Ford Frick, installed in 1951, knew the baseball business very well. During the early years of his National League presidency, he had to deal with the conditions of the Depression, which included cutting costs, leniency toward dues, and persuading the stronger to help (or at least not take advantage of) the weaker. Then came the lush postwar years, opening vistas of profit never imagined. Now attendance was down again but television was offering wider horizons. Frick understood the implications of population shifts thoroughly.

Yet he was also a lifelong baseball man on the emotional and professional side, steeped in the sport's traditions from the privileged position of writer and broadcaster, sensitive to what the fans really liked: the games and the stars, not the business.

Landis had eschewed empire building in the form of bureaucracy because he wanted to keep control. Frick avoided it because he didn't *want* control. He was hired to administer and mediate as necessary, not rule, and that was his personal inclination too.

The first three club moves did not cause much outrage. These were losing teams, failing where they were, and the enthusiasm in their new homes overrode everything else. Those who objected and asked why the commissioner didn't "do something" got the standard answer: "That's a league matter, not in my jurisdiction." That statement was perfectly true.

But the moves to California were something else.

First of all, the Giants and Dodgers were living symbols of tradition, a unique traditional rivalry based on same-city occupancy. Second, as of the spring of 1957, they had won seven of the last eight pennants, and Brooklyn in particular was universally known to be a center of profit as well as passion. Third, this was New York, where the populace had always been more interested in the National League than the American (which was not the case in Boston).

Fourth, both teams had been offered stadium deals to stay, and local buyers would have been plentiful if the teams were put up for sale. This hadn't been true in the previous cases, so the idea that the clubs were being "stolen" from local supporters gained credibility.

The moves became, in New York, a major political issue, which it had not been in the other three cases; there it was a hot political issue for the receiving cities, not the losing cities. Nothing could be done about preventing O'Malley and Stoneham from doing what they wanted with their private property in a free society; but a replacement for one of the teams *had* to be found. Moves could go in two directions, after all. Mayor Robert F. Wagner Jr., up for reelection, promptly named a commission to seek a National League team. At its head was a lawyer, well known in sports circles and a behind-the-scenes power among Democrats, named Bill Shea.

Shea approached Cincinnati, Pittsburgh, and Philadelphia about moving to New York, into a new stadium to be built by the city on the site of the 1939–40 and forthcoming 1964 World Fairs, in Queens. None accepted the invitation, among other reasons because doing so would raise political issues in their towns.

That set the stage for the next chapter.

Frick was in the middle of all these negotiations. His office as in New York. He and Shea knew the same people, moved in the same circles, hung out at Toots Shor's restaurant. He certainly appreciated the value—nay, the necessity—of a New York franchise to the National League. But he was in an awkward position. His job, nominally, was to protect "the best interests of baseball," and could anyone assert that moving into California wasn't good for baseball as a whole? Or deny that the three previous moves had been roaring successes? (Taking the three-year periods before and after each move, the Braves had tripled their attendance, the Kansas City A's and Baltimore Orioles more than doubled theirs.) On a practical (and in his eyes, moral) level, Frick was supposed to protect the interests of the men who hired him, and all club owners were benefiting from the moves. So he not only had to defend them in public statements, he had to do all he could to see that the transitions were as orderly as possible, minimizing disruption.

But in the New York context, his statement that "it's not in my jurisdiction" became a weapon in the hands of those unreconciled to their loss, a group that naturally included New York's newspapers. Frick was vilified, increasingly, for not wielding autocratic power he never had; for not doing "something" to preserve the status quo; for kowtowing to the "Lords of Baseball" (sportswriter Dick Young's phrase) instead of looking after the interests of the "fans." (Which fans? The ones in California or the ones in Brooklyn?)

Frick walked a tightrope and walked it well. He made positive statements, he looked after mundane details (like schedules and regulations, which could have become messy but didn't), and he did exactly what he was being paid to do along lines he personally believed in.

But everything has its price. Embroiled in franchise movement, Frick could not pay enough attention to two other areas that would get out of hand before the owners would confront them seriously, and to which he might have made constructive contributions, given his background and internal prestige at that time.

One was player relations. The other was centralized marketing.

The reforms of 1946, including the creation of the pension plan, had been frozen in place. There were player representatives on the pension committee, but their input was largely ignored. When there was a particular grievance, it still went up the club-league-commissioner ladder with no formal procedures and no recourse. General grievances about unreasonable scheduling, padded fences, travel expenses, severance, or anything like that went to a committee of owners and were simply ignored. The clubs, leagues, and minors had elaborate written regulations concerning their relationships, reconsidered every few years. The players as a group had nothing in writing except the pension; individuals had player contracts.

Allie Reynolds and Ralph Kiner were players on the pension committee. By 1953, they were asking for modest increases. Contemplating the terms then in effect and what the players sought gives us a basis for understanding what they did eventually and why.

Until a man played five full years in the majors, he wasn't entitled to any pension. After the age of 50, a five-year player would get $50 a month for life, a 10-year man $100, others in between. The players wanted to make it $80 and $150 and, since few played to the age of 40, change the age at which they could start collecting to 45.

Allowing for changes in inflation and life-style, it boiled down to this: the top pension would be $1,200 a year, when the average wage for a clerical worker was $4,000—and would be double that by the time a 1953 player in his 20's started collecting.

The owners' answer was a flat no. Kiner and Reynolds decided to get a lawyer to help them negotiate, and in August hired J. Norman Lewis. In December 1953, at the major league meetings in Atlanta, Frick agreed to meet with player representatives (one from each club) but flatly refused to have Lewis admitted. "But make sure your lawyer stays out in the foyer," we sang in the baseball writers' show, to the tune of Gershwin's "It Ain't Necessarily So."

The baseball community was particularly confident at that moment. On November 2 the Supreme Court had ruled 7–2 that the antitrust exemption should continue, despite its contradictions, until Congress changed it.

It wasn't until April of 1954 that an agreement was reached. The pensions would stay the same, but the pension fund would get guaranteed funding: all the All-Star Game receipts and 60 percent of the radio-television World Series money would go into it. The other request, that the minimum major league salary be raised from

$6,000 to $7,200? Rejected. Permission for more players to play more winter ball in the Caribbean? Rejected.

In July, during the All Star break, the Major League Baseball Players Association attained formal existence.

All concerned swore long and loud they had no intention of becoming a union. Unions were not for baseball, players agreed. This was strictly about pensions.

Frick was certainly no New Deal liberal in his own thinking, but he might have thought matters through a little better if the franchise moves weren't so center stage. He might—just might—have seen some wisdom in a policy of "give them the little they're asking for and leave them satisfied," since he did know ball players and how they felt and lived.

The marketing problem had a different dimension. Frick was the one charged with negotiating television contracts with the networks for the World Series—his only area of authority—and was qualified enough. But dealing with TV implied growing tie-in sales, creating and selling logo products, making package deals with advertisers. That world wasn't there yet, but one could see it coming. And *that* world did require a central bureaucracy, professionals adept at such activities working directly under someone's supervision. That someone could only be the commissioner, since there was no one else, and they would require extensive staff and expense structures. This commissioner had minimum staff and wanted it that way. The result was that much pioneering work in this direction wasn't done, at a time when baseball was still supreme in sports prestige. Over the next 10 years, baseball fell far behind football in developing this area, but might have upstaged football if it had taken full advantage of its position early enough.

That's hindsight, but hindsight is what lets us see what happened more clearly than we could at the time.

Meanwhile, the money was rolling in—in the new cities, club by club from radio and television, in concessions. Players, bound by the reserve system, would take what they were given. Neither they nor outside promoters could use the antitrust threat. Cities that wanted teams were eager to talk about building ball parks, and so were the old cities trying to keep teams. Certain columnists might ridicule Frick, but his employers liked the way he operated. They renewed his contract for another seven years starting in 1958.

THE *NEW* NEW STARS

The Korean War ended in 1953, and the twice-departed Ted Williams was back by August. He got into 37 games, hit .407, and socked 13 homers. Others drifted back about the same time, and those who were simply selective service draftees were now part of a rotating pool.

But the spotlight was being taken by new names: Mantle, Mays, Robin Roberts, Eddie Mathews, Henry Aaron, Lew Burdette, Frank Robinson, Al Rosen, Harvey Kuenn, Rocky Colavito, Ernie Banks, and on and on. Their density was as great as in the past, since there were still only 16 teams, relocated or not. Their exposure was greater than ever, thanks to television. Their production of homers was higher than ever—fans loved homers—while the glamorous pitchers were still working every fourth day and completing their games. Survivors of the 1930's may have been unwilling to call it a Golden Age, but the young fans knew better and had no doubts, laying the foundations for the collector craze that would blossom when they grew up and treasured memories of the 1950's.

This was, as it turned out, the last such intense cycle of star formation precisely because there were still only 16 teams.

Then there were the managers. Their role was changing as hand-held microphones appeared in so many hands. The manager had always been the club's official spokesman. Now more and more of his time and attention, especially before and after games, had to be devoted to that role. The demand for quotes—the only product the electronic media had to offer, forcing the print journalists to imitate and keep pace—became insatiable. The publicity and damage-control capabilities of the manager became a major part of his responsibility and effectiveness.

Casey Stengel, Leo Durocher, Charlie Dressen, and Birdie Tebbets had the personalities and skills to make the most of manipulating the media. McGraw and Mack and their counterparts, in their day, had done that by dealing with a relatively small group of regular writers, much as President Roosevelt handled a White House press corps face-to-face with mutual trust and the potent weapon of ostracism to be used against troublemakers: to be excluded from the inner circle meant professional and social failure. But mobs of strangers with dozens of outlets, inundating the regulars ("my writers," as Stengel called them), made the old method obsolete. Stengel's doubletalk, Durochers's anecdotes and name-dropping, Dressen's disingenuous egotism and baseball cleverness, Birdie's nonstop chatter sprinkled with insights—these not only got the job done in the new environment, they put the fans into a new relationship. The manager had been perceived, from the beginning, as the general of the army, the captain of the ship (to this day, "skipper" is still a way to address a manager). He was admired or skewered for the way he made decisions, and how they turned out. Now he was also a prime source of entertainment and information, expected to be accessible to all.

In various ways, according to their natures, managers Paul Richards, Fred Haney, Al Lopez, Lou Boudreau, Eddie Stanky, Bobby Bragan, Mayo Smith and in due course Walter Aston and Bill Rigney became media celebrities during the 1950's in ways their predecessors had not.

And there were, at any given moment, only 16 of them.

THE MINORS

While the majors thrived, the destruction of the minors was under way. The forces for expansion automatically downgraded the high minors. Each new major league territory eliminated what had been one of the most important minor league territories. The Pacific Coast League, which had sought semimajor status for itself, became a dead issue instantly when the Giants and Dodgers came into California, surviving in name but not in substance. Milwaukee and Kansas City had been mainstays of the American Association, Baltimore the most distinguished franchise in the International League for half a century. Replacing them with Toledo, Denver, and the like was bad enough for the Association and the International, but the Coast League had four teams wiped out, Hollywood as well as Los Angeles, Oakland as well as San Francisco, and their places were taken by Phoenix, Salt Lake City, Spokane, and Vancouver (which actually supplanted Oakland in 1956).

Here is the domino theory applied. The new Triple-A cities had been strong Double-A cities, which had to replace them with what used to be Single-A cities, and so on down the line. In terms of population centers, prestige, and historical attachments, there was debilitation all the way down the line.

Worse still was the economic impact on all minor league territories of the radio broadcasts and now telecasts of major league games. The minor league fan base, once the farm systems were established, developed loyalties to the parent clubs. One accepted the loss in mid–pennant race of one's favorite player because his promotion to the majors, for the sake of the parent club, was deemed a legitimate priority. So one rooted for the parent club, wherever it was, as well as the local one. Now if the big-league club's games could be experienced directly through radio and television, the impulse to attend the local game weakened—and the possibility of getting local radio money for the minor league games dried up altogether.

The minors did more than beg for restrictions on broadcasts, at least in direct competition with their playing times. They sued, claiming invasion of their territories had cost the minors $50 million in five years, and introduced an antitrust bill in the Senate aimed at the St. Louis farm system's control of clubs. (Cardinal broadcasts had the biggest impact on minors in Middle America.) But the Supreme Court decision made all that moot.

During the 1950's, however, the quality of play in the high minors remained stable. That's why the new stars were reaching the majors with adequate preparation. This would cease to be true after further expansion at the top and further contraction of the minors, making more haphazard. But as long as there were only 16 teams with only 400 major league jobs; as long as major league pay was so low that a Triple-A career was not unreasonable for a player in his 30's; as long as *all* player movement was totally under club control, the training function of the minors was preserved.

The 1950's, however, did mark the beginning of decline. From the lowest point of the depression in 1933 to prewar 1941 the number of leagues operating had grown from 14 to 41. After the war, the number jumped to more than 50. Then:

	Leagues	Farm Clubs
1950	58	210
1954	36	156
1958	24	157

So the clubs that began disappearing once movement-expansion in the majors began were the independents.

And here's what happened to the Triple-A circuits:

	1950	1960
International League	Toronto*	—
	Montreal*	—
	Jersey City	—
	Buffalo	—
	Baltimore*	Miami*
	Rochester	—
	Syracuse	Richmond
	Springfield	Columbus
American Association	Milwaukee*	Houston*
	Kansas City*	Denver*
	Minneapolis*	—
	St.Paul	—
	Louisville	—
	Indianapolis	—
	Columbus	Charleston, W. Va.
	Toledo	Dallas–Ft. Worth*
Pacific Coast League	Los Angeles*	Vancouver
	Hollywood*	Tacoma
	San Francisco*	Spokane
	Oakland*	Salt Lake City
	San Diego*	—

1950	1960
Sacramento	—
Portland	—
Seattle*	—

*Eventually replaced by a major league team

SEASONS 1953–57

1953

The Yankees and Dodgers won again in 1953, with far less resistance, and the Yankees won a fifth straight World Series in less dramatic fashion than in 1952.

NL—With Mays still in the army and Maglie and Jansen suffering from ailments that started the year before, the Giants were unable to challenge the Dodgers. The only opposition came from the transplanted and transformed Milwaukee Braves, but they were no serious threat after midseason, when the Dodgers got rolling. Brooklyn won 46 and lost only 14 during July and August, and finished first by 13 games with 105 victories. Philadelphia and St. Louis also finished ahead of the Giants, who fell 14 games below .500.

At Brooklyn, Snider came into his own with 42 homers, while Campanella hit 41 and Hodges 31. Furillo was batting champion at .344 (to Musial's .337). Jim Gilliam arrived and took over second base, so Robinson divided his time between left field and third base. Campy's 142 runs batted in led the league, Gilliam hit a league-leading 17 triples, Snider hit .336 and Robinson .329, and the team led the league in stolen bases.

With that, and excellent fielding, the pitching staff could do without Newcombe, who was in the army. Carl Erskine was 20–6, Russ Meyer 15–5, Billy Loes 14–8, and Preacher Roe 11–3, giving him a three-year stretch of 44–8.

The Braves had Spahn 23–7 and Burdette (obtained for Sain) 15–5, followed by two youngsters, Bob Buhl and left-handed Johnny Antonelli. Eddie Mathews, their 21-year-old third baseman, led the league with 47 homers. Bill Bruton, their new center fielder, led in stolen bases with 26. Joe Adcock, a first baseman with awesome right-handed power, and Del Crandall, 23, an outstanding catcher, were clearly foundation stones in a great future. (That's what made O'Malley so nervous.) Managed by Grimm, in the Milwaukee that loved him so much, drenched in adulation, this group would indeed dethrone the Dodgers eventually.

Stanky, as Cardinal manager, lacked the kind of pitching and defense that would make his approach to baseball work, although Harvey Haddix, a little left-hander, was 20–9. Durocher, once out of contention, seemed to lose interest and let players like Dark practice managing in late-season games. Hornsby, given another chance to manage by Cincinnati late in 1952, couldn't quite finish 1953, leaving with eight games to go after fighting all season with his players and the local press.

In Pittsburgh, Rickey still concentrating on building a farm system, found his timetable stretched out by the military draft. The hapless parent club was still guided by Fred Haney and lost only 104 games, eight fewer than in 1952.

AL—Ford was out of the army and went 18–6 for the Yankees, making his career record 27–7. Sain and Reynolds, both starting and relieving regularly, produced 27 victories and 22 saves. Lopat was his old self (16–4), but Raschi wasn't (13–6). Mantle had established himself in center. Bauer and Gene Woodling flanked him, no longer being platooned. Billy Martin had taken over second base in Coleman's absence. Berra was the home-run leader with 29 (to Mantle's 21). It was the easiest season Stengel ever had.

In Cleveland, Rosen had a year for the ages. With 43 homers and 145 runs batted in, he missed the Triple Crown because Mickey Vernon, in Washington, hit one point higher than his .336. The Lemon-Garcia-Wynn trio won 56 games, and Doby contributed 29 home runs. Richards brought the White Sox in third again. The Red Sox were fourth, even though Parnell had a 21–8 season, and the Senators under Harris were fifth despite Vernon and Bob Porterfield's 22–10. Dykes was going nowhere in Philadelphia, and Marion managed the Browns to last place in what everyone acknowledged was a lame-duck season en route to Baltimore.

All-Star Game—The Nationals made it four straight with an uneventful 5–1 decision as Roberts, Spahn, Simmons, and Murry Dickson held the American Leaguers to five hits.

WS—They took up where they left off. The Yankees won the opener at Yankee Stadium 9–5, featuring a two-out, three-run triple by Martin in the first inning and later homers by Berra and Joe Collins, while Sain relieved Reynolds in the sixth. Then Lopat defeated Roe 4–2 on Mantle's two-run, tie-breaking homer in the eighth, after Martin had hit a solo homer in the seventh to tie.

At Ebbets Field, however, Brooklyn's Erskine set a World Series record by striking out 14 and won 3–2 on Campanella's homer off Raschi in the eighth. Then the Dodgers pounded Ford for a 7–3 victory, and the fifth game was a true Ebbets Field slugfest. Mantle hit a grand slam early, Martin added a two-run job later, and the Yankees took a 10–2 lead into the eighth before surviving 11–7.

Erskine started on two days' rest at the Stadium (no travel days in a Subway Series) and fell behind 3–0 in the first two innings. Ford left after seven with a 3–1 lead, but Furillo's two-run homer off Reynolds with one out in the ninth tied it. Then Martin untied it with a single to center with one out and two on, and the Yankees had their unprecedented—and as yet unmatched—fifth straight World Series triumph.

Martin had 12 hits, a record for a six-game series and equal to the mark for seven- and eight-game sets also.

1954

Just when it seemed the Yankees and Dodgers would take permanent possession of the World Series, Cleveland and the Giants intervened with once-in-a-lifetime seasons that dethroned both in 1954.

NL—Choosing pragmatism over sentiment, the Giants traded Bobby Thomson—*the* Bobby Thomson—to Milwaukee for Johnny Antonelli. They had other everyday players, especially with

Mays back from the army, but they needed pitching desperately. They guessed right. Antonelli's 21–7 anchored a pitching staff bolstered at the other end by a relief tandem of Hoyt Wilhelm, knuckleballer, and Marv Grissom, hard thrower. This pair accounted for 22 victories and 26 saves. Mays, with 36 homers, was on a Ruthian home-run pace in August, then was told by Durocher to concentrate on getting on base, so he proceeded to raise his batting average to .345, beating out teammate Don Mueller (.342) and Snider (.341) for the batting title, while settling for 41 homers (Ted Kluszewski of Cincinnati led with 49). Thomson, meanwhile, broke his ankle in spring training and didn't play at all until August.

O'Malley made the same choice in Brooklyn, with worse results. Dressen had just finished first three years in a row counting the play-off year, got on well with his players, was well liked by the fans, and had long, impeccable baseball credentials. But when he had the nerve to ask for a three-year contract, O'Malley wouldn't even give him a chance to retract the request. He promoted Walter Alston, who had worked his way up the system to Montreal, and signed him to what would be the first of 23 consecutive one-year contracts. But the Dodger veterans didn't relate to Alston at all, and those who had played for him in the minors weren't that fond of him. The New York media spotlight was not comfortable for the quiet Alston, and worst of all, the players had no confidence in him. The Dodgers struggled and sputtered until August before starting to play well, and by then it was too late. They finished five games out with 13 fewer victories than the year before.

Milwaukee started fast, had a horrible June, then made it a three-team race for a while until the Giants took command in late August. They played a 20-year-old rookie, Hank Aaron, in right field, since Thomson was unavailable. Spahn went 21–12, Mathews hit 40 homers, but it just wasn't enough. All the other teams finished under .500.

AL—Cleveland's pitching had been overpowering for years, its offense productive, its defense good enough behind such hard-to-hit pitchers. Now Lopez got the missing piece: stifling relief. Like the Giants, the Indians had a tandem, lefty Don Mossi and righty Ray Narleski.

The result was the best record of the modern era (1920 on). The Indians won 111 games, lost

43, for a .721 winning percentage—one game better than the fabled 1927 Yankees. It was eight games better than the current Yankees, who won 103, the most they ever had or would under Stengel; but when they went 44–14 through July and August and found themselves a game and a half further back than when they started, they knew they were done.

At Cleveland, Doby's 32 homers and 126 runs batted in led the league. Bobby Avila's .341 gave the second baseman the batting crown. Lemon, Wynn, and Garcia won 65 games, Art Houtteman added 15, and Feller, at 35, went 13–3. Since starters finished exactly half their games (77), the bull pen had a reasonable workload, and whatever the two rookies didn't mop up, Hal Newhouser did (7–2 with 7 saves).

There has never been another pitching staff of such distinction in its totality.

Jimmy Dykes had left the A's to manage first-year Baltimore, but after the season Paul Richards moved in to take charge, having finished third again with the White Sox. Eddie Joost managed what would be the last year of the Athletics in Philadelphia, and they ran true to form: 103 defeats, eighth place.

All-Star Game—In Cleveland's Municipal Stadium, before a crowd of 69,000, the Americans won 11–9. There were 31 hits and six homers, two by Rosen. Trailing 9–8 in the eighth, Doby tied it with a pinch home run, and a looping single with two out by Nellie Fox scored Mantle and Berra with the winning runs.

WS—The Indians, of course, were lopsided favorites. They had won 14 more games than the Giants, they had the pitching, they had more power. On paper, it was no contest. On the field, it turned out to be no contest—the other way. The Giants swept.

The Polo Grounds contours were the key. In the first game, the Indians got a two-run triple from Vic Wertz in the first inning. The Giants tied it on three singles and a walk in the third. In the eighth, the first two Indians got on, and Wertz, who already had three hits, drove one about 440 feet to almost dead center—where Mays, his back to the plate, made a spectacular catch that has become one of the most reshown plays in baseball history. The Indians proceeded to fill the bases, but Grissom kept it 2–2 with a strikeout and a fly.

In the tenth, Durocher sent his favorite pinch-hitter, left-handed Dusty Rhodes, to bat for Irvin against Lemon. Dusty popped up—260 feet down the right-field line into the first row for a three-run homer and a 5–2 victory.

That was the Polo Grounds: hit it 440 feet, nothing; 260 feet, home run and ball game.

The next day, Al Smith hit Antonelli's first pitch over the roof, but Cleveland never scored again. In the fifth, Rhodes hit for Irvin again, singled home the tying run, stayed in, and hit a homer in the seventh. Giants, 3–1.

The next day, in Cleveland, Leo sent Dusty up in the *third* inning, bases full, one out. First pitch, two-run single for 3–0 lead. Giants won 6–2.

The next day, the Giants made it 7–0 with a four-run fifth and closed it out 7–3.

And the national television audience saw every bit of it.

1955

Fun's fun, but the Yankees and Dodgers reclaimed their apparent birthrights in 1955, and this time Brooklyn got what it had failed to get in 1889, 1916, 1920, 1941, 1947, 1949, 1952, and 1953—the World Series championship.

NL—It was a runaway. The Dodgers won their first 10, went to 22–2, to 52–19, and coasted. Newcombe was back in form, 20–5, and as a pinch-hitter, hit seven home runs, hitting .359. All the regulars had their usual numbers. The only open spot, since Pafko had gone to Milwaukee, left field, was now occupied by Sandy Amoros, with Robinson staying at third.

Milwaukee, still wowing its followers, came in 13½ games behind. The Giants, their pitching shot, could not regain the 1954 magic, and Durocher was on his way out. (Stoneham was ready to fire him at the start of 1954, but the older players talked him out of it and were proved right.) Mays, left to his own devices, hit 51 homers. Philadelphia's new manager, Mayo Smith, had a .500 club, with Roberts, 23–14, winning 20 for the sixth straight year. Stanky, who had been hired before Busch bought the Cardinals, was fired by him May 28 and replaced by Harry Walker, who had been managing at Rochester.

AL—With the aid of an 18-player trade with

Baltimore, giving up prospects for major leaguers, the Yankees were revamped. Bob Turley and Don Larsen, right-handers, were the principal figures, joining Ford and Tommy Byrne in the rotation. Bill Skowron was now at first, McDougald at second (with Martin in the army for the second year), Billy Hunter sharing shortstop with the aging Rizzuto, Andy Carey at third. Mantle was flanked by Bauer and Noren, Woodling having gone to Baltimore. Berra, winning his second straight and third altogether MVP Award, caught 145 games, putting his six-year average at 142—a remarkable workload that would continue for one more year.

An exciting three-way race developed with Cleveland and the White Sox, now directed by Marion. On September 13, Cleveland led by two games, but the Yankees started an eight-game winning streak while Cleveland lost five straight, and the Yankees finished three games up.

Mantle blossomed with 37 home runs, the league's best, while Jackie Jensen, now in Boston, had 116 runs batted in and Al Kaline, in his second season at Detroit at age 20, became the league's youngest batting champion (.340) since Cobb in 1907. Not one pitcher won 20 games.

All-Star Game—In Milwaukee, the Nationals scored three runs with two out in the eighth to create a 5–5 tie, which stood until Musial hit Red Sox Frank Sullivan's first pitch of the 12th inning over the right-field screen.

WS—Right until the end, it seemed like Same Old Yankees, Same Old Dodgers. The first two games were at Yankee Stadium and the Yankees won them 6–5 and 4–2, with Collins hitting two homers in the first game to help Ford over Newcombe, and a four-run, two-out rally in the fourth inning of the second. Byrne, who pitched a five-hitter, knocked in the two deciding runs with a bases-loaded single.

But the next three games were at Ebbets Field, and Yankee pitchers couldn't cope with that. The Dodgers won 8–3 behind Johnny Podres, their left-handed rookie celebrating his 23d birthday; 8–5 as Campanella, Hodges, and Snider hit home runs; and 5–3 as Snider hit two more for rookie Roger Craig (six innings) and Labine (three).

The last two games, however, would be in the Stadium, and Ford promptly made sure it would go to the seventh game with a 5–1 four-hitter. In the showdown, Podres produced an eight-hit shutout, while the Dodgers scored two runs on their five hits, and at last—after 67 years of trying—Dem Bums were Champeens of the Woild.

The key moment came in the bottom of the sixth. Trailing 2–0, the Yankees got the first two men on and Berra hit a line drive curving toward the left-field corner. Amoros, who had just entered the game, made a spectacular catch and McDougald was doubled off first. It was a play that would live forever in Brooklyn Dodger history—which, no one knew then, would be over forever in less than two years.

1956

The Yankees and Dodgers made it to the World Series again in 1956, the Yankees in a runaway, the Dodgers by squeaking through by one game over Milwaukee, and this time, with even more melodrama than the year before, the Yankees prevailed.

NL—Actually, this was a three-team race, including Cincinnati. Tebbetts had become manager of the Reds in 1954, under Gabe Paul, and they added pitching to a traditionally powerful offense, itself boosted by the addition of 20-year-old Frank Robinson, whose 38 homers tied a rookie record set by Wally Berger back in 1930. Brooks Lawrence, the pitching leader at 19–10 of an otherwise deep but unspectacular staff, was black, like Robinson. Here in the most southern of major league cities, across the Ohio from Kentucky, was the most vivid proof yet that performance was being chosen over prejudice, even while prejudice still expressed itself.

The Milwaukee Braves, who had put in place an imposing lineup with even better pitching, changed managers in May, replacing Grimm with Fred Haney. He had managed the Browns and Pirates as hopeless tailenders and now found real talent at his disposal for the first time. His team took off, actually winning at a better pace (.630) than the Dodgers (.604). Their rising black star, Hank Aaron, 22 in his third season, wound up as batting champion (.328).

Alston, no longer a nobody and Brooklyn's darling now that he had accomplished what Uncle Robby, Lippy Leo, Burt Shotton, and Cholly Dressen had been unable to, had some problems.

Podres, the Series hero, was in the navy. Jackie Robinson, at 37, was now a utility man used at four positions, an uncomfortable role. Campanella played all year with a damaged hand, not treated properly, which reduced his average to .219. But Newcombe produced his greatest year, 27–7 and the MVP Award, and Snider's 43 homers led the league, as did Labine's 19 saves.

But the difference turned out to be Sal Maglie, in another loyalty-wrenching switch that marked the Giant-Dodger rivalry. The most feared Dodger tormentor since Hubbell had been cut loose by the Giants at the end of 1955 and, at 39, had drifted to Cleveland. In May, he joined the Dodgers and delivered a 13–5 season with a 2.87 earned run average, bettered only by Burdette, Spahn, and Antonelli.

The Braves led most of the way, and in the final week led by a game. On September 25, Maglie pitched a no-hitter in Philadelphia, and the final weekend began with the Dodgers one behind with three to play. Friday they were rained out at home while the Braves lost in St. Louis. Saturday afternoon, Maglie and Labine beat Pittsburgh 6–2 and 3–1. That night, Spahn was beaten in 12 innings 2–1, leaving the Dodgers ahead by one. Sunday, Snider and Amaros hit two homers apiece in an 8–6 victory that nullified Milwaukee's 4–2 victory in St. Louis.

Three of the other teams had new managers in 1956, all of whom would become prominent. Bill Rigney took over the Giants, Fred Hutchinson the Cardinals, and Mayo Smith the Phillies. But relatively little attention was paid to the most significant indicator of all: the Dodgers did, as O'Malley had promised, play seven of their home games in Jersey City, and the wheels of drastic change were already turning.

AL—The full flowering of Mickey Mantle was the central fact of this American League season. He hit .363 with 52 homers and 130 runs batted in, a Triple Crown with the highest home-run total any triple-crown winner ever had. That and a pitching staff bolstered by recent farm products helped the Yankees to a 29–13 start, a small but persistent lead over Cleveland and Chicago through July, and a pullaway to final margins of 9 and 12 games over them.

The managerial shuffle was interesting in itself. The White Sox under Marion had done pretty much the same as under Richards, whose Baltimore Orioles (nee St. Louis Browns) were sixth. Boudreau's A's fell to last, pushing Dressen's Senators to seventh. Bucky Harris, three decades beyond his Boy Wonder stage, was fifth with Detroit, and Pinky Higgins fourth with Boston. All five were in their second season in place. Only Richards and Higgins would survive one more.

At Cleveland, Wynn, Lemon, and the new left-handed fireballer, Herb Score, won 20 each. Billy Pierce did that in Chicago and Billy Hoeft in Detroit, where Frank Lary led everyone with 21. But the Yankees' Ford, 19–6 and the earned run leader at 2.47, was emerging as the league's best pitcher in a year featuring lefties.

All-Star Game—At Washington, the Nationals won 7–3, in a game that contained four home runs, by Mays, Mantle, Williams, and Musial. That's what fans came to see and what television paid for, in an "exhibition game" still not really welcomed by the baseball establishment.

WS—The Yankee-Dodger rematch, which proved to be the last Subway Series (although few suspected it yet), followed the usual pattern. At Ebbets Field, the Dodgers mauled Yankee pitching 6–3 and 13–6, especially Don Larsen, knocked out in a six-run second inning of the second game. At the Stadium, the Yankees won 5–3 and 6–2, behind Ford and Tom Sturdivant. Again, the fifth game seemed pivotal.

Maglie faced Larsen, who pitched a perfect game, 27 up, 27 down, the only one in Series history. He almost had to, to beat Maglie, who yielded only five hits, one a homer by Mantle. But while the baseball world was still buzzing about this unique thrill, the teams went back to Ebbets Field and played an equally remarkable game. Turley and Labine went through nine innings 0–0, and the Dodgers won in the 10th when Jackie Robinson, with two out and two on, hit a line drive over the head of Enos Slaughter, New York's annual late-season pickup.

Poised for another championship, with Newcombe starting against 22-year-old Johnny Kucks, the Dodgers wound up with one of their greatest disappointments. Berra hit a pair of two-run homers in the first three innings, Elston Howard's homer finished Newk, and Bill Skowron added a grand slam off Craig in a 9–0 rout.

1957

In 1957, rumors and ultimate confirmation that the Giants and Dodgers were going to California shared attention with on-field events all season long, as the Milwaukee Braves finally overtook the Dodgers, and the Yankees kept rolling.

NL—Just as 1956 was the blossoming of Mantle, 1957 was the blossoming of Aaron. His .322 average wasn't good enough for the batting title, which Musial took at .351, but his 44 homers and 132 runs batted in led the league and the Braves to a decisive victory. And it was a strong team, bolstered in June by the addition of Red Schoendienst from the Giants, with Mathews providing the one-two lefty-righty power punch in front of Aaron. Spahn (21–11), Bob Buhl (18–7), and Burdette (17–9) headed the league's best pitching staff. Haney, so late in his baseball life, was reliving Stengel's experience of finally managing players who could play.

Hutchinson's Cardinals were the ones who had to be fought off, as the Dodgers began showing age, suffering injury, and reacting to the uncertainties of moving (They tried to trade Jackie Robinson to the Giants, but he retired instead.) Led by Musial, Ken Boyer, and Wally Moon, the Cards could not, in the long run, match Milwaukee's pitching. Half a game out at the end of July, they had a 14–16 August to Milwaukee's 19–7, and that was that. They finished eight games out, the Dodgers 11, the Reds 15.

AL—This race was equally undramatic. Even with Ford injured and a bewildering series of personnel changes, the Yankees posted 21–9 records in both June and July and won by eight games over Chicago and 16 over Boston, while Cleveland, its talent running out, fell to sixth.

Mantle's .365 was not good enough for another batting title, as Williams hit .388 at the age of 38, and Roy Sievers, with last-place Washington, led in homers (42) and runs batted in (114). But statistics are only that, and it's winning that counts, and now Mantle was established as the core of Yankee winning. (He had 34 homers and was walked 146 times in 144 games.) DiMaggio had played in six World Series his first seven seasons; now Mantle would play in his sixth in *his* first seven. The glamour had been transferred successfully.

Only two pitchers won 20, Pierce in Chicago and Jim Bunning in Detroit, while no one else won more than 16. Score's career was cut short when he was hit in the eye by a line drive in May; his vision was saved, but eventually he developed arm trouble after being rehabilitated. The two bottom teams changed managers, Cookie Lavagetto succeeding Dressen in Washington early in the year and Harry Craft taking over from Boudreau in Kansas City in August, without changing their fates.

All-Star Game—The Americans won 6–5 at St. Louis, but that wasn't the story. In 1956, Cincinnati fans had stuffed the ballot box, electing five of their players as starters and making three others runners-up in the voting. Now they voted Reds into seven of the eight starting positions, conceding only first base to Musial. Commissioner Frick stepped in and ordered Mays and Aaron to replace Wally Post and Gus Bell, and the practice of having fans vote was abolished as too subject to abuse. The new system would have players, coaches, and managers doing the voting. In the game itself, the Americans took a 3–2 lead into the ninth, scored three runs, then withstood an answering three-run rally ended by Minnie Minoso's running catch of a Gil Hodges line drive.

WS—The Braves had set a National League attendance record of 2,215,404 and were the country's sentimental favorite as they came to New York to face the Yankees. Ford outpitched Spahn 3–1 in the opener, but Burdette, whom the Yankees had given up, beat them 4–2. So the Series moved into an excited Midwest all even. Except for a few games in Cleveland in 1948 and 1954, this was the first time since 1946 that Series games were played away from the Eastern Seaboard.

The latest Yankee rookie, Tony Kubek, a native of Milwaukee, hit two home runs in a 12–3 Yankee triumph, but the Braves evened the Series 7–5 in a dramatic fourth game. A three-run homer by Elston Howard with two out in the ninth gave the Yankees a 4–4 tie, and they took a 5–4 lead in the 10th, but the Braves tied it and won on a two-run homer by Mathews. And when Burdette beat Ford 1–0, the Braves went back to New York one game from victory.

They didn't get it right away, losing 3–2 to Turley, but the travel day enabled Burdette to start the seventh game with two days' rest, and he produced another shutout, winning 5–0 on the strength of a four-run third inning off Larsen.

For the second time in three years, the Yankees had lost the seventh game, and for the third time in four, they were not World Champions. The dynasty was certainly not overthrown, since they had won eight of the last nine American League pennants, but it was beginning to seem vulnerable.

But the Series itself was upstaged by the official announcement, on the off day before the sixth game, that the Dodgers would be playing in Los Angeles in 1958. The Giants had committed publicly to San Francisco back in August. The unthinkable had become undeniable.

Within a year, the Yankees would be champions again. Within two, the Los Angeles Dodgers would be. Within three, it would be the hapless, hopeless, laughable Pittsburgh Pirates. Within four, there would be two new teams, and within five, a new New York neighbor for the Yankees, the Mets.

Within seven, the Braves would be abandoning Milwaukee.

The terrain was changing faster than anyone then imagined.

AFTERMATH

At the time, baseball saw itself as unassailably popular, prosperous, safe from legal challenge, possessing a privileged status in U.S. culture that other sports, and other entertainments, could not approach. The response of the new cities was further proof of this supremacy. It felt invulnerable. The television future promised new untold riches. The game on the field was spectacular.

All those facts intensified a great conflict. The 16 clubs already in wanted above all no additions: each had one-sixteenth of a good thing, and none wanted a smaller fraction. Outsiders, always ready to imitate success, could not start up on their own (as some had in the past) because all professional players, down to the youngest in the lowest minors, were already controlled by the existing monopoly, just sanctified by the Supreme Court. Yet the clubs faced unprecedented support, in as-yet-unoccupied communities, for efforts to gain entry because of the vivid example the five franchise moves had provided.

So the price of success was what it had always been, from the 1880s on: pressure from outsiders to share in it. That was the most visible fallout of club movement. (Look again at the chart on page 258.)

Less visible, but in the long run more important, was the attitudinal fallout. The successful moves fed arrogance and sanctified the utter shortsightedness that characterized them. As population patterns indicated, expansion in some form was inevitable, but it went forward without any general plan, without thought of consequences and how to deal with them, driven only by expediency, personal preference (and vindictiveness), and local self-interest. Any questions about the effect on the whole were brushed aside.

In the same way, the leadership failed to confront the real, predictable, obvious, and growing determination of the players to get a better deal than they had. The postwar players as a group were better educated, more secure, more aware (through military service) citizens of a prospering society than their predecessors had been. It would have been easy, and wise, to give them the crumbs they were asking for—indeed, to sugarcoat them—and even more important, to treat their requests with respect and dignity. It wouldn't have taken much to keep them satisfied then. Instead, owners kept throwing "I'm the boss and don't you forget it" in the face of a group of individuals they themselves had selected for competitive fire. The organizational strength the players ultimately achieved could have been nipped in the bud at that point—and at many later points, for that matter.

Why wasn't it? Because of the arrogant attitude built into the system. Both the franchise shifts and the government had just demonstrated to the owners that they could do whatever they wanted and benefit from it. Players? There were plenty of them out there to replace those who weren't satisfied, and there always would be.

The owners didn't understand that expansion would change that too.

CHAPTER 19

Challenge

THE CONTINENTAL LEAGUE

Even before the Giants and Dodgers played their first games in California in April 1958, a search for a New York replacement was underway and leading to far more momentous consequences.

In December 1957, two months after O'Malley's public commitment to Los Angeles, New York's Mayor Wagner appointed a four-man committee to bring another National League team to the stadium the city was now willing to build in Queens. The committee's composition was revealing.

Wagner was a Democrat facing reelection, son of a U.S. senator who had been a major figure under President Franklin Roosevelt. He chose James Farley, one of Roosevelt's early political managers and then postmaster general, now an elder statesman in the party that had lost the presidency to General Eisenhower, recently reelected; Bernard Gimbel, whose famous department store made him an ultraprominent representative of the retail community; Clint Blume, a real-estate big shot who had once played some ball; and Bill Shea, a lawyer who had the strongest insider democrat connections and a well-known sports background as college player and minor league promoter.

There it was, a political-commercial alliance that proved how much more than "just baseball" was at stake. Getting a team, having failed to keep a team, was vital for business and for votes.

Shea, from the start, functioned as a one-man committee; the other three were window dressing. He was a doer, and he knew his stuff.

He approached Crosley in Cincinnati, Galbreath in Pittsburgh, and Carpenter in Philadelphia about moving their teams to New York. The first two gave it some thought, then declined. Carpenter was not interested, period. Within a few weeks, Shea could see that getting an existing club wouldn't work, so the only answer would be expansion.

To the existing 16 club owners, overwhelmingly Republican, the Democratic ties of the Shea-Wagner group meant less than nothing. But Congress was still controlled by Democrats, and for the last seven years, Congress had been tinkering with the antitrust exemption the Supreme Court had so recently, and so unexpectedly, upheld. All concerned were aware of what Congress could do if it wanted to, and that the number of senators from states that might want teams was significantly large. California had just gone into the "have" column, but even so, the 16 teams occupied only 10 states, or 20 votes out of 96 (with Alaska and Hawaii in the wings). The House was more complicated mathematically, but no more secure.

Potential Democratic clout could not be ignored.

Shea acquired two important allies. Edwin Johnson, a former governor of Colorado and U.S. senator as a Democrat, although extremely conservative and anti-Roosevelt, had long been active in baseball as president of the Western League. He was based in Denver and still had personal ties to members of the present Senate. Branch Rickey, semiretired as an advisor to the Pirates, was willing to join Shea in a effort to make baseball expand.

How? By creating a third league, of course. Since 1900, the eight-team 154-game league had seemed ordained by nature. The one serious attempt to enlarge the market was the Federal League of 1914–15, and it had not failed in any artistic sense, only financially and as a competitor of the other two. A third league *accepted* by Organized Baseball would work—if it could get accepted.

That's what Shea and Rickey decided to pursue. The name they gave it was the Continental League, because it would include cities in Canada.

All through 1958, while an eventful baseball season played itself out, Shea kept developing his third-league idea. In Cleveland, where internal ownership strife had brought William Daley to the fore, it was declared that the Indians would leave after 1958, although a bid to move to Houston was rejected. In Philadelphia, the Phillies threatened to move across the river to New Jersey, near Garden State Racetrack, if a new ball park could not be built in Philadelphia proper. In Pittsburgh, late in the year, the Pirates sold off Forbes Field (staying as a tenant) and began looking for a new home.

And Congress was busy. It appropriated $8 million for a multipurpose stadium in Washington, to be called D.C. Stadium and shared by the football Redskins and baseball Senators. It considered a bill by Rep. Emanuel Celler (D-Brooklyn) that would limit baseball's antitrust exemption to only what was was "reasonably necessary," and another by Rep. Kenneth Keating (R-upstate New York) that would exempt baseball from virtually everything. Keating's actually passed the House late in the session, but the Senate never took it up.

Meanwhile, Sen. Estes Kefauver (D-Tennessee), head of the antitrust subcommittee of the Judiciary Committee, held midsummer hearings on the television issue. Frick declared that "radio-TV is wrecking the minors" and that in 10 years, baseball wouldn't exist—unless the majors were allowed to act collectively on broadcasting deals outside antitrust restrictions.

It was in these sessions that Stengel gave his famous incomprehensible monologue, which Mantle followed with, "I agree with everything Casey said."

Back in Los Angeles, in June, the Dodgers narrowly survived a referendum on the Chavez Ravine site the city had given them, 52 percent to 48, clearing the way for their permanent residence and the building of Dodger Stadium. At the end of the season, no less than half the teams made managerial or general-manager changes. At the December winter meetings, the clubs considered a draft of all first-year players—aimed at the Yankee system's ability to sign and lock up top prospects because they *were* the Yankees with their World Series promise—and rejected a bold demand by the major league players (through their pension-oriented association) to have 20 percent of gross receipts set aside for player compensation.

Imagine! If 20 percent could be rejected out of hand, what must the actual percentage have been? Thirty-five years later the owners would be offering 50 percent, and the players would spurn it. This was an example of the myopia mentioned in the last chapter, the refusal to give a little to save a lot later, and it had a direct consequence. Three months later the players dropped J. Norman Lewis as their legal representative—the lawyer who had to stay out in the foyer—and hired Frank Scott as a business agent (to line up appearances and endorsements) and Judge Robert Cannon of Milwaukee as a *pro bono* legal advisor.

Finally, at the December meetings, Harridge retired as American League president, to be succeeded by Joe Cronin, who had been running the front office of the Red Sox. And in March 1959, Veeck was back in action, buying controlling interest in the White Sox for a group that included Greenberg (ousted in Cleveland's internal fight) and a Chicago real-estate man named Arthur Allyn.

As the 1959 season began, therefore, the ferment in the existing leagues was intense. Since everyone on all sides was well aware of what others were doing and thinking—not always accurately or completely, but close enough in an industry where true secrecy is simply impossible—the prospects of a third league did not seem unrealistic. Undesirable, to the existing 16, yes; unrealistic, no.

In May, they tried to come to terms with the idea among themselves. The 16 owners, Frick, Giles, and Cronin got together on Galbreath's farm near Columbus in a secret meeting—secret in the sense that they made no announcement of it. Sensitive to the tacit threat in Congress, they outlined the conditions that would make a third league acceptable to them.

1. Each team's owners and financial arrangements would have to be approved by them.
2. Each new city would have to be at least as large as the smallest existing city (Kansas City, with a metropolitan-area population of about 800,000) and would have to provide a ball park with at least 35,000 capacity.
3. The new league would have to accept and sign all existing Major and Major-Minor regulatory agreements, standard player contracts, the pension plan, and other obligations, including a $7,000 minimum salary, and adopt a 154-game schedule.
4. All its plans would have to be a submitted for approval at least 10 months before its teams began play.

As arrogant as those conditions were, they were not inherently unacceptable to Shea, whose only desire at this point was to get a third league functioning so that New York could have a team in it. But they left unanswered two basic questions. How would three league champions take part in a World Series, whose traditional form was considered as sacrosanct as the 154-game schedule? And where (or how) would the new teams get players, since all existing professional players were under the control of the existing 16 teams through their farm systems?

Fans and commentators were agitated by the first question, but Shea knew that the second was the one that really mattered.

On July 27, the Continental League made its formal announcement. It would begin play in 1961 as an eight-team circuit. Five franchises had been awarded, three more would be. The five:

New York, owned by a consortium that included Joan Whitney Payson, of the immensely wealthy and powerful Whitney family also prominent in horse racing

Denver, to be run by Bob Howsam, an experienced baseball executive who was ex-senator Johnson's son-in-law

Toronto, owned by entrepreneur Jack Kent Cooke, who already owned the International League Maple Leafs there (since 1951) and had developed a friendship with Rickey

Houston, whose ownership group was led by Craig Cullinan Jr., a grandson of the founder of Texaco, and the man who had offered $6 million for the Indians to get them to move to Texas (Before that, he had tried to buy the A's in Philadelphia and the Cardinals.)

Minneapolis–St. Paul, where the ownership group was not yet well-defined, as local conflicts existed

New York, Toronto, and Houston would have new stadiums; Denver would upgrade its long-established minor league park; and the Twin Cities had had the new one in place, ready to be expanded, since 1956—the one to which Stoneham was going to take his Giants, and Griffith wanted to take his Senators.

On July 28, the day after the announcement, Senator Kefauver opened a new set of antitrust hearings, focusing now on player availability. He pointed out that some teams now controlled up to 400 and more players, and he wanted this cut to 80. But the rest of his proposed bill was, by subsequent standards, extremely benign: it would legalize the reserve system for the 80, exempt territorial rights and combined TV deals from antitrust, and allow anything that could be construed as necessary for "the preservation of public confidence in the honesty of sports contests." But it would subject baseball to the law on the same footing as other sports.

The first witness was Keating, now a senator. He opposed Kefauver's bill, pushing his own, the one the House passed in 1958. Others opposed one feature or another. The hearings lasted until July 31.

On August 2, Newark applied for the sixth Continental League franchise.

On August 18, Rickey was named president of the Continental League and predicted that in its third season it would be ready to participate in a World Series.

Now the minors started to complain. They wanted indemnities for cities taken over by the majors, pushing smaller cities up into higher leagues and aggravating the problem of major league games broadcast into minor league territories. When the moves of the 1950's occurred, they could be brushed off because (1) the major league teams owned the minor league territories they entered, and (2) on all issues, the majors simply ignored, stifled, or overrode minor league complaints (as they had been doing all century long) by using the interlocking provisions of the major-minor agreement. But if a third league—"outsiders"—was now moving in, the minors could ask more stridently.

The majors took a different tack. If the Kefauver or any other limits on player control were to go through for the sake of stocking a third league, there was now a real reason to oppose the league altogether. Maybe internal expansion would be the lesser evil.

So in October 1959, the American League announced that it would add Minneapolis as a ninth team if the National would add New York and arrange interleague play. (A league with an odd number of teams must have interleague play to avoid having one team idle every day.)

The National didn't reject the idea until December 7.

The next day, the Continental League announced that Atlanta would have its sixth franchise, with Dallas next. And in January, it completed its lineup by adding Buffalo.

But now Minneapolis was wavering, and others had private hopes. Wouldn't it be better to join the existing moneymakers than to run the risks of a wholly new league? If they were amenable to expansion, isn't that what we wanted in the first place?

Chronology tells the rest of the story.

May 6, 1960—Kefauver introduces a new bill that would limit a system's control to 100 players, free new teams from paying indemnities for territory, but make any action to oppose or interfere with a new league (any new league) an explicit antitrust violation.

May 17—The owners meet in Chicago to support Frick's opposition to the bill. Stoneham and Crosley change their votes against National League expansion, meeting that league's unanimity requirement.

May 24—Key provisions of the Kefauver bill are gutted by a fellow committee member, Senator Philip A. Hart (D-Michigan), a brother-in-law of Spike Briggs, who used to own the Tigers, and himself a former vice-president of the Tigers and current legal advisor to the National Football League Lions.

June 28—The Senate kills the bill altogether, 73–12. Continental gives up hope of a 1961 start and aims for 1962.

July 10—The American League revives its nine-team plan. The National is still opposed.

July 11—The National agrees to expansion in principle.

July 18—The American League votes for 10 teams in 1961, 12 within three or four years. The National votes for 10 starting in 1962. The Continental League is asked if it will give up its own plans in return for having four of its groups granted expansion franchises.

July 20–21—The Continental and the major leagues negotiate the indemnity question, settling on modest amounts.

August 2—The Continental agrees to dissolve. But Shea has carried out his mission.

THE ALTERNATIVE

The real reason the American League had started pushing for expansion is that it was so badly outmaneuvered and outmanaged by the National League in the 1950's.

The National was way ahead in recruiting the available and future black stars, while the American seemed reluctant and half-hearted (except for Veeck in Cleveland) about accepting them. The Yankees, biased enough but not out of proportion to mainstream attitudes, simply didn't need to change, winning perpetually with an endless supply of white players. The rest of the league ranged from hostile, in Boston and Detroit, to passive.

At the same time, the National's moves into Milwaukee, Los Angeles, and San Francisco had been runaway successes overnight, while the American's moves into Baltimore and Kansas City were merely modest improvements over terrible situations. Milwaukee was hard to explain, but there was simply no comparison in market potential between the two California cities and Baltimore and Kansas City.

And, by the end of the decade, serious efforts to provide new ball parks were underway in four of the five "old" cities, excepting only the self-satisfied Cubs in Wrigley

Field. In the American, the only new park planned was the one in Washington, which the existing Senators didn't intend to use anyhow as they sought to move to Minneapolis.

And on top of everything, the National was maintaining its long tradition of close pennant races with different and unexpected winners from year to year, while the American had become more than ever an appendage of the Yankees.

The results were striking. From 1948 through 1952, the last five years before any movement, the American had outdrawn the National by 7.3 million, nearly 1.5 million a year. In the next three years, attendance was almost exactly the same, as Milwaukee alone made up the difference. Then, from 1956 through 1960, with California added, the National outdrew the American by 6.6 million, or 1.3 million a year.

The All-Star Game, a poor real measure of anything but with great symbolic impact on fans, also shifted. The American had won 12 of the first 16, through 1949. The National then won six of the next nine, with its black stars increasingly prominent. The implication was that it was playing a better brand of baseball, with only the uniqueness of the Yankees preventing the World Series from reflecting the same trend. But even there, from 1947 to 1953, the Yankees and Cleveland (once) had run off seven straight; from 1954 to 1960, National League teams won five of the seven.

National League owners, led by O'Malley, did not try to hide their contempt for the American League (as an entity, not individual owners). And the American League owners knew they had to try something. So they were open to, and eager for, expansion, which offered new markets and some sort of ready cash as an entry fee (although this was a minor factor).

Once the nine-club idea was killed, it was a matter of choosing the best new members.

The National lived up to its commitment. It took in New York and Houston with their Continental League backers, Mrs. Payson for the Mets and Cullinan for the Houston Sports Association. A week later, on October 26, 1960, the American reneged on its promise. It ignored applications from Toronto and Dallas–Fort Worth, let Griffith move from Washington to Minneapolis (cutting out that Continental group), and placed new franchises in Los Angeles and Washington.

But it wasn't that simple. Back in August, the Yankees had insisted that if a National League team went into New York, an American League team must go into Los Angeles, the number-two market. (That Del Webb, co-owner of the Yankees, had strong California and Nevada ties was not a coincidence.) Since there was no Los Angeles applicant in the Continental group, the franchise was up for grabs. The league asked Greenberg to organize a group, while O'Malley protested the very idea.

As for Washington, the Senators had drawn 740,000 in 1960, their highest attendance since the postwar boom days of 1949, and they had an improving team whose fifth-place finish matched its best showing in 14 years. But its radio-TV rights brought well under $200,000, especially since the Orioles were next door in Baltimore. Minneapolis was offering a five-year guarantee of a million tickets a year, and $500,000 for broadcasting, plus a new stadium in a virgin area dying for major league membership. How could a family business like the Griffiths' resist that?

So the Washington Senators became the Minnesota Twins, and the new Washington franchise was given to a group headed by General Elwood P. Quesada, who had been head of the Ninth Air Force during World War II and was now head of the Federal Aviation Agency (from which he promptly and properly resigned). The new team took the old name, Senators, which would have been confusing if more people cared more than they actually did.

That was settled by November 17, but the Los Angeles situation was not.

The American offered to wait until O'Malley's Taj Mahal was ready for the Dodgers in Chavez Ravine, if the National would go along with a nine-team interleague plan in the interim. No thanks, said the National Leaguers.

At the December meetings in St. Louis, they finally got things straightened out.

First, the owners had to rewrite their own rules to legitimatize the moves into New York and Los Angeles. Then they gave the Los Angeles franchise to Gene Autry, the one-time singing-cowboy movie star, now the owner of a major chain of radio stations along the West Coast, and Bob Reynolds, once a Stanford football star, now Autry's business associate. These people had impeccable Hollywood credentials and their finger on the future: broadcasting. That the Tigers had passed into sole control of John Fetzer in October did no harm, because Fetzer, too, was a radio magnate in the Midwest.

With this group, O'Malley could make a deal. The new team, to be called the Angels like their Pacific Coast predecessors, would play one year at Wrigley Field, which O'Malley had bought form the Cubs and then turned over to the city as part of his deal for Chavez Ravine, and then become his tenant in Dodger Stadium for four years, with an option for four more.

It was now December 7, with the start of the 1961 season only four months away. A 10-team league could not use a 154-game schedule, and the new teams had to be stocked with players. Contingency plans were in place, but the Nationals thought the Americans were foolish to rush ahead. They would take their time, add their teams in 1962 and play 1961 the old way.

In 154 games, each team played seven rivals 22 times each. Now each would have nine rivals, and playing them 18 times each would make 162 games. Why 18? Because that's nine home, nine away, and a three-game series is the best pattern for baseball, the right balance between too much traveling and overstaying your welcome as a visiting attraction. Three trips to each city would work out fine.

The player plan worked this way: Each team would submit 15 of its 40-man roster for selection, at least seven of them from the 25-man active list of September 1, 1960. Every team must lose three players but not more than four. Each expansion team must choose 28—10 pitchers, two catchers, six infielders, four outfielders, and six more without regard to position. It could then choose one player from each farm system, if that player were eligible for the minor league draft, and take part in the minor league draft.

Each of the 28 players would cost $75,000, with draftees bringing regular draft prices.

The franchise itself would cost nothing.

The whole entry fee would consist of the purchase price of players. (Weird? Not at all. Tax advantages, pure and simple.)

On December 14 in Boston, where Cronin had established the league office because he lived there (as Harridge had in Chicago and Giles still did in Cincinnati), the expansion draft took place. When it was over, the Angels had 30 players for $2,150,000, the new Senators 31 for $2,175,000.

In the mix, the Angels got some good young talent (Jim Fregosi, Buck Rodgers, Dean Chance). The National Leaguers shook their heads and smiled. By acting so quickly, the American League had not given its teams a chance to juggle rosters and keep good prospects off the draft list. The Nationals would make sure no such valuable goods slipped through, with a full year to arrange their own drafting procedures.

They did it this way: each team had to list seven of its active 25 as of August 31, 1961. Each new team could take two of these at $75,000 apiece. Also listed would be eight players from each team's optionees or others on the 40-man list. The new teams must take two of these, and a third if they wished, at $50,000 each. Once these selections were made, each existing team would put up two more players from its August 31 list as "premium" picks at $125,000 each, and the new teams could pick four each from this group, but no more than one from any team.

On October 10, 1961, in Cincinnati, right after the World Series, the Mets chose 22 players for $1,800,000 and the Houston Colt .45's, known as the Colts, 23 players for $1,850,000. Events would prove the National Leaguers right: no talent slipped through.

After four years, the National League was back in New York, the American League was in Los Angeles, and both the face and the nature of the baseball business had been changed forever, more thoroughly than anyone seemed to realize.

SEASONS 1958–60

1958

Just as in 1956, a return match in 1958 went to the Yankees. The Yankees won the last three games to take the World Series from the Braves after a sum-

mer in which neither defending champion was seriously challenged in his own league.

NL—Even as current world champions, the Braves were pushed out of the limelight by the California story. The San Francisco Giants and Los Angeles Dodgers played each other in the first six games, Tuesday, Wednesday night, and

Thursday in San Francisco, Friday night, Saturday, and Sunday in Los Angeles. They split—and sold about 220,000 tickets in six days. Seals Stadium, the minor league park that the Giants had to use while their new park was being built, had only 22,500 seats, but the famous Los Angeles Coliseum, a football and Olympic venue, could hold 90,000. The Giants wound up with 1.2 million, almost double their 1957 Polo Grounds total in a building two and a half times as big. The Dodgers, despite the unattractiveness of half the Coliseum's seats for baseball, ended with 1.845 million, exceeding their best ever in Brooklyn—with a collapsing team that finished seventh.

The Giants, however, got off to a flying start, led until June, didn't fade until August, and finished third. Five rookie regulars, including Orlando Cepeda, excited San Francisco while Bill Rigney, the manager who was a native of Oakland, was considered a hometown boy. Also loaded with young talent, the Pirates overtook the Giants in September and finished second, but eight games behind the Braves.

No one could match Milwaukee's pitching. Spahn (22–11) and Burdette (20–10) headed a staff of exceptional depth. Mathews hit 31 homers and Aaron 30 (with a .326 average), and the defense was solid. Pittsburgh's Bob Friend (22–14) was the only other 20-game winner, while for all the fuss about rookies, Willie Mays was San Francisco's mainstay with .346, a league-leading 31 stolen bases, and 29 homers.

But individual honors were spread around. Richie Ashburn, with last-place Philadelphia, beat out Mays for the batting title at .350. Chicago's slim shortstop, Ernie Banks, hit 47 homers, knocked in 129 runs, and won the MVP, although his Cubs finished fifth. And San Francisco's Stu Miller, starting 20 games and relieving in 21, used his tantalizing slow deliveries to lead the league in earned run average (2.47).

Three of the eight managers didn't make it through the season. The Phils brought back Eddie Sawyer to replace Mayo Smith in July, Birdie Tebbetts gave way to Jimmy Dykes in Cincinnati in August, and Fred Hutchinson turned the Cardinals over to Stan Hack in the final two weeks.

AL—A Yankee runaway was aided by a rainy spring, which allowed Ford and Turley to start an exceptional proportion of the games played in April and May, when both had hot streaks. After a 9–4 April, the Yankees won 16 of their first 18 May games, and at 25–6 they had a nine-game lead by May 25. They finished July ahead by 15, then lost one more than half their remaining games to wind up with their largest margin (10 games) and worst record (92 victories) of Stengel's regime. Al Lopez, who had moved to the White Sox the year before, brought them in second again, with Boston third. The Indians switched in midseason from Bobby Bragan to Joe Gordon, and the Tigers from Jack Tighe to Bill Norman, while Paul Richards was still putting things together in Baltimore and finishing sixth.

Williams won the batting title with an unusually low .328, nosing out teammate Pete Runnels (.322) and Detroit's Harvey Kuenn (.319). Mantle led with 42 homers (and hit .304), but Jackie Jensen, who batted in 122 runs with Runnels and Williams hitting in front of him, won the MVP. Turley was the only 20-game winner (21–7), but Ford led in earned run average (2.01) and shutouts (7).

Alone in New York for the first time, and with no pennant-race suspense whatsoever, the Yankees drew 1,428,000, their lowest total since World War II. The year before, even with the departure of the Giants known and of the Dodgers suspected, New Yorkers had bought more than 3 million baseball tickets. None—absolutely none—of the National League interest had been transferred to the Yankees, so Shea's search for a replacement gained urgency.

All-Star Game—In Baltimore, the Americans won 4–3 as Gil McDougald produced a tie-breaking single in the sixth and Billy O'Dell, of the Orioles, set down nine men in order over the last three innings.

WS—It started in Milwaukee, and Spahn won the opener in 10 innings 4–3, outlasting Ford and Ryne Duren, New York's latest relief specialist, who took over in the eighth. Then the Braves knocked out Turley in a seven-run first inning and let Burdette coast to a 13–5 rout, in which Mantle hit two homers and Burdette one.

At Yankee Stadium, Larsen and Duren delivered a six-hit shutout while Hank Bauer knocked in all four Yankee runs with a two-run homer and two-run single. But Spahn trumped that with a 3–0 two-hitter against Ford. The Yankees seemed finished.

However, Turley produced a third straight shutout game, a five–hitter, and a 7–0 Yankee victory sent the Series back to Milwaukee. Spahn started against Ford, who didn't get through the second inning but the Yankees managed to tie 2–2 in the sixth and won in the 10th. They scored twice, the Braves got one back against Duren, and Turley had to come in to get the final out in a 4–3 decision.

For the fourth straight year, a seventh game was needed, the only such streak in Series history to this day. It was Burdette against Larsen. In the third, with the Yankees leading 2–1 on unearned runs, Turley replaced Larsen with two on and one out and held the lead until Del Crandall homered with two out in the sixth. With two out in the eighth, Berra doubled, Elston Howard singled him home, Andy Carey scratched a hit off Mathews's glove, and Bill (Moose) Skowron hit a three-run homer that meant a 6–2 victory and another Yankee championship.

1959

The Los Angeles Dodgers, who had lost the only two pennant-tie play-offs the National League had ever had, won one in 1959 from the Milwaukee Braves and went on to dispose of the White Sox in a World Series that didn't include the Yankees for only the second time in 11 years.

NL—After two years of relative calm, the league enjoyed one of its wildest three-team races, just as in the old days. The Dodgers, with a revived pitching staff, the San Francisco Giants, with their sophomore class, and the Braves came into the final week one game apart. The Giants, who had just been swept in a three-game series by the Dodgers in San Francisco, lost two more in Chicago, while the Dodgers split in St. Louis and the Braves took two of three from Pittsburgh at home. On Friday, September 25, the Dodgers won, the Braves lost, and the Giants were rained out. On Saturday, the Dodgers lost in Chicago while the Braves beat Philadelphia, so they were tied while the Giants, winning in St. Louis, remained alive. On Sunday, first the Dodgers and then the Braves won, eliminating the Giants, who proceeded to lose a doubleheader.

The two-of-three play-off began in Milwaukee. The teams had been dodging raindrops for a week, and more rain delayed the start of Monday's game for nearly an hour and held attendance to 18,000. A sixth-inning homer by John Roseboro gave the Dodgers a 3–2 victory, secured by Larry Sherry's relief turn of 7⅔ innings. Both teams immediately flew to Los Angeles and played the next afternoon, when Burdette took a 5–2 lead into the ninth. But the Dodgers rallied to tie, even as Don McMahon and Spahn relieved, and won 6–5 in the 12th against Bob Rush.

It was a remarkable turnaround for the Dodgers, whose Brooklyn stars were all in eclipse. The Coliseum contour had finished Snider and all other left-handed power hitters. To make the diamond fit inside the oval, left field was only 251 feet down the line to a 42-foot-high screen, while right center ranged from 380 to 440 even with a false fence. Hodges and Reese were aging, Campanella had never made it to California because of a car crash that left him paralyzed in January of 1958, Newcombe and Robinson were gone. So victory was fashioned by a flock of young pitchers— Johnny Podres, Don Drysdale, Sherry, Stan Williams, Danny McDevitt, and a still undeveloped Sandy Koufax—and a batting order anchored by Wally Moon, a left-handed hitter who had mastered an inside-out swing to pepper that left-field screen.

Aaron was batting champion at .355 and hit 39 homers. Mathews led with 46 homers to 45 for Banks, who led with 143 runs batted in. Spahn and Burdette were each 21–15 (as was Sam Jones for the Giants). But the two most remarkable pitching performances belonged to the Pittsburgh Pirates. Elroy Face, never starting a game and relieving in 57, posted an 18–1 record, plus 10 saves. And on May 26 in Milwaukee, Harvey Haddix pitched the best single game ever—before or since—and couldn't win it.

The little left-hander pitched 12 perfect innings, retiring 36 batters in a row against a historically powerful batting order, going through it four times. Because his team couldn't score against Burdette, even though it got 12 hits, Haddix went into the bottom of the 13th still 0–0, with no chance to win yet.

The perfect game evaporated when Don Hoak threw low to first on Felix Mantilla's grounder. But it was still a no-hitter as Mathews sacrificed and Aaron was purposely passed. Then Joe Adcock hit

a long high fly to center, hard to follow in the drizzle and mist. It cleared Bill Virdon's leap and fell
just beyond the fence, apparently a three-run
homer. Mantilla trotted home but Aaron, thinking
the ball had hit in front of the fence instead of over
it, touched second and headed for the dugout. Adcock, continuing toward third, was therefore out
for passing a runner and only Mantilla's run
counted. The final score, by ruling of the league
president, was 1–0; Adcock lost a homer, and
Haddix, regardless, had the least rewarding and
most admirable pitching performance in major
league history.

AL—Inconsistent pitching finally undid the
Yankees, who were no factor after July, and the
White Sox beat Cleveland by five games down the
stretch. Lopez put together veteran pitchers with
a running offense short on power, and it all
worked in Veeck's first year as owner. Chicago's
Comiskey Park was a festival all summer long.

Luis Aparicio, a brilliant shortstop, stole 56
bases, until then a total exceeded only twice since
1920 in either league. (Ben Chapman in 1931 and
George Case in 1943 had stolen 61.) Aparicio
would lead the league in steals for nine consecutive years, 1956–64, the longest such streak on
record. Nellie Fox, his partner playing second, hit
.306 and displayed all the vital "little" skills, hitting
only two home runs. The team batted only .250
and was the only one with fewer than 100 homers.

But its pitchers didn't need a lot of runs. Early
Wynn, at 39, was 22–10 and Bob Shaw 18–6.
Pierce, 32, added 14 victories and the bull pen
was taken care of by Turk Lown, 35, and Gerry
Staley, 38. Shaw was the baby at 26.

No other staff matched that quality. Cleveland
had the home-run cochampion, Rocky Colavito,
with 42, matching Harmon Killebrew's total with
Washington. Detroit's Kuenn was batting champion at .353.

Dykes took over managing the Tigers after
Norman started 2–15, and Pinky Higgins was replaced by Billy Jurges halfway through the season
in Boston.

All-Star Games—Still thinking primarily about
pensions, the Players Association was seeking
more funding. The only source was World Series
television money and All-Star Game receipts. A
second All-Star Game was the most obvious and
practical way to increase income. As purists and

commentators scoffed, customers simply bought
it and the players made the "sacrifice" of playing
an extra game.

The "regular" game was scheduled for Pittsburgh on July 7, and the Nationals won 5–4. Ford
took a 4–3 lead into the bottom of the eighth, but
Ken Boyer pinch-hit a single, Dick Groat sacrificed, Aaron singled for the tie, and Mays tripled
for the lead—an all-star rally if ever there was one.

The second game was scheduled for the Los
Angeles Coliseum on August 3, shoehorned into
a schedule that had not anticipated a second interruption. It drew 55,000 and netted $260,000,
achieving its purpose. This time the Americans
won, 5–3.

WS—Rat race is as good a description as any of
what the Dodgers went through to win their second championship in 70 years of club history and
their first in only two years as Californians. They
had finished the regular season on Sunday in
Chicago, played Monday in Milwaukee and Tuesday afternoon in Los Angeles in the playoff. Now
they headed back to Chicago for a World Series
opener on Thursday. Not quite awake, they lost
11–0 to Wynn, who was backed up by Ted
Kluszewski's two homers. But they righted themselves the next day, Podres beating Shaw, and the
teams headed back to Los Angeles. There, Drysdale won 3–1, after which an eighth-inning tie-
breaking homer by Hodges gave the Dodgers a
5–4 victory on Monday.

A victory Tuesday would avoid another trip
back to Chicago, but Shaw prevented it with a
nine-hit shutout and a 1–0 victory over Koufax,
the run scoring on a fourth-inning double play after two of the five singles the Sox got. So it was
back to the airport.

The travel day provided a respite, at least, and
sending Podres against Wynn, the Dodgers
wrapped up things early with a two-run homer by
Snider in the third followed by a six-run fourth.
The game ended 9–3, and the seventh-game streak
was broken.

Even in six games, however, World Series
records were set with an attendance of 420,784,
receipts of $5.63 million, a winner's share of
$11,231.18, and a loser's share of $7,275.17. Suddenly, one was hearing few complaints from players and management about how "ridiculous" the
Coliseum was for baseball.

1960

As talk of a third league and expansion filled the air, the 1960 season itself provided plenty of drama as the Yankees returned to the World Series but lost to a Cinderella team, the Pittsburgh Pirates, in the most eventful seventh game yet.

NL—What Rickey had envisioned when he took over the Pirates in 1951 finally came to fruition. A farm system whose development had been held back by the military draft and by a wild bonus-baby market paid off under the direction of Joe L. Brown and manager Danny Murtaugh. Last or next-to-last for eight straight years, the Pirates had jumped to second in 1958, slipped to fourth in 1959, and now took command with an 11–3 start. In first place at the end of every month, the Pirates held off a September drive by the Braves and finished with a deceptively small three-game margin.

Their own system had produced shortstop Dick Groat (a basketball star at Duke who came directly to the majors), second baseman Bill Mazeroski, first baseman Dick Stuart, and pitchers Bob Friend, Elroy Face, and Vernon Law. Rickey had plucked Roberto Clemente out of the Dodger system when it tried to hide him from the draft and got Yankee-trained Bill Virdon for center field by trading for him after the Cardinals got him for Enos Slaughter. Don Hoak at third and Gino Cimoli in left were Dodger-system discards, catcher Hal Smith Yankee surplus because of Berra and Elston Howard. Pitchers Haddix and Vinegar Bend Mizell were older Cardinal-system products. Rickey's fingerprints were everywhere.

Groat emerged as batting champion at .325 in a close race with Dodger Norm Larker, Mays, and Clemente. Banks led Aaron in homers, 41 to 40, but Aaron (126) and Mathews (123) led his 117 runs batted in. Law (20–9) and Friend (18–12) were among the league's pitching elite, represented by Ernie Broglio (St Louis, 21–9), Spahn (21–10), and Burdette (19–13), and San Francisco's Mike McCormick, whose 2.70 earned run average beat out Broglio's 2.75. Drysdale led in strikeouts, 246 in 269 innings, and Dodger shortstop Maury Wills, who had taught himself to be a switch-hitter so that he could get on base, stole 50 bases, a total not attained in the National League since 1923, when Max Carey had 51.

What the figures of Aaron, Wills, and Drysdale portended was universally ignored. The first two were setting themselves up to break "unbreakable" records, while Drysdale was showing teammate Koufax what an intimidating fastball could do.

AL—Before the Athletics moved there from Philadelphia, Kansas City was the top Yankee farm club. Under the ownership of Arnold Johnson and direction of Parke Carroll, it was ridiculed as continuing in that role. Time after time the Yankees sent prospects and discards to the A's in exchange for players they could use. In 1959, the A's had acquired a promising slugging outfielder from the Indians named Roger Maris. Now he went to the Yankees in a seven-player deal that included such names as Larsen, Bauer, and Marv Throneberry (to become celebrated as a Met).

In three American League seasons, Maris had averaged 19 homers a year and hit .249, so he wasn't exactly ready-made. As a Yankee, though, he hit 39 home runs (batting in front of Mantle, whose 40 led the league), hit .283, led the league in runs batted in (112, while Mantle had 94), played right field brilliantly, and won the MVP Award.

With so powerful an offense and a new airtight infield of Bobby Richardson at second, Tony Kubek at short, and Clete Boyer at third, the Yankees pieced together an odd pitching staff on which Art Ditmar's 15–9 was the best record. Challenged strongly by the White Sox and Orioles through July, they went 44–18 the rest of the way and finished eight games ahead of Baltimore. Even so, the Orioles caught and passed them right after Labor Day, but the Yankees swept a four-game series from them September 16–18 and went on to a 15-game winning streak through the final day.

Richards, at Baltimore, had finally fashioned the pitching staff he had always sought. His "Baby Birds," all 22 or 21 years old, were Chuck Estrada, Milt Pappas, Jack Fisher, Steve Barber, and Jerry Walker. Only Pappas went on to above-average success in career terms, but they set a standard for Baltimore pitching that became a tradition for three decades.

Elsewhere, strange things happened. Cleveland's general manager was Frank Lane, a flamboyant and tireless trader. On April 17, he traded

Colavito, the home-run cochampion, to Detroit for Kuenn, the batting champion. Both players were revered where they were, unwelcome where they went; but neither minded getting away from his manager, Gordon in Cleveland, Dykes in Detroit. But in August, Lane and Bill DeWitt, who was running the Tigers, traded managers—the only time this has ever been done—so Colavito wound up working for Gordon again in Detroit and Kuenn playing for Dykes in Cleveland. Kuenn hit his .308, Colavito his 36 homers, but their efforts didn't do much for either team.

All-Star Games—This time the two games were built into a single break in the schedule, played at Kansas City July 11 and Yankee Stadium two days later. The Nationals won both, 5–3 and 6–0, with Mays batting leadoff and getting three hits in each game, including a home run at New York, where he also stole a base. Even so, the second game drew only 30,000, less than half the Stadium capacity. Maybe two wasn't such a great idea after all.

WS—"The 1960 World's Series was the wackiest ever played." That's how Fred Lieb begins his account in the 1961 *Official Baseball Guide,* and Lieb was a legendary and prolific baseball writer who had begun his fandom in the 1890s and had been covering baseball since 1910. He was right.

The Pirates won the first, fourth, and fifth games by scores of 6–4, 3–2, and 5–2. The Yankees won the second, third, and sixth 16–3, 10–0, and 12–0, with Ford pitching the two shutouts after Stengel decided not to use him in the first two games at Pittsburgh. He would say later it was the biggest mistake he had ever made as a manager.

That meant it came down to a seventh game again, at Forbes Field. The Pirates knocked out Turley in the second inning and built a 4–0 lead. Law, who had won the first and fourth games with Face's help, held it until Skowron hit a homer in the fifth, and was knocked out in the sixth as the Yankees took a 5–4 lead on Berra's three-run homer off Face. They made it 7–4 in the eighth, but Cimoli opened the home half with a single, and Virdon's apparent double-play grounder to Kubek took a bad hop and hit him in the throat, forcing him out of the game. Two more singles and a three-run homer by Smith off Jim Coates completed a five-run inning, and Pittsburgh had a two-run lead, 9–7.

Richardson and Dale Long started the ninth with hits off Friend, and Haddix came in. He got Maris to foul out, but Mantle's single scored Richardson and put a runner on third. When Rocky Nelson, playing first, backhanded Berra's grounder and stepped on first, eliminating any force, Mantle scrambled safely back to first while the tying run scored. If Nelson had tagged Mantle first and then touched the bag, the Series would have been over.

So Ralph Terry faced Mazeroski, leading off the bottom of the ninth—and Mazeroski hit the second pitch over the left-field wall. Pittsburgh had won 10–9, and for the first time a World Series had ended with a game-winning homer.

The Yankees had hit .336 as a team, outscored Pittsburgh 55–27, set a dozen Series records including 10 homers and 142 total bases on 91 hits—and lost. The Pirates posted a staff earned run average of 7.11—and won. Wacky was right. Few World Series events have been rehashed as often as Mazeroski's homer.

It was a fitting climax for the end of stability.

AFTERMATH

The unraveling of a familiar baseball universe that was taking place in meeting rooms was reflected in 1960 in the ball parks. The trading of managers was only one example of how unstable things could become.

Sawyer quit as manager of the Phillies after the first game—the first game!—of the season. Gene Mauch, who had been managing in Minneapolis for the Red Sox, replaced him. On May 4, the Cubs decided that Grimm, who had started his third cycle as their manager less than a month before, should be replaced by Boudreau, who had become one of their broadcasters since his last managing job—and sent Grimm up to the booth. On June 18, the Giants fired Rigney, who had brought them within one day of a pennant nine months earlier, and made Tom Sheehan, their garrulous scout and drinking buddy of Stoneham, manager. On July 3, the Red Sox fired Billy Jurges and brought Pinky Higgins, whom they had promoted to the front office when hiring Jurges the year before, back to the dugout. On August 3, the Gordon-Dykes exchange took place.

It got worse. When the season ended, the Yankees discarded Stengel as "too old" (he was 70) so that coach Ralph Houk, their next choice, would not leave to manage elsewhere. They also dropped Weiss, using the same excuse of retirement age, and gave his post to Roy Hamey, who had left the Phillies.

The Cubs went further. They decided not to have a single manager at all, but a board of coaches—one of who would be Grimm, while Boudreau returned to to the microphone. Bob Scheffing, who had managed the Cubs in 1959, became Detroit's manager, Gordon having been named on October 5 to succeed Bob Elliott in Kansas City, a team in the process of being sold.

Rigney, having been considered for the Detroit job, signed on with the newly formed Angels in time to take part in the expansion draft. The new Senators hired Mickey Vernon, who had a strong Washington identity as a player but no managerial experience. (He was a Pittsburgh coach in 1960.)

This game of musical chairs reflected the process of upheaval, and it went right to the top, the ownership level. On October 11, John Fetzer, part of an 11-investor group that bought the Tigers from Briggs in 1956, took over full control, whereupon DeWitt resigned. But DeWitt could take charge of Cincinnati because Gabe Paul resigned to be general manager of the new club in Houston. Meanwhile, John McHale had left Detroit (under DeWitt) to become general manager of Milwaukee—which then hired Birdie Tebbetts as a vice-president, blurring its line of command and creating discomfort for Dressen, who had been made manager in 1960 after Haney's play-off loss of 1959. The Angels, once organized by Autry, made Haney, once popular as Hollywood's manager, their general manager.

And Kansas City had been up for sale since the death of Arnold Johnson in the spring of 1960. His estate faced tax problems. In December, the American League approved the purchase of the club by a Kansas City group. But within days, a higher bid came in from Charles O. Finley, a self-made insurance millionaire from Chicago, who had tried to buy the Tigers and a Los Angeles franchise. Finley bought the 52 percent interest Johnson had held for just under $2 million and acquired the other 48 percent in February.

In opening up California, the baseball establishment had also opened a Pandora's box of un-foreseen changes. It's not that expansion could have been, or should have been, avoided; it's that it proceeded without any coherent plan or consideration of consequences and needs. And once traditional patterns were shattered, new structures to replace the old were not easy to find. A third league might have fit familiar procedures. Enlarged leagues could not.

When the unthinkable is actually done, like leaving Brooklyn and scheduling 162 games, other unthinkables become thinkable.

If new cities were gold mines, why not more gold mines?

If Congress was going to look at antitrust, why not use baseball's clout to fashion favorable legislation, not merely oppose restriction?

If one All-Star Game is good, aren't two better?

If you can trade players, why not managers?

The most important fallout from abandoning traditional forms was not recognized by anyone at the time: it started players thinking.

Except for the brief revolt of 1890 and the momentary alternatives offered by the Federal and Mexican League escapades, players had accepted their total subservience as an inevitable condition of the business. Unionism, when mentioned in 1946, was a dirty word to them. It still was, but if the owners could jerk around cities and schedules as they pleased, couldn't players do *something* to get a better break? They couldn't generate all that money without players, could they?

Four aspects of their experience in the 1950s all pushed them in the same direction.

1. Through firsthand experience with the pension plan, they learned the full extent of management arrogance and indifference, and of their own powerlessness as individuals.

2. By interaction with their new black teammates, they raised their consciousness about the nature and manifestation of injustice. This was subtle but real. Black players, by life experience, were sensitive to what constituted exploitation and mistreatment in a way most whites weren't. But white players, seeing what blacks were subjected to in everyday life—not on the ball field so much, but in hotels and in transit and especially in the minors—became more receptive to explanations of how they themselves, in other ways, were being mistreated. At a time when civil-rights issues were beginning to permeate society, and discrimina-

tion was coming under attack *in principle,* players in the 20s began thinking about their own "rights" and about the difference between begging and getting leverage.

3. The new television contracts, the new cities, and the attendance records made more visible how much money was really pouring into the baseball business. In 1957, Jerry Coleman said he could foresee a distant future when the *average* player might be making $75,000 a year. It seemed outlandish when the average was under $15,000. But Jerry was no labor radical, just an intelligent man who could do arithmetic and yet not even imagine what was really going to happen in his lifetime.

4. If there were going to be more major league teams, in three leagues or in whatever way, there would be more major league jobs.

And that was the one that counted. The first three awarenesses were abstractions. The fourth was concrete.

Expansion created a completely different outlook in a different proportion of players. With 16 teams and 24 Triple-A farm clubs, the pressure on most major leaguers was great. There were 400 roster spots. The top 100 players, in terms of ability, were pretty secure: if one team didn't want them, another would. But the other 300 lived on the edge. An injury, a slump, or anything that displeased management could get them replaced by a Triple-A player not that much inferior. One could get sent to and buried in the minors simply as punishment.

But suppose there were 600 major league roster spots (as there soon would be). Now not only the top 100, but the next 200 or 300 would be fairly secure. The bottom 200 could still be staring at demotion, but now the group confident enough to ask for more would be half or more of the player population, not one-quarter—enough to start *doing* something.

More than anything else, this consequence of expansion created the conditions that led, step by step, to the management-labor conflicts that would dominate the rest of the century.

PART VI

EXPANSION

CHAPTER 20

Ten-Team Leagues

DEMOGRAPHICS

Baseball, like all other human endeavors, does not operate in a vacuum. The dispersal and expansion of the major leagues was part of a larger set of forces affecting related industries in similar ways. In 1959, the four major professional team sports had 42 teams—16 baseball, 12 football, eight basketball, six hockey. Ten years later, there were 87—24 baseball, 26 football, 25 basketball in two leagues, 12 hockey. By 1972, with another hockey league, there were 107. (In 1997, there were 115, consolidated into one league per sport, with more on the way in each sport.)

To understand what was happening to baseball, one must look at the whole picture. It is best displayed in the form of a chart. The city populations are for their metropolitan areas (as defined by the census then) in millions.

City	1960 Metropolitan-Area Population (in millions)	Teams in 1959	Teams in 1969
New York	14.7	Baseball, football, basketball, hockey	2 Baseball, 2 football, 2 basketball, hockey

(Continued)

City	1960 Metropolitan-Area Population (in millions)	Teams in 1959	Teams in 1969
Los Angeles	6.7	Baseball, football	2 Baseball, football, 2 basketball, hockey
Chicago	6.7	2 Baseball, 2 football, hockey	2 Baseball, football, basketball, hockey
Philadelphia	4.3	Baseball, football, basketball	Baseball, football, basketball, hockey
Detroit	3.7	Baseball, football, basketball, hockey	Baseball, football, basketball, hockey
San Francisco	2.7	Baseball, football	2 Baseball, 2 football, 2 basketball, hockey
Boston	2.6	Baseball, basketball, hockey	Baseball, football, basketball, hockey
Pittsburgh	2.4	Baseball, football	Baseball, football, hockey
St. Louis	2.0	Baseball, basketball	Baseball, football, hockey
Washington	2.0	Baseball, football	Baseball, football
Cleveland	1.8	Baseball, football	Baseball, football
Baltimore	1.7	Baseball, football	Baseball, football, basketball
Minneapolis	1.4	Basketball	Baseball, football, basketball, hockey
Buffalo	1.3	—	Football
Milwaukee	1.2	Baseball, football*	Football, basketball
Dallas	1.1	—	Football, basketball
Cincinnati	1.1	Baseball, basketball	Baseball, football, basketball
Seattle	1.1	—	Baseball, basketball
Kansas City	1.0	Baseball	Baseball, football
Houston	1.2	—	Baseball, football, basketball
Atlanta	1.0	—	Baseball, football, basketball

*Green Bay Packers

(Continued)

City	1960 Metropolitan-Area Population (in millions)	Teams in 1959	Teams in 1969
San Diego	1.0	—	Baseball, football, basketball
Miami	0.9	—	Football, basketball
Denver	0.9	—	Football, basketball
New Orleans	0.9	—	Football, basketball
Phoenix	0.7	—	Basketball
Indianapolis	0.7	—	Basketball
Louisville	0.7	—	Basketball
Syracuse	0.3	Basketball	—
Montreal	1.6	Hockey	Baseball, hockey
Toronto	1.4	Hockey	Hockey

The expansion process would continue through the 1970s, 1980s, and 1990s.

This table will be relevant from now on. (We'll update it in the 1990s.) Note the following:

In 1959, only New York and Detroit are represented in all four sports, and none of the markets smaller than Boston have more than two. Then competition for the sports dollar, especially as premium seat prices go up and luxury boxes are invented, intensifies *among* sports, making more vital a winning record *within* a sport. In 1969, three or four teams are competing for customers in 15 cities.

In 1959, at a baseball owners' meeting, 12 of the 16 votes come from the top 12 markets, or three-quarters. In 1969, only 16 of 24 are from the top 12, or two-thirds—a significant difference. That majority will continue to shrink, increasing the conflicts of interest *among* the clubs, and will lead to the disaster of the 1990's.

Below the top three (New York, Los Angeles, Chicago), the absolute number differences among the remaining cities are not so great as to be crucial in 1959. But as all cities grow, some much faster than others, over the next 30 years, the *gaps* between various markets get larger, exacerbating diverging interests.

The full force of these demographic trends will make itself felt only gradually, but cumulatively over many years. In 1960, hardly anyone in the baseball business pays any attention to them.

THE NEW TEAMS

The hasty draft arranged for the American League expansion teams allowed them to get some capable players. In 1961, the Angels won 70 games, finishing eighth, and the Senators won 61 to tie Kansas City for ninth. They weren't any worse, relatively, than second-division clubs had been for years. And in their second season, the Angels actually stayed in the pennant race until September and finished third. They finished above .500 in three of their first seven years.

The National Leaguers had a whole year to make sure that the draft-eligible portions of their major and minor league rosters contained no one they really wanted. More familiar names turned up on the Mets and Houston than on the Angels and Senators, because so many had outlived their usefulness in the eyes of their original clubs. So the Mets, with Ashburn (once a batting champion), Hodges (with bad knees soon forcing retirement), Snider (in their second season), and others with past credentials couldn't keep them from losing 120, 111, 109, and 112 games in their first four years. But good *young* talent was withheld.

Promotionally, however, the Mets were an enormous success. They brought in Stengel as manager, Weiss as club president (but actually general manager, a title prohibited by his Yankee retirement terms). Stengel's wit and salesmanship overrode everything else, and the patently unfair selection process worked in their favor: the Mets were *created* inferior, so sophisticated fans could enjoy the gallantry of the team's spirited but ineffectual efforts. When they moved into their new Stadium in 1964—named after Bill Shea—they outdrew the Yankees by 400,000, even though they remained dead last while the Yankees had won another pennant in dramatic come-from-behind fashion.

Stengel's gift for fascinating remarks appeared at the draft meeting, the day after the Yankees had won another World Series in Cincinnati. His first choice was Hobie Landrith, a respected defensive catcher nearing the end of a career in which he hit .233. Why?

"You have to start with a catcher," explained Casey, "or you'll have all passed balls."

Impeccable logic was combined, soon enough, with brutal honesty. After the umpty-umpth self-inflicted disaster, he greeted "his" writers, as they came to the clubhouse, with a quintessential Stengel evaluation: "We're a fraud," he said.

He was touching on a real issue. Was expansion a fraud? Was diluting "major league" caliber of play undermining the meaning of the phrase? Most professional baseball people felt that way, were embarrassed by it, and went about their business making the best of it. But expansion certainly meant a shift in values. No matter how proficient additional newcomers might be, the 50 or 100 best players, whoever they were in relative terms, were now spread among more teams. Neither batting orders nor pitching staffs could be as effective; it was safer to pitch around the dangerous hitter, and possible more often to make hay against a larger number of second-line pitchers.

Adding four teams to 16 was bad enough, but in 1969 they added four more. The major league population had increased by 50 percent, from 400 roster spots to 600. Obviously, one-third of all the regulars would have been substitutes, or minor leaguers, in a 16-team setup.

On the other hand, did it matter? They were still the most proficient baseball players alive, playing against each other, and the games and pennant races were close, and all things are relative, so what was the complaint? Cities that acquired teams reveled in their status as members of the major league club. The old cities retained self-esteem. More teams meant more action, and more games ("product," to the commercial world) to sell to television.

Houston did better than the Mets, but not much. The Colts, under Harry Craft, lost only 96 and finished eighth, six games ahead of the no-manager, coaching-staff Cubs the first year. But the next three years they lost 96, 97, and 96 and finished ahead of only the Mets.

Fraud or simply a new product? Expansion produced both, but the question itself was irrelevant. By the old standards, baseball today was certainly a diluted product, but the whole outside world in which the old standards had become "normal" was going through fundamental changes, so how could baseball cling to them? The degree to which American life took new directions during the 1960s doesn't need elaboration here, but indifference to history, rebellion against established proprieties, focus on the immediate, and pursuit of more self-centered goals certainly affected the baseball world directly. The real difference was that baseball was no longer in a class of its own at the top of the commercial sports pyramid, but only the oldest and biggest among successful challengers. The cause of the difference was television, which made any event it carried equal to all others while it was on—football, Olympics, basketball, boxing, whatever. In the scramble for public attention, baseball was subjected to a type of competition it never had before—not from rival baseball producers, but from other sports.

Before World War II, any superior athlete who wanted a professional career turned to baseball. (Of course, he had to be white, but that was also true in other sports and the society as a whole at that time.) In the 1960s credible and profitable careers were open in football and basketball, and no one will ever know how many and which potentially great baseball players were channeled into other sports as teenagers. A small hint was provided by Dave DeBusschere and Gene Conley, solid pitchers who were also National Basketball Association regulars. Later, Bo Jackson would be a more vivid example as he starred in football and baseball, and after him Dieon Sanders.

Fandom was even more subject to this broadening of interest, again because of television. All major events could be seen, each new one crowding out the last one, so why wouldn't children growing up in that environment relate to all? And wouldn't that make wallowing in comparisons to the past, so ingrained in previous generations of baseball fans, less necessary or attractive?

An era had begun in which, contrary to the song, the fundamental things did *not* apply as time went by. The extent to which the break with eight-team, 154-game competition would alter all perceptions was not realized, then, even by those who bemoaned it. But in a very real sense, "baseball as we know it" ended in 1961 for those who knew it before that. Yet when the next total upheaval came in 1969, within the decade, that would be the end of "baseball as we know it" all over again, because we had quickly become accustomed to the 10-team leagues. The radically new becomes the normal very quickly. What was hard to grasp, and uncomfortable, were the unfolding truths that the *new* normalities would never again stay the same very long, and that a perpetual shifting of standards would be the nature of the future.

The new American League clubs didn't do so well. The second-year success of the Angels aroused false expectations; the new Senators didn't arouse anything. The National League newcomers did worse. The Mets finished last five times and ninth twice in their first seven seasons, averaging 105 losses per year. But Houston, even when it started playing in its Astrodome, never got higher than eighth and wound up in the seventh year finishing 10th behind the Mets.

But the expansion clubs were not the ones guiding baseball into new paths. A new owner of an old club was.

Enter Charles Oscar Finley.

Flamboyant and cantankerous, Finley was a self-made Chicago millionaire in the insurance business, who had tried to buy a team for years. He finally secured the Kansas City Athletics between December 1960 and February 1961, after the expansion draft. Its roster was as weak as those of the expansion teams, as events would prove. But Finley was full of ideas for promotion and team improvement, a born maverick endowed with boundless energy. Over the next 15 years, his strong-willed decisions about his own property would force the entire baseball business into situations other owners did not want but could not escape.

At the same time, other important ownership changes were taking place. Powell Crosley died in March, 1961, and by December the Reds had been acquired by Bill DeWitt. In June, Veeck, who was ill, sold full control of the White Sox to Arthur Allyn, one of his hitherto silent partners, who became sole owner in May of 1962. In November 1962, Perini sold the Braves to a group of Chicagoans led by John McHale and Bill Bartholomay for $6 million. Four days later, the Cleveland Indians passed into the hands of Bill Daley and Gabe Paul, whose association with the Houston team had not worked out well. Eight days after that, full control of the Houston club went to Judge Roy Hofheinz, one of the original investors, who had pushed the idea of a domed stadium from the beginning.

And early in 1963, General Quesada's interest in the new Washington Senators was bought out by two of his partners, James Lemon and James Johnston.

Suddenly, at an American League meeting, six of the ten owners were men who had not been in charge of their clubs less than three years before, and so were four of the ten National League owners. What's more, Commissioner Frick's term was expiring in 1965, and he had made his determination to retire explicit, while Cronin, as American League president, had been in office only since 1959. At a joint meeting of the two leagues, more than half the decision makers were people new to one another.

The unprecedented scale of such turnover made Finley's actions harder to deal with.

By the end of his first year, 1961, Finley was in a bitter fight with Kansas City authorities over better lease terms and his demand for a new ball park. Early in 1962, he threatened to move the team to Dallas–Fort Worth. (Meanwhile, in Dallas, Lamar Hunt, one of the founders of the new American Football League, was preparing to move his Dallas Texans to Kansas City, where the same city leaders gave him the kind of terms, in the same Municipal Stadium, they were denying Finley. The Texans became the Kansas City Chiefs in May of 1963, intensifying the fight with Finley.)

Now Finley threatened to move to Atlanta or Oakland, where plans to build a stadium were underway. Cronin actually offered some support for the Oakland idea, because he favored having a second team on the West Coast to balance the Angels, a move for which Autry lobbied tirelessly. Cronin had grown up in San Francisco and "knew the territory."

Disliked by the other owners, who considered him an outsider and a loudmouth, Finley was not about to get permission to move anywhere. But when the new owners of the Braves, whose McHale was highly respected and well liked by the Establishment, announced that they were listening to offers from Atlanta, the possibility of another franchise move became real.

From a peak of 2.2 million in 1957, Milwaukee attendance had dropped to 767,000 in 1962. This was the same Braves organization that had gone from 1.4 million to 281,000 in Boston between 1948 and 1952, so evidently it knew how to do that. The new owners were young, wealthy, investment-world operators who had neither Milwaukee roots nor any intention of pouring money into a franchise that was being offered millions in radio-television money and a new stadium in Atlanta. That would be major league baseball's first foray into the South, comparable to the opening up of the West Coast.

San Diego also expressed interest in the Braves but couldn't match the TV offer, although it did have a new stadium in the works.

In 1964, Finley was threatening to move to Louisville, declaring he would play there in a cow pasture if no park were available. The others pressured him, successfully, to sign a lease in Kansas City.

But on August 13, a real blockbuster shook the baseball world. The Yankees were sold to the Columbia Broadcasting System.

Finley and Allyn raised the loudest objections. The Yankees had won 13 of the last 15 pennants and had the most powerful farm system. How could anyone compete with them if they now had the limitless resources of a huge corporation? Wasn't CBS one of the chief buyers of baseball telecasts? Wasn't this a conflict of interest? Wasn't it an antitrust question?

The Senate thought so and called hearings. But the chairman of the subcommittee was now Senator Philip Hart (D-Michigan), friend of the Tigers and Lions, who had defused Kefauver's bill in 1959. The Senate accepted assurances from both the Yankees and CBS that nothing was wrong with their arrangement, and Commissioner Frick testified that he agreed.

So the National League approved the request of the Braves to move to Atlanta, but not until 1966 because the lease in Milwaukee ran through 1965. On November 10, the Braves signed their deal with Atlanta, making 1965 a lame-duck season in Milwaukee, something the five previous moving franchises had managed to avoid.

By now, Cleveland was threatening to move to Seattle, if not Oakland or Dallas, but ultimately voted (October 16) to stay in Cleveland.

The unthinkable had become not merely thinkable but fashionable.

The Yankee deal left Dan Topping in charge of operations, retaining a minority interest. CBS, by the time it exercised its option for 100 percent ownership in 1966, paid $14.2 million, by far the highest price ever paid for a sports franchise. And that was only for the ball club and minor league holdings; Yankee Stadium itself and the land under it had been sold and leased back to the club long ago.

In 1965, Milwaukee put up a fight. It filed an antitrust suit in state court under Wisconsin's antitrust laws, since the federal exemption shut off that avenue. Meanwhile, a group of local business leaders organized the Brewers, using the old minor league name, to seek a replacement franchise, either through expansion or the move of another club. In February 1966, there was a trial in which Milwaukee won as the Braves were opening the season in Atlanta. But higher courts overruled that verdict, and the Braves remained in Atlanta.

In August of 1966 the Indians were purchased by Vern Stouffer, frozen-food and hotel magnate, from Daley and Paul for $8 million. CBS bought out Topping in September and put Michael Burke, himself a charismatic character, in charge of the Yankees. In December, DeWitt sold the Reds to a 13-man group of Cincinnati businessmen led by Frank Dale, publisher of the *Cincinnati Enquirer,* for $7 million.

Of the eight American League owners who had tried to get the National to go along with a ninth-team expansion plan in 1959, only one—Boston's Tom Yawkey—was still in place seven years later. But six of the eight National Leaguers who had rejected it, and president Warren Giles, were still there. The rift between the two leagues had grown wider.

At that point, Finley—remember Finley?—dragged all of them where they did not want to go, into another expansion, in the messiest fashion yet.

Finley's relations with Kansas City authorities had deteriorated beyond repair. The city had plans for a modern baseball-football complex (with sliding roof, no less) but didn't want to go ahead until Finley agreed to terms or, preferably, sold out. The fact that he chiefs were a big success and played in the first Super Bowl game in January 1967 didn't help. Finley wasn't going to sell, so he had to move his Athletics.

At a special meeting in Chicago, October 18, 1967, he sought permission to move to Oakland, whose Coliseum complex was complete. He needed six of the other nine owners' votes, plus his own, for the required two-thirds. He got five. But Baltimore (now owned entirely by Jerry Hoffberger) voted against, while the Yankees, Cleveland, and Washington abstained. Part of the proposed deal was that the league would place an expansion team in Kansas City in due course.

There was a break, but not an adjournment, and then another vote. This time the Yankees voted yes, with Baltimore still opposed and the other two still abstaining. But that was enough. The A's could go to Oakland immediately, for 1968, and Kansas City could have a new team in 1971.

It was later widely believed but never proved that the Yankees switched because Autry, the radio-network man, called William Paley, head of CBS, to tell Burke to change his vote. Autry, more than anyone, wanted a second West Coast team, and network operators can understand one another's needs, can't they?

In any case, the deal was announced at about 11 P.M: A's to Oakland in 1968, expansion including Kansas City in 1971.

A block away, the Kansas City delegation was furious, and it included Senator Stuart Symington (D-Missouri), one of the Senate's most influential figures. They rushed over to Cronin, told him off, and used the magic word "antitrust," which sounded a lot worse coming from Symington's mouth than in the press. Kansas City was only too glad to be rid of Finley, but it wanted another team *now*.

The other owners had scattered. (The first order of business at any league meeting had always been to arrange transportation to leave.) Cronin got enough of them together to reopen the question. The Kansas City people would go along with a 1969 start. The league voted yes and announced the adjustment after midnight.

But an 11th team needs a 12th team.

Groups from Dallas, New Orleans, and Seattle were on tap. The first two confessed they weren't ready to move so quickly. Seattle wasn't ready either, but it said yes, with the promise of a domed stadium to come.

The National was miffed. Again, the American had acted precipitately, without thought or preparation, and had committed a double sin. It was letting Finley move into what the National considered San Francisco's exclusive territory, and it was taking Seattle, on which the National had its eye for future occupancy. But the National couldn't do much but bluster. By the December annual meetings, it was agreeing to go to 12 teams without specifying where or when.

By then (December 1) the Seattle franchise had been awarded to Daley (who had tried to move the Indians there), allied with Dewey Soriano, president of the diminished Pacific Coast League, and his brother Max, an attorney. In reference to Seattle's maritime setting, the team would be called the Pilots.

The Kansas City franchise was awarded in January 1968 to Ewing Kauffman, whose fortune came from pharmaceuticals and whose civic activities in Kansas City were well known. The team would be called the Royals.

Each new club would take 30 players (three from each of the exiting 10 clubs) at $175,000 apiece, pay a $100,000 membership fee, and contribute to the pension fund, making the entry cost about $5.5 million—almost triple the 1961–62 level.

The National had applications from Dallas, Buffalo (whose group included DeWitt), Milwaukee, San Diego, Toronto, Montreal, and Denver. Hoffheinz promptly vetoed Dallas, considering all of Texas his territory.

In April 1968, the National finally agreed that it, too, would expand in 1969. On May 27, it awarded franchises to San Diego, whose co-owner was to be Buzzy Bavasi, O'Malley's general manager of the Dodgers since the Brooklyn days, and Montreal, whose group of Canadian big-businesspeople included McHale. Insider trading was running true to form, with DeWitt, in Buffalo, shut out because there were too many insiders. But the entry fee was $10 million, with $4 million of it for the franchise itself. The Nationals considered themselves a much more valuable property than that other league. The new names were Padres in San Diego and Expos in Montreal.

What the National would not do, it swore loudly, citing tradition, was to split into divisions. The American, which had been considering splitting into two fives since 1965, had recommended a split in August of 1967, but the National was not interested, and you couldn't make interlocking schedules (for the two-team cities, to avoid games on the same day) unless both leagues did it. Now the American was going to split into two sixes, no matter what. "You can't sell a 12th-place team," declared Cronin for the American, but for the National Giles insisted, "We will play as a 12-team league"—as if this very league hadn't found in the 1890's why that doesn't work.

Not until July 10 did the National accept the inevitable and also split into two divisions.

On December 3, 1968, the Washington Senators were bought for $10 million—five times their entry fee of eight years before—by Bob Short of Minneapolis.

The new club lineup was complete.

THE NEW PARKS

New cities had to provide ball parks and, since they were starting from scratch, produced modern buildings stressing unobstructed views. Old cities, to keep their teams, had to provide new parks along the same lines to replace the outmoded parks built before World War I. Lou Gehrig had played all 2,130 of his games in just nine parks, two in Cleveland; from 1916 through 1952, the National League had played all its games in only eight. Between 1960 and 1968, major league baseball was played in 11 new venues. This was the sequence:

1960—San Francisco: Candlestick Park, 42,000; fan-shaped (narrower at home plate) double deck to both foul poles, open to the Bay behind outfield.

1961—Los Angeles: Angels use Wrigley Field, 20,000, old Pacific Coast League park, temporarily.

   Minnesota: Metropolitan Stadium, 31,000 (to 40,000 in 1964), in Bloomington, adjacent to the Minneapolis–St.Paul International Airport. Also home for the new football Vikings.

1962—Los Angeles: Dodger Stadium, 55,000, the "Taj Mahal on the Freeway." Eight levels curving out to behind right and left fields, open bleachers behind outfield, fan-shaped for baseball, Stadium Club overlooking right field. Angels also move in as a tenant.

   Washington: D.C. Stadium, 43,500. Double-deck complete circle with movable sections for multipurpose use, also home of the football Redskins.

   Houston: Colt Stadium, 32,000. Temporary structure adjacent to site where Astrodome is being built.

   New York: Refurbished Polo Grounds used by Mets.

   St. Louis, Pittsburgh, Philadelphia: New parks approved.

1963—Atlanta: New park approved.

1964—New York: Shea Stadium, 55,000, multipurpose oval, open behind outfield. Also home to football Jets.

   Anaheim, Dallas–Fort Worth, Oakland: Construction begun.

1965—Houston: Astrodome, 46,000, first indoor stadium, multipurpose oval, also home to football Oilers.

1966—Atlanta: Fulton County Stadium, 51,000, circular multipurpose, also home to football Falcons.

   Anaheim: Anaheim Stadium, 44,000, lovely scaled-down version of Dodger Stadium, near Disneyland.

   St. Louis: New Busch Stadium, 49,000, opens May 12; multipurpose oval, also home to the football Cardinals.

   Houston: Artificial turf installed in Astrodome because grass died when translucent roof, blinding fielders, had to be painted over.

1967—San Francisco: Approves enlarging Candlestick for football.

   Philadelphia: Approves new stadium.

   San Diego: Opens new stadium.

1968—Oakland: Athletics move into Oakland Coliseum, 50,000, multipurpose oval, also home to the football Raiders.

1969—San Diego: Padres use San Diego Stadium, 50,000, multipurpose oval, also home to football Chargers.

> *Montreal:* Jarry Park, 3,000-seat recreational facility enlarged to 28,000 open seats, to be used by Expos until a promised stadium could be built. (When the franchise was awarded, it was intended to use the Expo Autostade, a 25,000-seat structure built for the Expo '67 World's Fair, which is why the team was named the Expos. But plans to convert it for baseball, with a roof, proved too expensive.)

> *Seattle:* Sick's Stadium, 18,000 expanded to 25,000 in June, a 56-year-old minor-league park to be used until a domed stadium could be built.

> *Kansas City:* Municipal Stadium, abandoned by the A's, to be used until a new sports complex on the city's outskirts can be completed, also home to the football Chiefs.

1970—Cincinnati: Riverfront Stadium, 51,000, multipurpose oval, opens June 30, artificial turf, also home to the football Bengals.

> *Pittsburgh:* Three Rivers Stadium, 50,000, multipurpose oval, opens July 16 (the site is that of Exposition Park, used between 1882 and 1915 by teams in four different major leagues, including the Pirates, 1891–1909), artificial turf, also home to football Steelers.

> *St. Louis:* Busch Stadium installs artificial turf.

1971—Philadelphia: Veterans Stadium, 56,000, multipurpose oval, artificial turf, also home to football Eagles.

> *San Francisco:* Candlestick's doubledecking completed all the way around, making a lopsided multipurpose oval with movable sections and artificial turf, baseball capacity now 58,000, also home to the football 49ers.

All these parks have been tinkered with endlessly, altering exact seating capacity, moving interior fences, and so forth. But that had been just as true of the old parks. Essentially unchanged from the 1950's, as of 1970, were Yankee Stadium, Boston's Fenway Park, Cleveland's Municipal Stadium, Detroit's Tiger Stadium (called that starting in 1961), Chicago's Comiskey Park and Wrigley Field, and Kansas City's Municipal Stadium.

In other words, in 1970, the National League has new facilities for 11 of its 12 teams, although Montreal's is unsuitable and temporary, while the American League has only three of its 12 (Washington, Minnesota, Anaheim) in modernized homes, with Kansas City on the way.

That was one more reason why the National Leaguers looked down upon, and disrespected, the "Junior Circuit" that had outstripped them in the 1930s and 1940s and was now clearly second fiddle. Pendulums do swing.

THE NEW COMMISSIONERS

Frick, insisting he would retire in 1965, agreed to serve until a successor was actually installed and pressed for an adjustment in the commissionership. After Landis, no absolute powers were granted Chandler or Frick, and in all the engagements with Congress it became obvious that the impotence of the commissioner, with respect to club-owner whims, damaged arguments for the antitrust exemption. Frick persuaded the owners to give back to the next commissioner one vital weapon, their agreement not to take any dispute with him to court. This, too, would have strange and unanticipated consequences without really changing anything directly, since the whole concept dealt with public relations and perceptions, not actual exercise of ruling power.

On March 29, 1965, a screening committee was set up. On July 21, it said it had winnowed down a list of 50 to 15, and by October 20, to ten. On November 17, the choice was announced.

William D. Eckert.

Who?

Gen. William D. Eckert, a three-star general in the air force, concerned primarily with contract and procurement matters.

"Good God!" cried Larry Fox, a baseball writer working that day in the office of the *New York World-Telegram*. "They've named the Unknown Soldier." It was a line that popped into many minds simultaneously.

Exactly why and how the owners chose him remains a mystery to this day, at least to me. One story was that some of them thought they were getting Eugene Zuckert, secretary of the air force, a better known Washingtonian. But whatever the actual details and internal politics, they were really getting what they wanted, someone so completely out of touch with their business that there would be no danger of his interfering, while projecting the image of leadership. Wouldn't a respectable air force general project that?

What they also wanted, of course, was efficient administration of a commissioner's office getting deeper every day into television and marketing negotiations. Contracts, get it? But in this they had guessed wrong. Eckert was hamstrung not only by his total ignorance of the baseball world and its manipulative members, but by his own natural caution and sincere desire to do right, which meant putting off most actions until he could learn more about the problem or hope it went away.

So they tried to help him. They persuaded Lee MacPhail to give up the presidency of the Orioles (who were on the verge of great success) and become the commissioner's administrative aide. They hired Joe Reichler, the Associated Press' most experienced and ubiquitous baseball writer, to be his public-relations man; Reichler would write his speeches (down to such mundane declarations as "Good morning") and shepherd him around the baseball map.

Eckert's cautious frame of mind was revealed at his first major press conference. Trying to glimpse his inner personality Harry Jupiter of San Francisco asked him what he liked to read. Eckert reeled off various sections of a newspaper and mentioned comics.

"Which comic strip do you like best?" Jupiter asked.

"I'd rather not single one out," said Eckert.

Late in 1966, when CBS took full control of the Yankees and put Mike Burke in charge, Lee MacPhail joined them as operating head of the baseball side (general manager, in effect). He and Ralph Houk, the Yankee manager, had always been close. Lee had gone to Baltimore from the Yankees after apprenticeship under Weiss, and he was, after all, the son of the legendary Larry. He simply wanted to get back into action.

His place as Eckert's guide was taken by McHale, who had finished presiding over the move of the Braves to Atlanta.

Television negotiations were no problem, because John Fetzer, the highly respected owner of the Tigers, was an expert on such matters, and many of the other owners were also knowledgeable and good negotiators. Back in 1964, Fetzer had suggested that they make a national television deal for Monday-Night Baseball, which aroused no interest among fellow owners or television executives. Six years later, the same idea would carry football to its greatest heights.

But the worst aspect of the Eckert fiasco was competitive. The National Football League, in 1961, had chosen a young commissioner named Pete Rozelle, whose background and expertise were in public relations in its most modern form. He presided over the rise of his league to television primacy and helped lobby Congress to permit a merger with the American Football League in 1966, restoring his industry's monopoly. And the National Basketball Association was being led by Commissioner Walter Kennedy, a public-relations professional in his own right, who had embarked on a program of expansion and pursued constructive labor relations with a militant group of players. When baseball was still unchallenged as the only true major sport, say in the 1930s or 1940s, an ineffectual commissionership might have done little harm. In the 1960s, it was a masterpiece of bad timing.

By the end of 1968, the owners could see that they couldn't drift this way any longer. In three seminal matters—the transformation of the Players Association into an actual labor union in 1967, the Finley-to-Oakland furor, and the working out of expansion to 12-team leagues during 1968, the commissioner had proved totally irrelevant. He wasn't asked for any input, and he offered none. He wasn't doing any good as a spokesman. Even if all they really wanted was a figurehead, they had to have one who could *be* a credible figurehead.

At the December 1968 annual meeting in San Francisco, they fired him. His seven-year contract still had four years to run.

Now they needed a successor, and they were sure they wanted one of their own. Turning over the business to an outsider like Landis had brought increasing difficulties, but only Yawkey and Wrigley among the 20 owners went back that far, and everything was so different now that comparisons were pointless. But most of them knew, either firsthand or from associates, that outsider Chandler had not worked out well, while insider Frick was pretty good and outsider Eckert a terrible mistake. It was time to turn to an insider again.

More attention to their own history, of course, could have told them that outsider Landis had been chosen in the first place because the insider regime of Ban Johnson and Garry Herrmann had failed so badly, but who needs history?

So they walked right in—like walking nose first into a closed door in the dark— the very dilemma that had led to Landis.

An insider—any insider—must have closer connections to one league than to the other. And neither league is willing to have their joint overseer come from the other one. Especially when the two leagues had so much mutual distrust on current matters, like expansion.

When they met in Chicago on December 20, 1968, they embarked on a stalemate that lasted more than seven weeks. That afternoon, they convened at four o'clock in the afternoon and had a 13-hour session that lasted until 5 A.M. To be elected, a candidate had to get nine of 12 votes in *each* league, not merely 18 of 24. After 19 ballots, they gave up.

There were four real candidates. MacPhail got nine American League votes but only four in the National. Chub Feeney, general manager of his uncle Horace Stoneham's Giants, got all 12 National League votes but only five in the American. Michael Burke, newcomer though he was, got six American and two National votes, then backed off.

The other was McHale, popular and the possessor of fine credentials. He had been a major league player (a first baseman), had run the Tigers and the Braves, had served as Eckert's deputy. But had now undertaken to run the expansion Montreal club and couldn't very well leave it high and dry—nor would his fellow National Leaguers really want him to. So when the American was ready to give him 11 votes, he withdrew without ever having the National vote on him.

At least three other names came up in the discussion: Cronin; Judge Cannon, recently cut loose from the Players Association; and Supreme Court justice Whizzer White.

But the only conclusion they reached was that they'd have to change the voting rules. Then they scattered for the holidays.

They didn't meet again until February 4, 1969, at Miami Beach.

Nothing had changed. The buzz word was "restructuring," but the reality was still two leagues. They needed neutrality and more time, but they were running out of time and only an outsider could be convincingly neutral. And they didn't want an outsider.

Then they did something truly creative. They made one of their lawyers a *tempo-*

rary commissioner, to "just run the office" for a few months until they could get this sorted out. They adopted that idea unanimously in a matter of minutes.

The lawyer they chose was Bowie K. Kuhn. At 41, he was one of the younger members of the Wall Street law firm (Willkie Farr Gallagher) that had represented the National League for many years. He had handled the Milwaukee antitrust case successfully. He was the one who dealt with the new union leader, Marvin Miller, until a professional management negotiator (John Gaherin) had been hired 17 months before. Nominally, he was a National Leaguer, but in a lawyer that didn't seem to matter. And anyhow, he was only going to be commissioner pro tem, an interim caretaker until they got a real one.

Bowie was tall, vigorous, an authentic baseball fan from childhood in Washington, a Princeton man, a forceful speaker. In the image department, he'd do fine.

And now they could get down to the business of restructuring, of making expansion work, of living with two divisions and a pre–World Series playoff. They had solved a problem the way they liked best, by going around it.

THE NEW SCHEDULE

The principles of schedule making, worked out by trial and error in the 19th century, were: each team needs its fair share of "good" dates (weekends and holidays); no team should stay on the road too long, creating too big a gap in its home schedule; a one-day or two-day visit to a city is too short, causing too much travel, so a series of three or four games is ideal; the climate (in the Northeast, where all the teams were then) prevents you from starting before mid-April and playing beyond mid-October; as much as possible, you want a game every day.

With eight teams, that settled into 154 games, 22 against each of seven rivals—11 home, 11 away. Once an Atlantic Seaboard team went west, it was both economical and practical to hit all four western cities on the same trip (Cleveland and Detroit in the American, Pittsburgh and Cincinnati in the National, Chicago and St. Louis in both) and vice versa (to New York, Boston, Philadelphia, and Washington). Traveling by train, three such trips a year meant playing sets of 4-4-3; the intrasectional games could be scheduled more flexibly if one wished. After World War II, a four-trip pattern (3-3-3-2) was adopted and added variety to the home menu. Essentially, this was ("baseball as we know it") from 1903 to 1960.

The adjustment to 10-team leagues was relatively easy. If each item made three three-game visits to each of nine opponents, you'd wind up with 9 times 18, equals 162 games. But while fans and writers thought in terms of 154-game and 162-game seasons, managements think of "openings," that is, home dates. If these had to go from 77 to 81 to make things come out even, why complain about four extra home dates?

But 12 teams in two divisions is another story. First of all, to give divisions *competitive* validity, you need a different number of games with your own set of opponents than with the other set. Otherwise, you have random collections and no justification for giving a team its divisional championship while three teams in the other division have better records against the same opposition, faced as frequently.

Then, you want to keep the number to 162, because a whole decade has been spent establishing it as the new norm for the important matter of comparative statistics. Fewer means giving up home dates. More won't be agreed to by the players, who now have a collective-bargaining contract. And anyhow, you have to stay within the six-month window while inserting a divisional play-off before the World Series.

Well, if you play five fellow division members 18 times each (three-game sets, home and away) and the six teams in the other division 12 times (two three-game sets, home and away), you've got it. That's 90 inside your division, 72 outside, for 162, with enough difference to make separate division races valid.

The American split by geographic logic: Anaheim, Oakland, Seattle, Minnesota, Kansas City, and Chicago in the West; New York, Boston, Baltimore, Washington, Cleveland, and Detroit in the East.

The National screamed long and loud that its divisions were not "geographical" and shouldn't be called East and West. One had Los Angeles, San Francisco, San Diego, Houston, Cincinnati, and Atlanta; the other had New York, Philadelphia, Pittsburgh, Montreal, Chicago, and St. Louis. Obviously, it would make more sense to have St. Louis and Chicago "west" and Atlanta and Cincinnati "east," but the Mets wanted it this way. They were being deprived of three home games each with the Giants and the Dodgers, who had been filling their park every time they came to New York. The next best attraction was St. Louis, having won the last two pennant races. And Chicago had to be paired with St. Louis because it wanted to be and after all had a historic rivalry with "New York," even if that preceded the Mets. The Mets wanted the Cards and Cubs for the extra games, not the Reds and Braves. They got their way.

For years, baseball people had sneered at postseason play-offs as fit only for the minors and other sports. So when the two division winners meet for the right to advance to the World Series, don't you dare call it a "play-off series." It's the League Championship Series (eventually LCS), and don't you forget it.

All that was set in place July 10, 1968, for the 1969 season.

THE NEW RULES

In 1961, the American League played the first 162-game season, and it got everyone very upset.

Roger Maris had the nerve to hit 61 home runs, one more than the hallowed 60 Ruth had hit in 1927, the record that had withstood so many assaults.

Commissioner Frick took it personally. It wasn't that he had once ghostwritten stories for Ruth, that they had been good friends, that Ruth was a central subject in what he had written and broadcast. It was that Ruth's persona and records represented the essence of the "baseball as we know it" that was dissolving before his eyes, with his participation. The very stability being lost was embedded in the "great" records, and Ruth's 60 was the most magical of them all.

Maris was a fine player, an unobjectionable person, a credit to the game. But if he were going to surpass Babe Ruth—Babe Ruth!— he'd better "really" do it.

Whereupon Frick, an intelligent man, did a remarkably foolish thing. He tarnished, at a key moment, what all baseball should have been celebrating. As July ended, with both Maris and Mantle approaching 40 homers and threatening the record, he issued an edict. To "count," the 61st homer would have to be achieved by game no. 154. Beyond that, it would be whatever it was, but it wouldn't "break" Ruth's mark.

What was wrong with that? Well, to begin with, there had never been any "official" records sanctified by the commissioner or any other baseball authority. Publishers of record books listed whatever they wished, fans and commentators accepted whatever they accepted, but no "official" mechanism existed.

Then, from a promotional point of view, this edict was suicidal. It made the last eight games meaningless when they could have been built up into sellouts, and it cost the industry untold dollars.

Finally, it was illogical, unreasonable, unfair, and inconsistent. A "season" record was whatever happened in a season. If you wanted to count games, at bats, plate appearance's, or even swings, you were welcome to, but that would simply be another category. (In fact, it would turn out that although Ruth's schedule called for eight fewer games, he actually went to the plate in 1927 only six fewer times than Maris did in 1961.)

Frick's "asterisk" ruling—he never used that term, but that's what was pinned on ⋅ it (from the use of asterisks to denote special circumstances concerning a record)— turned what should have been a climax into a premature race against time and created endless controversy. If ever he should have claimed "that's not in my jurisdiction," this was the occasion.

But it had worse consequences. Maris did hit 61, Mantle wound up with 54, Harmon Killebrew and Jim Gentile hit 46 each, Rocky Colavito hit 45, and Norm Cash 41. The league's total of 1,534 was a record 40 percent above the previous high—and in 1962, the league hit 1,552. Whether or not one blamed expansion, offense had jumped. The same thing was happening in the National League, with eight teams in 1961 and 10 in 1962.

Once the idea had been raised that there was something "wrong" with these numbers, and that they could be blamed on a longer schedule, it was easy to slip into the next foolish step.

The Rules Committee decided to redefine the strike zone in favor of pitchers.

The committee, headed by Frick's top lieutenant, Charles Segar, had impressions that were contrary to the facts. The aggregate batting average and amount of scoring in 1961 and 1962 was exactly what they had been all through the 1950's. The increase in homers was part of a long-term trend, and not out of line with a 15-year graph. The offense-defense balance was fine.

But these were old men acting on myth, letting nostalgia override reason. (Proof of their irrationality was on hand: in that same 1961 season, Sandy Koufax had set a National League record by striking out 269 batters, surpassing by two the 267 Christy Mathewson recorded in 1903, and Koufax did it in 154 games; what neither Frick nor Segar nor anyone else bothered to note was that 1903 had been a 140-game season. If Maris needed an asterisk, didn't Koufax? But not a word was said about that.)

What the Rules Committee did say was this: we're "restoring" the strike zone to top of shoulders, bottom of knees, as it was before the book was completely recodified in 1950.

Even that wasn't true. The 1949 book had said simply "not lower than his knees, not higher than his shoulders," without pinpointing tops and bottoms. The 1950 revision said "between the batter's armpits and the top of his knees when he assumes his normal stance." It just tried to describe more accurately what had been actual practice for 30 years and continued to be, eliminating some vagueness by adding "normal stance." The 1963 book now said "between the *top* of the batter's shoulders and his knees" in a normal stance.

Trouble was, the strike zone never was, and never will be, a geometrical construct defined precisely in words or diagrams. It's whatever a professional umpire says it is. Every batter's stance is different, and every umpire has his own angle of vision. Professional pitchers and hitters adjust automatically, asking only for consistency: the same pitch should be called the same way throughout a game.

The words didn't matter that much, but if the bosses tell the umpires, unmistakably, to "make the strike zone bigger," they do it. In practice, they started to widen it rather than stretch it vertically, but the point was that it became fuzzier and larger.

The result was devastating. For 15 years, the norms had stabilized at an aggregate batting average around .258, with both teams producing just under 9.0 runs a game. In 1963—the very next season—the average dropped to .246 and the runs to 7.89. There were 1,400 fewer walks and 1,200 more strikeouts.

Suddenly, the runs per game were the lowest since 1919, except for the one war year of 1943.

Pitchers, and especially managers, caught on fast. (One manager gave orders never to throw the first pitch within the strike zone, because there was a 50–50 chance it would be called a strike anyhow.) Offense continued to die.

By 1968, the runs were down to 6.84, the level of 1908. The batting average was .237, lower than 1908, the lowest ever. One of every five games played, 21 percent, ended as a shutout. Carl Yastrzemski won the American League batting championship at .301, the only man in the *league* to hit .300. Pete Rose led the National at .335, but only four others made .300—five men on 20 teams. In 1962, there had been 23. Fifty years of attractive offense-defense balance had been undone.

What it all meant was dull games. A two-run lead seemed insurmountable, even early in a game. A great pitching duel between stars now and then is wonderful. A daily diet of 3–1, 4–2 and 2–0 games is soporific.

Hadn't the owners learned that lesson back in 1920 and become rich?

They couldn't ignore it any longer, especially with four new cities coming in. So they redid the book again. Actually, they made it worse, inserting "top of knees," but the message to the umpires was "tighten it up." They also lowered the mound. Back in 1904, the maximum height had been set at 15 inches to establish some sort of limit. Now everyone had it that high, unless they cheated and made it higher. The new rule lowered it to 10 inches.

The lowered mound did some good. The strike zone remained fuzzy. Offense revived only a little bit, to 8.16 runs and .248. By 1972 it was down again to 7.38 and .244. The more drastic measures that were needed had been tried in the minors for several years.

In 1973, the American League adopted the designated hitter.

Gradually, offense worked its way back to 1950 levels but did not match them entirely until the 1990s

THE NEW PLAYERS ASSOCIATION

Preoccupied with all those other problems and changes, the owners paid insufficient attention to what was developing on the labor front and then reacted to it with uniform impatience, arrogance, underestimation, and blind stubbornness, all of which led to self-inflicted defeat.

It all began with the snubbing of J. Norman Lewis, when all that the players wanted was some pension improvement. Judge Cannon, as their pro bono representative, saw himself as a baseball insider, a benign friend of the establishment simply conveying player requests. The tacit assumption was that all concerned were truly and exclusively devoted to "the good of the game."

In 1962, a new and vastly improved pension plan was adopted. A player with five years of service could, at age 50, collect $125.50 a month for life, up from $88; a 10-year man could get $250, a 20-year man (of whom there would be very few) $300. If the 20-year man waited until age 65 to start collecting, he would get $723.25, up from $550, every month for life. But until a player completed five years on the active major roster, he had no pension at all.

This was touted as one of the best pensions in any industry, spoken of as a dazzling amount of money. And it didn't sound bad in 1962.

But Players and their advisors can do calculations that fans and writers might not bother with. Those 1962 dollar amounts would not go to any immediate retirees, as in other industries; they would begin only far in the future. If a player retired (or returned permanently to the minors) after only five years, he would probably be only 30 years old. If he did that in 1966, he'd be looking at $1,500 a *year* for life starting in 1986. Big inflation hadn't hit yet, but one could imagine that this might not be much by then. If a player played for 20 years, retired at age 40 in 1980, and waited until he was 65, he could receive the maximum, $8,859 a year—starting in the year 2005.

One didn't have to be a genius to figure out that the *present* numbers in a *prospective* pension didn't mean much unless they were constantly upgraded in every new negotiation every few years. It might be a decent pension *now,* but nobody was going to get it now (except an already retired group not directly represented). If some player didn't figure this out, a teammate would be sure to explain it.

The owners evidently thought they wouldn't

Then there was the half-hearted, quickly dropped, suggestion that 20 percent of the gross be earmarked for player compensation. The congressional hearings had provided documentation, now open to all, that back in the 1930's, player salaries accounted for 37 percent of all expenses, so 63 percent had gone to something else, including profits if any. Now the player payroll was down around 16 percent of revenue and still shrinking, so 20 percent seemed a reasonable share for the people who were not merely the workforce but the product itself. No big fuss was made about the rejected idea at the moment, but it showed what players were beginning to think.

Nobody was mad at Judge Cannon. No one doubted that owners would give as little as they could get away with—players hadn't doubted that since the 1880's. But there had to be a better way to get action.

In 1964, the basketball players held up the start of their nationally televised All-Star Game in Boston until Commissioner Kennedy gave a personal promise that he'd fix their (much smaller) pension plan. The next year, they threatened to strike the play-offs just as they were about to start. Management promptly made a satisfactory agreement, there was no stoppage, and there still has never been one in the National Basketball Association.

But the basketball players made no bones about it: their Player's Association was a union, ready for collective bargaining on all work-related issues, including pensions.

Well, baseball players weren't about to see themselves as union workers, but perhaps more professional advice wouldn't be so bad.

Robin Roberts, National League player representative and a Philadelphia celebrity, had contacts at the University of Pennsylvania's famous Wharton School of Business. These led him to one Marvin Miller in Pittsburgh. Miller was an economist (not a lawyer, as he has been persistently misdescribed since) working for the steelworkers' union, with the highest degree of training and experience in labor negotiation, endowed with exceptional negotiating skills. He believed completely in the collective-bargaining process, using all the detailed mechanisms of labor law, as the only effective way for workers to get fair treatment and appropriate compensation.

Miller was also, by nature, an outstanding teacher. If he took on the baseball job, he would have to educate his membership in the methods and necessity of formal bargaining.

The players hired him at $50,000 a year, effective July 1, 1966. His title was executive director of the Major League Baseball Players Association. He brought with him a younger lawyer, Dick Moss, whom he knew from Pittsburgh. In ten years, they would have a greater impact on changing the nature of the baseball business than all the owners and commissioners put together, and Miller more than any individual since Spalding.

For the first time, the Players Association would have a functioning office in continuous operation. But it had to be paid for, along with Miller's salary. The ordinary way was to finance such an office with union dues, collected by the employer as a payroll deduction. Up to now, the clubs themselves had been paying all expenses of the Players Association out of the pension-plan funds, including Judge Cannon's expenses and Norman Lewis' fees. But now that the Association was going to engage in labor negotiation, that system was illegal: an employer cannot fund a union.

The owners, who wanted to have nothing to do with a union anyhow, hoped it would starve itself out of existence. Dues were only $50 a player, amounting to $25,000 a year, not enough of a budget even if every player sent in his check on time.

But the players were also paying $344 a year each as a contribution to the pension plan. In most industries, employee contributions had been phased out long ago; management footed the whole bill. If baseball switched to a noncontributory plan, and the $344 per player were used to fund the Association office, everything would work out. If the $344 became union dues, each player would actually save $50, since that old dues payment could be abandoned. And it wouldn't cost the clubs anything, since it all came from pension-fund money, which couldn't be used for anything else.

It made sense—but it would also make life too easy for the Association and this new radical, Miller. The clubs refused to use the checkoff; let Miller get each of 500 players to send him the $344 check, ha ha ha!

By making an issue of refusing to take the routine step of withholding dues, the owners got formal labor relations off to a bad start that presaged future deterioration. It began a process of teaching the players, again and again with increasing intensity, that management was an enemy eager to use any of its powerful weapons against the collective interests of the players, a lesson Miller could never have gotten across simply by words. It took six months for Miller to collect individually signed authorizations from players for the withholding mechanism, and by that time each such contact had become a rudimentary educational experience.

Even so, this money would arrive only during the 1967 season. To raise funds faster, Miller launched a group licensing program—selling the rights to all players' pictures and autographs—that would become a phenomenal success in its own right. The first deal, with Coca-Cola, brought $60,000 a year for two years. Coke could use any or all of the 500 players for pictures inside bottle caps. But a player's baseball cap contains a team logo on its front, and when the clubs refused to give permission for the logo's use, it had to be airbrushed out. This delayed but did not kill the deal—and provided more education for the players.

In all that followed, when Miller's objective was something he couldn't quite reach through his own efforts, one or more owners would do or say something that would help him get it.

So far, all this was happening under the Eckert commissionership. To the extent that Miller had a specific opposite number, it was Kuhn, the National League lawyer. By the middle of 1967, however, the owners needed a more formal setup to deal with Miller as he pressed for a true collective-bargaining agreement—an actual labor-relations contract spelling out players' rights, the very written relationship the owners had been avoiding successfully for 90 years. They created a Player Relations Committee (essentially the two league presidents and an owner from each league) and hired a professional negotiator as its "consultant." He was John Gaherin, an experienced management-side negotiator who promptly became the butt of jokes because of his previous connection with devastating railroad and newspaper strikes in New York. Nevertheless, he was a capable and well-qualified representative with one fatal handicap: his employers looked upon, and treated, him as a messenger rather than a true deal maker, so that he couldn't say yes to anything until the committee said he could, and the committee needed prior approval from at least an influential group among the disunited owners in two leagues. Miller and Moss could make a deal on the spot, within broad lines set by their player representatives, and then get it ratified; Gaherin needed ratification of every word and comma beforehand and could respond to any suggestion or adjustment only by taking it back to his principals. This pattern would persist from now on, no matter who the management negotiator or Miller's successor turned out to be.

During the fall of 1967, Miller tried to fashion a "basic agreement"—a labor contract. The owners had other issues in mind. The Finley-Oakland expansion mess was on their hands, the complications of the Milwaukee-to-Atlanta move still had ramifications in Milwaukee, McHale had replaced MacPhail as Eckert's guide, new ballpark projects were underway in several cities, and they were beginning the process of playing catch-up to football in television and marketing arrangements. The players were talking about minimum salaries and expense money and scheduling and petty grievances. The habit of taking them for granted was hard to shake.

At the December meetings, held in Mexico City, the owners told Miller and the 20 player reps that they were "too busy" to meet with them, even though they had invited them down for that purpose. Any players who hadn't known about the "keep your lawyer in the foyer" policy of the previous decade knew it now. Their response was to call their own press conference and announce that they had extended Miller's contract for two years, through 1970.

Finally, on February 21, 1968, the first labor agreement was adopted. It was for two years, and its provisions reveal what the players *didn't* have up to that point.

1. Minimum salary up to $12,000 from $7,000
2. Increases in per diem on travel days ("meal money," tips, laundry, etc.) to $15, and spring-training allowances (when there is no salary) to $40 a week
3. Moving expenses for a player called up from the minors, sent to the minors, or traded, and uniform regulations (covering all clubs) for hotel and travel accommodations
4. A set of grievance procedures and rules for arbitrating disputes, with the commissioner as arbitrator
5. Scheduling guidelines to prevent a doubleheader, a night getaway game before a day game the next day, or a regular or exhibition game (except for charity) during the All-Star break
6. No changes in any regulation affecting player benefits or obligations during a season, and then only such changes consistent with existing agreements and after discussion with the Players Association
7. No salary cut bigger than 20 percent (instead of 25 percent)
8. Joint studies to be made of "possible alternatives to the reserve clause as now constituted" and of length of schedule
9. An increase to $4.1 million, from $2.25 million, for funding the pension plan, in line with the increased value of All-Star and World Series television rights

Look at No. 4 and No. 6. Those are the key provisions opening the door to future gains. The rest, in hindsight, are remarkably modest, even within the economy of 1967.

And Number 9, the pension plan, will be the next battleground.

So as 1968 comes to an end, with 12-team leagues and divisional play on the horizon and with the commissioner question completely unresolved by two leagues split more seriously than at any time since 1920, the Players Association has established itself as what it no longer denies or feels ashamed of: a labor union.

We should note the names of the negotiators of this first agreement. On the management side, Cronin and Giles and their lawyers, Sandy Hadden and Bowie Kuhn, and Gaherin; on the player side, Miller and Moss and 12 players. The players were:

Jim Bunning, who will become a congressman
Joe Torre, Bob (Buck) Rodgers, and Russ Nixon, who will become big-league managers
Tim McCarver, who will become a high-ranking telecaster
Steve Hamilton, who will become a college athletic director
Jack Fisher, Dick Hall, Bill Freehan, Ed Kranepool, Jim Pagliaroni, and Milt Pappas

That's six catchers, five pitchers, and a first baseman (Kranepool) who will become a stock broker. Draw your own conclusions about where baseball's "brains" lie.

SEASONS 1961–68

1961

Under a new manager, the Yankees turned out to be more dominant than ever, while Cincinnati emerged as the surprise winner of the National League's last eight-team season.

NL—The Reds held off the Dodgers, by a final margin of four games, on the full blossoming of new stars: outfielders Frank Robinson, 25, and Vada Pinson, 22, and pitchers Joey Jay, 25, and Jim O'Toole, 24. Robinson's .323 with 37 homers and 124 runs batted in made him MVP; Pinson hit .343 and with 23 stolen bases (to Robinson's 22) trailed only Maury Wills, who stole 35. Jay was 21–10, the only 20-game winner besides Spahn (21–13), while O'Toole, the left-hander, was 19–9. Fred Hutchinson did what a manager is supposed to do—hold things together during a bad start (last place in May)—and finally reached a World Series in his third year with his third team.

The Braves and Cardinals changed managers in midseason, Milwaukee from Dressen to Tebbetts, the Cardinals from Solly Hemus to Johnny Keane, while the Cubs, with their rotating coaches, finished seventh. They avoided last place only because the Phillies, in their first full year under Gene Mauch, lost 107, including a 23-game losing streak, then and now the second longest in major league history. (Those 1899 Cleveland Spiders lost 24 straight.)

Roberto Clemente was batting champion at .351, and Sandy Koufax, starting to control his startling fastball, had an 18–13 season with the Dodgers, who were playing their last season in the lopsided Coliseum. At Milwaukee on April 28, Spahn pitched a no-hitter against the Giants, and two days later Willie Mays hit four homers off three other Milwaukee pitchers. The stars were shining brightly.

AL—The Maris-Mantle pursuit of Ruth's record, especially after the misnamed asterisk ruling, overshadowed everything else in the first 10-team, 162-game season. With a record team total of 240 homers, the Yankees played at a .700 pace from June on, because they also had a revitalized pitching staff. Houk let Ford start every fourth day, and Ford posted a 25–4 record with a league-leading 209 strikeouts, making maximum use of reliever Luis Arroyo, who won 15 games and saved 29 others.

Even so, the Yankees remained in a tight race with Detroit, managed now by Bob Scheffing, until they managed a three-game sweep of the Tigers September 1–3 at Yankee Stadium, drawing 177,000 for the series. They went on to win 13 straight to clinch the pennant the night Maris hit number 59 in game no. 154 in Baltimore. The third-place Orioles, in their last season with Richards as manager, finished 14 games back.

In their first season in Minnesota, the former Washington Senators replaced Cookie Lavagetto with Sam Mele in midseason, while Finley, taking over Kansas City, fired Joe Gordon and made Hank Bauer manager in June. The A's, who played at a .377 pace under Gordon, played .380 for Bauer, using 52 players in the process. Their problem was talent, not managing.

All-Star Games—For the third year, there were two games. On July 11 in San Francisco, the National won 5–4, scoring twice in the bottom of the 10th after falling behind in the top half. They needed just four batters: Aaron singled, Mays doubled, Robinson was hit by a pitch, and Clemente singled. Talk about all-stars; but the game is remembered more for a ninth-inning walk by Stu Miller, the league's top reliever, who was caught in midmotion by a furious gust of typical Candlestick Park wind. The instant myth became that he was "blown off the mound," an image whose poetic truth transcends its literal inaccuracy.

On July 31 in Boston, equally typical weather conditions, East Coast variety, intervened more directly. A 1–1 tie was called at the end of the ninth inning when it started to rain hard. It was and is the only All-Star Game not played to a decision, but everyone concerned had planes and trains to catch, so it was called off after waiting only 30 minutes.

WS—The Reds were no match for the Yankees in this Series, winning only the second game, 6–2, behind Jay at New York. Ford's two-hit, 2–0 shutout in the opener and his six scoreless innings in the fourth game (which ended 7–0) enabled him to break Ruth's record of consecutive scoreless innings in World Series play—without asterisk complications. Ruth had pitched 29 innings for the Red Sox without allowing a run between 1916–18. Ford now had 32. "It's been a tough year for the Babe," Whitey quipped. The Yankees won the third and fifth games at Cincinnati by scores of 3–2 and 13–5.

1962

The National League's first 10-team season produced a spectacular pennant race ending in another three-game play-off won in the last inning by the Giants from the Dodgers; but also, in 1962 just as in 1951, the Yankees were there to win the World Series.

NL—In their magnificent new Dodger Stadium, the Los Angeles Dodgers seemed headed for glory until Koufax, with his record at 14–5, went on the disabled list in mid-July because of numbness in his pitching hand. Don Drysdale, who would finish 25–9, was not enough to prevent the September slide that let the Giants catch up. From a September 11 tie, the Giants had a seven-game losing streak, but the Dodgers lost 10 of their last 13 so the Giants forced a playoff by winning three of their last five. On the final day, the Dodgers lost 1–0 to the Cardinals, while Mays hit a homer for a 2–1 victory over Houston in San Francisco.

Koufax started the first play-off game at Candlestick but lasted only seven batters as Mays and Jim Davenport hit homers, and the Giants won 8–0 behind Billy Pierce. At Dodger Stadium, the Dodgers came from behind to win a four-hour game 8–7, and in the third game they took a 4–2 lead into the ninth. Eleven years before, the Giants had beaten them with a four-run ninth at home; now they had a four-run ninth on the road and won 6–4. History hadn't repeated exactly, but close enough.

Even so, this Dodger team had more significant assets than the Giants had. The team was built on pitching and nonhomer run manufacture, in a pitcher-friendly park, signaling major changes in baseball style. Wills stole 104 bases. As unassailable as Ruth's 60 homers had seemed the year before, Ty Cobb's 1915 record of 96 stolen bases had been considered by baseball insiders even more unapproachable. And Tommy Davis, a "singles hitter" whose .346 led the league, produced 153 runs batted in, the only time the 150-plateau was reached in 47 years from 1949 through 1995.

To put Wills's base stealing in perspective, we must note that the runner-up, teammate Willie Davis, stole 32 bases, while the American League leader, Luis Aparicio, had 31.

The Dodger pattern would dominate the next few seasons, but the Giants were at a one-year peak. Jack Sanford won 16 straight in a 24–7 season. Pierce was 12–0 at Candlestick in a 16–6 year. Juan Marichal, in his second full season, was 18–11. Billy O'Dell, providing perfect lefty-right balance with Pierce for the two right-handers, was 19–11. Mays hit 49 homers, Orlando Cepeda 35, Felipe Alou 25, and Willie McCovey, in only 229 at bats, 20.

Cincinnati gave it a good try, winning 98 games (to 101 by the other two before the play-off), with Robinson just behind Tommy Davis at .342 (with 39 homers), and right-handers Bob Purkey (23–5) and Jay (21–14) doing their best. Meanwhile Musial, at 41, hit .330 for the sixth-place Cardinals in what would be his last season as a regular.

AL—Houk's second pennant was actually easier, though far less glamorous, than his first. The Yankees won only 98 games, not 109; Maris and Mantle hit 33 and 30 homers, not 61 and 54. Ford was 17–8, not 25–4, and Arroyo was out of business with a sore arm. But Detroit fell off dramatically, Cleveland collapsed after an early drive, and the two teams staying close into September were Minnesota and the second-year Angels. Despite a 17–18 August between a 23–8 July and 17–9 September, the Yankees had no real problems, and their top pitcher was now Ralph Terry (23–12), the 1960 victim of Mazeroski's World Series homer.

The new top slugger was Harmon Killebrew of the Twins, with 48 home runs and 126 runs batted in, while Boston's Pete Runnels nosed out Mantle for the batting title, .326 to .321.

Had expansion inflated offensive statistics? Well, the aggregate averages for 20 teams in 1962—runs per game, batting average, home runs per game—were almost identical with those of 1956. Whatever problem the strike-zone tinkerers thought they were about to solve, expansion was not its cause.

All-Star Games—The two-game All-Star idea had outlived its welcome, and this would be its last year. On July 10, in Washington's new stadium, the Nationals won 3–1, allowing just four hits. On July 30 at Chicago's Wrigley Field, the Americans won 9–4. Press and public were showing less interest in the diluted showcase, and it was decided to return to a single game in 1963.

WS—The Yankees won the opener at Candlestick 6–2, as Ford's scoreless streak ended at 33 when the Giants scored in the second inning on a two-out bunt single by Jose Pagan after singles by Mays and Davenport. Yankee Clete Boyer's homer broke a 2–2 tie in the seventh. Then the Giant's Sanford pitched a three-hit, 2–0 shutout the next day, beating Terry.

In New York, the Yankees won 3–2, then lost 7–3 to a grand-slam home run by Chuck Hiller, San Francisco's second baseman who had hit just three homers all year. After a rainout, the Yankees won the fifth 5–3 on a three-run eighth-inning homer by Tom Tresh.

Preceding the rainout, Commissioner Frick's lieutenants kept reporting, "It's clearing in Jersey," where the west wind came from. But in San Francisco, the west wind was off the Pacific Ocean, and it rained steadily for three days before the Series could be resumed. When it did, Pierce beat Ford 5–2, so the Yankees went into a seventh game for the sixth time in their last seven World Series. Terry faced Sanford. In the fifth, the Yankees filled the bases with none out, and manager Dark decided to concede a run for a double play, into which Tony Kubek obligingly hit. So it was still 1–0 when Matty Alou opened the bottom of the ninth by beating out a drag bunt. Terry struck out the next two, but Mays doubled to the right-field corner, where fast fielding by Maris made Alou stop at third. Manager Houk let Terry pitch to the left-handed McCovey, with right-handed Cepeda up next and first base open, and McCovey hit a savage line drive right at second baseman Bobby Richardson. If it had gone through, it would have been the first result-reversing final hit (as distinct from tie-breaking) in World Series history. As it was, Terry had vindication for 1960.

The cultural impact can be imagined from the "Peanuts" comic strip that appeared many weeks later, showing Charlie Brown sitting on the curb, silent for three panels, then saying, "Why couldn't McCovey have hit it one foot higher?"

1963

This time the Dodgers had a healthy Koufax all year long, and the result was their second World Series triumph in as many tries since coming to Los Angeles.

NL—Koufax had his first superseason, 25–5, a record 306 strikeouts, 11 shutouts, a 1.88 earned run average. The rest of a strong Dodgers pitching staff, for which Drysdale was 19–17, could rest on the relief work of Ron Perranoski, 16–3 with 21 saves. Koufax and Drysdale started 82 games—one more than half the schedule—and pitched more than 300 innings each, while Perranoski worked in 69 games. For that kind of pitching, Frank Howard's 28 homers, Tommy Davis's .326 for another batting title, and Wills's modest 40 steals provided sufficient offense. In July the Dodgers won 17 of 20 and opened a seven-game lead. Then the Cardinals, rebuilt with productive trades as well as a revived farm system, won 19 of 20 and closed to within one game as the Dodgers came to St. Louis September 16. But Podres won 3–1, Koufax 4–0, and Perranoski, working six scoreless innings, 6–5 in a game that went 13 innings. The sweep effectively ended the race.

Koufax, who had pitched a no-hitter against the Mets in 1962 shortly before his hand went dead, pitched another on May 11 against the Giants and Juan Marichal, who pitched a no-hitter a month later himself. Podres won three of the 53 games in the majors that ended 1–0. The new strike zone was having an immediate effect, but neither the press nor the public seemed to notice.

AL—The Yankees, apparently stronger than ever, took command with a 17–9 May and won by 10½ games with 104 victories. Al Lopez brought the White Sox in second with Mele's Minnesota third. Boston's Carl Yastrzemski won his first batting title at .321, with teammate Dick Stuart leading in runs batted in with 118, while Killebrew remained home-run king with 45.

In the only midseason managerial change, the expansion Washington Senators replaced Mickey Vernon with Gil Hodges in May but finished last anyhow.

The new strike zone had its effect in this

league too. Ford's 24–7 and Jim Bouton's 21–7 led the Yankees, Camilo Pasqual was 20–9 for the Twins, Steve Barber 20–13 for Baltimore, Bill Monbouquette 20–10 for seventh-place Boston. In 1962, Baltimore's 3.69 earned run average had been good enough to lead the league; now half the teams, five, posted lower marks as the White Sox led with 2.97.

All-Star Game—In Cleveland, the Nationals won 5–3, as the aftereffects of the two-game experiment became vividly clear. The game drew only 44,000 in a 74,000-seat building.

WS—Another Yankee-Dodger series, the first since the Brooklyn days, caused immense anticipation. But it didn't last long. Koufax fanned 15, a Series record, in a 5–2 victory at Yankee Stadium, and Podres, on the scene of his 1955 triumph, won the second 4–1 with Perranoski's help in the ninth. At Dodger Stadium, Drysdale beat Bouton 1–0, making a first-inning run stand up, and Koufax faced Ford in the fourth game. Frank Howard's homer in the fifth was matched by Mantle's in the seventh, but an unearned run gave the Dodgers a 2–1 lead in the bottom half, when Joe Pepitone lost sight of a throw to first from third. With the tying run on first and one out in the ninth, Koufax struck out Mantle and completed one of the greatest seasons any pitcher ever had.

1964

Perhaps the most eventful single season in baseball history, 1964 can be given only a telegraphic summary here. Excellent books about it are abundant.

NL—The Dodgers collapsed right at the start, went through a succession of slumps and injuries, and finished a distant sixth. Koufax, 19–5 by August 16, pitched no more because of a damaged elbow.

The Phillies, who still had many survivors of the 23-game losing streak of 1961, got off well, battled the Giants for the lead up to August, then pulled away and had a 6½-game lead with 12 to play.

Cincinnati's manager, Hutchinson, suffering from cancer which would soon prove fatal, had to turn over the club to Dick Sisler in August, but it hung on and passed the slumping Giants in pursuit of the Phillies as September began.

The Cardinals, after their 1963 run, were in turmoil. Owner Busch was dissatisfied with the performance of his front office. He had hired Branch Rickey as an advisor, and with the club in fifth place in August, fired Bing Devine, his general manager for the last seven years, and brought in Bob Howsam, associated with Rickey's Continental League enterprise. Busch denied Rickey's influence but didn't deny that he was seeking Leo Durocher to replace manager Johnny Keane, Devine's protege.

But just before trading deadline, June 15, Devine had sent pitcher Ernie Broglio to Chicago for left fielder Lou Brock, and with that piece in place the Cardinals began to win.

Nevertheless, with two weeks to go the Phillies seemed safe at 90–60, with St. Louis and Cincinnati 83–66 and San Francisco 83–67. But the Phillies lost the next 10—three to Cincinnati and four to Milwaukee at home, then three in St. Louis. The Cards took a five-game winning streak into their Philadelphia series and swept it 5–1, 4–2, 8–5. That enabled them to pass Cincinnati as well as the Phils.

On the final Friday, with plans in place to untangle a four-team tie, the Cards lost to the hapless Mets while the Phillies finally won at Cincinnati. On Saturday, the Mets walloped the Cards 15–5, while the Giants eliminated themselves by losing at Chicago. The Phils and Reds were idle, so the final day dawned with the Cards and Reds tied at 92–69 and the Phils alive at 91–70. The Phils beat the Reds 10–0, but the Cardinals won the pennant by beating the Mets 11–5.

And through all this, the Braves were trying to leave Milwaukee for Atlanta; the Cubs had abandoned their coaching board to let Bob Kennedy manage; the Mets were as bad as ever in their new Shea Stadium but drawing 1.7 million; and the Giants had decided in August to discard manager Dark but let him finish the year as the race developed.

Jim Bunning, who pitched the league's first perfect game in 84 years against the Mets on June 21 (Father's Day), was Philadelphia's leading pitcher, 19–8. Mauch used him, Chris Short, and Art Mahaffey in a three-man rotation down the stretch, and it didn't work, as it hadn't for Lopez in Cleveland in 1952. Power was provided by Johnny Callison, 31 homers, 104 runs batted in, and a 22-year-old rookie, Dick Allen, 29 homers, 91 runs batted in.

The Cards had Bill White at first, Dick Groat at short, Brock in left and Curt Simmons (a Philadelphia Whiz Kid in 1950, now 35 years old) to pitch, acquired in trades; and Ken Boyer at third, Curt Flood in center, Tim McCarver catching, and Julian Javier at second, from their own system. Musial had retired, so right field was filled by Mike Shannon, brought up from the minors in midseason. And their top two pitchers, left-hander Ray Sadecki and right-hander Bob Gibson, were also homegrown Devine products, who had played for Keane in the minors.

For the Giants, Marichal had come into his own (21–8), while Mays hit 47 homers and Cepeda and Jim Ray Hart 31 apiece. Robinson, Pinson, and Deron Johnson gave Cincinnati lots of offense, but the pitchers faltered. Clemente led the league with .339, Boyer with 119 runs batted in, Wills with 53 stolen bases, Mays in homers. Larry Jackson pitched 24 victories for the eighth-place Cubs, and Koufax finished with a 1.74 earned-run average.

And the other league was no less intriguing.

AL—The Yankees, ultimate symbols of victory, boasting 13 pennants in the last 15 years, were annoyed at being upstaged by the Mets, ultimate symbols of defeat, under the leadership of Stengel and Weiss, their own discards. Roy Hamey, Weiss's successor, wanted to retire. Topping was preparing to sell. Why not let Houk become general manager and Yogi Berra the manager in the dugout? Stengel talked funny, and Yogi was quoted as talking funny; wouldn't that be a public-relations standoff? The team was so good it could win with anyone managing, and Houk could pull strings when and if needed as general manager.

It was an idea that would accomplish what the entire American League had been unable to do for 40 years: dismantle the Yankee empire. But not immediately.

Given the traditionally difficult task of managing his own teammates, with no previous managerial experience anyhow, Yogi had his troubles. By spring training Topping had called him an idiot. The players ran behind his back to Houk with every grievance. The White Sox, under Lopez, and the Orioles, now managed by Hank Bauer, pro-

vided formidable opposition. The Yankee pitching staff was wearing out, with Ford hurt by midseason. The farm system had stopped producing.

Even so, the Yankees entered August in first place, 61–38, percentage points ahead of Baltimore. But soon they were losing 10 of 15 to the White Sox and Orioles, and it would have been worse if not for Mel Stottlemyre, called up from the minors on August 12 and an instant success.

Two days later, the sale of the club to CBS was announced, a deal that "shook baseball as it had never been shaken before by a change in club ownership," according to the *1965 Baseball Guide*'s review of the year.

At that point, Houk had already decided that Berra would have to go, no matter how this year turned out, and he began searching for a new manager.

But on August 22 the Yankees started to win. Mantle came back from an injury. Stottlemyre would finish 9–3. On September 5, Houk got Berra the reliever he sorely needed, and Pedro Ramos saved eight games. They went 26–8 to clinch on the next-to-last day, finishing one game ahead of Chicago and two ahead of Baltimore.

Minnesota's Tony Oliva was the new batting champion, his .323 beating out Baltimore's Brooks Robinson's .317 while Brooks led with 118 runs batted in, and Killebrew was still home-run champion with 49. Aparicio, in Baltimore since 1963, stole 57 bases and was setting the same example in this league that Wills was in the National. Only Gary Peters, 20–9 with the White Sox, and Dean Chance, 20–8 with the Angels, won 20 games. Only the Athletics' owner, Finley, changed managers in midseason, switching from Eddie Lopat to Mel McGaha, but the A's still finished last.

All-Star Game—Played at Shea Stadium, the game produced ninth-inning drama as the Nationals, once trailing 12–4 in the series, pulled even at 17 victories each with a 7–4 decision. Dick Radatz, Boston's relief ace, took a 4–3 lead into the bottom of the ninth. He walked Mays, who promptly stole second and provoked a wild throw home on Cepeda's looping single to right. After an intentional pass, Radatz fanned Aaron but yielded a three-run homer to Callison, which mandated references to the one by Williams in Detroit in 1941.

WS—The Cards won in seven games, but the aftermath was even more exciting. The Yankees fired Berra. Busch asked Keane to stay, but Keane stuck by his resignation. Then Houk hired Keane, against whom he had managed in the minors, to manage the CBS Yankees. And Yogi joined Stengel as a player-coach with the Mets, who also hired Bing Devine as assistant and heir apparent to Weiss. The Cardinals made Red Schoendienst, a hometown favorite, their manager, counting on nostalgia to nullify the loss of Keane.

The World Series games were hot stuff in themselves. The Cards outslugged the Yankees in the first game in St. Louis 9–5, but the Yankees struck back, 8–3 behind Stottlemyre, and the teams went to New York even. Bouton and Simmons went 1–1 to the ninth at Yankee Stadium in the third game, and when Barney Schultz, a relief hero during the Cardinal stretch run, came in to start the ninth, Mantle greeted him with a home run, his 16th in World Series play, breaking another record held by Ruth.

But the Cards won the next two, 4–3 on a grand slam by Ken Boyer off Al Downing and 5–2 on a 10th-inning three-run homer by McCarver after a two-run homer by Tresh had tied the game in the bottom of the ninth.

In St. Louis, the Yankees forced a seventh game as Bouton won 8–3, backed by a grand-slam homer by Pepitone. Finally, Gibson survived home runs by Mantle, Clete Boyer, and Phil Linz in a 7–5 victory that made the Cardinals champions for the first time in 18 years.

In retrospect, 1964 was a year that changed baseball's direction in many ways, especially in off-field power alignments and in the end (not then expected) of Yankee domination. But perhaps the most important occurence took place in January and involved no one in baseball. The American Football League (AFL), struggling to survive as a challenger to the established National Football League, got a $36 million television contract from NBC, assuring its future. That set in motion pro football's ascendancy in the sports marketplace during the rest of the decade and into the 1970s, with consequences from which baseball has never recovered. One piece of fallout was the AFL's ability, early in 1965, to give college star Joe Namath a package widely advertised as $400,000. It raised the consciousness of everyone

in sports to what riches might lie ahead, and the more mature baseball players who were struggling with pension arrangements and wondering how to strengthen their Players Association were not unaware of the implicit message.

1965

A Koufax able to pitch a full season brought the Dodgers to new heights, while the unforeseen collapse of the Yankees left the Minnesota Twins as American League champions. The Twins provided their new city with a World Series in their fourth year; the Braves had delivered one to Milwaukee in their fifth, the Dodgers to Los Angeles in their second, the Giants to San Francisco in their fifth. Baltimore hadn't made it yet but had become a perennial contender within seven seasons. Whatever the fate of expansion teams, the benefits of moving an old franchise were becoming self-evident.

NL—A four-team scramble settled into a Giant-Dodger race in September. The Giants started the month with a 14-game winning streak, but just as it ended, the Dodgers began a 13-game run. In the final week, Giant pitching collapsed, and the Dodgers won by a two-game margin.

Koufax was 26–8, with a record 382 strikeouts in 336 innings, eight shutouts among 27 complete games, allowing only 216 hits. His earned run average was 2.08. Drysdale, 23–12 with seven shutouts, worked 308 innings, and Claude Osteen, the third starter, 287. Their ERAs were 2.78 and 2.79. With Wills stealing 94 bases, a team batting average of .245 proved sufficient, as the Dodger run total of 608 was the lowest in the league except for expansion Houston and the Mets.

The Giants got 52 home runs from Mays and 39 from Willie McCovey, but beyond Marichal (22–13, 10 shutouts, 2.14 ERA) had only mediocre pitching. Their new manager was Herman Franks, who had been Leo Durocher's top lieutenant in the Polo Grounds days and had played for Leo in Brooklyn before the war.

The Braves, having announced that they would be leaving Milwaukee, suffered at the gate even though they stayed in the race through August before finishing fifth, managed by Bobby Bragan. Sisler's Reds, scoring 825 runs (217 more than the

Dodgers) also were in contention until September, but their pitching was too thin beyond Sammy Ellis (22–10) and Jim Maloney (20–11). Pittsburgh, managed by Harry Walker, was never in the race but finished third by winning 27 of their last 38, and Clemente was batting champion again at .329. Milwaukee's Tony Cloninger went 24–11 but wasn't even among the top 15 qualifiers for the earned run leadership.

Spahn, at 44, had left the Braves to be pitcher-coach for the Mets, but when he wouldn't assign himself to the bull pen, he got released and finished the year with the Giants. Shortly after he left, Stengel suffered a broken hip and then formally retired, turning the Mets over to Wes Westrum.

AL—The Twins marched to a pennant the way the Yankees used to: 27–15 the first two months, 38–22 the next two, 37–23 the rest of the way. Oliva was batting champion at .321 (only two others, in the whole league, Carl Yastrzemski and Vic Davalillo of Cleveland, hit .300). Killebrew was hurt half the year and hit only 25 homers, but there was balanced offense and strong pitching: Mudcat Grant 21–7, Jim Kaat 18–11, and a deep staff. Shortstop Zoilo Versalles was MVP and Earl Battey a solid catcher. The margin over Chicago was seven games.

Keane was the wrong man to handle New York's publicity pressures or the team's aging stars, in a situation compounded by injuries. The front office was a mess, with Topping nominally still in charge but lines of authority to CBS unclear, so the farm system deteriorated some more. Stottlemyre went 20–9 in his first full season, but Ford was wearing out, Bouton had a bad arm, Maris missed 119 games, and Mantle 54. Finishing sixth at 77–85, the Yankees had their first losing record and lowest finish in 40 years, since 1925, the year of Ruth's famous rebellion.

All-Star Game—At Minnesota, the Nationals won 6–5 and took the lead in the series for the first time. Mays, as always an all-star among all-stars, opened the game with a homer, then scored the winning run in the seventh after the Americans had pulled even from a 5–0 deficit. Oliva opened the bottom of the ninth with a double, but Gibson caught the pop-up of an attempted bunt and fanned Killebrew and Pepitone to end the game.

WS—The Dodgers' Koufax could not start the first game, in Minneapolis, because of his observance of Yom Kippur, the most holy Jewish holiday. So Drysdale did and got knocked out in a six-run third that led to an 8–2 victory for Grant. Then Koufax fell behind Kaat 2–0 in the sixth, and the Twins won again, 5–1.

In Los Angeles, it was another story. Osteen pitched a 4–0 four-hit shutout, Drysdale won a 7–2 five-hitter, and Koufax followed with a four-hit 7–0 shutout with 10 strikeouts.

But Grant won the sixth game 5–1 against Osteen, and Koufax—whose arthritic elbow was well publicized—had to start the seventh game on two days' rest. He was overpowering. The Dodgers got two runs off Kaat in the fourth, enough for a 2–0 three-hitter with 10 strikeouts. The Brooklyn Dodgers had won one World Series in 10 tries; the Los Angeles Dodgers were now three for three.

1966

The big story in spring training was a joint hold-out by Koufax and Drysdale, asking for a three-year million-dollar contract to be divided equally. Koufax settled for one year at $125,000 and Drysdale for $110,000, and the weakness of their bargaining position had a significant effect on attitudes about the hiring of Marvin Miller, then in the works. They then produced another Dodger pennant but were swept in the World Series by the Baltimore Orioles.

NL—This was another Giant-Dodger race, this time also involving the Pirates, right down to the last day.

The final weekend began with the Dodgers in Philadelphia, two games ahead of Pittsburgh and 3½ ahead of the Giants, who had three to play in Pittsburgh and a possible makeup game in Cincinnati. On Friday, the Dodgers lost, while the Pittsburgh game was rained out. On Saturday, the Dodgers were rained out, while the Giants swept their doubleheader 5–4 and 2–0, eliminating the Pirates. On Sunday, the Giants won again, 7–3 in 11 innings, while the Dodgers lost their opener 4–3 with Drysdale.

Now the Giants sat in the Pittsburgh airport waiting for reports of Koufax pitching the second game in Philadelphia. If the Dodgers lost, the Giants would have to go to Cincinnati, where, by winning one game, they could create a pennant play-off with the Dodgers. But Koufax, on two days' rest, won 6–3 and the Giants flew home to San Francisco to disband.

That made Sandy's record 27–9 with a 1.73 earned run average, 317 strikeouts in 323 innings, 27 complete games, five shutouts. In four years, since his arm trouble began in 1962, he had worked 1,192 innings, struck out 1,228 batters, completed 60 percent of his starts (89 of 150), allowed only 6.2 hits per nine innings pitched, and thrown 31 shutouts, which meant holding the opposition scoreless in every fifth start. His won-lost record was 97–27, a .782 pace, and when asked to relieve three times, he posted three saves. No comparable stretch of pitching superiority exists in the lively-ball era that began in 1920, but at that point, at age 31, he decided to retire because he was unwilling to take the increasing doses of medication needed to keep him going.

He, Drysdale, Osteen, and a rookie named Don Sutton started 154 of the 162 Dodger games this season. (Joe Moeller started the other eight.) And when they needed relief, they got it from Phil Regan, who added a 14–1 won-lost record to his 21 saves, earning the nickname "Vulture."

The Giants had Marichal, 25–6, and Gaylord Perry, 21–8, but a sharp drop-off in the rest of their pitching. They also had home-run power: Mays 37, McCovey 36, Hart 33, Tom Haller 27. Pittsburgh had a new batting champion, little Matty Alou, whose .342 included only two home runs (while Clemente hit 29 homers in his .318). But Pirate pitchers, led by the intimidating Bob Veale, 16–12, couldn't match the Dodger and Giant staffs.

Gibson, 21–12, and Philadelphia's Chris Short, 20–10, were the other 20-game winners. Aaron, in Atlanta, found himself in a favorable home-run park and hit 44, marking the start of his drive to surpass Ruth's career total. His 127 runs batted in led the league.

Durocher, who had been a broadcaster and Dodger coach since leaving the Giants in 1955, returned to managing with the Chicago Cubs—and earned the distinction of being the first manager to finish below the Mets. Westrum, his catcher on the miracle 1951 Giants, brought the Mets in ninth, still behind Houston but 7½ games ahead of Durocher's Cubs, who lost 103 games.

In Houston's Astrodome, artificial turf was used for the first time this season, because painting the roof to cut glare had killed the grass. In St. Louis, the new Busch Stadium was not ready when the season began, so the Cardinals didn't move in until May 12. They played their first 10 games (losing seven) at what had been Sportsman's Park, a site housing major league baseball for the preceding 90 years.

AL—The Orioles had traded a promising pitcher, Milt Pappas, to Cincinnati for Frank Robinson, a proven commodity, in December of 1965. Robinson proceeded to tear up his new league and lead the Orioles to their first pennant by a large margin. They had a 13-game lead before the end of July and wound up nine games ahead of Minnesota.

Robinson won the Triple Crown as well as the MVP Award. He hit .316 with 49 homers and 122 runs batted in. Boog Powell added 34 homers and Brooks Robinson 23, giving ample support to four young starters: Jim Palmer (20), Dave McNally (23), Wally Bunker (21) and Steve Barber (27), none of whom won more than Palmer's 15 but all of whom worked effectively until relievers Stu Miller and (after coming from the White Sox) Eddie Fisher could take over. Bauer, who had chafed under Stengel's platooning as a player, turned out to be a pretty good platooner himself when he managed.

Kaat had a 25–13 season for the Twins, and the Tigers came up with a 22-year-old righty, Denny McLain, whose 20–14 helped them place third. Eddie Stanky succeeded Lopez as manager of the White Sox and brought them in fourth, while Finley hired Alvin Dark, for the Athletics let him manage the entire season, and was rewarded with a rise all the way to seventh place. In Detroit, the year was tragic: Dressen had a heart attack in May, and his successor, coach Bob Swift, came down with lung cancer in July. Dressen died in August, Swift in October.

The final demise of the Yankee dynasty was the other big story. After a 4–16 start, Houk fired Keane and returned to the dugout. The team spurted for a month, then finished dead last, half a game behind the Red Sox—and one slot lower than the ninth-place Mets across town. A September 22 game at the Stadium that drew 413 spectators highlighted an attendance drop to 1.1 million, 800,000 less than the Mets. In mid-

September, Topping departed, Mike Burke took over for CBS as president, Houk became permanent manager, and Lee MacPhail—who had built the Orioles but was not there to share the triumph because he had agreed to baby-sit Commissioner Eckert—came back as general manager. Fears that CBS "resources" would solidify Yankee power were no longer heard.

All-Star Game—Awarded to St. Louis out of turn in honor of the new Busch Stadium, the game was played on July 12 in 105-degree heat that reached 130 degrees down on the field. (Asked to comment on the new stadium, Casey Stengel declared "it holds the heat well.") The game went 10 innings, the Nationals winning 2–1 on a single by McCarver, a sacrifice, and a single by Wills.

WS—Baltimore's sweep was one of the most efficient ever, and the Dodger performance one of the weakest. Both Robinsons hit homers in the first inning off Drysdale in Los Angeles, and when the Dodgers closed to within 3–2 in the third inning, Moe Drabowsky relieved McNally and allowed only one more hit. The Dodgers never scored again.

Palmer's four-hitter in the 6–0 second game, against Koufax, was decided when Willie Davis made three errors on two plays in center field in the fifth inning, giving the Orioles their first three runs. In Baltimore, Bunker beat Osteen 1–0 on Paul Blair's fifth-inning homer, and McNally beat Drysdale 1–0 on Frank Robinson's fourth-inning homer. The Dodgers had hit .142, which remains the lowest for a club in a World Series.

Still not widely discussed, the widened strike zone, was being reflected in these numbers. The American League had hit .240, and only Robinson and Oliva (.307) hit .300. The National was normal enough at .256 but would fall into line next year.

1967

The Red Sox accomplished their "Impossible Dream" by winning the pennant on the last day, coming off a ninth-place finish the year before, but couldn't carry it to the final step against the Cardinals, who had run away from the rest of the National League.

NL—Stan Musial had become active general manager of the Cardinals when the new owners of the Cincinnati Reds had hired Bob Howsam in January. His buddy Schoendienst had some talent to work with. Orlando Cepeda and Roger Maris had been acquired in trades, young pitchers like Steve Carlton and Nelson Briles bolstered the staff led by Dick Hughes (16–6), and Gibson, Flood, McCarver, Shannon, Javier, and Brock were 1964 champions still going strong They finished 10½ games ahead of the Giants and 14 ahead of the Cubs, quickly turned into a winning mode by Durocher.

Clemente won another batting title at .357, while Cepeda was MVP with 111 runs batted in and a .325 average. Flood hit .335, and Brock stole 52 bases. (Aaron, now the real home-run king, led with 39 for Atlanta.) But in general, beyond less than a dozen outstanding hitters, offense was dying. The league average fell to .249.

The Dodgers, without Koufax, Wills (traded to Pittsburgh), and Tommy Davis (traded to the Mets), fell all the way to eighth, as Drysdale showed wear and tear also. The Mets slipped back to 10th and discarded Westrum, hiring Gil Hodges from Washington for 1968. The Pirates replaced Walker with Danny Murtaugh, their 1960 hero, midway through a .500 season. The only 20-game winners were Mike McCormick, 22–11 in San Francisco and the Cy Young Award winner, and Ferguson Jenkins, 20–13 for the Cubs.

AL—Stretch-drive drama equal to 1908, 1948, 1949, and other legendary races focused on the Red Sox, Twins, Tigers, and White Sox, enhanced by managerial personalities. Dick Williams, a feisty newcomer, was vigorously ending the "country-club atmosphere" of the Boston clubhouse. Mayo Smith, a nonstop talker, had taken over the Tigers. Stanky had the White Sox, and Bill Rigney, whose Angels would play a key peripheral role, was always good copy. Only the Twins, who replaced Mele with Cal Ermer June 9, had no lively spokesman, but they had rumors of dissension going for them.

The last two days started with the Twins in Boston, the Angels in Detroit, and the White Sox eliminated as the result of a doubleheader loss in Kansas City Wednesday and a 1–0 loss to Washington at home on Friday. The Twins were 91–69 and Boston 90–70 with two to play. The Tigers were 89–69 facing two doubleheaders because of rain on Thursday and Friday.

Saturday, Boston won 6–4 on a three-run homer by Carl Yastrzemski, while the Tigers, after winning 5–0 behind Mickey Lolich, ran into a six-run eighth in losing the second game 8–6. By winning the final doubleheader, the Tigers could tie whoever won the Boston game and force a play-off.

Sunday the Red Sox won again, 5–3. The Tigers also won, 6–4, and led in the second game. But once again they couldn't hold the lead, and when the Angels won 8–5 at 7:42 P.M. Eastern time, the Red Sox listening to the radio in their clubhouse for the last two hours were pennant winners for the first time in 21 years, and only the second time in 49.

Yaz was the man: batting champion (.326 to Frank Robinson's .311), tied with Killebrew at 44 homers, leader with 121 runs batted in, MVP. George Scott, 23-year-old first baseman, hit .303 (and the only other .300 hitter in the league was Al Kaline). Jim Lonborg was the pitching man, 22–9 on a staff for which no one else won more than 12. The other contenders actually had deeper pitching—Earl Wilson (22–11), McLain, Lolich, and Joe Sparma in Detroit, Dean Chance (20–11) and Kaat in Minnesota, Joel Horlen and Gary Peters in Chicago. But the Red Sox had the "Impossible Dream" theme drawn from the current hit musical based on Don Quixote, and that's what myths are made of.

Baltimore's pitching went to pieces, Hodges got Washington up to seventh, Joe Adcock got nowhere managing the Indians, Houk's Yankees finished ninth; but it was Kansas City, last again, that provided a key development, thanks to Finley.

A complaint about rowdy behavior on a commercial flight led Finley to fine an accused player, Lew Krausse; to ban the serving of liquor on future flights; and to criticize his players in general. They answered with an outraged public statement. Finley decided that Dark was siding with his players against him and fired the manager, then reinstated him. When Ken Harrelson, one of his best hitters, spoke out publicly for Dark against Finley, the owner "retaliated" by firing him—that is, giving him his release. The issue of Krausse's fine led the players to ask Miller to arrange a hearing before Commissioner Eckert, claiming abuse of employees by Finley. Miller filed an unfair-labor-practice claim with the National Labor Relations Board, which was withdrawn when Finley backed down on all counts.

The two important long-range results were: (1) all players learned they had a union that could go to bat for them with a grievance, instead of trying to argue one-on-one with an employer, and (2) Harrelson, a free agent because of his release, promptly got a $75,000 bonus-salary package from the Red Sox, joining them in time to take part in the pennant run and World Series—showing all players what it could mean to be free of the reserve system.

All-Star Game—Awarded to Anaheim, again in honor of the new ball park occupied by the Angels the year before, this game became a farce. It started at about 4:30 P.M. California time for the sake of prime-time television back East and was soon being played in twilight, an edge the world's best pitchers didn't need. It went 15 innings containing a total of 17 hits and 30 strikeouts, with only two walks (both to Yaz). Dick Allen hit a homer in the second off Chance, Brooks Robinson matched it off Jenkins in the sixth, and it stayed 1–1 until Tony Perez hit one off Catfish Hunter, working his fifth inning, in the top of the 15th, for a 2–1 victory.

WS—The Red Sox gave it a good try, but the Cardinals' Gibson and Brock were too much for them. Gibson's six-hitter won the opener 2–1 at Fenway, as Brock got four hits, stole two bases, and scored both runs on groundouts by Maris. Lonborg responded with a 5–0 one-hitter, only the fourth in Series history. Yastrzemski hit two homers, and Javier broke up the no-hitter with a two-out double in the eighth.

In St. Louis, the Cards won 5–2 behind Briles and 6–0 behind Gibson, but now it was Lonborg's turn again and he produced a 3–1 three-hitter. Back at Fenway, Rico Petrocelli hit two homers and Yaz and Smith one apiece in an 8–4 victory that forced a seventh game. Lonborg tried it, against Gibson, on two days' rest, but didn't have it. Gibson pitched a three-hitter, hit a homer, and won 7–2, as Javier's three-run shot settled matters. Brock hit .414 and set a Series record with seven stolen bases, surpassing a mark set by Honus Wagner in 1909 and reviving mention of Pepper Martin in 1931. The fabric of historical reference was still intact for the baseball public.

1968

The Cardinals won their pennant easily again in 1968, but the Tigers ambushed them in the World Series by winning the last three games. However, the real story of the year was the Death of Offense, which finally had everyone's attention.

NL—Same team, same result. The 1968 Cards were just like the 1967 edition at eight positions. The only significant change in pitching was that Hughes was hurt and Ray Washburn took up the slack behind Gibson and Briles, with Carlton coming along. Again the margin was substantial over the Giants (9 games) and Cubs (13 games). Brock stole 62 bases, Flood hit .301 (fifth in the league). When a pitching staff posts a 2.48 earned run average, as this one did, not much more offense is needed.

Finishing second for the fourth straight year, Herman Franks had had enough. He said he'd leave if he didn't win the pennant, and he didn't, so he did. The Dodgers, still in transition, were bogged down in seventh, well below .500. The Mets, under Hodges, had their best season ever, moving up to ninth place and finally beating out Houston. Pete Rose was batting champion at .335, McCovey the chief power producer with 36 homers and 105 runs batted in.

Now about the pitchers.

Gibson, 22–9, and a 1.12 earned run average, breaking a National League record (1.22) set in 1916 by Grover Cleveland Alexander, better than the best (1.14) by Walter Johnson in 1913. He outdid top-grade Hall of Famers working in dead-ball days. He pitched 13 shutouts and completed 28 of his 34 starts.

Marichal, 26–9, wasn't far behind. He finished 30 of his 38 starts and had a 20–4 record by August 1. Although Jenkins, at 20–15, was the only other 20-gamer, the real measure of universal effectiveness was the fact that among the 16 highest qualifiers for the earned run title (162 or more innings pitched), the *highest* ERA was 2.74. The *league* figure was 2.99. The league batting average was .243.

And wait 'til you see what the American Leaguers did.

AL—The Tigers shrugged off their near miss of 1967 and won by 12 games over Baltimore, with Boston fourth, Minnesota seventh, and Chicago ninth. Deny McLain won 31 games and lost six, the first 30-game winner in the majors since Dizzy Dean in 1934, and the first in this league since Lefty Grove in 1931. He started 41, finished 28, and posted an earned run average of 1.96, which was only good enough for fourth place. Luis Tiant (21–9, Cleveland) led with 1.60, Sam McDowell (also Cleveland, 15–14) had 1.81, and Dave McNally (22–10) 1.95. Mel Stottlemyre was 21–12 with the Yankees, who pulled themselves back up to fifth. The league's ERA was 2.98, its batting average .230, nine points below its previous low of 1908, in the deadest of dead-ball days.

Yastrzemski repeated as batting champion—at .301. He wasn't merely the only one over .300, he was the only one over .290. That Frank Howard, now in Washington, could hit 44 home runs (with 106 runs batted in) and Harrelson 36 in Boston (with a league-leading 109 runs batted in) marked them as truly exceptional.

Meanwhile, Finley's true skill at spotting good ball players and hiring the right people to develop them was paying off. In their first season in Oakland, the Athletics came in sixth, over .500 (82–80), their best finish since 1949 back in Philadelphia under Mack. Finley's starters, all under 25, were Jim (Catfish) Hunter, John (Blue Moon) Odom (nicknames ordained by Finley), Jim Nash, and Chuck Dobson. (The fifth starter, Krausse, was 25.) Fresh out of college were outfielders Rick Monday and Reggie Jackson and third baseman Sal Bando. His shortstop, a 26-year-old four-year veteran from Cuba, was Dagoberto (Bert or Campy) Campaneris, who had played all nine positions in one game as a stunt in 1965, and who led the league with 62 stolen bases in 1968. Not yet regulars were Joe Rudi and Dick Green and catcher Dave Duncan. A utility man named Tony La Russa got into 23 games, while a 21-year-old pitcher named Rollie Fingers got into one.

All would soon be famous.

The sinking White Sox brought Lopez back out of retirement when Stanky left in midseason. The Indians had hired Dark when Finley fired him again, and they came in a strong third.

And everyone knew, by summer, that this would be the last 10-team single-standing season.

All-Star Game—In the Astrodome, the growing power outage was most noticeable. The last two All-Star Games had ended 2–1 in extra innings. This one was over in nine, 1–0. Mays opened the bottom of the first with a ground single off Tiant, took second on a wild pickoff attempt, third on a wild-pitch ball four, and scored as McCovey bounced into a double play. That was it. The best hitters in the world collected eight hits in 63 trips to the plate. And the Nationals had won for the 10th time in the last 11 decisions.

WS—Tigers manager Mayo Smith made one of the gutsiest decisions a manager could make going into a World Series spotlight. He had won a pennant easily with Ray Oyler at shortstop and Mickey Stanley in center, both first-rate defensive players. But Oyler had hit .135 (yes, *one* thirty-five) in 111 games and Dick Tracewski, his alternate, had hit .156. So Smith told Stanley to play shortstop, allowing Al Kaline, who had been injured the first half of the season, to return to right field with Jim Northrup in center and Willie Horton in left, leaving Norm Cash at first. Those three had hit 82 home runs, nine more than the entire St. Louis team.

If Stanley had messed up in the infield, Smith could never have lived it down. But he did fine. And he got two of Detroit's five hits when Gibson pitched a 4–0 shutout and set a Series record by striking out 17. But the Tigers got 13 the next day in an 8–1 victory by Lolich.

In Detroit, the Cards won 7–3 on three-run homers by McCarver and Cepeda, and apparently had command after a 10–1 rout in which Gibson pitched another five-hitter. When the Cards scored three runs off Lolich in the first inning of the fifth game, Smith made another gutsy move: he left Lolich in. The Cards never scored again, and Detroit won the game 5–3, sending the Series back to St. Louis.

McLain, who had been hit hard in two starts, started again. Backed by two runs in the second and 10 in the third (including a grand slam by Northrup), he coasted home 13–1, setting up a Gibson-Lolich seventh game. They were scoreless for six innings. Then the Tigers scored three, with the aid of a triple by Northrup that Flood misplayed, and closed it out 4–1.

And that was the last time a team could win the World Series by winning only one postseason series.

AFTERMATH

The true meaning of the 1960s, dimly perceived at the time if at all, is the inescapability of change. Baseball authorities and fans alike tried to cling to traditional formulations and attitudes in new circumstances that made them impossible. In almost all other aspects of life, people understood from 1945 on that the postwar world would be fundamentally different from what they had been used to before. Whatever one liked or didn't like, hoped for or feared, moved away from or into, one understood that the conditions of life, of work, of social relationships, physical surroundings, governmental functions, unexamined stereotypes, and fashion would not be resumed exactly as they were before the war. Whether or not one articulated that realization, it was felt on almost every level.

But not in sports and not in baseball, for excellent reasons. After all, the whole appeal of sports was based on its continuity, its reproduction of situations one had related to from childhood on. In other sports, not so long and so well entrenched, adjustment to new realities was easy: the broken pattern not so firmly established, the innovations were seen as improvements. In baseball, the perception of perfection had been instilled during the 1920s and 1930s, with the 1940s regarded as an interruption. Any deviation was to be resented and resisted.

Gradually through the 1950s, into the cold war and baby boom, people accepted the world's new directions. But baseball tried to cling to its old patterns against all odds. It would not admit that new population patterns, transportation and communication capabilities, economic competition, and unprecedented leisure industries required appropriately altered patterns of doing business. It kept trying to force new developments into old molds, thereby missing the opportunity to find new molds that fit.

Frick's response to Maris was deeply indicative of this frame of mind, an attempt to preserve former *frameworks* at any cost, instead of honoring them as history and welcoming the new. Baseball resisted expansion in the form of a third league, resisted the groping of its workers toward what all other workers had, resisted creative use of the new media and marketing methods, resisted internal restructuring that cried out for abandoning the Landis-czar model, resisted considering the health of the minors on which their system rested, resisted anything and everything that didn't suggest, however falsely, that what applied in 1940 applied now.

Trying to impose 154-game standards on records and schedules, or to somehow "reconcile" them by edict or by manipulative arithmetic, revealed the underlying denial going on. It must remain "baseball as we know it," even if it never really was that way and couldn't be in the future even if it had been.

So the expansion, the relations with the players, the new ball parks, the legal struggles, the shifting marketplace—all were dealt with reactively, too late, with insufficient thought of actual consequences, under pressure, amid petty squabbling, without a *plan*. It's not surprising that such a transition period did not go smoothly; it's amazing that it went as smoothly as it did.

But by 1969, the truth could be evaded no longer: baseball would have to change. Enlarged leagues had to split into divisions and adopt playoffs. Employment practices had to observe the laws of the land. Television's needs, as well as its effects, had to be taken into account. If playing rules and practices had made the game less entertaining, something had to be done, even if it involved that unthinkable concept "change."

The 10-team leagues of the 1960s demonstrated, beyond argument and belatedly, that the old patterns were untenable and couldn't really persist even if you pretended they did. One could present baseball indoors, on an artificial surface, with a longer schedule, in places with radically different seasonal climates, and then send the picture into homes where people did not buy tickets. How would a Landis or a Ruppert or a Ban Johnson or a Wrigley respond to that? (We know how Phil Wrigley did respond: "No lights on my building, ever!") Spalding? I suspect he would have been a highly creative and constructive adapter; but there were no Spaldings in 1960.

In 1901 and in 1920, the change had been abrupt and permanent. In the 1960s, a comparable degree of change was drawn out over a full decade, with no guarantee that some new pattern would be comparably permanent.

CHAPTER 21

Divisions and Play-Offs

The beginning of Bowie Kuhn's commissionership coincided with the start of divisional play, which represented a complete break with baseball's past. Regardless of emotions and mindsets, the question was no longer how to keep things the same, but how to make new arrangements work and pilot the industry through uncharted waters. It also coincided with the Players Association's first behavior as a true labor union, acting collectively in pursuit of its goals and monitoring adherence to its written contract. Furthermore, it coincided with new alignments among the owners: there were four new clubs (this is, new votes) and some significant changes in leadership among the older clubs. So a totally fresh start was under way on the field, in the structure of competition; in player relations; and in administration.

The commissionership itself was at a crossroads. The autocracy of Landis had not been permitted Chandler. Frick, without it, had been on the same wavelength as his owners and had advocated giving his successor more power. But whatever Eckert's contract did or didn't say, his regime created a complete vacuum. By making Kuhn commissioner pro tem the owners acknowledged that they didn't really know what they wanted the commissioner to be.

So it was up to Kuhn to carve out his own path.

How he chose to do it laid the groundwork for more strife than could be anticipated even by those who anticipated strife.

Kuhn was highly intelligent, well educated, articulate, and alert. He knew the baseball business from the inside very well. He was also a deeply sincere, knowledgeable and, authentic "fan of the game"—"baseball as we know it," of course—and comfortable with the government and business leaders with whom baseball was more and more enmeshed. And, as a lawyer, he was certainly qualified to fill the more central role legal advisers were taking throughout the sports and entertainment industries.

With all that going for him, Kuhn had one terrible flaw that undid all his assets. He was remarkably insensitive to the reactions of other people. He would be arrogant, aloof, downright insulting, and appallingly self-righteous—no doubt unconsciously so most of the time—while apparently (and in his own eyes) behaving courteously and properly. He made a good first impression that usually went downhill with increasing contact. It was as if he believed that whatever conclusion he came to about anything, others must accept it and willingly go along with it simply because *he* saw it that way. No further explanation or discussion was needed. The voice from Olympus had spoken. Anything he declared was so simply because he said it was.

Combine that with failure to think through thoroughly enough the full consequences of actions that seemed expedient, and resistance to seeking or taking advice, and you have a formula for the kind of mess that eventually brought him down and still permeates baseball affairs.

AN ACTIVE COMMISSIONER

The day Kuhn was elected, February 4, 1969, a crisis already existed. Hundreds of players were refusing to sign their 1969 contracts while Miller and Gaherin fought over the terms of a new pension agreement covered by a separate contract, not part of the general collective bargaining agreement. There would be four new teams, so obviously the pension plan would need more money. How much more, and how to calculate the right amount? Miller urged his players not to sign 1969 contracts until the pension matter was settled, since the pension rights (and medical coverage) were a significant part of their compensation. How could one agree to salary terms without knowing what the rest of one's entitlements would be?

Signing a new contract was not a mere formality. What made the reserve system work was the one-year option clause, which let a team unilaterally renew the existing signed contract. Without a signed 1969 contract, the option clause from 1968 would hold the player only through 1969, making him a free agent after that. Therefore, the clubs had rigorously enforced rules that no one could play or even report for practice without a signed *current* contract. The signing boycott was a threat to spring training.

In their first show of solidarity, about 125 players gathered in New York on February 3 to reaffirm a threat to strike spring training if no pension deal were made by then. (March 1 was the official reporting date, although pitchers and catchers went in earlier.) They had already rejected management offers by votes of 491–7 and 461–6, but it was their physical presence (traveling at their own expense) that got attention and bolstered their own morale. The next morning, in Florida, the owners decided they couldn't go on being rudderless and named Kuhn commissioner.

As soon as he returned to New York, Kuhn called Miller. As commissioner, he was now the focus of public pressure to "do something," and he brokered an agreement quickly. On February 24, the 24 player reps met with Miller all night long, and the next morning an agreement between the players and the Players Relations Committee was announced. Kuhn's backstage intervention had worked. Spring training would start immediately.

What Kuhn had done, essentially, was persuade the owners to give the players what they'd been asking for in the first place. The hang-up had been caused by the new setup and a new TV contract. Since 1905, the "players' share" of the World Series had been 60 percent of the gate receipts of the first four games, distributed as prize money to the first-division clubs. The pension plan, which came in 1950, was funded by the World Series television rights and the All-Star Game receipts. But the new and huge national television package didn't distinguish between regular-season games (of little interest to the networks) and postseason. The World Series was the real reason for the tie-in sale. The owners now insisted no tie existed between World Series and pensions: they would settle on some flat sum, and where it came from was nobody's business. The players finally settled for vague language that the TV source was unchanged—leaving the issue open— but got exactly the same one-third of the total package they had before: $5.45 million of the $16.5 million national TV deal, instead of $4.1 million of $12.3 million.

They also got increases in the payout schedule, reduction from five years to four years to qualify for the pension plan, retroactive inclusion of players back to 1959, and a severance provision for players that could cover the time between retirement and age 60. The five-year requirement had left out 59 percent of those who reached the majors. Four years would include more than 50 percent.

As a management negotiator before Gaherin, Kuhn had been unyielding. As commissioner, in three weeks he pushed compromise because (on the facts of the case) only a reasonable settlement could get the players to come in, and the commissioner's prime responsibility—to his own public image—was to get them to play.

Here it was, right at the start, the dilemma that would confront the owners with increasing force. The commissioner, their own employee, was bound to go against them in any strike or lockout situation because the one thing a commissioner could not tolerate was no baseball. (Kuhn would try to ride out a couple of stoppages, but his successors would not.)

For his intervention, Kuhn was widely and loudly praised by press, public, and Miller. In private, the owners were not so sure an interventionist commissioner was such a good idea.

But Kuhn liked intervening.

On February 28, a player named Donn Clendenon announced his retirement. He had been taken by Montreal in the expansion draft in October and traded to Houston in January for Rusty Staub, a Houston hero, and Jesus Alou, the youngest of the three brothers. Clendenon had accepted the trade and agreed to terms in Houston but now, more than a month later, decided not to play.

Montreal, having promoted Staub as a mainstay of the new team, wanted to keep him, and the rest of the league didn't want to tamper with the fragile new franchise, its first in Canada. So on March 8, league president Warren Giles rejected Clendenon's retirement letter and ruled that the deal stood; Houston was out of luck.

Kuhn jumped in, talked to Clendenon, said that he might agree to play, and that he still belonged to Montreal; he affirmed that Staub was needed in Montreal and urged Huston to accept some other form of compensation. The commissioner had absolutely no authority to involve himself in any trade, and all sorts of actual rules and precedents were being violated by not canceling a deal in which a player didn't report.

On March 20, Clendenon reaffirmed his retirement.

On March 24, Houston's Judge Hoffheinz sued Montreal and called Kuhn names for abusing his powers.

On April 3, Clendenon agreed to play for Montreal—for $50,000 a year instead of the $36,000 he was to get at Houston.

The players got the point immediately.

"Great, if I'm traded, I'll retire before I report," declared Kranepool, one of the signers of the general agreement.

Kuhn didn't get it. Within three weeks, he did it again. The Red Sox traded Harrelson—who had made a bundle being released by Finley less than two years before—to Cleveland. "The Hawk," as this 27-year-old idol of the mod set was now called, announced his retirement. He couldn't afford to go to Cleveland, he explained, because he stood to make $750,000 in nonbaseball activities as a popular figure in New England.

That was on April 19. By April 22, Kuhn, who actually said, "Baseball needs you," persuaded Harrelson to join the Indians—for $100,000, double his Boston salary.

In public-relations terms, Kuhn was doing fine. He was visible, forceful, and enthusiastic as commissioner, and his decisions weren't bothering any players or fans. And he got the chance to sound righteous as an upholder of "the integrity of the game" when *Sports Illustrated* ran a story showing that Finley, owner of the Athletics, had some stock in a company that did business (hotel laundry) in Las Vegas. Kuhn ordered Finley to sell the stock in accordance with "guidelines I will soon issue." (Atlanta's Bill Bartholomay also had some stock.) If any guidelines ever appeared, or if any stock was ever sold, no headlines ever told that part of the story.

But Kuhn's big triumph came in July. Professional baseball's centennial, based on the 1869 Red Stockings of Cincinnati, was being celebrated in Washington at the All-Star break. A lavish dinner and visit to the White House was hosted by President Nixon, a truly passionate baseball fan, and Kuhn was a centerpiece in all the ceremonies. Flaunting his Washington status, Kuhn got grudging acceptance even from owners who hadn't liked his other actions, and of course he scored high with the public.

So in August, he made his push. He called the annual summer meeting for Seattle, where Daley, the absentee owner from Cleveland, was already trying to sell the team (halfway through its first expansion season) to Milwaukee or Dallas. Kuhn spoke publicly in favor of not allowing this to happen; privately, he concentrated on turning his pro tem into a seven-year contract, and he succeeded because (1) his popularity was high and (2) the owners couldn't afford the public-relations consequences of having him resign.

Ford and Eckert had been paid $65,000. Kuhn had been given $100,000 temporarily. Now he had $150,000 for seven years and was the "regular" commissioner.

His year ended on a high note, as the World Series, which is the commissioner's only on-field province, included the Miracle Mets.

But 1970 wasn't so good.

He couldn't save the Pilots in Seattle, and they were sold to Milwaukee, triggering a lawsuit that would force another unwilling expansion in 1977. The actual move wasn't made until April 1, six days before the home opener in Milwaukee.

In February, he preempted a *Sports Illustrated* story by investigating Denny McLain, the 31-game winner, for being part of a bookmaking operation. He got McLain to confess, then decided (on April 1) to suspend him until July 1, drawing ridicule from all sides. If McLain really was in the gambling business, he should have been barred for life; if not, he shouldn't have been suspended at all. Kuhn's excuse was that the business had failed, and his analogy about the distinction between "murder and attempted murder" didn't help much.

In January, Kuhn's response to Curt Flood's refusal to be traded to Philadelphia set in motion an antitrust suit focused on the reserve issue itself. A highly publicized full-scale trial took place in New York between May 19 and June 10, filled with celebrity witnesses, leading to Judge Irving Ben Cooper's preordained decision that he had no jurisdiction because of the Supreme Court's exemption. But that set appeals in motion. And provided a trial record of testimony.

Meanwhile, there was umpire trouble. The National League umpires had formed a union back in 1965. American League umpires were trying to form one in 1968 when two of the leaders, Al Salerno and Bill Valentine, were fired by league president Cronin at the end of the season. They filed an unfair-labor-practice charge, and hearings before the National Labor Relations Board (NLRB) went on during July. It wasn't until November that the labor board ruled in favor of the American League, citing insufficient evidence of motive related to organizing activity.

By then, however, the umpires of both leagues had struck the divisional play-off games in Pittsburgh and Minnesota on October 3 over play-off and World Series pay. A settlement was reached while substitute umpires worked the first game. The American League umpires subsequently joined the Nationals in what is now the Major League Umpires Association.

The players, too, had significant play-off-money issues to deal with. The CBA (as we'll call the collective bargaining agreements from now on) had expired at the end of 1969. A new agreement, not ratified until June, included severe (in fact, crucial) curtailment of the commissioner's power in arbitrating disputes.

By September, McLain was being suspended again, once for throwing ice water on writers, once for carrying a gun.

One might say that Bowie—by now, everyone referred to him as "Bowie" rather than "Kewn" or "Koon"—had experienced a great rookie year followed by the sophomore jinx.

For the commissioner, 1971 was relatively quiet, but 1972 was a lot worse than 1970. The pension plan was up for renewal, and it led to the first actual strike since 1890. The final weekend of spring training and the first 13 days of the regular season were wiped out. This time, Commissioner Kuhn stayed out of it and neither hurt nor helped the situation, a circumstance that didn't enhance his image. In June, contrary to most expectations, the Supreme Court again sustained the antitrust exemption— against its own better judgment, it acknowledged—but the winning strategy, to which Bowie contributed, contained seeds of defeat. Baseball argued, before the Court, that the reserve issue was really a question of labor negotiation, now that there was a union, and not an antitrust matter at all. The Court bought the argument, which meant that the reserve now became a subject of mandatory bargaining in the next contract, ending the stonewalling that had protected the reserve since 1888.

This would turn out to be the pivot point of all the revolutionary events that followed.

Through all these developments, Kuhn developed another pattern that would eventually undo him. He plunged full-bore into internal politics. A commissioner is the creature of the owners, and owners fall into factions, and Bowie became enmeshed in playing one group against another in seeking support for his position on various matters. Since you can never please all of them, your support must come from whichever group or individual seems more potent at the time. The trouble is, alliances and interests shift from time to time and issue to issue, so you wind up displeasing almost everyone at some time on some point. And people, especially powerful people, tend to remember being thwarted more than favors, so that vindictiveness lasts longer than gratitude.

There is nothing unusual about such game playing, and it's done successfully all the time. But Kuhn's insensitivity and arrogance, as described above, led him to make more enemies than necessary and create fewer loyalists than he needed. The problem was not that he was too political—no commissioner could avoid that—but that he wasn't good at it in the long run.

In 1973, the focus was back on the game itself, as the American League adopted the designated hitter while the National League rejected it. That put the commissioner, who had to make World Series rules, in the middle. And that particular World Series produced another noisy confrontation with Finley, who tried to suspend one player in order to activate a better one.

By 1975, when it was time to consider renewing Kuhn's contract, a substantial segment of the owners was ready to ditch him. But in the early 1970s, he started with favorable public image, which began to deteriorate from the McLain case.

Probably, the turning point occurred at the owners' December meetings of 1969, again in Florida. Having shed the pro tem label in August and now sure of his position, Kuhn pushed for adoption of a "restructuring plan" developed at the Wharton School of Business in the aftermath of the previous year's deadlock on choosing a successor to Eckert. This blueprint would concentrate all power in the commissioner's office and reduce the already weak league presidents to figureheads carrying out assigned duties; they would give up their independent offices (Cronin's in Boston, Giles' in Cincinnati) and move into a centralized headquarters in New York.

Landis, in 1920, was in a position to get anything he demanded from a group of owners who saw him as a potential savior and most of whom had baseball as their primary business. Kuhn had no such leverage with the 20 big-business operators of 1969. They knew a power grab when they saw one. So the National League elected Chub Feeney, Stoneham's nephew and nearly commissioner, to succeed Giles, who was retiring, and that effectively shelved restructuring. Feeney, who believed completely in "baseball as we know it," set up the National League office in San Francisco, his new home. Kuhn made no fuss about his defeat and proceeded to execute a lot of step-by-step centralization that was inevitable anyhow, and badly needed. But the owners as a group would remember what Kuhn appeared to forget or ignore: Remember who's boss.

An active commissioner makes waves. The owners had to remind him, "We make the waves."

AN ACTIVE UNION

The players were also ready to make waves of their own.

The show of solidarity in the 1969 pension dispute established the credibility of Miller and greatly strengthened the Players Association's hand in CBA negotiations that followed. Even for the first set of divisional playoffs in 1969 while the old contract was in force, agreements had to be made. What would be the prize money for the new pre–World Series round? What about first-division money, which used to go to teams finishing second, third, and fourth? How would gross or net, from which player shares would be calculated be defined? But the 1969 formulas would be a one-year deal in any case; permanent arrangements had to be included in the CBA.

But that was just money. The owners, in all their dealings with the players, always concentrated on the money: how much (or little) must they give, how much can they keep. They always assumed that players were as obsessed, individually, as they were about dollars. Anything could be settled with the right amount of dollars, and loss of dollars would be the ultimate weapon of intimidation.

Players loved money, and thought selfishly, as much as anyone. But they also understood, under Miller's tutelage, that other items were more important in determining how money would eventually flow.

And in the 1970 CBA, they got a provision that would, in due course, make it possible to blow up the whole system. Or, to stick with the wave-making metaphor, engulf and sink the whole reserve-clause ship.

The new contract, ratified 541–54 by the players in June, was retroactive to the start of 1970 to run through 1972. The minimum salary, $10,000 in 1969, would rise by steps to $13,500 in 1972. The players would get 60 percent, up from 50 percent, of the play-off-money pool, and that would be from the total before expenses connected with the play-offs. Termination pay had been zero for a man cut in spring training and only 30 days (a sixth of the year's total, calculated on a 182-day season) after that. Now it would be 30 days in spring training and 60 days after that, and in 1972 it would become a full year's pay for anyone cut after May 15.

These were nice little gains, and the players gave up their request to have the schedule reduced back to 154 games. It would stay at 162.

But the real deal didn't involve money. The provision that counted changed the arbitration machinery. In the first CBA, the players got the right to take a grievance to an arbitrator, but the arbitrator was still the commissioner. Now it would be an outsider, unless the case at issue involved "the integrity of the game" (like McLain's bookmaking). That subject would still belong to the commissioner.

This was a mammoth change. It meant that any dispute involving a player would go before a professional arbitrator who would weigh the case on its merits without obligation to either side. Part of the Landis myth was that a player who felt mistreated—not paid on time, disciplined unfairly or excessively, locked up in the minors, traded or sold contrary to regulations—could "appeal" to the commissioner for redress. But how could a commissioner chosen by, paid by, and in two cases out of four fired by the owners be the judge in a case against them? The conflict of interest was explicit. Look back at the Sisler case (chapter 9) to see how clearly the impossibility of resolving such conflicts was demonstrated to the three-man commission. The basic relationships had not changed.

Why did management accept the grievance-arbitrator provision so easily? Commissioner Kuhn supported it because he would no longer be in the position of ruling for one owner's interest against another's. An outside arbitrator would get him off that nasty hook. And other management minds didn't grasp the full implications of this change.

Miller's faith in this provision rested on the historic one-sidedness of all baseball regulations since 1903. Players would win most grievances before an impartial judge because the facts would be on their side. The existing rules were a stacked deck. There was no way players could legislate anything or enforce observance, and there is a limit to how many items could be bargained at the table once every few years. A grievance procedure gave players a mechanism for self-protection, and an impartial judge a good chance to prevail.

This was the key victory in the entire history of the Players Association.

At the moment, however, it made little difference. Its only immediate effect was the filing of a grievance about the 1969 prize money, which had been set unilaterally by the owners—a violation of the old CBA. Arbitrator David Cole eventually found that the players were underpaid a total of $82,000, which provided a few hundred dollars apiece for those on the teams that had finished second in each division.

Also of no effect was the Flood case, launched early in 1970 (whose details will appear in the next section). The top stars—Frank Robinson, Yastrzemski, Frank Howard, Willie Mays, Hank Aaron, and Bob Gibson—were getting about $125,000 a year, while Pete Rose, Clemente, Marichal, and McCovey were also at the $100,000 level. In the preceding five years, the war between the football leagues, leading to their merger, had produced multiyear individual player packages worth up to $800,000, underlining the lesson taught by Harrelson and Clendenon about an individual's bargaining power. In basketball—a bush-league sport, to hear baseball people talk—competition between two leagues gave the top college player, Lew Alcindor of UCLA, a $1.4 million package before he ever played a pro game. That baseball players were behind the curve was plain enough, and the ironbound reserve was the reason.

At the end of 1971, the pension agreement had to be renewed. The fund now had a surplus. The players wanted increased input, to finance better medical coverage, whose cost was increasing. The clubs said, "Not one cent more." Once again, strike talk swirled over spring training in 1972. Throughout March, amid more and more acrimonious rhetoric from both sides and almost daily reports of meetings and strike votes, the difference boiled down to $1 million more sought by the players and up to $400,000 being offered by the clubs, who now acknowledged that inflation existed.

The regular season was to start April 5. On March 30, the players voted 663–10 to authorize a strike. Now we need another chronology:

April 1—Miller suggested using $800,000 of available surplus, already in the pension fund, to cover the increases. Since that would mean *no* increased contributions by the clubs, it was tantamount to surrender. Meanwhile, the players did strike the remaining exhibition games, hoping this would hasten agreement in time to open the season.

April 2—The owners rejected Miller's suggestion.

April 4—At an emergency meeting in Chicago, the owners reconsidered Miller's plan and rejected it again, calling it "imprudent"—although some of them had not been informed of this possibility (using the surplus only) until this meeting.

April 5—The Houston-at-Cincinnati opener was canceled. From then on, games were canceled day by day.

April 7—The players offered to start playing for two or three weeks, and if no agreement were reached by then, to accept binding arbitration of the dispute. The owners said no.

April 9—President Nixon called in both sides to meet with federal mediator J. Curtis Counts. The clubs promptly agreed to use $400,000 of the surplus funds—the very deal they could have made before the strike. But they insisted the players had to forfeit their pay for the missed games, yet make up the games during the season. To that, the players said no: either pay us for made-up games, or don't pay us and don't make up the games.

April 10–13—For four more days, they argued about the back-pay question, even though agreement on the original issue of pension funding had been reached. Finally, the owners abandoned (with Kuhn's urging) their attempt to "punish" the strikers. There would be no back pay and no games made up.

April 15—Play began, picking up the original schedule as it stood. Some teams wound up playing 153, others as many as 156. But the world did not end.

A pattern had been set. The owners wouldn't believe that the players would stick together in a strike, then hoped they'd give in if they were made to miss a paycheck. Miller, deeply afraid that the players might not stick together in an untested situation, had tried to avoid the test by offering a rational, yielding solution before it started. He had been rebuffed. The squabble over how to resume convinced him further that the owners' willingness to bargain couldn't be trusted. The owners were furious at being forced to lose income for no good reason and believed Miller was mesmerizing unsophisticated players into following his lead for his own aggrandizement. These attitudes would persist, fester, grow, and become a bigger problem than any substantive issue.

And now, at the end of 1972, a new CBA had to be negotiated.

The owners had told the Supreme Court in oral arguments in March that the reserve rules were a matter of collective bargaining. Now they had to bargain. Labor agreements are exempt from antitrust restrictions if unions accept them.

The crux was salary negotiation. A reserved player had zero bargaining power, undeniably. If he were never a free agent, he could never learn, let alone get, his true market value (as the multileague football, basketball, and hockey players could). So an escape hatch of some sort was needed. What about arbitration? If club and player couldn't agree on salary, an impartial arbitrator could decide whose figure was more reasonable—encouraging the club to make a reasonable offer, discouraging the player from making an unreasonable demand.

That left the owners with one of two choices. They could loosen the reserve (the players talked of free agency after nine or ten years of major league service), or they could accept arbitration.

They chose arbitration.

The players also got another important concession, the "five and ten rule." A 10-year veteran who had spent the last five years with the same club could veto being traded. And a player could not be sent to the minors without his consent after five years (instead of the previous eight-year requirement) in the majors. He would have to be released, becoming a free agent.

Both salary arbitration and the 5–10 rule were alternatives to free agency, intended to alleviate the worst effects of the lifetime reserve. The 5–10 rule alone would have pre-empted Flood's suit.

This agreement was reached February 25, in time to start spring training. It would run for three years, through 1975.

THE FLOOD CASE

Curt Flood was 31 years old as the 1969 season ended, a 12-year veteran with a .293 lifetime average, participant in 21 World Series and three All-Star Games, an outstanding center fielder. He earned $90,000 a year and had played for the St. Louis Cardinals since 1958 after coming up through the Cincinnati system and being traded to St. Louis.

On October 7, the Cardinals traded him, Tim McCarver, and two others to Philadelphia for Dick Allen, a pitcher and an infielder.

Flood balked. He felt demeaned by having no choice about where he practiced his profession. For him as a black, the word "slavery" had overtones not felt by most whites, and the reserve had been likened to slavery since the 1880s. All he could do was challenge the reserve in court, as others had done before him, and he felt strongly enough to do that.

The Players Association was not ready, in 1969, to confront the reserve head on. The vast majority of baseball people, writers, fans, and even lawyers accepted the system as a necessity for orderly competition. But if Flood were to take it to court and lose, all players would be saddled with the consequences of the defeat.

Because they had been snubbed at the winter meetings in 1967 in Mexico City and 1968 in San Francisco, the players had called their own annual meeting for Puerto Rico instead of Miami (where the clubs were busy rejecting the restructuring plan and electing Feeney National League president). Flood appeared before the player reps, who were wary about his intentions. Did he mean it? Would he stick it out? Was he just trying to better himself financially?

Flood convinced them he was sincere, and that he would press his suit with or without their support.

They decided to support him.

On December 24, Flood wrote to the commissioner asking that he be allowed to negotiate with all clubs: "I do not feel that I am a piece of property to be bought and sold irrespective of my wishes."

Kuhn's reply, December 30, was respectful, but pointed out that the terms of assignment were in all the contracts Flood had signed for 12 years and had been left intact by the collective bargaining process. It was a pro forma, and correct, denial of his request.

On January 16, in New York, Flood sued the commissioner and 24 owners for $1 million, claiming his rights were violated under federal and state antritrust laws and the constitutional provision against indentured service. The Players Association provided financial support and had found Arthur Goldberg—former Supreme Court justice, secretary of labor, UN ambassador, and graduate of the steel workers' union—to represent him.

Everyone understood that the Supreme Court antitrust exemption could not be overturned until and unless the case got back there. This was the first step toward that end.

It also got the Players Association off dead center in trying to raise the issue of reforming the reserve. (When Jim Bouton, irrepressibly facetious, had suggested at a bargaining session that a player be made a free agent at the age of 65, Chub Feeney had said, "No, because that would give you a foot in the door.") They could deal with other matters while this worked its way through. Most believed the Supreme Court would refuse to hear it; few believed the Court would uphold the exemption again if it did. It was the belief, or at least the fear, that the Supreme Court would not act so illogically a third time that led the owners into the labor-issue strategy, which was where the players had wanted the argument to be all along but had no way to get there through their own efforts.

So Flood, through his own determination, with minimum encouragement, at the sacrifice of his still productive career, and with immense cost to his personal life, created the circumstances that maneuvered the owners into giving the players that "foot in the door."

It is important to realize that this was not—and has never been—a good guys versus bad guys conflict. The owners were never wrong in their basic contentions that (1) baseball as a business has special characteristics; (2) players, who come and go in short careers, with necessarily selfish concerns in every individual, can't be given managerial control; (3) the rules they had evolved over a century had created, out of nothing, a prosperous industry and cultural asset whose primary beneficiaries were the players themselves; (4) the present owners were the only people who had put up their own money and taken on the obligation to pay all bills, including salaries, in good times and bad; and (5) the maintenance of traditional practices, based on illusion or not, was an essential feature of what they were selling, and what served the public interest.

Nor were the players wrong in their long-held beliefs that (1) the rules as they evolved were open to abuse, often exercised; (2) the "slavery" element of a perpetual reserve, regardless of pay scales, ran counter to this society's most fundamental principles of marketplace freedom and personal choice; (3) the rules were enforced by employers acting together in ways all sorts of laws had been passed to prevent; (4) for all of management's organizational skills and financial risk, it was only the special abilities of exceptional players that made the game itself marketable; and (5) fair treatment and fair pay could be achieved only by collective action, which their new union finally made possible.

So everything boiled down to matters of degree. Of course controls were needed over which players played where; but how much control, how administered? Of course players, who were the product as well as the employees, had to be given a "fair share" of the profits generated; but what was a fair share, and how could it be determined? Of course regulations had to promote "competitive balance"; but what really produced it? Which regulations were actually needed to achieve the legitimate goals of all concerned (including fans), and which gave excessive control to one side or the other?

Since the players in the 1960s were starting from the zero end of the scale in bargaining power, anything and everything they gained meant the owners were giving up something. But where was the reasonable middle range?

The owners argued, whether or not they privately believed it (as many did), that each concession was the beginning of the end of "baseball as we know it."

The players knew, at that stage, that what they were asking for were minor adjustments that couldn't and wouldn't upset the whole. In 1890, 1901, 1914, and 1946 and 1959, when rival leagues of one sort or another had entered the picture, the pendulum of leverage had swung in their direction. In the 1960s, it was swinging toward the players in three other major sports. Since the antitrust exemption made that route impossible in baseball, another had to be found.

Flood's antitrust suit, merely by its existence, provided one.

The failure on the owner side consisted of unwillingness to give a little when a little would have been accepted. By resisting unwisely, unnecessarily, for too long, the owners ended up giving more than was asked for originally. They kept losing these battles not because they had evil motives, mean impulses, or excessive greed, but because they had bad judgment.

And the players kept winning not because they had become immensely powerful or were more wealthy or because Miller had good judgment (which he did), or were more worthy, but because the owners kept handing them victories by defending unreasonable positions for so long that when they collapsed they were overrun.

All this was the true subtext of the Flood case. The trial, part circus, was also a great educational experience, the way the Celler hearings of 1951 and later congressional hearings had been. When the Supreme Court finally surprised everyone in June 1972 by upholding the 1922 and 1953 decisions and insisting that it was up to Congress to straighten out the "anomaly" Congress had never created in the first place, Flood's defeat was already counterbalanced by the strike that spring and the transfer of the reserve issue to the bargaining table.

In 1973 the owners chose salary arbitration as a means of preserving the permanent reserve. But the arbitrator would be an outsider, not the commissioner. That was the key concession won by the players in 1970. And outside arbitrators had to be given guidelines. Here another Miller proposal was adopted, an either-or system. Player and club would each submit a figure, and the arbitrator would have to choose one or the other, not split it. On what basis? By comparing the salaries of players in similar categories (experience, statistics, position) and choosing the figure closest to that norm.

The idea was to promote individual compromises *before* arbitration. But if the figures went to an arbitrator, a club that tried to lowball (in comparison to "market value") would lose. And player agents quickly became more adept at calculating the correct high end than general mangers, accustomed to no resistance, were at estimating an acceptable low end. So players won most arbitrations, and salary levels for everyone soared. Simply the availability of arbitration made clubs offer more in the first place. In that sense, players won *all* arbitrations before they started.

All that was because of Flood, who didn't play in 1970, tried to come back in spring training of 1971 with the Washington Senators, left after a couple of weeks, and dropped out of sight. Most players, other than those who served as player reps, never understood what they owed him. And baseball management, for whom Flood would have made an excellent coach and perhaps someday a manager, naturally refused to have anything to do with him.

But no player, other than Spalding and Ruth, changed the course of baseball history as much as Curt Flood.

AN ACTIVE SCENE

If acceptance of change is the theme of the early 1970s, it was operating on all levels.

The new division began, in 1969, this way:

AL East	NL East
Boston	Montreal
New York Yankees	New York Mets
Baltimore	Philadelphia
Washington	Pittsburgh
Cleveland	Chicago Cubs
Detroit	St. Louis

AL West	NL West
Seattle Pilots	San Francisco
Oakland	Los Angeles
California (Anaheim)	San Diego
Kansas City	Houston
Minnesota	Cincinnati
Chicago White Sox	Atlanta

In 1970, Seattle became the Milwaukee Brewers, remaining in AL West. In 1972, the Washington Senators became the Texas Rangers, who moved into AL West while Milwaukee moved into AL East.

In 1977, Seattle re-entered AL West as the Mariners, and Toronto joined AL East, forming two seven-team divisions.

The divisional races and the play-offs that followed them proved immensely popular, especially on national television. There were now four pennant races to follow instead of two, with that much more chance that some would be close. (The first NL West race in 1969 had five teams within two games of the lead with only three weeks to go.) The play-offs became two mini–World Series, and apprehensions that the World Series itself would be somehow diminished by its preliminaries proved totally groundless.

That change and a bunch of new ball parks made attendance soar. Cincinnati and Pittsburgh moved into their new stadiums in the middle of 1970, Philadelphia at the start of 1971. San Diego's was also new. In 1968, attendance had been 1.15 million a club for 20 clubs. By 1973, it was 1.25 million, an increase of almost 10 percent, comparable to the jump in 1958 and 1959 when the Giants and Dodgers had opened up California.

The ownership group itself was changing. At the 1969 meeting that elected Kuhn, there were six new members: the four expansion teams, Cincinnati (represented by Frank Dale for the past year or so), and Washington. The last mattered most.

Bob Short had bought the Senators—this was Senators II, the expansion team—on January 28, 1969, one week before the Kuhn appointment. He was treasurer of the Democratic National Committee and operator of a trucking business and hotel in Minneapolis, but also well-known in sports. In the 1950s, he had parlayed a $10,000 investment in the Minneapolis Lakers into full control of the basketball team, then sold it for $5 million to Los Angeles. If the commissioner and union were now "active," Short was by nature hyperactive.

The first thing he did was persuade Ted Williams to become the team's manager, a masterstroke of public relations.

The second thing he did was fight with the District of Columbia over lease terms, while boosting attendance from 550,000 to 900,000 the first year.

Then he sought a better local TV deal and failed, because Baltimore—a pennant winner in 1966, 1969, and 1970—was blanketing the area.

So after the 1971 season, in which attendance slipped back below 700,000, he moved the team to Texas.

Abandon the nation's capital? Unthinkable.

But this was a time when everything was thinkable. Besides, baseball had abandoned Washington several times during the 19th century with no ill effects.

Short had paid $10 million in 1969 and had debts. The Texas deal included $7 million up front for local radio-television rights. Arlington, Texas, was between Dallas and Fort Worth, and it had built a stadium suitable for expansion to major league requirements during its pursuit of other teams (like the Athletics and Pilots). The Washington Senators II became the Texas Rangers, still owned by Short, still managed by Williams, still featuring Frank Howard (whose home-run output went from 44 to 26 to 9 from 1970 to 1972). And part of the deal was Short's agreement to sell to local owners.

How could the American League let him do this? How could it not? It had already let the original Senators go to Minneapolis, the Browns to Baltimore, the A's to Kansas City and from there to Oakland, while accepting four new teams, of which Short's was one. If the league wanted a team in Washington, all it had to do was give the city another expansion team, as it had before. Owners don't stop other owners from moving, because they might need that vote to move themselves some day—unless it's Finley, and ultimately they let him go too.

Also in 1972, the Cleveland Indians were sold to Nick Mileti, who also owned the NBA basketball team there, as part of an eight-man group. Within a year, Mileti turned the reins over to Ted Bonda, another member of that group.

On January 3, 1973, CBS sold the Yankees to a 17-man syndicate headed by George Steinbrenner and Gabe Paul of Cleveland, retaining Mike Burke as president. By April Burke was gone and Paul was in charge of daily operations. The sales price was an astounding $10 million, 29 percent less than CBS had paid less than nine years before. And that was less than the $10.8 million Milwaukee had paid for the bankrupt Pilots in 1970.

Within 10 years, the going price for a franchise would double, and 10 years after that it would be 10 times the Yankee price tag. It wasn't only the players who would soon have unimaginable prosperity rain down upon them.

SEASONS 1969-72

1969

NL—The Miracle Mets, in their second year under Hodges and led by second-year pitchers Tom Seaver and Jerry Koosman, fought off Durocher's Cubs in early September and won 100 games, winning NL East by eight games. They started winning early but made their real drive from mid-August on. Atlanta also took command down the stretch out of a five-team scramble, as the Giants, now managed by Clyde King, placed second for the fifth straight year.

The Mets swept a high-scoring play-off, 9–5 and 11–6 at Atlanta, 7–4 at New York. The best-of-five format gave the odd home game to the team that had to open on the road.

Pete Rose beat out Clemente for the batting title, .348 to .345, while McCovey outhomered Aaron, 45–44. Aaron's career total was now 554, trailing only Ruth and Mays, and his chance of catching Ruth was starting to be noticed.

AL—Baltimore, now managed by Earl Weaver, won AL East by 19 games over Detroit and swept Minnesota, winner of AL West by nine games, in the play-offs. The Twins were Billy Martin's first managing assignment, but he was fired at the end of the year anyhow. So was Hank Bauer by Finley in Oakland, even though the rapidly maturing A's rose all the way to second place.

The Twins had the batting champion in Rod Carew (.332) and the home-run leader in Killebrew (49), but the Orioles had the best pitching. Mike Cuellar (23–11), McNally (20–7), and Palmer (16–4) helped produce a 2.83 team earned run average almost half a run better than anyone else's.

The lowered mound and still ambiguous strike zone brought the combined major league batting average to .248, up 11 points from 1968, and runs per game to 8.16 from 6.84—a big improvement, but still low by historical standards.

All-Star Game—The centennial dinner and other celebrations were marvelous, but the Tuesday-night game was washed out by a furious rainstorm. They played Wednesday afternoon, when McCovey's two homers led the Nationals to a 9–3 victory, their seventh straight.

A conflux of cosmic forces added to the aura of happy excitement that suffused the occasion. The Mets, who had acquired Clendenon in mid-June and were acting like believable contenders while winning two series from the first-place Cubs in early July, had reached All-Star break with two victories in Montreal, while the world watched the first men to walk on the moon. If that moon walk didn't suggest that anything was possible, what could?

WS—Truly one of the great upsets, in terms of unexpected result, in sports history, the first "extended" championship was won by the Mets, a remarkable counterpart of the football Jets' triumph in Super Bowl III just 10 months before. Seaver lost the first game to Cuellar 4–1, but Koosman beat McNally 2–1, holding the Orioles to two hits.

In Shea Stadium, Met victories by 5–0, 2–1 in 10 innings, and 5–3 were marked by spectacular game-saving catches by outfielders Tommie Agee and Ron Swoboda and displayed the depth of the young Met pitching staff. Gary Gentry and a 22-year-old second-stringer named Nolan Ryan combined on the third-game shutout, then Seaver and Koosman followed with complete games.

1970

NL—Now respectable contenders, the Mets ran third behind Pittsburgh and Chicago as the Pirates pulled away from a three-way traffic jam in mid-September. They won 14 of their last 20 while the Cubs went 9–9 and the Mets 7–12. In NL West, the Reds ran away and hid, finishing 14½ games ahead of the Dodgers and launching the legend of the Big Red Machine.

The play-off, however, was dominated by pitchers as Cincinnati won 3–0 in 10 innings, 3–1, and 3–2. Sparky Anderson, the new Cincinnati manager who operated a bull pen by committee, earned the name "Captain Hook" as he used seven pitchers, two of them twice, to hold the Pirates to three runs in 28 innings.

Both Mays and Aaron reached 3,000 hits during the season, the ninth and tenth players to do so. Mays now had 628 homers and Aaron 592. Atlanta's Rico Carty hit .366, the league's highest average in 22 years, while Gibson and San Francisco's Gaylord Perry each won 23 games.

AL—Baltimore and Minnesota, now managed by Bill Rigney, won handily again, by 15 and nine games, and the play-off was another three-game sweep for the Orioles. The scores were 10–6 and 11–3 in Minnesota, 6–1 in Baltimore. The Orioles had three 20-game winners in Cuellar (24–8), McNally (24–9), and Palmer (20–10) and posted 108 victories, one less than in 1969. The Twins had too little backup for Jim Perry (24–12) and Kaat (14–10).

Alex Johnson, and outfielder with the Angels, nosed out Yastrzemski for the batting title, .3289 to .3286—16 more hits in 48 more at bats. And Yas's 40 homers weren't enough for power honors, as Frank Howard, with the Senators, hit 44 homers and batted in 126 runs. For Minnesota,

Oliva was in the batting race at .325, and Kille-brew provided 41 homers.

The search for more offense had prompted Commissioner Kuhn to propose widened foul lines (not tried) and a super-lively ball called X-5 (used in 22 spring games). Also rejected was Fin-ley's advocacy of a colored baseball. (Larry MacPhail had tried a yellow ball before World War II, but the dye came off.) But without gim-micks, the 1970 offense figures were up to a .254 average, 8.68 runs, and 1.76 homers a game—al-most exactly the same numbers as in 1960, the last year of 16 teams. Perhaps the offense-defense bal-ance was correcting itself.

All-Star Game—The activist Commissioner, aware of the stagnating interest in this game and its importance to the pension package, returned player selection to the fans, making a deal with Gillette (the World Series TV sponsor) to distrib-ute punch-card ballots. This would avoid, it was hoped, the kind of ballot-box stuffing that newspaper-conducted polls had produced in the 1950s, killing fan participation then. It was an im-perfect plan, but it did work and has been in place ever since. Once again, fans had a better idea of what they wanted from this game than the pro-fessional baseball people did.

Played July 14 at Cincinnati's new Riverfront Stadium, into which the Reds had moved only three weeks before, the game proved one of the most competitive of the entire series. The Ameri-cans took a 4–1 lead into the ninth, but the Na-tionals rallied to tie. In the 12th, with two out, Pete Rose singled, went to second on a hit by Billy Garbarkewitz, and set sail for home on Jim Hick-man's single to center. He bowled over catcher Ray Fosse with a shoulder block just as Amos Otis' throw was arriving, and the National had a 5–4 victory, its eighth straight.

WS—Embarrassed by their loss to the Mets the year before, the Orioles let nothing spoil their perfect season and polished off the Reds in five games. They won 4–3 and 6–5 in Cincinnati, where Brooks Robinson's defensive skills at third shone more brightly than ever on the artificial turf. In Baltimore, a 9–3 game behind McNally gave them an iron grip, and although the Reds prolonged matters with a three-run eighth that gave them a 6–5 victory in the fourth game, Cuel-lar closed it out 9–3 the next day.

1971

NL—Pittsburgh won again, more easily this time, seven games ahead of St. Louis as the Cubs and Mets dropped into a tie for third, 14 games out. In the West, the Reds fell out of contention while the Giants, finally, prevailed by one game in a race to the wire with the Dodgers. Los Angeles cut an 8½-game lead to one between September 5 and 14, but the Giants hung on.

San Francisco won the first playoff game at home 5–4 but lost the next three. Bob Robertson hit three home runs in a 9–4 decision at Candle-stick and hit one off Marichal in Pittsburgh, in what turned into a 2–1 Pirate victory when Richie Hebner homered in the eighth. The next day, a four-run sixth capped by Al Oliver's three-run homer broke a 5–5 tie and sent the Pirates to the World Series, 9–5.

The Cardinal challenge to Pittsburgh had been led by Joe Torre, now playing third base, who hit .363 with 137 runs batted in and was MVP. But Clemente's .341 and Willie Stargell's 48 homers gave Pittsburgh plenty of power. (Robert-son hit 26 homers.) The other Cardinal top assets were Steve Carlton, now 26 years old, who put his 20–9 alongside Gibson's 16–13, and Brock, who stole 64 bases. Other top pitchers were Jenkins (24–13 for the Cubs), Seaver (20–10), and Al Downing (20–9 for Los Angeles).

AL—Baltimore made it three straight pen-nants with another three-game sweep in the play-offs. Weaver's Orioles won 101 games, making it 318 in three years, the kind of stretch the Cubs had enjoyed in the first decade of the century, the Yankees in the 1920s, the A's shortly after that, and the Cardinals during World War II. This time, the play-off victim was the Oakland Athlet-ics, coming into its own with Dick Williams as the manager and all those young players matured, bolstered by a rookie left-hander, Vida Blue, who went 24–8, led the league with a 1.82 ERA and eight shutouts, struck out 301, and won both the MVP and Cy Young Awards.

This time, the Orioles had four 20-game win-ners: McNally, 21–5, Palmer, 20–9, Cuellar, 20–9, and Dobson, 20–8. The first three beat Oakland 5–3, 5–1, and 5–3.

Oliva regained the batting title at .337, while 33 home runs by Chicago's Bill Melton were enough to lead the league, as its average dropped again to .247. Alvin Dark was replaced as Cleveland manager in midseason by Johnny Lipon, and Billy Martin had taken over the Tigers, who finished second by 12 games to Baltimore.

All-Star Game—The Americans broke their losing streak, 6–4, in a game at Detroit in which all the runs came on homers. Reggie Jackson hit the most memorable one, high into the light tower in right center field, estimated at 520 feet. In the 1950s, they called them tape-measure jobs; now it was "a moon shot." Johnny Bench, with one on, and Aaron gave the Nationals a 3–0 lead, but Jackson and Frank Robinson, each with a man on, made it 4–3 in the third. Killebrew's two-run homer in the sixth made Clemente's solo shot in the eighth harmless.

WS—At long last, Clemente, the most underrated player by the public (but not by his peers) of his era, had a chance to strut his stuff on the World Series stage. Did he ever.

Baltimore, now considered unbeatable, looked that way at home, winning 5–3 with McNally and 11–3 with Palmer. But Steve Blass, against Cuellar, let no one but a Robinson hit safely (homer and single by Frank, single by Brooks) in a 5–1 game at Pittsburgh. A three-run homer by Robertson nailed it down.

The Pirates won again, 4–3, getting eight innings of one-hit pitching from the bull pen after Baltimore had a three-run first, and moved ahead as Nelson Briles pitched a two-hit 4–0 shutout. Robertson hit his sixth homer in nine postseason games so far.

Clemente had 10 hits by now, none particularly dramatic, and when the Series returned to Baltimore, he tripled in the first inning but was stranded. He hit a homer in the third. But the Pirates couldn't add to or hold a 2–0 lead, and although Clemente's fast fielding prevented the winning run from scoring in the bottom of the ninth, he couldn't help in the tenth when, with Frank Robinson on third, Brooks had the sense to fly out to center instead of right. The Orioles won 3–2.

Blass faced Cuellar in the seventh game, and Clemente broke a scoreless tie with a homer in the fourth. Both teams scored in the eighth, but Blass completed a four-hitter and won 2–1. Clemente had hit .414 with a .759 slugging average, and shone afield. No one could be unaware of his status now.

1972

NL—Tragedy marked the start and finish. In West Palm Beach, where the Mets trained, Gil Hodges dropped dead of a heart attack while returning from the golf course the first day of the strike. Yogi Berra, who had remained as a coach under him and Westrum, was named manager. On December 31, Clemente was killed in a plane crash on a mercy mission. He was flying to Managua, Nicaragua, with relief supplies for earthquake victims in that city, where he had coached an amateur team. On the final day of the regular season, Clemente had collected his 3,000th hit. He was voted into the Hall of Fame the following year, the five-year waiting period being waived as it had been for Lou Gehrig.

The Pirates made it three NL East titles in a row, even though Murtaugh had stepped down and Bill Virdon was a rookie manager. They finish 11 ahead of Chicago, where Durocher was pressured to turn over the reins to Whitey Lockman in midseason, and 13½ ahead of the Mets under Yogi. Cincinnati returned to the top in the West, by a 9½-game margin over Houston, which hired Durocher to replace Harry Walker in the final month.

This play-off series went to the limit for the first time. Pittsburgh won 5–1 and lost 5–3 at home. It won 3–2 and lost 7–1 at Cincinnati and led 3–2 in the ninth inning of the fifth game. But Bench greeted Dave Giusti, the relief ace, with a homer, and two singles brought Bob Moose in from the bull pen. A deep fly moved a runner to third, a pop-up provided the second out, and Moose made a wild pitch that let Cincinnati's winning run score.

There were remarkable individual performances around the league. Carlton, traded to the Phillies, went 27–10 for a last-place team that won only 32 other games, posting a 1.98 ERA with eight shutouts and 308 strikeouts, turning in 30 complete games. Bench led with 40 homers and 126 runs batted in, rare feats for a catcher. Billy Williams of the Cubs was batting champion at .333, and Brock stole 63 bases.

AL—The strike, it turned out, determined the AL East race. Detroit finished 86–70, Boston

85–70, since none of the canceled games were made up—and four of the unplayed games were Boston versus Detroit. But the Tigers did clinch by beating Boston twice for a 1½-game lead with one to play (which Boston won). In AL West, the A's won comfortably by 5½ games over Chciago.

This play-off also went the limit. The A's won at home 3–2, with two runs in the bottom of the 11th, and 5–0 behind Blue Moon Odom. The Tigers won at home 3–0, behind Joe Coleman, and pulled out the fourth game 4–3, with a three-run 10th after the A's had scored twice. But the A's won the deciding game 2–1 and headed for the club's first World Series since 1931.

Carew's .318 was good enough for another batting crown, as the .300 population dwindled again to six players and the league average to .239. Dick Allen, now with the White Sox, hit 37 homers, knocked in 113 runs, and was MVP. Gaylord Perry, traded by the Giants to Cleveland for Sam Mc-Dowell, went 24–16 with a 1.92 ERA, but Boston's Luis Tiant had 1.91 in half as many innings. Lolich was 22–14 in Detroit, Catfish Hunter 21–7 in Oakland, Palmer 21–10 in Baltimore; but the real wonder was Wilbur Wood, a knuckleballer, at Chicago, where Chuck Tanner was the free-thinking manager. Wood started 49 games, sometimes with two days' rest, worked 377 innings, won 24 games, lost 17, and put up a 2.51 ERA. Teammate Stan Bahnsen, a fastballer, was 21–16 as the White Sox finished second behind the A's.

The pitchers were reasserting control.

All-Star Game—In Atlanta, an anticipated home-run derby never developed. The Nationals tied it 3–3 in the ninth, against Wood, and won it in the 10th on Joe Morgan's single off McNally. It was the seventh extra-inning All-Star Game, all won by the National League.

WS—The A's went into the World Series as underdogs, getting more attention for their noisy internal squabbles and for the mustaches Finley was now paying them to wear. But they won the opener in Cincinnati as Gene Tenace, who caught sometimes and played first base at others, hit two home runs, one with a man on, in a 3–2 game secured by scoreless relief pitching by Rollie Fingers and Vida Blue. Then they won the second 2–1, as Fingers got the last out for Hunter.

The third game, at Oakland, was set back a day by rain. Then the Reds won it 1–0, but the A's went up three games to one with a ninth-inning rally the next day, scoring twice after falling behind 2–1 in the eighth. Facing elimination, the Reds won a wild fifth game 5–4, overcoming an early three-run homer by Tenace with single runs in the eighth and ninth. Tenace now had four home runs, tying a World Series record held by Babe Ruth.

Back in Cincinnati, the Reds seemed to assert themselves in an 8–1 pounding, so it was down to one game. Tenace knocked in a run with a first-inning single. The Reds tied it in the fifth. Two-out doubles by Tenace and Sal Bando gave the A's a 3–1 lead in the sixth. In the eighth, Fingers relieved with men on second and third and nobody out, escaped with only one run scoring on a fly, and closed out the ninth. He had relieved in six of the seven games, and neither team had a complete game.

It had taken 12 years, but Finley's team was champion of the baseball world. A legendary dynasty was in the making, perhaps the last.

AFTERMATH

The first four years of divisional play established three facts: The divisional races and play-offs worked; the low-offense problem had not been solved; and the days when club owners could do whatever they felt like were over.

Three grievance cases in 1971 showed how far the players had come from submission to Landis-style arbitrariness and subservience in general. And three player-contract cases in 1972 showed where they had to go next.

Case 1: Alex Johnson, the 1970 batting champion, started behaving erratically in spring training with the Angels. He would fail to run out grounders or to make ordinary effort in the field. He would play brilliantly for several games, then relapse. He was hostile to teammates. By June, he had been fined 29 times and benched five times by manager Lefty Phillips. On June 13, during a game at Anaheim, he had a confrontation with teammate Chico Ruiz, also black. Both had already been used as pinch-hitters and were alone in the clubhouse. Johnson claimed Ruiz pulled out a gun and threatened him. General manager Dick Walsh investigated and announced he found no gun, implying Johnson had lied. Johnson played a few more games and, after being benched for the fifth time June 26, was suspended for the rest of the season without pay. The charge was "not hustling," an authentic baseball crime.

Johnson consulted Miller, who filed a grievance on his behalf. That meant the impartial arbitrator would have to hear the case, with formal testimony being taken. Meanwhile, Miller urged Johnson to undergo psychiatric examination. The Players Association's position was: if the player was deliberately malingering, discipline, and suspension were justified, but if he acted that way because he was emotionally disturbed, he should be placed on the disabled list, as with any physical illness or injury.

At the hearing, Walsh confessed that he had found Ruiz's gun and lied about it. Johnson testified for three hours, and two eminent psychiatrists reported that Johnson was "emotionally incapacitated." The arbitrator ruled that his remaining salary, about $30,000, had to be paid, but that the $3,750 in fines stood.

The result was considered important in that it established that a mental illness was as legitimate an incapacity as a physical injury, with explicit safeguards against actual malingering. But it was even more important for its indirect effect. It showed all players that they had an effective advocate to turn to when in trouble. Johnson was unpopular with other players, incomprehensible to his employers, unsympathetic in the eyes of the public. But the new grievance system could deliver just treatment even to him.

Case 2: Tony Conigliaro had been a Red Sox hero (160 homers in six years) and teenage idol until hit in the left eye by a pitch in 1967. He missed the whole 1968 season and in 1971 wound up as a member of the Angels, as unaccepted by his teammates as Johnson, talking of retiring. On July 10, he left the club and went home to Boston. His salary stopped. But a medical exam showed his vision had deteriorated over the past year. The Players Association filed a grievance August 4. This time, a quick settlement was reached without a hearing, and the Angels paid Conigliaro the $40,000 the rest of his contract called for, minus two days' pay for jumping the club.

Case 3: Clete Boyer, at 34, had become a home-run hitter in Atlanta but didn't get along with the boss, Paul Richards, whom he criticized

publicly in May. Richards said he'd release him if Boyer would write a check for the 60 days' severance the club would have to pay him. The club gave him $15,000, and he gave it $10,000. In effect, he had bought his release.

The Players Association, which saw this as a violation of the provision about termination pay, filed a grievance, and Commissioner Kuhn had to tell the Atlanta club that it was violating the CBA and to return the money. But Kuhn also fined Boyer $1,000 for betting on football and basketball games (which Boyer admitted), and no other club would hire him, so it was a Pyrrhic victory.

What bothered management, of course, was the implied precedent of buying out a contract to become a free agent. It settled for the letter of the labor agreement quickly to avoid pursuing the issue, then quietly blackballed Boyer, who spent a year playing in Japan before returning to a long career as a major league coach.

Case 4: Vida Blue, the biggest star of 1971 as a rookie, held out for more money in 1972. His 1971 salary had been $14,750, a bit above the minimum. Now he asked for $115,000, later scaled down to $92,500, a figure his attorney said represented the average salary of baseball's top pitchers. Finley's top offer was $50,000. When Blue said he would retire (he was 22), Finley scoffed at the idea and offered an argument whose irony apparently escaped him. "I stand to lose $500,000 at the gate if Vida doesn't play," he said. Hmmm.

On April 27, two weeks into the strike-delayed season, Kuhn intervened and brokered a $63,000 deal. He "ordered" Finley to keep the deal open until May 2, whereupon Finley blasted Kuhn for involving himself and exceeding his authority. But on May 2, Blue signed—and Kuhn fined and reprimanded Finley for remarks "not in the best interests of baseball." The Finley-Kuhn war was on full blast. It would become important.

Case 5: With virtually no publicity, Ted Simmons, the Cardinal catcher, was allowed to play without signing a 1972 contract. He had asked for a 100 percent raise, to $35,000 (after catching 130 games and hitting .304). The club unilaterally paid him $25,000 and let him play while negotiation continued. It wasn't until August 9 that he signed a two-year contract worth $75,000.

Case 6: Willie Mays, past 40, was slowing down. Horace Stoneham, for whom he had played his entire career, was the epitome of the paternalistic owner; he had inherited the team from his father. Stoneham believed completely in rewarding friends and exiling enemies, and he truly loved Willie. He was paying Mays $165,000 but couldn't afford to keep doing it because the A's had moved into Oakland and ruined the Giants' business.

So he traded Mays to the New York Mets, who had plenty of money. There Willie could finish his career in the city that had originally idolized him and still did, and be paid $165,000 as long as he played. What's more, the Mets offered him $225,000 for three years after he stopped if he would remain as a coach.

The first three cases demonstrated the value, to the players, of the grievance procedure and its manifold uses. The last three showed how nervous management was about breaches of the reserve, and how the players might work around it. If Simmons had actually completed the season without signing, he could have claimed he had played out that one-year option and was free.

Simmons didn't, but someone would.

PART VII

THE NEW AGE

CHAPTER 22

Free Agency

The stage was set. In four short seasons, from 1973 to 1976, the entire structure of baseball would change more than it had in the preceding 90 years. It had been happening gradually—franchise moves starting in 1953 after 50 years of stability, expansion starting in 1961, a players union in 1968, divisional play in 1969, an actual strike in 1972. The accelerating pace of change was obvious enough. Nevertheless, at the end of the 1972 season, the reserve system was every bit as rigid and intact as it had been since the player revolt of 1890; the playing rules had been essentially unchanged since 1903; the scale of operation, as measured by attendance, salary scales, sales price of a team, and general revenue (including television) had been increasing naturally by manageable increments in line with economic and population growth, but well within the range of what was considered normal development.

But now came the true upheaval, a shattering of all the remaining traditions. A new CBA in 1973, instituting salary arbitration, altered payroll structure. That season, the designated hitter not only made a radical change in the game itself, but broke the bond of common rules for the two leagues attained in 1903. By 1976, the entire reserve system was wiped out completely, to be replaced by a *negotiated* set of restrictions that would become the subject of unceasing labor war.

At the same time, both attendance and television revenue would climb to heights that few, if any, anticipated, feeding the economics of an evolving system. The changes that culminated in 1976 led by 1980 to constant turmoil, which soon became a perpetual distraction taken for granted by public and participants alike. In 1977, the American League added two more teams, so that the leagues had not only different rules but different sizes, a situation last encountered in 1884, and it didn't seem to bother anyone as prosperity kept skyrocketing. The ambiguity of the commissionership's function was highlighted by a major lawsuit by an owner against the Commissioner, the first such large-scale attack on the nature of the hierarchy itself since the days of 1919 that had produced Czar Landis.

And, by 1980, the strike-lockout method of bargaining made such crises seem not only routine but inevitable.

All this took place against a background of explosive growth in all spectator sports. Football took command of television. Basketball and hockey more than doubled in size. Team tennis came and went. College football bowl games and basketball tournaments proliferated, with the NCAA basketball championship tournament attaining an impact (on television) comparable to the Super Bowl and World Series. The Olympics, spilling out of amateurism's bonds, shared that rarefied atmosphere. The marketing of logoed merchandise, the concepts of luxury box and preferred seating, the stimulation of commercialized collecting, all opened new economic vistas. Baseball, moving faster than it had ever moved before, could hardly keep pace.

The 1770s had seen the birth of the United States of America. The 1870s had marked the birth of professional baseball in organized form. The 1970s gave birth to new patterns as fundamentally different from what had gone before as those other seventies.

There were six main themes, or story lines:

1. The designated hitter and its effects
2. The full effect of an impartial arbitrator on player bargaining power, bringing down the reserve system
3. The antecedents and consequences of the American League's expansion to 14 teams in 1977
4. Bitter bargaining replete with strike threats
5. The climax of the Kuhn-Finley conflict, which had to be settled in court and which altered permanently the internal politics of commissioner-owner relationships
6. Escalation of every respect of baseball economics, especially salary levels and value of franchises

We'll take them one by one.

THE DESIGNATED HITTER

The designated-hitter rule as adopted had been tried in the minors as far back as 1969. A permanent pinch-hitter, who did not play in the field, batted instead of the pitcher. Only if the designated hitter (DH) or his substitute were put in the field during the game would a pitcher bat for the remainder of the game in the slot of the fielder removed.

It was not adopted unanimously. The American League voted 8–4 to try it. The National, by inaction, did not prevent it. (If the leagues had split on a formal vote, the commissioner would break the tie, and Kuhn was in favor of it.) There is no mention of the rule in the *Official Baseball Rules* for 1973, 1974, and 1975. Not until the 1976 book is rule 6.10 added, describing the DH's use and declaring, "Any League may elect to use the Designated Hitter Rule."

It was also not well thought out.

If the goal was to increase hitting by not having helpless pitchers take a turn at bat, the best solution would have been to have an eight-man batting order. Simply don't let the pitchers bat. That would bring up the best hitters, in the middle of the batting order, one more time in every game. A star like Aaron or Yastrzemski might get 100 extra at bats a season that way.

As it was, the rule contained a self-canceling feature. It sent a better hitter to bat in the ninth slot, but allowed the opposition to avoid removing an effective pitcher for a pinch-hitter. Offense would benefit, but only a little.

The manager had to make his decision before handing in the batting order. If it didn't contain a DH, none could be used in that game. One might think that a manager would make that choice, day by day, according to the hitting ability of his starter. A starting pitcher who could hit like Red Ruffing or Don Newcombe or Wes Ferrell would be allowed to bat, with the player who would be the DH available to pinch-hit at a vital moment instead of being locked into one batting-order slot.

One might think that—but managers didn't think it. The rule had been tried in the International League back in 1969, and not a single manager chose to let his pitcher hit. The rule didn't, and still doesn't, require a team to use a DH. But all managers do. In 23 years through 1996, no American League manager has chosen not to use the DH except in isolated instances, perhaps once or twice a year in the entire league.

The net effect was easy to predict. One of the nine slots in the batting order would now hit .250 instead of .150, so one could expect one-ninth better production, roughly 10 percent. It's hard to translate that into batting average, but a rise of 20 points or so seemed reasonable. In 1972, the league had hit .239, and sure enough, in 1973 it hit .259. Run production jumped by 29 percent over 1972, but was only 11 percent higher than in 1971, a more valid comparison because 1972 was abnormal.

In fact, the effect on pitching was greater than the effect on hitting. By not being forced out for a hitter, better pitchers worked a greater number of innings, removed only for ineffectiveness or fatigue. The American League had been averaging, since going to 12 teams in 1969, seven 20-game winners a season; in 1973 it had 12.

But that wouldn't last, because the rule helped pitching in another way. A DH allowed you to have a thinner bench, since you'd need an orthodox pinch-hitter less often and consequently fewer occasions for a defensive replacement. Therefore, you could carry one more pitcher instead of a utility player, and that meant a deeper bull pen that could be reorganized with better set-up men preceding a closer; or, perhaps, more rest and better spotting for nonstar starters. So from 1977 through 1980, even with the number of teams increased to 14, the league averaged only four 20-game winners a year.

The other side effect, not talked about beforehand but quickly recognized, was the opportunity provided to aging or injured good hitters. They could function as a DH without being a liability in the field. Big-name hitters with gate appeal could stay in action an extra couple of years at the end of a career. Younger players with talented bats but poor fielding ability could also be used this way and developed into semi-stars.

But as a cure, it was very mild. In 1974, for instance, the National still outscored the American (for the last time). It took three or four seasons for American League managers to settle into the best way to make full use of a DH (day to day, that is), and for teams to sign individuals best suited for it. Still, it did what it was supposed to do to a degree: league scoring went up and attendance with it. Whether these elements would have evened out anyhow over time, no one will ever know.

Meanwhile, everyone but the National League adopted the DH rule—minors, colleges, amateurs. Any pitcher with natural hitting ability saw that ability atrophy from high school on.

The biggest strategic difference was this. In a DH lineup, a manager looked upon every inning as a potential scoring inning when anyone got on, able to hit-and-run and make other standard offensive maneuvers in any part of the batting order. When pitchers hit, one or two innings are usually written off as a total or partial loss. If a pitcher leads off, hits second with one out, or is due up with two out with men on base, you might as well concentrate on the next inning. Your odds are better when the pitcher makes the third out and the top of the order starts the next inning, than when a pitcher gets on with two out, the leadoff man makes out, and a less favorable sequence follows.

In the final analysis, the DH rule turned out to make surprisingly little *practical* difference, while it remained an inflammatory subject for aesthetics and debate. When you added it all up, after 25 years (through the 1997 season) the DH was producing one additional run every three games for the team using it. If the World Series, where the DH was in use in some games and not in others, the American League had a theoretical disadvantage (being forced to have a pitcher bat), it didn't show up in games won and lost. The American League won 12 of the 22 World Series (none in 1994) and—except for the 1987 and 1991 Series in which the Minnesota Twins won all eight home games (with the DH and in their dome) and lost all six on the road (without the DH)—won more non-DH games than they lost.

It simply was no big deal. If you went to 10 DH games and 10 non-DH games, you'd see three more homers and three fewer strikeouts with the DH, and three more sacrifice bunts without it. Since the game is played by alert humans, they simply adapt to whatever the rules require and play the percentages as they come to know them.

But as a topic of passionate conversation, pro but mostly con, the DH became a permanent big deal, expounded on by commissioners, club owners, and managers as well as by commentators and fans. What it really demonstrated was baseball's greatest innate virtue: it's the greatest talking-reading-arguing sport ever invented.

ARBITRATION

The impartial arbitration procedure, inserted with so little outside notice in the 1970 CBA, was the lever that brought down the whole reserve structure.

Salary arbitration was the first step. The clubs chose it as the lesser of evils to retain what they looked upon as perpetual reserve rights. If they insisted (as they had to the courts) that a zero-power bargaining position for the employee was needed for the industry's health, they had to give him some kind of escape from take-it-or-leave-it salary negotiations.

The method adopted, urged by Miller, was either-or. Any arbitrator tends to split the difference. But if each side submits a figure and he has to choose one or the other, without the power to change it, there is pressure on both sides to be reasonable. A club offering obviously too little (in comparison to the "market") will lose, as will a player asking for obviously too much. The mere existence of such a procedure will push both club and player to exchange honest "best offers" and then to split the difference voluntarily to avoid the arbitration risks.

But in such a procedure, the player always wins before he starts. The club's offer is *always* higher than it would have been, for the sake of winning or avoiding the arbitration, and must be based on some sort of objective standard. So the player who *loses* his arbitration case invariably ends up with much more than the club would have given him before salary arbitration existed, even if the player was the biggest star and willing to hold out (as Koufax and Drysdale had).

So the salary-arbitration cases, no matter how they came out, accelerated the upward thrust on salaries begun by the mere fact of expansion. And with a union watchdog on their side to see that all procedures were followed properly, the players finally had a weapon with which to fight for "their fair share" of the rapidly growing revenue.

In 1973, the year after the strike, Dick Allen got a record salary of $250,000 from the White Sox. Hank Aaron, one home run away from Babe Ruth's career record of 714, was at $200,000. At $100,000 or higher were 28 other players. The average salary was $36,500, nearly double what it had been when Miller was hired seven years before; the minimum was $15,000 under the new agreement.

The first arbitration cases were heard going into the 1974 season, 29 of them, and the clubs "won" 16—but in fact of course lost all. The real effect was that higher salaries were being offered to *all* players, averting arbitration in most cases.

But salary was not the only thing now subject to arbitration. *Any* dispute about the meaning of a contract, or living up to one, could get there through the grievance procedure.

In preserving the reserve system, the owner relied, as they had since 1880s, on what was called "the reserve clause."

It said, simply, that this year's compensation included the consideration for the club's right to retain the player's services for the following year as well, at its discretion—its "option"—without the player's agreement.

The clause had to be included in every player's contract, or the league would not approve the contract. (Spalding and Hulbert understood this back in 1876—it was a foundation stone of the "league" idea, the mechanism by which blacklisting could be enforced.)

As long as the clubs insisted that a player sign a new current contract before playing, the reserve clause automatically renewed itself perpetually: each contract committed the player to the next year as well.

But in the 1960s, it became harder to insist on preplay contract signing. All the other sports had adopted the classic baseball model for their contracts. But in their conflicts over rival leagues, they generated court cases that made it clear that a one-year option was exactly that, one year. If a player sat out that year (as some cases permitted), there was still a bit of ambiguity about unfulfilled obligations; but if he *played out* that year, he was free.

Now, if the *club* prevented him from fulfilling the option-year obligation by not letting him play without a new contract, it would be arguing against itself. Either the option committed him to play that year or it didn't, but it said nothing about signing another contract. If the player wanted to play and the club (or league) prevented him, wouldn't the club be the one breaking the contract?

At the same time, the signing boycott of 1969 over the separate issue of the pension negotiation showed both sides that players could refuse to sign contracts in a timely manner and yet not refuse to play. So from that point on, rigid adherence to the no-sign, no-play policy began to unravel. Several players went through the training season and beyond before signing.

For the clubs, the vital point was that a player sign at *some* point during the current season, so that the "option year" could not be played out completely. Until that happened, baseball would not have to test its fallback position, its theory that the "option year" incorporated all the terms of the original contract (except salary) *including* the option clause. Therefore, the option would automatically renew itself forever simply by the contract's being activated.

Miller was eager to test such reasoning. It involved, indisputably, interpretation of what the contract meant, and such interpretation was, under the CBA, a matter for an arbitrator. But no test could arise until some player actually did play out a full option year without re-signing.

Ted Simmons was on that path in 1972 but signed in August (for a satisfactory raise). During 1973, seven players started the season unsigned. Four of them signed shortly afterward, making their following-year status moot. The other three were simply given unconditional releases, making them the kind of free agents that had always existed—players not in demand, that is, unemployed and looking for work. Two of them caught on with other clubs in June and July (but without the kind of bonuses Harrelson had wangled), while the third went back to the minors.

In 1974, even with the salary-arbitration process now available, two players decided to hold out—Sparky Lyle, the left-handed relief ace of the Yankees, and Bobby Tolan, the San Diego outfielder. Lyle played the whole season before signing, on the final day, a contract that covered 1974 and 1975 (for more money). But Tolan never signed, and on October 17 the Players Association filed a grievance claiming he should now be a free agent. A test case was at hand.

However, an entirely different case usurped it the same month. James (Catfish) Hunter had become the leading pitcher on the Oakland team that was now winning (in October 1974) its third straight World Series. He had signed a two-year contract at the beginning of 1974 calling for $100,000 a year, but, for tax purposes, $50,000 each year was to be paid to a third party, named but not controlled by Hunter, for an annuity that would pay off later.

As the World Series began, news emerged that there was a dispute. Finley had not paid the other $50,000 in the stipulated manner, and Hunter was pursuing a grievance.

In baseball's early years, well into the 20th century, nonpayment of salary due was a recurrent and serious issue. The leagues and the commissioner's office always took the position that they would guarantee payment if an owner reneged. Rules about this were strict and observed. For decades, a player in such a situation had been made whole, one way or another, by the league if necessary.

But the standard player contract, it turned out, offered a player a choice of *two* remedies if its payment provisions (or other provisions) were not met. One was to have the payment made in full. The other was to claim that the contract had been broken and no further obligations existed.

Hunter chose the second remedy.

It would make him a free agent.

Finley had been derelict from May on (for his own tax reasons). Hunter had protested, in writing, in September. Finley had not responded. Finally, on October 4 (during the play-offs), Finley had offered Hunter a $50,000 check. Hunter, advised all along by Miller, Moss, and his own attorneys, refused it; it was supposed to be deposited to an annuity fund, not to him.

Lee MacPhail, the new American League president, considered this a good-faith gesture on Finley's part, and eventual full payment only a technicality.

Hunter and the Association rejected that view. They weren't seeking restitution by late payment; they were claiming the contract had been abrogated, and they were content to have it that way.

The grievance went to arbitrator Peter Seitz. On December 13, 1974, he issued his ruling.

Hunter was a free agent. The conditions of his contract had not been met. He could have, Seitz took pains to point out, filed a grievance seeking restitution, but he didn't. Instead, he chose the other course that the contract gave him, to have the contract terminated. He had that right, he had exercised it, and the contract was voided.

He was now the only player available to all 24 clubs, who could bid for his services—and he was the top pitcher in baseball. (The Tolan grievance had been dropped when the Hunter case came up.)

How much would he be worth on the open market?

How about a five-year package giving him $3.2 million?

That's what he accepted from the Yankees after a two-month circus. Baseball appealed Seitz's decision to the courts, who upheld it. (Only some impropriety on the part of an arbitrator is cause for overturning his or her decision, and here there was none.) At least 48 baseball executives made pilgrimages to Hunter's North Carolina farm, offering more and more money. Rumors and reports flooded the sports pages. Hunter signed with the Yankees on New Year's Eve.

In and of itself, the Hunter case did nothing to the reserve system. It was a special circumstance, a foul-up by one club owner of one contract. It didn't challenge or alter any contractual provision, merely took advantage of noncompliance.

But its practical and psychological effects were earthshaking. Hunter's Yankee deal, averaging more than $600,000 a season, was far more than double what anyone had ever received, and its five-year length was unheard of. (Hunter, at 29, would be likely to finish his career with the Yankees and in fact did.) It showed the players, more vividly than ever, how far below "true market value" their pay scale had always been.

And it terrified the owners. Here was another instance of what they'd been struggling to avoid since 1876: competing against each other for star players. O.K., this had happened; but to contemplate further weakening of the reserve in the upcoming CBA negotiation was impossible. Salary arbitration might be bad, but free agency was to be avoided at all costs.

In that climate—emboldened players, appalled owners—the reserve clause itself was still unsettled.

The Hunter case had sidetracked the Tolan grievance (he signed in December), but would there be others?

Yes. Pitchers Andy Messersmith (Dodgers) and Dave McNally (Baltimore) went into the 1975 season without signing new contracts, ready to play out their option year.

McNally, who had had such great success for 13 years in Baltimore, had been traded in December 1974 to Montreal. He was 32, plagued frequently by arm trouble, and in June he retired, walking away from the remainder of a $125,000 salary and higher offers to return. His name remained in the grievance, but his case was moot.

Messersmith had a 19–14 season for the second-place Dodgers, ranking second in the league in earned run average at 2.29. His original disagreement over contract terms, in the spring of 1975, was over his request for a no-trade clause. The Dodgers exercised the option clause and gave him a $25,000 raise to $115,000. When the season ended, they offered him a three-year package worth $540,000. But by that time he felt committed to going through with the test case. Like many stars, he took seriously his position of leverage. Only stars could win gains for the rest of the players, even though their own situations were prosperous. Kiner and Reynolds had done that in the early pension dealings, the stars of the day had done it back in 1890. In star-driven entertainment industries, "labor" can gain or lose only what the stars are willing or unwilling to back. Messersmith wasn't facing the degree of risk or emotional investment that Flood had; but, like Flood, he was willing to think beyond his own immediate bank account.

Baseball's management has always found this hard to believe and has often made costly miscalculations as a result. It assumes player cynicism similar to its own.

On October 7, 1975, the Players Association filed a grievance asking that Messersmith be declared a free agent and that all 24 clubs be notified of his availability.

On October 24, the clubs replied that the issue raised was outside the province of the arbitration panel and without merit anyhow.

On October 28, Ewing Kauffman, owner of the Royals, filed a civil suit in Kansas City, asking the U.S. district court to restrain the Players Association from proceeding with its grievance. The other 23 clubs were ready to join as plaintiffs.

Kauffman argued that his $6 million investment in the club in 1969 was made in reliance on the continuation of the reserve system. If the system were subject to arbitration, his investment would be threatened, while the status quo wouldn't hurt the players. Moss argued that 16 arbitration cases involving reserve issues had been argued since 1970, with no attempt on management's part to enjoin them, and urged the judge to order the grievances to be heard as scheduled.

Judge John W. Oliver persuaded the owners to go ahead with the grievance procedure, with the proviso that the clubs could contest the grievance panel's jurisdiction if dissatisfied with the outcome.

Hearings were held November 21 and 24 and December 1. The panel (Miller, Gaherin, Seitz) met December 5, 8, 13, and 20. Miller and Gaherin, their votes always known in advance, were simply advocates. The arbitrator, Seitz, would be the sole determinant.

The clause he had to interpret was painfully clear. "If prior to March 1, player and club have not agreed . . . the club shall have the right . . . to renew this contract for the period of one year."

One year, argued Miller, meant one year.

Renew the contract, argued Gaherin on behalf of the clubs, meant renew the option clause also, for the year after that.

Anyone who could read English could see the contradiction between "one year" stated explicitly and "forever" implied by the club interpretation.

Seitz was aware of the magnitude of the stakes. For nearly a century, it had been taken for granted that the reserve was needed for orderly baseball operation. No one could tell what would follow its destruction. He urged Gaherin to take the case out of his hands and negotiate some acceptable compromise directly with the players— making it clear that if forced to rule, he'd have to rule against the clubs. He could withhold his decision for months. But the clubs insisted they wanted a ruling now.

So on December 23, he issued it. One year meant one year. Messersmith and McNally were free agents.

Within minutes, the owners issued their prepared statement that Seitz was fired as arbitrator. Either side had the right to do that (but not until any case already begun had run its course), and Seitz was the first of the four who had served to be dismissed.

The clubs immediately went back to Judge Oliver in Kansas City, challenging Seitz's jurisdiction. On February 4, Judge Oliver upheld Seitz and praised his conduct and reasoning. Once the clubs signed the first CBA in 1968, he said, they became subject to the labor-management laws, which favor arbitration of all labor disputes.

The owners appealed to the Eighth U.S. Circuit Appeals Court, which upheld Judge Oliver.

There it was. Any and every player who played through 1976 without signing a new contract would be a free agent the day that season ended. The only exceptions would be players who had multiyear contracts extending beyond 1976, and they would be free whenever those contracts expired.

All players.

The last time such a situation existed was 101 years ago. No one knew what it would lead to. Everyone was in shock (even the players). Some system, somehow, would have to be put in place. But how?

Why, by negotiation.

That's all that the players had been asking for in the first place, as far back as 1888.

What the Seitz decision did, therefore, was force the issue to the bargaining table, the step the owners had been stonewalling all along. Some regulation of how players could move from team to team had to exist; no one denied that. But the regulation would now have to be agreed on, in some kind of give-and-take bargaining, not unilaterally imposed. (What that bargaining produced we'll see later in this chapter.)

New guidelines would have to be bargained in the context of the momentary chaos of "everyone free," instead of in the context of "loosening" the old totally restrictive system, as Seitz had urged. Why the clubs pushed him to a decision then, instead of negotiating from strength, was never made clear either at the time or in later analyses and revelations and was probably unclear in the minds of those who made that decision then. It remains inexplicable in retrospect.

MORE TEAMS

The expansion to 24 teams had worked well. The two six-team divisions in each league made coherent pennant races of their own, and the League Championship Series playoffs had been a big hit without detracting from the World Series. The pattern of 18 games with each team in your own division (three visits to each) and 12 games with those in the other division (two visits) was easily grasped by fans, practical in every respect, and quickly establishing its own traditions.

But there were three trouble spots. Seattle, having lost its team to Milwaukee after only one year, had taken its case to court. Washington, abandoned for a second time and left without any team at all in 1972, looked like a significant emptiness, not only symbolically as the nation's capital (missing from "the national game"?) but as a lobbying center when legislative and federal court issues were on baseball's front burner. Most of all, however, the Oakland–San Francisco situation demanded immediate attention.

The Giants, in their first nine years in San Francisco, averaged 1.5 million customers a year. In 1968, the year the Athletics moved into Oakland, each team drew 840,000. And the pattern never changed. The area total kept hovering around 1.6 million, with the majority shifting toward whichever team was winning more. The A's, even when finishing first five years in a row and winning three World Series, could not average a million. The Giants, without Mays and Marichal for glamour and sinking competitively, were down to the 500,000 level by 1974.

Heck, that was less than they had their last year at the Polo Grounds, when they had already told New Yorkers they were leaving.

The A's, at least, had a championship team. The Giants had nothing. Horace Stoneham could no longer afford the team his father had bought 55 years before. He had to put it up for sale.

No one in San Francisco was ready to buy it.

So he sold it to the Labatt brewery people in Toronto. His 30-year lease on Candlestick Park had 13 years to go. Toronto was willing to give him $8 million for the team and put aside an additional $5 million to buy out the lease or fight it in court.

The city went to court to prevent breaking the lease, although it was obvious that the only issue was the amount of money that would make a fair settlement. You couldn't force anyone to operate a business where he didn't want to, or prevent him from making a legitimate sale of his own property. Going to court was a delaying action, giving a local buyer a chance to respond to the crisis.

A local buyer did. Bob Lurie, heir to a real-estate fortune and a minority stockholder in the Giants since their arrival, was willing to put up $4 million. So was Bob Short, in Minneapolis. He had just sold his Texas Rangers and wanted to get back into baseball. But before the deal could be completed, Short suffered a serious injury in a fall on the ice at home, and Lurie found another partner, Bud Herseth, a cattleman in Phoenix. Short had wanted to run the club and had already alienated Lurie. Herseth was happy to be a silent partner, and Lurie emerged as a major league club owner, with all the status and attention that implied. (In a couple of years, he bought Herseth out.)

So the Giants would stay in San Francisco, and to stimulate memories of better days, Lurie brought Bill Rigney back as manager.

All this was early in 1976, when the Messersmith case was in the appeals process and neither the public nor the club owners had given full attention to its consequences. Lurie thought he was buying into reserve-system baseball.

Meanwhile, trouble in San Diego had seemed to work itself out. C. Arnholt Smith, who had been awarded the expansion franchise in 1969, had run into financial trouble, namely, a $22 million debt to the Internal Revenue Service. By May of 1973, he succeeded in selling the team for $12 million to a group in Washington, which would move it there for 1974. Commissioner Kuhn, who grew up in Washington and who was so involved in inside-the-beltway social and political affairs, welcomed this development.

It turned out, however, that the Washington people didn't really have the money available, and San Diego mayor Pete Wilson had also used the lawsuit delaying tactic. In October, Smith announced he had a buyer who would keep the team in San Diego—Marge Everett, who was a prominent racetrack operator, whose father had been one famous in Chicago. But Marge had enemies, among them owners John Galbreath in Pittsburgh and Mrs. Payson in New York, who were racetrack people themselves, and Kuhn, who declared privately if not publicly that Everett would be "unacceptable" as a club owner for unspecified reasons.

After much soap-opera maneuvering, it seemed in late December that the move to Washington was on again, and on January 9, 1974, the National League formally rejected Everett 9–3. But Washington still hadn't come up with the money.

Suddenly, on January 23, Ray Kroc came forth and gave Smith $12 million in cash for the club, so that it could remain in San Diego. Kroc, who had made his fortune in McDonald hamburger franchising, was a colorful personality. The Padres were the most unsuccessful of all the expansion teams, having finished last five years in a row and averaged 600,000 in attendance. (Even the Mets had escaped the cellar after four years, although they fell back into it.) Kroc, grabbing the public-address microphone to "apologize" to the fans for his inept players, boosted the attendance to over a million in 1974 (while finishing last again) and to 1.2 million, double the Smith regime average, in 1975 in response to a fourth-place finish and a record 71 victories—20 games under .500.

But that left Washington, D.C., along with Seattle, restless about broken promises and aroused expectations.

Now the deal to keep the Giants at San Francisco put Toronto in the same excited and unsatisfied state. It couldn't go back to its traditional Triple-A team, one of the most successful in baseball, any more than Milwaukee could have in 1953 after Veeck talked about bringing the Browns there. Besides, Toronto was a metropolis of 3 million people, bigger than Montreal, too good a market to pass up. The National League wanted it badly.

Kuhn's idea was to add two more expansion teams. Put a National League team in Washington, D.C., an American League team in Toronto, and have the 13-team leagues play interleague games. (With an odd number of teams, you need interleague play to have each team have a game every day; that problem doesn't exist in football, basketball, or hockey, which have plenty of off days to accommodate staggered scheduling.)

The Nationals told Kuhn to stuff it. They didn't want interleague play, they wanted Toronto. And Baltimore didn't want anyone back in Washington, D.C., in either league.

What the National really wanted was Toronto *and* Seattle, and for the American to accept two lesser expansion markets—any two. But the American was feeling feisty under MacPhail and had twice gone its own way without waiting for the National. It had jumped the gun on expansion to 10 teams in 1961 a year early, and it was using the DH happily without the National's approval or participation. It was ready to move now.

Seattle's lawsuit was persistent, and antitrust issues were inherent in it. The domed stadium promised back in 1968 was now a reality, the Kingdome, and the National Football League had put a team into it to begin play in the fall of 1976.

The American League's solution was: we'll put a team in Seattle in return for it dropping the suit, and we'll put one in Toronto, and we'll have a 14-team league with two seven-team divisions. If the National wants to stay with 12 teams, let it.

And that became the baseball map in 1977.

In addition to the two new venues, altered playing fields were coming on line. In 1972, Candlestick's open outfield area was filled in by double decking all the way around, completing a lopsided oval, so that the football 49ers could move in. This was now a 62,000-seat building—more than the Giants needed—with artificial turf. In 1973, Yankee Stadium was 50 years old and now owned by the city. The football Giants, who had moved in as tenants in 1956 from the Polo Grounds and had sold out every game since, were leaving to go to their own stadium being built for them across the Hudson River in New Jersey. The Yankees, who had seen the city build Shea Stadium for the Mets before they existed, threatened to go to the Jersey complex also unless something were done for them. So at the end of the 1973 season, Yankee Stadium was completely rebuilt inside, leaving only the shell intact, to eliminate vision-blocking poles and increase luxury seating. During the two years it would take to complete the renovation, the Yankees would share Shea Stadium with the Mets.

In Montreal, the Expos had been playing in jerry-built Jarry Park. When the 1976 Olympic Games ended, Stade Olympique became available and the Expos moved in for the 1977 season. Grandiose plans for a moveable roof did not pan out, but the stadium held 60,000 instead of Jarry's 28,000. It had artificial turf. (The moveable roof was finally installed and made to work in 1989.)

And in Kansas City, the new ball park was ready for the 1973 season. It was a jewel in appearance and layout, its service areas connected underground to the adjacent beautiful football stadium. But even though it was a baseball-only outdoor park, it used artificial turf. The Kansas City area was notorious for sudden summer rain-storms, and the market depended heavily on hinterland customers, coming from a large circle extending into three or four states (as was the case with Cincinnati, St. Louis, and Minneapolis). The artificial turf could drain so quickly that most games interrupted by rain could be resumed, and few would have to be canceled by early morning or afternoon rain. Assuring customers that there would *be* a game, regardless of threatening weather, had become an important element in baseball market-ing. All in all, the proper word for Royals Stadium was "gorgeous."

THE NEW RESERVE SYSTEM

Distrust and bitterness marked the bargaining that produced the new arrangements made necessary by the Messersmith ruling, and they increased and congealed over the next 20 years. To see why this happened in an era of burgeoning prosperity, one must recognize the climate created by public and private statements. Two themes endlessly repeated by management were that teams would go out of business if an-other penny of player expense were added, and that "Svengali" Miller was being fol-lowed blindly by naive and ignorant players while making demands designed to jus-tify and glorify his own role as their negotiator.

"Baseball cannot function under the Messersmith decision," declared Commis-sioner Kuhn early in 1976.

"We're going to have to stop spending money like drunken sailors," said Cubs owner Phil Wrigley in 1973—before salary arbitration, before free agency, when the average salary had reached $36,500.

A year before that, John Holland, Wrigley's general manager, commented on the fact that his Cubs now had two players making $100,000. "I know we have reached the saturation point. If our payroll goes any higher, we can't make it."

Dick Young, the most influential of all baseball columnists, who had become a spokesman for management on labor issues, wrote on the eve of the 1972 strike that Miller "brainwashed" the player reps, with his "steel trap mind wrapped in a butter melting voice. . . . With few exceptions, they follow him blindly, like Zombies."

Dozens of similar comments, especially those predicting financial disaster, poured forth daily.

In response, the players claimed that the owners were simply lying—about their finances, about their true projections for the future, and about player attitudes. And if some on the management side really did believe what they were saying, the situation was even worse.

In fact, too often, management negotiators *were* lying, not only to the public and to the players, but to their own employers. They reported back what they thought would fit their principals' preconceptions and desires. Time after time, their financial figures proved false and had to be corrected. In the 1972 strike, some owners first heard that there *was* a pension-fund surplus for the first time four days into the strike.

Trouble was, many players, on a rotating basis, attended bargaining sessions and saw for themselves the evasive and stonewalling tactics used against them, while rarely if ever did any owner have firsthand knowledge of what went on. The players trusted Miller because almost everything he told them, about facts and figures and likely next steps, turned out to be true—not because Miller was some sort of paragon of virtue, but because the facts happened to be on his side.

As Aesop had noted so many centuries ago, crying wolf was a practice eventually dangerous to the cryer.

The concerted effort to demonize Miller had a perverse effect on the players, unifying them behind him as they found his advice repeatedly valid. Also, and worse, it deflected the owners' attention from confronting the true issues. In trying to defend every inch of their own turf, they wound up giving more ground than they had to and misconceived their own best long-range interests.

Forcing Seitz to make a decision was one example. The new negotiation provided a bigger one.

As of February 1976, with the Seitz decision upheld by Judge Oliver, the situation was this: any player who hadn't signed a 1976 contract could be a free agent at the end of the season; anyone who had could be a free agent at the end of the 1977 season (or later, whenever a multiyear contract ran out). Multiyear contracts were rare up to then.

The clubs, arguing that the Seitz decision applied only to Messersmith and Mc-Nally specifically, refused to proceed with anything until a new system was agreed to. That included refusing to start spring training.

Miller claimed he had a problem. If he bargained away the free agency already achieved, he would be sued by his own members for representing them improperly. Would the clubs undertake, in writing, to assume all liability for any judgments against him and the Players Association? Or to get players, one by one, to sign waivers of the free-agent rights?

No way, said the clubs. Here's our offer: a player can become a free agent after his ninth season in the majors, with the rule to be retroactive covering all present players.

That wouldn't do, but it included an element Miller wanted.

He had drawn the right conclusion from the Hunter case. One free agent, 24 teams, meant bidding went through the roof. If there were 600 free agents and 24 teams, it would be the players competing against each other for jobs instead of teams competing for desirable players. Total free agency would reverse the supply-demand situation. It would be best for the players if the supply of free agents at any one time was somehow limited, guaranteeing them a seller's market.

The formula settled upon was:

1. A player could declare himself a free agent after his sixth major league season. Once he did, he couldn't do it again for another five years.
2. Players not yet eligible for free agency could go to salary arbitration.
3. Those who wanted to retain their right to play out 1976 or 1977 could do so.
4. A free agent would have the right to negotiate with no more than 12 of the 24 clubs, who would go through a "free agent draft" procedure to list the players they wanted to deal with. (That is, as many as 12 clubs could list a particular player.)

The first point seemed a straightforward compromise between the nine years offered and nothing.

The second was merely a continuation of what had been accepted as necessary in 1973.

The third was easily resolved: pay the player you care about enough to make him sign, putting him under the retroactive provisions of the new system, or let him go.

The fourth seemed to be a concession to management's passion for limitations, without hurting a player's possibilities to any significant degree. As long as several clubs could bid, he could bargain.

Finley, for one, saw through it. "Make 'em all free agents," he cried. Many uninvolved commentators agreed with him. But the mindset of control, limitation, restriction, regulation, and protection of "my" player (i.e., property) was too deeply ingrained to be yielded up. Even if it was illusory and created a counterproductive market force, some sort of partial reserve was a constant craving.

A partial reserve also kept alive the hope that it could be amplified in future agreements. And that's where the real trouble came in.

Agreement was close enough by March 19 to have spring training camps open, and the season began on schedule on April 8. The actual agreement wasn't nailed down until July 12, the day before the All-Star Game, and not finally approved by the players until August 9.

The new CBA, covering 1976 through 1979, had other new provisions as well. The pension plan funding was now up to $8.5 million a year. The minimum salary went up to $19,000 and to $21,000 after two years. If a player were released after the season began, he was guaranteed his full year's pay; if during spring training, 30 days. A player completing his fifth year in the majors could demand to be traded, and if he wasn't, would become a free agent immediately (instead of a year later).

At the end of the 1976 season, 24 players went through the free-agent draft, Reggie Jackson leading the way with a five-year $3 million package from the Yankees. In 1977, there were 54, in 1978 there were 42, in 1979 there were 44. The top man in 1979 was Nolan Ryan, who left the Angels for the Houston Astros (near his Texas home) for a four-year $4.5 million package. The $1 million-a-year baseball player had arrived.

And by 1979 the average salary was around $120,000, six times what it had been when the players hired Miller 12 years before. No wonder they believed in him. The limited supply of free agents was working.

And no wonder the owners were more convinced than ever that "this can't go on."

A new CBA had to be negotiated during 1979.

Actually, management's feelings of desperation were not justified. In 1979, attendance broke all records for the fourth straight year, reaching 43.5 million, and the new national television package, which began in 1976, now brought $23.25 million a year, roughly 30 percent more than the previous pact. Ticket prices had started to rise, too. In 1973, subtracting $28 million from a $200 million gross left $172 million for all other expenses and profits, after player payroll and pension-fund costs were met. In 1979, payroll and pension costs were up to $88.5 million, but the gross was up to $300 million, so the "surplus" was $211.5 million, or $39.5 million more than it had been. In 1973, the Yankees and Reds had sold for $10 million; in 1977, the Red Sox sold for a record $17 million, and in 1979 the Houston Astros for $19 million.

Aware of such numbers, and now kept well informed by their individual agents as well as by their union, players didn't see why disaster was impending and drastic change had to be made. The owners, however, were hung up on the idea of reasserting "control of player movement." They focused on a particularly discredited device.

They wanted "compensation" to a club that lost a free agent from the club that signed him, in the form of a player of comparable value.

That system, in football, had been called "the Rozelle Rule." Subject to antitrust laws, football didn't prevent a player from being a free agent when a contract expired. But if he went to another club, and the two involved could not agree on compensation (in players, draft choices, or money), the commissioner—Pete Rozelle—would decide what the appropriate compensation would be to make a team "whole" for its loss. Since everyone understood that he could (and would) make the compensation excessive at worst and a standoff at best, free agents found themselves getting no offers, and for years there was no free-agent movement. When the football players finally took their problems to court, in the late 1960s and early 1970s, the courts declared in no uncertain terms that the Rozelle Rule was flat-out illegal.

A version of the Rozelle Rule is what the clubs wanted added to their new free-agent system in 1980.

They tinkered with various formulations, but that was the essence. The players, of course, would have nothing to do with it. One might force it on them, if one could; but they would never accept it voluntarily.

Through 1979, that was a sticking point. The owners had fired Gaherin and made Ray Grebey their negotiator, a man whose reputation in labor-negotiation circles stressed his "toughness" in applying a tactic called "Bulwareism." It was "This is our offer and it won't change, and we'll keep insisting on it until you give in."

The other proposal was even less acceptable: a flat salary scale, according to years of service, for the first six years, wiping out arbitration. Neither side considered this a serious proposal.

Miller's counterproposal on compensation was interesting. Compensation did exist: it was an amateur draft choice, not significant in baseball's scheme of things. Miller suggested the clubs set up a fund to which all clubs contributed, from which the team losing a player could draw some appropriate amount of money.

By rejecting that offer, the owners made the battle line definite. They wanted to lower salaries, period. The stalemate got more and more acrimonious. On March 4, 1980, the player reps voted 27–0 to strike April 1, with the season scheduled to open April 9.

On March 18, the owners dropped their salary scale proposal. By then, the players had voted 967–1 to go ahead and strike.

On March 27, Grebey called for federal mediation, and Ken Moffett was the veteran mediator assigned.

On March 30, his nine-hour meeting with both sides produced no movement.

On April 2, the player reps voted to cancel the 92 remaining exhibition games and to start the season, but to set May 23 as their strike date if no agreement had been reached.

By May 9, there had been 11 fruitless meetings, with everyone admitting there was only one issue: compensation.

On May 15, Miller suggested sending that issue to a committee, agreeing on everything else, and taking a year to study all the ramifications of the free-agent system. The owners said no, they want it settled now.

On May 18, Moffet reported, "No progress, and the climate is highly charged."

On May 19, Commissioner Kuhn, always involved through back channels, publicly took a mediation role.

On May 22, in New York, the negotiators started meeting at 11:15 A.M. The teams playing that day did not know whether they would proceed to the next stop after the game or begin a strike. The drama lasted through the night. At 5 A.M., May 23, after a seven-hour session, they announced they had reached a four-year agreement.

The terms?

The compensation issue would be put off for a year, to be studied by a joint player-management committee.

The minimum salary would go up to $30,000 and $35,000 in 1983. The pension fund would get $15.5 million annually, allowing larger pension payouts and insurance coverage. Salary arbitration would be available to any player after two years in the majors, and to those with more than six years whenever they were not eligible for free agency. Once again, the players had made tremendous gains.

The memorandum of understanding about the compensation issue was a time bomb. It provided that, if no resolution had been found, the owners could declare between February 15 and February 20, 1981, that they would put their proposal into effect. The players would then have until March 1 to set a strike date, to be no later than June 1.

The owners ratified this agreement June 5, 1980, but were split 21–5. A strong faction wanted a strike, convinced the players would lose it. "Take a strike" became a slogan with a segment of management that grew with time. The players, who wanted the status quo and had gotten more, ratified the agreement July 8 virtually unanimously.

Both sides had prepared for a strike. The owners had a $30 million strike-insurance policy with Lloyds of London. The players had collected a fund of more than $1 million from their gum-card and other endorsement money, to be used to help lower-paid players. Both those war chests grew during 1980.

The "study group" was a farce. It met but got nowhere. It was plain that the management side was merely marking time until it could impose its plan unilaterally in February. If the players wanted to strike then, fine; the owners wouldn't let them off the hook—as the hard-liners saw it—again.

Meanwhile, two other developments panicked owners and tilted support toward the "let's take a strike, once and for all" idea. In February of 1980, Bruce Sutter, relief ace of the Cubs, had won a salary arbitration that gave him $700,000 a year; the

Cubs had offered $350,000. Again, the day before the hearing on February 25, the Cubs had rejected Sutter's request to take more time to negotiate. Demanding a decision "now"—and losing—had become a pattern. Then, in January 1981, Dave Winfield, a free agent after six years in San Diego, was signed by the Yankees for $1.3 million a year for 10 years—a $13 million package.

This *can't* go on, the owners cried, although they were the ones doing it.

Why not? the players wanted to know.

But it couldn't. Not without a fight.

FINLEY VERSUS KUHN

Bowie Kuhn, the interventionist commissioner so lionized in his first year, was having a tough decade. His handling of the McLain matter had raised doubts about his judgment. He had given owners in Houston, Pittsburgh, Montreal, Cleveland, and Boston reason to be displeased in cases involving players. He had been unable to save Seattle, or arrange a smooth transition to Milwaukee, in 1970. He had not been able to prevent, or settle quickly, the unnecessary 1972 strike. He had been of no use, or source of helpful advice or leadership, in the Hunter and Messersmith cases. He was one of the architects of the "it's a labor matter" defense in the Flood case, now backfiring. But most noticeably of all, he fought publicly with Charley Finley.

That was one of the things other owners liked, because they didn't like Charley. When Vida Blue had held out in 1972, Kuhn had stepped in and made Finley shell out more than he wanted to. In 1973, Kuhn suspended George Steinbrenner for two years because he had been indicted and convicted of illegal contributions to President Nixon's election campaign. Some thought this made Steinbrenner the commissioner's enemy, but others saw it as a slap on the wrist under the circumstances. What did "suspending" an owner mean? Could he be kept away from all telephones? Did the people working for the club not know he was still their boss? Finley, who had spent his baseball career sniping at the Yankees and now had a championship team while the Yankees had fallen, had a low opinion of anything Kuhn did, and he didn't hesitate to express it.

The commissioner's seven-year term was to expire in August 1976. Rules required the owners to consider rehiring him 12 to 18 months before that. By June 1975, there was a "Dump Bowie" movement led by Finley.

To be reelected, Kuhn needed a 9–3 vote in each league. Since Walter O'Malley was one of his biggest backers, the National League was no problem. But Finley and Baltimore's Jerry Hoffberger were strongly anti-Kuhn, and the Yankees were willing to vote with them. (On whose say-so? the suspended Steinbrenner said, with a straight face, he had no right to take part in any baseball business.) Then Finley got Eddie Chiles, who had just bought the Texas Rangers, to go along. The day after the All-

Star Game in Milwaukee, the American League voted for Kuhn 8–4—not enough to renew.

O'Malley managed to hold off the joint meeting, which would formalize the matter overnight. Texas and the Yankees were persuaded to switch their votes. Kuhn's contract was renewed for another seven years (after 1976) by votes of 10–2 and 12–0.

In the ensuing press conference, Kuhn and Finley traded insults. Their mutual antagonism deepened.

Then came the Messersmith decision and free agency.

Finley knew he couldn't survive in a free-agent system. He had always operated on a shoestring, but always in the black. He had fought with and abused most of his players, over money and other matters. He had an all-star team, all of whom knew they could get more money elsewhere and would be glad to be rid of him. His first championship manager, Dick Williams, had walked out. Finley fired his successor, Alvin Dark, right after he lost the 1975 play-off to the Red Sox. If the sale of the Giants to Toronto had gone through, at least Finley would have had the whole Bay Area market to himself. As it was, when the 1976 season began with free agency looming at its end, he knew what he had to do.

The only way he could raise money would be to sell his stars, the time-honored method used by the venerable Connie Mack with this very same franchise, the sainted Clark Griffith in Washington, and others. He could use the money to finance a search for new, young, unknown, low-priced talent, as he had done successfully in Kansas City in gathering his present crop of stars. His ability to build a winner was a matter of record.

In 1974, in the first salary arbitration, Reggie Jackson and Sal Bando had won six-figure awards. In 1976, most of Finley's players didn't sign at all, to play out their options. So just before the season opened, he traded Jackson and pitcher Ken Holtzman to Baltimore. Then, just before the trading deadline of June 15, he sold Vida Blue to the Yankees for $1.5 million and Joe Rudi and Rollie Fingers to the Red Sox for $1 million each.

Commissioner Kuhn voided the June deals.

He claimed it was "not in the best interests of baseball" to weaken a team (Oakland) just for money. A "trade" had to imply comparable player values, to preserve "competitive balance."

He had no right whatsoever, under baseball regulations, to take such a step, nor any justification in logic or precedent. It was partly vindictiveness, his character flaw; partly a hope that finances would force Finley out of baseball—a hope many club owners shared, and therefore a good move politically—and partly outrage, shared by all other owners, at so publicly establishing the true market value of these (and therefore other) players. Even so, many owners said openly that the commissioner was out of line.

Finley's only recourse was to sue. He sought $10 million in damages, charging

Kuhn with conspiracy to deprive him of his money and various civil rights, and listing the two leagues, the executive council, and the Yankees and Red Sox as codefendants.

A 15-day trial took place in Chicago in March 1977, before federal judge Fred McGarr. The key issue was how much discretionary power the Major League Agreement gave the commissioner. The words themselves were open to various interpretations, so the case hinged on the testimony of club owners—who hired the commissioner—concerning the "legislative intent" of certain clauses and how much power they *intended* a commissioner to have.

The owners were in a strange position. They knew they didn't intend the commissioner to have unlimited powers—they had made sure, since Landis, that he wouldn't have. But if Finley prevailed, *they* would have to pay; the only money in league and commissioner coffers was theirs. The players had already slipped out of their control. The public relations need for a "strong" commissioner was clear. If they undercut his authority now, what other chaos might follow?

They testified that they believed he did have the authority to act as he did. The judge ruled for Kuhn, saying Finley had not proved Kuhn's action was "capricious."

In this backhanded manner, the commissionership regained, at least theoretically, powers it hadn't had since Landis, with little danger that Kuhn would exercise them against the establishment's will. But strengthening the public impression that the commissioner did have such power would haunt the owners. Kuhn's successors believed it, and ultimately the owners were forced to get rid of commissioners altogether.

As a way of getting rid of Finley, it worked. He started looking for a buyer immediately, tried twice to sell the team to Denver, and finally, in 1980, found someone willing to keep it in Oakland as a matter of civic loyalty. Walter Haas Jr., of San Francisco's Levi-Strauss jeans family, took it over for $12.7 million.

The rest of the owners, having reelected Kuhn and granted him, by testimony, powers he didn't have by contract, never trusted him wholeheartedly again.

PROGRESS

The eight-year period that started with the Designated Hitter, worked its way into free agency, and ended with a truly serious strike threat included plenty of isolated historic developments as well.

Homer Number 714—Hank Aaron had finished 1973 with 713 homers, one less than Babe Ruth's total. With maximum buildup amid unprecedented television exposure, he hit number 714 his first time at bat in the April 4 opener at Cincinnati, and number 715 in Atlanta April 8 off Al Downing of the Dodgers. He finished the year with 733 and moved on to Milwaukee, where he could take advantage of the designated-hitter rule for two more years, and ended his 23-year career with 755.

First Black Manager—On October 3, 1974, the Cleveland Indians hired Frank Robinson as their manager, the first black to be given that responsibility, 27 years after the arrival of Jackie Robinson. He had already joined the Indians as a player, on September 12, in a waiver deal with the California Angels. He had schooled himself for such an opportunity by managing the five previous winters in Puerto Rico's Winter League, where many major leaguers and top minor prospects played. He would also serve as a designated hitter.

Robinson's Indians finished fourth, just as they had the year before under Ken Aspromonte. They were fourth again in 1976, inching above .500, and Robinson was fired less than halfway through 1977, when the club went on to finish fifth (and sixth or seventh for the next eight years). He finished that year as a coach with the Angels, spent the next three in the Baltimore organization as a coach under Earl Weaver (with a brief managing turn at Rochester), and took over the San Francisco Giants in 1981. By then he was accepted not as a pioneer or a symbol, but as just another manager—and a very good one at that.

The Bronx Zoo—Steinbrenner took command of the Yankees at the beginning of 1973, with the Burke-MacPhail-Houk triumvirate still in charge. He dumped Burke within weeks, putting his Cleveland partner, Gabe Paul, in charge. By the end of the season Houk was determined to leave, no matter what, and MacPhail was being tabbed as successor to retiring league president Cronin. (Houk was promptly hired by Detroit.)

Dick Williams quit the Athletics during the World Series, with private negotiations to take the Yankee job already in progress. Since his A's had just beaten the Mets in the World Series, he was all the more desirable in Yankee eyes. But Finley insisted on getting something in return and his demands were too great; so after Cronin (in his last ruling) upheld Finley's rights to Williams, Paul hired Bill Virdon, who had been dropped in midseason by the Pirates.

So Virdon managed the Yankees in 1974, as they played at Shea Stadium, and nearly brought them in first for the first time since 1964. They lost out to Baltimore only on the final weekend, by two games. Paul knew how to put together good teams and was doing it; he had acquired Catfish Hunter among others.

On September 2, 1975, Texas fired Billy Martin, who had been hired by Short as successor to Ted Williams before Short sold the team to local interests. Within a week, Paul fired Virdon and hired Martin, not only because Martin was so highly regarded but because the next season would open back in the new Yankee Stadium, where Martin's ties to past Yankee greatness could be exploited for much-needed nostalgia promotion.

Now Steinbrenner's suspension was over, and he became the prototype and national symbol of the abusive, meddling, harassing boss—worse than Finley. The Yankees won the 1976 pennant but got swept in the the World Series by the Reds. Steinbrenner signed free-agent Reggie Jackson, upping the ante for everyone as he had with Hunter. Martin and Jackson fought each other from the start, but the Yankees won the 1977 World Series with Jackson as the big star.

By 1978, even Paul couldn't deal with Steinbrenner, and he had taken an opportunity to buy into and run the Cleveland club. Al Rosen was the new general manager. In August, Martin exploded, saying Jackson and Steinbrenner deserved each other ("one's a born liar, the other's convicted"), and quit before he could be fired. Rosen brought in his old teammate Bob Lemon to manage, and the team won another World Series.

Now Steinbrenner hit his stride. Early in 1979, he fired Lemon and brought back Martin. Then he fired Martin and made Dick Howser manager for 1980. Howser won 103 games but lost the playoff to Kansas City, so he fired Howser. Gene Michael managed the first half of 1981, then was replaced by Lemon, who wound up in the World Series again but lost it. In the next nine seasons, Steinbrenner made 11 more managerial changes—including Martin, twice—but never finished at first again.

Records—Maris had surpassed Ruth's 60 homers, Wills had surpassed Cobb's 96 stolen bases, and now Aaron had surpassed Ruth's 714. The unbreakable records were being broken, and it didn't stop there. The 1974 season that began with Aaron's homer ended with Lou Brock stealing 114 bases, surpassing Wills's "impossible" 104. In the sixth and last game of the 1977 World Series, Jackson hit three home runs, giving him five for a single Series and wiping out another Ruth record. In 1978, Pete Rose electrified the season by making the best run ever at DiMaggio's 56-game hitting streak, reaching 44, which left him with a share of the National League record set by Willie Keeler in 1897, the mark DiMaggio had chased so dramatically.

In 1974, Bob Gibson became the first pitcher since Walter Johnson to reach 3,000 strikeouts. But in 1973, Nolan Ryan had broken Koufax's single-season strikeout record with 383, one more than Koufax had accumulated in 10 fewer innings, and, unlike Koufax, Ryan did it in a designated-hitter league in which he had no opposing pitchers to strike out. In 1973–75, Ryan produced four no-hitters, tying Koufax for that distinction, and he wasn't yet 30 years old.

Finances—As playing records fell, so did money and attendance records. A table sums it up:

	1970	1973	1977	1980	% Increase 1970–80
Attendance per club (in millions)	1.20	1.25	1.76	1.93	60
Gross revenue (in millions)	$137	$200	$260	$333	144
National TV package (in millions)	$9.6	$18	$23.25	$41.575	355

(Continued)

	1970	1973	1977	1980	% Increase 1970–80
Top sale price of club (in millions)	$10.8	$10	$17	$21.1	100
Average salary	$29,300	$36,500	$87,300	$140,000	377
To pension fund (in millions)	$5.45	$6.15	$8.5	$15.5	282
Residue after player and pension costs (in millions)	$114	$174	$202	$216	90

Did these figures substantiate the predictions of disaster that accompanied every change in the 1970s? Much was made of the fact that the salary *percentage* increase rose faster than other percentages; but the *dollar* picture was different, with twice as many dollars available *after* players were paid as before. The contrast between these openly available numbers and the continued owner demand for reversing course accounted for the bitterness that would erupt with greater force than ever in the 1980s.

SEASONS 1973–80

1973

The Oakland A's, amid well-publicized internal squabbling, retained their world championship in 1973, beating back the Mets, who had survived the closest of all pennant races.

NL—On August 17, the Mets were in last place in NL East, but only 7½ games out. Into the final week, five teams (except the Phillies) were only 2½ games apart. The Mets prevailed with an 82–79 record, with the last game unnecessary, the closest to .500 any first-place team ever finished. Meanwhile the Reds, winning 99 games, held off the Dodgers by 3½ games in NL West—and proceeded to lose the League Championship Series (LCS) to the Mets, held to eight runs in the five games by Met pitching. Thus Yogi Berra, the "joke manager" in the eyes of the former Yankee brass, became only the second manager to reach the World Series from both leagues (Joe McCarthy was the first), and he had done it in only three years of managing. Pete Rose was batting champion, Willie Stargell hit 44 homers, and Brock stole 70 bases.

AL—The A's and Orioles won their divisions decisively, and the A's won the fifth play-off game at home on a shutout by Hunter. Reggie Jackson was MVP; Hunter, Holtzman, and Blue won 21, 21, and 20 as starters, and Fingers presided over a deep bull pen.

The DH enabled some outstanding hitters with serious leg problems to extend their careers: Oliva in Minnesota, Frank Robinson with the Angels, Orlando Cepeda in Boston, Tommy Davis in Baltimore. All the designated hitters hit .257, the whole league .259; but the batting title went to Rod Carew of the Twins, who hit .350 in a league in which no one else hit higher than .306. The 12 winners of 20 games represented nine different clubs.

All-Star Game—In Kansas City's new stadium, the National won 7–1, giving the league a 25–18 lead in the series.

WS—After Oakland won the opener 2–1, the second game lasted 4 hours and 13 minutes before the Mets nailed down a 10–7 decision with a four-run 12th inning. As the teams moved on to New York, Finley, incensed at two errors made by A's second baseman Mike Andrews, tried to have him plead injury so that he could be replaced. Commissioner Kuhn wouldn't allow that and fined Finley for trying, while Oakland players were also outraged on behalf of their teammate. Meanwhile, word of Williams's intention to quit leaked out. Amid the distractions, the A's won the third game in 11 innings 3–2 but were stifled in the next two games by Jon Matlock (6–1 five-hitter) and Jerry Koosman (2–0 three-hitter).

Back in Oakland, Berra started Seaver on short rest, trying for a clincher, but lost 3–1 to Hunter and Fingers. In the seventh game, two-run homers by Campaneris and Jackson in the third inning off Matlack powered a 5–2 A's victory.

1974

Under Al Dark, brought out of limbo by Finley, the Oakland Athletics became the only club to win a third straight championship since the last Yankee dynasty ended in 1964.

NL—Bolstered by an influx of farm-system talent, including a whole infield (Steve Garvey, Davey Lopes, Bill Russell, Ron Cey), the Dodgers finished four games ahead of the Reds while the Pirates, again under their favorite leader, Danny Murtaugh, held off a late drive by St. Louis. A 20–8 August by the Pirates withstood an 18–9 September by the Cardinals. Then the Dodgers won the first two games at Pittsburgh, behind Don Sutton and Messersmith. The Pirates won in Los Angeles, but Sutton closed it out 12–1.

Messersmith's 20–6 with a 2.59 earned run average was the most impressive pitching line, while Ralph Garr of Atlanta led all hitters with .353, a 32-point margin over the runner-up, Pittsburgh's Al Oliver.

AL—The A's did as well for Dark as for Williams, winning their division by five games, and squared off again with the Orioles, who were pressed surprisingly hard by Virdon's Yankees, after making up an earlier eight-game deficit to the Red Sox. The Orioles won 25 of their last 31 games. But after winning the first play-off game in Oakland, they lost three straight, 5–0, 1–0, and 2–1 to Holtzman, Blue, and Hunter.

Carew won his third straight batting title, his fourth in six years, with .364, while Hunter's 25–12 was matched by Ferguson Jenkins, now with the Texas Rangers.

All-Star Game—The Nationals won again, 7–2 at Pittsburgh, making it 11 victories in the last 12.

WS—The A's were rolling. Even with the Hunter contract story circulating and agents giving pregame interviews on the field, they polished off the Dodgers in five games in businesslike fashion. At Los Angeles, they split 3–2 decisions, the Dodgers winning the second. At Oakland, Holtzman-Fingers won 3–2, Hunter-Fingers 5–2, and Blue-Fingers 3–2. The final tie-breaking run was a homer by Joe Rudi off Mike Marshall, the Dodger relief specialist appearing in his 113th game that season: 106 in the regular season, two in the play-offs, and all five World Series games.

1975

Cincinnati's Big Red Machine peaked in 1975, winning 108 games and a dramatic seven-game World Series from the Red Sox.

NL—Cincinnati's margin over the Dodgers in NL West was 20 games. Pittsburgh won comfortably enough by 6½ over Philadelphia. But the play-off was no contest, an 8–3, 6–1, 5–3 sweep. Chicago's Bill Madlock won the batting title at .354, and Philadelphia's Mike Schmidt was home-run leader for the second straight year, with 38. Lopes stole 77 bases, and hardly anyone noticed.

AL—After winning their fifth straight division title, the A's fell to the Red Sox, who didn't let the Orioles catch them this time. Oakland finished seven games ahead of Kansas City, but it no longer had Hunter, so it had to start the playoffs in Fenway Park with two left-handers, Holtzman and Blue. Both lost, 7–1 and 6–3, and in the next game at Oakland, the Red Sox ended it, 5–3. Boston's new generation of heroes included outfielders Fred Lynn and Jim Rice, first baseman George Scott and catcher Carlton Fisk, all outstanding hitters.

Carew put up another batting title at .359. Hunter won 23 games for the third-place Yankees, and Jim Palmer 23 for Baltimore.

All-Star Game—The National League's 6–3 victory at Milwaukee was upstaged by the unsuccessful palace revolt against Commissioner Kuhn and speculation about Messersmith actually playing out his option.

WS—This was the last World Series played

with no DH at all, and it mattered. The Red Sox split at home, winning 6–0, losing 3–2. Cincinnati won in 10 innings at home 6–5, lost 5–4, and won 6–2, returning to Boston in need of one victory.

Rain put off the sixth game for three days, and it was played at night on October 21 in a New England autumn, starting at 8:32 P.M. Trailing 6–3, the Red Sox tied it in the eighth on Bernie Carbo's three-run homer. The game went into extra innings, past midnight, and it was 12:34 A.M. when a huge television audience saw Fisk frantically trying to wave his long drive fair as he pranced toward first. It hit the left-field foul pole, and Boston had a 7–6 victory and a shot at the seventh game.

It was 3–3 in that game's eighth inning when the DH rule proved significant. Boston's pitcher was James Willoughby, its most effective reliever against the Reds. In three games, he had allowed just three hits in 6⅓ innings and had entered this game with two out in the seventh. He had ended the rally, which tied the game, and set down three Reds in order in the eighth. But it was his turn to hit with two out in the bottom of the eighth. Manager Darrell Johnson sent up a pinch-hitter, which under World Series rules took Willoughby out of the game. (With the DH rule the Red Sox used all year, that would not have been necessary.) The next pitcher, Jim Burton, walked two men and yielded a game-winning single to Joe Morgan. That wasn't "the reason" Boston lost, and Johnson's decision could be second-guessed. But the situation underlined the subtlety and importance of every playing rule, and the self-canceling feature of the DH as an aid to overall offense. It let better pitchers, as well as better hitters, stay in action.

1976

The Reds won again in 1976, with a World Series sweep, and took their place among baseball history's most dominant teams.

NL—A 10-game margin over the Dodgers, being managed for the 23d and last time by Walter Alston, and 102 victories marked the last season this Red team would win. Johnny Bench, Pete Rose, Tony Perez, Joe Morgan, George Foster, Dave Concepcion, Ken Griffey (not yet having to be identified as "senior"), Cesar Geronimo—they

were truly an all-star lineup. None of their pitchers, over the years, had been as consistently outstanding, but there were a lot of them, smartly used by Captain Hook Sparky Anderson. Free agency was coming and they would scatter, although not right away.

In NL East, the Phillies supplanted the Pirates, who had won that division title five times in six years. Danny Ozark, a Dodger-system graduate, was now their manager, and the Phils finished nine games ahead of Pittsburgh. Schmidt led the league in homers for the third straight year, with 38, but the biggest lift came from Steve Carlton, the left-hander, who was 20–7. Madlock was batting champion and Morgan the MVP, both for the second straight year.

The play-off looked like a straight-set tennis score: Cincinnati 6–3, 6–2, 7–6. In the third game, at Cincinnati, the Phils took a 6–4 lead into the bottom of the ninth, only to have Foster and Bench wipe it out with successive homers. A single, two walks, and a single by Griffey ended it.

AL—The Yankees, under Martin, ran away with AL East by 10½ games over Baltimore. Kansas City, under Whitey Herzog, dethroned the A's, now managed by Chuck Tanner. For 12 days after Commissioner Kuhn blocked the sale of the A's Blue, Fingers, and Rudi, Finley wouldn't allow them to play, until his other players threatened to strike. The A's won seven of the 12, so their 2½ game margin behind the Royals at the end can't be ascribed to that period; the psychological effect was harder to judge.

The play-off was terrific. Hunter opened with a 4–1 five-hitter at Kansas City, but the Royals won 7–3 the next day. It was 5–3 Yankees and 7–4 Royals at Yankee Stadium, setting up the deciding fifth game. A three-run homer by George Brett tied the score at 6–6 in the top of the eighth. When Chris Chambliss opened the Yankee ninth with a game-winning homer, fans staged a near riot that prevented him from circling the bases and did $100,000 worth of damage to the refurbished Stadium.

Brett emerged as batting champion with .333, one point ahead of teammate Hal McRae, two ahead of Carew. The earned run leader was a colorful rookie in Detroit named Mark Fidrych, nicknamed "the Bird," who talked to the baseball before throwing it. The television camera loved that habit even more than his fans did, who accounted for half the total Tiger attendance on the days Fidrych started. He was 19–9 with a 2.34 ERA.

All-Star Game—Played at Philadelphia as part of the nation's bicentennial celebration, this one was a 7–1 rout that gave the Nationals 13 victories in the last 14. They started with two runs off Fidrych by the first three batters.

WS—The Reds were playing, as people were starting to say, at a higher level. They won 5–1 and 4–3 at home, 6–2 and 7–2 in frigid Yankee Stadium. Bench hit .533 with two homers, Foster .429, the whole team .313. The DH, used by both teams, was a nonissue.

1977

A livelier ball in 1977 produced unusual hitting statistics. The explanation given was that the manufacturing contract had been shifted from Spalding to Rawlings; that Spalding, over the years, had become less than meticulous about meeting specifications; that Rawlings, anxious to make a good impression, went strictly by the book; and that a livelier ball resulted. Whatever the reason, the fact was undeniable. Foster hit 52 home runs, the first player to reach 50 since Mays in 1965, and knocked in 149 runs, the most since Tommy Davis in 1962. Aggregate batting averages were up 10 points from the preceding year, runs were up 13 percent, homers up 50 percent, shutouts down 33 percent—statistical shifts of a size historically associated with changes in the ball or pitching rules, and not otherwise.

The Yankees won another pennant and faced the Dodgers in a World Series for the first time since 1963.

NL—Tommy Lasorda, who had been coaching at third and had managed most current Dodgers in the minors, succeeded Alston and won right away. From a 17–3 start, the Dodgers never looked back and beat Cincinnati by 10 games. Garvey hit 33 homers, Reggie Smith 32, Cey and Dusty Baker 30 each—the first time any team had four 30-homer men the same year. Their leading pitcher was Tommy John, a 34-year-old left-hander coming back from radically new reconstructive surgery of his arm (which has since become standard). He was 20–7 with a 2.78 ERA.

The Phillies won NL East again, five games ahead of the Pirates (now managed by Tanner), but once again failed in the playoff. They won the first game in Los Angeles 7–5 but lost the next three 7–1, 6–5, and 4–1. The last game was played in a steady, cold rain, but postponing it might have messed up the World Series television schedule.

Pittsburgh's Dave Parker was batting champion at .338.

AL—The Yankees and Royals had a play-off rematch, with the same result. The Yankees, with Jackson added, fought off the Red Sox and Orioles, who tied for second 2½ games back (with Detroit next, 26 games out). The Royals were a comfortable eight games ahead of Texas as the denuded A's, with almost everyone leaving to take advantage of free agency, fell to last, even behind expansion Seattle. Tenace and Fingers were in San Diego, Bando in Milwaukee, Rudi in Anaheim.

In New York, the Yankees lost 7–2, won 6–2. In Kansas City, the Royals won 6–2 and had the upper hand with two more home games. But the Yankees won them, 6–4 and 5–3, the last with a three-run ninth. Reliever Lyle was the winner in both games.

Carew, flirting with .400, won another American League batting title at .388. That gave him six, tying Ted Williams and second only to Ty Cobb's 12. Rice led in homers with 39, and it was now seven years since any American Leaguer had hit 40—DH or no DH.

All-Star Game—Yankee Stadium was the site, and the Nationals kept winning. They made their point with a four-run first inning and coasted in, 7–5.

WS—The Yankee-Dodger rematch after so many years—New York and Los Angeles—was television's ratings dream. And it lived up to expectations. The first game, at Yankee Stadium, went 12 innings before the Yankees won 4–3. In the second, Burt Hooten held the Yankees to five hits while four home runs gave him a 6–1 victory. In Dodger Stadium, the Yankees defeated John 5–3 and won 4–2 behind Ron Guidry, as Reggie Jackson doubled to start a three-run second and homered in the sixth. But the Dodgers stayed alive in a 10–4 game, in which Jackson hit another homer, so the teams went back to New York.

Hooten started and was given two runs in the

first. But he walked Jackson to start the second and Chambliss hit a two-run homer. The Dodgers made it 3–2, but when Thurman Munson opened the fourth with a single, Jackson followed with a two-run homer. In the fifth, facing Elias Sosa, Reggie hit another two-run homer with two out for a 7–3 lead that seemed convincingly decisive. But Jackson came up again, leading off the eighth against knuckleballer Charley Hough, with every-one wondering if he could do it again. He could. He hit the first pitch into the center-field bleach-ers. The final score was 8–4.

1978

The Yankees and Dodgers made it to the World Series again in 1978, with the same result: the Yankees in six.

NL—There were rematches all around. The Dodgers fought off Cincinnati by 2½ games, the Phils beat Pittsburgh by only 1½. The Dodgers won in Philadelphia 9–5 and 4–0 (a four-hitter by John), got hammered at home 9–4, then won in the 10th inning 4–3 after a mishandled line drive with two out.

Parker repeated as batting champion (.334) and Foster as power leader (40 homers, 120 runs batted in).

AL—AL East had its most dramatic race so far. By July 19, the Yankees were 14 games behind the Red Sox. A week later, Martin was gone and Lemon, fired only three weeks before by the White Sox, took over the Yankees. September 7–10 in Fenway Park, they beat the Red Sox 15–3, 13–2, 7–0, and 7–4, tying for first place. They fell three back after that, but on September 30 they had a one-game lead with one to play. A loss to Cleveland while the Red Sox won created the one-game play-off needed to settle the first division-race tie.

Guidry, his record 24–3, faced Mike Torrez, his Yankee teammate the year before, in Fenway. Boston led 2–0 in the seventh when Bucky Dent hit a three-run homer into the screen, and the Yankees went on to win 5–4. Memories of 1948 and 1949 devastated Boston.

The Royals, AL West winners by five games over California and Texas, were waiting in Kansas City. The Yankees won 7–1, the Royals 10–4, and it was back to Yankee Stadium. Brett hit three solo

homers in the third game, but a two-run shot by Munson gave the Yankees a 5–4 victory, and Guidry, with Goose Gossage's help, won the fourth game 2–1. Signed as a free agent, Gossage replaced and surpassed Sparky Lyle.

Guidry's 25–3 (the division play-off game counts in regular-season statistics) and 1.74 ERA, with nine shutouts and 248 strikeouts in 274 in-nings allowing only 187 hits, constituted one of the finest pitching records ever compiled. Carew won his seventh batting title (.333), and Rice hit 46 homers with 139 runs batted in. The desig-nated hitters, however, hit .253 in a league whose overall average was .261.

All-Star Game—Scene: San Diego. Date: July 11. Score: National League 7, American League 3. What else is new?

WS—Yankee-Dodger hype was bursting all bonds. The Dodgers won the opener, with John, 11–5, although Reggie Jackson hit another homer, giving him six in this last four Series games and breaking a record held by Lou Gehrig. Trailing 4–3 in the ninth inning of the second game, the Yankees got two on with one out, and Lasorda brought in a right-handed rookie, Bob Welch, to face Munson. Munson lined out to right field, and Welch stayed in to face Jackson. In a minidrama replayed on television for the next two decades, Jackson fouled off three two-strike pitches—then fanned on a 3–2 count. The Dodgers were two games up.

But the Yankees swept the New York games 5–1, 4–3 in 10 innings (marked by defensive hero-ics at third base by Graig Nettles), and 12–2. In Los Angeles, the Hunter-Gossage combination ended it, 7–2. Steinbrenner was on top of the baseball world. Lemon was thrilled. And Stein-brenner would wait eight whole months before firing Lemon and bringing back Martin.

1979

Pittsburgh and Baltimore returned to the top of their divisions in 1979 and produced one of those rare World Series in which the winner—in this case Pittsburgh—comes back from a 3–1 deficit.

NL—Even though the Big Red Machine was starting to break up—Rose had gone to Philadel-phia and Perez to Montreal, and manager An-derson had been fired—Cincinnati won NL West in a tight race with Houston. Virdon, who had become manager of the Astros shortly after the Yankees dumped him for Martin in 1975, had put together a team with outstanding pitching to take advantage of the Astrodome's hostility to hitting. The new Cincinnati manager was John McNamara, who had contributed to the early development of the Champion A's. The Astros had a 10-game lead at one point but faded badly in the last six weeks. The final margin, in doubt to the last weekend, was a game and a half.

The Pirates returned to the top, pushed by Montreal, not Philadelphia. Expos manager Dick Williams, when blocked from the Yankee job in 1974, had surfaced as manager of the Angels by midseason, and left in midseason of 1976. He took over the Expos in 1977. Now they were 10 years old and had never been higher than fourth in a six-team division. But they started 29–15, hung on, and weren't formally eliminated until shut out by the Phillies' Carlton on the last day. Their 23–11 September was a strong finish, but not enough to catch the Pirates, who were 61–30 the last three months.

Keith Hernandez of the Cardinals (.344) led in hitting, with Rose (.331) second. Dave Kingman, with the Cubs, hit 48 homers, denying that department's title to Schmidt, whose 45 was more than he ever had before. Houston's James Rodney Richard was the year's most fearsome pitcher, 313 strikeouts in 292 innings, 18–13, league leader with a 2.71 ERA.

The Pirates swept the play-off in three games, but the first two were close, 5–2 in 11 innings and 3–2 in 10, both in Cincinnati. Back home in Pittsburgh it was 7–1.

AL—Baltimore returned to the top, 102 victories providing an eight-game margin over Milwaukee, as the Yankees fell to fourth. The California Angels, managed since early the previous season by Jim Fregosi and strengthened by the free-agent acquisition of Carew, won their first AL West championship by three games over Kansas City, five over Texas, and six over Minnesota. The Oakland Athletics hit bottom while Finley appeared to have them sold to Marvin Davis of Denver: 108 defeats, home attendance of 306,000—one-eighth of what the Yankees, Red Sox, Angels, Reds, Dodgers, and Phillies did, less than an 11th of the record 3.3 million the Dodgers had drawn the year before. Then the sale fell through.

Fred Lynn was batting champion with .333; Milwaukee's Gorman Thomas hit 45 home runs; Kansas City's Willie Wilson stole 83 bases. Tommy John, now a Yankee, was 21–9, but Guidry, leading the league again with a 2.78 ERA, was 18–8 for a two-year total of 33–11.

Baltimore won the play-off opener at home on a three-run two-out pinch homer by John Lowenstein in the 10th inning, 6–3. The Orioles took a 9–1 lead in three innings in the second game and barely held on, 9–8. They had a 3–2 lead in the ninth at Anaheim and lost 4–3, but an 8–0 six-hitter by Scott McGregor wrapped it up.

All-Star Game—This was the 50th game of the series (how time flies!), in the Seattle Kingdome before 59,000 spectators, and unusually entertaining. The Nationals won, of course, but only by scoring single runs in the top of the eighth and ninth innings for a 7–6 decision.

WS—Willie Stargell, at 38, was the spiritual and physical leader of the Pirates, who adopted a song called "We Are Family" as their theme. They lost the opener at Baltimore 5–4 and won the second 3–2, but then lost twice at home, 8–4 and 9–6, before sending the Series back to Baltimore with a 7–1 decision. There a 4–0 victory evened the Series. In the sixth inning of the seventh game, Stargell's two-run homer, his third of the Series, gave Pittsburgh a 2–1 lead in what became a 4–1 victory. Stargell had hit .400 and was named Series MVP, but the real story was that seven different Pittsburgh pitchers held the Orioles to two runs in the last three games.

1980

The Phillies, who had not reached a World Series since 1950 and before that only in 1915, emerged as champions of the baseball world in 1980 after their series of play-off failures in recent years.

NL—One race went to the wire, and the other beyond it. In NL West, the Dodgers swept a final three-game series from Houston in Los Angeles, each by one run, to create a first-place tie, forcing the Astros to stay over for a play-off game—which Houston then won 7–1. In NL East, September began with Pittsburgh, Philadelphia, and Montreal virtually tied, but Pittsburgh dropped out (losing 13 of 15) and the Expos came to the final Friday tied with the Phillies and facing them in

Montreal. That night Schmidt drove in both runs in a 2–1 Philadelphia victory, and on Saturday his 48th home run in the 11th inning won the game 6–4 and clinched first place.

The Astros, flying east across the country—the "wrong" way in terms of time zones—and losing three hours, lost the play-off opener to the Phillies' Carlton 3–1. But they won the next day with a four-run 10th, 7–4, and in Houston won 1–0 in 11 innings. The Phillies then won two more 10-inning games 5–3 and 8–7, closing out the most closely contested League Championship Series ever played.

Schmidt's 48 homers and 121 runs batted in made him a unanimous MVP choice, only the second in the history of the award. (Orlando Cepeda was unanimous in 1967.) Bill Buckner, now with the Cubs, won the batting title at .324, nosing out Hernandez by three points. Montreal's Ron LeFlore stole 97 bases—one more than what was once Cobb's once unmatchable magic number—without attracting much attention. Carlton's 24–9 with a 2.34 ERA, surpassed only by Don Sutton's 2.21, was the best pitching record.

AL—Even though Baltimore won 100 games, the Yankees, now under Dick Howser, won 103 and stayed ahead of the Orioles all season. Kansas City, having discarded Herzog for Jim Frey, for many years Earl Weaver's right-hand man in Baltimore, ran away with the AL West title by 14 games. Martin, surfacing as manager of Oakland (his hometown), brought the recently hopeless A's in second, creating excitement that helped convince the Haas family to buy the team from Finley.

Herzog had been dropped because he lost the play-off to the Yankees three times. Now Frey produced a three-game sweep, 7–2, 3–2, 4–2—so Steinbrenner promptly fired Howser. Managers were getting less and less tolerance from owners.

Brett, flirting with .400 even more seriously than Carew had three years before, wound up at .390, the highest batting average since the .406 of Ted Williams in 1941. Reggie Jackson and Milwaukee's Ben Ogilvie shared the home-run lead at 41, while Rickey Henderson, allowed to run at will by Martin in Oakland, stole 100 bases, finally erasing Cobb's American League record. The A's also had a rookie pitcher, Mike Norris, who went 22–9, while Steve Stone was 25–7 for Baltimore, Tommy John 22–9 for the Yankees, and Scott McGregor 20–8 for the Orioles.

All-Star Game—At Dodger Stadium, the Nationals won 4–2, making it nine straight, 16 of the last 17, and 32–18 in the series.

WS—The Phils won at home 7–6 and 6–4, and so did the Royals, 4–3 in 10 innings and 5–3. But the fifth game was different. The Royals took a 3–2 lead into the ninth, when Schmidt's single triggered a two-run rally and a 4–3 Philadelphia victory. Back home, the Phillies wrapped it up 4–1, with Tug McGraw, the relief hero for the 1973 Mets, nailing it down for Carlton in the last two innings. McGraw had appeared in nine of the 11 postseason games—saving four, winning one, losing two—after putting up 20 saves, five victories, and a 1.47 earned run average in 57 appearances during the regular season.

AFTERMATH

In the long run, the most lasting effect of the revolutionary changes of the 1970s was atmospheric pollution.

The right emotional atmosphere is the essence of sports promotion. Unless you can create it, you have nothing to sell. The followers—only some of whom buy tickets, but all of whom contribute to economic viability by demonstrating their interest—must be and must remain persuaded that the activity is worth investing their emotions in. Results matter only to those who care. Nonparticipants care only if they choose to, only if the net result of caring is somehow satisfying.

Followers must be able to believe the games are on the level. That's basic.

But they must also be able to "identify." The club name and city affiliation are "ours." The batter or pitcher can be "me" in vicarious association. Realistically, I understand that his skills are beyond my capacity, but in my imagination I can share his triumph, defeat, and accomplishment once I attach my interest to his identity. In that sense, the player becomes my "hero," especially when I am a child or adolescent first forming my attachment to the game in its major league context.

The degree to which I worship or take in stride my sports hero varies. But the feeling itself can come only as a result of active promotion, through publicity and comment and word of mouth. No child shouts, "I'm Willie Mays" without indoctrination absorbed unconsciously.

And that feeling, one way or another, must be positive. That is, I have to *like* the image that's presented to me. If I dislike or even am indifferent to the person as perceived, I will no longer choose to invest my emotions.

For 100 years, baseball—and all other sports, by imitation—had assiduously concentrated on glorifying the star athlete. The discovery that this could be done had launched professional sports in the first place. Later, communications technology brought the process to its 20th-century height. As many must lose as can win, but the "heroes" must appear "heroic."

So the tactics adopted by management in the 1970s, when confronted by serious labor opposition for the first time, contained a suicidal element.

Management started bad-mouthing its own product, the players.

Regardless of the merits, either way, of specific disputes, it was management that had overwhelming control of forming public attitudes. It had the publicity machinery and the ear of opinion makers. It had control of what happened, to the point of forcing or avoiding a stoppage of play. It determined how its product—the players—was perceived.

In trying to sway public opinion to its side of the labor disputes, management began painting the players as greedy, ungrateful, overpaid, insufficiently productive, and innocently misled individuals who, by their selfishness, were depriving *you,* the fan, of the orderly tradition you were used to enjoying.

But if that's how players were, how could they be my heroes?

It was a fundamental miscalculation, because it could have no effect on actual negotiations. Once established as a bargaining unit, the union couldn't be swayed much by public opinion: it would accept or not accept any deal only on the basis of its own analysis, not what outsiders thought. If anything, bad publicity only made players circle the wagons. Persuading fans that owners were "right" didn't persuade the players.

The miscalculation went further. By fomenting public hostility to the players, the owners were creating irreparable divisions. The brunt of insult and antagonism from the public was borne not only by players themselves, but by their wives in the supermarket and their children in school, day by day, as civilian noncombatants in war. Such wounds don't heal easily, if at all.

Management was not being insincere. The vast majority of experienced baseball executives, as well as owners, honestly felt that the union was "going too far," "getting too much," destroying "baseball as we know it"; that there was "no place in baseball for unions"; that the way things had always been was the only way they could be.

Why wouldn't they feel this way? They were the ones who had grown up and advanced within the system. Those who had other visions had always dropped out, from the 1880s on. Just as high-ranking colonial officials throughout the world believed passionately in the empires they represented, baseball officials of the 1970s believed in the baseball world they had inherited.

But two conditions were dramatically different.

First, by the 1970s, the character and capability of news media had changed. Everything was open to scrutiny and to immediate publicity to a degree never before possible.

Second, the money being generated went off the scale.

Traditionally, player salaries had been a private matter. Buzzie Bavasi, in the 1960s, could tell eight different Dodgers that each was the second-highest-paid player on the club and get away with it. The pay of big stars was publicized, but no one knew what was hype and what was real. Even so, a $100,000 player making five to ten times as much as an ordinary fan was not inconceivably rich, just lucky. One could envy but still relate to such earning power.

With formal labor bargaining, and especially with arbitration, documented salaries became a matter of public record. And when this became a matter of millions, a fan could not relate. A player getting $2 million was taking down 50 to 100 times what his rooters were making, and that's a different story. When he makes out, the fan feels betrayed and becomes vituperative.

This combination, of actual increase and management harping on "excessive" demands, created a rift between fan and player that kept growing ever wider.

Then came free agency, which had a damaging psychological aspect.

In terms of justice, economic and otherwise, some degree of free agency was clearly right in a proudly free-market society loudly proclaiming its disdain for the restrictions of the socialist societies it opposed in the cold war. And simply in terms of a fair share of a profitable industry, what the players were attaining by 1980 was certainly justified.

But under the reserve system, the only way players changed teams was by trade, and the assumption (by the fan) in every trade is that it will help our team win. It may not, but that's the intent. Every move was accepted as being in the common interest of the club and the fan: we want our team to win.

Under free agency, the player moved because it was better for *him,* with no return to the team he left. That team's fans resented the "desertion" as much as management did.

This was unrealistic. First of all, statistics would show that from 1961, the beginning of expansion, through 1993, the movement of players from one major league team to another was exactly the same, a range of 4 to 6 players per team per year. Since trades still existed, the free-agent movement was something less than that. Nor was it a matter of second-line players moving and stars staying put. A check of all the Hall of Famers who played before 1960 would show that more than a third of them had been traded during career peaks in the "old days."

The difference was, the *team* decided who would be traded; the free agent moved for his personal purposes, not for the benefit of "my" team.

Of course, "my" team could benefit by acquiring a star free agent, and fans never complained when that happened. As statistics would prove, free agency greatly increased "competitive balance" by spreading championships around. But here again, perception was more important than reality. The "loss" of a free agent caused lasting bitterness; the acquisition of one was taken for granted, but with an undertone of hostility that

said, "Okay, show me you're worth all that money."

These negative by-products of free agency were inescapable. What the owners did, however, was magnify them by harping on player "disloyalty" and their own (untrue) financial hardship. Among other things, they convinced fans that higher ticket prices were needed to pay higher salaries, which was untrue both theoretically and practically. In theory, tickets to anything are priced automatically at whatever the market will bear: if too high, they don't sell, and if too low, they are resold to speculators. In practice, the new revenue was coming from television and marketing, not from ticket prices, which in fact lagged behind inflation and other sports' prices.

The antagonism bred in the 1970s between players and owners and, by owner propaganda, between fans and players would never be repaired and would eventually get out of hand. Never again would players receive undiluted adulation the way Christy Mathewson, Walter Johnson, Babe Ruth, Lou Gehrig, Joe DiMaggio, Mickey Mantle, Stan Musial, Willie Mays, and so many others did in their day. The current star would always be lionized for achievement as a star, but with a residue of skepticism, and could turned against viciously when productivity fell or off-field trouble arose.

The enormous influx of money from expansion and television caused three other side effects that took root in the 1970s and kept growing. The money attracted player agents, who became a third force exacerbating all labor-management difficulties; it inflated the value of franchises, attracting owners oriented toward financial speculation more than toward baseball operations; and, through immediate prosperity encouraged neglect of fan-creation in children, which had always been a conscious primary goal of past ownerships.

And the last-minute agreement in 1980, of course, had only postponed the explosion that was bound to come.

CHAPTER 23

Strike Two

The compensation plan study group consisted of Frank Cashen and Harry Dalton, general managers of the Mets and Milwaukee, and players Bob Boone (Philadelphia, a Stanford product and son of a former major leaguer, Ray Boone) and Sal Bando (Milwaukee, survivor of Finley's A's, Arizona State). Four more knowledgeable, intelligent, experienced, down-to-earth, practical-minded baseball people would be hard to find.

They got absolutely nowhere and knew full well they had no power to go anywhere. The deadline for management to announce its adoption of its own compensation plan was February 19, 1981. These meetings were a charade. In late January, they announced they had no agreement.

Ray Grebey for management and Marvin Miller for the union took up the negotiations. After two weeks, nothing had changed. On February 19, Grebey announced implementation of management's compensation plan.

The players had until March 1 to respond by announcing a strike date, which could be no later than June 1. On February 25, the player reps met in Tampa and announced Friday, May 29, as the day to strike. They took pains to say this was a procedural step, hoping it would hasten a negotiated settlement before then.

The compensation plan was:

1. A player who ranked in the top half of his league's players at that position in plate appearances or innings pitched would be considered a "ranking player."

2. If a ranking player was named by at least eight teams in what was now called the "re-entry draft," he would be subject to compensation to his old team from his new team.

3. If the player ranked in the top 33 percent (in plate appearances or innings pitched), the club that signed him could protect 15 of the 40 players on its roster, and the old club could pick one of the others; if he ranked between 34 and 50 percent, the new club could protect 18.

This plan would effectively discourage any club from signing any "ranking" free agent, since it would have to give up a player of significant value, and it would certainly decrease the dollar value of any free agent it did sign. The 50 percent provision would cover all worthwhile players, and clubs would see to it that eight teams would list every available name whether they wanted the player or not.

No one could believe the players would simply accept such a proposal. But as a starting point for negotiation, it was also management's finishing point: that's what Grebey was supposed to be an expert on.

The season began with much fan excitement. Pete Rose was going to break Stan Musial's National League record of 3,630 hits, Carl Yastrzemski was going to get his 3,000th hit, and Gaylord Perry was headed for his 300th pitching victory. The Dodgers unveiled a Mexican left-hander, Fernando Valenzuela, who had a spectacular start and turned on the Los Angeles Latino community as never before. Tim Raines, a rookie outfielder at Montreal, started out as if he would break every base-stealing record there was. And good pennant races were shaping up.

But more and more news coverage shifted to hotel meeting rooms.

Mediator Ken Moffett started a series of meetings with Grebey and Miller April 20. They got nowhere.

On May 5, a flap developed over the news that Dalton had been fined $50,000 for violating a "gag rule" that Grebey had persuaded the owners to adopt. (It could go as high as $500,000.) Dalton had told Tom Boswell, the *Washington Post*'s baseball writer, "I hope management is really looking for a compromise and not a victory. I'm not sure that's the case. The Players Association is genuinely looking for a compromise if we'll just give them something they can accept without losing too much face."

This was, as later events would prove, the absolute truth—but not what the owners wanted the public to think. The fine was never paid and eventually rescinded. But that was the crux of the situation: owners, feeling they had "lost" every previous confrontation, desperately wanted a "victory" in the eyes of the public (and the business community) as well as at the table. And they were sure that striking players, after missing a paycheck, would cave in.

On May 7, the players filed an unfair-labor-practice charge with the National Labor Relations Board. Management was not bargaining in good faith, it said, and should turn over financial data to support its claim that free-agent sweepstakes were bankrupting any club at all. The law required opening books if any claim of "can't af-ford it" were made.

Grebey immediately denied that the clubs had ever claimed financial hardship as the result of free agency.

Then what was the fight about? Players wondered. Just beating the union to show who's boss? Hmmm.

On May 27, just 36 hours before strike deadline, the NLRB announced it would seek a temporary restraining order to postpone the strike and put off the compen-sation issue to 1982. Miller and Grebey agreed to hold off until the request could be heard, so the May 29 strike date was off.

In the hearing, on June 3 in Rochester, Commissioner Kuhn, Grebey, and Miller were the only witnesses. Kuhn spoke of financial difficulties created by free agency. Grebey followed by declaring, "At no time in my dealings with owners have any ex-pressed the inability to pay salaries" and emphasized that Kuhn was not speaking for the owners.

The commissioner, not speaking for the owners?

Distrust deepened.

On June 6, while waiting for Judge Henry Werker's decision, Miller offered a compromise. Let all clubs protect a certain number of players and put the rest into a pool. The club losing a free agent could select one from this pool, so the club sign-ing him wouldn't necessarily be the one giving compensation, but the affected club would get something.

Grebey said no.

On June 10, Judge Werker issued his decision: no restraining order. Evidence didn't support a finding that compensation presented "an economic issue."

Miller immediately activated the strike resolution. Starting Friday, June 12, no games would be played until a settlement was reached and approved by the players.

Moffett called a last-ditch bargaining session that lasted all day on June 11. It ended at 12:30 A.M. with Miller announcing that the strike was on, and that he would stay out of future bargaining sessions because the owners considered him an imped-iment to settlement. Negotiations would be conducted by elected player reps and at-torneys Donald Fehr and Peter Rose (no relation to the player). By now, Moss had left the Players Association to become a player agent. (It was he who got Nolan Ryan his $1 million contract in Houston.) Fehr, from Kansas City, had first dealt with the Players Association when the Messersmith case was appealed there, and had suc-ceeded Moss as its counsel.

Miller, of course, would still be chief strategist and advisor, but he said his phys-ical absence might lower the temperature.

The playing season stopped after June 11.

At that point, four tight pennant races were in progress. The Yankees led Balti-more by two games, Milwaukee by three, Detroit by 3½; Oakland led Texas by 1½ and

Chicago by 2½; Los Angeles led Cincinnati by half a game; and Philadelphia led St. Louis by a game and a half.

Pete Rose had tied Musial's record. Raines had 50 stolen bases in 55 games, a pace that would break Brock's 118. Valenzuela pitched five shutouts in his first eight decisions, helping the Dodgers average 46,238 a game at home. Attendance was 1.1 million ahead of the previous year's at the same point, on track to shatter the record of 43.5 million set in 1979.

That weekend, 66 games were canceled, and players on the 13 teams caught on the road had to pay their own way home. But it was widely believed the strike would not last long. The 1972 strike had produced agreement within a few days.

However, this time the clubs had that strike-insurance policy, and the Players Association had its war chest. Players had already collected five of their 12 semimonthly paychecks (including June 15) at the high level salaries had reached. Immediate economic pressure was not a factor. The strike insurance came to $50 million; the players had no insurance, but several million dollars from endorsements to distribute as needed.

Negotiations continued sporadically. Boone, Steve Rogers, and Mark Belanger were the chief player reps; Grebey, league presidents Feeney and MacPhail, and lawyers Barry Rona, Lou Hoynes, and James Garner were the management team. Miller rejoined the talks on July 1, his absence having had no effect.

On July 4, after a five-hour session, the talks broke off.

"There's a philosophical difference," Moffett explained, "pool arrangement versus direct compensation."

The difference was, and would remain for years, revealing. The pool arrangement addressed the problem the clubs claimed they had—restoring competitive balance. The direct compensation went to the heart of what they really wanted—discouraging free agency.

There was an even deeper psychological difference.

Businessmen—owners, lawyers, administrators—tend to look upon money not collected as money lost. ("I lost a million dollars that year," said Walter O'Malley in all seriousness when the Dodgers drew 2.5 million, "because we should have drawn three million.") Baseball people believed that players not getting paid would not stay out and would abandon theoretical principles for a resumption of income. (Agents think the same way—money not collected is money lost—but figure they'll get it back in the next contract or with the next client.)

Players, on the other hand, are not a random sample of the population. They have been selected and trained for one quality above all others, their competitiveness. Once the labor-management issue was drawn as a conflict, they were precisely the sort of people who resist giving in and "losing." That's what made them big leaguers. They also had lifelong training and experience in teamwork, in sticking together, in learning that you win and lose only as a team. No less selfish than anyone else, they had more *practice* in hanging together in a fight than the owners had. As for money, they (like most of us) thought of getting it or not getting it without dwelling on "potential" revenue. And they also knew that at any moment, one injury can end a career, so they had to make what they could while they could.

So the two groups arrived at opposite conclusions. The owners thought, The more they make, the more they're losing by staying out. The players thought, Now that I've been paid so much, I can afford to stay out for a while if that's what it takes to avoid getting less later.

Older baseball people in particular were caught in the mindset of the paternalism of the past. They remembered when players didn't earn enough to avoid off-season jobs and were always asking for (and getting) advances on next year's pay. They didn't recognize how much easier it is to stay on strike when you have money in the bank than when you need the next paycheck to pay for food; they thought the already high pay scale would make players more malleable, not less.

These psychological gaps would persist and widen through the next 15 years.

The summer dragged on. Players were restless but determined. Fans were frustrated. Local economies suffered, wailed city officials, from the layoff of stadium workers, absence of ancillary business activity, ball-park rent, and so forth. The All-Star Game, scheduled for July 14 in Cleveland, was called off.

After three postponements, the NLRB began its hearing on the unfair-labor-practice charge—the one asking for economic data, about which Judge Welker had refused to block a strike—on July 6 in New York. It would last four days.

On July 9, the 26 club owners, who had not met since the strike began, got together in New York. There were dissidents among them, but the group gave Grebey a vote of confidence. How could they have done anything else?

On July 15, Raymond J. Donovan, the secretary of labor, entered the discussions alongside Moffett, expressing President Reagan's concern. Donovan urged them to move the talks to Washington. They did. July 20–25 a series of meetings took place under a news blackout, with owners or top club officials actually taking part for the first time: Ed Fitzgerald of Milwaukee, Joe Burke of Kansas City, young Clark Griffith of Minnesota, Bob Howsam of Cincinnati, John McHale of Montreal, Dan Galbreath of Pittsburgh.

They got nowhere. The strike itself had raised new issues. Players got credit for days on the major league roster during a season, days that determined their seniority rights toward free agency, pension entitlements, trade-veto rights, salary arbitration, and so forth. Would the strike days count? If not, many would lose a whole year out of a short career. What about the pension fund, whose money came from the All-Star Game? What about the umpires who weren't working and weren't on strike: should they get paid? If the strike were settled, how would play resume?

Amid deepening pessimism, Miller called a meeting of his player reps for July 27 in Chicago, and the owners called a meeting in New York on July 29.

On Thursday, July 30, Moffett called for a meeting of the negotiators. But Miller and Fehr, Grebey and MacPhail, were already meeting secretly at the National League office. They broke at 5 P.M. for consultation with their sides, reconvened at 6:30 P.M., called in the full negotiating committees at midnight, had an agreement in principle by 1:30 A.M., and locked up the details by 5 A.M.

At 6 A.M., Friday, July 31, they went over to Moffett's hotel (the Doral Inn, a few blocks away) to announce that the strike was over.

Play would resume Sunday, August 10, with the All-Star Game in Cleveland, giving players a week to gather and prepare. League play would resume August 11.

On the key question of compensation, the clubs accepted what Miller had suggested on June 6, nearly eight weeks before: a player pool instead of direct compensation. On other matters (we'll list them in a moment), the players made significant gains, in some ways more than they had been asking for when the 1979 negotiations began.

Why? How did the great philosophical difference on compensation suddenly evaporate? Why did the apparently honest gloom of July 25 in Washington turn into serious bargaining within a few days?

Simple. The strike-insurance money ran out.

No longer subsidized by the insurance, the owners didn't want to stay shut any longer. Remember, money not taken in is money lost. While it was being taken in from insurance, it was replacing the gate (at least to some degree). When that stopped, it was time to open up.

So they agreed to terms they could have had without a strike a year earlier.

This was the deal.

Compensation:

1. Type A is a player who ranks in the top 20 percent of those at his position over the last two years, according to a complex and fairly inclusive statistical formula. Type B is in the 21–30 percent range.

2. A team losing a Type A player gets one from the compensation pool plus an amateur draft choice. For a Type B player, it gets two amateur draft choices. For all others, one amateur draft choice if four or more clubs claim the right to deal with the free agent.

3. To fill the compensation pool, clubs can protect 26 of their 40-man-roster players, putting all the others into the pool, with exceptions.

4. The exceptions are: a maximum of five clubs can elect to be excluded from the procedure for three years, neither signing a Type A free agent nor contributing to the pool; of the remaining teams, one that signed a Type A could protect only 24, not 26.

5. No team can lose more than one player from the pool each year. Once it loses a player, its other players are removed from the pool for two years or until it signs a Type A free agent itself.

6. A team losing a player also gets $150,000 from a fund to be set up by all the clubs.

7. There is no limit on the number of teams taking part in the reentry draft.

8. In 1981, only seven Type A players will require a professional player as compensation if 21 to 23 teams take part in the pool process, or eight if 24 or more teams participate. In 1982 and 1983, that number will be nine players if all 26 teams participate. Additional Type A free agents, if there are that many, will be compensated for by additional amateur draft choices.

Does any of that make sense?

Is any of it necessary?

Isn't it simply rhetorical face-saving for management's two-year demand that it get "compensation"? It certainly wouldn't inhibit in any significant way the appeal of or competition for quality free agents.

Was it worth a 50-day strike?

Look at the other provisions:

1. All the strike days will count as credited service time; no deductions.

2. The CBA is extended a year, through 1984, with a $40,000 minimum salary that year.

3. The pension benefit plan will get $2.14 million from the All-Star Game, whether it's played or not.

4. Incentive bonus clauses based on 1981 statistics will be prorated as to performance and bonus if the original figures are not reached.

5. The owners can decide how they want the season to finish, but if they choose a split season—separate standings for the second half, with an extra round of play-offs—60 percent of the gate receipts of the divisional play-offs would be shared equally by the eight teams involved, and each player would get an extra five days' pay.

The owners did decide on a split season. As it happened, about one-third of the schedule had been played before the strike, and about one-third had been wiped out by it. What was left on the schedule would be picked up as is, with no attempt to adjust for inequality in home-road games or opponents faced. The standings of June 12 would be considered the complete first half. The second half would start with each team's record 0–0. In the divisional play-off, the winners of each half would meet in a three-of-five play-off. What if the same team won both halves? It would face the team with the next best record for both halves. But that, Chicago manager Tony La Russa (a lawyer) pointed out, might make it advantageous to lose on purpose to the first-half winner, to make sure it won again. Embarrassed, Commissioner Kuhn subsequently changed it so that a winner of both halves would play its second-half runner-up, but with an extra home game.

Not all the owners liked the settlement, and with reason. Hard-liners who wanted a full test of player resolve hadn't gotten one. Others thought a tougher compensation rule than the one adopted was attainable.

The two comments cited in the *Official Baseball Guide* of 1982 proved to be dead wrong.

Said Doug DeCinces, one of the more involved player reps: "I very seriously doubt that the owners will try to challenge the players again."

Said Hank Peters, Baltimore's general manager: "If we ever let a strike happen again, kiss baseball goodbye."

One misread owner mentality, the other underestimated baseball's resilience.

THE REST OF THE 1981 SEASON

The Yankees, A's, Phillies, and Dodgers were guaranteed first-round play-off berths as first-half winners. None of them won the second half. The A's came closest, losing by one game to Kansas City, which played four more games than Oakland and had to win a makeup game in Cleveland on October 5, the day after the regular schedule ended, to clinch first place. Milwaukee won the second half of AL East by a game and a half over Boston and Detroit. In the National League, Montreal beat out St. Louis by half a game and Houston finished a game and a half ahead of Cincinnati.

So Cincinnati, whose 66–42 record was the best in either league, and St. Louis, whose 59–43 was the best in NL East, got shut out of the play-offs altogether.

What about the public reaction? Were fans turned off? Embittered? Indifferent?

The All-Star Game was played as intended that Sunday in Cleveland, and 72,000 turned out. The Nationals won 5–4 on Schmidt's two-run homer in the eighth.

The next night, in Philadelphia, Rose had his first chance to break Musial's record, and 60,000 showed up to watch him try. He did it with an eighth-inning single off Bruce Sutter of the Cardinals, for number 3,631.

There were plenty of small crowds too, of course, but when the season ended the average was 1.05 million per club for two-thirds the normal number of openings, a per-game average not remarkably different from the 1980s.

The two rounds of pre–World Series didn't sell out every single game but were robust enough. The 26 games averaged 45,000. The six-game World Series was a flat-out sellout, 56,000 a game.

So much for public vindictiveness.

Statistics, naturally, were hard to translate into "normal" terms, since simple projections are notoriously invalid. But exceptional events stood on their own feet. On

May 15, with strike talk heating up, Len Barker had pitched a 3–0 perfect game on a cold and rainy night in Cleveland against Toronto. Five days before that, in Montreal, Charlie Lea had pitched an "ordinary" no-hitter against San Francisco. Appropriately enough, Lea was born in France, where his father had been on military duty. French Canada liked that.

Then, on September 26 in Houston, Nolan Ryan pitched a no-hitter against the Dodgers—the fifth of his career, something no other pitcher had ever done. It left him with a league-leading 1.69 earned run average, half a run better than anyone else's.

And batting titles were legitimate. Bill Madlock, now in Pittsburgh, led the National League with .341, and Boston's Carney Lansford led the American with .336. Raines wound up with 71 stolen bases in 88 games.

The play-offs were eventful. Three of the four in the first set went the full five games, and so did the National League's Championship Series.

The Yankees won their first two games in Milwaukee 5–3 and 3–0, then lost two at home 5–3 and 2–1, provoking a blast at everyone from Steinbrenner. (The manager was Bob Lemon again, Gene Michael having been demoted at the start of September.) A 7–4 victory that included a home run by Reggie Jackson restored order.

Billy Martin's A's, featuring four young starters on a staff that produced 60 complete games in 109 starts, stifled Kansas City in three straight, 4–0, 2–1, 4–1. What Martin lacked was a bull pen.

The Dodgers had their hands full with Houston, losing 3–1 and 1–0 in 11 innings at the Astrodome. But they won the next three at home, 6–1, 2–1, 4–0.

And Montreal, after its two near misses, finally won the NL East championship. After a pair of 3–1 victories at home, the Expos went to Philadelphia and lost two, 6–2 and 6–5 in 10 innings. But Steve Rogers pitched a 3–0 six-hitter to beat Carlton in the deciding game. The Expos had fired Dick Williams early in September and were being managed by Jim Fanning, a former catcher who stepped down from the front office, where he was in effect the general manager under McHale.

In the regular LCS, the Yankees polished off Oakland in three straight, 3–1, 13–3, 4–0, while the Dodgers couldn't get past Montreal until the final inning. After they won the opener at home 5–1, they lost 3–0 and, in Montreal, 4–1, before winning 7–1. The fifth game was 1–1 after eight innings (Valenzuela against Ray Burris, who had shut out the Dodgers in Los Angeles). Burris went out for a pinch-hitter in the eighth, so in came Rogers, who had beaten the Dodgers in the third game and Philadelphia twice. With two out, Rick Monday hit a home run, and when Welch got the third out for Valenzuela in the bottom of the ninth, the Dodgers had another pennant.

So the year that had been so terribly disrupted wound up with another Yankee-Dodger World Series.

When the Yankees won the first two games at Yankee Stadium 5–3 and 3–0 with Guidry and John starting and Gossage saving both, it seemed like the same old story. But it wasn't.

Valenzuela, allowing nine hits and seven walks, battled through to a 5–4 victory at Dodger Stadium. In a wild one, the Dodgers broke a 6–6 tie against John, being used in relief, and evened the Series with an 8–7 decision. Then, in a pitching duel between Guidry and Jerry Reuss, Pedro Guerrero and Steve Yeager hit successive homers in the seventh inning for a 2–1 victory and the lead, three games to two.

Back in Yankee Stadium, the Dodgers pounded John and five other pitchers 9–2, ending the season.

By then the strike was all but forgotten.

Someone had said it back in the 19th century, and now they were saying it again: "Baseball certainly must be a great game to be able to survive the people who run it."

CHAPTER 24

Rolling in Money

What followed the strike, perceived as such a disaster, was incredible prosperity. Over the next decade, labor-management relations remained terrible and got worse. The threat of strike or lockout seemed to become endemic. But the dollars rained down from heaven (where the broadcast airwaves were) in ever increasing quantities. Those who believe that money can't buy happiness need cite no better example than the baseball community.

Much of the story is told most clearly in tables. We start with demographics. In the first table, the populations are for standard market areas, not city boundaries.

	Population (in millions)		
	1960	1992	Year of New Ball Park
New York	14.7	18.1	1964, 1976
Los Angeles	6.7	14.5	1962, 1966
Chicago	6.7	8.1	1991
San Francisco	2.7	6.3	1960, 1968
Philadelphia	4.3	5.9	1971
Detroit	3.7	4.7	— (1912)
Boston	2.6	4.2	— (1912)
Washington	2.0	3.9	1962
Cleveland	1.8	2.8	1994

(Continued)

	Population (in millions)		
	1960	**1992**	**Year of New Ball Park**
St. Louis	2.0	2.4	1966
Baltimore	1.7	2.4	1992
Pittsburgh	2.4	2.2	1970
Cincinnati	1.1	1.7	1970
Milwaukee	1.2	1.6	— (1953)
Kansas City	1.0	1.6	1973
Houston	—	3.7	1965 (dome)
Atlanta	—	2.8	1966
Montreal	—	2.9	1977 (roof)
San Diego	—	2.5	1969
Seattle	—	2.6	1977 (dome)
Toronto	—	3.1	1989 (roof)
Dallas–Ft. Worth	—	3.9	1972, 1994
Minneapolis	—	2.5	1982 (dome)
Total in Majors	54.6	104.4	13 since 1970

Note: Two-team cities are Chicago, Los Angeles since 1961, New York since 1962, San Francisco since 1968. Washington has no team after 1972 but can be considered part of a single Baltimore-Washington area of 6.3 million.

As of 1992, cities with teams in all four major sports (baseball, football, basketball, hockey), with the total number of teams in parenthesis, are: New York (9), Los Angeles (7), Chicago (5), San Francisco (5), Philadelphia (4), Detroit (4), Boston (4), Baltimore-Washington (4), and Minneapolis (4).

In the table, note how little growth took place from 1960 to 1990 in Cleveland, St. Louis, Cincinnati, Milwaukee and Kansas City, and that Pittsburgh actually had a decrease.

Note that the top five markets (New York, Los Angeles, Chicago, San Francisco–Oakland, and Philadelphia) have more total population than the total of the remaining seventeen.

We can see how "resource equality" is breaking down, why revenue sharing has become a bigger issue than before, and how the proportion of haves to have-nots is changing.

Now look at franchise values.

Year	Club Sold	Announced Price (in millions)
1976	San Francisco	$8
	Atlanta	$12
	Seattle	$6.5 (expansion entry fee)

(Continued)

Year	Club Sold	Announced Price (in millions)
1976	Toronto	$7 (expansion entry fee)
1977	Boston	$17
	Cleveland	$12
1979	Houston	$19
	Baltimore	$12.3
	Cleveland	$12
1980	N.Y. Mets	$21.1
	Oakland	$12.7
1981	Philadelphia	$30
	Chi. Cubs	$20.5
	Chi. White Sox	$20
	Seattle	$13.1
1983	Kansas City	$23
	Pittsburgh	$21
	Detroit	$43
1984	Minnesota	$47
	Cincinnati	$22
1985	Pittsburgh	$22
1986	N.Y. Mets	$80.5
	Philadelphia	$51
	Texas	$50
	Cleveland	$35
1989	Baltimore	$70
	Seattle	$77
	Texas	$79
1990	San Diego	$75
	Kansas City	$68
1991	Montreal	$100
1992	Seattle	$125
	San Francisco	$100
	Houston	$90
	Detroit	$85
1993	Baltimore	$173
	Florida	$95 (expansion entry fee)
	Colorado	$95 (expansion entry fee)

These are the announced dollar figures and cannot be taken too seriously. They don't indicate how much down, how much is paid out how and when, whether they may be inflated for business purposes (and it's certainly good for all the others to have announced prices as high as possible).

But the *pattern* is unmistakable and undisputed. In 20 years, ball clubs increased 10 times in sales value—the same 20 years during which a crescendo of wolf crying and predictions of financial disaster never let up.

Between 1940 and 1960, a 21-year period, 11 of the 16 clubs changed hands a total of 16 times. From 1961 to 1971—half as many years—five of the 16 were sold seven times, and eight new teams were added. But from 1972 through 1986—15 years—19 of the 24 teams were sold 28 times with only two added, one of which was resold. In the five years 1989–93, there were 11 more sales involving 10 teams.

The 1961–62 entry fee was about $2 million. In 1968 it was between $6 million and $10 million. In 1976, for Seattle and Toronto, it was about $7 million. But in 1993, for Colorado and Florida, it was $95 million, and the next jump, in 1995, would be to $130 million. Inflation? Sure. But not *that* much.

The business of *selling* a team was taking precedence over *running* a team. The emphasis had shifted from "making a product"—creating a winning team in a good competitive context—to "maximizing asset value."

And the balance of interests within the group had changed significantly. Refer back to the population table. In 1960, before expansion, the "larger" markets (more than 2.5 million population) had eight teams and the "smaller" also eight. In 1992, with 26 teams, the "larger" (more than 5 million) were also nine—but the "small" were 17. That change in the arithmetic of voting is enough to explain, aside from other factors, what happened in the 1990s.

However, as any homeowner knows, selling a property after years of possession can look better on paper than it is in reality. What about actual income, year by year, and expenditure? We had a snapshot of it in the 1970s. Here's what happened after the 1981 strike:

Year	Attendance	National TV	Gross Revenue*	Player Costs	Residue
1982	44.6	$53.4	$422	$185	$237
1984	44.7	$163	$600		
1986	47.5	$181	$746	$317	$429
1988	53.0	$197	$958	$335	$623
1990	54.8	$365	$1,336	$494	$842
1991	56.8	$351	$1,537	$695	$842
1992	55.9	$377	$1,668	$950	$718
1993**	70.3	$377	$1,880	$1,052	$828

*All figures in millions
**28 teams instead of 26

Again, the exact numbers in the table may be unreliable, as they are taken from pubic statements, but the *scale* and *proportion* are accurate. Patterns and trends were unmistakable. Money was pouring into the industry, more and faster than anyone had ever fantasized, even a decade before.

Well, if the potential market size had doubled, if the value of clubs went up 10 times, the total revenue four to five times, and the salaries of 700 players averaged $1 million a year instead of $15,000 a year for the 400 players in the 16-club days, what was so terribly wrong?

Ah, but what about the famous competitive balance? Everybody knew that the "rich" clubs would gobble up all the best players and never lose, while the "poor" clubs would be consigned to perpetual tailending. That was just common sense, wasn't it? It might not happen overnight, but it would sooner or later. And if only a few clubs monopolize the championships year after year, how can the others stay in business?

Well, one could look at the record.

From 1901 through 1968, when each league had only a single standing, there were 68 pennant races in each.

In the American League, one team—the Yankees—won 29 of them. Philadelphia won nine, Boston, and Detroit eight each. That's 54 of the 68, or 79 percent, by four of the eight teams. (Never mind the two late starters in 1961.) The other four won 14 times among them.

In the National League, the Giants won 16, the Dodgers 14, the Cards 12, and the Cubs 10—52 by the top four clubs, or 75 percent.

Evidently there wasn't such wonderful competitive balance in those days.

Starting in 1969, we had two races in each league. Instead of "pennant winners," who now had to win a short play-off, let's count "first-place finishers," who represent season-long success.

We'll take to 12-year segments that make comparison easy. From 1969 through 1980, the reserve system is still in place until 1977, and because free agency is limited to six-year veterans, it takes a few seasons for any introduction of free agency to take effect. We'll call 1969–80 a continuation of the reserve system.

In AL East, Baltimore and New York won 10 of the 12. In AL West, Oakland and Kansas City won 9. In NL East, Pittsburgh and Philadelphia won 10. In NL West, Cincinnati and Los Angeles won 9. So just eight of the 24 teams took 79 percent of the division titles.

That's suggestive. Before divisions, the top half of the teams finished first 77 percent of the time. Afterwards, the top one-third did it 79 percent. The similarity is striking. In 80 years of the reserve system, success was not very evenly distributed. Half the teams had three-quarters of the success.

And where were the habitually successful teams? Chicago, New York–San Francisco, Brooklyn–Los Angeles, and St. Louis in the Nation; New York, Philadelphia, Detroit, and Boston in the American.

Do you detect a "big market" tilt?

Well, let's say that by 1981 the free-agent system has had time to take effect. What happened over the next 12 years?

All 12 National League teams finished first at least once.

Of the 14 American League teams, 11 finished first at least once. (And two of the other three, Cleveland and Seattle, would finish first in 1995, the first year of three divisions. Only Texas remained shut out.)

The top two teams in three of the four divisions accounted for seven titles, or 58 percent; in NL East, Pittsburgh and St. Louis accounted for six.

So division dominance by two teams, in adjacent 12-year periods that differ only by the advent of free agency, dropped from 79 percent to 56 percent.

Is that more "competitive balance," or less?

There's one other way to measure dominance. Count the number of repeaters, the times a previous year's winner wins again.

From 1901 to 1968 it was 36 percent—one of every three races was won by the defending champion.

From 1969 to 1980, it was 36 percent.

From 1981 to 1992, it was 17 percent.

Why dwell on this?

Because the difference between what was really happening and what official baseball was telling the public was happening accounts for the great contradiction that characterizes the rest of the 1980s and leads to the disaster of the early 1990s. Reality was almost all positive—more money, better competitive distribution, a steady stream of spectacular and historic on-field achievements, more extensively seen, via television, than ever before. But *description* was increasingly negative. Players were greedy, disloyal, not trying their hardest, not "earning" their huge salaries. That message, disseminated as a labor-war tactic, was picked up by a significant portion of the public. It was also seized upon by competitors for the entertainment dollar, with their own publicity machines, whose self-interest in magnifying baseball's "decline" was manifest.

External developments aggravated the problem. Commercialized autograph and memento collecting created a vested interest in nostalgia, which can be stimulated by demeaning the present. The gum cards were an example. Earlier generations of kids who collected and traded them had prized those of current and new players; but the dollar value of collectibles now rested on glorifying the past. As player participation in card shows, for big money, became widespread, the "purity" of autograph collecting shifted from a moment of contact—a "brush with fame"—to a stock-market transaction, resented by the noncollecting fan. At the same time, if a player's signature and his willingness to give it had acquired substantial value, why wouldn't a player ration his free autographs? The club officials who criticized him weren't giving out free tickets, nor were indignant columnists turning in columns for free. The atmosphere became more polluted, and more energy poured into the cycle of mutual antagonism between performer and spectator.

Television, while supplying so much money, also had inherently antibaseball aspects. Improved technology made highlight shots a staple of news broadcasts and, when

ESPN came into being, all-day sports programs. But five-second highlights of football and basketball action are incomparably more exciting than any baseball action a camera can catch. The makers of commercials using sports figures, and producers of news shows and specials, naturally gravitated to the most exciting visuals. Football and basketball promoters began to exploit and service those tendencies by consciously building up the glamour of their stars. Baseball promoters, out of habit or ignorance, lagged behind in organizing their own campaigns—and not only failed to glamorize their top stars industry wide, but actually criticized them to combat their economic leverage.

In trying to win the public-relations battle in labor negotiations, management set in motion forces that undermined the larger public-relations purpose of glamorizing the product.

More and more baseball "news," therefore, dealt with off-field conflict at the expense of on-field description, even though there was more and more on-field activity that was worth—by traditional measures—a baseball fan's interest.

The poisoned atmosphere was filled with commissioner politics, drug problems and other personal misbehavior, labor conflict settling into guerrilla warfare between CBA battles, threats of teams moving, and generalized verbal sniping.

COMMISSIONER TURNOVER

The owners had backed Bowie Kuhn in the Finley lawsuit, but they hadn't liked what he had done or the position it left them in. He had followed up his veto of the sale of Oakland's players with an edict that $400,000 was the maximum allowable transaction in exchanging a player for cash—a baseless, capricious, and irrelevant standard. He had given as a rationale for preventing the "demolition" of the Athletics the need to maintain "competitive integrity," claiming that teams like the Yankees and Red Sox shouldn't be able to "buy" pennant-producing stars and "distort" a pennant race. This was fatuous on its face. Didn't depriving the acquiring teams of those players distort the race just as much? Even his supporters were embarrassed. And since when was it considered wrong to improve your team by buying a better player? Like Babe Ruth, for instance?

Before the 1977 season, Finley sold a pitcher, Paul Lindblad, to Texas for $400,000. Kuhn tried to block the sale but could find no grounds to do so, although he accused Finley of "cannibalizing" the A's. That's how the $400,000 became the frozen allowable price. That December, Finley sold Vida Blue to the Reds for $1.75 million—more than the Yankees had offered in 1976—and a minor league first baseman. Kuhn voided the deal. The hearing he held in January 1977, and the arrogant, ill-reasoned report he issued from it, wiped out whatever credibility he still had among the owners. In March 1978, Blue was sold to the Giants for six minor leaguers and $390,000 (officially; in fact, who knows?) when the Giants were talking of contributing $1 million to a $4 million plan to buy out the Oakland lease so that the A's could move to Denver, and leave San Francisco to the Giants. Kuhn saw nothing to investigate in that, and Blue won 18 games for the Giants while the Reds finished 2½ games behind the Dodgers in a presumably "undistorted" NL West race.

In 1979, Walter O'Malley died. Even in retirement, with his son Peter running the Dodgers, he had been Kuhn's chief protector as the most influential figure among the other owners. Whatever his opinion of Kuhn's particular actions and abilities, O'Malley grasped the importance of the *appearance* of strength in the commissioner's office, and Bowie was the one they had. O'Malley's support, even tacit support, carried a lot of weight with the other owners because they knew how well he understood the business, and they trusted his judgment.

It became clear that Kuhn's second term, due to run out in 1983, would be his last. In the political game of shifting factions among owners on various issues, he had lost out to virtually all.

The irony was, in his later years he became a much better commissioner. He negotiated three big increases in national television deals. He organized and expanded the previously neglected marketing and administrative structures of the commissioner's office. He learned to stay out of the line of fire in labor negotiations. His arrogance was muted as internal opposition to him solidified. He certainly knew the game's history and business practices, and his love for it was genuine. He had consolidated the league offices in New York, when MacPhail succeeded Cronin (whose American League office had been in Boston) and Feeney was persuaded to bring the National League headquarters back to New York from San Francisco. If he had acted as constructively in the 1970s as he started to in the 1980s, he might not have generated the opposition that finally dismissed him. In objective terms, things might have gone better in the rest of the 1980s if the owners had renewed his contract again, because they certainly didn't go well, or even as well, under his successors.

The last two talent searches for a commissioner had been fiascos. The one in 1965 produced Eckert and the one in 1968 led to deadlock and the eventual Kuhn compromise. This time the search went well. The proceedings were orderly; factionalism was at a minimum. So many clubs had changed hands since 1968 that there were fewer carryover frictions than there used to be. Of the 24 unanimous votes for Kuhn "pro tem" in February of 1969, only seven were in the same hands when it came time to vote for a successor in 1983.

In 1982, a move to extend Kuhn's contract for three years was rejected. Some were coming over to his side, but not enough. The "usual suspects" were subjects of rumors—MacPhail, McHale, other "baseball men," prominent politicians. But since no real agreement existed, when Kuhn announced he would no longer seek reelection, they promptly extended his tenure for another year.

Then they found someone who impressed them.

Peter Ueberroth was a hot commodity. He had made his fortune in the travel-agency business, acquired good political connections (primarily Republican), and had become head of the Los Angeles Olympic Organizing Committee (for the 1984 Games) in 1979. Amid much fanfare and praise, this was to be the most successful Olympics ever staged, producing a profit instead of a loss. The chief mechanism, exploited fully for the first time under Ueberroth's leadership, was private-company sponsorship as a fund-raising device; that is, selling the rights to put logos and product names on every conceivable bit of paraphernalia, on buildings, on events, and on procedures. This strategy not only raised a lot of money, it obscured the even larger amount of government subsidization (local, state, and national) that makes an Olympics possible at all. Ueberroth also negotiated a fat television contract.

The 47-year-old Ueberroth was smart and presented a favorable public image. He was authoritarian, not to say dictatorial, in mindset, manner, and method. He was highly efficient and well organized at whatever he undertook, adept at self-promotion, unconcerned with long-range consequences in dealing with a one-shot event like the Olympics. He didn't hesitate to ignore or antagonize anyone who didn't want to follow the rules he set down, nor did he worry about popularity as such. He could zero in effectively on his objective, whatever that was. Wherever he operated, he was going after power, not adulation.

And he had nowhere to go once the Olympics were over.

The owners elected him commissioner unanimously on March 3, 1984.

He would not take office until October 1, after the Olympics. He would get $300,000 a year, doubling the previous salary. His term would run through December 31, 1989. Kuhn, whose contract had actually expired August 13, 1983, would stay on through September 30, 1984, the last day of the regular schedule.

For the first time since Landis the owners were choosing someone they thought they needed, instead of simply filling an office they wished was unnecessary. That gave Ueberroth leverage similar to (although not as great as) what Landis had in 1921. So he could insist on certain provisions, with the advice and support of Kuhn, who knew the lay of the land so well.

1. He would be formally recognized as baseball's chief executive officer, with everyone, including league presidents, reporting directly to him, outranking any committee of owners, including the Executive Council.
2. For his reelection, the three-quarters-in-each-league rule would have to go. A simple majority of the 26, with a minimum of five from each league, would be enough.
3. The rules against taking a commissioner's decision to court would be strengthened.
4. The maximum fine he could impose on a club would be $250,000 instead of $5,000.

Those demands were accepted. He took the job.

He made no pretense of lifelong passion for baseball, nor did he claim any deep knowledge of its intricate procedures and traditional practices. Exactly the opposite. He was going to show it how to thrive in the modern world, using his business acumen and expertise.

In reality, both he and his employers were starting from a false premise. Exactly the qualities that made him successful in the Olympic operation were handicaps in the baseball world. In the Olympics, the authorities have total, absolute control—over athlete eligibility, site selection, credentials, security, and doling out privileges. Anyone who wants anything must submit to their rulings. Decisive, even ruthless, application of whatever has been decided is not only feasible but, for all practical purposes, irresistible. Those offended are unimportant, because in any particular venue, this is a once-in-a-lifetime event, and these people won't have to be dealt with again. And as an international festival, the Olympics have greater power than any single government, as proved by its ability to go ahead in 1980 in Moscow without the United States and in 1984 in Los Angeles without the Soviet Union.

Baseball life was nothing like that. It depended on long-lasting support in the same cities for decades, where people had memories, traditional privileges, various kinds of leverage over the ball club, and a sense that the game belonged to *them*. Each club was an independent fiefdom, outranking central authority. It was a product its purveyors were trying to sell to the public 365 days a year, every year, over and over again, dependent on their continuing affection. In the Olympic hierarchy, once given authority, Ueberroth could expect to have his directives carried out. In baseball, the commissioner's primary job was to listen to, cater to, and, it was hoped, guide constructively the 26 independent and all-powerful club owners. A commissioner's "edict" was only as good as their willingness to abide by it—and the public and media were totally *out* of his control.

Whatever Ueberroth's capabilities, the Olympic *techniques* could not work in baseball. When, on top of everything else, Ueberroth didn't bother to hide his contempt for the club owners as a group, his chances of leading them constructively evaporated quickly. He was not Landis, they were not the shell-shocked group of 1920, and this was not the world of half a century before when baseball was the only major league sport in the marketplace.

The mismatch got off to a flying start.

Back in 1979, the umpires had held out en masse for the first seven weeks of the season, seeking higher pay. All games were played as scheduled, with minor league and other substitute umpires taking their place. They returned that May 19 after agreement was reached on a new system. Instead of each umpire, like a player, having an individually negotiated contract (with the league president), a salary scale based on years of service was adopted. The agreement also provided for rotation of postseason assignments, to spread those payments around. In 1982, they had signed a new four-year agreement after a strike threat settled just before opening day, which provided more money but returned to a merit system for postseason and All-Star appointments. It also permitted a reopening of salary negotiation after two years.

The umpires' union representative, Richie Phillips, had been responsible for those gains. Now he wanted postseason pay to be tied to gate receipts, the way player prize shares were. The package he was seeking would cost an additional total of $340,000.

After three months, his negotiations with Feeney and Bobby Brown (in his first year as American League president) had broken down. On October 1—the day Ueberroth took office—Phillips announced the umpires wouldn't work play-off games, starting the next day, without an agreement.

The league presidents held fast. The umpires struck. The first round of the playoffs was played with substitute umpires.

On October 7, both sides agreed to accept binding arbitration from the commissioner. The umpires went back to work immediately.

On October 15, arbitrator Ueberroth issued his decision. They had asked for a $340,000 package. He gave them $480,000 for each of the next three years, plus back pay, plus rotation.

As an outsider, even with no particular interest in baseball, Ueberroth could see that it was ridiculous for a $600 million industry to get hung up over what amounted to $23,000 per club; that games can't be played without umpires; that a major league label on players needs a major league label on umpires; and that to let such an issue vie for public attention during the showcase week of the entire season was stupidity of the highest order. He quickly disposed of something that should never have reached such a point of confrontation. At the same time, it's hard to believe Phillips agreed to arbitration without some idea of how it would go.

But his ruling did more. It shocked the owners that he had gone "against" them on a money matter. It usurped the last remnant of a league president's power, control over umpires, putting Feeney and Brown firmly in their places—low in the pecking order—for all other issues as well.

Back in the days of Spalding and Ban Johnson, it was the league president who was "czar." It had taken Landis six years to finally break Johnson's remaining power, in the Cobb-Speaker gambling case. Ueberroth had established his commissionership's internal supremacy in two weeks.

And it was a type of success that, by repetition, would drive him out.

Ueberroth was shocked to learn that baseball finances, so jealously kept secret from the public and grudgingly given to Congress and the union bit by incomplete bit, were also being kept secret internally. Clubs were withholding financial data from each other, and hence from the central office. How in the world could there be coherent control of promotion or expense if the parts didn't know what the whole was doing, and vice versa? He got them to start sharing information.

When it came time for the next negotiation with the players, in 1985, the kind of figures the players had sought in 1981 were now available, presumably making bargaining easier. Of course, the figures submitted were way off and had to be corrected, so they exacerbated distrust instead of building it. But the owners were still concentrating on salary caps more than dollars. When the moment for another strike arrived, in August 1985, Ueberroth undercut the management position with a public statement that a salary cap wasn't important and "forced" both sides to a quick settlement very favorable to the players. We'll see the details later, but that strike lasted one day.

Ueberroth followed that move by "showing" the owners how to act "sensibly," holding down salaries by not going after free agents—entirely as individual clubs independently making rational business decisions, or course. They followed his advice, which constituted collusive action of a sort specifically forbidden in the collective-bargaining agreement—originally at the insistence of the owners—and subject to grievance. The eventual settlement, after he was gone, cost $280 million.

He negotiated a new television contract for still greater numbers—roughly 1.5 *billion* for the years 1990–93—but in a fragmented form among networks and cable. That deal would cause its own problem.

He ruled (as Kuhn had in his last couple of years) inconsistently in some ugly drug cases, which were coming to the surface in all sports in those years, then declared he had "solved" the drug problem.

He brought immense, and constructive, organization to baseball's marketing arm. He made a good impression in public. He avoided lawsuits. He ran business meetings like an autocrat, something owners weren't accustomed to but a climate their lawyers, who now outnumbered them in such sessions, probably welcomed.

And, by 1988, knowing he had no chance of being reelected, he announced that he would be leaving at the end of his contract because he had "straightened out baseball" and had better things to do (like run for the Senate, maybe?). At that point, June 1, the owners did offer him a five-year extension. He said he was flattered but refused it.

In plain language, each side was glad to be rid of the other, and the owners didn't have to look far for a successor. Back in 1983, when a replacement for Kuhn was first being sought, support had developed for A. Bartlett Giamatti, the president of Yale, no less. A tremendous and highly visible baseball fan, especially around the Red Sox, this professor of literature had much to recommend him, including a tough stand against striking workers at Yale. It was just talk then, but when Chub Feeney decided he'd retire at the end of the 1986 season, Giamatti astonished both academic and sports worlds by accepting the presidency of the National League. He was elected in June and took office in December.

A man of such intellectual breadth, wit, and formal distinction was not something baseball people were used to in their inner councils, nor did they expect, until they dealt with him, such a person to have the regular-guy charm and camaraderie Gia-matti projected. If the commissionership was open, here was the man to fill it. They elected him September 8, 1988, to a five-year term starting April 1, 1989. Ueberroth was perfectly happy to leave his post nine months early, since the job was filled and no one wanted a lame-duck regime. Had Giamatti's National League presidency been a holding pattern and indoctrination session for the commissionership from the start? Probably.

But Giamatti had one fatal flaw among his countless assets: he was a fan. He re-ally was. He had absorbed the romance, myths, written rules, and visible traditions of baseball. He knew absolutely nothing about the reality of the business, its never-spoken laws, its true business objectives (to avoid competition at all costs), or the true nature of athletes and their behavior.

He had a fundamentally distorted view of what a commissioner was, based on the dedicated fan's perceptions of what Landis was supposed to have been. He really did worship great players, he really did think ball parks were green cathedrals, and he had always believed that club owners were "sportsmen," although a few months as Na-tional League president had started to disabuse him of the last illusion. But that was the key word, "illusion." Selling sports is selling an illusion—that the outcome of the game matters to the fan—and the magician cannot afford to believe that the illusion he creates is real. Giamatti was a very bright man, a fast learner, able to grasp quickly complex and subtle situations—but, coming in, a prisoner of the fan viewpoint.

Exactly five months after he took office, on September 1 Giamatti died suddenly of a heart attack. He was only 51.

What kind of commissionership he might have had, and where he might have led baseball in the 1990s, can never be known. My own opinion, which reflects the con-ventional wisdom of the time and the general impression of insiders, is that his tenure might have been very good indeed. He would have shed, or at least tempered, his ro-manticism. He had persuasive powers, people skills, the ability to establish positive relationships, and certainly the intelligence to deal with the real difficulties. His pub-lic persona was ideal, his rhetoric would be on the fan's wavelength instead of mind-less like Eckert's, transparently self-serving like Kuhn's, or coldly distant like Ueber-roth's. He might have become the best of all the commissioners.

Actually, however, Giamatti's five short months were dominated by two actions that were the direct result of his fan's psychology. One was the prosecution of Pete Rose for gambling. The other was his choice of Fay Vincent as his deputy.

The Rose case will have its own discussion further on, but the essential point in this regard was Giamatti's overreaction to the word "gambling." Perhaps he saw Rose's activities as similar to, and as dangerous as, the Black Sox scandal. Every fan had been taught to believe that Landis and Babe Ruth had saved baseball from the scandal's wreckage (which wasn't the way it was, as we saw in Chapter 11). Almost cer-tainly Giamatti felt he had to prove his case (that Rose bet on baseball) by courtroom-quality evidence, which was very hard to do. He could have, within the bounds of baseball law, simply suspended Rose on the spot, for however long he wished, for "undesirable contacts" that Rose never denied (and couldn't). Instead, the drawn-out case that could not be proved overrode everything else during an eventful baseball season, and tarnished it.

The trouble with Vincent was that he, too, had a fan's viewpoint, without Giamatti's idealism or depth. Giamatti did what most leaders do, bring to his side a trusted friend to act as sounding board and to see to the details of his decisions. What he needed in that role was a most experienced baseball man. MacPhail and McHale had been supplied to Eckert, who was beyond help, and whatever even keel was kept then was due to them. Giamatti, given his sharp mind and ability, could have made excellent use of such support. Instead, he was merely reflecting and magnifying his own viewpoints with Vincent, who became his chief overseer of the Rose case and professed to be equally starry-eyed about "the game."

That was bad enough. But it created a strange situation when Giamatti died. Vincent had broad experience in the world of finance (to mixed reviews, it must be admitted, among those who dealt with him in the movie business, but with a record of financial success). Baseball insiders, in September 1989, knew him only as Giamatti's man, when respect for Giamatti was at its peak.

In the shock of the sudden loss of Giamatti, the owners were in no condition to face another commissioner search or to deal with an interregnum. A World Series was on the horizon; another player negotiation was coming up; there was lots of unfinished business. Promoting the deputy was the natural and easy thing to do. On September 2, they named him "acting commissioner." On September 13, they elected him unanimously, 26–0, to the rest of Giamatti's term, which would run to March 31, 1994.

So Francis T. (Fay) Vincent, also 51 years old, became the eighth commissioner, the fourth in five years. He was a graduate of Williams (a fellow alumnus of George Steinbrenner) and of Yale Law School. He had worked in corporate law in Washington and New York, served briefly with the Securities and Exchange Commission in 1978, then became CEO of Columbia Pictures. Coca-Cola bought Columbia in 1983, and Vincent stayed on as executive vice-president until July of 1988, so he was "free" when Giamatti brought him into baseball.

Trouble was, he believed *completely* in the commissioner myth that fans took for granted. He saw himself as the protector of the game's integrity (chasing down Pete Rose); as the custodian of public interest, responsible to "the fans" for baseball's purity; as arbiter of all internal conflicts among owners; as the architect of "what's best for the game" when questions of scheduling and organizing arose; as the embodiment of baseball law the way a king or queen of England is the embodiment of the Crown. In practice, he wanted to emulate Ueberroth. He would be CEO, club owners his department heads.

Vincent's first appearance on the stage was an unqualified success. A major earthquake interrupted the World Series between San Francisco and Oakland just as the third game was about to start in Candlestick Park. In the week that followed, he said and did all the right things; he didn't cancel the Series but kept baseball in perspective. He waited for order to be restored, for the structure to be pronounced safe, for the important civic functions to be taken care of, then calmly had play resumed and the championship completed. In countless television appearances, his identity as commissioner of baseball was firmly established.

In 1990, however, another agreement with the players was to be negotiated. The owners were taking another crack at testing the union and locked the players out of spring training. Owners remained convinced that when players missed a few of those ever greater paychecks, they would yield. It would be painful to "take a strike," but worth it in the long run.

But how could the "custodian of public interest" let a lockout happen? With fans and media clamoring for delivery of their entertainment, how could a man who said and *believed* "my prime obligation is to the fans" sit by? Wasn't that what the public blamed Kuhn for in 1981, and cheered Ueberroth for preventing in 1985?

By backdoor intervention, Vincent forced a settlement in time to start the season a week late, with adjustments to the schedule to get in the full 162 games. He did this by getting the newest indigestible element—a proposed salary cap—off the table, the way Ueberroth had done in 1985. The agreement that followed was once again more favorable to the players than they expected.

Vincent's success, in his own and the public's eyes, was his failure. Once again, an attempt to "really test" player resolve had been aborted. The salary cap, like the compensation issue in the past, had been put there *because* it was unacceptable. Removing it, or postponing it, negated the test.

The owners would have to get rid of Vincent before the next negotiation. Then he made it easy for them. All through 1990, he prosecuted a case against Steinbrenner the way he had against Rose. It resulted in a "lifetime" suspension that (a) had provisions that weren't carried out, (b) led to lawsuits, and (c) lasted just two years. The issue was a tangled one: in a long-running contract dispute with Dave Winfield, Steinbrenner had made payments to a "gambler" who had been threatening both of them with derogatory publicity and who was eventually convicted of extortion. How and why this mess, whatever it was, merited expulsion of the owner was never clear, but Landis had expelled an owner in 1943 for betting on baseball games, hadn't he? Subsequently, in cases involving the drug-use suspension of Steve Howe, now pitching for the Yankees, Vincent evidently displayed Napoleonic characteristics when he questioned and threatened Yankee employees.

Vincent's role in the Rose case had forecast his tendency to make rigid judgments. Giamatti was the principal actor, but Vincent and the prosecutor, a Washington trial lawyer named John Dowd, with strong inside-the-beltway connections, were the scriptwriters.

Rose, like countless other players and baseball officials, liked to bet, on horses and sports events. A sports bettor is usually driven by the idea that he can guess right, more than by the idea of winning money (which he bets again until he loses). Betting by officials and players implies an eventual falling into debt and being forced, or enticed, to fix a game at some point. So the baseball contract specifically forbids betting on baseball. Rose, arrogant and competitive as he was, engaged in his betting activity more extensively and more openly than others and developed close associations with bookmakers and gamblers.

The one thing he staunchly denied was betting on baseball. After extensive investigation, Dowd concluded that he was lying, but he couldn't prove it.

In February, when Rose's situation first became known, Ueberroth could have suspended him for consorting with felons and gamblers, which Rose could not and did not deny. But Ueberroth was on his way out and left the case to Giamatti, who subsequently delegated Vincent to oversee its progress. Dowd then did his digging and submitted a report on which Giamatti acted on August 24, after months of ugly stories littering the baseball landscape while Rose continued to manage the Reds.

Giamatti announced that Rose was banished from baseball "for life" because he had engaged "in a variety of acts which have stained the game." Rose had signed an agreement that he would not challenge the penalty in court, but the document also said specifically that the commissioner would make no finding about Rose betting on baseball, and that nothing in the agreement could be deemed admission or denial by Rose.

When Giamatti read this statement to the press, he was asked immediately if he thought Rose bet on baseball and the Reds. He said he did, on the basis of Dowd's report. Rose subsequently insisted that this was a betrayal, since he wouldn't have signed the agreement had it included the baseball betting charge. But the point was that, for all of Dowd's 225 pages of report and seven volumes of exhibits, *proving* that Rose bet on baseball was very hard to do in a court of law—and totally unnecessary for baseball's purposes.

Could Rose be reinstated? "The burden to show a redirected, reconfigured, rehabilitated life is entirely Pete Rose's," said Giamatti. Soon afterwards Rose went to jail for tax evasion, but that finding had to do with unreported payments from autograph and card shows, not gambling. He served his time and turned to radio commentary and more card shows.

Vincent, however, was married to the Dowd report, so there would never be a question of Rose seeking reinstatement from him. At issue was Rose's eligibility for the Hall of Fame. Until and unless he was reinstated, the player who got more hits than anyone else could not be in it.

But these were sideshows. So were conflicts Vincent generated concerning realignment of the National League's divisions, how games carried on cable should be handled, and how the Colorado and Florida expansion fees should be split. The real issue was dealing with the players. The last three commissioners had frustrated attempts to have it out once and for all. In June 1992, the Players Relations Committee—the owners' bargaining arm—sought formal exclusion of the commissioner from any labor negotiation. Vincent refused to yield his place. In July, the realignment squabble ended with the Cubs getting an injunction against Vincent's version. In August, the Players Association filed an unfair-labor-practice complaint against him for his handling of the Howe case. The two league presidents invited him (in writing) to a special owners' meeting to discuss "the office and duties of the commissioner." Vincent's August 20 reply was, "I will not resign—ever."

"Ever" turned out to be less than three weeks. On September 3, the owners convened in Chicago and produced an 18–9 no-confidence vote. On September 7, Vincent issued his resignation, calling it "my final act as commissioner 'in the best interests of baseball.' "

A fan's illusions die hard.

Governance passed to the Executive Council, which made Bud Selig, owner of the Milwaukee Brewers and a leader of past search committees, its chairman. In due course, he became "acting commissioner," with a salary but no real authority.

There would not be—could not be—another commissioner until the labor war was settled one way or another. What Giamatti and Vincent misunderstood, what Ueberroth didn't want to put up with, what Kuhn couldn't manage, was the true nature of the position. An employee is paid to look after the interest and carry out the purposes of the employer—no more, no less. A commissioner is the employee of the clubowners, his sole employers, in any and every sport. If he can persuade them to act according to his view of what's "in the best interest" of that business, fine. But he must persuade; he can't possibly force. And his view of "best interest" can't be essentially contrary to theirs. If his judgment is good and his employers are willing to follow him, a commissioner can be highly effective. If it's not, or they're not, the office itself becomes a detriment.

In deposing Vincent, the owners disposed of the czardom myth so vigorously developed by Ban Johnson and Judge Landis, and so successfully publicized and swallowed for so long. In that sense, there would never again be a commissioner. The title could remain, but the illusion of its independence could not.

THE LABOR FRONT

The Players Association came out of the 1981 strike with its power established and material gains. More important, it had beaten back the first full-scale attempt to undo free agency in the form it had been achieved. From now on, the association would be more concerned with maintaining a status quo working in its favor, with marginal adjustments, than with changing the system, its original objective now attained.

At the end of 1982, Miller, approaching 65, retired. The players chose Moffett, who had acted as federal mediator during the long strike, as their new executive director. It was a brief and bad marriage. He had no feel for their problems and desires, no firsthand knowledge of their past battles, and none of the special qualities Miller had displayed as educator and strategist. For their part, the players had become dependent on the kind of painstakingly detailed leadership Miller and Moss had given them. In December, they elected Fehr, who had succeeded Moss and had been involved with them since the Messersmith case in 1976, as their new leader.

In 1984, the new CBA negotiation began. There were two sticking points: the clubs wanted a salary cap, and the players wanted an increase in pension funding proportional to a much larger national television package. Grebey was gone, so the chief management negotiator was Lee MacPhail (who had just turned over the American League presidency to Bobby Brown), assisted by Barry Rona, longtime counsel to the Players Relations Committee. Fehr was the chief spokesman for the players, with Miller at his side as an advisor. These meetings were less acrimonious than in the past, especially because of MacPhail and his essentially conciliatory nature. But on substance they got nowhere.

Ueberroth had begun collecting and analyzing financial data. Show the players whatever figures they needed, he ordered. The exchange of information that followed became a comedy but did permanent harm.

For example, management submitted a chart (March 12) that showed that the entire industry of 26 clubs had last showed a profit in 1978—a total of $4,568, an average of less than $200 per club. (Honest. There are no zeroes missing). The next year, according to the chart, they lost $600,000. In 1982 they lost $92,094,948 (and how many cents?), the next year $66.6 million, and the incomplete figures for 1984 showed the same rate of flow of red ink.

In other words, the *losses* for a five-year period were on the order of $300,000,000 (let's keep the zeroes straight). The known revenue for those years was about $1.8 million.

In other words, they claimed *losses* of about $300,000,000 for the six-year period (including 1984) when their known revenue was about $2,500,000,000. Since the player payrolls and pension-fund payments in that time came to less than $1,000,000,000—figures the players knew themselves—that meant $1,800,000,000 must have been spent on something else. On what? And how was the $300,000,000 "loss" made up? Had owners written checks for that amount?

Keeping financial data secret was merely stonewalling. Submitting numbers like these was an insult to the intelligence of the adversary, guaranteed to produce anger and distrust. Management also "projected" losses of $420,000,000 for 1985–88. Then they revised that, when challenged, to $218,000,000. Then they produced, in a press conference, an independent expert to prove their point—and his estimate of their 1984 losses was 40 percent *less* than their own.

This virtuoso performance of crying wolf made all subsequent negotiations more difficult and hostile.

On May 20, management finally put forth a firm proposal: the salary cap would be the 1985 average, forbidding trades or free-agent signings that put a club over the cap, and salary arbitration awards could not go higher than double the player's previous year's pay.

On July 15, the players set August 6 as their strike date.

On July 30, management added its pension-fund proposal, essentially freezing contributions at the present level.

On August 1, Ueberroth called a news conference, and branding the management proposals "frivolous" and saying the owners should "stop asking for the players to solve their financial problems." His suggestion: forget salary caps, get the players to accept no salary arbitration for the first three years of a man's career (instead of two, as it was), compromise on the pension, and get on with it.

For this, the owners were paying him $300,000 a year?

His statement made a strike unnecessary, but an owner committee on August 2 couldn't bring itself to give in. Meetings on August 4 and August 5 didn't close the gap, and the games of August 6 were canceled. That day and the next, however, all-day sessions got it done, especially in private talk between Fehr and Rona. At 10:45 P.M., August 7, the settlement was announced. Play resumed August 8 with a flock of doubleheaders, and a full 162-game season was completed.

The settlement? No caps of any kind; three years instead of two to qualify for arbitration; doubling the pension contribution; minimum salary up to $60,000 from $40,000, with future cost-of-living increases built in; an upward adjustment in World Series prize money.

And what about compensation for losing a free agent, the issue that had caused the real strike in 1981?

No compensation, both sides agreed. No reentry draft. A free agent can deal with anyone, but if his last team wants to retain its negotiating rights it must offer him salary arbitration.

How could so big a deal as compensation evaporate so fast? Well, it had backfired. In 1981, the owners had accepted Miller's alternative of a player pool instead of direct compensation from the club that took the free agent. In 1983, Tom Seaver, the first and greatest of Met superstars, had returned to them from Cincinnati after a bad year there, and had a bad year with them too, at the age of 38. The Mets saw no reason to protect him from the compensation pool. The White Sox, upon losing Dennis Lamp as a Type A free agent to Toronto, took Seaver—who proceeded to win 15 games for them in 1984 and posted the 300th victory of his career with a flourish at Yankee Stadium two days before the 1985 strike began. Meanwhile, the Mets, with nothing to show for the transaction either way, finished second both years and could have used Seaver.

The 1985 CBA would run through 1989. It contained a provision first sought by the clubs in memory of the Koufax-Drysdale holdout in pre–free-agent days. Players agreed that they would not act collectively in any salary negotiation—and neither would the clubs. In other words, players could not agree among themselves on where to sign (and for how much), and clubs could not agree among themselves on whom to sign (and for how much). To do so would constitute "collusion."

Remember that word.

When the 1985 season ended, there was the usual number of free agents—players with at least six years of major league service. But suddenly they weren't getting any offers except from their own team. The market had dried up, noticeably. Of course, every club had a perfect right to decide it didn't want a particular, or any, free agent. And wasn't it simply sound business practice not to break your own budget? By the same reasoning, it followed that multiyear contracts were no longer being offered, not only to the current crop of free agents but to those players who soon would be.

It was an amazing display of sudden and simultaneous fiscal prudence on 26 fronts. Club owners had taken Ueberroth's advice to heart and were acting "responsibly."

"They're in collusion," cried Fehr—and filed a grievance. Thomas Roberts, who had been appointed arbitrator (the position once held by Seitz) late in 1985, took on the collusion case in June of 1986 while finishing up his deliberations on a drug-testing grievance (which will be dealt with in the next section). On July 30, he issued his ruling, for the players and against the owners on the question of mandatory drug testing.

A week later, the Players Relations Committee fired Roberts, who was digging into the collusion case.

Either side had the right to fire the arbitrator, for any reason, but not while he was deciding a case. So the firing became a grievance in itself. The owners had fired Seitz, and the players had fired four other arbitrators (including one Richard I. Bloch), but always *between* cases. Once submitted to an arbitrator, a case must be seen through by that arbitrator.

In September, an arbitrator—Bloch, as it turned out—ruled that Roberts could not be fired from the collusion case. By then, the two sides had chosen another arbitrator, George Nicolau, for all future cases. But Roberts would stay with the collusion case.

Let's cut to the chase. The clubs, despite denials, did conspire to ignore or limit free-agent opportunities after the 1985, 1986, and 1987 seasons. Essentially, a club would let all others know, "Don't touch this one, I still want him," and they observed each others' requests. Trouble was, they left something of a paper trail and, by asking some players to sign an "I won't sue" clause, proved that there was something to sue about.

In September 1987, Roberts found that collusion had taken place. The collective-bargaining agreement, which called for free agency, had been violated by "a common understanding that no club would bid for a free agent until and unless his former club no longer desired to sign that free agent." In January 1988, he declared seven players affected by the 1985–86 off-season collusion to be free agents again, then and there. There were 132 others who felt entitled to damages in dollars. It took two more years, until August 31, 1989, to calculate what the monetary damages should be—$10.8 million, to be apportioned in further hearings of individual cases.

By that time, Nicolau was dealing with Collusion II and Collusion III, covering the off-seasons of 1986–87 and 1987–88. At that point, after Robert's first finding that collusion existed, the practice had stopped. Nicolau also granted some players another crack at free agency, and ultimately the bill for all three collusion years came to $280 million and "new look" free agency for 15 more players. When this amount was determined, in October of 1990, it came to just under $11 million per club.

More than one baseball official said privately—very privately—"We came out ahead."

But the ongoing collusion cases had an important effect on the 1990 CBA negotiation.

When negotiations began in 1989, Ueberroth was gone, collusion had stopped, and salaries were skyrocketing. Limited free agency and salary arbitration had a ratcheting-up effect. Top-grade free agents were in short supply (thanks to the six-year limitation), and their prices were bid up. Arbitrators had to follow formulas according to "comparable" categories of players, which included high-priced free agents, tilting "normal" levels higher. The next free agent was negotiating off the higher base for everyone, in turn lifting the arbitration level, and so forth. But the players received every suggestion for change remembering that the owners had violated the last agreement as soon as they signed it. How could they assume "good faith" about new proposals?

The chief management negotiator now was Chuck O'Conner, a lawyer. He laid out a new approach:

1. Of baseball's total revenues, 39 percent would be set aside for players. (But the formula was easy to rig downward.)
2. For the first six years in the majors, there would be a set salary scale based on length of service and performance rankings in four groups of players (starting pitchers, relievers, catchers and middle infielders, the rest).
3. After six years, they would be free agents, as now.
4. Each team would have a payroll cap. If it was at the cap or higher, it could not sign a free agent without getting under the cap.

The first point would freeze the player share at where it was in 1989. (It had risen to 39 percent of gross revenues from 12 percent in the 20 years since the first CBA. But how to define gross revenues? Thirty-nine percent of what?)

The second was a variety of "classification"—set salaries—that had provoked revolt exactly 100 years before.

The third was made meaningless by the fourth.

Management called this "an innovative Baseball Partnership."

Fehr called it another attempt to roll back the free-agent system adopted in 1976 when the Seitz decision had killed the old reserve system.

To prevent another strike once the season began, the owners would not open training camps until there was an agreement. Since it was obvious there could not be one along these lines, Commissioner Vincent stepped in, suggesting:

1. Forget revenue sharing and salary caps.
2. Leave free agency as is.
3. Limit salary arbitration awards to a maximum of 75 percent above the previous contract.
4. Settle the collusion cases.

In short, leave the players alone and play ball.

Agreement wasn't reached until March 18. Camps would open March 20, exhibitions would start March 26, and the season would start a week late and extend three days late, squeezing in 162 games without delaying postseason play. The terms:

1. Minimum salary up to $100,000 from $60,000
2. Pension contribution up to $55 million from $34 million
3. Raises in meal money and other allowances
4. Some of the players with less than three years of service allowed to go to salary arbitration (the 17 percent with most service)
5. No caps, no arbitration limits, no changes in free agency

And then these troublemakers:

1. Either side can reopen the contract on major issues after three years (in a four-year pact running through 1993).
2. If found guilty of collusion again, the owners will pay the union treble damages (as antitrust penalties provide).
3. A group of experts would be set up to study revenue sharing and industry economics in general.

Chalk up another bargaining-table defeat for the owners. There was no test of player resolve. There was no escape from a commissioner's public-relations clout. It wasn't *his* money that was buying peace. Never again.

Planning for the next showdown began immediately. The National League would be adding two teams for 1993, Florida (Miami) and Colorado (Denver). In various analyses, there were now three groups of teams, according to revenue resource: the top eight, the middle 10, and the bottom eight. Internal politics now focused on exploiting the splits to gain adherents to one policy or another.

The hot issue was revenue sharing, which now meant sharing among the clubs. If the rich gave more to the poor, the poor would use it to bid against the rich, helping no one; if the disparity grew unchecked, the poor would fall behind, competitively and financially; but if payrolls could be capped, then more money to the poor could not be used to bid against the rich, and the money not paid in salaries by the rich could be shared with the poor.

One didn't need an advanced degree in political science to grasp the following:

If you propose some formula for sharing total revenue more equally among the clubs, the vote might be 18–8, or 20–6, or 16–10, or something like that, either for or against.

If you propose taking the money from the players to spread around the clubs, the will be 28–0 in favor.

Guess which scenario appealed to the clubs.

Assuming the players would accept a salary cap of some kind, the owners had to agree on a formula for sharing revenue among themselves. They already shared a good deal. National TV and radio money was split equally. Visiting teams got roughly 20 percent of the gate. When superstations brought games through cable into another area (as the Cubs, Braves, and Mets had for a long time), some payments went into a central fund. Some postseason money was distributed. Revenue from Major League Baseball–logoed merchandise was shared equally.

But the big items were local radio-television, and especially cable; luxury boxes and other premium seating; whatever concessions arrangements the local club had; signage and other in-the-park revenues; and things like corporate sponsorships. The home team kept all such money. Since the Yankees, for instance, had a local cable package worth about $50 million a year while others had none at all, the disparities were greater than ever.

In December 1992, the clubs notified the players that they intended to reopen the contract in 1993, but made no specific proposal. Their new chief negotiator was Richard Ravitch, and he presided over a new strategy, of which Chicago's Jerry Reinsdorf and Milwaukee's Bud Selig were portrayed as the leaders.

Step 1: Get the owners to agree on a sharing formula.

Step 2: Get them to require a three-quarter vote (21–7) to approve any *change* in what's agreed to.

Step 3: Present it to the players and hold fast.

Step 4: When the players keep rejecting it, declare that an impasse has been reached in bargaining (as the labor laws allow) and impose the plan anyhow.

Step 5: The only legal and practical response the players can make is to strike. If they do, let's see how long they stick to it; but this time we'll stick too. And we can hold out longer than they can. Besides, so many of them make so much money now that they won't strike, and if they try, it will split their ranks.

Once again, sheer chronology tells the story better than discursive description.

December 7, 1992—Owners vote 15–13 to reopen the contract, at the winter meetings in Louisville.

December 8—Owners give official notification of a possible lockout if agreement is not reached.

February 17, 1993—Owners vote that revenue sharing among clubs is linked to player acceptance of a salary cap: no cap, no sharing.

August 12—Unable to agree on a revenue-sharing formula, owners promise no lockout and no unilateral imposition of any plan through the end of the 1994 season.

August 16—Players pledge not to strike in 1993, but that's all.

December 31—The 1990 CBA expires.

January 18, 1994—Owners approve, 28–0, a revenue-sharing formula (details still secret) to be carried out only after players agree to a salary cap. This will be known as the Fort Lauderdale plan.

January 19—Owners eliminate the Players Relations Committee, make the commissioner's office the bargaining agent, and suspend the search for a new commissioner until a CBA is attained. The acting commissioner is Selig, with Ravitch reporting directly to him.

March 7—At the first collective-bargaining session, in Tampa, Ravitch tells players a salary cap is an absolute must.

June 8—Owners decide it will take a 21–7 vote to approve any collective-bargaining agreement reached during a strike.

June 14—Owners formally present their proposals, which include many takebacks in a seven-year agreement.

July 18—Players reject the proposals and ask minor improvements in the present system.

July 27—Ravitch rejects players' counterproposal.

July 28—Players set August 12 as strike date.

Here we need an explanation. The players had been discussing strike strategy all year. Some wanted to strike the All-Star Game (July 12 at Pittsburgh) to get maximum television attention, as a warning shot across the bow. Others wanted to strike only the postseason. But if a July strike kept going, players would lose half a year's pay, and the pension fund would lose the All-Star money. If they waited until October 1, everyone would have a full year's pay, but only the eight play-off teams would bear the brunt. They settled on August 12 because they believed—hoped, wished, gambled— that this would leave enough time to hammer out an agreement and still be able to resume play (say, by Labor Day) in time to settle pennant races and start play-offs.

The fact was, the players simply did not believe the owners would forego either the play-offs, in which most of their national television money was concentrated, or the traditional impact of the World Series.

Why strike at all? Well, if they completed the season, and the owners then declared impasse and imposed a salary cap for 1995, they would be stuck. They couldn't strike during the off-season and would have no way to escape the effects of a cap. The owners' promise not to impose, made a year before, would expire at the end of the season. Another such promise would make a strike unnecessary while bargaining continued, but the impasse strategy precluded that approach.

Both sides miscalculated. Owners didn't believe players would stick to a strike into postseason, players didn't believe owners would give up a postseason.

Back to chronology:

August 2—At a bargaining session, players learn that the $7.8 million dollar payment to the pension fund, from the All-Star Game just played, has not and will not be made. The sense of betrayal and distrust attached to the collusion experience increases.

September 2—After several fruitless bargaining sessions, Selig announces that September 9 is the deadline for canceling the rest of the season.

September 8—Players present a counterproposal to the salary cap in the form of a "tax" on the largest payrolls and markets.

September 9—Owners reject this as ludicrously inadequate, but Selig postpones canceling the season.

September 14—Owners cancel the rest of the season, including the World Series.

September 29—House Judiciary Committee passes a bill that would remove part of the antitrust exemption, the players testifying that they would end the strike and take their chances in court. But the Senate version loses in committee and is withdrawn.

October 14—President Clinton appoints a prestigious federal mediator, W.J. (Bill) Usery.

November 10—John Harrington, CEO of the Boston Red Sox, replaces Ravitch as chief negotiator.

November 17—Owners make a new proposal, replace the salary cap with a prohibitive payroll tax.

November 29—Owners say they will declare impasse December 7 and impose the salary cap, and that they are prepared to open spring training with "replacement players."

November 30—Usery persuades owners to withdraw the December 7 impasse threat.

December 10—Players make a comprehensive proposal including a payroll tax, free agency after four years, no salary arbitration, set minimum salaries for players with less than four years—and a voice in choosing the commissioner, negotiating television contracts, realignment, and expansion. That would be a "partnership" between players and owners.

December 11—Owners make a counter proposal for a higher tax with none of the partnership items.

December 14—The proposals are mutually rejected and talks break off, while the

National Labor Relations Board says it will issue a complaint against the owners for their failure to make the All-Star payment on August 1.

December 15—Owners vote 25–3 to declare impasse December 22.

December 22—Players make another tax proposal.

December 23—Owners declare impasse, impose the salary cap, eliminate salary arbitration.

December 27—Players file an unfair-labor-practice charge, seeking injunction against what they claim is an illegal implementation of impasse and salary cap.

We'll leave it at that point, January 1995. If you feel up in the air, that's exactly how everyone in baseball and everyone with the slightest interest in it felt at that time.

The 1994 World Series had not taken place, the first time in 90 years this had been allowed to happen.

Nearly a thousand players, some in the minors, did not know what their personal contract status was for the coming year.

Club owners didn't know whether the new regulations they had just promulgated would mean anything or not, since baseball doesn't exist until it's time to play.

Who might yet sue whom over what was a great unknown.

Perhaps half of all ball-club employees were off the payroll, temporarily or permanently.

"Replacement baseball," as the owners called it, or "scab baseball," as the players called it, was being promised for all of 1995 if necessary, causing a great deal of divisive discussion and public disgust.

Spring-training communities in Florida and Arizona, hard hit by the 1990 showdown, were bracing for another economic blow.

And obituaries for "our national game" filled the airwaves, the the print media, and private conversations.

We'll pick up the thread in the next, and last chapter.

DRUGS

The word "drugs" resonates differently in different times and social settings. We don't apply it, ordinarily, to tobacco, alcohol, and caffeine products, although these are certainly drugs by any technical definition. We do apply it to medications that are considered benign in proper doses and dangerous otherwise, but not morally repugnant. In common usage, we consider "drug use" reprehensible when we're referring to the voluntary use of mind-altering, mood-altering, or behavior-altering substances to produce some sort of pleasure or enhance capability.

In American society, drug use in this last sense became widespread in mainstream life in the 1960s, as part of that decade's social revolution. But it reached professional sports both earlier and later. In the social sense, drug use did not become a serious issue until well into the 1970s and 1980s, well after hippyism flourished. But the groundwork was laid back in the 1950s, by the medical establishment itself.

Professional athletes operate under enormous emotional stress with constant, and often severe, physical pain. After World War II, there was an explosion of miracle drugs (like penicillin) that relieved injury and illness much faster and better, enabling a player to perform. Also becoming easily available were uppers, downers, and other loosely identified pills to pep you up, let you sleep, help you cope. Team doctors and trainers dispensed them freely and—before their side effects became fully understood—often encouraged their use. Steroids, especially in the the football and track-and-field communities, became the most common of the "performance-enhancing" drugs.

When one grows accustomed to pills and shots in the locker room for approved purposes, the step to "recreational" drugs is that much easier to take. If those who could get visibly drunk on beer or hard stuff were considered "manly," and tobacco chewed and spat even more than smoked was also a sign of "manhood," what could be wrong with marijuana at a party? Or, if available, cocaine? Or something even more exotic?

In the show-business world, illegal recreational drugs had been commonplace for generations, as they were among the more rebellious elements of "the idle rich." They differed from liquor and tobacco mainly in being more expensive to obtain.

And when more and more young athletes got big money faster, they could afford what the Hollywood crowd had always taken for granted.

Drug-use scandals, therefore, became highly publicized aspects of professional sports from the 1970s on. Street drugs in the inner cities were becoming more widely recognized, and feared, as terrible national social problems. The apprehensions thus aroused made it seem all the more reprehensible when drug use involved these favored individuals—sports heroes. The clash of images made it worse: the words "clean" and "sport" had always been linked. Star athletes were "role models" in the "All-American boy" formulation. My favorite ball player a druggie? What an awful revelation!

I won't try to catalogue specific names here for two reasons. One is that those caught, by the law or simply by the media, were only the tip of the iceberg; it is misleading, as well as unfair, to single them out. The other is that the record and rumors are so entangled, incomplete, and immersed in self-serving accounts that to rely on them would also be misleading, unfair, and unreliable.

What matters here is the general situation that developed.

Display of one's righteous opposition to drug use was more important, as a public relations need, than any actual attempt to curb the practice. "Mandatory testing" became the war cry. It became, in the 1970s and early 1980s, a major political issue throughout society, and in sports on the high school and college level, especially.

Among the pros, football and basketball had the more visible problems. But it was soon recognized that it was a problem for baseball too.

The first line of discipline is the club. Drug abusers hide their habit well, but a sure sign is showing up late, missing a practice or a bus, and eventually missing a game. The club's recourse, after trying ways to help, is suspension without pay.

Once there was a labor contract, however, there were limits on the length of suspensions and the amount of fines, and a way to monitor their proper application. The Alex Johnson case had shown how the union could protect a player's right to fair treatment even in adverse circumstances. To the public, the line between defending rights and condoning misbehavior is hazy and unwelcome, but to those involved it is valid. The next level of discipline is the commissioner, and when Commissioner Kuhn had to deal with such cases, he and the Players Association could wind up in adversarial roles.

Nevertheless, the Association and its leadership wanted as much as anyone to deal with the problem constructively, as did the vast majority of its members. So it concentrated on procedures. Obviously, it would be best for the Association and the commissioner to work together to set up a joint program for drug treatment, education, and, when necessary discipline.

Such a program was set up in June of 1984. What the Association and its members did not want, however, was random or mandatory testing. Violation of privacy, the possibility of error, and the opportunity for disciplinary threat or abuse did not seem warranted by the scale of the problem, just for the public-relations benefit of being able to say it was being done. Management saw it differently, as a reasonable price to pay for essential public image. That disagreement could not be bridged. The cooperative program was dropped soon after the 1985 strike because agreement on what it ought to be could not be reached.

Ueberroth, as the new commissioner fresh from the Olympics, where drug testing was mandatory (primarily for steroids), instituted random testing for all baseball personnel under his jurisdiction—administrators, club front offices, minor leaguers, everyone but major league players.

In general, all concerned had slipped into a reasonable posture. When a player got involved with the law, baseball followed up with some kind of disciplinary action. Where there was no arrest or formal charge, the club emphasis was on rehabilitation or release, with little if any formal punishment. This didn't hold true in every case, but it was the pattern.

Thus Commissioner Kuhn had imposed sanctions (limited suspensions) on Willie Wilson, Vida Blue, and others actually convicted (usually of possession), who were welcomed back and who played again, some very effectively for a long time. The public-relations damage got worse when former big names like Denny McLain, Maury Wills, and Joe Pepitone surfaced in drug cases, but they were out of baseball's jurisdiction.

In May of 1985, Ueberroth installed his mandatory-testing program, which didn't include major league players. By then, a major drug investigation had been going on for months in Philadelphia, and in September it resulted in a highly publicized criminal trial. A caterer who served the clubhouses, home and visitors, was convicted of dealing drugs. Players testifying against him were granted immunity from prosecution, but several confessed to drug use and implicated many other players.

Ueberoth thereupon sent letters to all players appealing for approval of mandatory testing. Many players agreed, but the Players Association resisted on two grounds: (1) there was a cooperative program in place and it was working, and (2) such a major change had to be part of collective bargaining. When no agreement on this point could be reached, the owners pulled out of the program October 22. They then tried putting drug-testing clauses into individual contracts, but this violated the CBA, which specified what could be in a contract.

In February 1986, Ueberroth took punitive action against 23 players and one coach involved in the Pittsburgh trial. Seven players, including such stars as Keith Hernandez, Dave Parker, and Joaquin Andujar, would be suspended for a year unless they (1) donated 10 percent of their 1986 salaries to drug programs, (2) accepted random testing for the rest of their careers, and (3) did 100 hours of community service over the next two years. The others got lesser penalties along the same lines. Then the commissioner sent a letter to all players outlining a drug-testing plan of his own, to replace the program abandoned the previous October.

The Players Association filed two grievances, one on behalf of the penalized players, challenging the nature of the punishment, and one against the letter, calling it an attempt to evade the collective-bargaining process by dealing directly with the players.

On July 30, arbitrator Roberts upheld the union's claim about bargaining (but did not overturn the individual penalties)—the decision the owners tried to use to justify firing Roberts in the middle of the Collusion I case he had already undertaken. Three months later, another arbitrator made a similar ruling against the National Football League for putting in a program without union approval.

And there the matter rested. The flood of drug cases ebbed. No joint program was bargained in future contracts. When a specific punishment was challenged as too severe or following improper procedure, the union usually prevailed. But as players learned that protracted drug use damaged their performance (as Dave Parker confessed), they either rehabilitated themselves or disappeared, while younger players, better warned and more closely watched, did not fall into the habit as frequently. By the 1990s, the drug question had become simply part of the fabric of American life, no different in sports than elsewhere: when it appeared, it was dealt with somehow, but shock and hysteria were no longer the standard response.

OWNERSHIP TURNOVER

The final big story of the 1980s was the shift in the identity and nature of club ownerships.

In 1980, the Tribune Company of Chicago, a media conglomerate that published
the *Chicago Tribune* and other newspapers and operated WGN radio and television
stations in Chicago and others elsewhere, bought the Cubs from the Wrigley family,
which had owned it since 1920 and had given the ball park the name Wrigley Field
in 1926. The acquisition was too new for the Tribune Company to be an influential
factor in the strike of 1981, but because of WGN and the corporation's political
power in Chicago and Illinois, it became a more important player in baseball affairs
as time went on.

In 1976, Ted Turner had bought the Atlanta Braves (for $12 million) when his
broadcasting empire consisted only of one Atlanta station. But the Braves games it
carried were then sold to cable systems all across the country. WGN, which carried
Cubs games, did the same, and the Tribune Company also owned the *New York Daily
News* and the television station that carried Yankee games. In New York, the Mets were
on Station WWOR, a "superstation" like Turner's and WGN, carried by cable systems
everywhere. When Turner's Cable News Network became an international phenomenon, he, like the Tribune Company, had corporate interests that transcended baseball. As time went on, teams with direct television and cable connections would become a subconstituency to be dealt with in all baseball business.

In 1981, Ruly Carpenter, who had inherited the Phillies (acquired by the
DuPont family in 1943), sold them for $30 million to a syndicate headed by Bill
Giles, Warren's son, born, bred, and brought up in baseball affairs. The Seattle
Mariners, brought into existence only five years before for $6.5 million, were sold
for $13 million to George Argyros, a real-estate operator from Southern California.
The White Sox, who had been reacquired by Bill Veeck in 1976, were purchased by
a syndicate headed by Jerry Reinsdorf (real estate) and Eddie Einhorn (television
sales and programming) for $20 million, in a deal that included the ball park and
its land.

In 1983, Ewing Kauffman, original owner of the expansion Kansas City Royals
since 1969, sold 49 percent to a Memphis real-estate man, Aaron Fogelman, giving
him an option to buy control. The Galbreaths, who had acquired full control of the
Pittsburgh Pirates in 1949, sold 48 percent to Warner Communications. And in October, John Fetzer sold the Detroit Tigers (for $43 million) to Tom Monaghan, who
owned a chain of pizza restaurants.

In 1984, after threatening to move the team to Tampa, Calvin Griffith sold the
Twins to Carl Pohlad, a banker who would keep them in Minneapolis. The Griffith

family had owned the team, the former Washington Senators, since 1920. The price was $47 million. In Cincinnati, Marge Schott, an automobile dealer, acquired majority interest in the Reds from the Williams brothers, retaining Bob Howsam as the team's baseball head.

In 1985, the Galbreaths got out altogether. A consortium of private investors and the city of Pittsburgh took over the Pirates for $22 million, half the value being sought, contrary to the trend of all other sales.

You get the picture. The Wrigleys, Carpenters, Fetzers, Galbreaths, Veecks—long-term influential baseball people—were being replaced by "investors" with non-baseball agendas.

There were exceptions, but not enough to alter the trend. When the Haas family bought the A's from Finley in 1981, to keep them in Oakland, the team acquired an ownership as dedicated to baseball as Finley was and infinitely more dedicated to the community. When Nelson Doubleday bought the Mets from Payson's heirs in 1981 for $21 million, it was for the publishing house that bore his name; but in 1986, he and Fred Wilpon bought it as a private partnership—for $80.5 million—out of mostly baseball (and I suppose tax) motivation.

Why were the old owners getting out? Whatever other motives each may have had, no one can doubt that they weren't enjoying baseball the way they once did. Free agency changed the climate as well as the economics. The uncomplimentary way to put it (as player advocates did) was that the fun of being a "plantation owner" dealing with "his" players was gone when players acquired a choice of employers. A kinder and more accurate way to put it was that the tearing apart of traditional contexts and practices—by expansion, by television, by a different world on so many levels, including more hostile news media—took the fun out of it, entirely apart from free agency and player independence.

The owners of the "old days," just like the fans and players of their time, had become uncomfortable not so much with the baseball world of the 1980s, but with the *whole* world of the 1980s. What they missed was the totality of the 1950s, not simply the baseball experience of that time. Such nostalgia was creating a whole collectibles "industry"—but not for them.

So the game of owner musical-chairs went on and picked up speed.

Steve O'Neill (not the former player and manager) had acquired majority control of the Indians in 1978. He died in 1983. After other deals fell through, Richard and David Jacobs bought control in July of 1986. They were real-estate and shopping-mall developers involved in major efforts to revive the entire downtown Cleveland community.

Eddie Chiles, whose business was servicing oil wells and based in Fort Worth, had acquired full control of the Texas Rangers in 1980. Seeking financial help in 1986, he tried to sell some of it to a cable-television operator, but the league wouldn't approve. In 1988, he tried to sell to a group that wanted to move the franchise to Tampa, but that also fell through, and in 1989 he sold the club—and Arlington Stadium with its surrounding 114 acres—to a large local syndicate that included President George Bush's son George. His aborted 1986 deal had been for $50 million; this one was for $79 million.

Also in 1989, Argyros sold the Seattle Mariners to Jeff Smullyan, a radio-station operator from Indianapolis, for $77 million—just about six times what he had paid eight years before. And the Baltimore Orioles, acquired by Washington attorney Edward Bennett Williams from Hoffberger in 1979 for $12.3 million, were sold by his widow for $70 million to a group led by Eli Jacobs, a New York investor.

In 1990, Ray Kroc's survivors sold the San Diego Padres to a syndicate headed by Tom Werner, a television-show producer, for $75 million, and Ewing Kauffman reacquired sole ownership of the Kansas City Royals in a transaction that pegged the club's value at $68 million.

The Twins had stayed in Minnesota after flirting with Tampa. In 1988, the Cubs, overcoming much local opposition, installed lights at Wrigley Field (to make it suitable for postseason television commitments), while the White Sox, in deteriorating Comiskey Park (built in 1910), threatened to move away. St. Petersburg, Florida, was building a domed stadium, and the White Sox seemed headed there until the state of Illinois kicked in with financing for a new Comiskey Park across the street from the old one.

By now the pressure for a team in Florida was all but irresistible. In June 1990, the National League announced that it would award two expansion franchises in 1991, with four Florida sites in contention: Tampa, St. Petersburg, Orlando, and Miami–Fort Lauderdale, where a new football stadium was suitable for a baseball tenant as well. Meanwhile Smulyan, who had just bought Seattle, where the team had never been successful financially or competitively, wanted to move it to St. Petersburg.

The climax of ball-club shuffleboard came in 1992.

In June of 1991, the National League had awarded its new franchises to Denver and Miami (to be called Colorado and Florida), giving each league fourteen teams. Bob Lurie had been trying to get his Giants out of Candlestick Park, always a flawed facility but made worse when expanded to accommodate the football 49er's, since 1985. But two ballot measures in San Francisco, one in San Jose, and one in Santa Clara (adjacent to San Jose) had failed to approve ball-park projects, so on August 7, 1992, Lurie agreed to sell the team for $115 million to the Tampa area, to play in the St. Petersburg building.

The 1993 National Circuits became:

NL East–Montreal, New York Mets, Philadelphia, Pittsburgh, Chicago, St. Louis, Florida (Miami).

NL West–San Francisco, Los Angeles, San Diego, Colorado (Denver), Houston, Atlanta, Cincinnati.

By that time, Smulyan had already sold Seattle for $125 million to a local syndicate whose major financing came from Japan; Monaghan had sold the Detroit Tigers for $85 million to Michael Illitch, a rival pizza-chain owner who also owned the hockey Red Wings; and John McMullen had finally sold the Astros and the Houston Astrodome complex for $90 million to Drayton McLane, second-largest stockholder in the Wal-Mart Enterprises retail chain.

The National League did not want to abandon San Francisco, didn't like the Tampa purchasers, and helped promote a local buyout of Lurie. A group was formed, headed by Peter Magowan of Safeway supermarkets (and a member of the Merrill family so prominent in stock trading) and Walter Shorenstein, a real-estate mogul with considerable political clout in the Democratic Party nationally, in San Francisco civic affairs, and in the theater world. Magowan would run the baseball operation.

It wasn't until November that the league formally rejected the move to Florida, 9–4, whereupon Lurie accepted a $100 million offer from the Magowan group, retaining a 10 percent interest. That sale triggered an antitrust action by the spurned Tampa purchasers, intended as much to guarantee consideration for the next round of expansion or franchise moves as for courtroom victory. The lessons taught by Kansas City in 1968 and Seattle in 1976 were there for all to see.

Amid such instability at the ownership level, it's not surprising that labor negotiations became so difficult. The chief negotiator on the labor side, Fehr, had personal experience with all that had been done and said back to the beginning of free agency in 1976, and perpetual access to Miller himself. His chief lieutenant, Gene Orza, was equally well versed in the history and dynamics of these exchanges. On the ownership side, there was virtually no institutional memory left, and where it did exist, it was ignored by a majority of newcomers and their lawyers, equally ignorant and insensitive concerning past encounters. It was harder and harder to talk on the same wavelength.

Nor is it surprising that public relations were in bad shape, that the commissioner's office and function had become chaotic, and that real financial problems had arisen. A $100 million franchise, unlike a $10 million one, involves crushing debt burden. Most of it has to be borrowed, and what you pay in cash ceases to produce income, which has the same effect as paying interest. The larger portion of operating expenses devoted to debt service changes everything, and it alters relations between clubs even more than size of home market area does.

And yet, amid all this turmoil—finances, labor war, drug problems, tarnished image, growing competition for the entertainment dollar, local ball-park politics, threats to move—the game itself, on the field, was providing one glorious season after another.

SEASONS 1982–92

1982

The fan response to the 1981 strike was an all-time attendance record in 1982 (44.6 million). A St. Louis–Milwaukee World Series marked only the second time in 37 years that two mid-American representatives faced each other. (There had been a St. Louis–Detroit pairing in 1968.) And all four divisions produced terrific pennant races.

NL—With two days left, Atlanta (managed by Joe Torre), Los Angeles (Lasorda), and San Francisco (Frank Robinson) were alive in NL West. On Saturday, the Dodgers eliminated the Giants, beating them 15–2 at Candlestick, while the Braves won at San Diego. On Sunday, the Braves lost, giving the Dodgers a chance to create a tie— but a half hour later Joe Morgan's three-run homer for the Giants killed the Dodgers, 5–3. It was this Atlanta campaign, seen nationally by cable viewers all season, that established the "superstation" phenomenon.

In NL East, the Cards took command with an eight-game winning streak in mid-September, most of it on an eastern trip, and finished three games ahead of Philadelphia. Ozzie Smith, acquired from San Diego, came into full glory as the best shortstop of his time. Bruce Sutter, discarded by the Cubs the year before, anchored the bull pen. Joaquin Andujar was spectacular during the last seven weeks as a starting pitcher, and went on to dominate the postseason. Willie McGee was a brilliant rookie, Keith Hernanadez a star at bat and at first base. Manager Whitey Herzog had a deep pitching staff and speed—Lonnie Smith had 68 of the team's 200 stolen bases—and the Cards went on to sweep Atlanta (7–0, 4–3, 6–2) and win the World Series even though they had the smallest total of homers (67) of any team in the majors. That feat had been managed before only by the 1965 Dodgers.

Al Oliver, traded to Montreal by Texas, won the batting crown at .331, while Philadelphia's Carlton, 23–11, was the only 20-game winner in either league. Montreal's Tim Raines stole 78 bases.

AL—In AL West, the Angels got catcher Bob Boone from Philadelphia, shortstop Tom Foli from Pittsburgh, and Doug DeCinces from Balti-more to join previously acquired Rod Carew, Don Baylor, and Fred Lynn—then signed Reggie Jackson as a free agent when his Yankee contract ran out. The result was manager Gene Mauch's first taste of a first-place finish in 22 years of managing, despite spotty pitching. The Angels outlasted Kansas City by three games and Chicago by six, clinching first on the final Saturday.

Milwaukee went to Baltimore for the final four games with a three-game lead in AL East and proceeded to lose the first three. But on the last day, Don Sutton, acquired from Houston only a month before, produced a 10–2 victory over Jim Palmer for the Brewers. Thus Earl Weaver, who announced he'd be retiring, missed another shot at the postseason, while Harvey Kuenn, who had replaced Buck Rodgers as Milwaukee manager on June 2, got one in the fourth month of his managerial career.

Now Kuenn went up against Mauch, the most experienced and highly ranked (by his peers) of all active mangers. The Angels won at home 8–3 and 4–2 and were mentally gearing up for the World Series as they went to Milwaukee. But Sutton beat them 5–3, and the Brewers evened the series 9–5, pounding Tommy John, whom the Angels had acquired from the Yankees when the Brewers got Sutton, and who had also helped their stretch run. In the deciding game, a two-out, two-run, looping single by Cecil Cooper in the seventh inning gave Milwaukee a 4–3 victory, and Mauch had fallen short again.

It was an eventful year in other ways. The Yankees, while dropping to fourth, had three managers, five pitching coaches, and three batting coaches as Steinbrenner outdid himself in disruptive club ownership. In July, Texas fired Don Zimmer, replaced him with Darrell Johnson, then dropped Johnson at the end of the season. Also gone at the end of the year were Martin in Oakland, Dave Garcia in Cleveland, Mauch, and Clyde King, the last of the Yankee trio.

Meanwhile, Gaylord Perry had recorded his 300th victory (for Seattle against the Yankees on May 6), only the 15th man to do so and the first since Early Wynn in 1963. Rickey Henderson raised the stolen-base record to 130, passing Brock's 118 before August was over. Robin Yount, Milwaukee's shortstop, missed the batting title by one point behind Willie Wilson's .332 but was MVP with 29 homers and 114 runs batted in, while teammate Gorman Thomas tied Reggie Jackson for the home-run lead (39), and Wilson's Kansas City teammate Hal McRae led in runs batted in with 133, a rare example of a player knocking in more than 100 more runs than his homer total (27).

All-Star Game—The 53rd was played outside the United States for the first time, in Montreal's Olympic Stadium, but won by (who else?) the National League, 4–1, for the 19th time in the last 20.

WS—For television-ratings analysts, a St. Louis–Milwaukee World Series was not what they dreamed about, but for honest baseball fans, it was fine. The Brewers, who had already hit 221 home runs to 68 for the Cardinals, won the opener 10–0, in St. Louis. But the Cards pulled out the second game 5–4, after falling behind 4–2, and won the third 6–2, with Sutter saving Andujar. Then the Brewers produced a six-run seventh for a 7–5 decision in the fourth game and won the fifth game 6–4, so they went back to St. Louis leading three games to two.

There a 13–1 pounding of Sutton evened matters, and in the seventh game, the Andujar-Sutter combination locked it up for the Cardinals, 6–2. Andujar's earned run average for 20 postseason innings was 1.80, and Sutter had a hand in five of the seven victories. "Pitching," an astute analyst intoned, not for the first time, "is the name of the game."

1983

Less dramatic than the previous season, but producing a new attendance record anyhow, 1983 ended with Baltimore winning another championship under a new manger, Joe Altobelli.

NL—The year before, the Braves had taken a big early-season lead but had to hold off the Dodgers on the final day. This time, the same pattern wound up with the Dodgers overtaking the Braves by three games. The Phillies, after Paul Owens came down from the front office to replace Pat Corrales as manager on July 18, pulled away from Pittsburgh by winning 14 of their last 16 to win by six. In the regular season, the Phils had lost 11 of 12 to the Dodgers; in the play-off,

after splitting two games in Los Angeles, they knocked them off at home 7–2 and 7–2.

Bill Madlock, in Pittsburgh, won his fourth batting title at .323, while Philadelphia's Schmidt had a 40-homer year. In April, Nolan Ryan (in Houston) surpassed Walter Johnson's "unapproachable" record of 3,508 strikeouts in a career, but by the time the season ended Carlton had 3,709 and Ryan 3,677. On September 23, Carlton won his 300th, becoming No. 16 on that list. Steve Garvey, having beaten the National League record for consecutive games played held by Billy Williams, ended that streak at 1,207 games when he suffered a broken thumb.

AL—Altobelli, who had spent most of his career working in the Oriole system except for his chance to manage San Francisco 1977–79, was Weaver's natural in-house successor and brought the team home by a six-game margin over Detroit. In AL West, Tony La Russa's White Sox won 70 of their last 100 games to win that division race by 20 games. But Chicago scored only two runs in the play-offs, winning the first game 1–0 at Baltimore, then losing 4–0, 11–1, and 3–0 in 10 innings.

In Boston, Wade Boggs, in his second big-league season, hit .361, giving the league a new batting champion, while Carl Yastrzemski retired after 23 seasons with 3,308 games played, surpassing a record held by Hank Aaron. Jim Rice led with 39 homers and tied Cecil Cooper with 126 runs batted in, but the Red Sox finished a distant sixth anyhow. Steinbrenner's Yankee manipulations continued. He brought back Martin as manager in January, got a third-place finish one game behind Detroit, and fired him in December in favor of Yogi Berra, who had been working as one of his coaches. The Indians hired Corrales two weeks after the Phils dropped him, replacing Mike Ferraro, who had started the season.

All-Star Game—Just how routine the extravaganza had become was shown by the fact that the American League—the *American*—finally won an All-Star Game, and it caused barely a ripple in the baseball firmament. It was played in Comiskey Park to celebrate the first game in 1933, and a grand-slam homer by Fred Lynn—the first in All-Star play—produced a 9–1 lead in three innings of a game that ended 13–3.

WS—After the Phillies won the first game 2–1,

the Orioles reeled off four straight: 4–1, a three-hitter by Mike Boddiker; 3–2; 5–4; and 5–0, a five-hitter by Scott McGregor. The two teams hit .204. Pitching is the name of the game.

1984

Sparky Anderson, fired by Cincinnati after the 1978 season, had taken over the Detroit Tigers in the middle of 1979 and in 1984 became the only manager to win the World Series for each league.

NL—The Cubs had not finished in first place in 39 years, since the eight-team league of 1945. The San Diego Padres, born in 1969, had never finished higher than fourth in their six-team division. The Cubs, managed by Jim Frey, held off a challenge by the rebuilt Mets, managed by Davey Johnson, and won NL East by 6½ games. The Padres, having finished at exactly .500 in their first two seasons under Dick Williams, went to 92 victories and a 12-game margin in NL West. The heavily favored Cubs won the first two games at Chicago 13–0 and 4–2, but the Padres rose up at home 7–1, 7–5, 6–3 and went on to the World Series.

New stars were emerging. San Diego had Tony Gwynn, in his first full season, hitting .351, beating anyone else in the league by 30 points. Dwight Gooden, a 19-year-old right-hander with the Mets, struck out 276, a rookie record, and placed second (to Alejandro Pena of the Dodgers) in earned runs with 2.60, winning 17 games. (The year before, the Mets' Daryl Strawberry had been Rookie of the Year.) In Philadelphia, Juan Samuel's 72 stolen bases was a record for rookies, second this season only to Tim Raines's 75, making Raines the first ever to have 70 or more for four straight years.

Former Yankee stars Graig Nettles and Goose Gossage and ex-Dodger Garvey were part of the Padre package. The Cubs had Ryne Sandberg at second, the league's MVP, ending a two-year hold on that award by Dale Murphy, Atlanta's home-run hitter. Rick Sutcliffe, joining the Cubs after starting 5–4 in Cleveland, went 16–1 for them.

As the season wore on among the disappointed teams, the Giants fired Frank Robinson, the Reds dropped Vern Rapp and made Pete Rose player-manager, and Montreal fired Bill Virdon before he could complete his second season there.

AL—Newcomers shone here too. Don Mat-

tingly, Yankee first baseman, won the batting title on the last day, making four hits to nose out teammate Dave Winfield, .343 to .340. Mark Langston, a left-hander in Seattle, led the league with 204 strikeouts and won 17 games. (Only Boddiker won 20.)

But the Tigers blotted out everyone else. They won their first nine games, including a no-hitter by Jack Morris at Chicago. They were 35–5 by May 24, the best record for the first 40 games any team had ever had, were 55–21 at the end of June, and coasted to 104 victories. Morris wound up 19–11, Dan Petry 18–8, and Milt Wilcox 17–8, and Captain Hook found a bull-pen "hammer" (as manager Sparky Anderson called a dependable closer) in left-handed Willie Hernandez, who finished 68 games with credit for 32 saves and nine victories. Power was provided by Kirk Gibson, catcher Lance Parrish, and what would become a historic keystone combination of Alan Trammell at short and Lou Whitaker at second.

Kansas City, under Dick Howser, had a bad start while Wilson was sitting out his drug suspension but came on and held off California and Minnesota, who finished three games back, tied for second. John McNamara had followed Mauch as manager of the Angels. Billy Gardner was manager of the Twins, surrounded by rumors of moving to Tampa while the club's sale by the Griffith family was being completed. Entering the final week, the Twins were tied with the Royals for first place with seven to play. They won the first game of their trip in Chicago, for Frank Viola's 18th victory, but lost the remaining six.

The play-off figured to be no contest and it wasn't. Detroit swept the Royals, although after an 8–1 first game, the other two were battles—3–2 in 11 innings and 1–0 (Wilcox-Hernandez).

Meanwhile, on the final day of the regular season, California's Mike Witt pitched a perfect game at Texas, only the 13th in major league history. He struck out 10 and won 1–0, thanks to a run driven in by Reggie Jackson.

All-Star Game—Candlestick Park, where the wind had upstaged the players in 1961, was the site, and this time the hitters produced the breeze. A total of 21 of them struck out in a 3–1 National League victory. Three of the four runs were solo homers by George Brett, Gary Carter, and Dale Murphy; the other was unearned.

WS—The Tigers didn't let anything spoil their perfect season, and the Padres had gone as far as they could go. Morris won the first game, at San Diego, 3–2. San Diego won 5–3, as relievers Andy Hawkins and Craig Lefferts shut out the Tigers for eight innings after a three-run first. But in Detroit, 5–2, 4–2, and 8–4 closed it out.

1985

The Kansas City Royals, so close to ultimate victory for 10 seasons, finally got it in 1985, as the divisional system delivered four more tough pennant races and two memorable play-offs.

NL—The Dodgers had the easiest time, taking command with a 20–7 July, but their lead was down to 4½ with two weeks to go and not safe with the Reds coming on. Then they won nine of 11 to clinch. In NL East, the Cards had a 14–1 September spurt to pull four games ahead of the Mets, but then lost two of three in Montreal and the first two at home to the Mets before winning the last game of that series and the next two to clinch, with one day to go.

The Cards had a rookie outfielder, Vince Coleman, who led off and stole 110 bases, a rookie record. McGee, hitting next, won the batting title (.353) and the MVP, with 54 stolen bases of his own. Right behind them was Jack Clark, a home-run hitter. The Dodger strength was pitching: Orel Hershiser, 19–3; Bob Welch, 14–4; Fernanado Valenzuela, 17–10; a good bull pen; and a 2.96 team ERA. But the Cardinals had John Tudor, 21–8, and Danny Cox, 18–9, and a team ERA of 3.10, almost as good.

The League Championship Series play-off pattern was expanded to best of seven this year, with a World Series type of 2-3-2 home-field pattern. The Dodgers started out by winning 4–2 and 8–2 at home, then lost 4–2 and 12–2 in St. Louis. The pivotal fifth game was 2–2 when Tom Niedenfuer took over for Valenzuela to start the ninth. Coleman's leg had been injured before the first game by the machine that operates the tarp used to cover the infield, and he was unable to play, so McGee led off and Ozzie Smith hit second. Niedenfuer got McGee out, but Smith—who had hit only 13 home runs in his career in 4,253 at bats—hit one now down the right-field line.

In Los Angeles, the Dodgers took a 4–1 lead

into the seventh, but the Cards knocked out Hershiser in the seventh, and Smith tripled off Niedenfuer to tie the score. In the ninth, the Dodgers led 5–4, and Niedenfuer faced Clark with two on, two out, and first base open. Put him on? Lasorda decided not to. Clark hit a three-run homer, and the 7–5 final score sent the Cards to the World Series and Lasorda to second-guesser's paradise.

Television magnified these events as never before, but there had been great events all season long. On September 11, Rose broke the record for hits with No. 4,192—exactly 57 years to the day after Ty Cobb had played his last game with 4,191. And the best pitcher of all had been New York's Gooden: 24–4, eight shutouts, a 1.53 ERA, and 268 strikeouts. (Tudor had 10 shutouts and was second with a 1.93 ERA.) And on July 11, Ryan had recorded his 4,000th strikeout.

AL—On August 4, with the strike scheduled to start in two days, Seaver won his 300th game in dramatic fashion in New York, scene of his greatest triumphs (although this time in Yankee Stadium, not Shea), while in California, Rod Carew got his 3,000th hit against the Minnesota team with which he had spent most of his career.

To have such "baseball" upstaged by the labor war was a perfect illustration of the concept of "self-inflicted harm." When the strike ended in less than 48 hours, more goodies poured forth. Boggs won another batting title at .368, but Mattingly—third at .324, with 35 homers and 145 runs batted in—was MVP. (Brett hit .335.) Mattingly's RBI total was the highest in the league in 32 years. And on the final day of the regular season, Phil Niekro, now with the Yankees, posted his 300th victory.

At the same time, two pennant-race dramas played themselves out. In AL West, Mauch was back in charge of the Angels, McNamara having moved to the Red Sox. The Angels were involved in a season-long battle with Howser's Royals. With seven games to go, the Angels were ahead by one, but lost three of four in Kansas City. When they lost again at Texas while the Royals beat Oakland, they were two down with two to go, and Kansas City clinched by beating Oakland in 10 innings, while the Angels won their last two. In AL East, Bobby Cox had built Toronto into a team that led most of the way. The Yankees, who had replaced Berra with

Martin in April, had a 30–6 stretch that brought them within a game and a half on September 12. Then they lost eight straight but won 10 of 12 to get back within two games, with two to play at Toronto. But Doyle Alexander beat them 5–1 the next day, and Niekro's 300th left them two behind.

The new play-off went the full seven games. In Toronto, the Blue Jays won 6–1 and 6–5, a 10-inning game in which the Royals tied in the ninth and went ahead in the tenth, before Toronto came back with two runs in its half.

Kansas City struggled to a 6–5 victory at home but lost the fourth game as it had the first, to starter Dave Stieb and reliever Tom Henke, 3–1, the Blue Jays scoring three in the top of the ninth. But Toronto couldn't close it out. Danny Jackson shut them out 2–0 and sent the teams back to Toronto. There the Royals won twice more, 5–3 and 6–2, and advanced to the World Series.

All-Star Game—In the Metrodome in Minneapolis: Nationals 6, Americans 1, five National League pitchers allowing a total of five hits. The American League winning streak ended at one.

WS—St. Louis and Kansas City, the opposite ends of the state of Missouri, made an even more mid-American matchup than 1982's. They called this the I-70 Series, after the interstate highway connecting the two cities.

The Cardinals won the first two games on the road 3–1 (Tudor) and 4–2 (Cox), and although Andujar lost in St. Louis 6–1, Tudor's 3–0 five-hitter put the Royals down again, one game to three. The Pirates had overcome such a handicap in 1979, the Tigers in 1968, the Yankees in 1958 and the Pirates in 1925, so it can be done, but rarely. The Royals did it.

Jackson's five-hitter won the fifth game 6–1. Trailing 1–0 in the bottom of the ninth of the sixth game, the Royals scored two runs after a disputed call at first base opened the inning, and won 2–1. And they won the final game 11–0 behind Bret Saberhagen's five-hitter, as both Herzog and Andujar, relieving, threw tantrums and were ejected by the umpires in a tumultuous six-run fifth inning.

Twenty of a possible 21 postseason games had taken place, and all but the three in Toronto's oddly shaped and about to be abandoned Exposition Stadium had sold out. Complaints about divisional play-offs violating tradition had died away.

1986

The New York Mets rose to the top of the baseball world in 1986, but they had to come back from the brink of defeat at the hands of the Red Sox, who were there after teetering on the brink of elimination in the play-offs.

NL—The Mets won NL East by 21½ games, the largest margin since divisions began and exceeded in all major league history only by the Pittsburgh Pirates of 1902, when there was no World Series to go to. Their 108 victories were accumulated in monthly records of 13–3, 18–9, 19–9, 16–11, 21–11, and 5–0. Houston won NL West by 10 games over Cincinnati and gave the Mets a hard time before yielding in six games in the play-off. But some brilliant individual performances made up for the lack of pennant-race excitement.

Met starters were Gooden, 17–6; Bob Ojeda, 18–5; Sid Fernandez, 16–6; and Ron Darling, 15–6. Their closers (as "firemen" were called now) were Roger McDowell, 14–9 with 22 saves, and Jesse Orosco (21 saves, 8–6). Keith Hernandez, at first base, and Gary Carter, the catcher, had established their all-star status elsewhere before becoming Mets. Houston's Mike Scott, 18–10, led the league with a 2.22 ERA and 306 strikeouts and made his last regular-season start a no-hitter. Valenzuela's 21–11 and Mike Krukow's 20–9 for San Francisco were all the more impressive because their teams were not contenders.

In a tight race for the batting title, Montreal's Raines won at .334 to .332 for Steve Sax (Dodgers) and .329 for Tony Gwynn. Coleman stole 109 bases for St. Louis, but Raines reached 70 for the sixth straight year, an unprecedented feat.

Spectacular pitching marked the playoff. In the Astrodome, Scott beat Gooden 1–0, but Ojeda answered with a 5–1 decision over Nolan Ryan. Lenny Dykstra's two-run homer in the ninth gave the Mets the third game, at home, 6–5, but Scott stopped them again, 3–1 on three hits. In the fifth game, Ryan and Gooden were 1–1 through nine innings, and the Mets won in the 12th when Carter, in a 1-for-21 slump, singled home the winning run.

The sixth game was the classic. Houston got three in the first, the Mets three in the top of the ninth. In the 14th, the Mets scored, but in the bottom half Billy Hatcher's homer tied it again. In the 16th, the Mets scored three runs, but the Astros scored twice and had the tying run in scoring position when Jesse Orosco, the left-handed half of the closer corps, struck out Kevin Bass. So the Mets didn't have to face Scott in a seventh game. Orosco wound up with credit for three of the four Met victories.

AL—The races produced clear-cut winners—the Red Sox by 5½ games over the Yankees, the Angels by five over Texas—but the play-off was even better than the National League's.

Mauch's Angels took a 3–1 lead in games this time. They won 8–1 and lost 9–2 in Boston, then went home and won 5–3 and 4–3 in 11 innings after scoring three in the bottom of the ninth. And they took a 5–2 lead into the ninth inning of the fifth game. But two-run homers by Don Baylor and Dave Henderson off Donnie Moore put Boston ahead. In their half, the Angels tied it but left the bases loaded with two out. Then Henderson's scoring fly in the 11th gave the Sox a 7–6 victory.

They talk of shifts in momentum, and this was a historic one. The Angels had been one strike away from the World Series in both halves of the ninth inning. In Boston, they were beaten 10–4 and 8–1, and Mauch never did get to a Series as a manager.

Boggs beat out Mattingly .357 to .352 for the batting title. Jesse Barfield had a 40-homer year for Toronto. Joe Carter, in Cleveland, led in runs batted in with 121. Henderson, traded to the Yankees, stole 87 bases and scored 130 runs. But the Red Sox had Roger Clemens: 24–4, the best ERA at 2.48, and seven strikeouts short of the pitching triple crown only because Seattle's Mark Langston posted 245 to his 238. There was no shortage of individual brilliance in this league either.

There was also tragedy. Dick Howser, manager of the defending champion Royals and of a winning All-Star team on July 15, was diagnosed two days later with a brain tumor. Mike Ferraro, one of his coaches, handled the team the rest of the year. After chemotherapy, Howser tried to resume managing in 1987 spring training but had to quit after four days. He died that June.

All-Star Game—In the Astrodome, Clemens, whose record was 14–0 at that point, set down the first nine National Leaguers in order and the

Americans went on to win 3–2, on a two-run homer by Lou Whitaker off Gooden and a solo shot by Frank White of the Royals off Scott.

WS—A classic, pure and simple. Boston wins the opener in New York 1–0, scoring on a walk, wild pitch, and booted grounder. It wins the second 9–3, getting 18 hits in a game started by Gooden, even though Clemens doesn't last either. At Fenway, the Mets win 7–1 and 6–2, but Bruce Hurst outpitches Gooden in the fifth game and wins 4–2.

The sixth game is 3–3 into extra innings, and in the 10th Henderson's homer, a double by Boggs, and a single by Marty Barrett put Boston ahead 5–3. The first two Mets go out. One more out and the Red Sox will have their first Series championship since 1918—when they still had Babe Ruth, 68 years ago. But Carter singles. So does pinch-hitter Kevin Mitchell. Ray Knight loops a single to center, and it's 5–4. Bob Stanley comes in to face Mookie Wilson and makes a wild pitch on a 2–2 count, letting Mitchell score from third. It's 5–5, Knight on second. Wilson hits a slow, squiggly bouncer alongside first. It goes through Bill Buckner's legs. Knight races home. Mets win, 6–5.

Seventh game. Red Sox take a 3–0 lead in the second. The Mets get three in the sixth. Knight leads off the seventh with a homer, and another three-run inning results. When Dwight Evans socks a two-run double in the eighth, the Red Sox are within 6–5. But Strawberry opens the home eighth with a homer, and Orosco drives in another run himself, then completes a two-inning save. Score, 8–5.

The Mets have finally relived 1969. Buckner is an immortalized goat in a class with Merkle and Snodgrass and Heinie Zimmerman and others the fans of the 1980s never heard of. And Boston begins contemplating what will become known as "The Curse of the Bambino," the occult explanation for New England's failure to enjoy a World Series triumph. Is it punishment for trading away the Babe to the hated Yankees and establishing New York's dynasty? They lost seventh games of the World Series in 1946, 1967, and 1986, a pennant playoff in 1948, a last-day, pennant-deciding game in 1949, and a divisional play-off game in 1978. What Red Sox fan could accept all that as mere coincidence?

1987

A new Cinderella team, the Minnesota Twins, emerged as unexpected World Champions in 1987, while the Cardinals repeated their 1985 experience of not being able to win just one more game.

NL—A new regime with the Giants—Al Rosen as general manager, Roger Craig as field manager—brought San Francisco its first divisional title since 1971, by a six-game margin over Cincinnati. The Mets, who found almost their entire pitching staff crippled by injury (and Gooden involved in drug rehabilitation), did well to challenge St. Louis in September, but the Cards won a crucial series from them at that point and went on to win by three games.

The Cards had, basically, their 1985 team, while the Giants were loaded with newcomers like Will Clark, Robbie Thompson, and Jeffrey Leonard. In midseason they got left-hander Dave Dravecky and ex-Met Kevin Mitchell from San Diego, and that made the difference.

After the Cards won the opener at St. Louis 5–3, Dravecky pitched a 5–0 two-hitter. And after the Cards won at Candlestick 6–5, the Giants won 4–2 and 6–3 and went back to St. Louis full of hope. But they never scored again, as Tudor and Cox beat them 1–0 and 6–0.

Gwynn's .370 was the highest National League batting average since Musial's .376 in 1948. It was an abnormally heavy-hitting year, especially in homers, and Andre Dawson, with the Cubs, led with 49. (Both leagues set records for homers, totalling 4,258.) Only Sutcliffe (18) and Cincinnati's Shane Rawley (17) could win more than 16 games, while the Cards, league champions, had no one with more than 11. Nolan Ryan, at age 40, had an 8–16 won-lost record but led the league with a 2.76 ERA and struck out 270 batters in 212 innings.

AL—Detroit fought off Toronto in a dramatic final series to win AL East, while Minnesota won AL West by two games over Kansas City with only 85 victories, a total exceeded by the top four eastern-division teams and four National League teams. The Tigers and Blue Jays (managed by Jimy Williams, who had been Cox's top coach before Cox went back to Atlanta as general manager), played seven of their last 11 games against each other. Toronto won the first three, Detroit the last four. All were one-run decisions. The last one, which was decisive, ended 1–0 as Larry Herndon's home run off Jimmy Key gave Frank Tanana the only run he needed.

The Twins, meanwhile, were defying all sorts of conventional wisdom. They had a rookie manager, Tom Kelley, and a young general manager, Andy MacPhail—Lee's son, Larry's grandson. MacPhail got a top reliever, Jeff Reardon from Montreal, to back up Frank Viola and Bert Blyleven, and young talent like Kirby Puckett, Kent Hrbek, Gary Gaetti, and Tom Brunansky made the most of the Metrodome's hitter-friendly atmosphere in a homer-happy year. (Those four produced 125 home runs.) They simply brushed the Tigers aside in the play-off, 8–5 and 6–3 at home and, after a 7–6 setback in Detroit, 5–3 and 9–5 there.

Wade Boggs hit .363, Milwaukee's Paul Molitor .353, Alan Trammell .343, Puckett .332, Mattingly .327. Toronto's George Bell had 47 homers and 134 runs batted in, making him MVP, while Oakland's Mark McGuire set a rookie record of 49. Clemens was 20–9, Oakland's Dave Stewart 20–13 while Key, 17–8, was the ERA leader (2.76) with Viola next (2.90 and 17–10) and Clemens third (2.97). The new stars were shining brightly.

All-Star Game—On July 14 at Oakland, this was a farce. Amid much talk of a "lively ball" because of the widespread home-run outburst, the game turned out to be scoreless through 12 innings, partly because television's desire for eastern time zone prime time made it start in West Coast twilight at 5:40 P.M. Finally, in the top of the 13th, when it was dark enough to see, Tim Raines hit a two-run triple and the Nationals won 2–0.

WS—Home teams won all games. Minnesota started out 10–1 and 8–4, with a seven-run fourth in the first game and a six-run fourth in the second. At St. Louis, the Cards won 3–1, 7–2, and 4–2. Back in the dome, it was Minnesota 11–5. In the seventh game, Reardon nailed down a 4–2 victory for Viola.

The team with the ninth-best regular-season record had won the World Series—without a peep of protest from purists, perhaps because the regular-season attendance of 52 million set a record for the fifth time in six years since the long strike, and all 19 postseason games were virtual sellouts.

1988

The Mighty Mets seemed headed to a repetition of their 1986 triumph in 1988 until an under-rated Dodger team, led by Orel Hershiser, de-railed them in the play-offs and went on to win the World Series.

NL—With 100 victories, the Mets won NL East by 15 games. The Dodgers led NL West by only 2½ games at All-Star break, but then used an 11–5 road trip and a 10–2 spurt in August to open a siz-able lead in September, and Hershiser took it from there. On August 30, in a 4–2 victory at Mon-treal, he held the Expos scoreless the last four in-nings, then didn't allow another run the rest of the season. He pitched five straight shutouts and 10 scoreless innings in his final start, for a string of 59 consecutive scoreless innings, breaking the record of 58 set 20 years before by Don Drysdale, who was now up in the broadcasting booth de-scribing Hershiser's feat. His season record was 23–8 with a 2.26 earned run average. But New York's David Cone was 20–3 with a 2.22 ERA. The Mets also had Gooden at 18–9 and Darling at 17–9, and the league's leading offense. They went into the play-offs heavily favored, having beaten the Dodgers 10 of 11 during the season.

They looked even better after the first game in Los Angeles. Hershiser took a 2–0 lead into the ninth, but the Mets scored three off him and Jay Howell. The Dodgers won the next game 6–3, but form seemed to be holding when the Mets won 8–4 with a five-run eighth and led 4–2 into the ninth inning of the fourth game, with Gooden working on a three-hitter. Then Mike Scioscia fol-lowed a walk with a two-run homer, tying the score. When Kirk Gibson hit a homer in the 12th, Lasorda needed three pitchers to preserve the 5–4 victory, including Hershiser to get the final out with the bases loaded.

By now, even weekend World Series games were being played at night, less in worship of prime time than to escape conflict with televised football games. That one, on Sunday, October 9, lasted 4½ hours, well past midnight. The next af-ternoon the Dodgers won 7–4 and headed home with the lead. The Mets' answer was Cone's 5–1 five-hitter, so it was up to Hershiser again in the seventh game. Backed by a run in the first and five more in the second, when the Met defense

cracked, he produced another shutout, a 6–0 five-hitter.

After the heavy hitting of 1987, the pendulum swung the other way. Gwynn's .313 was good enough for another batting crown. Strawberry's 39 homers led the league, and only one other man hit as many as 30 (Al Davis of Houston). And on September 16 in Cincinnati, Tom Browning pitched baseball's 14th perfect game, against the Dodgers.

AL—When the Haas family bought the A's from Charley Finley to keep them in Oakland, the chief asset was Billy Martin, who had them play-ing "Billyball." But after the 1982 season, Martin went back to the Yankees, and the A's began building a sound organization from the ground up, the way Finley never had. By 1986 they had a well-stocked farm system and a brilliant manager, Tony La Russa, cut loose by the White Sox in a front-office shuffle after the 1985 season. Al-though fourth at exactly .500 in 1987, they had finished only four games behind the champion Twins. In 1988 they were ready. Strong in every department, they won 104 games and finished 13 games ahead of second-place Minnesota.

It was a different story in AL East, with four teams finishing only two games apart. The Red Sox had Joe Morgan, long a manager in their farm system and now a coach, replace McNamara at the All-Star break, when the team was nine games behind. They won 19 of the first 20 games he managed, then hung on to nose out Detroit by one and Milwaukee and Toronto by two. Clemens, who was 12–5 before the break, was made ineffective by injuries after that, but the team thrived on its new-hero-a-day pattern.

It could not, however, match the A's, who swept the play-off 2–1 and 4–3 in Boston, 10–6 and 4–1 at home.

Boggs, for his fourth straight batting title, hit .366, with only Puckett (.356) within 40 points. Oakland's Jose Canseco made much of becoming the first 40–40 man—42 homers, 40 stolen bases—while Henderson, still a Yankee, stole 93. Canseco was MVP. Oakland pitching was led by Dave Stew-art, 21–12, and Dennis Eckersley, for years a starter on other clubs, converted into a supercloser by La Russa and Dave Duncan, his pitching coach. Eck had 45 saves in what would be the start of a re-markable five-year run to Hall of Fame status. For

Minnesota, Viola was 24–7, and for Kansas City, Mike Gubicza 20–8, both with sub-3.00 ERAs.

All-Star Game—When the All-Star idea started in the 1930s, a rule was made limiting pitchers to three innings, to prevent overwork or one-day dominance. In the American's 2–1 victory at Cincinnati, each side used eight different pitchers, and the 16 men allowed 11 hits and three walks. One hit was Oakland catcher Terry Steinbach's home run off Gooden, the only pitcher to work three innings.

WS—Kirk Gibson, a favorite in Detroit because he was a football star at Michigan before going on to the 1984 champion Tigers, was one of those who gained a second-look free-agency opportunity in the collusion rulings. His career had gone downhill because of injuries, but when he signed with the Dodgers his leadership qualities and fierce competitiveness outweighed ordinary statistics and he was voted National League MVP in their winning year. Now, with the World Series starting, his leg was so bad that he couldn't play at all.

That's why Mickey Hatcher started in left field—and hit a two-run homer off Stewart in the first inning. Canseco trumped that with a grand-slam homer in the top of the second, and the A's got to the ninth inning with a 4–3 lead and Eckersley coming in to do his thing. The first two outs were routine, but he then walked Mike Davis, and up to the plate limped Gibson, barely able to walk, to pinch-hit. He fouled off three pitches after two strikes, wincing visibly each time—then hit a home run on a 3–2 pitch. As he hobbled around the bases to make the 5–4 victory official, Jack Buck, the television announcer, summed it up perfectly: "I don't believe what I just saw," he cried. Destiny had made its statement.

The next night, Hershiser made his: a three-hit 5–0 shutout.

In Oakland, the A's almost reversed the procedure. The third game was 1–1 in the ninth with Jay Howell, the main Oakland reliever whose place Eckersley had taken, on the mound for the Dodgers. Mark McGwire hit a homer with one out to win the game 2–1. But Howell came in and got the last seven outs to preserve a 4–3 Dodger victory in the fourth game, and it was Hershiser's turn again. Hatcher, the journeyman who had been out of work when the season began, hit another first-inning two-run homer. Hershiser did yield a run on a sacrifice fly in the third, but Mike Davis promptly hit another two-run homer for him, and the pitcher went on to complete a 5–2 four-hitter that ended the season.

In postseason play, Hershiser had posted a 1.08 earned run average in seven appearances. In the last 135 innings he pitched, going back to August, he allowed nine earned runs, an ERA of 0.62 under maximum competitive pressure. His entire year's work amounted to 310 innings, 26–8, a 2.09 ERA, and 10 shutouts.

1989

The A's were dominant again in 1989, and not even an earthquake could prevent them from winning the World Series this time.

NL—The Giants regained their 1987 form, only better, even though they lost Dravecky to arm cancer, which eventually required amputation. Their final margin over San Diego was three games, but only because the Padres finished with a nonthreatening rush. In NL East, the Cubs returned to first place, six games ahead of the Mets, under the managership of Don Zimmer, a Dodger teammate of Giants field manager Roger Craig 30 years before in Brooklyn, when they were young farm products. Zimmer had previously managed San Diego in its early days, the Red Sox when they lost the play-off to the Yankees in 1978, and Texas.

In a heavy-hitting and eventful play-off series, the Giants won in five games, winning three straight at home (5–4, 6–4, 3–2) after splitting the first two in Chicago (an 11–3 victory, a 9–5 loss). Will Clark was the star, hitting .650, while he, Kevin Mitchell, Thompson, and Matt Williams, the new third baseman, hit two homers each.

Clark had lost the batting title on the last day to Gwynn, .336 to .333, but Mitchell had led the league with 47 homers and 125 runs batted in, earning the MVP Award. Scott Garrelts, converted from reliever to starter by Craig, nosed out Hershiser for the ERA leadership, 2.28 to 2.31, with Langston, now in Montreal, a close third at 2.39, but their respective won-lost records were only 14–5, 15–15, and 12–9. The league's biggest winner was a Cub right-hander named Greg Maddux, 19–12.

AL—Winning 99 games, the A's had no trouble finishing seven games ahead of Kansas City in their division, but AL East provided excitement. Frank Robinson had become manager of Baltimore during the first week of the 1988 season, while the Orioles were opening their campaign with a 21-game losing streak en route to 107 defeats. But they started 1989 sticking to and above .500 while Toronto, after a 12–24 start, fired Jimy Williams and made Cito Gaston manager. By mid-July, the Orioles had a 7½-game lead and even after a 1–13 slump didn't yield first place until September 1. Then Toronto overtook them, with a 28–10 stretch up to September 12. But the Orioles hung on and reached Toronto for the final three games with a chance to tie. Only when the Blue Jays won the first two, 2–1 in 11 innings and 4–3, coming from behind in both, was the race settled. Thus the Orioles almost accomplished a historic last-to-first turnaround.

The A's, however, were too much for anyone. They had Rickey Henderson, back from the Yankees early in the season; Dave Henderson in center, Canseco and McGwire, Dave Parker as their designated hitter, Steinbach to catch, Carney Lansford at third, and a pitching rotation of Stewart, Bob Welch, Mike Moore, and Storm Davis backed up by Eckersley. Stewart was 21–9, Davis 19–7, Moore 19–11, and Welch 17–8, while Eckersley, in the process of notching 33 saves and four victories despite missing 40 games because of injury, walked just three batters all year and struck out 55 in 58 innings. Lansford's .336 was second only to Kirby Puckett's .339 (with Boggs third at .330). McGwire's 33 homers were exceeded only by the 36 Fred McGriff hit for Toronto, and Joe Carter's 35 in Cleveland, while Rickey Henderson stole 77 bases, second to no one. (But the best pitcher in the league was Kansas City's Bret Saberhagen: 23–6, a 2.16 ERA.)

So the A's rolled right over Toronto in five games. It was 7–3 and 6–3 at home, a 7–3 loss in the Skydome, then 6–5 and 4–3.

Through all this, Nolan Ryan was still going strong at 43. He had moved to the Texas Rangers, and his 301 strikeouts brought his total above 5,000.

All-Star Game—At Anaheim, the National League scored twice in the top of the first. Then Bo Jackson, the great football player who also played baseball for Kansas City, led off the bottom half with a tremendous homer. Boggs followed with another, and the Americans went on to win 5–3. Winning pitcher: Ryan.

WS—October 14, at Oakland, Stewart's five-hitter marked a 5–0 Oakland victory over the Giants. October 15, Moore allowed only four hits but needed help to finish a 5–1 victory. Even though this was the first time since the 1950s in New York that the whole Series was being played in a single metropolitan area, an open ("travel") day followed, as the television schedule required.

The third game, on October 17, was to start at 5:30, San Francisco time, in Candlestick. At 5:04 P.M., just as the introductions were about to start, the earthquake hit. It registered 7.1 on the Richter scale, but, amazingly, none of the 60,000 in the ball park were injured or even threatened. Many expected the game to go on anyhow. But with serious damage throughout the region, Commissioner Fay Vincent, in office only six weeks, said and did all the right things. He called for calm and patience, didn't cancel the Series, said there would be time enough to decide how to resume when important matters of real life were taken care of, and eventually was able to keep the World Series record intact.

So game three was played 12 days later, on October 27. Stewart pitched again, and Oakland won 13–7. Then Moore won 9–6. Eight different A's had hit nine home runs in the four games.

If there was going to be another dynasty, it looked like the A's were the ones who would have it.

If, that is, the owners let them play.

1990

The lockout that disrupted spring training and made the 1990 season start a week late had a devastating effect on the anticipatory enthusiasm that made the start of a new baseball season the modern counterpart of ancient spring fertility rites. Instead of talking about a team's prospects, trades, and possible records, what one heard was money-money-money, with an undercurrent of drug use and other misbehavior, and expressions of mutual disrespect between owners and players.

But when the games actually began, the pure "baseball news" included:

April 16—Nolan Ryan pitched the 12th one-hitter of his career.

April 27—Wally Backman of the Pirates got six hits in a game, the first player to do so in 16 years.

April 29—Greg Maddux set a record for pitchers by getting seven putouts, all while covering first base.

May 18—Ryne Sandberg, Cub second baseman, made an error—his first in 124 games, the longest errorless streak for any infielder other than a first baseman.

May 22—Andre Dawson of the Cubs was walked intentionally five times, a record, with Cincinnati manager Lou Piniella giving the orders.

May 29—Rickey Henderson broke Ty Cobb's American League career record by stealing a base for the 893d time.

June 4—Ramon Martinez of the Dodgers struck out 18 Atlanta Braves—one short of the record—all in the first eight innings.

June 9—Eddie Murray hit homers lefty and righty in the same game for the 10th time, tying a mark held by Mickey Mantle.

June 12—Cal Ripken's 1,308th consecutive game put him second only to Lou Gehrig's 2,130 in that category.

July 17—The Minnesota Twins became the first team ever to make two triple plays in the same game—and lost it to the Red Sox 1–0.

July 18—Now the Twins made six double plays and lost again, 5–4, as the Red Sox made four for a two-team record of 10.

July 25—George Brett hit for the cycle (single, double, triple, homer) for the second time in his career.

August 15—Mark McGwire hit his 30th homer, becoming the only player to hit at least that many in each of his first four seasons.

August 17—Carlton Fisk's 329th homer broke Johnny Bench's record for catchers.

August 26—Bo Jackson, who had hit three successive home runs on July 17 before sustaining a shoulder injury that put him on the disabled list, hit Randy Johnson's first pitch for a 450-foot homer, thus tying the record for home runs in four consecutive at bats.

August 31—The Griffeys, Ken Sr. and Ken Jr., became the first father-son pair to play together in the majors. Each singled and scored in the first inning of their Seattle team's 5–2 victory.

September 25—With eight successive hits good for eight runs in the first inning, the Yankees equaled two records in a 15–3 victory.

Wait. That's the incidental stuff, the little things.

There were nine no-hitters pitched, including one by Nolan Ryan, who also posted his 300th victory. Detroit's Cecil Fielder, who had played the previous year in Japan, joined the Tigers and hit 51 home runs, only the third player in 29 years to hit that many. Willie McGee won the National League batting title while playing in the American League with Oakland, to whom he'd been traded August 29. And the Yankees, finishing last with a 67–95 record, had their worst season in 77 years.

That's the kind of entertainment the labor war was obscuring, and it provided an object lesson about sports promotion that would be ignored four years later: Your business is to stage the games. If you do that, everything else takes care of itself; the games automatically manufacture what people enjoy. If you don't play, there's nothing to sell or for people to take an interest in.

The no-hitters began on April 11, the third day of the delayed season. Mark Langston, who had just joined the Angels, and Mike Witt combined to beat Seattle 1–0 at Anaheim.

On June 2, Randy Johnson, the 6-foot 10-inch left-hander who had gone to Seattle from Montreal the preceding May as part of a trade for Langston, tossed one against the Tigers.

On June 11, Ryan pitched his sixth, against the champion A's in Oakland, no less, striking out 14. He already held the record with five.

On June 29, Dave Stewart threw one for the A's at Toronto, and a few hours later Valenzuela completed one for the Dodgers against St. Louis. Never before had there been two no-hitters the same day.

On July 1, only a day and a half later, Andy Hawkins pitched a complete game of eight hitless innings for the Yankees at Chicago. He didn't have to pitch the ninth because three errors in the eighth inning made him a 4–0 loser—only the second pitcher ever to lose a complete-game no-hitter.

On July 12, Hawkins was the loser again as Chicago's Melido Perez pitched a rain-shortened six-inning no-hitter, winning 8–0.

On August 15, Terry Mulholland just missed a perfect game. He gave the Giants no hits and no walks, but Charlie Hayes, the third baseman, made an error in the seventh. Mulholland and Hayes had both been traded by the Giants to Philadelphia the previous June.

And on September 2, Toronto's Dave Stieb, who had lost a no-hit bid in the ninth inning on four previous occasions, was able to finish one in a 3–0 victory at Cleveland.

And oh yes, there were a couple of pretty good pennant races.

NL—For the first 15 years of NL East, the Pirates were perpetual contenders, finishing first or second 10 times. Then they fell to the bottom for three straight years, replaced Chuck Tanner with Jim Leyland in 1986, were sold, tried to rebuild. Suddenly, in 1990, they made it. Barry Bonds and Bobby Bonilla suddenly blossomed and ran one-two in the MVP balloting. Doug Drabek won the Cy Young Award. They got the jump with a 31–19 start while the favored Mets were 21–26, held up against the challenge when the Mets went 38–18 in June and July, and produced a 19–10 September to New York's 15–15 to finish four games up. Bonds hit 33 homers, Bonilla 32, and they drove in 234 runs. Drabek went 22–6.

Cincinnati, in NL West, led wire to wire, starting 9–0 and going to 33–12. The Reds fought off moves by the Dodgers and Giants, and their .500 pace the last four months was enough to win the division by five games. Then they played in October the way they had in April. They beat Pittsburgh in six tight games.

Pittsburgh won the opener at Cincinnati 4–3 before Drabek lost to Browning 2–1. The Reds won 6–3 and 5–3 in Pittsburgh before Drabek beat Browning 3–2. Then the Reds ended it 2–1. They had three nasty relievers—Randy Myers, Norm Charlton, and Rob Dibble—so starters Browning, Danny Jackson, and Jose Rijo could get help early and daily if needed. Among them, they held Bonilla and Bonds to six singles, a double, and one run batted in, and a .180 batting average.

The batting title went to McGee because he went to the other league with his average at .335 for 125 games, and no one got closer than Eddie Murray, now a Dodger, who finished at .330. Sandberg hit 40 homers, and Matt Williams, the youngest Giant slugger, led the league with 122 runs batted in.

AL—The A's rolled over everyone again, winning 103 games, finishing nine ahead of Chicago. The Red Sox amazed everyone, including themselves, by beating out Toronto by two games even though Clemens and Reardon got hurt late in the season. Boston's 19–9 August was enough to withstand Toronto's 17–10 September. Then the A's swept Boston, as they had two years before, this time with four straight one-run pitching performances: 9–1, 4–1, 4–1, and 3–1.

Welch had a Cy Young year with 27–6. Stewart was 22–12, Scott Sanderson 17–11—and Eckersley 4–2 with 48 saves. This time he walked only four and struck out 73 in 73 innings, allowing just 41 hits. Henderson's .325 gave Brett a run for the batting crown (Brett hit .329), and with 65 stolen bases, he was MVP despite Fielder's home runs. Clemens, 21–6, led in ERA with 1.93.

All-Star Game—At Wrigley Field, 15 pitchers, nine from the National League, took part and allowed just two runs, both scored in the seventh by the American League on Julio Franco's double off Dibble. The National Leaguers got just two singles. That's right, the wind was blowing in from Lake Michigan at Wrigley that night.

WS—In one of the all-time shockers, the Reds swept the A's. Rijo and two of the relievers won the first game 7–0, then the Reds tied in the eighth against Welch and scored in the 10th against Eckersley to take the second game 5–4. In Oakland, a seven-run third inning gave them an 8–3 victory, and Rijo beat Stewart 2–1, with Myers getting the last two outs for him.

So much for dynasties.

1991

The new Collective Bargaining Agreement, so abrasive to the owners, let fans and media concentrate on baseball for a while in 1991. An interesting season, in which little went according to form, produced an unforeseen Minnesota-Atlanta World Series, which the Twins won again in the seventh game.

The glut of no-hit games continued, eight of them making a total of 17 in two years. In the entire decade of the 1980s there had been 10. Ryan started it on May 1, against Toronto. Then it was Tommy Greene of the Phillies, May 23 at Montreal; four Oriole pitchers combining against the

A's, July 13; Mark Gardner of Montreal, who completed nine hitless innings in a scoreless game at Dodger Stadium but gave up two hits in the 10th and lost 1–0 on July 26; his teammate, Dennis Martinez, who held the Dodgers hitless and beat them 2–0 two days later; Wilson Alvarez of the White Sox at Baltimore, 7–0 on August 11; Bret Saberhagen in Kansas City against the White Sox, 7–0 on August 26; and three Braves pitchers against San Diego on September 11 in a 1–0 game.

NL—Bobby Cox had returned to Atlanta to be general manager, but after two sixth-place finishes he went back to managing midway through 1990, when the Braves finished last again. But they had been collecting pitchers, developing rookies, and making wise midlevel free-agent choices. At All-Star break, they trailed the Dodgers by 9½ games, overtook them gradually, and, with an eight-game winning streak, took first and clinched it with one day to go. Meanwhile, the Pirates made it two straight in NL East by a 14-game margin and got off on the right foot in the play-off by beating Tom Glavine (20–11) at Pittsburgh 5–1.

But the Braves won 1–0 the next day, and 10–3 at Atlanta. Then the Pirates won 3–2 in 10 innings and 1–0 against Glavine, so they returned to Pittsburgh primed for a World Series. But 21-year-old Steve Avery outpitched Drabek 1–0, as the Braves scored a ninth-inning run after failing to score for 26 straight innings, and John Smoltz gave the Braves another shutout, 4–0, ending Pittsburgh's season. Bonds, after another fine season (he was MVP runner-up to Atlanta's Terry Pendleton), hit .148 in the series.

The batting championship went to Pendleton at .319, while Cincinnati's Hal Morris hit .318 and Gwynn .317 (and McGee, now with San Francisco, .312). No one hit more than the 38 home runs produced by Howard Johnson of the Mets. Glavine and Pittsburgh's John Smiley (20–8) were the only 20-game winners.

AL—The Braves had gone from last to first in a six-team division; the Twins did it in a seven-team division. What's more, they did it in a division in which every team finished at .500 or higher. Their 95 victories left them eight games ahead of Chicago. Their chief free-agent addition was Jack Morris, who had pitched so well for Detroit, and he delivered 18 victories. Toronto, surviving chal-

lenges from Detroit in August and Boston in September, won AL East by seven games.

As usual, the first two games were split, Minnesota winning 5–4 and losing 5–2 at home. But then the Twins won 3–2 (in 10 innings), 9–3, and 8–5. They had a heavy-hitting team, and it didn't let up.

Wade Boggs, hitting .332, fell short of the batting title again, trailing Julio Franco's .341. Fielder and Canseco hit 44 homers each, and Henderson stole 58 more bases. But he was the center of attention early in the season, when he passed Lou Brock's career record of 938. He finished the year with 994.

All-Star Game—The Americans, finally seeming to get the hang of things, won 4–2 in the Toronto Skydome, on Cal Ripken's three-run homer off Dennis Martinez.

WS—The 88th modern World Series was a worthy climax to an interesting season, melodramatic to the final moment. Morris started off the Twins with a 5–2 victory, and Glavine was beaten in the second game, 3–2. But in Atlanta, the Braves won three straight: 5–4 in 12 innings, 3–2 with a run in the bottom of the ninth, and finally a "laugher," 14–5.

The sixth game, with increasing tension, went 11 innings, until Puckett led off the bottom of the inning with a home run for the Twins, his third hit of the game. That left it up to Morris and Smoltz in the seventh game, and they matched zeroes through nine innings. The Twins had lined into a double play with the bases full and one out in the eighth; they had left men on first and third in the ninth; but in the 10th, with the bases full and one out and the outfield as well as the infield drawn in, Gene Larkin, pinch-hitting, lined a hit to left center that settled matters.

The final victory brought Morris's postseason record to 7–1, the kind of statistic that made Lefty Gomez, Red Ruffing, and Bob Gibson famous.

1992

The Braves got back to the World Series in 1992, but lost it again, to Toronto. The A's got back to the top of their division but lost the League Championship Series to Toronto.

NL—The Braves repeated the previous year's pattern, falling far behind with a 20–27 start, then pulling away from the field by wining more than two-thirds of their remaining games (78–37). Second-place Cincinnati finished eight games behind. The Pirates also won again, for the third straight year, by nine games over Montreal, only to run into their most frustrating play-off defeat.

Beaten 5–1 and 13–5 at Atlanta and 6–4 at home after a 3–2 victory, the Pirates seemed finished. But they won the last home game 7–1, and game six in Atlanta 13–4 with an eight-run second inning. And with Drabek facing Smoltz, they went into the ninth inning of the seventh game with a 2–0 lead.

Then that rarest of melodramas occurred, a reversal of who would be champion on the final pitch. Pendleton's double, an error, and a walk filled the bases for the Braves with none out. Stan Belinda relieved Drabek and yielded a run on a scoring fly, walked a man to reload the bases, and made pinch-hitter Brian Hunter pop up. The only pinch-hitter Cox had left was Francisco Cabrera, who had been to bat only 12 times all year, and he lined a single to left field. Sid Bream, chugging around from second base, just did beat Bonds's throw home with the winning run and a 3–2 final score.

Nevertheless, Bonds was the MVP, hitting .311 with 34 homers, and Leyland was Manager of the Year. Chicago's Greg Maddux, 20–11 with 2.18 earned run average, won the Cy Young Award, and Gary Sheffield, a rising star in San Diego, the batting championship at .330. Teammate Fred McGriff, who had led the American League in homers three years before, now led the National with 35. Only Kevin Gross, with the Dodgers, pitched a no-hitter—against the Giants, August 17 in Los Angeles.

AL—Eckersley won both the MVP and Cy Young Awards as the A's returned to first place despite a wave of injuries and a midseason trade of Canseco to Texas. This time he had 51 saves, a 7–1 won-lost record, and 93 strikeouts in 80 innings, walking 11. Over a five-year span, he had walked only 38 men in 360 innings—and 12 of those walks had been intentional. He had recorded 220 saves in 247 opportunities and a 24–9 won-lost record. Relief pitching of such effectiveness had never been seen.

McGwire, hurt late in the season, finished second in homers with 42 to the 43 Juan Gonzalez hit

for Texas. Edgar Martinez of Seattle was the new batting champion at .343. Henderson passed 1,000 in stolen bases, but Cleveland's Ken Lofton was the league leader with 66, and Fielder led with 124 runs batted in.

Clemens had the best ERA, 2.41, in an 18–11 year, while Chicago's Jack McDowell went 20–10 and Kevin Brown of Texas 21–11. Boston's Matt Young produced the only no-hitter—an eight-inning complete game 2–1 loss at Cleveland, allowing seven walks and six stolen bases.

In AL East, Toronto had signed Jack Morris and Dave Winfield as free agents, and for late-season pennant insurance got David Cone from the Mets. The Blue Jays held first place from June 20 on, and a final push by Milwaukee fell four games short.

The A's started the play-offs as expected, winning 4–3 in Toronto on a ninth inning home run by Harold Baines off Morris, with Stewart starting and Eckersley finishing. But then it all changed.

Cone won the second game 3–1. In two outstanding seesaw games on the weekend in Oakland, the Blue Jays won 7–5 and 7–6 in 11 innings. Eckersley could not cut short a three-run eighth, which started with the A's leading 6–1, and gave up a two-run homer to Roberto Alomar in the ninth, tying that game. Stewart prolonged the series with a 6–2 victory the next day, but back in Toronto the Blue Jays got six runs in the first three innings of a 9–2 victory that sent them, finally, to a World Series.

All-Star Game—In San Diego, the Americans pounded out a 13–6 victory, their fifth straight.

WS—Good pitching is supposed to beat good hitting, so Atlanta was favored. Glavine outpitched Morris in the first game, as each gave up three singles and one home run—but Damon Berryhill's off Morris in the sixth came with two men on, so Atlanta won 3–1. And Smoltz had a 4–2 lead into the eighth of a game Cone started, until Ed Sprague's two-run homer in the ninth off Jeff Reardon won it for Toronto, 5–4.

The first two games in Toronto were just as tight. Candy Maldonado broke a 2–2 tie in the bottom of the ninth with a bases-loaded, one-out hit, giving Toronto a 3–2 victory, and Jimmy Key, saved by Henke, beat Glavine 2–1 for a commanding lead. The Braves sent the series back to Atlanta, 7–1 behind Smoltz, where the sixth game became an epic struggle. The Braves had to score a run with two out in the bottom of the ninth to send it into extra innings, 2–2. In the top of the 11th, Winfield, at the age of 41, hit a two-run double past third, the first extra-base hit in a World Series game in his entire career. The Braves could score only one in their half, and the 4–3 decision gave the World Series to a team from outside the United States for the first time—a very tiny, very belated justification of the word "world" in World Series.

AFTERMATH

The period between 1982, after the long strike, and 1993, when a new strike was made all but inevitable by disposing of the commissioner and announcing the reopening of the labor contract a year early, included a lot of scene setting for the upheavals to come.

The most pervasive, and gradual, change was atmospheric. An undercurrent of resentment and hostility was felt—and increasingly expressed—by players for management, management for players, by both for the media and by the media for them, by players for umpires, by umpires for the league offices, and most of all, by the public for the whole business. Fans generally bought into management's position that players were overpaid and, through free agency, "disloyal." The growing attitude was, no player is worth millions of dollars, but it he's getting that much and is on my team, he'd better hit a home run every time up. Oddly enough, this attitude didn't keep fans from buying tickets or from consuming ever more printed and broadcast material about baseball; it just made them enjoy it less, like smokers or dieters saying they want to quit while slavishly sticking to their habit.

But there were specifics, too.

One consequence of replacing Ueberroth with Giamatti was the need for a new National League president so soon after appointing one. The job was offered to Bill White, who had been broadcasting Yankee games as Phil Rizzuto's television partner since ending his own distinguished playing career in 1969. He would be the first "African-American"—the term then coming into use—to hold so high an administrative position in baseball. He had some misgivings, but he accepted. Now, at the beginning of 1989, both leagues had former major league players as president for the first time, since Bobby Brown was the American League president. One might think that this would help player-management relations but, ironically enough, it coincided with a time when the office of league president had long been stripped of power and influence. White, however, was a more forceful person on baseball matters than Brown, who had returned to the game after retiring from a post-playing career as a cardiologist. It may even be that their baseball backgrounds worked against them in the eyes of the new owners, who had so little regard for "baseball as we know it" in their finance-driven world. If they didn't respect players, why would they respect ex-players?

On the other hand, the runaway prosperity of the industry as a whole—bargaining statements aside—and constant talk of more expansion stimulated a new wave of ball-park construction, producing the best parks yet. The multipurpose ovals designed in the 1960s, with their artificial turf, were recognized as mistakes. The Skydome in Toronto, opened during the 1989 season, still fit that designation, but it was so advanced technologically (with a retractable roof) and so marvelous in other respects (a hotel behind the outfield!) that it was a huge success. But the ones going on the drawing board for Baltimore, Cleveland, and Texas, more so than the new Comiskey Park in Chicago, would prove to be a perfect blend of traditional values and modern conveniences. They would not come online until the 1990s, but they were being planned in the 1980s, because cities and states were willing to put money into using the baseball team to revitalize downtowns and to keep their major league labels from going elsewhere.

In San Francisco, where voters refused to approve a new park, Bob Lurie decided to sell. Finding no buyers at home, he sold to a group in Tampa. During the 1992 season, that seemed like a done deal. But the league didn't want it to happen, and White was instrumental in backstage maneuvers that finally produced San Francisco buyers. The whole story, however, merely underlined the point: if you build one, they may come, but if you don't, they'll go. The new owners of the Giants would succeed in getting a new park approved.

The squabbling over financial statements led to the formation of a blue-ribbon committee of four economic experts, unconnected with baseball, to study and report on the industry's financial state. The Players Association chose two (with the wonderfully resonant baseball names of Feller (David) and Aaron (Henry J.), and the owners chose two, Paul Volcker (former chairman of the Federal Reserve Board) and Peter Goldmark. More distinguished academic and financial world names would be hard to find.

Their conclusions were ignored.

Pressure for expansion also grew because of the imbalance in the two leagues. Since 1977, the American had 14 members and the National still only 12. At first, there was a dispute because the national television and marketing money had always been split evenly between the two leagues, then passed on to the members. That system gave each National League club more money, so they changed the split in order to even distribution 26 ways. But a 14-team league is unwieldy and unsatisfactory on many levels, and the ideal solution eventually would be 16 teams in each. The next step would have to be, however, two more in the National.

It had already been decided, in 1991, that the two new teams would be placed in Denver (called Colorado) and Miami (called Florida). Part of the opposition to moving the Giants to Tampa came from Miami (vigorously denied, of course), which wanted exclusivity in Florida for awhile, to establish its identity.

Finally, there was the matter of competitive balance. Was it a real problem or just a talking point? The 1991 World Series, between two teams that had finished last the previous year, certainly indicated that competitive opportunities were wide open, and it had never happened before free agency. In fact, it happened in 1991 only with the aid of free agency. But anecdotal and isolated examples are never good enough. What did the record actually show?

Years	A.L. Pennants Won	N.L. Pennants Won
1901–20	Philadelphia 6	New York 6
	Boston 6	Chicago 5
	Chicago 4	Pittsburgh 4
	Detroit 3	Brooklyn 2
	Cleveland 1	Philadelphia 1
	Three teams 0	Boston 1
		Two teams 0
1921–40	New York 11	New York 7
	Philadelphia 3	St. Louis 5
	Washington 3	Chicago 4
	Detroit 3	Pittsburgh 2
	Four teams 0	Cincinnati 2
		Three teams 0
1941–60	New York 14	Dodgers 8
	Cleveland 2	St. Louis 4
	St. Louis 1	Braves 3
	Detroit 1	Giants 2
	Boston 1	Chicago 1
	Chicago 1	Philadelphia 1
	Two teams 0	Pittsburgh 1
		Cincinnati 0
1961–80	New York 7	Dodgers 6
	Baltimore 5	Cincinnati 5
	Oakland 3	St. Louis 3
	Boston 2	Pittsburgh 2
	Minnesota 1	Mets 2
	Detroit 1	Giants 1
	Kansas City 1	Philadelphia 1
	Seven teams 0	Five teams 0

That's a fairly lopsided distribution of success in 20-year segments, and even worse if you look at the long stretches of no championships for the teams that have a "1" or "2" after their names.

And what happened from 1981 on, with the free-agency system starting to take hold? This is for 1981–92:

American League	National League
Oakland 3	St. Louis 3
Minnesota 2	Dodgers 2
Boston 1	Braves 2
Kansas City 1	Philadelphia 1
Detroit 1	San Diego 1
Baltimore 1	Giants 1
Milwaukee 1	Mets 1
New York 1	Cincinnati 1
Toronto 1	

So in 12 seasons, nine different American League teams won and eight different National League teams.

Is that less competitive balance than before, or more?

There's also the "big market" and "small

market" discrepancy. Oakland, Minnesota, Kansas City, and Milwaukee, generally classified as "small" (Oakland sharing the Bay Area with San Francisco), represented the American League in seven of the 12 years; New York, Los Angeles, and Chicago, a total of once. St. Louis, Atlanta, San Diego, and Cincinnati accounted for seven of the 12 National League participa-tions; New York, Los Angeles, and Chicago for four.

Does that remind you of the glorious 1950s, when the players knew their place and 15 of the 20 World Series teams were from New York?

This ever-widening gap between perception—or assertion—and reality was about to make real trouble.

CHAPTER 25

Strike Three

We are nearing the end of the story. The "baseball as we know it" in the largest sense, as conceived by Spalding and Hulbert in the winter of 1875–76 and elaborated thereafter into "our national game" at the turn of the century and the prototype of major sports promotion after that, entering the fabric and language of American life as a universally understood cultural characteristic—that particular "baseball as we know it" embarked on a course of self-destruction in 1993.

Its shape had been changing, of course, bit by bit through the decades, each change deplored by those who were comfortable with their era's familiar pattern, mourning the passing of "baseball as we knew it." Yet each new detail, each altered format, was quickly absorbed into an adjusted "baseball as we know it *now*," unequivocally connected to its past.

This time, however, two fundamental changes would occur that could not be undone or ignored. The inviolable connection to the past would be broken, and the separation of baseball business from baseball on the field would no longer be possible in the consciousness of anyone thinking about it, especially those *not* involved in the business. The second was even more important than the first. The perception of baseball's *romance* as distinct from its business operations was permanently tarnished if not totally erased.

Baseball did not "die" in the third great strike that mangled the 1994 and 1995 seasons. What died was the capability taken for granted for generations, of being a fan *only* of its on-field aspects. The game-business would certainly continue, expand, become more prosperous and attention commanding than ever, and in many of its facets thrive. It would go on producing stars, melodramas, thrills, victories, defeats, and, no doubt, scandals. But it would not be the same, in that following its results without following its financial arrangements would no longer be possible.

That's the sense in which our story is ending. History can deal only with something that is essentially complete; ongoing events are the province of journalism. And just as the end of the Roman Empire was not the end of history for Italy or the Mediterranean world, "the end of baseball as we knew it" does not imply the end of baseball history. What the third strike did was to complete the story we began, and to begin something else. What will follow is another story for later historians to deal with.

Nothing that happened on the field in 1993, 1994, and 1995 could be separated from the business issues raised, in the consciousness of players, club officials from owners through clubhouse attendants, mature fans or children, or even casual viewers of the evening news on television. Personalities and games became inextricably linked with dollars, and disposition of dollars, *consciously,* became a factor in understanding outcomes and one's reaction to the outcome of games played.

Purity, once lost, is not restorable. It may not even be desired, or necessary. Life without it may turn out to be rewarding in different ways. But it cannot be regained.

1993: AVERTING DISASTER

Before the 1993 season began, even in training camp, war had been declared, publicly. Reopened talks about the Collective Bargaining Agreement that would run out December 31 began in January, and the declaration by Richard Ravitch, the management negotiator, that he would recommend "no lockout in 1993" was as upsetting as the opposite would have been. Memories of the 1990 disruption and delay was fresh. All but the youngest fans and players remembered the severed season of 1981, even if the brief interruption of 1985 had faded away. Plenty of people, especially Fehr himself, all managers and coaches and most executives, and a substantial portion of media members remembered the first strike of 1972 only too well. Ravitch's saying he wouldn't ask for a lockout merely brought the word "lockout" to the surface.

In February the owners put forth their salary-cap proposal. Anyone who followed baseball at all knew it would not be accepted by the players, whose only weapon of resistance was a strike. They might or might not be forced, one way or another, to accept a salary cap (which is what the owners hoped), but they would never accept one voluntarily, without a fight.

So strike-lockout was in the air as spring training began.

There was another contentious issue that impinged on the fan's daily awareness: the schedule.

Florida and Colorado were ready to start play, making the National a 14-team league, as the American had been since 1977. Florida was added to the Eastern Division, Colorado to the Western, but the attempt to realign the composition of the divisions had been killed by the Cubs. It seemed to be a perfect opportunity to correct the 1969 absurdity of grouping Cincinnati and Atlanta with the three West Coast teams and Houston. Moving them to the Eastern Division and Chicago and St. Louis into the Western Division would serve geography, logic, and travel practicalities. But the Cubs (that is, the Tribune Company conglomerate) did not want their WGN television schedule disturbed by some extra games in the Pacific time zone, two hours different from Chicago's. So Atlanta and Cincinnati stayed put.

The WGN television schedule? Why should a baseball fan have to think about that, instead of about who's going to pitch?

Now, the seven-team divisions (as the American League had learned) demanded a "balanced schedule." Since there had to be at least one interdivision game every day (because it takes two teams to make one game), everybody had to play everybody else roughly the same number of times. The formula came out to 13 games with six teams in your own division (78), 12 with the other 7 (84), to make the total 162. Clearly, this wasn't as good, competitively, as the 18-inside, 12-outside formula National Leaguers were used to, but it had been working in the other league and was tolerable.

But it was also intended to be temporary. The idea was to split each league into three divisions starting in 1994—a five, a five, and a four—and have a wild-card team (the second-place finisher with the best record) join three division leaders in an extra round of play-offs.

Then it would be possible, again, to have the teams within a division play each other significantly more often than they played outside teams, restoring validity to the divisional race.

But an extra round of play-offs was something the Players Association would have to agree to, and it would have to be incorporated in the new CBA. The players welcomed the idea in principle, but what would be the prize money? That would have to be bargained.

Meanwhile, the 1993 season began with no assurance that it would be completed. It wasn't until August 12 that the owners, having failed to agree among themselves on a revenue-sharing formula, pledged no lockout in 1994 and no attempt to make unilateral changes in rules before the end of the 1994 season. At that point, the players pledged no strike for the rest of 1993, and only then was the postseason competition assured.

It was still the old system, however. Only the winners of the two divisions would meet in the League Championship Series, the winners going on to the World Series.

As it happened, Atlanta and San Francisco in NL West engaged in one of the greatest of all season-long pennant races. The Giants, under their new ownership, had signed Barry Bonds, as a free agent, to a six-year package worth $43,750,000, setting a record at an annual average of $7 million plus. Added to Will Clark and Matt Williams, Bonds gave the Giants imposing power and brilliant outfield play. They opened a 9½-game lead over the Braves by early August. The Braves had added free agent Greg Maddux, who chose them over the Yankees for less money, to their already brilliant pitching staff, and on July 18 bolstered their offense by trading for Fred McGriff, the home run–hitting first baseman. From that point on they started cutting into the Giant lead, although the Giants kept winning too. Going into the final five days of the season, the teams were tied with 100 victories apiece. On Thursday, the Giants lost at Colorado while the Braves beat Houston at home and moved ahead, but on Friday the Giants won at Los Angeles and the Braves lost to Houston, so they were tied again. The Giants had three more in Los Angeles, the Braves three at home with the expansion Rockies.

Both won Friday. Both won Saturday. The Braves won again Sunday, but an exhausted Giant pitching staff collapsed in a 12–1 loss, and the Braves won the race.

It was superb theater. But if the sensible reorganization plan had gone through, both teams would have been runaway winners of different divisions and ready to square off in the play-off. Instead, the Giants were done, and Atlanta had to play Philadelphia, winner of NL East by three games over late-closing but unthreatening Montreal. The Phils, under the balanced schedule, had lost eight of their 12 games with the Giants and had wound up with six fewer total victories—yet they proceeded to knock off the Braves, four games to two. As "fair" competition, this was not ideal, but it had happened before (see the 1987 Minnesota Twins), and it was a temporary, transitional circumstance.

But that's where competition and negotiation butted heads again. The owners and players, who couldn't agree on anything, couldn't agree on how the payoff from the extra playoff series in 1994 should work. Without the extra play-off, you couldn't have three divisions. As the winter dragged on, the clubs had to make and issue schedules not knowing whether the grouping would be two divisions or three. That meant only a balanced, two-division schedule could be drawn up. The main purpose of three divisions was to make divisional competition better by having more intradivision games; if every team played every other team the same number of times (give or take one), three arbitrary groupings were even more unfair than two. Eventually, as was inevitable, agreement was reached on the play-off payoff before the 1994 season began, but by then everyone was stuck with a repetition of the 1993 schedule pattern— 12 games with everyone, a 13th game with some.

Again, the competition itself was being driven by extraneous economic factors. The new divisions were:

American League East	American League Central	American League West
Toronto	Cleveland	Seattle
Boston	Chicago	Oakland
New York	Milwaukee	California
Baltimore	Minnesota	Texas
Detroit	Kansas City	

National League East	National League Central	National League West
Montreal	Cincinnati	San Francisco
New York	Chicago	Los Angeles
Philadelphia	St. Louis	San Diego
Atlanta	Pittsburgh	Colorado
Florida	Houston	

In 1993, Toronto had won the Eastern Division by seven games over the Yankees, with Detroit and Baltimore tied three games farther back and Boston five games behind them. That group was now intact in the three-division system.

Cleveland was of special interest. The Indians had been putting together an impressive team, signing young players to long-term contracts under a vigorous general manager (John Hart) and a field manager with no previous experience (Mike Hargrove). In their seven-team division, the Indians had been sixth or seventh 12 times and no higher than fourth for 17 consecutive years going into the 1993 season, and had finished sixth again, 10 games below .500 for the second straight year. But they were presenting exciting individuals as hitters, and the new downtown ball park was visibly under construction. In cavernous Cleveland Stadium, with its 75,000 seats, they had averaged barely one million a year in attendance for 15 years going into 1993, and much less than a million for the 27 years before that. Then, in 1993, the prospect of the new park, with not yet improvement in victories, brought their gate to 2.2 million.

And now, for 1994, they would be in a Central Division, away from those eastern powerhouses they had been trailing for two decades. Minnesota, Kansas City, and Chicago had enjoyed rotating success in the 1980s but were less imposing opposition. Milwaukee, which did have some moments of glory in the Eastern Division but had fallen to seventh in 1993, was also coming into the new division. The Indians might be instant contenders.

As for the new four-team Western Division, it represented the worst feature of the balanced schedule. Its teams would play each other only 13 times the whole season, so that only 39 of a team's 162 games would be against its own pennant-race foes. More than 75 percent of its games would be against outsiders. It would be theoretically possible to finish first—and make the play-offs—with a 20–142 won-lost record if all four teams lost all outside games and one of them won one more than half the 39 inside. This was a ridiculous example, but mathematically possible, and an indicator that the divisional winner might realistically be well under .500.

In the National League, the new alignment separated the Braves and Giants and broke the Dodger-Cincinnati connection that had produced so many storied struggles since divisional play began. It also separated the Pittsburgh-Philadelphia tandem that had dominated the Eastern Division for much of the 1970s and 1980s. And putting the expansion Rockies in with the Dodgers, Giants, and Astros made that Western Division, for all practical purposes, a three-team division.

Strangely enough—and frighteningly, to those who saw the implications—there was a universally passive reaction to these changes. Instead of arguing about how the new alignments would work, or whether they were fair or not, or how they could have been done otherwise, or what each team's prospects actually were, most commentators and fans talked only about salaries, the threat of a stoppage, and the insult to "purity" of having a second-place club make the play-offs.

In this climate, much of what was wonderful about the 1993 season, while noted, didn't "take" in the collective imagination the way baseball drama used to. The Atlanta–San Francisco race got full appreciation, while it was on. The play-offs were hot on television, and the World Series more so. But as soon as they were over, they were obliterated by daily communiques from the labor battlefront and by the nagging question, will there be a stoppage? Neither strike nor lockout was "unthinkable," and the owners' refusal to even look for a new commissioner sent a message all too clearly understood. If Selig, the owner of a "poor" club, had emerged as the spokesman for the ownership side, who could possibly be looking after the "public interest"? Since Fehr was being demonized as tirelessly as Miller had been and had none of Miller's historical credentials or personal force to counteract any of the attacks, and since most of the top-level players were perceived as spoiled and selfish (and too often behaved in ways that strengthened that impression), it was easy to say "a plague on both their houses"—which may or may not have been a fair distribution of blame but would have been an inconceivable response toward baseball in the past. The hundred-year tradition had been for the public to admire, not revile, both owners and players.

Here's a small example of what was going wrong. Murray Chass had become, by the 1980s, the most experienced baseball writer on the *New York Times,* with top seniority. He had covered baseball for the Associated Press before coming to the *Times* in the 1960s, in the process becoming rich in background, adept at interpreting statistics, familiar with all playing and front-office personnel, and a qualified observer-describer of baseball games to the highest degree. But in the 1990s, he was virtually excluded from covering any games or traveling with a ball club. Almost all his assignments, all year round, dealt with labor negotiations, commissioner politics, lawsuits, congressional hearings, arbitrations, salaries, and other business affairs—important matters, dealt with thoroughly, well explained, conscientiously followed, but offering no "baseball" nourishment.

Other newspapers weren't always as serious-minded as the *Times,* but Chass' situation was replicated all across the country by columnists as well as beat writers (and radio and television news reporters). The most qualified "baseball writers" were not writing about "baseball" but about the business affairs of baseball people.

How could a fan's sense of romance thrive on that? And how could that possibly attract new fans?

Yet what was actually transpiring in that 1993 season was as good raw material for "just baseball" as any past season had ever offered.

Maddux, 20–10 for Atlanta with a league-leading 2.36 earned run average, won the Cy Young Award for the second straight year, the first to do so since Sandy Koufax in 1965–66, the first ever to do it with different teams. His teammate, Tom Glavine, who had preceded him as Cy Young winner in 1991, was 22–6, and Steve Avery 18–6. A trio like that was reminiscent of the Lemon-Wynn-Garcia firing line of the Indians back in the 1950s.

Atlanta's Dave Justice hit 40 home runs and McGriff hit 19 in his 68 games with the Braves for a season total of 37, while Ron Gant, the left fielder, added 36.

Bonds, in his first season as a Giant, hit .336 with 46 homers, knocked in a league-high 123 runs, ignited and kept driving their 103-victory season, and won the MVP for the third time in four years, something no one else had ever done. Matt Williams hit 38 homers for the Giants, while Bill Swift (ERA leader the year before) went 21–8 and John Burkett 22–7 for rookie manager Dusty Baker, a great story in himself and Manager of the Year.

Andres Galarraga, a former Montreal star now with the expansion Rockies, beat out Tony Gwynn for the batting title, .370 to .358, after flirting with .400 for a while.

The Phillies didn't have comparable individual standouts, but they did win 97 games in Jim Fregosi's third year as their manager and overcame the Braves. After squeezing out the first game in 11 innings 4–3 at home, they absorbed 14–3 and 9–4 defeats, then eked out two more one-run victories, 2–1 and 4–3 in 10 innings after the Braves had scored three in the ninth to tie. A 6–3 victory over Maddux then put them in the World Series. They were stocked with colorful characters: Lenny Dykstra, John Kruk, Darren Daulton, and, above all, reliever Mitch (Wild Thing) Williams, who got the victories in both extra-inning games and saves in the other two winning games.

The American League had its own headliners. Toronto's John Olerud (.363), Paul Molitor (.332), and Roberto Alomar (.326) ranked one-two-three in batting average, another unprecedented situation. Juan Gonzalez led in homers again, with 46, while Albert Belle, an emerging Cleveland star, hit 38 and led with 129 runs batted in. But the brightest star of all was Ken Griffey Jr. in Seattle: 45 homers, .309, and more pure flair than anyone. Cleveland's Lofton stole 70 bases. And better than anyone, in the eyes of many, was big Frank Thomas of the White Sox: 41 homers, 128 runs batted in, .317, and a unanimous choice for MVP.

A new generation of pitchers was taking over. Jack McDowell, 22–10 in Chicago, took the Cy Young, but Kevin Appier of Kansas City, 18–8, was the ERA leader at 2.56. Chicago's Wilson Alvarez, 15–8, was the only other under 3.00 (at 2.95). Randy Johnson, in Seattle, was 19–8 and struck out 308 men; he was by far the most intimidating pitcher. Eckersley still had his magic, with 36 saves and 80 strikeouts in 67 innings (although he was getting "wild"—13 walks). But Kansas City's Jeff Montgomery and Toronto's Duane Ward posted 45 saves each.

The White Sox won AL West, under manager Gene Lamont, on the strength of their pitching. (Alex Fernandez, the third starter, was 18–9.) But they couldn't hold the Blue Jays in the play-off. Toronto won 7–3 and 3–1 in Chicago, and although the White Sox evened the series with 6–1 and 7–4 victories that gave visiting teams four straight, Toronto's 5–3 victory over McDowell in the fifth game restored control. The Blue Jays had acquired two famous former A's, pitcher Dave Stewart and Rickey Henderson, and Stewart, who had won Game two, who was the winner again in a 6–3 decision nailed down by Ward.

The World Series opened in Toronto with an 8–4 Toronto victory, but the Phillies bounced back 6–4, with Williams getting another save. Toronto won 10–3 at Philadelphia, and then came the highest-scoring World Series game ever played, four hours and 14 minutes of television that fascinated those who could stay up late enough to watch it all. Toronto led 3–0 in the first, but the Phils answered with four runs in their half, led 6–3 an inning later, and trailed 7–6 an inning after that. Then the Phils made it 11–7 and led 14–9 in the eighth, when they called upon Williams again. There's a saying about going to the well too often, and this was the time. With two out, a two-run single by Henderson and a two-run triple by Devon White capped a six-run inning that produced a 15–14 victory after Ward got the last four outs.

Now Curt Schilling had to keep the Phils alive. He pitched a five-hit shutout, made two early runs stand up, and the 2–0 victory sent the Series back to Toronto. The Blue Jays built a 5–1 lead for Stewart, but he gave out in the seventh as the Phils scored five and took a 6–5 lead. They still had it when Williams went out to pitch the ninth. He walked Henderson, got White out but yielded a single to Molitor. Up came Joe Carter and hit one into the left-field seats for a three-run homer that won the game 8–6, won the World Series, made a great TV moment, and wrecked the career of Williams, who never recovered his effectiveness.

It was also a season in which Mark Whitten, a Cardinal outfielder, hit four home runs and knocked in 12 runs in a single game (September 7 at Cincinnati), an RBI record. Carlos Baerga of the Indians hit home runs lefty and righty in the *same inning* against the Yankees on April 8, the first player ever to do that. Griffey tied a major league record with a home run in each of eight consecutive games, Anthony Young, pitching for the Mets, lost a record 27 games in a row (over two seasons). There were three no-hitters—Chris Bosio for Seattle against Boston April 22, Jim Abbott for the Yankees over Cleveland September 4, and Darryl Kile for Houston over the Mets September 8. And Sparky Anderson won his 2,000th game as a manager.

Such a wealth of baseball events should bring out the fans, and it did. In Denver, the Rockies were using the 76,000-seat Mile High football stadium while a true ball park was being built for them, and they pulled in the astonishing total of 4.48 million, more even than Toronto's 4.1 million in the Skydome. They *averaged* more than 50,000 a game. The Florida Marlins, in their first year, drew 3.06 million. Baltimore, in its magnificent new Camden Yards park, had 3.6 million, Atlanta 3.8 million, the Dodgers and Phils 3.1 million each. The two-league total reached 70.3 million—the ninth time in 12 years that it hit a record high.

To put a sour taste on all that required extra effort, but the owners and players managed to make it.

By the very nature of sports promotion, those staging the events control the tenor and content of the publicity they get. They determine what will be written about and discussed by what they say and do. Ads would be shrugged off as self-serving. They must live off "news."

Look back at chapter 5, where Spalding, writing in 1911, describes how he manipulated reactions to his $10,000 sale of King Kelly in 1886.

Trouble is, successful manipulation is a two-edged sword. It will cut through whatever you thrust at, and if you thrust it in the wrong direction it will run through your friend as fatally as through your enemy.

And the 1990s were not the 1880s, in that the technology and scale of publicity machinery had become so different, so much greater, and so much more immediate.

Whatever promoters and players talked about, the media magnified. When they talked about games, the on-field drama became bigger than life by repetition and exaggeration. When they talked only about money, mutual antagonism, and the possibility of not playing at all, that's what monopolized the public's attention—by repetition and exaggeration.

All the elements that made baseball so popular in the first place as a "talking and reading" sport were now turned against it.

The hot-stove-league winter of 1993–94, which could have been devoted to reliving and amplifying the marvels of 1993, anticipating 1994, and trying to calculate the fascinating permutations three divisions might bring—speculating about trades and other player movements, wondering how the two new teams would progress, wallowing in the promised glory of the new parks opening up in Cleveland and Texas that would rival Baltimore's gem—all this was obliterated by the constant threat of strike, lockout, and intransigence. And the very issue being argued—whether millionaire players or billionaire owners would prevail in adopting regulations no one could understand or care about—was a huge turnoff in itself.

What emerged was an all too clear battle line.

The owners were determined to roll back salaries through some salary-cap arrangement, curtail if not eliminate salary arbitration, and cut down on some of the other gains the players had made. If the players would not accept this voluntarily by the time the 1994 season ended, the owners would declare a bargaining impasse under the labor law and impose the new rules unilaterally.

At that point, the players would have no way of using their only weapon—a strike—because there would be nothing to strike until the spring of 1995, and by that time all the 1995 contracts would have been entered into under the owners' new rules. So if they were to act at all, it would have to be a preemptive strike during the 1994 season.

What a wonderful thing for fans to look forward to in spring training, eh?

One of the subjects obscured by the damper put on "just baseball" talk was an aspect of what actually transpired on the field in 1993.

Offense, as measured by runs scored, batting averages, and home runs, had soared, suddenly and significantly. Such figures, on a leaguewide basis, fluctuate within a relatively narrow range from year to year, although a steady series of small changes in the same direction will make a trend. But enormous jumps, up or down, from one season to the next were rare and always reflected a major change in rules (like the pitching distance in 1893) or equipment (like the livelier ball in 1930) or both (as in 1920). From 1977 through 1992, the 15 years in which 26 teams were playing, there were "hitters' years" and "pitchers' years," but the general level was well established: about 8.5 runs and 1.6 homers a game (by both teams) and a .259 batting average.

But from 1992 to 1993, the batting average jumped from .256 to .266; runs from 8.23 to 9.20; homers from 1.44 to 1.77. Instead of 14 percent of all games producing a shutout only 9.6 percent did—the lowest such figure in 63 years, since the super-lively ball of 1930.

Such a variation could mean only one thing. The rules hadn't changed, so the ball must have.

The games played in 1994 and 1995 would bear this out, as the offensive figures went even higher.

Now it doesn't matter whether the ball is juiced up on purpose or by some unintended or even unrealized change in the manufacturing process, the materials used, or both. Whenever it is, baseball fans love it. Higher-scoring games have two unmistakable virtues: they provide more action in running bases and chasing down batted balls; and they heighten the tensions that make the game so enjoyable for spectators, by increasing the number of potential scoring situations and the actual changes of lead in the story line of any game. The effect, over time, is to enhance the spectators' ability to *believe* that a three-or-four-run rally is still possible (to be hoped for or feared), that any batter may hit a score-changing home run, that (literally) a ball game is never over until the last man is out. The degree of *likelihood* of a ninth-inning rally determines the intensity of the excitement in all the preceding innings as well.

That 15–14 World Series game was a perfect example.

By design or accident, the major leagues in 1993 were back to the kind of game that had been so popular in the 1920–60 era, which had settled into less offense since. This was one factor among many that helped account for the enormous attendance jump of 1993. Baseball's most stagnant period of attendance growth was 1963–72, a decade that coincided with the most dominant pitching (or weakest hitting) since 1920 and led to the designated hitter. A higher level of offense had coincided with a 53 percent increase in attendance between 1977 and 1992. And 1993 had taken this process to new heights.

But the labor war was undoing it all.

1994: DISASTER

The 1994 season began, as scheduled, with strike talk everywhere. The three-divisional standings were confusing at first and excoriated by most tradition-minded commentators. But the balls were flying over fences and runners were circling the bases at all-time high frequencies.

And that made the stoppage that much more painful.

A strike was expected around All-Star time, but the players, after considering that, decided to play the All-Star Game for the pension-fund money. The next target date discussed was around Labor Day, which would give the players all but their last two semimonthly paychecks. But ultimately that date was deemed to be too close to the end of the season to make resumption possible if a strike did lead to agreement. No one could even contemplate interfering with the World Series.

So the date chosen was August 12. At that point:

The Yankees had a 6½-game lead over Baltimore in AL East, the league's best record with 70 victories, and seemed headed for their first postseason participation in 13 years, since the strike year of 1981.

Chicago had a one-game lead over Cleveland and four over Kansas City in AL Central, but it was the Indians who were finally coming into their own and favored to win in the end.

Texas was leading AL West—with a 52–62 record, actualizing the fear that the new system might produce an under-.500 champion. Oakland, whose record on June 8 had been 17–41, was only one game behind Texas at 51–63, and Seattle, 49–63, was only a game behind that.

Montreal, at 74–40 the winningest team in baseball, had a six-game lead over Atlanta in NL East, but the Braves had proved three years in a row that they could make up that kind of deficit.

Cincinnati and Houston were only half a game apart at the top of NL Central, with third-place Pittsburgh 13 games out.

Los Angeles was 3½ games ahead of San Francisco in what was shaping up as another historic Giant-Dodger battle, with Colorado doing surprisingly well three games further back. But the Dodger record was only 58–56 and the Giants were 55–60, so a sub-.500 winner was possible here too.

Then, of course, there would be a wild-card team in each league, and it was too early to consider such possibilities, but at least 14 of the 28 teams had realistic hopes of winding up in the eight-team playoff somehow.

At this point, most teams had played 113 to 115 games, with only Colorado and San Diego at 117. That was just about seven-tenths of the 162 game schedule.

Matt Williams had 43 homers, Griffey 40, Jeff Bagwell of Houston 39 and Frank Thomas 38, all in a position to make a serious run at Roger Maris' record of 61, now

33 years old. (Ruth's 60 had been on the books for 33 years when Maris surpassed it in 1961.)

Tony Gwynn was hitting .394, with an honest shot at .400. Bagwell, hitting .368, had 116 runs batted in.

In the American League, a batting-title race involved Paul O'Neill (Yankees, .359), Albert Belle (Cleveland, .357), Thomas (.353), Lofton (.349), Boggs (.342), and Molitor (.341). Lofton already had 60 stolen bases, and Kirby Puckett 112 runs batted in.

Jimmy Key, with the Yankees, was 17–4 and Baltimore's Mike Mussina 16–5, while Maddux was 16–6 (with a 1.56 ERA) for Atlanta and Montreal's Ken Hill 16–5. David Cone, who had moved on to Kansas City, was also 16–5.

What kind of numbers might these players have put up in a full season? Nobody will ever know.

What's worse, nobody talks about what might have been.

The season was not resumed, so these became the final records of 1994, with some ambiguity about whether the division leaders should be called "champions." But Maddux and Cone were given Cy Young Awards, and Thomas and Bagwell were named MVPs, all eminently worthy—but tarnished.

Still, statistics were only statistics and had been adulterated by shortened seasons before—in 1918 by World War I, in 1972 and 1981 by strikes—without permanent damage to baseball's psyche.

Not having a World Series was something else.

Until mid-September, no one really believed this would happen. Even if the regular season could not be resumed, as the stalemate dragged on, it was possible to declare the August 11 standings official and get on with the playoffs.

What would it have taken? A pledge by the owners that they wouldn't declare impasse (as they had promised they wouldn't in 1993, and had kept their word.) The players were willing to play under an extension of the old contract while bargaining continued. But getting to impasse had been the owners' game plan from the beginning, and they stuck to it.

So, for the first time since 1904, when John T. Brush had hoped to stifle the infant American League by refusing to have his Giants grant it the prestige of equal status, there would be no World Series (and, of course, no play-offs leading up to it).

The cancellation, among other things, obscured the full effect of a misguided decision the owners had made about television.

National television (and radio) packages had always been sold as "rights." The carrier, network or station, paid some flat sum for the right to broadcast the games, then recouped by selling time to advertisers. In the last agreement, which expired with 1993, this had amounted to about $14 million per club per year.

That money, since it was distributed equally to all clubs, undermined the argument about the need for a "new system" of revenue sharing. Player negotiators could, and did, point to this package as a well-publicized cushion against other financial problems and argued that it could be, and should be, even larger in the future.

What if that guaranteed money weren't there? Wouldn't that justify the call for cutting back on salaries?

Not only for that reason, but certainly including it, the clubs embarked on an unprecedented arrangement. The Baseball Network would be a partnership between Major League Baseball (a registered trademark) and the ABC and NBC networks. There would be no rights fee at all. The networks and baseball would simply share whatever revenue the advertising brought in, and the joint enterprise would control the programming. There would be very few in-season weekend telecasts, virtually none before the All-Star Game. The play-off games would be "regionalized," played at the same time (prime time), and piped to predetermined areas presumably interested in only one of the four first-round games. Only the World Series itself could be seen by all fans everywhere.

Such an idea had two terrible flaws. The whole regular season was a buildup to the play-offs, and the League Championship Series had always used a staggered schedule so that all games could be seen on one network or another. And the importance of the traditional summer program of a national game every Saturday (or, originally, Sunday) afternoon was important to building up the season-long pennant races, far out of proportion to its actual ratings. To ration the play-off games could only frustrate and infuriate the public, and to assume that people in Denver wouldn't want to see a Yankee-Indian confrontation loaded with stars while being fed a "geographic" Dodger-Houston series was simply mindless.

On a deeper level, the plan undermined the famous "integrity of the game" concept in perception, if not in reality. A New York–Los Angeles World Series was worth more, to advertisers, than a Milwaukee–St. Louis World Series. How the pairing worked out was a risk the rights buyer always took, along with the risk of getting only four games instead of seven. Baseball, once it pocketed the flat fee for the rights, had no direct interest in which matchup turned up. But if official baseball was a partner in *selling* the ads, game by game, year by year, the pressure for a "good" matchup spilled over on it. As far back as 1905, baseball owners understood that the *public* needed assurance that players wouldn't "prolong" a Series for the sake of additional gate receipts and made a big proud noise about the fact that the players would share in the receipts "of the first four games only." The same principle applied here. It didn't get any attention because, in 1994, the Baseball Network never got off the ground.

But it had an important effect anyhow. The owners actually argued, to the public as well as the players, "We'll get millions less from television in 1994"—meaning *guaranteed* millions—"so we have to have a new salary system *now*."

The players replied that, if true, this was the owners' own doing; but rumor had it in August of 1994 that sales were going so well that the eventual total might match or exceed the 1993 revenue. Whether the rumors were true or not, they played a role in the player side's estimate of what would happen. Whatever money would come in was concentrated in play-off and World Series telecasts. The owners would never give that up, would they? Owners whose definition of "loss" was "what could have been made but wasn't"? The best chance to get them to give up the impasse idea, the players felt, was to make them face the threat of lost playoffs. That was the purpose of striking in August.

They were wrong. The owners were willing to give up immediate dollars this time for the sake of controlling salaries. If their control of salaries were institutionalized, it would further increase the value of every franchise. Where the owners were equally wrong was in clinging to the belief that the players would not stick together when confronted with (1) the loss of the postseason and (2) the new rules in the off-season with no collective action possible and their next year's income uncertain. The stars might stick it out, they thought, but certainly a majority of the others would yield.

So in October it became really astoundingly true. There was no World Series.

This was the defining moment. This is what "ends" the story that began in 1876. It was the first time that a season begun was not played through to some sort of conclusion that determined a "champion."

Why did this mean so much?

1. It broke continuity, the essential ingredient that fed a fan's interest from year to year. As betrayed as Brooklynites felt when the Dodgers went to California, the fabric of baseball itself had not been torn, even in their eyes. But to look down a list of champions and see "none," especially for an activity so intricately tied to records, memory, traditions, comparisons, and cyclical experience, was a shock that could never be erased. It might be forgiven, but it could never be forgotten.

2. It sent a message no one could ignore. The essence of deriving pleasure from the result of games is voluntary belief in the *supreme importance* of the outcome of the contest. Just as "willing suspension of disbelief" is necessary to the enjoyment of drama or fiction, "willing assumption of belief" is necessary to the enjoyment of a contest. You have to care who wins, and you have to believe that *the contestants care who wins*. The message sent by the cancellation was: "We don't think it's important enough to hold our championship showdown, when an argument over money has to be won." If *baseball* doesn't think it's all-important, why should we? How can we? When will we ever be sure that some other circumstance or private agenda won't override the importance of holding the next championship? How can we engage our emotions in the importance of an April result if it isn't a meaningful step toward October?

3. Both the broken continuity and the lesser-importance message went to the

heart of the *emotions* of the fan. Other entertainments engage our emotions temporarily, while we are experiencing them. We don't come away from a Shakespeare play, how ever deeply moved, with an ongoing feeling of loyalty to, and anticipation of, the next Shakespeare play. Being a sports fan involves a commitment and an assumption. The commitment is to adopted loyalty, since only that makes possible the vicarious sensations of victory and defeat. The assumption is that the competition, in recognizable form and related to a remembered past, *is always there.* If it's not going to be there, or we can't be sure it will be, we may still enjoy and patronize it whenever it is, but on a shallower level. We have been warned, "Don't commit."

Much of the handwringing that followed, therefore, was misplaced. There was never any danger that the industry would "die" or even fade away. It was too important, too entrenched, too embedded in all sorts of other powerful interests to be threatened. The crowds and money would return automatically whenever play was resumed.

What would not be resumed was the unquestioning sense of loyalty and personal need in those fans who felt betrayed, and the manufacture of such feelings in the fans to come. Future fans would enjoy baseball their way, on their terms, for the indefinite future—but not "baseball as we knew it." Some degree of emotional reservation would always be part of the involvement.

Before we pick up the thread of events in January 1995, we must note two developments concerning the All-Star Game and the Baltimore franchise.

The All-Star Game had grown into a two-day extravaganza, including an old-timers game, home-run contests, and other special events preceding the game itself. Baseball's marketing arm really showed its power here, and the tendency of players to skip the assignment had long since disappeared. The growth of the collectibles phenomenon, for autographs and memorabilia, had turned the occasion into a market fair and a convention for ancillary interests.

The game itself was being taken more seriously by participants. The 1993 game was played in Baltimore, in the justly admired Oriole Park at Camden Yards, and the American League won its sixth in a row, 9–3, with 14 pitchers taking part, none working more than two innings. In 1994, at Pittsburgh, the Nationals ended that streak, winning 8–7 in 10 innings after pulling even in the bottom of the ninth on a two-run homer by pinch-hitter McGriff off Lee Smith.

The series now stood at 38–26 in favor of the National League, with that one tie game in Boston in 1961.

The significance of the 1994 game was that the players decided to play it expressly for the pension-fund money. When the clubs then claimed they had the right to withhold the money (because the old CBA had expired), they caused bitterness that intensified the hostility in the strike situation and handed the players a weapon—a grievance that they won—that would weaken the owners' position later in the strike.

Hoffberger had sold the Orioles to Edward Bennett Williams for $12.3 million in 1979, and that quintessential Washington insider had been critical of his fellow owners in the 1981 strike, pressing for settlement. Williams's widow had sold the club in 1989 for $70 million to Eli Jacobs. In 1993, Jacobs went into personal bankruptcy (from matters not connected with baseball) and arranged to sell the team for about $140 million. But the bankruptcy court intervened and wanted the sale open to bids to establish the club's true market price. That turned out to be $173 million, from a group led by Peter Angelos, a Baltimore attorney known for, among other things, defending labor unions in court. Since this occurred on August 2, 1994, when the strike was scheduled to start nine days later, it did little to convince the players that baseball was facing a "financial crisis." The value of the franchise, determined in open bidding, was 14 times what it had been before the "devastating" strike of 1981, when players had been told the sport could not survive if salaries went any higher. And it had more than doubled in value in only four years.

The reason, of course, was the ball park, into which Baltimore and the state of Maryland had poured hundreds of millions of dollars. It promised to guarantee Oriole profits for many years, while, from the civic point of view, revitalizing a downtown area well enough to make the investment worthwhile.

Well, weren't there other new ball parks? What was the crisis? Positions hardened, distrust ballooned.

By December 1994, everything was coming to a head.

On December 14, talks broke off after each side had rejected the other's last proposal (a huge punitive "tax" on payrolls offered by management, a very low tax proposed by the players, which represented an acceptance of the principle but no economic impact in practice). The same day, the National Labor Relations Board announced that it had found against the owners on the question of withholding the August 1 pension-fund payment of $7.8 million.

Now it was beyond dispute that distrust was the central issue. From the owner point of view, the players were simply refusing to admit a problem existed. Whatever had happened in "ancient history" (which, one club executive told me, meant everything before 1990), the players had attained a position of bargaining power that inflated salaries beyond reason, and they were unwilling to give anything back to restore a fair balance. From the player point of view, the other side (1) had reneged on the 1985 agreement as soon as it was signed (by collusion), (2) had persistently lied about finances and still could not be believed, (3) wasn't making a credible case even with the numbers it submitted, and (4) was simply trying to "break the union"—or at least its power—with no intention of seeking an acceptable middle ground, let alone the "partnership" it talked about in public.

The sole issue had become surrender. Each side had the power to hurt the other financially and had used it; but neither could use it to the point of decision. The clubs could certainly close down long enough to make unpaid players abandon their union—

but that long a closedown would also break many clubs, which couldn't go that long without revenue, and with no games, there would be no revenue. By the same token, the players couldn't stay out indefinitely, since playing ball was their only livelihood.

So the owners played their last card to create pressure: they declared they would open the 1995 season on schedule using "replacement players"—strikebreakers, also known as scabs.

If there was any way to infuriate the players further and strengthen their resolve to stick together, this was it.

After all, the whole premise of "major league baseball" was that the performers were the "best available." To field teams, in major league uniforms, composed of players who had been explicitly rejected by these very clubs was professionally insulting and promotionally risky.

The portions of the public and media whose anger was directed at overpaid players who had stopped playing—very large portions, very vocal—were prepared to support "replacement ball." Advertisers and networks weren't so sure and had the sticky issue of their own union relationships to think about. The test could come only if the regular season began with the strike still on and replacement players in action. Would the customers come out? How many? For how long? Without doubt, if enough did, that would break the strike; if too few did, the players would emerge with more power than ever and the owners would have to give in. But how much would be enough? For which clubs? The Tribune Company, celebrated throughout the business and financial worlds for its defeat of other unions, might have the stomach and resources to close down the Cubs or have their replacement personnel play before empty seats; but what about Milwaukee (acting commissioner Selig's team, no less) and Seattle and Kansas City and Minnesota and San Diego and Pittsburgh and Cincinnati and other "smaller" markets without huge corporate ownership? Could they afford it? The ones for whom, presumably, the war was being fought?

Well, they were going to try. Only Angelos declared that Baltimore would refuse to use replacements, and Toronto was forbidden by Canadian law to do it. Angelos, with his background of dealing with organized labor, certainly understood the ugly overtones of using "scabs"; but more to the point, he had never been part of the original strategy, embarked upon before he bought the club, and the Orioles in Camden Yards were the surest money machine baseball had at the moment, if baseball were played.

On December 23, the owners declared an impasse existed and that their own rules were now in force: salary cap, no salary arbitration, a new class of "restricted" free agents.

The players promptly filed an unfair-labor-practice claim, denying that there was an impasse because no attempt at "good faith bargaining" had been made by management, and that it had refused to bargain over "wages," a mandatory subject of bargaining under the law.

There were no meetings in January. On February 1, the two sides met in Washington, at Usery's request, and again got nowhere. On February 7, President Clinton personally took a hand in the dispute, citing the effect on related jobs and businesses, and proposed binding arbitration of the disputed issues. Since the owners rejected that immediately, the players didn't have to commit themselves (but probably would have accepted).

At this time, it became clear that the NLRB was going to uphold the "failure to bargain" complaint, so the owners backed off on some of their newly imposed procedures concerning contracts. The legal situation was a mess: under the expired agreement, there were all sorts of dates in November, December, and January by which contracts had to be tendered or accepted, to establish a player's status, and for filing arbitration claims. All that had gone by the boards and no one really knew, on either side, who had what kind of rights or obligations.

On March 2, training camps opened with all clubs except Baltimore using replacement players—minor leaguers, semipro hopefuls, a few recently retired major leaguers. Some ambiguity existed. Was a nonunion member in training camp a "strikebreaker"? The union announced that those who played in exhibition games, when those began, would be considered strikebreakers. Aware of the explosive emotions this situation entailed, most clubs allowed their best minor league prospects to stay out, so as not to compromise their future—a wise enough step, but one that called further attention to how adulterated the replacement product would be.

Managers and coaches were in a difficult position. They were clearly management, obliged to fulfill contractual duties. But sooner or later the regular players would be back, somehow, so how could they avoid burning their bridges to them? Only Sparky Anderson, starting his 17th season as manager of the Tigers and 26th as a major league manager, would have no part of the "travesty." He took a leave of absence and stayed home in California, his status with the club to be determined later.

The exhibition games began. On March 15, the NLRB issued its ruling that the owners "had failed to bargain collectively in good faith." Such a finding eviscerated the strategy embarked upon three years before, just as Seitz's finding in December of 1975 had eviscerated the reserve system. However, just as then, the owners responded by hanging on, instead of seeking a prompt compromise.

On March 26, the NLRB voted 3–2 to allow its counsel to seek an injunction in federal court against management's use of any new regulations, and to reinstitute the terms of the expired CBA until a new one could be bargained correctly. The next day, the request was put before Judge Sonia Sotomayor.

Two days later the players voted to end their strike if the injunction were granted. Two days after that, March 31, Judge Sotomayor granted it, with some strong words:

"This strike has placed the entire concept of collective bargaining on trial. It is critical, therefore, that the Board assure and that I protect its assurance that the spirit and the letter of the Federal labor law be scrupulously followed."

1995: PICKING UP THE PIECES

The terms of the old CBA would remain in effect (free agency, salary arbitration, etc.), and if the owners wanted to try to declare impasse again, they would have to come to her for approval.

Since the players had offered to come back to work, continuing to keep them out would become a lockout, not a strike, with unknown liability possible. The owners scrapped the replacement plan, accepted the end of the strike on April 2, and quickly negotiated a plan for an extended spring training and a later start for a curtailed regular season.

But they also appealed Judge Sotomayor's ruling to a higher court, asking for a stay of the injunction on the grounds that it interfered with further collective bargaining.

When the Court of Appeals for Second Circuit upheld the injunction, it also scolded baseball's lawyers. In claiming that the injunction "is stopping you from negotiating a collective bargaining agreement, you're telling us something that isn't so," said Judge Jon Newman.

The truth was, there was not and never had been any plan for "good faith collective bargaining." There had been a plan to make the players "accept a new system," and it had now gone down in flames. For the rest of the calendar year, the owners made no serious attempt to bargain anything at all, proving the point. The players, at least for the time being, had no problem with the continuation of the old regulations.

The resumption plan was:

1. Allow three weeks of spring training for the regular players.
2. Start the season on April 25, picking up the schedule as originally drawn, simply dropping the first three weeks of games (as had been done in 1972).
3. However, to make the competition a bit more coherent, adjust individual games so that every team plays 144, with 72 at home and 72 on the road.
4. Begin the two-tier play-off as scheduled, on October 3, with a three-of-five first round, to be followed by the four-of-seven League Championship Series and the World Series opening October 21 in the National League city.

One reaction to this plan indicates how emotion overrides reason among baseball followers, and, emphasizes what was lost by the interruption. Many of the most experienced newspaper columnists and broadcast commentators lamented the decision to play 144 games.

"At least they could have made it 154," they wrote or said, in some form or other. "That way we'd have valid records."

Now, the 154-game schedule had been gone for 33 years. It had called for 22 games a year with seven opponents in an eight-team league. Suppose you did play 154 games with 14 teams in three divisions, what sort of "validity" would that produce? Besides, it was physically impossible to squeeze more than 144 or so into the calendar window that remained before the locked-in television play-off dates. Why would one even think of the number 154, let alone recommend it?

Because it represented, without analysis, "baseball as we know it."

It wouldn't any more. Baseball "as we know it" had been shifting and changing all along, over the decades, as we have seen, but the *yearning* for it never wavered.

That's what had suffered a crippling blow in the interruption: the yearning.

Meanwhile, the umpires had been having their own fight with management, among other things, about being on the payroll during the strike. They were locked out, the season began with replacement umpires (as had happened several times since the 1970s), and the regulars did not return until May 1.

As the 1995 season progressed, labor matters disappeared from the news. Baseball normality took hold quickly, once the clubs started playing games. Expressions of disgust, disillusion, and dissatisfaction were plentiful, in print and conversation, but none of the talked-about "boycotts" materialized. When it was all over, the 144-game season drew 50.3 million, slightly more than the 116-game 1994 season had produced. Since the 1994 average was 31,600 a game and the 1995 average 26,200, this was reported as a 17 percent drop. But it was due almost entirely to the fact that there had been no between-season ticket promotion possible, not to any reluctance of people to come to the games when they were actually put on. Furthermore 26,000 was an average baseball had never reached until 1989 and was substantially exceeded only in 1993 and 1994, so it could not realistically be called a rejection by the public. But here again, perception and presupposition outweighed actuality. Comment that baseball was "losing its public" proliferated.

It wasn't losing its "public." It was losing its "specialness," which is another thing entirely—and perhaps, in the long run, much more important.

The 1995 season, in fact, was just plain terrific.

The Cleveland Indians emerged as the class act of the American League. They won 100 games (of 144) and finished 30 games ahead of Kansas City in AL Central. The Red Sox, starting fast, held off the Yankees and won AL East by seven games, but the Yankees, with a 79–65 mark in second place, became the wild card. In AL West, Seattle and California finished in a flat tie after the Angels blew an 11-game lead in August, then made up a three-game deficit in the last five games. In the one-game play-off, Seattle's Randy Johnson beat them 7–1.

Atlanta handled NL East the way Cleveland did AL Central, winning by 21 games with a 90–54 record. Cincinnati took NL Central by nine games over Houston, while the Dodgers and Rockies staged a terrific race to the wire in NL West, the Dodgers finally winning by one game while Colorado salvaged the wild-card assignment, nosing out Chicago and Houston, who battled each other for it during the final week.

The Rockies, in only the third year of their existence, were playing in their new stadium, Coors Field, modeled after Camden Yards with significant local differences. It was an instant success, just as Jacobs Field in Cleveland and The Ball Park in Arlington, Texas, had been in 1994. Their first two years in Mile High Stadium, the Rockies had averaged nearly 60,000 a game. In Coors, capacity 50,000, they averaged 47,000. The Indians averaged 40,000 in "the Jake," the Orioles 46,000 in Baltimore, the Red Sox 30,000 in their 33,000-capacity, 83-year-old Fenway Park.

If this be bankruptcy, Patrick Henry might have said, make the most of it.

Seattle and the Yankees staged a spectacular play-off. The Yankees won at home 9–5 and 7–6 in a 15-inning game that lasted more than five hours. But Johnson was able to pitch in Seattle, three days after his play-off victory, and stopped New York 7–4. Then the Mariners broke a 6–6 tie with a five-run eighth for an 11–8 victory in the fourth game, and won the fifth 6–5 in 11 innings, scoring two in the eighth to tie against Cone and two in the 11th off McDowell after the Yankees had gone ahead in the top half. Griffey hit five home runs in this series.

Cleveland, meanwhile, disposed of the Red Sox in three straight. The Mariners then caused great excitement by winning two of the first three in the LCS, Johnson pitching the third in Cleveland. But the Indians won the next three and went on to their first World Series in 41 years.

Cincinnati rolled over the Dodgers in three straight, and Atlanta polished off Colorado in four, whereupon the Braves swept Cincinnati in four straight. And this time, when they got to the World Series, the Braves finally won, shutting down Cleveland's power. They won 3–2 and 4–3 at home, lost an 11-inning drama 7–6 in Cleveland before winning 5–2, were forced back to Atlanta by losing 5–4, then won a 1–0 one-hitter pitched by Glavine for eight innings and Mark Wohlers for one.

But all that is part of the next story, not this one, along with 1995s eye-opening individual feats: 50 home runs and 52 doubles by Albert Belle (never done before); a .356 batting title for Seattle's Edgar Martinez; 18–2 for Johnson, with 294 strikeouts in 214 innings and a 2.48 earned run average; Eddie Murray's 3,000th hit; Tony Gwynn's sixth National League batting title at .368; a fourth straight Cy Young award for Greg Maddux—unprecedented—for his 19–2 record with a 1.63 earned run average, almost a whole run lower than anyone else in the league; and the sensational Hideo Nomo, from Japan, 13–6 for Los Angeles and second only to Maddux in ERA; and many others.

No, our story ended when the 1994 World Series was not played. Everything after that is part of a new era, which will be seen in perspective only some decades into the next century. Its shape will depend on what sort of relationship—not mere agreement, but relationship—is arrived at by the players and owners. When 1996 began, they hadn't even exchanged meaningful proposals for 14 months and were no closer to resolution than three years earlier.

DENOUEMENT

Just how complete a break with the past had occurred, and how a distinctly different era had begun, was made evident by the events of 1995 through 1998.

The labor agreement was rebargained all through 1996. When finally signed in December, it was to cover 1996 through 2000, and continue through 2001 if the players wanted it to. It was another complete defeat of management goals: the free agent and arbitration rules stayed intact; there were substantial increases in minimum salary and minor perks; and the strength and unity of the union were demonstrated again.

But there were three revolutionary items.

First, a payroll "tax" on any team's payroll that exceeded a stipulated amount would go into a special fund.

Second, this fund would be used for revenue sharing among the clubs, to aid the smaller-revenue and smaller-payroll situations. And it would lump together the needs of all teams in both leagues instead of treating them separately.

Finally, the players agreed, as an experiment, to permit interleague games that would count in the standings in 1997 and (later) 1998 also—but only in those years.

All three—tax, revenue-sharing formula, interleague play—had been considered unsuitable for 120 years. The first two were precedent shattering in terms of the financial relationship among clubs, and in crossing league lines. But the third went to the heart of the competition directly visible to, and affecting, fans.

The interleague games were to be limited in number, no more than 20 for any one team, and concentrated in certain time periods. They would certainly, in their novelty, excite interest and comment. But they made a fundamental change in the idea of a league championship, which had always rested on "official" games between league members exclusively. That, after all, was the whole idea of a "league." Now the championship would also depend on how various contenders made out in games against *nonleague* opponents—and, what's more, games played under different rules (with a designated hitter in American League parks and without one in National League parks).

The World Series had always been a match between teams that had never faced each other during the season or had any common opponents. Now a World Series might be a rematch between teams that had met during the regular season.

It might work out very well—but it could never be "baseball as we knew it." The "specialness" was decreased.

This break in tradition also altered and complicated statistical records, so dear to the heart of the truest baseball fans. Now a batting title, earned run leadership, and every other category's listing would include performance against the "other" league. The solution chosen was the only practical one: anything done by a player or team would count according to affiliation, regardless of where the game was played, "affiliation" being determined by the uniform worn. Anything a National League team or player did would go in National League statistics, and the same for the American League.

In itself, all that was sensible and easily learned, But it was undeniably unprecedented, and one more blow to comparisons with the past. The quality of "continuity" was evaporating before our eyes.

The commissionership had been vacant for five years by the end of 1997, since Selig insisted that he was only "chairman of the executive council" and not "acting commissioner." While the future shape of the office was unclear, it was plain (and inescapable) that it would be different from what had evolved from Landis through Frick to Vincent. Many of its functions were split off in 1997 by the appointment of Paul Beetson of Toronto as "chief operating officer," devoid of any quasi-judicial and public-relations functions attached to the commissionership itself.

Here, too, was a major break with the pattern of the preceding 70 or 90 years (since Landis had been an extension of the three-man Commission that preceded him).

Then came the talk of "radical realignment" during 1997. Merely bringing up the subject was another shock to the baseball fan's psyche and one more unmistakable sign that the future would be entirely different from the familiar past. That it didn't happen, then and there, did not lessen the impact on one's sense of dissolving stability.

The problem was triggered by the scheduled entrance in 1998 of Phoenix and Tampa Bay. If you added one to each league, you'd have 15-team leagues, requiring an interleague game every day (just as seven-team divisions required an intradivision game every day, and therefore a balanced schedule). Nobody wanted that, and the players wouldn't agree to it even if management did. (The idea had been rejected back in 1976 when Kuhn was pushing it for 13-team leagues with a team back in Washington.) The only alternative was to put both teams in the same league, making a 16 and a 14. Such an imbalance had its deficiencies, but baseball had lived with a 14 and a 12 through 16 highly successful seasons (1977–92), so it wasn't unfeasible.

The "radical" proposal put forth by Selig in the spring of 1997 called for 13 to 15 clubs changing leagues, to arrange closer geographical groupings and heighten "local" rivalries (like New York's Yankees and Mets in the same division). This would totally destroy *all* relation to the past and throw away a century's worth of accumulated mental associations—and "denationalize" each new league into merely regional associations. It was a silly and impossible proposal from the start and soon fell of its own weight, but its message could not be ignored: to hell with the past, this is what television would like now.

The silliest aspect was that such a change was wholly unnecessary to achieve the stated goals. A shift by two or three teams to another division, and one to the other league, would be enough to satisfy geographic and local-rivalry requirements. That's what was finally adopted, as a temporary measure, for 1998. What was really needed, and inevitable, was the addition of two more teams for a total of 32, in 16-team leagues divided into four-team divisions, with only the four division champions going to the first round of play-offs. That would make a neat setup and work well, with or without interleague games. But it would be nothing like "baseball as we knew it."

That final step to 32 was being put off as long as possible because some teams wanted to keep "escape hatches" open, so that they could threaten to, or actually, move. It was their bargaining chip for getting their home cities to build them new ball parks, whatever the details of financing. The Giants were getting one in San Francisco, to open in 2000; Cincinnati, Pittsburgh, and Seattle had new ones promised, and more were being sought in Minnesota, Milwaukee, Houston, Detroit, Boston, and Oakland. Not all of these clubs talked of moving, but no matter how this came out, the face of baseball would be changed as thoroughly as when the steel-and-concrete parks were built before World War I.

During the 1990s, of course, all sorts of gradual changes were coming about, as they always had. But the key word is "gradual." The world of 1997, in every respect, was as different from the world of 1947 as 1947 had been from 1897. But the cancellation of the 1994 World Series was a breaking point. Popularity and prosperity returned quickly once play was resumed, but the *nature* of the baseball experience was altered forever.

That's why the central story line of this "concise" history is completed with the 1994 stoppage, and why future historical narratives can make a fresh start with 1995. Among other things, the identity of ownership underwent a major shift. Ted Turner's Atlanta Braves, always a subsidiary of his own television network, became part of vastly larger Time Warner when he sold his holdings to that conglomerate; the Cubs had become part of the Tribune Company in 1980; Disney had become the controlling interest in the Angels in 1996; and in 1997, Peter O'Malley announced that the Dodgers were being sold to Rupert Murdoch, whose news-and-entertainment conglomerate was as large as the others. Much was written about O'Malley representing "the last family ownership."

This shift, in turn, implied a different (and as yet undefined) role for the commissionership. Properly carried out, it rested on persuasion. The employee of the club owners can never *force* them to do anything but must make them willing to follow his lead for whatever policy he thinks is best for *them*. Landis did this arrogantly, Frick more subtly, and some failed altogether. But clubs had always been represented by one principal owner, however rich and powerful he might be in the outside world, and however many silent partners he had. Now the most powerful clubs were passing into the hands of conglomerates.

A commissioner, if wise and skilled enough, can earn the trust of individual owners and persuade them to follow a certain course. But no one can "persuade" a conglomerate: there are too many layers of private (and legitimate) agendas throughout their systems.

The canceled championship was not, by itself, the cause of the fall of the old structure. It was only the final straw, and it did break tradition's back.

From here on in, it would be a whole new ball game.

The Summation

Baseball, the game, began being systematized in New York in the 1840s, an amalgam of other stick-and-ball games going back to antiquity but more directly descended from the English games of rounders and cricket and their offshoots. By the beginning of the Civil War in 1861, widespread adoption of uniform rules was being stimulated by baseball (social) clubs through an annual convention.

Baseball, the business, began in the 1870's when professionalism became socially acceptable and spectator interest made it practical to charge admission to games played within enclosed grounds.

Baseball, the game, was fully developed by the early 1880s into rules we would recognize today, along with some basic techniques: pitch high and tight, low and away; fielders, especially at first base, lining up well wide of the base they were "covering"; aggressive baserunning to advance an extra base on hits as an even more valuable maneuver than stealing a base; change-of-pace and breaking-ball pitching; bunting as well as swinging away.

Baseball, the business, was put on a firm commercial (as distinct from merely professional) basis also in the 1880s, along a blueprint developed in 1876 by William Hulbert and Albert Spalding in Chicago, and Harry Wright in New England.

Baseball, the game, after rapid rule changes through the 1890s reached essentially its present form in 1903, with the adoption of the foul-strike.

Baseball, the business, took permanent form in 1903, when the newly formed eight-team American League and 27-year-old National League made a compact for mutual observance of contracts, regulations, and commercial practices.

Baseball, the game, changed in character (but not in rules) in 1920, when introduction of the lively ball and other procedural adjustments made the home run an integral and *common* part of the game.

Baseball, the business, went full-scale commercial during the 1920s, in the post–World War I expansion of American advertising, entertainment, mass-circulation publications, transportation, and leisure-time industries, partaking in the spread of "modern ideas" through the culture as a whole and in new relationships among social classes.

Baseball, the game, has undergone only minor and peripheral adjustments for the last 70 years on the professional level. Below that, it remains universally popular on the school, teenage amateur, and college levels, and recreationally in the form of softball. Of all the team sports, it has had the longest period of unchanging *basic* rules.

Baseball, the business, started to become an industry in the 1950's, when television and the money it generated began altering economic relationships and the cultural climate of the entire population.

Baseball, the business, became only one part of a rapidly expanding spectator-sports industry during the 1970s, facing commercial competition it never had before, but also facing commercial and marketing opportunities it didn't have before.

Baseball, the industry, became a part of multiindustry conglomerates on a large scale from about 1980 on, a financial instrument and bargaining chip in other agendas (notably television) as well as a game-presentation business.

Along the way, baseball, the business, developed powerful natural alliances with the sporting-goods industry, real estate, newspapers, local politicians, and foodstuff (including beer) providers.

Baseball, the game, provided the context for myth and symbolism, metaphor and fantasy, from the late 19th century on to writers, social critics, politicians, and, above all, children.

Players, once professionalized, entered into permanent conflict with baseball business operators over how much of the money generated should go to them.

The first attempt, the National Association of Professional Baseball Players, gave all decisive power to the players, and failed within a few years.

The National League of Baseball Clubs gave decisive power to the clubs, who were ongoing entities as business firms, simply hiring the players as employees.

Within a few years, these business firms devised a way, through interlocking agreements, to avoid bidding against each other for the better players, thus keeping salaries down. This became known as "the reserve system" and made practical the formation of a second league, the American Association.

The players, in 1890, rebelled against these restrictive arrangements, pulled out of the National League, and started their own. This oversaturation resulted in financial disaster for all three leagues, and within two years only one remained, the original National. As a monopoly, it controlled the movement of players and cut their salaries much more severely than in the preceding decade.

As player dissatisfaction grew, a new league, the American, provided an escape hatch from the reserve, and, through competition, raised salary levels dramatically in 1901.

Two years later the American joined the National in reinstating the reserve-monopoly system, and player compensation leveled off.

In 1912, a substantial number of players were ready to revolt again, but just then another new league, the Federal, created the escape-hatch, competition-for-talent circumstance that doubled the salary level again.

When the third league failed after the 1915 season, the two-league monopoly was restored.

Once World War I ended, players' dissatisfaction with their stifled bargaining power and relatively low pay was one factor (among other important ones) in the willingness of the Chicago White Sox to accept gamblers' bribes to throw the 1919 World Series.

During the 1920s, with the appointment of Judge Landis as a single commissioner, the internal affairs of baseball, the business, became more orderly. The monopoly, tighter than ever, did give individual players the recourse of appeal to the commissioner, but much more important was the rapidly rising level of prosperity through the 1920s. Players were being paid better because there was so much more money coming in than in the past.

In the 1930s, the Depression led to lower salaries within the iron-bound reserve, but in that era of widespread joblessness players were content to have any work at all, and it was plain that no great profits were being made anyhow. There was less player-management conflict than ever.

After World War II, in 1946, another explosion of prosperity raised baseball revenues to previously unimagined heights, and the upward movement of salaries by natural process relieved pressures for confronting the reserve.

By the late 1950s, the players, concerned primarily about pension arrangements at that point, began to think about organizing themselves (as the players of the 1880s had done) to bargain for a bigger share of the visibly expanding financial pie, and for better working conditions. Talk of a third league, which led instead expansion of the existing leagues, put an upward thrust on salaries (since more teams meant more major league jobs to be filled by players with major league salaries, and more demand for the most desirable players). But a bigger factor in raising pay scales was the competition from other sports, now that teenage athletes had opportunities in football and basketball that exceeded the rewards being offered by baseball.

Nevertheless, baseball, the business, was keeping an ever increasing slice of the pie. In the Depression years, more than 30 percent of the revenue was going to players; in the 1960s it was sinking below 15 percent.

At that point the players did organize, still focusing on pension benefits and working conditions (like minimum salary, some sort of severance pay, expenses when sent to another club, and so forth). By hiring Marvin Miller to head their Players Association, they got, for the first time, professional negotiating advice and leadership.

Baseball, the business, resisted every step of the way any suggestion that the reserve be loosened up even minutely, as it had for 90 years.

Functioning as a true bargaining unit, the players began to gain. A contract-signing boycott in 1969 and a strike in 1972 succeeded in strengthening the pension plan. A successful grievance in 1975 wiped out the reserve altogether. Having negotiated, in 1976, a free-agent system favorable to them, they fought off an attempt to emasculate it in a long strike in 1981. They fought off another such attempt in 1985, in two days. And they faced down a lockout in 1990 to preserve, once again, their gains.

And all this had turned into reality what the owners feared: in having to compete with one another for players, they were sending salaries sky-high and turning over to the players a larger and larger share of the pie (now unimaginably huge), up to 50 percent.

The 1990s, therefore, were merely a continuation of the tug-of-war that had begun in the 1870s. If players have too much control, the business doesn't prosper and it becomes difficult to promote. If players have no control or too little, they are soon subject to abuse, not only in level of pay but in countless demeaning exercises of authority against them in the name of "discipline." Some middle ground must be found somehow.

But what's the "right" level?

And is the adversary relationship of labor negotiation the proper way to determine it?

Those are questions, of course, that go far beyond baseball or sports, to the heart of our entire economic-social system. So far, we don't seem to have good answers in any field.

But consider the nature of the product.

Baseball, the game, is marketable *to spectators and followers* only if it is played with superior skill by the "best" practitioners in the world. That's the sense in which (as agents say) "the players are the game."

Baseball, the business, is the *staging* of the game in a context that will command the interest of spectators and followers. The *organizing* can be done only by clubs, as continuing entities with the authority to conduct the competition and with the resources to provide facilities, transportation, financial stability, and all the other essential activities of a promoter.

If the 18 most talented individuals in the world played each other in Central Park wearing sweatshirts without identifying marks, who would pay to watch them and how would they make any money?

If the club tried to present second-rate talent, calling it "big league" because it was dressed in the proper trappings inside some large stadium, it couldn't make much money either—and the out-of-work best players would be hired by someone else who would outfit them and generate money.

The symbiosis is total. But the perception on both sides is that "they" are living off "my" unique efforts. Both owners and players acknowledge the rewards should be shared. But how? How much to which? Under what rules?

That's what the fight has been about for 120 years, and that's what got out of hand in the 1990s.

And that's why the story we've traced ended, because it *did* get out of hand. The trauma of 1994 was so great that only some fundamentally new arrangement—a more realistic partnership in some form—can avoid a repetition. And if there does come a repetition, the trauma will be worse. So either way, the old tug-of-war is over. There will be either a new relationship, or new chapters of combat that lead to new leagues altogether.

Any new arrangement, whatever it is, will alter everything—attitudes, procedures, formats and (the main point here) the closeness of ties to the past.

The changes may, one fervently hopes, make baseball better than ever. Baseball, the game, is as near perfection as any athletic game ever devised (it says here, out of unabashed prejudice and person preference). But baseball, the business, will have to adapt to being only one entertainment among many, adopting formats consistent with the needs and tastes of an American culture radically different form its 19th-century roots and mid-20th-century glories.

What it will never be is "the same." The feelings, associations, mental constructs, and treasured lore we took for granted, assuming they would always be attached to it, won't be. And to whatever extent they survive, they won't be taken for granted. That's the most fundamental difference of all.

Whatever baseball's future course turns out to be, and whoever is part of conducting it, the story of how it got to here is relevant. Avoidable mistakes need not be repeated. Things that work need to be ignored, forgotten, or tinkered with. Decisions, should always follow careful consideration of likely consequences, and to explore those, the past is the best starting point we have—not perfect, not infallibly reliable, perhaps not even illuminating, but the only one available.

Our imaginary New Yorker of 1842 would be the great-great-great-great grandfather of an imaginary reader of this book now. If they could talk to each other across the gap of a century and a half, they would find, after suitable mutual explanations of detail, much to recognize in their shared passion for something called "baseball." And if the imaginary descendant in this imaginary exchange gave his imaginary forbear this book to read, I think our Knickerbocker Club member would be amazed to learn what became of his recreation activity, and marvel at how the story he helped start turned out.

And I believe, although this may be wishful thinking, that he would grasp the central point I hope the story makes: what really matters is what happens on the field when they play the games. All the rest—the physical effort, the mental machinations, the daily chores at all levels—is only the means of producing something that has no tangible existence but only the significance our minds attach to it: the content of scorebook and box score, of league standing and record book, of images replayed in the mind's eye, of excitement triggered only by our perceptions.

The function of baseball, game *and* business, is to manufacture memories— which can't be done unless you play the games.

That can't change.

Commissioners
and League Presidents

Commissioners		Years in Office
Kenesaw M. Landis	1920–1944	25
Albert B. Chandler	1945–1951	7
Ford C. Frick	1951–1965	14
William D. Eckert	1965–1968	4
Bowie K. Kuhn	1969–1984	16
Peter V. Ueberroth	1984–1989	4
A. Bartlett Giamatti	–1989	—
Francis T. Vincent	1989–1992	4

National League Presidents

Morgan G. Bulkeley	1876	1
William A. Hulbert	1877–1882	5
Arthur H. Soden	1882	1
Abraham G. Mills	1883–1884	2
Nicholas E. Young	1885–1902	18
Harry C. Pulliam	1903–1909	6
John A. Heydler	1909	1
Thomas J. Lynch	1910–1913	4
John K. Tener	1913–1918	4
John A. Heydler	1918–1934	16

Ford C. Frick	1934–1951	17
Warren C. Giles	1951–1969	19
Charles S. Feeney	1970–1986	17
A. Bartlett Giamatti	1987–1989	2
William D. White	1989–1994	6
Leonard S. Coleman Jr.	1994–	

American League Presidents

B. Bancroft Johnson	1901–1927	27
Ernest S. Barnard	1927–1931	4
William Harridge	1931–1959	28
Joseph E. Cronin	1959–1973	14
Leland S. MacPhail Jr.	1974–1983	10
Robert W. Brown	1984–1994	11
Gene A. Budig	1994–	

Note: From 1903 through 1920, the three-man National Commission consisted of the two league presidents and a chairman, who was Garry Herrmann, an owner of the Cincinnati Reds, throughout its existence. Landis then became the sole Commissioner.

Franchises

Listed alphabetically are the cities that have had a recognized major league team at any time. Los Angeles includes Anaheim, San Francisco includes Oakland, Minneapolis includes St. Paul (but Brooklyn is *not* included in New York); Denver is the home of "Colorado," Miami the home of "Florida."

The National League started in 1876.

The American League started in 1901.

The American Association operated from 1882 through 1891.

The Union Association operated only in 1884.

The Players League operated only in 1890.

The Federal League operated from 1913 through 1915.

Where there is a break in continuity and a new franchise awarded in the same city, this is indicated by a separate entry.

City	1876– National League	1901– American League	1882–91 American Association	1884 Union Association	1890 Players League	1913–15 Federal League
Altoona				1884		
Atlanta	1966–					
Baltimore	1892–99	1901–2	1882–91	1884		1914–15
		1954–				
Boston	1876–1952	1901–	1891	1884	1890	
Brooklyn	1890–1957		1884–89		1890	1914–15
Buffalo	1879–85				1890	1914–15
Chicago	1876–	1901–		1884	1890	1913–15
Cincinnati	1876–80		1882–89	1884		1913
	1890–					
Cleveland	1879–84	1901–	1887–88		1890	1913
	1889–99					
Columbus			1883–84			
			1889–91			
Dallas		1972–				
Denver	1993–					
Detroit	1881–88	1910–				
Hartford	1876–77					
Houston	1962–					

City	National League	American League	American Association	Union Association	Players League	Federal League
Indianapolis	1878			1884		1913–14
	1887–89					
Kansas City	1886	1955–67	1888–89	1884		1913–15
		1969–				
Los Angeles	1958–	1961–				
Louisville	1876–77		1882–91			
	1892–99					
Miami	1993–					
Milwaukee	1878	1901		1884		
	1953–65	1970–97				
	1998–					
Minneapolis		1961–		1884		
Montreal	1969–					
Newark						1915
New York	1876	1903–	1883–87		1890	
	1883–57					
	1962–					
Philadelphia	1876	1901–54	1882–90	1884	1890	
	1883–		1891			
Phoenix	1998–					
Pittsburgh	1887–		1882–86		1890	1913–15
Providence	1878–85					
Richmond			1884			
Rochester			1890			
St. Louis	1876–77	1902–53	1882–91	1884		1913–15
	1885–86					
	1892–					
San Diego	1969–					
San Francisco	1958–	1968–				
Seattle		1969				
		1977–				
Syracuse	1879		1890			
Tampa		1998–				
Toledo			1890			
Toronto		1977–				
Troy	1879–82					

(Continued)

City	National League	American League	American Association	Union Association	Players League	Federal League
Washington	1886–89	1901–60	1884	1884		
	1892–99	1961–71	1891			
Wilmington				1884		
Worcester	1880–82					

Club Sales

This list shows all the clubs sold and their sales price from 1940 through 1997. A "sale" is considered to have taken place when there is a major change in the "principal owners"—those who act as such in public and in league affairs—since almost all clubs have always had minority "silent" investors. The dollar figures are those publicly announced at the time and may not reflect the true nature of the transactions. Prices are shown in millions of dollars. Expansion franchises are shown in italics.

1940	—	
1941	Boston (NL)	0.75
1942	—	
1943	Philadelphia (NL)	0.4
1944	Boston (NL)	0.75
1945	New York (AL)	2.8
	St. Louis (AL)	1.4
1946	Pittsburgh	2.5
	Cleveland	1.6
1947	St. Louis (NL)	1.5
1948	—	
1949	St. Louis (AL)	2.0
	Cleveland	2.5
1950	Brooklyn	4.0
1951	St. Louis (AL)	2.2
1952	—	
1953	St. Louis (NL)	3.75
	St. Louis (AL)	2.5 (to Baltimore)
1954	Philadelphia (AL)	3.5 (to Kansas City)
1955	—	
1956	Cleveland	4.0
	Detroit	5.5
1957	—	
1958	—	
1959	Chicago (AL)	5.0

1960	Kansas City	3.8
	New York (NL)	1.8
	Houston	1.8
	Los Angeles (AL)	2.1
	Washington	2.1
1961	Chicago (AL)	7.8
	Cleveland	6.0
1962	Milwaukee	6.2
	Cincinnati	4.7
1963	Washington	5.0
1964	New York (AL)	14.2
1965	Baltimore	N.A.
1966	Cleveland	8.0
1967	Cincinnati	7.0
1968	*Montreal*	12.5
	San Diego	12.5
	Kansas City	5.6
	Seattle	5.6
1969	Washington	9.4
1970	Seattle	10.8 (to Milwaukee)
1971	Washington	11.0 (to Texas)
1972	Cleveland	10.0
1973	New York (AL)	10.0
	Cincinnati	10.0
1974	San Diego	12.0
1975	Chicago (AL)	10.7
1976	Atlanta	11.0
	Houston	N.A.
	San Francisco	8.5
	Toronto	7.0
	Seattle	6.5
1977	Cleveland	12.0
1978	Boston (AL)	17.0
1979	Houston	19.0

	Baltimore	13.0			Texas	80.0
1980	New York (NL)	21.0		1990	Montreal	86.0
	Oakland	12.7			San Diego	75.0
	Texas	N.A.			Kansas City	68.0
1981	Chicago (NL)	20.5		1991	Toronto	60
	Philadelphia	31.0			*Colorado*	95
	Chicago (AL)	20.0			*Florida*	95
	Seattle	13.0		1992	San Francisco	100
1982	—				Seattle	125
1983	Detroit	53.0			Detroit	85
1984	Minnesota	38.0			Houston	90
	Cincinnati	22.0		1993	Baltimore	173
1985	Pittsburgh	22.0		1994	San Diego	80
	Texas	50.0		1995	Pittsburgh	85
1986	New York (NL)	95.0			Oakland	85
	Cleveland	35.0			St. Louis	150
	Philadelphia	51.0			*Phoenix*	130
1987	—				*Tampa Bay*	130
1988	Baltimore	70.0		1996	—	
1989	Seattle	80.0		1997	Los Angeles	350

Finances

These tables show year-by-year attendance, revenue, player expense, salary level, and TV income for 1974 through 1997, with 1939 and 1969 for comparison. The figures are approximate and rounded off, drawn from various sources that often don't agree. Nevertheless, they reflect accurately the general relationship of these elements to each other and to the whole, giving a valid "snapshot" for the financial picture from year to year. Years in parentheses indicate incomplete seasons.

		Attendance (in millions)		Revenue (in millions)				Salary (in thousands)		TV Revenue (in millions)	
	Games	Total	Per Club	Gross	Payroll	Pension	Remainder	Ave.	Min.	National	Total
1939	1,232	9.0	0.56	12	3	0	9	7.3	0	0	0.9†
1969	1,944	27.2	1.13	125	15	5.5	104	24.9	10	16	37
1974	1,944	30.0	1.25	152	24.5	6.2	121	41	15	18	42
1975	1,944	29.8	1.24	160	26.8	6.5	126	45	16	18	44
1976	1,944	31.3	1.30	200	36	8.5	155	52	19	23	50
1977	2,106	38.7	1.49	230	49.6	8.5	172	82	19	23	52
1978	2,106	40.6	1.56	270	69.6	8.5	192	98	21	23	52
1979	2,106	43.5	1.67	300	80	8.5	211	114	21	23	55
1980	2,106	43.0	1.65	340	101	15.5	224	140	30	41	80
1981	(1,394)	26.5	1.02	280	130	15.5	134	186	33	41	89
1982	2,106	44.6	1.72	430	169	15.5	245	240	33	53	118
1983	2,106	45.5	1.75	520	203	15.5	301	290	35	59	154
1984	2,106	44.7	1.72	620	240	16	364	330	40	163	268
1985	2,106	46.8	1.80	700	250	16	434	370	60	162	277
1986	2,106	47.5	1.83	750	280	33	437	420	60	182	322
1987	2,106	52.0	2.00	900	280	33	587	420	63	197	351
1988	2,106	53.0	2.04	1,000	300	33	667	440	63	207	364
1989	2,106	55.0	2.12	1,200	360	93	801	500	69	247	479
1990	2,106	54.8	2.11	1,300	440	55	805	580	100	363	613
1991	2,106	56.8	2.18	1,500	640	55	805	850	100	368	615
1992	2,106	55.9	2.15	1,600	870	55	675	1,002	109	365	630*
1993	2,268	70.3	2.51	1,900	900	55	945	1,076	109	365	630*
1994	(1,600)	50.0	1.79	1,200	680	55	465	1,168	109	185	400*
1995	(2,017)	50.5	1.80	1,400	850	55	495	1,111	109	185	400*
1996	2,268	60.1	2.15	1,850	950	60	690	1,120	123	425*	800*
1997	2,268	63.1	2.25	2,000	1,100	60	840*	1,337	150	425*	800*

* Estimated
† Radio

Competitive Balance

In opposing free agency, the claim always was that without a reserve system, "all the best players would wind up on the richest (bigger market, bigger-spending) teams." Since free agency, the same dire forecast of "destroying competitive balance" has been routine.

The actual record tells a different story.

From 1901 through 1968, when each league had only one first-place team, four American League clubs won 79 percent of the pennant races, and four National League clubs won 75 percent.

From 1969 through 1981, when each league had two divisions but before free agency took full effect (starting in 1977), the top four first-place finishers took 81 percent of the division races in the American League, and 77 percent in the National.

From 1982 through 1997, all 14 American League clubs finished first at least once, with the top four accounting for 48 percent. In the National League, 11 teams finished first, excepting only Montreal and the two that started only in 1993, Colorado and Florida. But Florida won the 1997 World Series. The top four accounted for 55 percent.

COMPETITIVE BALANCE
ONE-STANDING PENNANT WINNERS

	AL	**NL**
1901–20	Philadelphia 6	New York 6
	Boston 6	Chicago 5
	Chicago 4	Pittsburgh 4
	Detroit 3	Brooklyn 2
	Cleveland 1	Boston 1
	New York 0	Philadelphia 1
	Washington 0	Cincinnati 1
	St. Louis 0	St. Louis 0
1921–46	New York 14	St. Louis 9
	Detroit 4	New York 7
	Philadelphia 3	Chicago 5
	Washington 3	Pittsburgh 2
	St. Louis 1	Cincinnati 2
	Boston 1	Brooklyn 1
	Chicago 0	Boston 0
	Cleveland 0	Philadelphia 0
1947–68	New York 15	Brooklyn–L.A. 10
	Cleveland 2	St. Louis 3
	Chicago 1	Bost–Mil 3
	Minnesota 1	N.Y.–SF 3
	Baltimore 1	Philadelphia 1
	Boston 1	Pittsburgh 1
	Detroit 1	Cincinnati 1
	Philadelphia–Kansas City–Oakland 0	Chicago 0
	California 0	New York Mets 0
	Washington 0	Houston 0
Summary	Top 4: 54 (New York, Philadelphia, Detriot, Boston)	Top 4: 51 (New York–San Francisco, Brooklyn–Los Angeles, St. Louis, Chicago)
	All Others: 14	All Others: 17

COMPETITIVE BALANCE
DIVISION WINNERS

	AL	**NL**
1969–81	Baltimore 6	Cincinnati 6
	Oakland 6	Pittsburgh 6
	New York 5	Los Angeles 4
	Kansas City 4	Philadelphia 4
	Minnesota 2	New York 2
	Detroit 1	Atlanta 1
	Boston 1	San Francisco 1
	California 1	Houston 1
	Washington–Texas 0	Montreal 1
	Cleveland 0	Chicago 0
	Chicago 0	San Diego 0
	Milwaukee 0	St. Louis 0
	Seattle 0	—
	Toronto 0	—
Summary	Top 4: 21 (Baltimore, Oakland, New York, Kansas City)	Top 4: 20 (Cincinnati, Pittsburgh, Los Angeles, Philadelphia)
	All Others: 5	All Others: 6
1982–97	Toronto 5	Atlanta 7
	Oakland 4	St. Louis 4
	Boston 4	Los Angeles 4
	Cleveland 3	Pittsburgh 3
	California 2	San Francisco 3
	Baltimore 2	San Diego 2
	Chicago 2	Cincinnati 2
	Detroit 2	Houston 2
	Kansas City 2	Philadelphia 2
	Minnesota 2	Chicago 2
	Seattle 2	New York 2
	New York 1	Montreal 0
	Texas 1	Colorado 0
	Milwaukee 1	Florida 0*

*Won World Series

Offensive Eras

Baseball offense, as determined by production, style of play, and rule adjustments, falls into eight distinct eras. Awareness of these differences is of use in comparing statistics from one era to another.

	Characteristics	Years	Games	Runs/Game	Batting Avg.	HR/Game
I	1903–19 Dead-Ball Era	17	20,607	7.68	.252	0.29
II	1920–41 Lively ball, trick pitches banned, Golden Age	22	27,096	9.69	.280	0.96
III	1942–45 Deader ball, Wartime Baseball	4	4,934	8.17	.257	0.81
IV	1946–62 Uniform ball, fairly lively, Postwar Golden Age	17	21,620	8.87	.259	1.60
V	1963–68 Enlarged strike zone, expansion to 20 teams	6	9,728	7.72	.245	1.59
VI	1969–1976 Divisional play, expansion to 24 teams	8	15,446	8.14	.253	1.47
VII	1977–92 Designated hitter in A.L. only, free-agent era, expansion to 26 teams	16	32,957	8.59	.259	1.60
VIII	1993–97 New lively ball, expansion to 28 teams	5	10,415	9.66	.268	2.02

Hitting

Changes in the ball itself have a visible effect on the hitter-pitcher balance. Until World War II, such differences in the liveliness of the *average* ball were discussed publicly by baseball officials, and the two leagues used different balls. From the late 1940s on, baseball officials have always denied that any change has ever been made. Nevertheless, changes have occurred, sometimes admitted later, sometimes not.

Equally important are changes in the interpretation of the strike zone, and certain pitching-rule changes. A chronology shows when the most dramatic changes took place—reflected in statistics, the testimony of practitioners, and styles of play.

Years	Ball	Strike Zone	Rules
1901–10	AL somewhat livelier than NL	Not lower than knees, not higher than shoulders, in "normal stance"	Ball used as long as possible
Late 1910– Early 1913	Cork-center ball makes both livelier		
1913–19	Deadened to 1910, AL still somewhat livelier		
1920–28	Lively ball, AL more than NL		Trick pitches banned, fresh ball at all times
1929–30	AL consistent, NL super-lively		
1931–33	AL consistent, NL deadened to 1928 level		1931: No more bounce-in homers; home run fair where it leaves field, not where it leaves umpire's sight
1934–37	Both agree on uniform ball, a little deader than old AL		
1938–41	NL reverts to deader ball		
1942–45	Ball deader with wartime material		
1947–49	AL and NL more nearly alike, livelier		
1950	AL, NL, and minors adopt uniform ball	Between armpits and top of knee, in "normal stance"	Mound maximum, 15 inches
1951–76	Very slow, gradual deadening		
1963		Top of shoulder and "knee," stance determined when swinging at pitch	

(Continued)

Years	Ball	Strike Zone	Rules
1970		Armpits to top of knees	Mound lowered to 10 inches
1977	New manufacturer makes ball much livelier		
1978–92	Deadened to 1976 standard		
1988		Midpoint between top of shoulders and belt to top of pants at the knees, as batter is "prepared" to swing—but diagram inconsistent with wording	
1993–97	Dramatically livelier		
1996		Midpoint between shoulder and pants and "hollow beneath the kneecap"—diagram even more ambiguous	

Sacrifice Fly	
1908–26	For scoring a runner
1926–30	For any baserunner advanced
1931–37	No sacrifice fly
1938	For scoring a runner
1939–53	No sacrifice fly
1954–	For scoring a runner

The Designated Hitter

The designated hitter has been the subject of intense controversy since the American League adopted it in 1973 while the National rejected it. It is now used in the minor leagues and almost universally in college and high school and in other countries. Those who prefer the National League version claim it's the only "pure" baseball; those who like the DH claim it makes games more interesting by increasing scoring and not having inept pitchers bat.

What is seldom noticed is how little difference the presence or absence of a DH really makes to the "profile" of the average game. A 25-year record exists, and that's a large enough sample from which to draw conclusions that wash out changes in personnel, team strengths, ball-park venues, schedules, and other factors.

Such analysis shows that:

1. The DH group, as a whole, has a *lower* batting average than the American League as a whole most of the time.
2. If you go to 10 DH games and 10 non-DH games, you are likely to see four more runs scored (by both teams in 10 games) in the American than in the National, and three more home runs; but you'll see two more sacrifice bunts and three more strikeouts in the National League games.
3. In the 13 years before the DH rule, the National had a higher batting average than the American in 12 of them. In the 25 years since, the American has outhit the National 25 years in a row. But the difference has been slight. The National averaged 7 points higher in its period, the American 7 points higher since. For any one team with a typical 6,000 at bats during a season, the difference between the American's .263 and the National's .256 amounts to 15 hits, or less than one hit every ten games.
4. In the World Series, some games have used the DH and some have not, under varying rules over the years. In games without the DH, the American League won 42, the National 39; with the DH, the American won 35, the National 26. Such differences are not significant—especially because almost the entire American League's advantage in games with the DH rests on 4–0 records posted by the Minnesota Twins in their domed stadium in 1987 and 1991.
5. One major anticipated result of the DH was that a starting pitcher, if doing well, would complete more games, since he would never have to be taken out for a pinch-hitter. That was true at first, but as the practice of using multiple pitchers became more prevalent in both leagues, the difference between them became less and less. In the years 1973–75, the American had 50 percent more complete games (per team per season) than the National; by 1989–90, they were virtually even. In 1997, for the first time, the National actually had more complete games than the American.

    What this shows is that National League managers, like their American League counterparts, were making their decisions on when to change pitchers on the basis of evaluating the pitching situation, regardless of rules about pinch-hitting.

PITCHING PATTERN IN THE DH ERA*

Year	AL Complete Games	AL Shutouts	NL Complete Games	NL ShutoutsDH
1973	51.1*	12.5*	37.3	12.8
1974	54.2	12.0	36.6	11.9
1975	52.1	11.4	35.2	10.8
1976	49.2	13.4	37.4	13.7
1977	41.9	8.4	26.8	10.1
1978	46.1	11.5	32.4	12.0
1979	39.4	8.3	30.2	10.1
1980	39.2	9.4	25.2	11.0
1981†	23.9	8.4	14.7	8.6
1982	32.9	8.7	24.9	9.7
1983	33.5	9.5	23.0	9.6
1984	28.4	8.8	19.5	10.8
1985	25.7	7.7	22.3	12.4
1986	25.4	8.8	18.7	9.4
1987	26.6	8.1	15.8	8.2
1988	25.1	9.9	22.5	12.8
1989	18.9	10.4	18.2	12.3
1990	16.2	10.3	16.7	9.7
1991	15.4	10.7	12.5	10.2
1992	17.3	10.1	14.8	13.1
1993	14.9	7.9	11.6	7.9
1994†	10.9	4.6	7.3	5.6
1995†	10.1	6.4	8.9	8.1
1996	11.6	5.6	9.1	8.4
1997	8.8	2.8	10.2	3.6

*Average number per club
†Less than 162 game schedule

COMPARISONS

	AL Avg.	DH Avg.	NL Avg.
1973	.259	.257	.254
1974	.258	.256	.255
1975	.258	.254	.257
1976	.256	.257*	.255
1977	.266	.264	.262
1978	.261	.253	.254
1979	.270	.262	.261
1980	.269	.270*	.259
1981	.256	.247	.255
1982	.264	.265*	.258
1983	.266	.266	.255
1984	.264	.256	.255
1985	.261	.240	.252
1986	.262	.256	.253
1987	.265	.253	.261
1988	.259	.251	.248
1989	.261	.255	.246
1990	.259	.251	.256
1991	.260	.257	.250
1992	.259	.258	.252
1993	.267	.262	.264
1994	.273	.273	.267
1995	.270	.275*	.263
1996	.277	.277	.262
1997	.271	.274*	.263
25-Year Average	.263	.259	.256

*When DH Exceeded League Average (5 of 25)

Ball Parks

Steel and concrete replaced wooden structures starting in 1909. This list contains all the new parks built for major league baseball use since then. It does not include temporary existing facilities used by teams moving to new cities, except where such a facility was turned into a permanent home field (like Baltimore in 1954, Kansas City in 1955, Montreal in 1969, and Toronto in 1977).

It should be remembered that virtually all these parks have had major changes in seating capacity, outfield dimensions, and structural features from time to time, as well as name changes.

All parks built after 1932 had lighting systems for night games as part of their original design.

New Ball Parks

1909	Philadelphia (AL)	Pittsburgh	
1910	Chicago (AL)	Cleveland	
1911	New York (NL)	Washington	
1912	Boston (AL)	Detroit	Cincinnati
1913	Brooklyn		
1915	Boston (NL)		
1916	Chicago (NL)		
1923	New York (AL)		
1932	Cleveland		
1953	Milwaukee		
1954	Baltimore*		
1955	Kansas City*		
1960	San Francisco		
1961	Minnesota		
1962	Los Angeles (NL)	Washington	
1964	New York (NL)		
1965	Houston†		
1966	St. Louis	Los Angeles (AL)	Atlanta
1968	Oakland		
1969	San Diego	Montreal	
1970	Cincinnati	Pittsburgh	
1971	Philadelphia		
1972	Texas		
1973	Kansas City		
1977	Montreal†	Toronto	Seattle†
1982	Minnesota†		
1988	Toronto†		
1991	Chicago (AL)		
1992	Baltimore		
1993	Florida		
1994	Cleveland	Texas	
1995	Colorado		
1997	Atlanta		
1998	Phoenix†	Tampa Bay†	

*Existing building adapted
†Indoor structure

Installation of Lights

1935	Cincinnati		
1938	Brooklyn		
1939	Philadelphia (NL, AL)	Cleveland	Chicago (AL)
1940	New York (NL)	St. Louis (AL, NL)	Pittsburgh
1941	Washington		
1946	New York (AL)	Boston (NL)	
1947	Boston (AL)		
1948	Detroit		
1988	Chicago (NL)		

EFFECT OF NEW BALL PARKS
Average Yearly Attendance and Ticket Sales (in Millions)

City	Old Park		New Park		% Change	Total Additional Tickets in 3 Years
	Last 3 Years	Avg. Attendance	First 3 Years	Avg. Attendance		
Houston	1962–64	0.8	1965–67	1.8	125	3
St. Louis*	1963–65	1.19	1967–69	1.93	62	2.2
Cincinnati*	1967–69	0.89	1971–73	1.7	91	2.43
Pittsburgh*	1967–69	0.79	1971–73	1.32	67	1.59
Philadelphia	1968–70	0.63	1971–73	1.43	127	2.4
Kansas City	1970–72	0.77	1973–75	1.22	58	1.35
N.Y. Yanks†	1971–73	1.1	1976–78	2.13	94	3.09
Montreal	1974–76	0.87	1977–79	1.7	95	2.49
Minnesota	1979–81	0.77	1982–84	1.13	47	1.08
Toronto*	1986–88	2.6	1990–92	3.97	53	4.11
Chicago WS	1988–90	1.4	1991–93	2.67	91	3.87
Baltimore‡	1989–91	2.5	1992–94	3.27	31	2.31
Cleveland	1991–93	1.48	1994–96	8.16	450	6.68
Texas	1991–93	2.27	1994–96	7.38	225	5.11

*Not including midseason move: St. Louis 1966, Cincinnati and Pittsburgh 1970, Toronto 1989
†Not including 1974–75 in Shea Stadium while Yankee Stadium was rebuilt
‡Third season cut short by strike; projected full season of 3.35 in 1994 would have made increase 40
   percent with 3 million extra tickets.
Note: These are all ball park changes in the *same city*. Only Kansas City (in town to outskirts) and Minnesota
   (outskirts to downtown) had significant differences in location.

Player Awards

Most Valuable Player (MVP)

1911–14	Chalmers Award (a car). One in each league.
1922–28	American League. No repeaters allowed.
1924–29	National League. No repeaters allowed.
1931–on	One in each league by Baseball Writers Association of America.

Cy Young Award

For pitcher of the year, by the Baseball Writers Association of America.

1956–66	One only.
1967–on	One in each league.

Rookie of the Year

By the Baseball Writers Association of America.

1947–48	One only.
1949–on	One in each league.

Gold Glove

For best fielder at each position.

1957	One only, by sportswriter special committee.
1958–64	One in each league, by major league players.
1965–on	One in each league, by coaches and managers.

Hall of Fame

1936–on	Players—at least five but not more than 20 years after retirement, by 10-year members of the Baseball Writers Association of America.
	All others—By special committees of veterans.

Elections have been held annually since 1966, at varying intervals before that.

Why "Pitching Is the Name of the Game"

The underlying pattern of baseball at the major league level is revealed by some generalized statistics, drawn from all the games played since 1903, when the foul-strike rule joined the 60-foot pitching distance to create today's game. All tactical and strategic decisions are made on the basis of a manager's opinion of how each particular matchup *varies* from these established "percentages":

Of all half innings (a team's turn at bat), 67 percent produce no runs, 20 percent one, and only 13 percent more than one.

Seventy percent of all plate appearances result in an out.

The best hitters make an out 60 percent of the time.

The worst pitchers retire 50 percent of the men they face.

Your three best hitters (whoever they are at any particular time) get to bat only 33 percent of the time.

Your two best pitchers (starter and closer) can face 100 percent of the batters in any game.

Over a full season, your three best hitters cannot bat more than 33 percent of the time. Your three best pitchers (two starters and a reliever) will work only 33 percent of the innings pitched. The rest of your staff must pitch 67 percent of the time.

Therefore, pitching *depth* is the key to success.

A hot pitcher can control 100 percent of any particular game, and can win 1–0. Three hot hitters can't control any game unless *their* own pitcher is effective enough.

Pitching *is* the name of the game.

Sources

No comprehensive bibliography is being attempted here. The following references are those on which I have depended most, and which contain vastly more material on matters touched upon in this book.

For overviews of baseball history up to the 1930s, Harold Seymour's *Baseball, the Early Years* and *Baseball, The Golden Age* remain supreme. Albert Spalding's *Our National Game* and David Pietrisza's *Major Leagues* are also invaluable. Of similar breadth and quality are the articles in the front sections of the *Total Baseball Encyclopedia,* fifth edition.

For complete player and team statistical information, covering all major league history, three encyclopedias are current: 1. *Total Baseball,* which is the most complete; 2. *The Macmillian Baseball Encyclopedia;* and 3. *The Sports Encyclopedia: Baseball,* which also contains brief summaries of each season's highlights. Each is organized differently, and they overlap, but at least one of them is indispensable to anyone interested in baseball. They are either updated or provide supplements from time to time.

For more thorough information on any one season, the annual Guides are basic. (A 1992 Guide covers the events of 1991). They have been published by the *Sporting News* since 1942, and by Spalding and Reach before that going back into the 19th century.

For records (in the sense of "setting a record"), the *Sporting News* publishes annually *The Complete Baseball Record Book* (once called *One for the Book*). The Elias Bureau, which processes most day-by-day statistics for football and basketball as well as baseball, annually publishes *The Book of Baseball Records,* whose earlier versions, such as *The Little Red Book,* go back further into the 1920s than the *Sporting News* versions. Both cover all baseball history.

For nonstatistical material on any particular season, person, city, or situation, literally dozens of excellent books are available, identifiable by the name of the person (as in biographies) or the year. Any large library can help track down your specific interests.

The Society for American Baseball Research (SABR) has published many monthlies, annuals, and special studies and can be contacted for guidance in any area, and for back copies of its publication.

The National Baseball Hall of Fame's library and archives, in Cooperstown, New York, can also identify where to find material according to one's special interest and suggest how to find it.

For information on ballparks, *Green Cathedrals* by Philip J. Lowry is uniquely thorough and fascinating.

For studies of baseball economics, various books written or edited by Paul Staudohar, Roger Noll, Gerald Scully, Andrew Zimbalist, James Quirk, and Rodney Fort are extremely informative.

In all these cases, information about correct titles, publishers and availability is best gained from consulting an experienced librarian. Many are out of print but are not hard to track down.

Strictly as a master of personal preference, the following books have been of special value to me:

Bill Veeck's *Veeck As In Wreck* and *The Hustler's Handbook.*

Lawrence Ritter's *The Glory of Their Times.*

Dave Anderson's *Pennant Races.*

Neil Sullivan's *The Dodgers Move West.*

David Halberstam's two books about the 1949 and 1964 seasons.

Jim Brosnan's *The Long Season* and its sequel, *Pennant Race.*

Robert Creamer's biographies of Babe Ruth and Casey Stengel.

Philip J. Lowry's *Green Cathedrals.*

John Warner Davenport's *Baseball Pennant Races.*

Index